CCT®/CCNA®

Routing and Switching

EXAM GUIDE

(Exams 100-490 & 200-301)

ABOUT THE AUTHORS

Glen E. Clarke, CCT, CCNA, MCITP, MCSE, MCSD, MCDBA, MCT, CEH, CHFI, CISSO, PenTest+, Security+, Network+, A+, is a technical trainer and owner of DC Advanced Technology Training (DCATT), an IT training company based out of Halifax, Nova Scotia. Glen spends most of his time delivering certified courses on Windows Server, Office 365, Hyper-V, SQL Server, Exchange Server, SharePoint, Visual Basic .NET, and ASP.NET. Glen also teaches a number of security-related courses covering topics such as ethical hacking and countermeasures, computer forensics and investigation, penetration testing, and information systems security officer. Glen also teaches a number of networking courses such as Cisco CCT, Cisco CCNA, and packet analysis.

Glen is an experienced author and technical editor whose published work was nominated for Referenceware Excellence Awards. Glen has authored numerous certification preparation guides, including the *CompTIA Network+ Certification Study Guide*, the *CompTIA Security+ Certification Study Guide*, the *CompTIA PenTest+ Certification for Dummies*, and the best-selling *CompTIA A+ Certification All-In-One for Dummies*.

When he's not working, Glen loves to spend quality time with his wife, Tanya, and their four children, Sara, Brendon, Ashlyn, and Rebecca. You can visit Glen online at www.dcatt.ca or contact him at glenclarke@dcatt.ca.

For almost 20 years, **Richard Deal** has operated his own company, The Deal Group, Inc., in Oviedo, Florida, east of Orlando. Richard has more than 25 years of experience in the computing and networking industry, including networking, training, systems administration, and programming. In addition to earning a B.S. in mathematics from Grove City College, he holds many certifications from Cisco and has taught many beginning and advanced Cisco classes. Richard is the author of *Cisco ASA Configuration,* an in-depth book on Cisco's ASA firewall appliances and their implementation, published by McGraw Hill. Richard is also the author of two books with Cisco Press: *The Complete Cisco VPN Configuration Guide* and *Cisco Router Firewall Security*; both books made it to Cisco's CCIE Security recommended reading list.

About the Technical Editor

Edward Tetz graduated in 1990 from Saint Lawrence College in Cornwall, Ontario, with a degree in business administration. Since that time, he has spent his career delivering certified technical training for a Microsoft Training Center and working as a service delivery professional in both Halifax, Nova Scotia, and Ottawa, Ontario. Over his career, Ed has supported Apple Macintosh, IBM OS/2, Linux, Novell NetWare, and all Microsoft operating systems from MS-DOS to Windows Server 2019, as well as hardware from most of the major manufactures. Ed currently works for Microsoft in Customer Success in Ottawa, supporting enterprise and government customers.

When not working with technology, Ed spends time with his wife, Sharon, and his two daughters, Emily and Mackenzie.

ALL·IN·ONE

CCT®/CCNA®
Routing and Switching
EXAM GUIDE
(Exams 100-490 & 200-301)

Glen E. Clarke
Richard Deal

New York   Chicago   San Francisco
Athens   London   Madrid   Mexico City
Milan   New Delhi   Singapore   Sydney   Toronto

To my beautiful wife, Tanya, who is constantly amazed that
I have the concentration to write a book, yet at the same time
I forget to take the garbage out each week.

—*Glen*

CONTENTS AT A GLANCE

CONTENTS

ACKNOWLEDGMENTS

I would like to thank the wonderful people at McGraw Hill for all the time and hard work they put into the creation of this book. A special thanks goes to Executive Editor Timothy Green for giving me the opportunity to write this book and for all his patience and support while I worked through the chapters. Thank you to Editorial Coordinator Emily Walters for keeping me focused on the next element I needed to work on, and the quick answers to all my questions! I look forward to our next project together!

Thank you to my close friend and former coworker, Ed Tetz, for his great feedback and encouraging ideas as the technical editor. Ed has helped me stay on track with the exam objectives and has also given me great ideas for adding value to discussions in the book. A needed thank you goes to copy editor Lisa Theobald for helping me find more direct explanations and wording. A big thank you to Patty Mon (Editorial Supervisor) and Revathi Viswanathan for their amazing work with the production of the book. It looks awesome!

A special thank you to my wife, Tanya, who has been extremely supportive and loving through the many hours of writing this book. I would also like to thank my four children, Sara, Brendon, Ashlyn, and Rebecca, for helping me remember the important things in life. I love the time I spend with all four of you!

Special thanks to Brendon Clarke for helping with some of the graphics in the book. You did an awesome job!

INTRODUCTION

Welcome to your first step in becoming Cisco certified! This book is designed not only to give you the background you need to manage Cisco devices, but also to provide a detailed certification exam guide for both the Cisco CCT and CCNA certification exams. Whether you are new to networking and looking to start a career in the field, or you are a seasoned networking professional who is looking for a book that gives you guidance on what to focus on for the exam, this book is for you!

This book covers a wide range of topics that you need to know about for the Cisco CCT and CCNA exams. Let's take a look at what you will learn in this book.

Chapter 1: Network Fundamentals   The book begins with a chapter on network fundamentals, which covers topics such as types of networks, network cabling, network architectures, network devices, and network protocols and applications.

Chapter 2: OSI Reference Model   You are then introduced to the OSI model and the different layers within the OSI model. You learn about what each layer of the OSI model does and the concept of encapsulation, as well as the types of communication that occur on a network.

Chapter 3: TCP/IP Protocol Suite   In this chapter you learn about the TCP/IP protocol suite, and the role that each protocol takes within the protocol suite. The protocols are identified at their networking layer and the TCP/IP model is compared against the OSI model.

Chapter 4: IP Addressing Basics   In this chapter you learn about IP addresses, subnet masks, and the default gateway setting. This chapter also introduces you to network IDs and host IDs and discusses how to convert binary to decimal and decimal to binary.

Chapter 5: Subnetting and VLSM   This chapter walks you through the purposes of subnetting and how to subnet an IP range to correspond to your physical network topology. This chapter also discusses the importance of variable length subnet masks (VLSMs) and the steps to calculate VLSM given a scenario.

Chapter 6: Cisco Device Basics   Chapter 6 starts the focus on Cisco devices. In this chapter you learn about the types of Cisco devices, hardware components, the different ports and interfaces, and how to install hardware modules into a device.

Chapter 7: Cisco IOS Basics   This chapter focuses on introducing the Cisco Internetwork Operating System (IOS), the different configuration modes, and the commands to apply a basic configuration to the Cisco device. You also learn commands to verify your configuration on the Cisco device.

Chapter 8: Cisco Device Management   Chapter 8 is an important chapter for the Cisco CCT exam; you learn about day to day management of a Cisco device including how to back up Cisco configuration files and IOS images and how to recover the Cisco IOS or configuration settings should something go wrong. You also learn about configuration registers and how to perform a password recovery.

Chapter 9: Switching Basics   This is the first of two chapters that focus on switches. In this chapter you are introduced to the functions and the basic configuration commands of a switch. You also learn about interface configuration, how to configure port security, and the important topic of virtual LANs (VLANs).

Chapter 10: Advanced Switching Features   In this chapter you learn about additional switching features such as the VLAN trunking protocol, Spanning Tree Protocol (STP), Rapid Spanning Tree Protocol (RSTP), and EtherChannels.

Chapter 11: Introduction to Routing   This chapter is a very important chapter for the Cisco CCNA exam and introduces you to the concept of routing. In this chapter you learn about static routing and floating static routes, and you are introduced to dynamic routing. You also learn about the routing process and how Cisco devices choose a route to a destination.

Chapter 12: OSPF Routing   This chapter is the second chapter focused on routing, but its purpose is to introduce you to Open Shortest Path First (OSPF) as a dynamic routing protocol. You will learn about how OSPF operates, how to configure OSPF, and how to troubleshoot OSPF.

Chapter 13: IP Services   This important chapter for the CCNA certification helps you understand the configuration of IP services in a Cisco environment. In this chapter you will learn about common network services such as Domain Name System (DNS), Dynamic Host Control Protocol (DHCP), and Network Time Protocol (NTP). You will also learn how to configure DHCP and Network Address Translation (NAT) on your Cisco routers.

Chapter 14: IPv6   In this chapter you learn about the changes made to the Internet Protocol (IP) with IPv6. You learn about the different address types, how to configure an IPv6 address on a device, and how to configure routing with IPv6.

Chapter 15: Wireless Networking   Chapter 15 discusses the basics of wireless networking, including the types of wireless networks, wireless standards, and wireless encryption protocols. You also learn about the purpose of the wireless LAN controller and the wireless access point modes.

Chapter 16: Security Fundamentals   This chapter introduces general security concepts to help you prepare for related questions on the CCNA exam. In this chapter you will learn about different types of attacks, authentication and authorization concepts, the need for passwords policies, and virtual private network (VPN) solutions.

Chapter 17: Implementing Security on Cisco Devices   This chapter is focused on implementing security on Cisco devices. In this chapter you will learn about configuring passwords on your Cisco device, encrypting those passwords, layer 2 security features on your switch, and access control lists (ACLs).

Chapter 18: Automation and Programmability   The final chapter in the book covers a new topic to CCNA, automation and programmability. In this chapter you learn about the importance of automation, and then you learn about software-defined networking (SDN) and Cisco Digital Network Architecture (DNA).

Online Content   Using your online code, you can access the online content that accompanies this book, including practice tests, the lab solutions PDF document, and more than 40 videos from the author demonstrating common configuration tasks on Cisco devices.

About the Exams

This book prepares you for two exams—the Cisco CCT certification exam and the Cisco CCNA certification exam. You can register for the Cisco exams at https://home.pearson-vue.com/cisco. Check the Cisco web site for the most up-to-date information on Cisco certifications. The following information is the most recent information as of the date of publication of this book.

Cisco CCT Certification: Exam 100-490

The Cisco Certified Technician (CCT) certification exam is focused on the job role of an IT technician who is supporting Cisco devices for customers or businesses. For this certification you must know how to support, configure, and troubleshoot a Cisco device on a network. Here are some details about the exam:

Exam Number:	100-490
Duration:	90 minutes
Number of Questions	60
Domains Percentages:	General Networking Knowledge – 25%
	Cisco Equipment and Related Hardware – 20%
	Cisco IOS Software Operation – 29%
	Service-related Knowledge – 26%

Cisco CCNA Certification: Exam 200-301

The Cisco Certified Network Associate (CCNA) certification exam is designed for network professionals who will be implementing Cisco devices on a network. The exam covers a wide range of topics, such as IP addressing, subnetting and VLSM, routing, wireless, IP services, and automation. Here are some details about the exam:

Exam Number:	200-301
Duration:	120 minutes
Number of Questions	102
Domains Percentages:	Network Fundamentals – 20%
	Network Access – 20%
	IP Connectivity – 25%
	IP Services – 10%
	Security Fundamentals – 15%
	Automation and Programmability – 10%

For a detailed listing of the exam objectives for both the Cisco CCT and CCNA certification exams, check out the Exam Readiness Checklists found in Appendix A of this book.

Taking the Exam at a Test Center or Online

When you register for the exam, you have a choice of taking the exam at a testing center or taking the exam online from the comfort of your own home or office.

If you are taking the exam at a testing center, be sure to show up 30 minutes early and bring two forms of ID with you, including one with a photo. You will not be allowed to take anything into the examination room with you.

If you are taking the exam online, you should log in 30 minutes before taking the test, because you'll need to perform some verification steps before the exam will start. As part of the verification process, you will need to upload a photo ID, and then take photos of your surrounding area and submit them. Ensure that there is nothing on your desk except the computer you are using to take the test. You must have a webcam focused on you at all times, and you are not allowed to leave the view of the webcam. I recommend that you take the test in a locked room, because you must be alone to take the test: no one else is allowed to enter the room or disturb you.

Recommended Steps to Prepare

I have taken a lot of certification exams over the years and one of the most common questions I am asked is, "How do you prepare for the exams?" So I want to share how I prepare for any certification exam I take.

- **Step 1: Read the entire book** Read the book from front to back. As you read, work through the exercises and the review questions, but at this point, don't worry about studying the book. This is your first pass through the book, so you just want to go through the topics without worrying about what you retain.

You can also watch the videos that accompany the book to see demonstrations of the topics covered.

- **Step 2: Read the book again**   This time, you should take time to study the book in a bit more detail and explore some of the topics that may not have accompanying exercises. I consider this trip through the book my play time. I am reading it again and experimenting with topics as I read.

- **Step 3: Read the book a third time**   At this point, you have a solid understanding of the topics, you've done the practice exercises a few times, and you've played on your own (hands-on is important). This third read will help you pick up on some of the finer details that you may not have focused on in your first two reads.

- **Step 4: Take the Practice Exams, three times**   It is important to note that you should not take the practice exams that come with this book until after you have read the entire book and have worked through the lab exercises. Many people like to take practice exams as they read, but I do not suggest that you do that, because you get used to those questions as you slowly work on them. To get a true assessment of how you will do on the real exam, you should wait until you've finished reading the entire book before you take the practice exams. The practice exams are designed to get your mind into "exam mode," so I recommend focusing on them at this stage. Four practice exams' worth of questions come with this book, including more than 100 practice exam questions for the CCT certification exam and more than 200 practice exam questions for the CCNA certification exam. You can generate tests based on chapter or exam domain and select how many questions you want, or you can generate timed practice exams in Exam Mode. (See "About the Online Content" at the end of the book for more information.) You can also take practice exams in open-book mode and read the explanations for each question to ensure that you understand why each choice is correct or incorrect. I typically take each practice exam three times as well, reading the explanations for any question I am unsure about or get wrong.

Network Fundamentals

In this chapter, you will

- Be introduced to common network services and devices
- Learn about network topologies
- Learn about types of cabling
- Take a look at access methods
- Learn about network architectures
- Learn virtualization fundamentals

This chapter offers a brief introduction to networking and some basic networking terms and concepts that you'll need to understand for the Cisco CCT and CCNA exams. You may already be familiar with this material; in that case, the chapter will provide a review of basic network concepts. For the exams, you should understand the various networking topologies used in networks, as well as different types of networks, such as local area networks (LANs) and wide area networks (WANs).

Introduction to Networks

A *network* includes all of the components (hardware and software) involved in connecting computers and applications across small and large distances. Networks are used to share information and services with users to help them increase their productivity. For example, a network may share a printer on the network so that everyone in your office can access it, instead of each user needing his or her own printer.

This section covers some of the components involved with networking, as well as the basic types of topologies used to connect networking components, including computers. Resources that are commonly shared in a network include data and applications, printers, network storage components (shared disk space), and backup storage components.

Network Characteristics

To design a successful network solution, you need to be familiar with the organization's needs and goals. Consider the following characteristics when designing a network:

- **Cost**   Includes the cost of the network components, their installation, and their ongoing maintenance.

1

- **Security**   Includes the protection of the network components and the data they contain and/or the data transmitted between them.

- **Speed**   Includes how fast data is transmitted between network endpoints (the data rate).

- **Topology**   Describes the physical cabling layout and the logical way data moves between components.

- **Scalability**   Defines how well the network can adapt to new growth, including new users, applications, and network components.

- **Reliability**   Defines the ability of network components to provide the appropriate levels of support and the required connectivity levels. The *mean time between failures* (MTBF) is a measurement commonly used to indicate the likelihood of a component failing.

- **Availability**   Measures the likelihood of the network being available to the users, where downtime occurs when the network is not available because of an outage or scheduled maintenance. Availability is typically measured in a percentage based on the number of minutes that exist in a year. Therefore, *uptime* would be the number of minutes the network is available divided by the number of minutes in a year.

 EXAM TIP   For the exam, you'll need to remember these important factors associated with designing and maintaining a network: cost, security, speed, topology, scalability, reliability, and availability.

Networking Components

Applications, the software that enables users to perform various tasks, make up a key component of networking. Many applications are *network-aware*, which means they enable you to access and use resources that are not stored directly on your local computer. While the number of networking applications ranges in the thousands, some of the more common networking applications in use in most organizations include e-mail applications for sending and receiving e-mail, File Transfer Protocol (FTP) applications for transferring files, and web applications for providing a graphical representation of information.

Protocols are used to enable systems to talk to one another on the network. Some protocols are *open standard*, meaning that many vendors can create applications that can interoperate with other applications using that protocol. Other protocols are *proprietary*, meaning that they work only with other applications created by a particular vendor.

The following is a list of common Internet protocols that we use on a daily basis to communicate over the Internet:

- **Simple Mail Transfer Protocol (SMTP)**   The Internet protocol for sending e-mails.

- **Post Office Protocol 3 (POP3)**   The Internet protocol for downloading e-mail from an e-mail server to your system so that you can read the e-mail.

- **Internet Message Access Protocol version 4 (IMAP4)** The Internet protocol used to read e-mail. IMAP4 supports additional capabilities and folder support over POP3.

- **File Transfer Protocol (FTP)** The Internet protocol for transferring files across the Internet.

- **Hypertext Transfer Protocol (HTTP)** The protocol used to deliver web pages from a web server to a web browser. All of the popular web servers such as Internet Information Services (IIS) and Apache are running an HTTP server.

Some applications, such as e-mail, require little bandwidth, while others, such as backup software, video software, and file transfer software, require a lot. Some applications operate in real-time, such as voice over IP (VoIP) and video; some operate interactively, such as instant messaging and database queries; and some operate in a batch mode, requiring little user interaction. Today's networks need to accommodate all these different types of resources and applications, including their specific requirements, such as bandwidth for large transfers or minimal delay and latency for VoIP and video. *Quality of service* (QoS) features are commonly used to meet these requirements.

 EXAM TIP Remember for the Cisco CCT and CCNA exams that VoIP and video traffic are sensitive to delay and latency. Therefore, QoS is commonly implemented to ensure that these applications have enough bandwidth and are prioritized throughout the network to limit the amount of delay they incur.

To build a network, you need three component categories:

- **Networking software** There are two types of software components—server software and client software. The server software offers some form of service to clients on the network (which is why we want the network). For example, the server software may share files or provide e-mail functionality. The client software connects to the servers to request to use the services.

- **Networking hardware** The network hardware components—such as hubs, switches, routers, firewalls, wireless access points, modems, and channel service units/data service units (CSUs/DSUs)—are responsible for moving information between the LAN and WAN.

- **Media type** Media types such as copper or fiber cabling are needed to connect the computers and networking components so that information can be shared between components. Wireless communication also falls in this category, because it is used to transmit data from one system to another on the network.

Network Locations

Network components are used in various locations. Table 1-1 shows some common terms used to describe the locations of network components.

Term	Definition
Small office/home office (SOHO)	Users working from a small or home office (a handful of people)
Branch office	A small group of users connected in a small area (LAN) that are geographically separated from a corporate office
Mobile users	Users who connect to a network from any location, via LAN or WAN
Corporate or central office	Where most users in an organization and their resources are located

Table 1-1 Networking Locations

Local Area Networks

Local area networks (LANs) are used to connect networking devices that reside in a close geographic area, such as a floor of a building, a building itself, or within a campus environment. In a LAN, you'll find a range of different types of devices, such as PCs, servers, switches, routers, multilayer switches, voice gateways, firewalls, and other devices. The media types used in LANs include copper and fiber cabling. They can also include Ethernet, Fast Ethernet (FE), Gigabit Ethernet (GE), Token Ring, and Fiber Distributed Data Interface (FDDI), which are different network architectures. Today, most networks use some form of Ethernet (discussed later in this chapter in the "Network Architectures" section).

NOTE Ethernet has become the de facto standard for LAN-based networks. Therefore, understanding its topology and workings is very important when it comes to implementation in a company's network. Hubs and bridges are rarely used in today's networks: they've been replaced with switches.

Wide Area Networks

Wide area networks (WANs) are used to connect multiple LANs together. For example, suppose you have an office in Boston (a LAN) and an office in Vancouver (another LAN); a WAN is used to connect these two LANs together so that users can communicate with other users and systems on both LANs. Typically, WANs are used when the LANs that must be connected are separated by a large distance. Whereas a corporation provides its own infrastructure for a LAN, WANs are leased from carrier networks, such as telephone companies and Internet service providers (ISPs). Four basic types of connections, or circuits, are used in WAN services: circuit-switched, cell-switched, packet-switched, and dedicated connections.

EXAM TIP For the exam, remember that LANs provide high-speed bandwidth connections to interconnect components in a geographically close location, such as a building or a campus. WANs provide lower speed bandwidth connections to interconnect multiple locations or sites. WANs involve paying recurring monthly costs to a service provider.

A wide array of WAN services are available to connect different office locations, including analog dialup, Asynchronous Transfer Mode (ATM), dedicated circuits, cable, digital subscriber line (DSL), Frame Relay, Integrated Services Digital Network (ISDN), and X.25. Analog dialup and ISDN are examples of circuit-switched services; ATM is an example of a cell-switched service; and Frame Relay and X.25 are examples of packet-switched services.

Circuit-switched services provide a temporary connection across a phone circuit. In networking, these services are typically used for backup of primary circuits and for temporary boosts of bandwidth. More commonly today, cellular wireless services (3G and 4G) are used for dial-on-demand applications or backup connections.

A *dedicated circuit* is a permanent connection between two sites in which the bandwidth is dedicated to that company's use. These circuits are common when a variety of services, such as voice, video, and data, must traverse the connection and you want guaranteed bandwidth available.

Cell-switched services can provide the same features that dedicated circuits offer, such as having a dedicated link, but one of its advantages over dedicated circuits is that it enables a single device to connect to multiple devices on the same interface. The downside of these services is that they are not available at all locations, they are difficult to set up and troubleshoot, and the equipment is expensive when compared to equipment used for dedicated circuits.

Packet-switched services are similar to cell-switched services, except cell-switched services switch *fixed-length* packets called cells and packet-switched services switch *variable-length* packets. This feature makes packet-switched services better suited for data services, but they can nonetheless provide some of the QoS features that cell-switched services provide.

Two other WAN services that are very popular technologies for high-speed Internet connections are digital subscriber lines (DSLs) and cable. DSL provides speeds up to a few megabits per second (Mbps) and costs much less than a typical WAN circuit from the carrier. It supports both voice and video and doesn't require a dialup connection (it's always enabled). The main disadvantage of DSL is that coverage is limited to about 18,000 feet, and the service is not available in all areas. Cable access uses coaxial copper and fiber connections—the same media used to provide television broadcast services. Cable supports higher data rates than DSL, but like DSL, it provides a full-time connection. However, cable has two major drawbacks: it is a shared service and functions in a logical bus topology much like Ethernet (discussed in Chapter 2), so the more customers in an area that connect via cable, the less bandwidth each customer has; also, because many people are sharing the medium, it is more susceptible to security risks such as eavesdropping on other subscribers' traffic.

Examples of networking devices used in WAN connections include cable and DSL modems, carrier switches, CSU/DSUs, firewalls, analog modems, and routers. You will learn more about these devices as we progress through the chapters.

Common Network Services and Devices

Although most of the questions you'll encounter on the CCNA exams will deal with proper implementation of features on a Cisco router or switch, you will see some networking questions that test your knowledge of basic concepts, such as the purpose of different network services and network infrastructure components. In this section you will learn about several network services and infrastructure components, such as routers and switches.

Types of Services

Networks today include many different servers that provide different types of services. Each service provides a specific function to the network, and it is important that you understand what those services are. You should be familiar with the following servers and services on the network:

- **DNS server**   This service is responsible for resolving fully qualified domain names (FQDNs) to IP addresses. For example, when you type an address such as www.gleneclarke.com in a browser window, your computer contacts a DNS server to determine the IP address of that friendly name.

- **DHCP server**   This service is responsible for assigning IP addresses to computers and devices when they connect to the network so that they can communicate with other systems on the network or surf the Internet.

- **HTTP server**   This service is responsible for hosting web pages that can be delivered to clients that connect to the web server.

- **File server**   This service is used to hold all of the data files for a company. A file server typically has lots of storage space and becomes the central point of storage for the company. It also becomes the central location of backup to ensure that company data files are backed up.

- **Application server**   This server has specified applications installed to provide services on the network. For example, a database product installed on the application server enables the server to provide application data out to the network; an e-mail server application installed on the server enables all users to connect to the server to send and receive e-mail.

- **SMTP/POP**   This service runs specific protocols that enable the e-mail software to send or receive e-mails. SMTP is the Internet protocol for sending e-mail, while POP is the Internet protocol for reading e-mails.

- **FTP**   This service can be installed on a host to enable someone to connect to the network and transfer files across the network or Internet. FTP uses TCP as the transport layer protocol and supports authentication.

- **TFTP**   The Trivial File Transfer Protocol service enables you to upload or download a file. TFTP uses the User Datagram Protocol (UDP) and does not support authentication.

- **Ping** This is not really a service, but a command-line tool that is used to test connectivity with another system. From a command prompt or terminal session on your system, you can use the command **ping** *<ip_address>* to send a test message to a remote system. If you can communicate with that system, you should receive a ping reply message.

- **Telnet** This service enables you to create a remote connection to a system, using the text-based interface of the system to perform remote administration. For example, network administrators may telnet into a switch or router to make configuration changes to that switch or router. Telnet sends all communication in clear text, including the username and password.

- **SSH** Secure Shell is the secure method of performing remote administration of a device on the network. SSH encrypts all communication including the username and password; it is designed as a secure replacement to telnet.

Network Infrastructure Components

Networks today use a number of different devices to aid in their functionality or security. Let's take a look at some common network devices you are sure to encounter on your network.

Hub

A hub is an older network device that you hopefully do not encounter on your networks, because they have been replaced by the more effective and secure switches. On an older network, all systems connected to the hub to provide network communication. A network hub had three pitfalls:

- **No filtering** When a system was to send data to another system, the hub would receive the data and then send the data to all other ports on the hub. The hub is a layer 1 device (you will learn about OSI layers in the next chapter), so it simply received the signal and sent it to all ports; it does not understand Media Access Control (MAC) addresses, but a switch does.

- **Collisions** Because any data sent was sent to all other ports, and because any system could send its own data at any time, this resulted in a lot of collisions on the network. A collision occurs when two pieces of data collide and then must be retransmitted.

- **Security** Because the data was sent to all ports on the hub, all systems receive *all* data. Systems look at the destination address in the frame to decide whether to process the data or discard it. But if someone was running a packet sniffer on a system that used a hub, he would receive all packets and be able to read them. This created a huge security concern.

The answer to the hub problem was to replace network hubs with switches, which have filtering capabilities that you will read about in the next section. Why do I bring up hubs if they have been replaced by switches? It is important that you know how a hub works, because it will help you understand the benefits of a switch. Switches reduce collisions, optimize traffic, and are better from a security point of view.

LAN Switch

Switches are one of the most common devices used on networks today. All other devices connect to the switch to gain access to the network. For example, you will connect workstations, servers, printers, and routers to a switch, so that each device can send and receive data to and from other devices. The switch acts as the central connectivity point for all devices on the network.

Layer 2 Switch   The switch tracks every device's MAC address (the physical address burned into the network card) and then associates that device's MAC address with the port on the switch to which the device is connected. The switch stores this information in a MAC address table in memory on the switch. The switch then acts as a filtering device by sending data only to the port that the data is destined for. For example, in Figure 1-1, computer A is sending data (a frame) to computer C. The frame enters the switch through the port that computer A is connected to (port 2). The switch reads the destination address of the frame and sees it is destined for cccc.cccc.cccc (computer C). The switch then checks the MAC table in memory to see what port has the MAC address of cccc.cccc.cccc. The switch notes that computer C is connected to port 4 and then forwards the data to port 4.

You will learn more about switches in Chapter 9.

Router

A switch is used to connect all systems together in a LAN type of setup, but what if you want to send data from your network to another network or across the Internet? That is the job of a router. A router sends, or routes, data from one network to another until the data reaches its final destination. Note that although switches look at the MAC address to decide where to forward a frame, routers use the IP address to determine what network to send the data to.

Figure 1-1
A switch is
a central
connectivity
device on the
network.

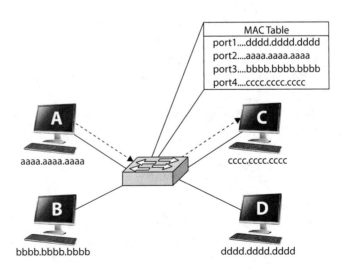

The router has a routing table, which is a list of all the networks that it knows how to reach. A router also includes a *gateway of last resort* (GWLR) setting that is used if the router does not have a route to the destination in its routing table.

Looking at Figure 1-2, you can see two routers labeled R1 and R2. Note that R1 does not have a physical connection to the 14.0.0.0 network. If computer A wanted to send data to computer D, here's what would happen:

1. The data would leave computer A's network card and go to the switch.

2. The switch would forward the frame to the R1 router.

3. The R1 router would look at the destination address of the data and note that the data is destined for computer D on the 14.0.0.0 network.

4. Router R1 would look at its routing table to determine whether it knows how to send data to the 14.0.0.0 network. In this case it does—R1 knows to route, or send, the data to router R2.

5. The data is then sent to router R2.

6. When router R2 receives the data, it looks at the destination address of the data and determines that it needs to send the data to computer D on the LAN.

You will learn more about switches and routers as we progress through the Cisco configuration topics, but at this point I want you to understand that switches are usually used in LANs, while routers are WAN devices. Also note that switches are layer 2 devices that work with MAC addresses, while routers are layer 3 devices that work with IP addresses. You will learn more about layers of the OSI model in the next chapter.

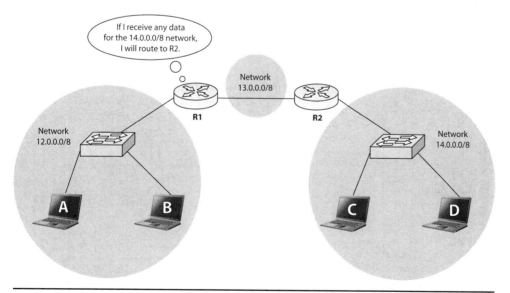

Figure 1-2   A router sends data from one network to another.

EXAM TIP The exam objectives expect you to understand the difference between a layer 2 switch and a layer 3 switch.

Layer 3 Switch A layer 3 switch performs all the functions of a layer 2 switch, but it also has the added functionality of *being a router*. Since most companies purchase a switch to connect their devices and then purchase a router to send data out to the WAN or Internet, Cisco includes layer 3 switches that serve as a router and switch, all in one device. As you will learn later in the "Network Design Models" section, the layer 2 switch is used at the access layer, while the layer 3 switch is used at the core layer.

Connecting to WAN with CSU/DSU

The *channel service unit/data service unit* (CSU/DSU) is a device that enables an organization to connect a high-speed data link from the ISP to the organization's router for access to and from a LAN or WAN. These high-speed connections are usually T1 or T3 connections or their European counterparts, E1 and E3. The CSU/DSU used will be specific to the speed of the line being connected to and from the service provider.

The CSU/DSU device handles signaling over the T1/T3 link, sending data between your router and the service provider. The CSU/DSU performs other functions as well, such as protecting against electrical interference from either side of the link. You may have an *external CSU/DSU* device that connects to the serial port on your organization's router and is used to connect the T1 line from your service provider (see Figure 1-3).

Many routers today come with an internal CSU/DSU module installed, which enables you to connect the router to the T1 line without the use of an external CSU/DSU. Figure 1-4 shows an integrated CSU/DSU built into a Cisco router.

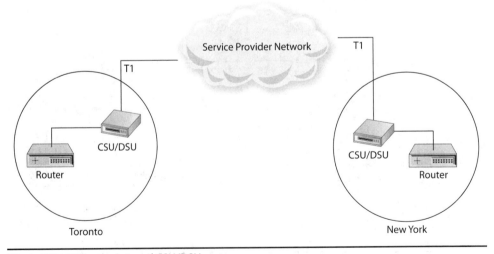

Figure 1-3 Using an external CSU/DSU

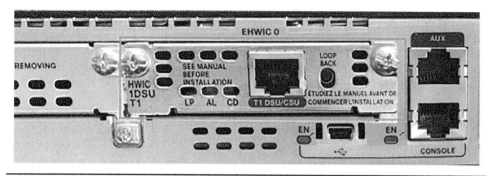

Figure 1-4 An integrated CSU/DSU on a Cisco router

You should be familiar with two other terms related to connecting your router to the WAN: *demarc* and *demarc extension*.

The *demarc*, also known as the *demarcation point*, is the point where the service provider's equipment connects to your building. The term is used to identify which party is responsible for a particular problem. For example, if the equipment that is faulty is on your company's side of the demarc point, it is your company's problem to fix; if the problem is on the service provider's side of the demarc point, the responsibility to solve the problem falls into the service provider's hands.

The term *demarc extension* (Figure 1-5) refers to the area between the connection into your building (from the service provider) and your company's communication equipment. The demarc extension is typically a patch cable that connects the service provider's line to your company's network equipment.

Figure 1-5
Demarcation
point and
demarc
extension

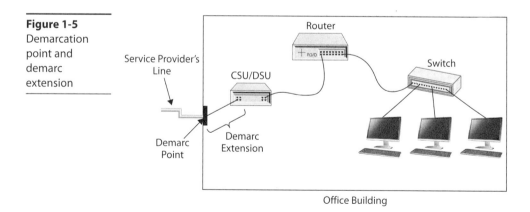

Firewalls

Firewalls control which traffic is allowed to enter a network or system and which traffic should be blocked. When configuring a firewall, you create the rules for allowing and denying traffic based on the protocol, port number, and direction of the traffic. Three major types of firewall are used:

- **Packet filtering firewall**   A packet filtering firewall can filter traffic based on the source and destination IP addresses, the source and destination port numbers, and the protocol used. The downfall of a simple packet filtering firewall is that it does not understand the context of the conversation, so it is easy for a hacker to craft a packet to pass through the firewall.

- **Stateful packet inspection firewall**   Like a packet filtering firewall, a stateful packet inspection firewall filters traffic based on source and destination IP addresses, the source and destination port numbers, and the protocol in use, but it also understands the context of a conversation and will not allow a packet through the firewall unless it suits a specific scenario. For example, if a hacker sends a packet to your network and tries to make it look like the packet is a response from a web site that someone visited, your firewall will know that no one visited that site, so it will not allow the traffic through.

- **Next-generation firewall**   A next-generation firewall (NGFW) is a layer 7 firewall that can inspect the application data and detect malicious packets. A regular firewall filters traffic based on it being HTTP or FTP traffic (using port numbers), but it cannot determine if there is malicious data inside the HTTP or FTP packet. An application-layer NGFW can inspect the application data that exists in the packet and determine whether there is suspicious content inside.

Intrusion Prevention System

An *intrusion prevention system (IPS)* is a security device that monitors activity, logs any suspicious activity, and then takes some form of corrective action. For example, if someone is doing a port scan on the network, the IPS would discover this suspicious activity, log the activity, and then disconnect the system that is performing the port scan from the network.

DHCP

DHCP is responsible for assigning IP address information automatically to systems on the network. The network administrator configures the DHCP server by configuring a *scope* (a range of addresses) that the server can assign addresses from. The DHCP service may configure a client with all the TCP/IP settings, including the subnet mask, the default gateway, and the address of the DNS server.

When a client starts up, it sends out a broadcast message looking for a DHCP server to receive an IP address from. The DHCP server replies with an offer, and the client then requests the address that has been offered. Finally, the DHCP service acknowledges that the client has the address for a period of time (known as the lease duration).

Network Address Translation

NAT enables us to hide our internal network structure from the outside world by having the NAT device receive all outbound packets, take the internal source address out, and replace it with the public IP address of the NAT device. This is beneficial because anyone who intercepts the data on the Internet will believe that the packet came from the NAT device and not the internal computer on the LAN. As a result, anyone who decides to attack the source of the packets will be attacking the NAT device instead, which will typically be a firewall product as well. You will learn more about NAT in Chapter 13.

Wireless Access Points/Access Points

An *access point* is a device added to your network that enables wireless clients to connect to the network. Many organizations that want to have the flexibility of offering wireless connectivity to clients will strategically place wireless access points throughout the building, enabling wireless clients to make connections to the network.

Wireless LAN Controllers

Configuring each access point on a network can be a time-consuming undertaking, with lots of potentials for errors. As a network administrator, you can centrally manage devices instead of needing to run around to each device and perform the configuration. Administrators can use a wireless LAN controller (WLC), or wireless controller for short, to manage access points centrally using the Lightweight Access Point Protocol (LWAPP). This removes the administrative burden of configuring each access point individually. You will learn more about wireless configurations in Chapter 15.

Cisco DNA Center

Cisco DNA Center is an appliance you can purchase that enables you to manage changes to your network devices centrally and simultaneously. The benefit of DNA Center is that you can use a number of software elements, such as scripts, to automate changes to all your devices at one time. You will learn more about Cisco DNA Center in Chapter 18.

Endpoints and Servers

Your network may include endpoints, which could be any number of devices, including the following:

- **Client** A client system, such as a Windows or Linux machine, connects to the network to access resources such as files, printers, or the Internet.

- **Server** A server system provides resources to the network. Examples of server types include a file server, an Active Directory server, a database server, and a web server.

- **Printer** A network printer may be connected to the network to enable other connected devices to print documents.

- **Mobile device** A device such as a laptop, tablet, or smart phone may be connected to the network to access resources.

Collision Domains and Broadcast Domains

The CCT and CCNA certification exams expect you to be familiar with *collision domain* and *broadcast domain*. Let's start with a quick definition of each and then I will expand on the two terms a bit:

- **Collision domain**   In this group of systems, simultaneous data transmissions can collide with one another.
- **Broadcast domain**   In this group of systems, each system can receive other systems' broadcast messages.

Collision Domain

In a collision domain, data transmission collisions can occur. For example, suppose you are using a hub to connect five systems to a network. Because traffic is sent to all ports on the hub, it is possible that if several systems send data at the same time, the data could collide on the network. For this reason, all network ports on a hub (and any devices connected to those ports) are considered parts of a *single collision domain*. This also means that when you cascade a hub off another hub, all hubs are part of the same collision domain.

If you were using a switch to connect the five systems together, each port on the switch would create its own network segment (like a bridge breaks the network down into different network segments). When data is sent by a system connected to the switch, the switch sends the data only to the port that the destination system resides on. For this reason, if another system were to send data at the same time, the data would not collide. As a result, each port on the switch creates a *separate collision domain*.

Broadcast Domain

A broadcast domain is a group of systems that can receive one another's broadcast messages. When using a hub to connect five systems in a network environment, if one system sends a broadcast message, the message is received by all other systems connected to the hub. For this reason, all ports on the hub create a *single broadcast domain*.

Likewise, if all five systems were connected to a switch and one of the systems sent a broadcast message, the broadcast message would be received by all other systems on the network. Therefore, when using a switch, all ports are part of the same broadcast domain as well.

If you wanted to control which systems received broadcast messages, you would have to use a router that does not forward broadcast messages on to other networks. You could also use virtual LANs (VLANs) on a switch, with each VLAN being a different broadcast domain.

 EXAM TIP   Be sure to know the difference between a broadcast domain and collision domain for the CCT and CCNA certification exams. Also, remember that a router is the device you use to create multiple broadcast domains.

Exercise 1-1: Identifying Network Components

In this exercise, you review the different network components by matching the component on the right with the definition on the left.

Definition	Component
_____ A layer 3 device responsible for sending data from one network to another	A. Switch
_____ A device that detects suspicious activity and then takes corrective action	B. Collision domain
_____ A layer 2 device used to connect all systems to the network	C. DHCP
_____ A group of systems that can receive one another's broadcast messages	D. Firewall
_____ A service that assigns IP addresses to other systems and devices on the network	E. Router
_____ The point where the service provider equipment connects to your building	F. Hub
_____ A group of systems in which separate data transmissions could potentially collide	G. IPS
_____ Used to protect a system or device from unwanted traffic	H. Demarc
_____ A layer 1 device used to connect all systems to the network	I. Broadcast domain

Network Design Models

A well-designed network is hierarchical in structure, where each layer in the hierarchy is focused on a specific job function. A well-designed network is also modular, in the sense that it is easy to add components to the network, so that as the company grows, the network can grow. The well-designed network should also be flexible and resilient, meaning that it is always available and includes some form of redundancy.

When designing Cisco networks, we usually follow two common design models: the *three-tier architecture model* and the *collapsed core architecture model*. Other network architectures are discussed here as well.

Three-tier Architecture

The three-tier architecture model is a common model used by Cisco network professionals to design a well-performing Cisco network. Following are the three layers:

- **Access layer** This layer is at the bottom of the hierarchy; it enables end users to connect to the network via switches. The access layer provides features that enable you to isolate traffic between different types of users and divide broadcast domains. A switch located on each floor of a building would represent this layer.

- **Distribution layer**   The second layer from the bottom, or the middle layer, enables you to control who can access what part of the network by using features such as routing, access control lists (ACLs), and network access policies. A distribution layer could be a central layer 3 switch residing in two buildings, in which each switch could access the layer 3 switch of the other building to connect.
- **Core layer**   The top layer of the model represents the backbone of the network. This layer is typically used to connect the networks of different buildings together. It includes a number of core routers that are responsible for delivering traffic to and from the network.

Collapsed Core (Two-tier) Architecture

A small organization may not need to use a three-layer model, so it can combine the distribution and core layers into a single layer known as a *collapsed layer*. This makes the collapsed core layer a two-layer model, comprising the *access layer* and the *collapsed distribution/core layer*. In a typical scenario, this may be used in a small company that uses only a few floors in a building for their network. Each floor would have a switch (access layer) that enables clients on that floor to connect to the network. Each floor switch would then connect to a central switch in the building, which is connected to a router to access the WAN or Internet.

Spine-leaf Architecture

Another example of a two-tier architecture is the *spine-leaf architecture,* in which the lower layer is the leaf layer that contains the access switches that enable devices to connect to the network. The leaf layer switches then connect to the spine layer switches, which connect all the switches to the rest of the network. The spine-leaf model is shown in Figure 1-6. Note that the leaf layer switches are access layer switches with a full mesh topology that connects to the spine layer switches.

Small Office/Home Office

A SOHO network is a totally different network topology that is designed for a very small number of devices that need access to a network and the Internet. A SOHO network typically involves a high-speed Internet connection into a home or office that connects

Figure 1-6
Spine-leaf
network
topology

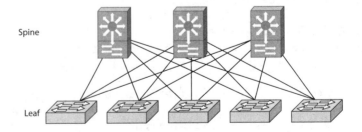

to an ISP's modem. The ISP's modem is connected to a WAN/Internet port on a wireless router, which usually has four switch ports that you can use to connect clients using unshielded twisted pair (UTP) cabling. A wireless router in a SOHO network could also provide a number of services, such as being a DHCP server, a NAT device, a firewall, or a wireless access point.

On-premises vs. Cloud

In most discussions of networking environments today, you will hear the terms *on-premises* versus *the cloud*. On-premises networking capabilities or devices exist on your physical network at your office location. If networking capabilities or devices reside in the cloud, this occurs at a cloud provider's network. For example, you may have a wireless LAN controller that is used to configure multiple wireless access points from a central point as an on-premises device (in your office), or you may use a cloud service, which means that these services are provided to your location by a cloud provider. One of the benefits of cloud-based solutions is that the provider typically handles issues such as high availability of the service so you don't have to.

Network Topologies

When you connect devices into a network, you need to decide which topology to use. The *topology* of the network is the layout of the network, and you can choose from a handful of network topologies. Figure 1-7 shows examples of four topologies used by different media types.

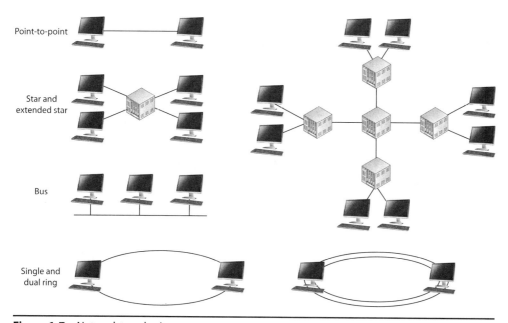

Figure 1-7 Network topologies

A *point-to-point* topology has a single connection between two components. In this topology, two components can directly communicate without interference from other components. These types of connections are not common when many components need to be connected together. An example of a point-to-point topology is two routers connected across a dedicated WAN link.

In a *star* topology, a central device has many point-to-point connections to other components. Star topologies are used in environments in which many components need to be connected. An example of a media type that uses a star topology is 1000BaseTx Ethernet. When connecting components together, you connect all of the devices, such as clients and servers, to a central switch. The main problem with a star topology is that if the center of the star fails, no components can communicate with others. To solve this problem, an extended star topology can be used. An extended star topology is basically multiple interconnected star topologies.

In a *bus* topology, all components are connected to and share a single wire. Bus topologies were common many years ago with network architectures such as 10Base5 and 10Base2 Ethernet. With a bus topology, if any system sends data on the wire, the data travels the entire length of the wire. Special types of connectors, or transceivers, are used to connect devices to the bus cabling. For example, in the old 10Base5, each device connected to the coaxial cable via a vampire tap. This device taps into the single strand of coaxial cable and provides the physical connection from a networking device to the single strand of cable.

In a *ring* topology, device one connects to device two, device two connects to device three, and so on to the last device, which connects back to the first device. Ring topologies can be implemented as a single ring or a dual ring. Dual rings are typically used when you need redundancy. For example, if one of the components fails in the ring, the ring can wrap itself, as shown in Figure 1-8, to provide a single, functional ring. FDDI is an example of a network architecture that uses a dual ring topology to connect systems to the network. Single ring topologies lack this type of redundancy feature and as a result, if there is a break in the ring, the network goes down.

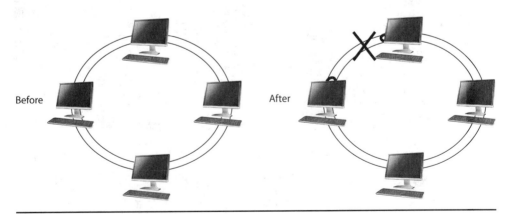

Figure 1-8   Dual rings and redundancy

NOTE   Token Ring and FDDI are examples of network architectures that use a ring topology. These are rarely used in networks today.

Physical vs. Logical Topologies

A *physical* topology describes how components are physically cabled together. For instance, 1000BaseT networks have a physical star topology and FDDI uses a physical dual ring topology. A *logical* topology describes how components communicate across the physical topology. The physical and logical topologies are independent of each other. For example, any variety of Ethernet uses a logical bus topology when components communicate, regardless of the physical layout of the cabling. This means that in Ethernet, you might be using 1000BaseT with a physical star topology to connect components together; however, these components are using a logical bus topology to communicate.

Token Ring is another good example of a network architecture that has a different physical topology from its logical one. Physically, Token Ring uses a star topology, similar to 1000BaseT Ethernet. This means that each system is physically connected to a central device, but logically, Token Ring components use a ring topology to communicate between devices. This can create confusion when you are trying to determine how components are connected together and how they communicate. FDDI, on the other hand, is straightforward. FDDI's physical and logical topologies are the same: a ring.

Table 1-2 shows common network architectures and their physical and logical topologies.

Fully and Partially Meshed Topologies

Meshing generically describes how components are connected together. Two types of meshed topologies are used: *partial* and *full*. In a partially meshed environment, every device is *not* connected to every other device. In a fully meshed environment, every component *is* connected to every other component. Figure 1-9 shows examples of these two types of topologies.

Note that, like physical and logical topologies, partial and full mesh can be seen from both a physical view and a logical one. For example, in a physical bus topology, all the components are fully meshed, since they are all connected to the same piece of wire—this is both a physical and a logical fully meshed topology and is common in LAN topologies.

Network Architecture	Physical Topology	Logical Topology
Ethernet	Bus, star, or point-to-point	Bus
FDDI	Ring	Ring
Token Ring	Star	Ring

Table 1-2   Examples of Physical and Logical Topologies

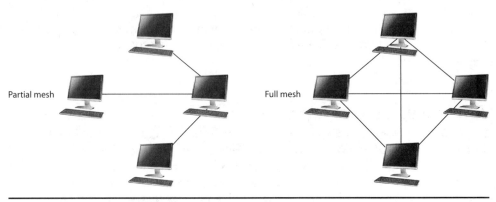

Figure 1-9   Partially and fully meshed topologies

WANs, on the other hand, because of their cost, commonly use partially meshed topologies to reduce the cost of connecting the components and locations. For example, in the partially meshed network shown at left in Figure 1-3, the top, left, and bottom components can all communicate via the device on the right. This communication introduces a delay in the transmission, but it reduces the cost, since not as many connections are needed.

 TIP   The formula used to determine the number of links needed to fully mesh a WAN is $N \times (N - 1) / 2$, where N is the number of locations. For example, if you had 10 locations, you would need 45 links ($10 \times (10 - 1) / 2$) to fully mesh these sites. In addition to cost being an inhibiting factor, the number of interfaces required on WAN devices as well as the management of these connections can quickly become overwhelming as you start interconnecting more and more locations.

Types of Cabling

LANs typically use either copper or fiber-optic cabling. Copper cabling can include one strand of copper across which an electrical voltage is transmitted, or it can be many strands of copper. Fiber-optic cabling uses light-emitting diodes (LEDs) and lasers to transmit data across a glass core. With this transmission, light is used to represent binary 1s and 0s: if light is on the wire, this represents a 1; if there is no light, this represents a 0.

Copper Cabling

Between copper and fiber, implementing copper cabling is less expensive. Three types of copper cabling have been used with networks over the years:

- **Thicknet**   Uses a thick coaxial cable (no longer used in today's networks)
- **Thinnet**   Uses a thin coaxial cable (no longer used in today's networks)

- **Unshielded twisted pair (UTP)**   Uses four pairs of wires in the cable, where each pair is periodically twisted

Of the three copper cabling types, UTP is the most common today, mainly because it is cheaper than the other two and is easier to install and troubleshoot. Given its advantages, copper cabling, including UTP, has two disadvantages:

- It is susceptible to electromagnetic interference (EMI) and radio frequency interference (RFI).
- Distances of the cable are limited to a short haul (100 meters).

UTP's internal copper cables are either 22- or 24-gauge in diameter. UTP for Ethernet has 100-ohm impedance, so you can't use just any UTP wiring, like the cable that is commonly found with telephones, for example. Each of the eight wires inside the cable is colored: some solid, some striped. Two pairs of the wires carry a true voltage, commonly called "tip" (T1–T4), and the other four carry an inverse voltage, commonly called "ring" (R1–R4). Today, people commonly call these *positive* and *negative* wires, respectively. A pair consists of a positive and negative wire, such as T1 and R1, T2 and R2, and so on, where each pair is twisted down the length of the cable.

UTP Categories

To help differentiate between the different kinds of UTP cabling, different categories were created. Table 1-3 shows the categories of UTP cabling.

Each of the endpoints of a UTP cable has an RJ-45 connector, which is a male connector that plugs into a female RJ-45 receptacle. The RJ-45 connector is similar to what you see on a telephone connector (RJ-11), except that the RJ-45 is about 50 percent larger in size and holds eight wires instead of four wires, as is the case with RJ-11.

Category	Description
Category 1	Used for telephone connections (not suitable for data)
Category 2	Used for data connections up to 4 Mbps—Token Ring
Category 3	Used for data connections up to 10 Mbps—Ethernet 10BaseT
Category 4	Used for data connections up to 16 Mbps—Token Ring
Category 5	Used for data connections up to 100 Mbps—Ethernet
Category 5E	Used for data connections up to 1 Gbps (gigabit per second)—Ethernet
Category 6	Used for data connections up to 1 Gbps (24-gauge)—Ethernet
Category 6A	Used in 10 Gigabit Ethernet networks with speeds up to 10 Gbps
Category 7	Used in 10 Gigabit Ethernet networks with speeds up to 10 Gbps

Table 1-3   UTP Categories

Pin	Color
1	White wire / orange stripe
2	Orange wire
3	White wire / green stripe
4	Blue wire
5	White wire / blue stripe
6	Green wire
7	White wire / brown stripe
8	Brown wire

Table 1-4 UTP Pinout Colors

Cabling Devices

With today's implementation of Ethernet over copper, two components make up the connection: an RJ-45 connector and a Category 5, 5E, 6, or 6A UTP cable. As mentioned earlier, the UTP cable has eight wires in it (four pairs of wires). Two types of implementations are used for the pinouts of the two sides of the wiring: *straight-through* and *crossover*. *Pinout* refers to the order of the wires and the pins they connect to within the RJ-45 interface. Two standards define the cabling pinouts: 568B is used for both straight-through cables and one end of a crossover cable. 568B wiring colors are listed in Table 1-4.

A straight-through Ethernet UTP cable has pin 1 on one end of the cable connected to pin 1 on the other end of the cable, pin 2 to pin 2, and so on. A straight-through cable is used to connect dissimilar devices together, for example, between a computer and a switch or a switch and a router.

EXAM TIP The CCT and the CCNA certification exams will test you on when to use a straight-through cable, and here is the golden rule to remember: Use a straight-through cable to connect dissimilar devices, such as connecting a computer to a switch, a computer to a hub, a switch to a router.

Figure 1-10 shows an example of straight-through connections between dissimilar devices.

Figure 1-10 Straight-through connections

PC/Server   Switch   PC/Server   Hub

Router   Switch   Router   Hub

Straight-through cable: ─────────

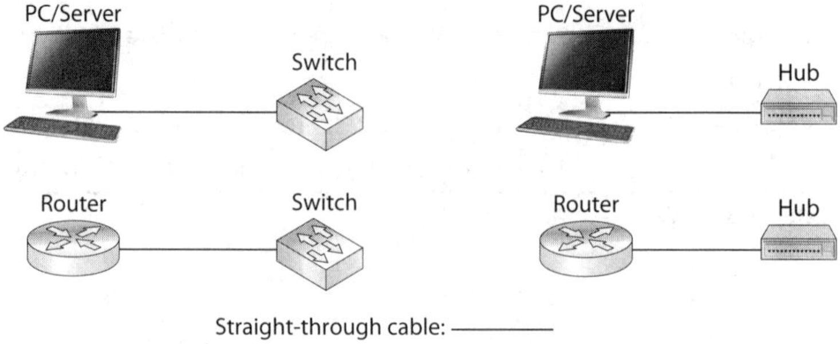

A crossover UTP Ethernet cable crosses over two sets of wires: pin 1 on one side is connected to pin 3 on the other side, and pin 2 is connected to pin 6. For the CCNA exam, remember that a crossover cable is used to connect similar devices together such as two computers together, two switches together, or a hub to a switch. You use a crossover cable when connecting similar devices together such as the following (shown in Figure 1-11):

- Computer to computer
- A hub to another hub
- A switch to another switch
- A hub to a switch
- A router to a computer
- A PC, router, or file server to another PC, router, or file server

EXAM TIP Remember for the CCNA exam when to use a straight-through and when to use a crossover cable. An Ethernet crossover cable crosses over pins 1 and 3 with pins 2 and 6 on one end of the cable.

Sometimes the Ethernet network interface card (NIC) female receptacle will give you a clue as to the type of cable to use. If an *X* appears on the port and the other port doesn't have an *X* label, use a straight-through cable. If neither device has an *X* or both have an *X*, use a crossover cable. In some instances, this setting can be changed in software with a command or in hardware through the use of a dual inline package (DIP) switch, which enables you to use the cable type that you currently have available.

Figure 1-11
Crossover
connections

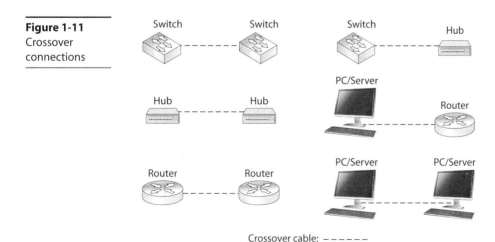

NOTE Many vendors' switches and devices support autosensing for the cable type. For example, you may be able to use a straight-through Ethernet cable between two switches. For exam purposes, however, you should know the information in the previous Exam Tips.

Fiber

Fiber-optic cabling is typically used to provide very high speeds and to span connections across very large distances. For example, speeds of 100 Gbps and distances greater than 10 kilometers are achievable through the use of fiber—copper cannot come close to these feats. However, fiber-optic cabling does have its disadvantages: it is expensive to implement, difficult to troubleshoot, and difficult to install.

EXAM TIP Fiber cabling is not affected by EMI and RFI, whereas copper cabling is. Because of issues of spanning copper between buildings in a campus network, fiber is the recommended cabling type.

Two types of fiber are used for data connections: multimode fiber (MMF) and single-mode fiber (SMF). MMF transmits 850- or 1300-nanometer (nm) wavelengths of light (light in the infrared spectrum, which you can't see with the naked eye). Fiber thickness for MMF is 62.5/125 microns. The core and cladding diameter (thickness of the actual cabling) is in the 50 to 100 micron range for MMF. The 850/1300-nm wavelengths equate to frequencies in the terahertz (THz) range. The light is transmitted using an LED. When transmitting a signal, the light source is bounced off of the inner cladding (shielding) surrounding the fiber. MMF's relatively large core diameter supports the propagation of multiple longitudinal modes (that is, different light paths) at a given wavelength; thus the term *multimode* is used. These multiple modes cause dispersion (signal spreading), which effectively limits the data speeds carried on the fiber to the hundreds-of-Mbps range. A good illustration of this process is when you turn on a flashlight close to a wall: as you move away from the wall, the diameter of the light gets larger and larger, showing dispersion.

SMF transmits 1300- or 1550-nm light and uses a laser as the light source. Because lasers provide a higher output than LEDs, SMF can span more than 10 kilometers in distance and have speeds up to 100 Gbps. Because of SMF's very small core diameter, only a single longitudinal mode is propagated at a given wavelength—hence the term *single-mode*. Since only a single mode is propagated, SMF exhibits less dispersion (that is, signal spreading) than MMF and can therefore support much higher data speeds than MMF (100+ Gbps).

The past decade has seen many advances in the use and deployment of fiber. One major enhancement is wavelength division multiplexing (WDM) and dense WDM (DWDM). WDM allows more than two wavelengths (signals) on the same piece of fiber, increasing the number of connections. DWDM allows yet more wavelengths, which are more closely spaced together: more than 200 wavelengths can be multiplexed into a light stream on a single piece of fiber. Obviously, one of the advantages of DWDM is that it provides flexibility and transparency of the protocols and traffic carried across the fiber.

For example, one wavelength can be used for a point-to-point connection, another for an Ethernet connection, another for an IP connection, and yet another for an ATM connection. Use of DWDM provides scalability and enables carriers to provision new connections *without* having to install new fiber lines, so they can add new connections in a very short period after you order them.

Let's talk about some of the terms used in fiber and how they affect distance and speed. *Cabling* provides the protective outer coating as well as the inner cladding. The inner cladding is denser to allow the light source to bounce off of it. In the middle of the cable is the *fiber* itself, which is used to transmit the signal. The index of refraction (IOR) affects the speed of the light source: it's the ratio of the speed of light in a vacuum to the speed of light in the fiber. In a vacuum, no variables affect the transmission; however, anytime you send something across a medium like fiber or copper, the media itself will exhibit properties that will affect the transmission, causing possible delays. IOR is used to measure these differences. Basically, IOR measures the density of the fiber; the denser the fiber, the slower the light travels through it.

The *loss factor* is used to describe any signal loss in the fiber before the light source gets to the end of the fiber. *Connector loss* occurs when a connector joins two pieces of fiber: a slight signal loss is expected. Also, the longer the fiber, the greater the likelihood that the signal strength will decrease by the time it reaches the end of the cable. This is called *attenuation*.

Two other terms describe signal degradation. *Microbending* occurs when a wrinkle in the fiber, typically where the cable is slightly bent, causes a distortion in the light source. *Macrobending* occurs when the light source leaks from the fiber, typically from a bend in the fiber cable. To overcome degradation over long distances, *optical amplifiers* can be used. These are similar to an Ethernet repeater or hub. A good amplifier, such as an erbium-doped fiber amplifier (EDFA), converts a light source directly to another light source, providing for the best reproduction of the original signal. Other amplifiers convert light to an electrical signal and then back to light, which can cause degradation in the signal quality.

Two main standards are used to describe the transmission of signals across a fiber: SONET (Synchronous Optical Network) and SDH (Synchronous Digital Hierarchy). SONET is defined by the Exchange Carriers Standards Association (ECSA) and American National Standards Institute (ANSI) and is typically used in North America. SDH is an international standard used throughout most of the world (with the exception of North America). Both of these standards define the physical layer framing used to transmit light sources, which also includes overhead for the transmission. Three types of overhead are experienced:

- **Section overhead (SOH)**   Overhead for the link between two devices, such as repeaters
- **Line overhead (LOH)**   Overhead for one or more sections connecting network devices, such as hubs
- **Path overhead (POH)**   Overhead for one or more lines connecting two devices that assemble and disassemble frames, such as carrier switches or a router's fiber interface

Common Term	SONET Term	SDH Term	Connection Rate
OC-1	STS-1	n/a	51.84 Mbps
OC-3	STS-3	STM-1	155.52 Mbps
OC-12	STS-12	STM-4	622.08 Mbps
OC-48	STS-48	STM-16	2488.32 Mbps
OC-192	STS-192	STM-64	9953.28 Mbps

Table 1-5 Fiber Connection Types

Typically, either a ring or point-to-point topology is used to connect the devices. With carrier metropolitan area networks (MANs), the most common implementation is through the use of rings. Auto-protection switching (APS) can be used to provide line redundancy: in case of failure on a primary line, a secondary line can automatically be utilized. Table 1-5 provides an overview of the more common connection types for SONET and SDH. Note that SONET uses Synchronous Transport Signal (STS) and that SDH uses Synchronous Transport Module (STM) to describe the signal.

The most common types of fiber-optic connectors, and their typical uses, are listed here:

- **Fiber Channel (FC)**   Used by service providers in their patch panels
- **Local Connector (LC)**   Used for enterprise equipment and commonly connect to small form-factor pluggable (SFP) modules
- **Standard Connector (SC)**   Used for enterprise equipment
- **Straight Tip (ST)**   Used for patch panels because of their durability

Traditionally, SC was the most commonly used connector type; however, LCs are becoming more and more common.

Table 1-6 briefly compares both the copper and fiber cable types.

Cable	Distance	Data Rates	Comparison
UTP	100 meters	10 Mbps–10 Gbps	Easy to install but susceptible to interference
Coaxial	500 meters	10–100 Mbps	Easy to install but difficult to troubleshoot (no longer used for Ethernet)
Fiber	10 kilometers	10 Mbps–100 Gbps	Difficult and expensive to install, difficult to troubleshoot, but can span very long distances and is not susceptible to interference

Table 1-6 Cable Type Comparisons

Access Methods

You now know that a network uses a topology—which is the layout of the network—and you know that some form of media such as cabling connects all hosts on the network. We have discussed the three major types of cabling: coax, twisted-pair, and fiber-optic cabling.

This section will identify various access methods. An access method determines how a host will place data on the wire: does the host have to wait its turn or can it just place the data on the wire whenever it wants? The answer is determined by three major access methods: CSMA/CD, CSMA/CA, and token passing. Let's look at each of these access methods.

CSMA/CD

Carrier-sense multiple access with collision detection (CSMA/CD) is one of the most popular access methods in use today. With CSMA/CD, every host has equal access to the wire and can place data on the wire when the wire is free from traffic. If a host wants to place data on the wire, it will "sense" the wire and determine whether a signal is already present. If it is, the host will wait to transmit the data; if the wire is free, the host will send the data.

The problem with the process just described is that if two systems "sense" the wire at the same time, they will both send data at the same time if the wire is free. When the two pieces of data are sent on the wire at the same time, they will collide with one another and the data will be destroyed. If the data is destroyed in transit, the data will need to be retransmitted. Consequently, after a collision, each host will wait a variable length of time before retransmitting the data (they don't want the data to collide again), thereby preventing a collision the second time. When a system determines that the data has collided and then retransmits the data, this is known as *collision detection*.

To summarize, with CSMA/CD, before a host sends data on the network, it will "sense" (CS) the wire to ensure that it is free of traffic. Multiple systems have equal access to the wire (MA), and if there is a collision, a host will detect that collision (CD) and retransmit the data.

CSMA/CA

Carrier-sense multiple access with collision avoidance (CSMA/CA) is not as popular as CSMA/CD, and for good reason. With CSMA/CA, before a host sends data on the wire, it will "sense" the wire to see if it is free of signals. If the wire is free, the host will try to "avoid" a collision by sending a signal out, letting all others know they should wait before sending data. This helps prevent collisions from occurring, but it involves sending more data out on the wire.

Token Passing

With both CSMA/CD and CSMA/CA, the possibility of collisions is always there, and the more hosts that are placed on the wire, the greater the chances of collisions, because you have more systems "waiting'" for the wire to become free so that they can send their data.

Token passing takes a totally different approach in determining how a system can place data on the wire. With token passing, an empty packet is running around on the wire—the "token." To place data on the wire, the system needs to wait for the token; once the system has the token and it is free of data, the system can place data on the wire. Since there is only one token and a host needs to have the token to "talk," it is impossible to have collisions in a token-passing environment.

For example, if Workstation 1 wants to send data on the wire, the workstation would wait for the token, which is circling the network millions of times per second. Once the token reaches Workstation 1, the workstation takes the token off the network, fills it with data, marks the token as being used so that no other systems try to fill the token with data, and then places the token back on the wire heading for the destination host.

All systems will look at the data, but they will not process it, since it is not destined for them. However, the system that is the intended destination will read the data and send the token back to the sender as a confirmation. Once the token has reached the original sender, the token is unflagged as being used and released as an empty token onto the network.

Network Architectures

Now that you have a better understanding of cabling, topologies, and access methods, let's examine how these are used to create the different network architectures. The following sections discuss the different implementations of Ethernet architectures used over the years and found in today's networks.

Ethernet

Many physical layer standards define the physical properties of an Ethernet implementation. One of the most common is IEEE 802.3 10Mb. Table 1-7 shows some of the 10-Mbps standards. The most common copper cabling for Ethernet is UTP.

Ethernet supports a bus topology—physical or logical. In a bus topology, every device is connected to the same piece of wire and all devices see every frame. For example, 10Base5 uses one long, thick piece of coaxial cable. NICs tap into this wire using a vampire tap. With 10Base2, the devices are connected together by many pieces of wire using BNC connectors, commonly called T-taps: one end of the T-tap connects to the

Ethernet Type	Distance Limitation	Cable Type	Interface Type	Physical Topology	Logical Topology
10Base5	500 meters	Thick coaxial cable—50 ohm (*thicknet*)	AUI	Bus	Bus
10Base2	185 meters	Thin coaxial cable (*thinnet*)	BNC	Bus	Bus
10BaseT	100 meters	UTP cabling (CAT 3, 4, 5, 5E, 6, and 6A)	RJ-45	Star (hub)	Bus

Table 1-7 10-Mbps Ethernet Properties

NIC and the other two connect to the two Ethernet cables that are part of the bus. Both endpoints of the cable must be terminated with a terminator cap. With 10BaseT, all devices are connected to a hub, where the hub provides a logical bus topology. All of these 10 Mbps Ethernet solutions support only half-duplex: they can send or receive, but they cannot do both simultaneously.

 EXAM TIP   For the exam, you should be familiar with these connection types. Half-duplex connections enable devices either to send or receive in both directions, but only one direction at a time. Additionally, devices such as a hub that are half-duplex devices experience a high level of collisions. Full-duplex connections can simultaneously send and receive without any collisions occurring. Switches are considered full-duplex devices and this is one of the reasons why they have replaced hubs on the network.

Fast Ethernet

Ethernet 10Base2 and 10Base5 haven't been used in years because of the difficulty in troubleshooting network problems based on the cabling they use. And 10BaseT networks have been supplanted by higher speed Ethernet solutions, such as Fast Ethernet and Gigabit Ethernet. All Ethernet standards uses CSMA/CD as the access method with Fast Ethernet running at 100 Mbps (while the older Ethernet ran at 10 Mbps). The older 10 Mbps Ethernet is half duplex, meaning you can send and receive data, but only one direction at a time. Fast Ethernet is full duplex (meaning you can send and receive data at the same time).

Table 1-8 shows the different implementations of Fast Ethernet. Fast Ethernet supports both half- and full-duplex connections. With full-duplex connections, a device can send *and* receive simultaneously but requires a point-to-point connection that doesn't involve a hub.

 EXAM TIP   For the exam be familiar with the Fast Ethernet and Gigabit Ethernet standards. You do not have to worry about the older standards such as 10Base2, 10Base5, and 10BaseT.

Ethernet Type	Distance Limitation	Cable Type	Cabling	Physical Topology	Logical Topology
100BaseTX	100 meters	UTP CAT 5, 5E, 6, 6A	RJ-45	Star	Bus
100BaseFX	400 meters half-duplex, 2000 meters full-duplex	MMF 62.5/125 micron with SC and ST connectors	RJ-45	Star	Bus
100BaseT4	100 meters	UTP CAT 3, 4, 5	RJ-45	Star	Bus

Table 1-8   Fast (100 Mbps) Ethernet Properties

Ethernet Type	Distance Limitation	Cable Type
1000BaseCX	25 meters	STP copper
1000BaseLX	3–10 kilometers	SMF
1000BaseSX	275 meters	MMF
1000BaseT	100 meters	CAT 5E and CAT 6 UTP (RJ-45)
1000BaseZX	100 meters	SMF

Table 1-9 1-Gbps Ethernet Properties

Gigabit Ethernet

Gigabit Ethernet is defined in IEEE 802.3z. To achieve 1-Gbps speeds, IEEE adopted the ANSI X3T11 Fiber Channel standard for the physical layer implementation. The physical layer is different from Ethernet and Fast Ethernet in that it uses an 8B/10B encoding scheme to code the physical layer information when transmitting it across the wire. The IEEE standard has been around for about a decade. Gigabit Ethernet connections are commonly used for uplink connections (switch-to-switch) and server applications. Table 1-9 shows the different implementations of Gigabit Ethernet.

10-Gigabit Ethernet

Standards for 10-Gigabit Ethernet (10,000 Mbps) have been developed that use fiber-optic cabling or UTP:

- **10GBaseSR**   Runs at 10 Gbps and uses "short-range" MMF cable, which has a maximum distance of 400 meters (depending on fiber type used)
- **10GBaseLR**   Runs at 10 Gbps and uses "long-range" SMF cable, which has a maximum distance of 10 kilometers
- **10GBaseER**   Runs at 10 Gbps and uses "extra-long-range" SMF cable, which has a maximum distance of 40 kilometers
- **10GBaseT**   Runs at 10 Gbps using CAT 6a UTP cabling, which has a maximum distance of 100 meters

 EXAM TIP   Be sure to be familiar with the Fast Ethernet, Gigabit Ethernet, and 10-Gigabit Ethernet architectures for the CCT and CCNA exams. Be familiar with the speeds, cable types, connectors, and maximum distance range of each architecture.

Serial, Optical, and Other Architectures

In addition to the very common Ethernet architectures, you should be familiar with other network technologies, including serial technologies, optical technologies, and Power over Ethernet (PoE). This section gives an overview of each of these different connection types and architectures.

Serial

Many network technologies deliver data in serial fashion, which means they deliver the data in a stream of bits, one after the other (versus a parallel technology that delivers multiple bits at one time). Serial connections are typically used with WAN connections, enabling your network to connect to other networks through a provider.

Optical

There are also special WAN versions of 10-Gigabit Ethernet that use fiber-optic cabling to connect to a SONET network:

- **10GBaseSW**   The 10-Gigabit Ethernet standard for short-range MMF cable, which has a maximum distance of 100 meters
- **10GBaseLW**   The 10-Gigabit Ethernet standard for long-range SMF cable, which has a maximum distance of 10 kilometers
- **10GBaseEW**   The 10-Gigabit Ethernet standard for extended-range SMF cable, which has a distance of up to 40 kilometers

Concepts of PoE

PoE is known as the IEEE 802.af standard and is a method of delivering power to devices using the Ethernet port. PoE has improved over time with what is known as PoE+, which is the 802.at standard. The benefit of PoE is that a device that supports PoE does not need a separate power cable to power the device; it can receive the power through the Ethernet port from the switch it is plugged into. Common examples of devices that can receive PoE are IP phones, wireless access points, and network cameras.

For PoE to work, the switch must have PoE-supported ports that the device would connect to. The device would also have to be a PoE-enabled device that can receive a PoE connection.

GBICs

A *gigabit interface converter* (GBIC) is an input/output (I/O) device that is plugged into a Gigabit Ethernet interface (and 10-Gbps connectors) and provides various interface connector types such as those listed in Table 1-9. The advantage of GBICs is that when you purchase a device that supports GBICs, your device comes with a Gigabit Ethernet port and you buy the appropriate GBIC interface connector based on the cabling you'll be using. This means that if you ever need to change your cable requirements, you need to swap only your current GBIC for one that matches your new cabling needs. Most GBICs are *hot-swappable*, but you should always check the device manufacturer's instructions before inserting or removing them.

 NOTE   You don't have to use one Ethernet media type and/or speed—it is very common to see a mixture of media types and connection speeds, based on specific needs. For example, it is common to see 100BaseTX using Category 5 or 5E cabling for user connections, 1000BaseTX with Category 5E cabling for server connections, and 1- or 10-Gbps fiber connections for switch-to-switch connections.

GBIC connectors are common in company networks, especially in data centers and for uplink connections in campus networks. The original standard, 802.3ak, in 2004 defined 10 Gbps over twin-axial cable, commonly called InfiniBand. 10-Gigabit Ethernet requires full-duplex connections. There are many different standards for 10 Gbps, and they primarily differ in the connectors, cabling, and how information is transmitted. The standard today is 802.3-2012, which accommodates all the 10 Gbps, 1 Gbps, and previous Ethernet standards. Note that GBIC ports and connectors have been superseded by *Small Form-factor Pluggable* (SFP) ports that you will see in Chapter 6.

Troubleshooting Interface and Cable Issues

When you're connecting devices to the network, a number of common issues may arise that deal with network connectivity and communication problems. The following are some common issues and how you can troubleshoot them.

Collisions

With Ethernet networks, it is possible for two systems to send data on the network at the same time and for that data to collide. This was a common issue when network hubs were used, because the hub would send the data to every port on the hub. Using network switches will help prevent collisions, because the switch sends the data only to the port that the destination system is connected to. Also, if the line is busy with traffic, the switch can store the packet until the line is free of a signal.

Errors

Network or packet errors can occur if there is a faulty network card or faulty cables. If corrupt packets are received, the sending system will need to retransmit the data, which in the end uses up more bandwidth.

Mismatch Duplex

The duplex setting on either end of the communication should match. As we progress into configuring interfaces on the Cisco devices, you will learn how to configure the duplex setting, but for now know that both ends of the communication should have the same duplex setting or network errors will occur. There are three types of duplexing:

- **Simplex** Data travels in one direction only, either sent or received by the interface.
- **Half duplex** Data can be sent or received by the interface, but not at the same time.
- **Full duplex** Data can be sent and received by the interface at the same time.

Speed

The speed of the network interface must match the speed at the other end of the communication. For example, the speed should be set to either 100 Mbps or 1000 Mbps, whichever matches the speed of the device you are connecting to. Network cards and ports on your Cisco devices include an autodetect setting that will automatically detect the speed that is being used.

Virtualization Fundamentals

Virtualization technology has taken off over the last few years, with companies consolidating many existing servers down to one physical server and running each server in a virtual machine. The virtual machine uses resources such as RAM and hard disk space from the actual physical server.

The benefit of virtualization technology is that, overall, companies use minimal resources such as memory, processor, and disk space on the actual physical servers they pay for. For example, suppose your company wants to have an e-mail server, so you spend thousands of dollars on this server, but once the e-mail server is installed and running, you are only using 30 percent of the RAM you purchased and 20 percent of the processing power. Then the company wants a database server and purchases a new physical server for you to install the database server software on. This doesn't make sense, though, because the original system you purchased is underutilized. In this day and age, you can use virtualization software that enables you to run both the e-mail server and database server on the same physical server. Products such as VMware and Microsoft Hyper-V enable you to run machines in a virtual environment.

Hypervisors

Virtualization of systems is provided by the *hypervisor*. Also known as the virtual machine monitor (VMM), the hypervisor is the software component that enables you to create and run virtual machines on the system. When you install the hypervisor on a system, that system is called the host system, while each virtual machine is known as a guest system.

There are two different types of hypervisors:

- **Type I**   This hypervisor type is software that runs directly on top of the hardware, which then has the host operating system running as a parent virtual machine. This enables the hypervisor to control access to the hardware from the host and the guest systems. These are also known as bare-metal hypervisors, because they run directly on top of the hardware. Microsoft Hyper-V and VMware ESXi servers are examples of type I hypervisors.

- **Type II**   A type II hypervisor involves having the OS installed on top of the hardware, and then installing virtualization software that will create VMs. Examples of type II hypervisors are VMware Workstation and Oracle VM VirtualBox.

Virtual Networking Components

With virtualization software, you can virtualize a number of different types of networking components. The following is a partial list:

- **Virtual switches**   Being able to create virtual switches enables you to place different virtual machines on different virtual networks.

- **Virtual routers**   You can connect different virtual switches together by virtual routers to route traffic between the different virtual switches (networks). Companies such as Cisco offer virtual versions of their routers and firewalls that you manage the same way you would the actual physical device.

- **Virtual firewall**   You can create virtual firewalls to control what traffic can enter or leave the different virtual networks.

- **Virtual NICs**   Virtualization software typically enables you to create virtual network cards in each VM and then connect those virtual network cards to a virtual switch, or map it to a physical network card so that the VM can participate on the real network.

- **Software-defined networking**   Software-defined networking (SDN) is a networking strategy that separates networking functionality into either a control plane (a routing mechanism) or a data plane (the different destinations). Using SDN creates a more dynamic and manageable network, because it is easy to change the configuration and move devices between networks.

- **Virtual desktops**   Companies can have users running virtual desktop systems, which are virtual machines stored on a central server and already configured for a group of applications the user would use. Virtual desktops use virtualization technology such as Hyper-V or VMware.

- **Virtual servers**   One of the most common virtualization technologies involves running multiple servers on one physical server, which saves on hardware cost and offers environmental benefits such as less power consumption due to the lower number of physical machines. Virtual servers use virtualization technology such as Hyper-V or VMware.

Chapter Review

This chapter focused on two topics: an introduction to networks and network topologies. A network connects components across a distance to enable the sharing of resources such as applications and data, printers, and network storage. Characteristics to consider when implementing and maintaining a network design include cost, security, speed, topology, scalability, reliability, and availability. Components common to a network include cabling, computers, switches, routers, firewalls, wireless access points, and others. Networks come in all shapes and sizes: central office, branch office, SOHO, and mobile users.

Network topologies describe how network components are physically cabled and logically how network components communicate with each other. Topology types include point-to-point, star, bus, and ring. Meshing describes how components are interconnected. In a fully meshed topology, every component has direct communication with every other component. In a partially meshed topology, not every component has direct communication with every other component; a component may need to communicate with an intermediate component to get information to the actual destination.

Quick Review

Introduction to Networks

- A network includes all of the hardware and software components used to connect computers across a distance to provide easy access to information and to increase productivity. To build a network, you need computers, networking devices, and media (cable or wireless connections).

- A SOHO (small office/home office) refers to a small company office or home office where only a few people work. A branch office involves a small group of users connected in a small area (LAN) that is geographically separated from a corporate office. Mobile users connect to a network from any remote location. A central or corporate office is the location of critical services and applications accessed by central office, branch office, SOHO, and mobile users.

Common Network Services and Devices

- Know the common network services: DHCP is a service that assigns IP addresses to systems on the network. A DNS server converts friendly names such as www.gleneclarke.com to IP addresses.

- A network-based firewall is used to control what traffic is allowed to enter or leave the network. The firewall filters traffic by analyzing the header of the packet and deciding if it is allowed in, based on the firewall rules.

- An access point is a device that connects to the network and enables wireless clients to connect to and gain access to the network.

Network Topologies

- A point-to-point topology uses a single connection between two devices and is typically used in WAN environments. In a star topology, a central device makes many point-to-point connections to other devices. A 10BaseT hub is an example of a central device in a star topology. A bus topology uses a single connection between all devices; Ethernet 10Base5 is an example of this topology. A ring topology connects one device to the next, where the last device is connected to the first. FDDI is an example of a ring topology.

- A physical topology defines how the computing devices are physically cabled together. A logical topology describes the method by which devices communicate across a physical topology. The two topologies can vary with the network technology/standard used.

- Meshing generically describes how devices are connected. In a partially meshed network, not every device has a connection to every other device. In a fully meshed network, each device is connected to all other devices.

Types of Cabling

- Copper cabling with Ethernet commonly uses UTP, a four-pair wire. It's cheap to use and easy to install and troubleshoot. UTP cabling, however, can span only short distances and is susceptible to EMI and RFI. UTP cables use RJ-45 connectors.

- Straight-through UTP cables are used to connect dissimilar devices, such as a computer to a switch or a switch to a router. Crossover UTP cables are used to connect similar devices (both hosts on the network), such as a computer to a computer, a switch to a switch, or a computer to a router.

- In fiber-optic cabling, a glass core carries pulses of light and is immune to electrical interference. Fiber-optic cabling is typically used as a backbone between buildings, but it can also be used at the workstation. Two implementations of fiber-optic include MMF for shorter distances and SMF for longer distances.

Access Methods

- CSMA/CD is the access method used by all Ethernet architectures and involves a system sensing the wire before sending data on the wire.

- In token passing, the system needs to wait for the token before it can pass a token on the wire; once the system has the token and it is free of data, the system can place data on the wire. Systems need the token before they can send data. Token ring network architectures used token passing as their access method.

Network Architectures

- There are different classifications of Ethernet architectures: *Ethernet* runs at 10 Mbps, *Fast Ethernet* runs at 100 Mbps, *Gigabit Ethernet* runs at 1000 Mbps (1 Gbps), and *10-Gigabit Ethernet* runs at 10 Gbps.

- For the CCT and CCNA exams, be familiar with the Faster Ethernet such as 100BaseTX, which uses UTP CAT 5/6/6A cabling, is a star topology, and runs at 100 Mbps. 100BaseFX uses MMF fiber-optic cabling to reach 400 meters and has a transfer rate of 100 Mbps.

- Some common Gigabit Ethernet standards are 1000BaseT, which uses UTP cabling with a maximum distance of 100 meters and has a transfer rate of 1000 Mbps. 1000BaseLX has a transfer rate of 1000 Mbps but uses SMF fiber-optic cable to reach up to 10 km. 1000BaseSX uses MMF fiber-optic cabling to reach shorter distances of around 275 meters.

Virtualization Fundamentals

- Virtualization is a method that enables you to better utilize resources on servers such as memory and processing power while using less power, because it requires less physical servers to run virtual servers.

- Know the different types of hypervisors and types of virtual components such as virtual network cards and virtual switches.

Questions

The following self-test questions will help you measure your understanding of the material presented in this chapter. Read all the choices carefully, as there may be more than one correct answer. Choose the correct answer(s) for each question.

1. Which of the following network characteristics is MTBF concerned with?

    A. Cost

    B. Security

    C. Reliability

    D. Availability

2. Which network topology typically involves a single network device that acts as a switch, router, and access point while providing services such as DHCP, NAT, and firewall functionality?

    A. SOHO

    B. Spine-leaf

    C. Collapsed-core

    D. WAN

3. Match each of the following technologies to either (1) LAN or (2) WAN:

    A. Switch

    B. Router

    C. 1000BaseT

    D. CSU/DSU

4. A _____ topology uses a central connectivity device to connect all systems to the network.

    A. Bus

    B. Star

    C. Point-to-point

    D. Ring

5. With the spine-leaf design model, what layer involves having the access layer switches in order for clients to connect to the network?

    A. Core

    B. Spine

    C. Distribution

    D. Leaf

6. What Gigabit Ethernet architecture uses single-mode fiber-optic cabling to reach distances of up to 10 km?
   A. 1000BaseT
   B. 1000BaseCX
   C. 1000BaseSX
   D. 1000BaseLX

7. Which of the following are characteristics of UTP cabling? (Choose two.)
   A. Carries pulses of light
   B. Uses multiple two-pair wires
   C. Is susceptible to EMI and RFI
   D. Is used between two campus buildings

8. You have run out of network ports on your switch. You purchase an additional network switch and want to connect the two switches together. What cable type would you use?
   A. Straight-through UTP
   B. Crossover UTP
   C. Serial
   D. Rollover

9. You need to connect a laptop to a switch, that same switch to another switch, and the second switch to a router. How many cables would you need and what types of UTP cables should you use?
   A. Two straight-through cables and one crossover cable
   B. Three straight-through cables and zero crossover cables
   C. One straight-through cable and two crossover cables
   D. One straight-through cable and one crossover cable

10. Which of the following is a connector used with 1000BaseT networks?
    A. ST
    B. DB-15
    C. RJ-45
    D. SC

11. Your company is running a Gigabit Ethernet network. Which of the following statements are true regarding when a device on the network can transmit data?
    A. When no other device is sending
    B. When the device has the token

    C. When the access point grants permission

    D. When the router is not busy

12. Which of the following represents the access method used by all Ethernet networks?

    A. CSMA/CA

    B. CSMA/CD

    C. Token Passing

    D. CSMA/TA

13. Which Gigabit Ethernet standard uses STP cabling to reach up to 25 meters?

    A. 1000BaseTX

    B. 1000BaseCX

    C. 1000BaseLX

    D. 1000BaseSX

14. Which of the following network services is responsible for translating a private IP to a public IP address?

    A. DHCP

    B. CSU/DSU

    C. NAT

    D. DNS

15. What network service is responsible for assigning IP addresses to endpoint devices on the network?

    A. DHCP

    B. CSU/DSU

    C. NAT

    D. DNS

16. A user on the network is complaining that she cannot connect to the web site of www.cisco.com. While troubleshooting, you can ping the IP address of the site, but not the FQDN. What could be the problem?

    A. DHCP

    B. CSU/DSU

    C. NAT

    D. DNS

Performance-based Questions

The Cisco exams have performance-based questions for which you must drag items from the left side of the screen to its proper place on the right side of the screen in order to answer the question. Following are some sample performance-based questions.

1. You need to crimp your own Ethernet cable using the 568B standard. Place the wires in the proper order by writing in the boxes.

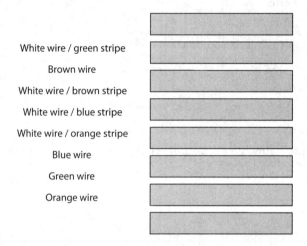

White wire / green stripe

Brown wire

White wire / brown stripe

White wire / blue stripe

White wire / orange stripe

Blue wire

Green wire

Orange wire

2. Looking at each of the scenarios, write above the line whether a crossover cable or a straight-through cable is used. Note that on the real exam, if this were a performance question, you would be expected to drag the appropriate cable type to connect the devices.

Answers

1. **C.** Mean time between failures (MTBF) is commonly used to measure reliability.

2. **A.** A small office/home office (SOHO) network involves having a single network device, such as a home router, that provides all network functions.

3. **A** and **C: 1 (LAN)**; **B** and **D: 2 (WAN)**. Ethernet architectures such as 1000BaseT and switches are LAN technologies, while routers and CSU/DSUs are components that enable you to connect to a WAN.

4. **B.** A star topology uses a central connectivity device to connect all systems to the network.

5. **D.** The leaf layer of the spine-leaf design topology involves having the access layer switches. This layer enables endpoints to connect to the network.

6. **D.** 1000BaseLX uses single-mode fiber-optic cabling to reach long distances of up to 10 km.

7. **B** and **C.** UTP, which uses multiple pairs of copper wires, is susceptible to EMI and RFI interference.

8. **B.** Crossover cables are used to connect similar devices together. Remember that straight-through cable connects dissimilar devices together.

9. **A.** The laptop-to-switch and switch-to-router connections need two straight-through cables; the switch-to-switch connection needs one crossover cable.

10. **C.** 1000BaseT uses UTP cabling, which uses an RJ-45 connector.

11. **A.** Ethernet networks use CSMA/CD as their access method, which means that a device can send data only when the wire is free of a signal (the cable is not being used).

12. **B.** All Ethernet architectures use carrier sense multiple access/collision detection (CSMA/CD). This access method involves a system checking the wire to ensure it is free of a signal before sending data. If the data collides with other data, the system will detect the collision and retransmit.

13. **B.** The 1000BaseCX uses STP cabling to reach a maximum distance of 25 meters.

14. **C.** Network Address Translation (NAT) is responsible for translating a private IP address in a packet to a public IP address so that it can travel over the Internet.

15. **A.** The DHCP network service is responsible for assigning IP address information to network devices so that they can communicate on the network.

16. **D.** The DNS service converts the FQDNs to IP addresses. If you cannot ping the FQDN, but you can ping the IP address, it could mean a problem with DNS converting the FQDN to an IP address. This typically means either the FQDN does not exist in DNS or you are configured to use the wrong DNS server.

Performance-based Answers

The following are the answers to the performance-based questions that are common on Cisco exams.

1. The following is the order of the wires for the 568B standard.

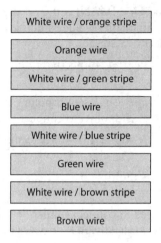

White wire / orange stripe
Orange wire
White wire / green stripe
Blue wire
White wire / blue stripe
Green wire
White wire / brown stripe
Brown wire

2. The following shows the correct type of cabling to connect different types of devices together. Remember that a crossover is used if the devices are considered similar devices (the exception being a router connecting to a computer).

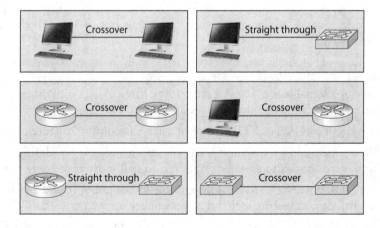

OSI Reference Model

In this chapter, you will

- Learn about the functions of the OSI Reference Model layers
- Learn about encapsulation and de-encapsulation

Before you can successfully configure Cisco switches and routers, you must understand the basic networking concepts outlined in this chapter and advanced concepts discussed in later chapters. The Open Systems Interconnection (OSI) Reference Model is the best place to start, since it will help you understand how information is transferred between networking components. Of the seven layers in the OSI Reference Model, you should understand how the bottom four layers of the OSI model function, because most networking components function at these layers. This chapter covers how traffic is generally moved between network components, and it uses the OSI Reference Model to illustrate the encapsulation and de-encapsulation process.

Layers of the OSI Reference Model

In the early 1980s, the International Organization for Standardization (ISO) defined a standard for manufacturers of networking components that would enable these networking components to communicate in dissimilar environments. The product of the standard is demonstrated in the seven layers of the OSI Reference Model, shown in Figure 2-1: application, presentation, session, transport, network, data link, and physical. Each layer is responsible for performing a specific process or role.

NOTE   A good mnemonic to use to remember the OSI Reference Model layers is "All people seem to need data processing" (application, presentation, session, transport, network, data link, and physical).

The functions of the first three layers—application, presentation, and session—are known as the *upper layers* of the OSI model, and they are typically controlled by the application software. These layers are normally not controlled or modified by a network administrator. Network administrators can use knowledge of the transport, network, data link, and physical layers to help troubleshoot network communication. These four layers, known as the *lower layers* of the OSI model, are the layers you should feel comfortable with as a network professional.

Figure 2-1
Layers of the OSI
Reference Model

Layer 7	Application
Layer 6	Presentation
Layer 5	Session
Layer 4	Transport
Layer 3	Network
Layer 2	Data link
Layer 1	Physical

Each layer of the OSI model is responsible for communicating with the layers directly above and below it, receiving data from or passing data to its neighboring layers. For example, the presentation layer will receive information from the application layer, format it appropriately, and then pass it to the session layer. The presentation layer will never deal directly with the transport, network, data link, or physical layers. The same idea is true for all layers with regard to their communication with other layers.

 CAUTION Understanding the functions of each of the OSI Reference Model layers is very important when it comes to troubleshooting network components and network communication. Once you understand these functions and the troubleshooting tools available to you at the various layers of the model, troubleshooting network-related problems will be much easier.

Network communication starts at the application layer of the OSI model (on the sending system) and works its way down through the layers to the physical layer. The information then passes along the communication medium to the receiving system, which works its way back up the layers, starting at the physical layer, as shown in Figure 2-2. (Be sure to refer to this figure frequently when reading through this section.)

When you're thinking of two devices communicating, such as two computers, it is important to understand that whatever action is done at one layer of a sending computer is undone at the same layer on the receiving computer. For example, if the presentation layer compresses the information on the sending computer, then the data is uncompressed on the receiving computer.

Let's look at the layers from the point of view of two computers that are sending data between each other. Computer1 and Server1 are exchanging data on the network. Computer1 is the sending computer, and Server1 is the receiving computer, as shown in Figure 2-3.

Figure 2-2
How packets
move through
the layers of the
OSI model

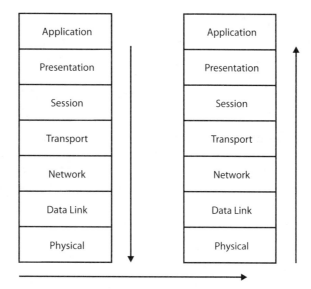

The data exchange starts with Computer1 sending a request to Server1 in the application layer. At Server1, the data moves back up through the layers to the application layer, which passes the data to the appropriate application or service on the system.

 EXAM TIP   The CCT exam is sure to test your knowledge of the OSI model and each of its layers, so be familiar with this for the exam! You should also note that the data has special terms assigned to it once it reaches different layers—at layer 4, the data is called a *segment*; at layer 3, the data is called a *packet*; and at layer 2, the data is called a *frame*.

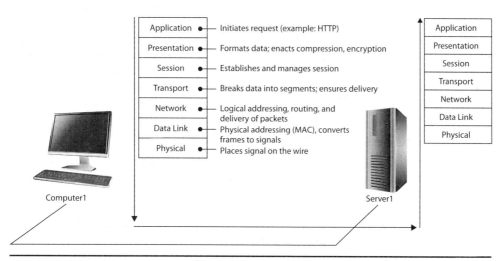

Figure 2-3   Identifying the function of each layer of the OSI model

Layer 7: The Application Layer

The application layer running on the sending system (Computer1) is responsible for initiating the actual request. This could be any type of networking request—a web request using a web browser (HTTP), an e-mail delivery request using Simple Mail Transport Protocol (SMTP), or a file system request using the network client redirector software. On the receiving system, the application layer would be responsible for passing the request to the appropriate application or service on that system. In our example, we will assume that you are sitting at Computer1 and you have typed the address of Server1 into your web browser to create an HTTP request.

There are many, many examples of protocols that run at the application layer. The most common are HTTP, telnet, Secure Shell (SSH), File Transfer Protocol (FTP), Post Office Protocol 3 (POP3), and Simple Mail Transfer Protocol (SMTP).

 EXAM TIP For the exams, remember that the top (seventh) layer of the OSI Reference Model, the application layer, provides the protocols and services that enable systems to initiate a request (sending system) or service a request (receiving system). Examples of application layer protocols include telnet, FTP, HTTP (for web browsing), SSH, POP3, and SMTP.

Layer 6: The Presentation Layer

After the request is made, the application layer passes the data down to the presentation layer, where it is formatted so that the data (or request) can be interpreted by the receiving system. When the presentation layer receives data from the application layer, it makes sure the data is in the proper format—if it is not, the presentation layer converts the data accordingly. On the receiving system, when the presentation layer receives network data from the session layer, it makes sure the data is in the proper format and once again converts it if it is not.

Formatting functions that could occur at the sending system's presentation layer include compression, encryption, and ensuring that the character code set can be interpreted on the other side. For example, if we choose to compress our data from the application that we are using, the application layer will pass that request to the presentation layer, but the presentation layer does the compression. At the receiving end, this data must be decompressed so that it can be read. When the data reaches the presentation layer of the receiving computer, it will decompress the data and pass it up to the application layer.

Layer 5: The Session Layer

The session layer manages the dialog between computers by establishing, managing, and terminating communications between them. When a session is established, three distinct phases are involved. In the establishment phase, the requestor initiates the service and the rules for communication between the two systems. These rules could include such things as who transmits and when, as well as how much data can be sent at a time. Both systems must agree on the rules; the rules are like the etiquette of the conversation. Once the rules are established, the data transfer phase begins. Both sides know how to talk to each other, what are the most efficient methods to use, and how to detect errors, all because of the rules defined in the first phase. Finally, termination occurs when the session is complete, and communication ends in an orderly fashion.

In our example, Computer1 creates a session with Server1 at this point, and they agree on the rules of the conversation.

 EXAM TIP For the exams, remember that the session layer is responsible for setting up, maintaining, and tearing down network connections. Examples of session layer techniques and protocols include Remote Procedure Calls (RPCs) and the Network File System (NFS).

Layer 4: The Transport Layer

The transport layer handles functions such as reliable and unreliable delivery of the data. For reliable transport protocols, the transport layer works hard to ensure reliable delivery of data to its destinations. On the sending system, the transport layer is responsible for breaking the data into smaller parts, called *segments*, so that if retransmission is required, only the missing segments will be sent. Missing segments are detected when the transport layer receives acknowledgments (ACKs) from the remote system upon receiving the packets. At the receiving system, the transport layer is responsible for opening all of the packets and reconstructing the original message.

Another function of the transport layer is segment sequencing. Sequencing is a connection-oriented service that takes segments that are received out of order and resequences them in the right order. For example, if I send you five packets and you receive the packets out of order (by their sequence number)—3, 1, 4, 2, 5—the transport layer will read the sequence numbers and assemble them in the correct order.

The transport layer also enables the option of specifying a "service address," known as a *port address*. The port address enables the services or applications that are running on the systems to specify what application the request came from and what application the request is headed for by having each application use a unique port address on the system. All modern operating systems run many programs at once, and each network program has a unique service address. Service addresses that are well defined (by networking standards, for example) are called *well-known addresses*. Service addresses also are called *sockets* or *ports* by protocols such as TCP/IP.

 EXAM TIP Remember for the exam that TCP is an example of a transport layer protocol responsible for reliable delivery, whereas User Datagram Protocol (UDP) is an example of a transport layer protocol responsible for unreliable delivery.

At this point, the request is broken into segments in preparation for being delivered across the network, and transport-layer information (such as the transport protocol being used and any additional transport information) is appended to the request. In this example, because we are dealing with a TCP/IP application, the source port and destination port are added.

Connection-Oriented Communication and Connectionless Communication

Connection-oriented communication ensures reliable delivery of data from the sender to the receiver. When establishing connection services, this form of communication requires that some sort of handshaking function be performed at the beginning of a communication session. During this process, the two computers determine the rules for communication, such as how much data to send at one time and which ports to use. Handshaking also determines the proper way to terminate the session when finished. This ensures that communication ends in an orderly manner.

A session is a reliable dialog between two computers. A session is like a telephone call: you set up a telephone call by dialing (handshaking), then speak to the other person (exchange data), say "Goodbye," and finally hang up when finished. Because connection-oriented services can provide reliable communication, they are used when two computers need to communicate in a session. Sessions are maintained until the two computers decide that they are finished communicating.

Connectionless communication is a form of communication in which the sending system does not "introduce" itself—it just fires off the data. Also, the destination computer does not notify the source when the information is received. This type of communication is considered unreliable because there is no notification to guarantee delivery. Connectionless communication can be faster than connection-oriented communication because the overhead of managing the session is not there, and after the information is sent, there is no second step to ensure that it was received properly.

Using a connectionless protocol at the transport layer means that the transport layer protocol is not guaranteeing delivery. Higher layer protocols, however, such as application layer protocols, may incorporate functionality to guarantee delivery.

It is important for the CCT/CCNA exams that you know the main functions of the transport layer:

- It sets up, maintains, and tears down a connection between two devices or systems.
- It can provide for the reliable or unreliable delivery of data across this connection.
- It breaks up data into smaller, more manageable segments.
- It multiplexes connections, enabling multiple applications to send and receive data simultaneously on the same networking device.
- It can implement flow control through ready/not ready signals or windowing to ensure that one component doesn't overflow another with too much data on a connection. Both of these methods are used to avoid congestion and typically use buffering.

EXAM TIP   For the exams, you'll need to know the five main functions of the transport layer: connection management, reliable and unreliable delivery of data, flow control, multiplexing, and segmentation.

Segmentation

Another function of the transport layer is to set up, maintain, and tear down connections for the session layer—that is, it handles the actual mechanics for the connection. The information transferred between networking devices at the transport layer is divided into segments. Segmentation is necessary to break up large amounts of data into more manageable sizes that the network can accommodate. A good analogy of this process is "it's easier to pour pebbles down a pipe than giant boulders."

EXAM TIP   Remember that data is broken into segments at the transport layer.

Connection Multiplexing

Because multiple connections may be established from one component to another component or to multiple components, some type of multiplexing function is needed to differentiate between data traversing the various connections. This ensures that the transport layer can send data from a particular application to the correct destination and application, and, when receiving data from a destination, the transport layer can get the data to the right local application. To accomplish connection multiplexing, a unique port number is assigned to each application. You will learn more about port numbers in Chapter 3.

Flow Control

Another function of the transport layer is to provide optional flow control. Flow control is used to ensure that networking components don't send too much information to the destination, overflowing its receiving buffer space and causing it to drop some of the transmitted information. Overflow is not good because the source will have to resend all the information that was dropped. The transport layer can use two basic flow control methods:

- Ready/not ready signals
- Windowing

EXAM TIP   For the exams, you should know that the purpose of flow control is to ensure that the destination doesn't get overrun by too much information sent by the source.

Ready/Not Ready Signals   When the destination receives more traffic than it can handle, it can send a *not ready* signal to the source, indicating that the source should stop transmitting data. When the destination has a chance to catch up and process the source's data, the destination responds back to the source with a *ready* signal. Upon receiving the ready signal, the source can resume sending data.

Two problems are associated with the use of ready/not ready signals to implement flow control. First, the destination may respond to the source with a not ready signal when its buffer fills up. While this message is on its way to the source, the source is *still sending* information to the destination, which the destination will probably have to drop because its buffer space is full. The second problem with the use of these signals is that once the destination is ready to receive more information, it must first send a ready signal to the source, which must receive it before more information can be sent. This causes a delay in the transfer of information. Because of these two inefficiencies with ready/not ready signals, they are not commonly used to implement flow control. Sometimes this process is referred to as *stop/start*, where you stop transmitting for a period and then start retransmitting.

Windowing   *Windowing* is a much more sophisticated method of flow control than using ready/not ready signals. With windowing, a window size is defined that specifies how much data (segments) can be sent before the source has to wait for an acknowledgment (ACK) from the destination. Once the ACK is received, the source can send the next batch of data (up to the maximum defined in the window size).

Windowing accomplishes two things: First, flow control is enforced, based on the window size. In many protocol implementations, the window size is dynamically negotiated up front and can be renegotiated during the lifetime of the connection. This ensures that the most optimal window size is used to send data without having the destination drop anything. Second, through the windowing process, the destination tells the source what was received. This indicates to the source whether any data was lost along the way to the destination and enables the source to resend any missing information. This provides reliability for a connection as well as better efficiency than ready/not ready signals. Because of these advantages, most connection-oriented transport protocols, such as TCP/IP's TCP, use windowing to implement flow control.

The window size chosen for a connection impacts its efficiency and throughput in defining how many segments (or bytes) can be sent before the source has to wait for an ACK. Figure 2-4 illustrates the importance of the size used for the window. The top part of the figure shows the connection using a window size of 1. In this instance, the source sends one segment with a sequence number (in this case *1*) and then waits for an acknowledgment from the destination. Depending on the transport protocol, the destination can send the ACK in different ways: it can send back a list of the sequence numbers of the segments it received, or it can send back the sequence number of the next segment it expects. The ACK from the destination has a number *2* in it. This tells the source that it can go ahead and send segment 2. Again, when the destination receives this segment, since the window size is 1, the destination will immediately reply with an

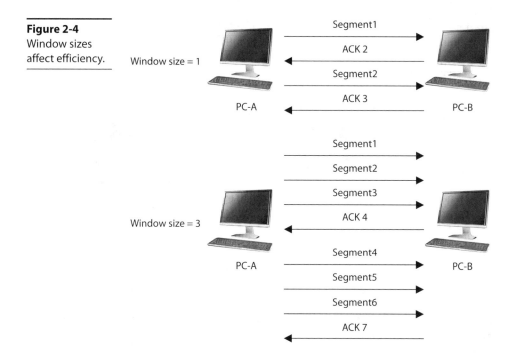

Figure 2-4
Window sizes
affect efficiency.

Window size = 1

Segment1
ACK 2
Segment2
ACK 3

PC-A   PC-B

Window size = 3

Segment1
Segment2
Segment3
ACK 4
Segment4
Segment5
Segment6
ACK 7

PC-A   PC-B

acknowledgment, indicating the receipt of this segment. In this example, the destination acknowledges back 3, indicating that segment 3 can be sent, and so on and so forth.

As you can see, with a window size of 1, the flow control process is not very quick or efficient. Let's look at an example with a window size of 3, as illustrated at the bottom portion of Figure 2-4. With a window size of 3, the source can send three segments at once before waiting for an ACK. Once segments are sent (each with its own unique sequence number: 1, 2, and 3), the source must wait for an ACK. In this instance, the destination sends an ACK back with the number 4 in it, indicating that the fourth segment is expected next. The source can then proceed to send segments 4, 5, and 6, and then wait for the destination's ACK. In this case, having a larger window size is more efficient: only one ACK is required for every three segments that are sent. Therefore, the larger the window size, the more efficient the transfer of information becomes.

This is not always the case, however. For example, let's assume that one segment gets lost on its way to the destination, as is shown in Figure 2-5. In this example, the window size negotiated is 3. PC-A sends its first three segments, which are successfully received by PC-B. PC-B acknowledges the next segment it expects, which is 4. When PC-A receives this ACK, it sends segments 4, 5, and 6. For some reason, segment 4 becomes lost and never reaches the destination, but segments 5 and 6 do arrive. Remember that the destination is keeping track of what was received: 1, 2, 3, 5, and 6. In this example, the destination sends back an ACK of 4, indicating that segment 4 is expected next.

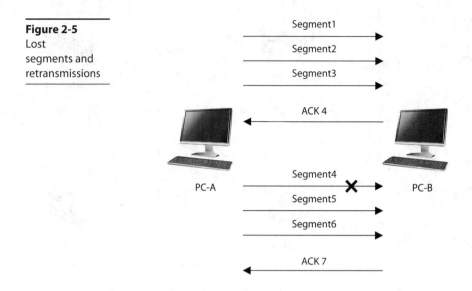

Figure 2-5
Lost segments and retransmissions

At this point, how PC-A reacts depends on the transport layer protocol that is used. Here are some possible options:

- PC-A understands that only segment 4 was lost and therefore resends segment 4. It then sends segments 7 and 8, filling up the window size.
- PC-A doesn't understand what was or wasn't received, so it sends three segments starting at segment 4, indicated by PC-B.

Of course, if two segments are lost, the first option listed won't work unless the destination can send a list of lost segments. Therefore, most protocol stacks that use windowing will implement the second option. Given this behavior, the size of the window can affect your performance. You would normally think that a window size of 100 would be very efficient; however, if the very first segment is lost, some protocols will have *all* 100 segments resent! As mentioned earlier, most protocol stacks use a window size that is negotiated up front and can be renegotiated at any time. Therefore, if a connection is experiencing a high number of errors, the window size can be dropped to a smaller value to increase efficiency. And once these errors disappear or drop down to a lower rate, the window size can be increased to maximize the connection's throughput.

What makes this situation even more complicated is that the window sizes on the source and destination devices can be *different*. For instance, PC-A might have a window size of 3, while PC-B has a window size of 10. In this example, PC-A is allowed to send ten segments to PC-B before waiting for an acknowledgment, while PC-B is allowed to send only three segments to PC-A.

NOTE Ready/not ready signals and windowing are used to implement flow control at the transport layer. Ready/not ready signals are not efficient, causing drops of unnecessary traffic and delays in the transmission of traffic. Windowing addresses these issues. With windowing, a window size is established, which defines the number of segments that can be transferred before waiting for an acknowledgment from the destination.

Layer 3: The Network Layer

The network layer is responsible for managing logical addressing information in the packets and the delivery, or routing, of those packets by using information stored in a routing table. The routing table is a list of available destinations that are stored in memory on the routers.

The network layer is responsible for working with logical addresses. Logical addresses uniquely identify a system on the network and, at the same time, identify the network that the system resides on. This is unlike a Media Access Control (MAC) address (the physical address burned into the network card), because a MAC address just gives the system a unique address and does not specify or imply what network the system lives on. The logical address is used by network-layer protocols to deliver the packets to the correct network.

In our example, the request is coming from a web browser and is destined for a web server, both of which are applications that run on TCP/IP. At this point, the network layer will add the source address (the IP address of the sending system) and the destination address (the IP address of the destination system) to the packet so that the receiving system will know where the packet came from.

EXAM TIP For the exams, remember that layer 3 of the OSI model handles logical addressing and routing. An example of a logical address is an IP address, which takes the form of 192.168.3.24. An IP address is also known as a layer 3 address.

The network layer is responsible for four main functions:

- Defines logical addresses used at layer 3
- Finds paths, based on the network numbers of logical addresses, to reach destination components
- Connects different data link layer types together, such as Ethernet, Fiber Distributed Data Interface (FDDI), serial, and Token Ring
- Defines segmentation via the use of packets to transport information

To move information between devices that have different network numbers, a router is used. Routers use information in the logical address to make intelligent decisions about how to reach a destination. Routing is discussed in Chapters 11 and 12, where you'll learn the details of routing. Basically, when a router receives a packet, it compares the destination address (from the layer 3 header of the packet, which is the destination IP address) in the packet to its routing table to determine whether the router knows how to send data to that destination network.

 EXAM TIP For the exam, remember that routers are considered layer 3 devices (network layer) and work with layer 3 addresses (IP addresses).

Layer 2: The Data Link Layer

At the data link layer, the data is converted from a packet to a pattern of electrical bit signals that will be used to send the data across the communication medium. On the receiving system, the electrical signals will be converted to packets by the data link layer and then passed up to the network layer for further processing. The data link layer is divided into two sublayers:

- **Logical link control (LLC)** This is responsible for error correction and control functions.
- **Media Access Control (MAC)** This determines the physical addressing of the hosts. It also determines how the host places traffic on the medium—for example, Carrier Sense Multiple Access/Collision Detection (CSMA/CD) versus token passing.

The MAC sublayer maintains physical device addresses (commonly referred to as MAC addresses) for communicating with other devices on the network. These physical addresses are burned into the network cards and constitute the low-level addresses used to determine the source and destination of network traffic. Note that the MAC address is used for communication on the local network segment, while the IP address is used for communication on different networks. You will learn more about IP addresses in Chapter 4.

 EXAM TIP For the CCT/CCNA exams, remember that a MAC address is the physical address assigned to the network card and is known as a layer 2 address. The MAC address is a 48-bit value displayed in hexadecimal format. An example of a MAC address is 00-02-3F-6B-25-13.

In our example, once the sending system's network layer appends the IP address information, the data link layer will append the MAC address information for the sending and receiving systems. This layer will also prepare the data for the wire by converting the packets to binary signals. On the receiving system, the data link layer will convert the signals passed to it by the physical layer to data and then pass the packets to the network layer for further processing.

EXAM TIP   Remember for the exams that the network access methods and architectures you learned about in Chapter 1 run at layer 2 of the OSI model. For example, Ethernet and Token Ring network architectures are defined at layer 2 of the OSI model.

Layer 2 Frames

The data link layer defines how a networking component accesses the media to which it is connected, and it also defines the media's frame type and transmission method. The frame includes the fields and components the data link layer uses to communicate with devices on the same wire or layer 2 topology. This communication occurs only for components on the same data link layer media type (or same piece of wire), within the same network segment. To traverse layer 2 protocols, Ethernet to Token Ring, for instance, a router is typically used.

EXAM TIP   Some questions on the exams will require you to know that most wide area network (WAN) protocols primarily function at the data link and physical layers.

Examples of layer 2 protocols and standards for local area network (LAN) connections include Institute of Electrical and Electronic Engineers (IEEE) 802.2, 802.3, and 802.5; Ethernet II; and FDDI. Examples of layer 2 WAN protocols and techniques include Asynchronous Transfer Mode (ATM), Frame Relay, High-Level Data Link Control (HDLC), Point-to-Point Protocol (PPP), Synchronous Data Link Control (SDLC), Serial Line Internet Protocol (SLIP), and X.25.

EXAM TIP   For the exams, remember that the data link layer defines hardware (MAC) addresses as well as the communication process that occurs within a media type. Switches, bridges, and network interface controllers or cards (NICs) are the primary networking components that function at the data link layer. For example, a switch prevents loops on the network using Spanning Tree Protocol (STP) or Rapid Spanning Tree Protocol (RSTP), which are considered layer 2 protocols. Examples of data link layer protocols and standards include IEEE's 802.2and 802.3; Ethernet II; HDLC; PPP; and Frame Relay. Error detection also occurs here, but not correction (no retransmission, only dropping bad frames).

The data link layer is also responsible for defining the format of layer 2 frames as well as the mechanics of how devices communicate with each other over the physical layer. The data link layer is responsible for the following:

- Defining the MAC or hardware addresses
- Defining the physical or hardware topology for connections
- Defining how the network layer protocol is encapsulated in the data link layer frame

- Providing both connectionless and connection-oriented services
- Verifying the checksum of the received frame to ensure it is valid (if it is invalid, it is discarded)

 EXAM TIP   Remember that the primary function of the data link layer is to regulate how two networking devices connected to the same layer 2 protocol communicate with each other. It also validates the checksum of the received frame to ensure it is valid. Frames are used to transmit information at the data link layer. If the devices are on different layer 2 protocols or segments, the network layer (layer 3) typically plays a role in the communication of these devices.

Data Link Layer Addressing

The data link layer uses MAC, or hardware, addresses for communication. For LAN communications, each machine on the same network segment or topology needs a unique MAC address. A MAC address is 48 bits in length and is represented as a hexadecimal number, 12 characters in length. To make it easier to read, the MAC address is represented in a dotted hexadecimal format, like this: *FFFF.FFFF.FFFF*. It is also common to see MAC addresses formatted in this way: *FF:FF:FF:FF:FF:FF*. Since the MAC address uses hexadecimal numbers, the values used range from 0 to 9 and A to F, for a total of 16 values for a single digit. For example, a hexadecimal value of *A* would be *10* in decimal.

 EXAM TIP   For the exams, you should remember that MAC addresses uniquely identify devices at layer 2. MAC addresses need to be unique only within a broadcast domain, which includes all layer 2–connected collision domains. MAC addresses enable communication between different devices on the same physical network (layer 2).

Each manufacturer of network cards is assigned a unique 24-bit vendor ID, which is then used as the first 24 bits of a MAC address for any network cards created by that vendor. Each vendor has one or more unique vendor IDs, with each making up the first half of a MAC address. These first six digits are commonly called the *organizationally unique identifier* (OUI). For example, one of Cisco's OUI values is *0000.0C*. The last six digits are used to represent the network interface card (NIC) uniquely within the OUI value. Theoretically, each NIC has a unique MAC address. In reality, however, this is probably not true. What is important for your purposes is that each of your devices has a unique MAC address on its network card within the same *network segment*. Some devices enable you to change this hardware address, while others do not.

 EXAM TIP   Remember for the CCT/CCNA exams that the first 24 bits of a MAC address is known as the OUI, which is a unique value used as the first part of the MAC address for all interface cards created by that vendor. You can have the same MAC address in different broadcast domains or virtual LANs, but not on the same network segment.

Communication Type	Description
Unicast	Represents communication to a single device on a segment
Broadcast	Represents communication to every device on a segment
Multicast	Represents communication to a group of devices on a segment

Table 2-1   Data Link Address Types

Communication Types

Different types of communication can occur on the network, and each of these uses a specific method of addressing to identify who a message is for. Each data link layer frame contains two MAC addresses: a source MAC address of the machine creating the frame, and a destination MAC address for the device or devices intended to receive the frame. The three general types of communication are shown in Table 2-1. The following sections cover each of these communication types in more depth.

Unicast   A frame with a destination *unicast* MAC address is intended for only one network component on a segment. The top part of Figure 2-6 shows an example of a unicast communication. In this example, PC-A creates an Ethernet frame with a destination MAC address that contains PC-C's address. When PC-A places this data link layer frame on the wire, all the devices on the segment receive it, but all systems except PC-C discard the frame because it is not destined for them. This gives us one-on-one communication with unicast.

Multicast   Unlike a unicast address, *multicast* communication represents communication to a group of devices on a segment. The multicast group can contain no devices up to every device on a segment. One of the interesting things about multicasting is that the membership of a group is *dynamic*—devices can join and leave the multicast group. (The detailed process of multicasting is beyond the scope of this book.)

The middle portion of Figure 2-6 shows an example of multicast communication. In this example, notice that the communication is sent to a few systems, but not all systems.

Broadcast   A *broadcast* message is sent to all systems on the network. The bottom portion of Figure 2-6 shows an example of a broadcast. In this example, PC-A puts a broadcast address in the destination field of the data link layer frame. The layer 2 representation of a broadcast address is *FF:FF:FF:FF:FF:FF*. This frame is then placed on the wire. Notice in this example that computers B, C, D, E, and F receive the broadcast message, and they *all* process it. It is important to note that a device on the network will process two frames: frames destined for its own MAC address, or frames destined for the broadcast address (*FF:FF:FF:FF:FF:FF*).

Layer 1: The Physical Layer

The bottom layer of the OSI hierarchy is concerned only with moving bits of data on and off the network medium. This includes the physical topology (or structure) of the network, the electrical and physical aspects of the medium used, and the encoding and timing of bit transmission and reception.

Figure 2-6
Unicast, multicast, and broadcast communications

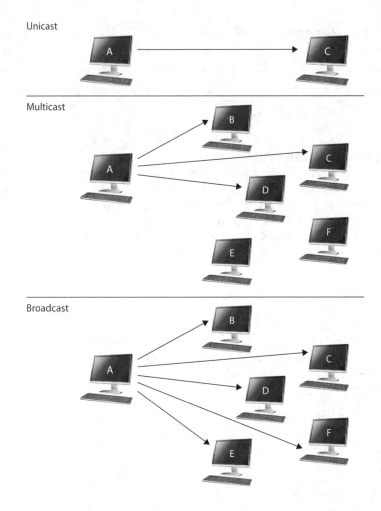

In our example, once the network layer has appended the logical addresses and passed the data to the data link layer, where the MAC addresses were appended and the data was converted to electrical signals, the data is then passed to the physical layer so that it can be released on the communication medium. On the receiving system, the physical layer will pick up the data off the wire and pass it to the data link layer, where it will ensure that the signal is destined for that system by reading the destination MAC address.

EXAM TIP Remember for the CCT/CCNA exams that anything that works with the electrical signal runs at layer 1 of the OSI model. This includes network cables and connectors.

The physical layer is responsible for the physical mechanics of a network connection, which include the following:

- The type of interface used on the networking device
- The type of cable used for connecting devices
- The connectors used on each end of the cable
- The pin patterns used for each of the connections on the cable
- The encoding of a message on a signal by converting binary digits to a physical representation based on the media type, such as electrical for copper, light for fiber, or a radio wave for wireless

The type of interface, or NIC, can be a physical card that you put into a computer, such as a Gigabit Ethernet card, or a fixed interface on a router, such as a Gigabit Ethernet port on a Cisco 1921 router.

The physical layer is also responsible for how binary information is converted to a physical layer signal and vice versa. For example, if the cable uses copper as a transport medium, the physical layer defines how binary 1s and 0s are converted into electrical signals by using different voltage levels. If the cable uses fiber, the physical layer defines how 1s and 0s are represented using a light-emitting diode (LED) or laser with different light frequencies.

Devices

When troubleshooting networking components, a network technician will find it useful to understand the layer of the OSI model at which the technology is running. Table 2-2 provides a reminder of the devices that function at three layers of the OSI Reference Model.

 EXAM TIP Remember for the exams that any technology that deals with logical addressing or routing is considered running at layer 3, anything that works with a MAC address is running at layer 2, and anything that works with an electrical signal runs at layer 1 of the OSI model.

Table 2-2
Devices and the Layers at Which They Function

Layer	Layer Name	Device
3	Network	Routers
2	Data link	Switches, bridges, NICs
1	Physical	Hubs and repeaters

Now that you have been introduced to the seven-layer OSI model, let's try an exercise to put your newfound knowledge to the test.

Exercise 2-1: Mixing and Matching OSI Model Definitions

In this exercise, you will match terms with their appropriate definitions. This exercise is designed to give you the opportunity to identify the purpose of each layer of the OSI model.

Definition	Layer
_____ Responsible for the logical addressing and delivery of the packets	A. Session
_____ Responsible for formatting the message	B. Physical
_____ Responsible for physical addressing and converting the data packets to electrical signals	C. Application
_____ Responsible for creating, managing, and ending a dialog	D. Network
_____ Responsible for reliable delivery, sequencing, and breaking the message into packets	E. Data link
_____ Responsible for placing or removing the signal on and off the wire	F. Presentation
_____ Responsible for initiating or receiving the network request	G. Transport

Encapsulation and De-encapsulation

The term *data encapsulation* refers to the fact that as data is passed down the seven layers of the OSI model, header information is added to the message. For example, when the information reaches layer 4 of the OSI model, a layer 4 header is added, which contains protocol information for that layer, such as the port number. On the sending system, the layer 4 header is added and then the data is passed down to layer 3, where the layer 3 header is added to the left side of the data and layer 4 header. The layer 3 header contains the layer 3 protocol information, such as the layer 3 source and destination addresses. Once the layer 3 header is applied, the message is then passed down to layer 2, where the layer 2 header is assigned and contains the source and destination MAC addresses (layer 2 addresses).

On the receiving system, the message is passed up the OSI model. The receiving system strips off the layer 2 header and reads the destination MAC address to ensure that this system is the destination of the message. Once the layer 2 header is read, the message is then passed up to the layer 3 protocol, which reads the layer 3 header (as shown in Figure 2-7). This process of *de-encapsulation* continues up the seven layers of the OSI model.

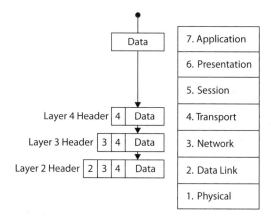

Figure 2-7
Each layer of the OSI model adds a header.

Generically speaking, *protocol data unit* (PDU) describes data as it passes through each layer of the OSI model. At each layer, a new header is added to the data. Table 2-3 describes the PDU terms used at the various layers. For instance, as data is passed from the session layer to the transport layer, the transport layer *encapsulates* the data PDU by adding a layer 4 header. At this point the data is now referred to as a segment. As the PDU information is passed down, each layer adds its own header, and at that point the data uses a different term in the model. For example, once the layer 3 header is added, the data is no longer termed a segment; it is now considered a *packet*. Likewise, once layer 2 header information is added, the data is known as a *frame*. This is important for you to understand, because when you read Chapters 9 and 10 you will notice that we do not use the term packet—a switch runs at layer 2, so therefore it works with frames instead of packets.

EXAM TIP You'll need to know the layer designations for the PDU terms in Table 2-3, and you should remember that computers deal with data in binary (bits). A quick mnemonic you can use to remember PDU terms is "Do Sergeants Pay For Beer?" (data, segment, packet, frame, bits).

Once the physical layer is reached, the bits of the data link layer frame are converted into a physical layer signal—a voltage, light source, radio wave, or other source according to the type of physical medium that is employed. When the destination receives the

Table 2-3
PDU Terms and Layers

PDU Terms	OSI Reference Model Layers
Data	Application, presentation, and session layers
Segment	Transport layer
Packet	Network layer
Frame	Data link layer
Bits	Physical layer

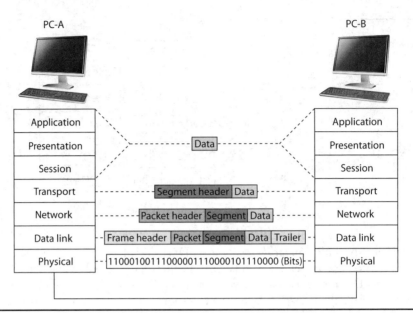

PC-A   PC-B

PC-A		PC-B
Application		Application
Presentation	Data	Presentation
Session		Session
Transport	Segment header │ Data	Transport
Network	Packet header │ Segment │ Data	Network
Data link	Frame header │ Packet │ Segment │ Data │ Trailer	Data link
Physical	11000100111000001110000101110000 (Bits)	Physical

Figure 2-8 Encapsulation and de-encapsulation processes

information, it goes through a reverse process of *de-encapsulating* information—basically stripping off the headers and trailers of the PDU information at each layer as the information is passed up from layer to layer of the OSI model.

Figure 2-8 shows an example of the processes used for encapsulating and de-encapsulating PDUs as data is passed down and back up the layers. In this example, you can see how the application, presentation, and session layers create the data PDU. As this information is passed down from layer to layer, each layer adds its own header (and possibly trailer, as is the case with most layer 2 protocols).

The next few sections will help you better understand the process that devices go through as information is transmitted between computers. The next section covers the details as to how information is encapsulated and sent down the protocol stack and then placed on the wire to the destination. The section following that covers the reverse process: how the information is de-encapsulated at the destination and delivered to the application at the application layer. The last part of the chapter looks at a more complex environment, where bridges, routers, and hubs are involved in the communication process to get information from the source to the destination.

Going Down the Protocol Stack

This section covers the basic mechanics as to how information is processed as it's sent down the protocol stack on a computer. Consult the diagram shown earlier in Figure 2-8 to follow along with this process as PC-A sends data to PC-B. In this example, assume that the data link layer is Ethernet and the physical layer is copper.

The first thing that occurs on PC-A is that the user, sitting in front of the computer, creates some type of information, or data, and then sends it to another location (PC-B). This includes the actual user input (application layer), as well as any formatting information (presentation layer). The application (or operating system) at the session layer then determines whether or not the data's intended destination is local to this computer (possibly a disk drive) or a remote location. In this instance, the user is sending the information to PC-B. We'll assume that the user is executing a telnet connection.

The session layer determines that this location is remote and has the transport layer deliver the information. A telnet connection uses TCP/IP and reliable connections (TCP) at the transport layer, which encapsulates the data from the higher layers into a segment. With TCP, as you will see in Chapter 3, only a header is added. The segment contains such information as the source and destination port numbers.

 CAUTION   Based on RFC standards, the TCP or UDP source port number really should be above 49,151, but not all operating systems follow this standard verbatim—in many cases, the source port number will be above 1023.

The transport layer passes the segment down to the network layer, which encapsulates the segment into a packet. The packet adds only a header, which contains layer 3 logical addressing information (source and destination address) as well as other information, such as the upper-layer protocol that created this information. In this example, TCP created this information, so this fact is noted in the packet header, and PC-A places its IP address as the source address in the packet and PC-B's IP address as the destination. This helps the destination, at the network layer, to determine whether the packet is for itself and which upper-layer process should handle the encapsulated segment. In the TCP/IP protocol stack, the terms *packet* and *datagram* are used interchangeably to describe this PDU. As you will see in Chapter 3, many protocols are involved in the TCP/IP protocol stack—Address Resolution Protocol (ARP), TCP, UDP, Internet Control Message Protocol (ICMP), Open Shortest Path First (OSPF), Enhanced Interior Gateway Routing Protocol (EIGRP), and many others.

The network layer then passes the packet down to the data link layer. The data link layer encapsulates the packet into a frame by adding both a header and a trailer. This example uses Ethernet as the data link layer medium, which was discussed in Chapter 1. The important components placed in the Ethernet frame header are the source and destination MAC addresses, as well as a field checksum sequence (FCS) value so that the destination can determine whether the frame is valid or corrupted when it is received. In this example, PC-A places its MAC address in the frame in the source field and PC-B's MAC address in the destination field. FCS is discussed in more depth in Chapter 1.

The data link layer frame is then passed down to the physical layer. At this point, remember that the concept of "PDUs" is a human concept that we have placed on the data to make it more readable to us, as well as to help deliver the information to the destination. However, from a computer's perspective, the data is just a bunch of binary values, 1s and 0s, or bits. The physical layer converts these bits into a physical property based on the cable or connection type. In this example, the cable is a copper cable, so the physical layer will convert the bits into voltages: one voltage level for a bit value of 1 and a different voltage level for a 0.

Going Up the Protocol Stack

For the sake of simplicity, assume PC-A and PC-B are on the same piece of copper. Once the destination PC receives the physical layer signals, the physical layer translates the voltage levels back to their binary representation and passes these bit values up to the data link layer.

The data link layer reassembles the bit values into the original data link frame (Ethernet). The network adapter examines the FCS to make sure the frame is valid and examines the destination MAC address to ensure that the Ethernet frame is meant for itself. If the destination MAC address doesn't match its own MAC address, or it is not a multicast or broadcast address, the NIC drops the frame. Otherwise, the NIC processes the frame. In this case, the NIC sees that the encapsulated packet is a TCP/IP packet, so it strips off (de-encapsulates) the Ethernet frame information and passes the packet up to the TCP/IP protocol stack at the network layer.

The network layer then examines the logical destination address in the packet header. If the destination logical address doesn't match its own address or is not a multicast or broadcast address, the network layer drops the packet. If the logical address matches, then the destination's network layer examines the protocol information in the packet header to determine which protocol should handle the packet. In this example, the logical address matches and the protocol is defined as TCP. Therefore, the network layer strips off the packet information and passes the encapsulated segment up to the TCP protocol at the transport layer.

Upon receiving the segment, the transport layer can perform many functions, depending on whether this is a reliable or unreliable connection. This discussion focuses on the multiplexing function of the transport layer. In this instance, the transport layer examines the destination port number in the segment header. In our example, the user from PC-A was using telnet to transmit information to PC-B, so the destination port number is 23. The transport layer examines this port number and realizes that the encapsulated data needs to be forwarded to the telnet application. If PC-B doesn't support telnet, the transport layer drops the segment. If it does, the transport layer strips off the segment information and passes the encapsulated data to the telnet application. If this is a new connection, a new telnet process is started up by the operating system.

Note that a logical communication takes place between two layers of two devices. For instance, a logical communication occurs at the transport layer between PC-A and PC-B, and this is also true at the network and data link layers.

 EXAM TIP For the exams, you should be familiar with the process of going down (encapsulation) and back up (de-encapsulation) the protocol stack when transferring data between devices.

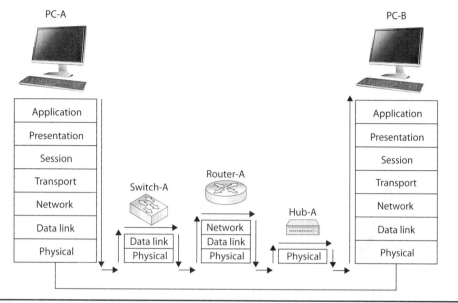

Figure 2-9 Multisegment communications

Layers and Communication

As you can see from the encapsulation and de-encapsulation process, *many* processes are occurring on both the source and destination computers to transmit and receive the information. This can become even more complicated if the source and destination are on different segments, separated by other networking devices, such as hubs, switches, and routers. Figure 2-9 shows an example of this process.

Let's take a look at the pathway of the information as it travels from PC-A to PC-B. In this example, PC-A wants to send data to PC-B. Notice that each device needs to process information at specific layers. For instance, once PC-A places its information on the wire, the switch connected to PC-A needs to process this information. Recall from earlier in this chapter that switches function at layer 2 of the OSI model. Whereas routers make path decisions based on destination layer 3 logical addresses, switches make path decisions based on layer 2 destination MAC addresses found in frames. Therefore, the switch's physical layer will have to convert the physical layer signal into bits and pass these bits up to the data link layer, where they are reassembled into a frame. The switch examines the destination MAC address of the frame and makes a switching decision, finding the port the frame needs to exit. The switch needs to forward the data to the router so it then sends the frame down to the physical layer, where the bits of the frame are converted into physical layer signals. (Switching is discussed in more detail in Chapter 9.)

The next device encountered is a router. Recall from earlier in the chapter that routers function at layer 3 (the network layer) of the OSI model. The router first converts the data (which is an electrical signal traveling the wire) into bits at the physical layer. The bits are passed up to the data link layer and reassembled into a frame. The router then examines the destination MAC address in the frame. If the MAC address doesn't match its own MAC address, the router drops the frame. If the MAC address matches, the router strips off the data link layer frame and passes the packet up to the network layer.

At the network layer on the router, one of the functions of the router is to route packets to destinations. To accomplish this, the router examines the destination logical address in the packet and extracts a network number from this address. The router then compares the network number to entries in its routing table. If the router doesn't find a match, it drops the packet; if it does find a match, it forwards the packet out the destination interface (the local interface designated by the router's routing table).

To accomplish the packet forwarding, the router passes the packet down to the data link layer, which encapsulates the packet into the correct data link layer frame format. If this were an Ethernet frame, for example, the source MAC address would be that of the router and the destination would be PC-B. At the data link layer, the frame is then passed down to the physical layer, where the bits are converted into an electrical signal at the physical layer once again.

 EXAM TIP When sending traffic between two devices on different segments, the source device has a layer 2 frame with its own MAC address as the source and the default gateway's (router) MAC address as the destination; however, in the layer 3 packet, the source layer 3 address is the source device and the destination layer 3 address is not the default gateway, but the actual destination the source is trying to reach. For the exams, remember that layer 2 addresses are used to communicate with devices on the same physical or logical layer 2 segment/network, and layer 3 addresses are used to communicate with devices across the network (multiple segments). Another way to remember this is that MAC addresses can change from link to link, but layer 3 logical addresses, by default, cannot.

Note that routers separate physical or logical segments, while bridges and switches don't. Therefore, if PC-A wants to send traffic to PC-B, PC-A uses the router's MAC (or layer 2) address to get traffic to the exit point of the segment, but it uses PC-B's logical (or layer 3) address to tell the router that this traffic is not for the router but for a machine on a different segment.

In Figure 2-9, the next device that receives these physical layer signals is the hub. Keep in mind that in today's day and age that is most likely going to be a switch, but I wanted to have a hub in the diagram to discuss how hubs handle data. Recall from earlier in the chapter that hubs and repeaters operate at the physical layer. Basically, a hub is a multi-port repeater: it repeats any physical layer signal it receives. Therefore, a signal received on one interface of a hub is repeated on all of its other interfaces. These signals are then received by PC-B, which passes this information up the protocol stack as described in the preceding section. Companies use switches instead of hubs today because hubs send the data (the electrical signal) to all ports, while a switch would filter traffic by only sending data to the port that the destination address is connected to.

For the CCT/CCNA Exams:
Things to Remember About the OSI Reference Model

For the exams, make sure you are familiar with the OSI Reference Model and why it was originally developed.

You should know the names and orders of the layers: application, presentation, session, transport, network, data link, and physical. You should also know the kinds of devices that work at various layers (router/network layer, switch/data link layer, and hub/physical layer) and some of the important functions these devices perform. For example, routers switch packets between network segments, they prevent the propagation of broadcasts, they can filter on layer 3 logical addresses, and they determine paths to destination logical networks. You should also be able to name example protocols that function at the various layers. For example, telnet and FTP function at the application layer.

Be especially familiar with the transport, network, and data link layers and their functions. The transport layer, for example, sets up, maintains, and tears down connections. It can provide reliable or unreliable delivery of data. It segments data into smaller, more manageable pieces. It can implement flow control through ready/not ready signals or windowing through the use of sequence and acknowledgment numbers to avoid congestion. It uses buffers to store incoming data and multiplexes multiple connections through the use of port numbers and layer 3 addresses. TCP and UDP are example protocols that operate at the transport layer.

The network layer defines logical addresses, finds best paths to destination logical addresses through the use of routing tables on routers, and connects different layer 2 link types together. Remember the advantages that routers provide, such as scalability through the use of hierarchical network designs and routing protocols, containment of broadcasts, intelligent path selection, and traffic filtering.

The data link layer defines how devices connect to a layer 2 media type and how these devices communicate with each other through the use of physical addresses, such as MAC addresses in Ethernet. Know what a MAC address looks like: it's 48 bits long and is represented in hexadecimal.

You should also be familiar with the PDU terms used at the various OSI Reference Model layers—segment/transport layer, packet or datagram/network layer, frame/data link layer, and bits/physical layer. You should also be able to describe how devices communicate with other devices at the various layers: what layer 2 or layer 3 addresses are used between various devices from the source to the destination. Remember that MAC addresses can change from link to link, but layer 3 addresses, such as TCP/IP addresses, typically do not.

Chapter Review

The OSI Reference Model defines the process of connecting two layers of networking functions. The application layer provides the user interface. The presentation layer determines how data is represented to the user. The session layer is responsible for setting up and tearing down connections. The transport layer is responsible for the mechanics of connections, including guaranteed services. The network layer provides a logical topology and layer 3 addresses: routers operate here. The data link layer defines MAC addresses and how communication is performed on a specific media type: switches, bridges, and NICs operate here. The physical layer defines physical properties for connections and communication: repeaters and hubs operate here. Wireless solutions are defined at the physical layer.

The transport layer sets up and maintains a session layer connection and provides for reliable or unreliable delivery of data, flow control, and multiplexing of connections. Reliable connections typically go through a handshake process to establish a connection. Acknowledgments are used to provide reliable delivery. Port or socket numbers are used for connection multiplexing. Ready/not ready signals and windowing are used to implement flow control. Windowing is more efficient than ready/not ready signals.

The network layer defines logical addresses, finds paths to destinations based on the network component of the address, and connects different layer 2 media types together. Routers are used to contain broadcasts. Routers use their routing table, which has a list of destination network numbers, to assist them when finding a destination. If a destination is not found in the routing table, the router drops traffic for this destination.

The data link layer defines hardware addressing. MAC addresses are 48 bits in length in hexadecimal. The first 24 bits (six digits) are the organizationally unique identifier (OUI). MAC addresses need to be unique only on a logical segment. In a unicast, one frame is sent to all devices on a segment, but only a single device will process it. In a multicast, one frame is sent to a group of devices. In a broadcast, one frame is sent to all devices.

A protocol data unit (PDU) describes data and its overhead. A PDU at the application layer is referred to as data, the transport layer PDU is called a segment, the network layer PDU is called a packet or datagram, the data link layer PDU is called a frame, and the physical layer PDU is called bits. As traffic goes down the protocol stack, each layer encapsulates the PDU from the layer above it. At the destination, a de-encapsulation process occurs as the traffic moves back up the protocol stack.

Quick Review

Introduction to the OSI Reference Model

- The OSI Reference Model provides the following advantages: it promotes interoperability, defines how to connect adjacent layers, compartmentalizes components, allows a modular design, serves as a teaching tool, and simplifies troubleshooting.

Layers of the OSI Reference Model

- The application layer (layer 7) is responsible for initiating a network request, or servicing that network request. The presentation layer (layer 6) defines the format of the information. The session layer (layer 5) is responsible for the setup and teardown of the dialog. The transport layer (layer 4) handles the mechanics of reliable or unreliable services. The network layer (layer 3) is responsible for logical addressing and routing. Routers function at layer 3. The data link layer (layer 2) assigns physical (MAC) addresses and defines how devices on a specific media type communicate with each other. Bridges, switches, and NICs operate at layer 2. The physical layer (layer 1) handles all physical properties for a connection. Hubs and repeaters function here.

- The data link layer defines MAC addresses, the physical or hardware topology, and the framing used; it provides for connection-oriented and connectionless services. MAC addresses are 48 bits in length and are represented in hexadecimal. The first six digits are the OUI (vendor code), and the last six digits represent the NIC within the OUI. A unicast is sent to one destination on a segment, a multicast is sent to a group of devices, and a broadcast (*FF:FF:FF:FF:FF:FF*) is sent to all devices.

- The network layer defines logical addresses, finds paths to destinations using the network number in the logical address, and connects different media types together. Routers function at the network layer. A routing table contains information about destination network numbers and how to reach them. Routers contain broadcasts, allow for scalability through hierarchical designs, make better decisions for reaching a destination than bridges, can switch packets on the same interface using VLANs, and can implement advanced features such as QoS and filtering.

- The transport layer sets up and maintains a session connection, segments data into smaller payloads, provides for reliable or unreliable transport of data, implements flow control, and multiplexes connections. Reliable connections use sequence numbers and acknowledgments. TCP is an example. Reliable transport protocols use a handshake process to set up a connection. Unreliable services don't use a connection setup process. UDP is an example. Multiplexing of connections is done with port or socket numbers. Flow control can be implemented with ready/not ready signals or windowing. Windowing is more efficient. The size of the window affects your throughput. Depending on the size, a source can send X segments before having to wait for an acknowledgment.

Encapsulation and De-encapsulation

- A protocol data unit (PDU) describes data and its overhead. Each layer has a unique PDU: as data is sent down the protocol stack, it is encapsulated at each layer by adding a header and, possibly, a trailer. The destination de-encapsulates the data as it goes back up the protocol stack.

- The transport layer PDU is a segment, the network layer PDU is a packet or datagram, the data link layer PDU is a frame, and the physical layer PDU is bits.

Questions

The following questions will help you measure your understanding of the material presented in this chapter. Read all the choices carefully, as there may be more than one correct answer. Choose the correct answer(s) for each question.

1. The OSI Reference Model provides for all of the following except which one?

   A. Defines the process for connecting two layers together, promoting interoperability between vendors

   B. Allows vendors to compartmentalize their design efforts to fit a modular design, which eases implementations and simplifies troubleshooting

   C. Separates a complex function into simpler components

   D. Defines eight layers common to all networking protocols

   E. Provides a teaching tool to help network administrators understand the communication process used between networking components

2. Put the following OSI Reference Model layers in the correct order, from high to low: (a) session, (b) presentation, (c) physical, (d) data link, (e) network, (f) application, (g) transport.

   A. c, d, e, g, a, b, f

   B. f, a, b, g, d, e, c

   C. f, b, g, a, e, d, c

   D. f, b, a, g, e, d, c

3. The _____ layer of the OSI model provides physical addressing.

   A. Transport

   B. Network

   C. Data link

   D. Physical

4. Sue has noticed that the first half of the MAC address (24 bits) is the same for all the network cards on your computers. What does the first 24 bits of a MAC address represent?

   A. AUI

   B. NIA

   C. RTP

   D. OUI

5. The network layer handles all of the following problems except _____.

   A. Broadcast problems

   B. Conversion between media types

   C. Hierarchy through the use of physical addresses

   D. Splitting collision domains into smaller ones

6. _____ are used to provide a reliable connection.

   A. Ready/not ready signals

   B. Sequence numbers and acknowledgments

   C. Windows

   D. Ready/not ready signals and windowing

7. Connection multiplexing is done through the use of a _____ number.

   A. Socket

   B. Hardware

   C. Network

   D. Session

Performance-based Questions

The Cisco exams have performance-based questions for which you must drag items from the left side of the screen to its proper place on the right side of the screen in order to answer the question. Following are some sample performance-based questions.

1. Match the device with the layer of the OSI Reference Model that the device functions at.

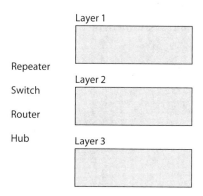

2. Match the PDU name with the OSI Reference Model layer at which it is used.

Layer 1

Layer 2

Packet
Segment
Frame   Layer 3
Bits

Layer 4

Answers

1. D. The OSI Reference Model is a seven-layer model, not an eight-layer model, that acts as a standard for all networking components including networking hardware and software.

2. D. From high to low, the OSI Reference Model has the following layers: application, presentation, session, transport, network, data link, and physical (f, b, a, g, e, d, c).

3. C. The data link layer provides physical addressing.

4. D. The first 24 bits of a MAC address identifies the vendor ID for the manufacturer of the network card. This ID is also known as an organizationally unique identifier (OUI).

5. C. The network layer creates a hierarchy through the use of logical, not physical, addresses. An example of a logical address is an IP address.

6. B. Sequence numbers and acknowledgments are used to provide a reliable transport layer connection.

7. A. Connection multiplexing is done through the use of a socket or port number.

Performance-based Answers

The following are the answers to the performance-based questions.

1. The following is layer of the OSI model that each device runs at.

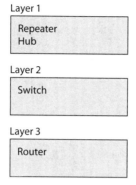

Layer 1

> Repeater
> Hub

Layer 2

> Switch

Layer 3

> Router

2. The following identifies the PDU name for the data at the different layers of the OSI model.

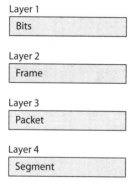

Layer 1

> Bits

Layer 2

> Frame

Layer 3

> Packet

Layer 4

> Segment

TCP/IP Protocol Suite

In this chapter, you will

- Learn about the layers of the TCP/IP model
- Understanding transport layer protocols
- Working with Internet layer protocols

The most popular protocol suite in use today is Transmission Control Protocol/Internet Protocol (TCP/IP). The Internet and most company intranets currently use TCP/IP because of its popularity, flexibility, compatibility, and capability to perform in both small and large network implementations. TCP/IP can connect a diverse range of hosts, from mainframes to handheld computers. The CCT and CCNA certification exams test your knowledge of TCP/IP quite heavily. Although TCP/IP is the most commonly used protocol, it is not the easiest to configure—or even to understand. This chapter gives you an in-depth understanding of TCP/IP, including the architecture, addressing issues, and configuration involved with its use. The CCT and CCNA exams will test your knowledge of the protocol, but most importantly, they will test your knowledge on the practical configuration of the protocol for different-sized networks.

 EXAM TIP TCP/IP is a protocol suite—meaning that there are multiple protocols within it. You will be required to know a number of these protocols for the CCT certification exam and as background information for the CCNA exam.

As you will learn in this chapter, each protocol in the suite has a specific purpose and function. It is not important for the CCT and CCNA exams that you understand the evolution of TCP/IP, so we discuss here the details of the protocol on which you are likely to be tested. Be sure to spend your time on the TCP/IP-related chapters, because this knowledge will help you as you work as a networking professional.

The TCP/IP Model

The TCP/IP model, also referred to as the TCP/IP Model, is a four-layer model similar in concept to the seven-layer OSI Reference Model. The four layers of the TCP/IP model map to the seven layers of the OSI version, but the TCP/IP model combines multiple layers of the OSI model, as shown in Figure 3-1. Several protocols direct how computers connect and

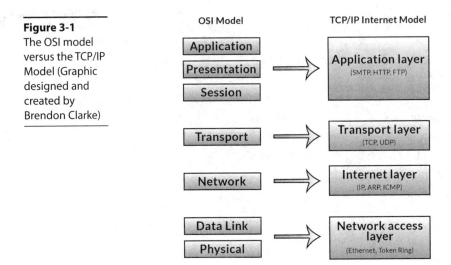

Figure 3-1
The OSI model versus the TCP/IP Model (Graphic designed and created by Brendon Clarke)

communicate using TCP/IP within the TCP/IP protocol suite, and each protocol runs on different layers of the TCP/IP Model.

Application Layer

The application layer is at the top of the TCP/IP model and corresponds to the application, presentation, and session layers of the OSI model. It is responsible for making network requests (sending computer) or servicing requests (receiving computer). So, for example, when a user submits a request from a web browser, the web browser responsible for the submission of the request is running at the application layer. When that web request reaches the web server, the web server running at the application layer accepts that request.

Following are popular application layer protocols:

- **Hypertext Transfer Protocol (HTTP)** Transfers HTML pages between the web server and the web browser
- **Hypertext Transfer Protocol Secure (HTTPS)** Delivers encrypted HTML pages from the web server to the web browser
- **Simple Mail Transfer Protocol (SMTP)** Sends Internet e-mail
- **Post Office Protocol (POP)** Reads or downloads Internet e-mail to your system
- **File Transfer Protocol (FTP)** Lets you download files from a system on the network or the Internet
- **Domain Name System (DNS)** Converts fully qualified domain names (FQDNs) to IP addresses
- **Remote Desktop Protocol (RDP)** Helps you operate a system remotely

Transport Layer

The next layer is the transport layer, which is responsible for both connection-oriented communication (a session is established) and connectionless communication (a session is not established). When the request comes down from the application layer, a transport protocol is chosen to handle it. The two transport protocols in TCP/IP are the Transmission Control Protocol (TCP) and the User Datagram Protocol (UDP). As data passes down the layers of the TCP/IP model, if connection-oriented communication is required, TCP is used as the transport layer protocol, but if connectionless communication is required, UDP is used.

Internet Layer

The Internet layer corresponds to the network layer of the OSI model. It is responsible for a number of important network activities, such as logical addressing, routing, and converting the logical address to the physical Media Access Control (MAC) address.

Here are examples of protocols that run at this layer:

- **Internet Protocol (IP)**   Handles all logical addressing (IP addresses) and routing functionality
- **Address Resolution Protocol (ARP)**   Converts the logical address (IP address) to a physical address (MAC address)
- **Internet Control Message Protocol (ICMP)**   Reports the status and any errors in the TCP/IP protocol suite

You will learn more about these protocols as we progress through the chapter.

Network Access Layer

The network access layer is sometimes referred to as the network interface layer or the link layer. The network access layer corresponds to the data link and physical layers of the OSI model. Examples of network access layer components are network architectures, physical addressing, cables, connectors, network media, and any other layer 2 and layer 1 network components. Because network access layer components were discussed in Chapter 1, we will focus on the protocols of TCP/IP in this chapter.

Transport Layer Protocols

Now let's take a look at the transport layer protocols in a little more detail. Remember that the transport layer includes the TCP and UDP protocols. In this section you will learn about the details of each protocol and examine the protocol header.

Transmission Control Protocol

TCP is responsible for providing connection-oriented communication and for ensuring delivery of the data (known as reliable delivery). Connection-oriented communication involves first establishing a connection between two systems and then ensuring that data sent across the connection reaches the destination. TCP will make sure that the data reaches its destination by retransmitting any data that is lost or corrupt. TCP is used by applications that require a reliable transport, but this transport has more overhead than a connectionless protocol because of the construction of the session and the monitoring and retransmission of any data across that session.

Another factor to remember about TCP is that the protocol requires that the recipient acknowledge the successful receipt of data. Of course, all the acknowledgments, or ACKs, generate additional traffic on the network, which reduces the amount of data that can be passed within a given time frame. The extra overhead involved in the creation, monitoring, and ending of the TCP session is worth the certainty that TCP will ensure that the data will reach its destination.

TCP ensures that data is delivered by using sequence numbers and acknowledgment numbers. A *sequence number* is a number assigned to each piece of data that is sent. After a system receives a piece of data, it acknowledges that it has received the data by sending an acknowledgment message back to the sender, with the original sequence number being the *acknowledgment number* of the reply message.

TCP Three-Way Handshake

Before a system can communicate over TCP, it must first establish a connection to the remote system. It does this through the TCP three-way handshake (see Figure 3-2).

The TCP three-way handshake involves three phases:

1. **SYN**   The sending system sends a SYN message to the receiving system. Each packet sent is assigned a unique sequence number. The SYN message contains the *initial sequence number* (ISN), which is the first sequence number to be used. In this example, Computer A is connecting to the web site on Computer B, so a SYN message is sent to port 80 on Computer B.

2. **SYN/ACK**   This phase acknowledges the first message, but at the same time indicates its initial sequence number. In this example, Computer B sends back the SYN/ACK message that is acknowledging that it has received packet 123 (by acknowledging that 124 is the next sequence number), but it has also specified that its ISN is 326.

3. **ACK**   The final phase is the acknowledgment message that acknowledges that the packet sent in the second phase has been received. In this example, Computer A sends the ACK to acknowledge that it has received packet 326 by acknowledging that the next packet will be sequence number 327.

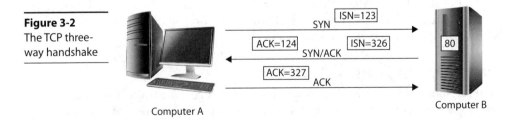

Figure 3-2
The TCP three-way handshake

Computer A

Computer B

Disconnecting from a TCP Session

Just as TCP uses a three-way handshake process to create a connection between two systems that want to communicate, it also has a process for a participant to disconnect from the conversation. Looking at Figure 3-3, you can see that if Computer A wants to disconnect from a TCP session, it must first send a FIN flag to Computer B to signal that it wants to end the conversation.

When Computer B receives the FIN message, it replies with an acknowledgment and then sends its own FIN message back to Computer A. As a final step to this process, Computer A must acknowledge that it received the FIN message from Computer B. This is similar to talking to someone on the phone—to end the conversation, you say goodbye and then wait for the other person to say goodbye before you hang up. I describe this as ending the conversation in a "polite" way.

There is also a way to end a conversation in an "impolite" manner. Back to the telephone analogy: You can end the conversation impolitely by hanging up the phone without saying goodbye. In the TCP world, you can "hang up" by sending a TCP message with the RST (reset) flag set.

TCP Ports

When applications use TCP or UDP to communicate over the network, each application must be uniquely identified by a unique port number on the system. A port is an address assigned to the application. When a client wants to communicate with one of these applications (also known as services), it must send the request to the appropriate port number on the system.

As a networking professional, you must know some of the port numbers used by popular services. Table 3-1 identifies common TCP port numbers you should know for the real world and the CCT/CCNA certification exams.

Both TCP and UDP support up to 65,536 port numbers that range from 0 to 65,535. The port numbers are divided into three different categories:

- **Well-known** These port numbers range from 0 to 1023 and are assigned by the Internet Assigned Number Authority (IANA) to application servers commonly used on the Internet, such as HTTP, DNS, and SMTP.

- **Registered** These port numbers range from 1024 to 49,151 and are assigned by IANA for proprietary applications, such as Microsoft SQL Server, Adobe Shockwave, Oracle software, and many others.

- **Dynamically assigned** These port numbers range from 49,152 to 65,535 and are dynamically assigned by the system, typically used by client software such as your web browser, FTP client, or telnet client.

Figure 3-3
Terminating a
TCP connection

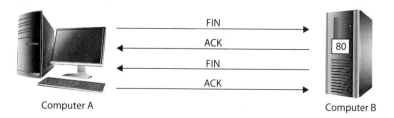

Computer A   Computer B

Port	Service	Description
20	FTP Data	Used by FTP to send data to a client
21	FTP Control	Used by FTP commands sent to the server
22	SSH	Used as a secure replacement protocol for telnet
23	Telnet	Used by telnet to connect remotely to a system such as a server or router
25	SMTP	Used to send Internet e-mail
53	DNS	Used for DNS zone transfers
80	HTTP	Used to deliver web pages to the browser
110	POP3	Used by POP3, the Internet protocol to read e-mail
143	IMAP	Used by IMAP, a newer Internet protocol to read e-mail
443	HTTPS	Used for secure web traffic
3389	RDP	TCP port used by Remote Desktop to manage a Windows system remotely

Table 3-1 Popular TCP Ports

TCP Flags

TCP uses TCP flags to identify important types of packets. Figure 3-4 displays the flags in a packet capture. Notice that instead of the actual flag being shown, the value is interpreted by Network Monitor and a description is shown. For example, instead of seeing the URG flag set to 0, you can see the first flag set to 0 with a description of "No urgent data."

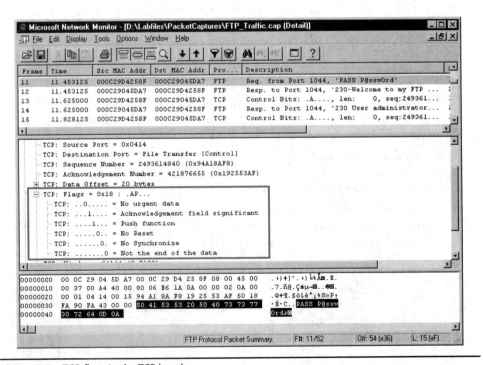

Figure 3-4 TCP flags in the TCP header

Following are the common TCP flags you should be familiar with for the CCT/CCNA certification exams:

- **SYN** The SYN flag is assigned to any packets that are part of the SYN phases of the three-way handshake.
- **ACK** The acknowledgment flag acknowledges that a previous packet has been received.
- **PSH** The push flag is designed to force data on an application.
- **URG** The urgent flag specifies that a packet is urgent.
- **FIN** The finish flag specifies that you would like to finalize, or end, the connection. This is how a TCP connection is ended the polite way—it is like saying goodbye to end a phone conversation.
- **RST** The reset flag is used to end a TCP conversation impolitely. This is like hanging up the phone without saying goodbye.

TCP Header

Every packet that is sent using TCP has a TCP header assigned to it, which contains TCP-related information such as the source port, destination port, and the TCP flags. Figure 3-5 displays the different fields in the TCP header.

Here are quick descriptions of each field in the TCP header:

- **Source Port** This 16-bit field identifies the port number of the sending system.
- **Destination Port** This 16-bit field identifies the port number the packet is destined for on the destination system.
- **Sequence Number** This 32-bit field identifies the sequence number of the packet.

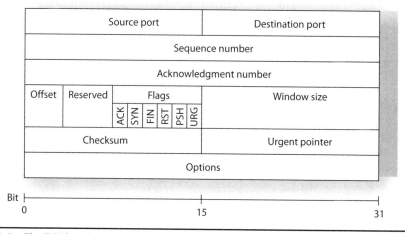

Figure 3-5 The TCP header

- **Acknowledgment Number** This 32-bit field identifies the packet that this packet is acknowledging.
- **Offset** This 4-bit field indicates where the data begins.
- **Reserved** This 6-bit field is always set to 0 and was designed for future use.
- **Flags** This 6-bit field is where the TCP flags are stored. There is a 1-bit field for each of the TCP flags mentioned earlier in this section.
- **Window Size** This 16-bit field determines the amount of information that can be sent before an acknowledgment is expected.
- **Checksum** This 16-bit field is used to verify the integrity of the TCP header.
- **Urgent Pointer** This 16-bit field is used only if the URG flag is set and is a reference to the last piece of information that was urgent.
- **Options** This is a variable-length field that specifies any additional settings that may be needed in the TCP header.

EXAM TIP Remember for the CCT certification that TCP and UDP are considered layer 4 (transport) protocols of the OSI model.

User Datagram Protocol

UDP is used by applications that are not concerned with ensuring that the data reaches the destination system. UDP is used for connectionless communication (unreliable), which means that data is sent to the destination and no effort is made to track the progress of the packet or determine whether it has reached the destination.

UDP Ports

Like TCP, UDP uses port numbers to identify different types of UDP traffic. Table 3-2 identifies a few examples of UDP traffic and the ports used.

Port	Service	Description
53	DNS	UDP port 53 is used for DNS queries.
67 and 68	DHCP	UDP port 67 is used by the DHCP service and port 68 is used by client requests.
69	TFTP	Trivial File Transfer Protocol is used to upload or download files without requiring authentication.
137 and 138	NetBIOS	UDP ports 137 and 138 are used by the NetBIOS name service and datagram service.
161	SNMP	UDP port 161 is used by the Simple Network Management Protocol.

Table 3-2 Popular UDP Ports

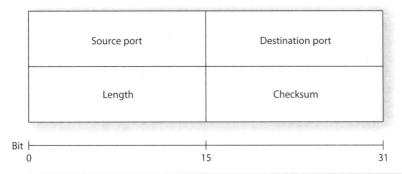

Source port	Destination port
Length	Checksum

Bit
0   15   31

Figure 3-6 The UDP header

UDP Header

Because UDP does not have to acknowledge the receipt of a packet, the structure of the UDP header is much simpler than that of the TCP header. For example, the UDP header does not need a sequence number or acknowledgment number; it also does not need flags to indicate special packets such as a SYN message, because there is no three-way handshake (UDP is connectionless). Figure 3-6 displays the UDP header.

The UDP header includes the following fields:

- **Source Port**   This 16-bit field indicates the port used by the sending application on the sending system.
- **Destination Port**   This 16-bit field indicates the port used by the application on the destination system.
- **Length**   This 16-bit field specifies the size of the UDP header in bytes.
- **Checksum**   This 16-bit field is used to verify the integrity of the UDP header.

Internet Layer Protocols

After a transport protocol has been selected, which is based on whether the communication should be connection oriented or connectionless, the information is passed to the Internet layer to determine who is responsible for its delivery. A few protocols run at the Internet layer, such as IP, ICMP, and ARP.

Internet Protocol

The Internet Protocol (IP) provides packet delivery for protocols in higher layers of the model. It is a connectionless delivery system that makes a "best-effort" attempt to deliver the packets to the correct destination. IP does not guarantee delivery of the packets—that is the responsibility of transport protocols; IP simply sends the data.

EXAM TIP   For the both the CCT and CCNA exams, you should remember that IP is a layer 3 protocol of the OSI model and is responsible for logical addressing and routing.

The Internet Protocol is also responsible for the logical addressing and routing of TCP/IP and, therefore, is considered a layer 3 protocol of the OSI model. The IP on the router is responsible for decrementing (usually by a value of 1) the TTL (time to live) of the packet to prevent it from running in a "network loop." Once the TTL of the packet is decremented to 0, the router removes the packet from the network and sends a status message to the sender (using ICMP); this prevents loops. Windows operating systems have a default TTL of 128, whereas most Linux operating systems have a TTL of 64 by default.

IP Header

The IP header in the packet contains information that helps the packet make its way from the source to the destination. Figure 3-7 displays the IP header structure.

The following is a listing of the fields in the IP header and their meaning:

- **Version**   This 4-bit field identifies the version of IP being used, for example, version 4 or 6.

- **Header Length**   This 4-bit field indicates the size of the IP header.

- **Type of Service**   This 8-bit field indicates how the packet should be handled by the system. For example, if the low delay option is specified here, it means that the system should deal with the packet right away.

- **Total Length**   This 16-bit field indicates the size of the IP packet.

- **Identification**   Because networks can handle only packets of a specific maximum size—known as a *maximum transmission unit* (MTU)—the system may break the data being sent into multiple fragments. This 16-bit field uniquely identifies the fragment.

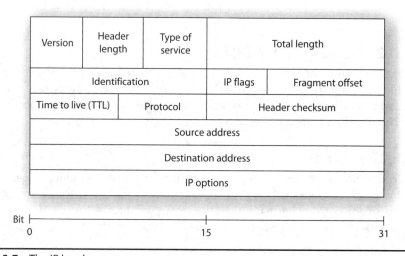

Figure 3-7   The IP header

- **IP Flags** This 3-bit field specifies how fragments are going to be dealt with. For example, a More Fragments (MF) flag indicates more fragments are to come. Also, a bit known as Don't Fragment (DF) specifies not to fragment the packet.

- **Fragment Offset** This 13-bit field specifies the order in which the fragments are to be put back together when the packet is assembled.

- **Time to Live (TTL)** This 8-bit field specifies when the packet is to expire. The TTL is a value that is decremented with every router the packet passes through. When the TTL reaches 0, the packet is discarded.

- **Protocol** This 8-bit field specifies what layer 4 protocol (TCP or UDP) the packet should use.

- **Header Checksum** This 16-bit field verifies the integrity of the IP header.

- **Source Address** This 32-bit field represents the IP address of the sending system. This is how the receiving system knows where to send the reply message.

- **Destination Address** This 32-bit field represents the IP address of the system the packet is destined for.

- **IP Options** This variable-length field is used to specify any other settings in the IP header.

Internet Control Message Protocol

The Internet Control Message Protocol (ICMP) enables systems on a TCP/IP network to share status and error information. You can use the status information to detect network trouble. ICMP messages are encapsulated within IP datagrams so that they can be routed throughout a network. Two programs that use ICMP messages are ping and tracert.

You can use ping to send ICMP echo requests to an IP address and wait for ICMP echo responses. Ping reports the time interval between sending the request and receiving the response. With ping, you can determine whether a particular IP system on your network is functioning correctly. You can use many different options with the ping utility.

 EXAM TIP Remember for both the CCT and CCNA exams that ICMP is the protocol in the TCP/IP protocol suite that is responsible for error and status reporting. Programs such as ping and tracert use ICMP.

Tracert traces the path taken to a particular host. This utility can be useful in troubleshooting internetworks. Tracert sends ICMP echo requests to an IP address while it increments the TTL field in the IP header by a count of 1, after starting at 1, and then analyzing the ICMP errors that are returned. Each succeeding echo request should get one unit further into the network before the TTL field reaches 0 and an "ICMP time exceeded" error message is returned by the router attempting to forward it.

Type	Code	Description
0 – Echo Reply	0	Echo reply message
3 – Destination Unreachable	0	Destination network
	1	Destination host unreachable
	2	Destination protocol unreachable
	3	Destination port unreachable
8 – Echo Request	0	Echo request message

Table 3-3   Common ICMP Types and Codes

ICMP Types and Codes

ICMP does not use port numbers, but instead uses ICMP types and codes to identify the different types of messages. For example, an echo request message that is used by the ping request uses ICMP type 8, while the ping reply comes back with an ICMP type 0 message.

Some of the ICMP types are broken down to finer levels with different codes in the type. For example, ICMP type 3 is a "destination unreachable" message, but because there are many reasons why a destination is unreachable, the type is subdivided into different codes. Each code represents a different message in the type (see Table 3-3).

ICMP Header

The ICMP header is a very small header compared to the IP header and the TCP header. Figure 3-8 displays the ICMP header, and a listing of the fields follows:

- **Type**   This 8-bit field indicates the ICMP type being used.
- **Code**   This 8-bit field indicates the ICMP code being used.
- **Checksum**   This 16-bit field is used to verify the integrity of the ICMP header.
- **Other**   This field stores any data within the ICMP header. For example, Microsoft operating systems place part of the alphabet in this field for echo request messages.

Also note that Internet Group Management Protocol (IGMP) is another Internet-layer protocol and is used for multicast applications.

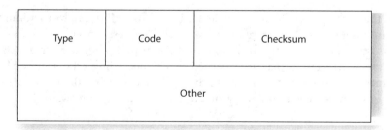

Figure 3-8   The ICMP header

Address Resolution Protocol

The Address Resolution Protocol (ARP) provides IP address–to–physical address resolution on a TCP/IP network. To accomplish this feat, ARP sends out a broadcast message with an ARP request packet that contains the IP address of the system it is trying to find. All systems on the local network see the message, and the system that owns the IP address for which ARP is looking replies by sending its physical address to the originating system in an ARP reply packet. The physical/IP address combo is then stored in the ARP cache of the originating system for future use.

 EXAM TIP   For the CCT certification exam, remember that ARP is responsible for converting an IP address (layer 3 address) to the physical Media Access Control (MAC) address (layer 2 address).

All systems maintain ARP caches that include IP address–to–physical address mappings. The ARP cache is always checked for an IP address–to–physical address mapping before initiating a broadcast. Let's take a look at how ARP works in a little more detail.

Single-Segment ARP Example

Let's start by discussing how ARP works on a single segment network, in which everyone exists on a single LAN. Figure 3-9 shows an example of the use of ARP.

In this example, PC-A wants to send information directly to PC-B. PC-A knows PC-B's IP address (or has DNS resolve it to an IP address); however, it doesn't know PC-B's Ethernet MAC address. To resolve, or convert, the IP address to a MAC address, PC-A generates an ARP request message. In the ARP request message, the source IP address is 10.1.1.1 and the destination IP address is 255.255.255.255 (the broadcast address, which means the data is destined for every device on the network). PC-A includes PC-B's IP address in the data field of the ARP datagram. This is encapsulated into an Ethernet frame, with a source MAC address of 0000.0CCC.1111 (PC-A's MAC address), and a destination MAC address of *FF:FF:FF:FF:FF:FF* (the local broadcast address) and is then placed on the Ethernet segment. Both PC-B and PC-C see this frame because it is destined for all systems (a broadcast message).

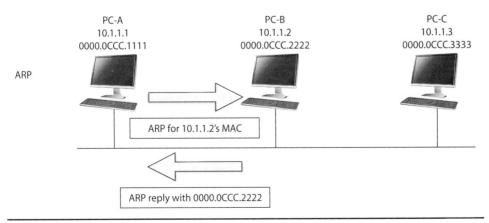

Figure 3-9   ARP on a single segment

Both devices' network interface cards (NICs) notice the data link layer broadcast address and assume that this frame is for them, since the destination MAC address is a broadcast, so they strip off the Ethernet frame and pass the IP datagram with the ARP request up to the Internet layer. Again, there is a broadcast address in the destination IP address field, so both devices' TCP/IP stacks will examine the data payload. PC-B notices that this is an ARP request and that this is its own IP address in the query, and it therefore responds directly back to PC-A with PC-B's MAC address. PC-C, however, sees that this is not an ARP for its own MAC address and ignores the requested datagram broadcast.

NOTE One important thing that both PC-B and PC-C will do is add PC-A's MAC address to their local ARP tables after they have received the initial broadcast message. They do this so that if either device needs to communicate with PC-A, neither will have to perform the ARP request as PC-A had to do. Entries in the ARP cache table will time out after a period of nonuse of the MAC address. This time period is dependent on the operating system used, but it can typically be changed by the user or administrator. Also, a device can generate a *gratuitous ARP*, an ARP reply that is generated without a corresponding ARP request. This is commonly used when a device may change its IP address or MAC address and wants to notify all other devices on the segment about the change so that the other devices have the correct information in their local ARP tables.

Two-Segment ARP Example

Figure 3-10 shows how ARP works across networks. This is very important for you to understand for the CCT and CCNA certification exams. In this example, PC-A wants to connect to PC-B using IP. The source IP address is 1.1.1.1 (PC-A), and the destination is 2.2.2.2 (PC-B). Because the two devices are on different networks, a router is used to communicate between the networks. Therefore, if PC-A wants to send something to PC-B, it has to be sent via the intermediate router. However, this communication does not occur at the network layer using IP; instead, it occurs at the data link layer.

The first thing that PC-A will do is determine whether the destination IP address is on the local network or a remote network (you will learn how this happens in Chapter 4). In this example, it is determined that the destination is on a remote network, so PC-A will need to know the MAC address of the default gateway router in order to send the data to the router. If the router's MAC address isn't already in its local ARP cache, PC-A will generate an ARP request for the default gateway's MAC address. This is shown in step 1 of Figure 3-10. In step 2, the router responds with the MAC address of its Ethernet interface connected to PC-A. In step 3, PC-A creates an IP packet with the source and destination IP addresses (the source is 1.1.1.1 and the destination is 2.2.2.2, PC-B) and encapsulates this in an Ethernet frame, with the source MAC address of PC-A and the destination MAC address of the *router*. PC-A then sends the Ethernet frame to the router.

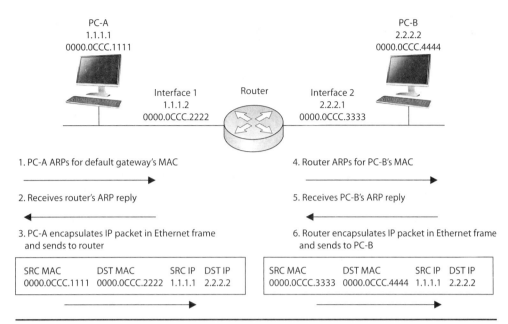

Figure 3-10   ARP example with a router

When the router receives the Ethernet frame, the router compares the frame to the MAC address on its Ethernet interface, which it matches. The router strips off the Ethernet frame and makes a routing decision based on the destination address of 2.2.2.2. In this case, the network is directly connected to the router's second interface. In step 4, if the router doesn't have PC-B's MAC address in its local ARP cache, the router ARPs for the MAC address of PC-B (2.2.2.2) and receives the response in step 5. The router then encapsulates the original IP packet in a new Ethernet frame in step 6, placing its second interface's MAC address, which is sourcing the frame, in the source MAC address field and PC-B's MAC address in the destination field. When PC-B receives this, it knows the frame is for itself (matching destination MAC address) and that PC-A originated the IP packet that's encapsulated based on the source IP address in the IP header at layer 3.

Note that in this example, the original IP addressing in the packet was not altered by the router, but two Ethernet frames are used to get the IP packet to the destination. Also, each device will keep the MAC addresses in a local ARP cache, so the next time PC-A needs to send something to PC-B, the devices will not have to ARP other intermediate devices again.

EXAM TIP   ARP is used to determine the layer 2 address in order to communicate with a device in the same broadcast domain. For the exams, be familiar with which device talks to which other device at both layer 2 and layer 3. With a router between the source and destination, note that the layer 2 addresses are changing each step along the communication pathway, but the source and destination IP addresses stay the same.

Exercise 3-1: Identifying TCP/IP Protocols

In this exercise, you will review the TCP/IP protocols by matching the protocol to the correct description.

Protocol	Description
___ TCP	A. Converts the logical address to the physical address
___ SMTP	B. Responsible for logical addressing and routing
___ ICMP	C. Responsible for reliable delivery
___ ARP	D. Application layer protocol used to download files
___ UDP	E. Responsible for error and status reporting
___ HTTPS	F. Internet protocol to send e-mail
___ FTP	G. Secure transmission of web traffic
___ IP	H. Unreliable delivery

Chapter Review

In this chapter, you learned about the fundamentals of TCP/IP and what makes this protocol so common in today's networking market. The following list summarizes what you learned:

- TCP/IP is a suite of protocols, the most popular of which are TCP, UDP, IP, and ARP. (The CCT/CCNA exams will definitely have several questions testing your knowledge of these protocols in real-world situations.)

- Application layer protocols are responsible for initiating a network request or servicing the network request. Example application layer protocols are HTTP, FTP, DNS, SMTP, and RDP.

- Transport layer protocols handle either connection-oriented communication (TCP) or connectionless communication (UDP). Internet layer protocols handle logical addressing and routing functions. IP performs logical addressing, ARP converts the logical address to a physical address, and ICMP is the status- and error-reporting protocol.

With a strong understanding of the material presented in this chapter, you will have no problems with any TCP/IP protocol-related questions on your exams. Not only is the material presented here important for the exams, but it will also be important after you ace the exams and continue on to a career as a networking professional.

Quick Review

TCP/IP Protocol Suite

- TCP/IP is a suite of protocols. Each protocol in the suite has its own set of responsibilities.
- TCP is used for connection-oriented, or reliable, communication. TCP uses sequence numbers and acknowledgment numbers to guarantee delivery.
- UDP is used for connectionless, or unreliable, communication and does not guarantee delivery.
- The Internet Protocol (IP) handles logical addressing and routing. It is responsible for packet routing and delivery.
- ARP, Address Resolution Protocol, is used to convert logical addresses to physical addresses.
- ICMP is the error-reporting or status-reporting protocol in the TCP/IP protocol suite.

Questions

The following questions will help you measure your understanding of the material presented in this chapter. Read all the choices carefully, as there may be more than one correct answer. Choose the correct answer(s) for each question.

1. Which layer of the OSI model does IP run at?

   A. Layer 2

   B. Layer 3

   C. Layer 4

   D. Layer 5

2. Which of the following protocols are layer 4 protocols of the OSI model? (Select all that apply.)

   A. TCP

   B. IP

   C. ARP

   D. UDP

3. Which protocol is responsible for converting the IP address to a MAC address?

   A. IP

   B. TCP

   C. ARP

   D. ICMP

4. Which protocol is responsible for connection-oriented communication?

   A. TCP

   B. IP

   C. UDP

   D. ICMP

5. Which protocol is responsible for error reporting and status information?

   A. ICMP

   B. TCP

   C. UDP

   D. IP

6. Which protocol is responsible for logical addressing and delivery of packets?

   A. ICMP

   B. TCP

   C. IP

   D. UDP

7. What two items are used by TCP to guarantee delivery of data? (Choose two.)

   A. Source port

   B. Acknowledgment numbers

   C. IP address

   D. Destination port

   E. Sequence numbers

8. What field in the IP header identifies the system that the packet came from?

   A. Source IP address

   B. Protocol

   C. Destination IP address

   D. Source port

9. What field in the TCP header is used to specify the target application that the packet is for?

   A. Source port

   B. Destination IP address

   C. Source IP address

   D. Destination port

Performance-based Questions

Performance-based questions are interactive questions that you will find on the Cisco exams where you must drag an object from one area of the screen to the other. The following are sample performance-based questions based on content found in this chapter.

1. Using the following exhibit, write the protocols found on the left into the appropriate box on the right to identify the layer that the protocol runs at. On the real exam you would be expected to drag and drop the items into the appropriate box.

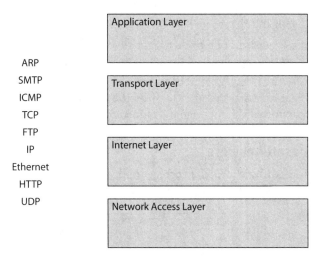

2. Looking at the following exhibit, identify the phases of the TCP three-way handshake by writing the phase name into the boxes. On the real exam you would drag the phase found on the left to the appropriate box on the right.

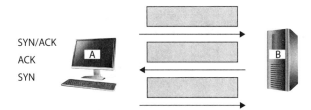

Answers

1. **B.** The Internet Protocol is responsible for logical addressing and routing, which is a function of layer 3 of the OSI model.

2. **A, D.** TCP and UDP are transport, layer 4, protocols. TCP is responsible for connection-oriented communication and error-free delivery, whereas UDP is responsible for connectionless communication.

3. **C.** The Address Resolution Protocol (ARP) is responsible for converting an IP address to a MAC address so that communication can occur.

4. A. TCP is responsible for connection-oriented communication in the TCP/IP protocol suite.

5. A. ICMP is responsible for reporting errors and sending back status information when communicating over TCP/IP.

6. C. IP is responsible for packet delivery and logical addressing.

7. B, E. The sequence number and acknowledgment number are used by TCP to guarantee delivery of data. Each message has a sequence number assigned to it, and when it is received by the destination, an ACK message is sent back with an acknowledgment number.

8. A. The source IP address of a packet identifies what system the packet was sent from. This is important, because the receiving system knows who to reply to because the sender's IP address is in the source IP address field.

9. D. The destination port is used to identify the port number of the application on the target system that the message is destined for.

Performance-based Answers

1. The following exhibit shows the correct application layer, transport layer, Internet layer, and network access layer protocols.

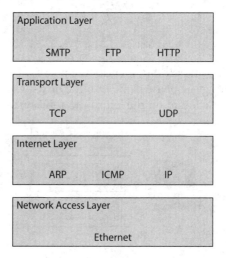

2. The following exhibit shows the correct stages of the TCP three-way handshake.

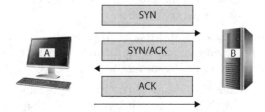

IP Addressing Basics

In this chapter, you will

- Review TCP/IP fundamentals
- Learn about TCP/IP addressing
- Learn how to configure IP address settings
- Learn about the pathway of communication

Reading this chapter will give you an in-depth understanding of TCP/IP addressing, something you want to know well before you read Chapter 5 on subnetting. The CCT/CCNA exams will test your knowledge of address configuration for different-sized networks, starting with address classes and working into subnetting. You should have a strong understanding of the information presented in this chapter and the next chapter before taking the CCT/CCNA exams.

Configuring TCP/IP

You have learned about some of the popular protocols that exist in the TCP/IP suite. This section will introduce you to the configuration of TCP/IP by discussing the addressing scheme and rules for assigning an address to a system. To configure TCP/IP properly, you must know the settings for the IP address, subnet mask, and default gateway. Let's start with the IP address.

IP Address

The IP address is a 32-bit value that uniquely identifies the system on the network (or the Internet). The IP address is divided into four numbers, with each number separated by a period (for example, 192.168.1.15). Each of the four numbers is made up of 8 bits, and there are four numbers of 8 bits each, equaling 32 bits.

Each of the 8-bit values is called an *octet* (for example, the 192 or the 168 in the preceding example is an octet). There are four octets in an IP address. The four octets in an IP address are divided into two parts: a network ID and a host ID. The network ID portion of the IP address is a unique number that identifies the particular network, and the host ID portion is a unique number that identifies the computer or device on that network. The subnet mask determines the number of bits that make up the network ID and the number of bits that make up the host ID. Let's see how this works.

	Octet 1	Octet 2	Octet 3	Octet 4
IP address	192	168	1	15
Subnet mask	255	255	255	0
Address portion	N	N	N	H

Table 4-1 Identifying the Network ID and Host ID Portions of an IP Address

Subnet Mask

The subnet mask is used by TCP/IP to determine whether a host is on a local or remote network. When a 255 is used in an octet, then the corresponding octet (the octet in the same position) in the IP address represents the network ID. So, if my IP address is 192.168.1.15 and my subnet mask is 255.255.255.0, the first three octets of the subnet mask (255.255.255) would represent the network ID (corresponding to 192.168.1) and the last octet (0) would represent the host ID (corresponding to 15). Again, the network ID assigns a unique address to the network itself, while the host ID uniquely identifies the system on the network.

To use a different example, if a subnet mask is 255.0.0.0, it would mean that the first octet of the IP address (192 in our example) is used as the network ID portion, while the last three octets (168.1.15) are the host ID portion of the IP address.

Table 4-1 summarizes the first example. You can see that the network ID (represented with an "N" in the lowermost row) is 192.168.1, and the host ID is the last octet with a value of 15. This means that this system is on the 192.168.1 network and any other system on the same network will have the same network ID.

So what is the purpose of the subnet masks? Or better yet, why do we have a subnet mask that breaks the IP address into a network ID and a host ID? When a system such as 192.168.1.15 with a subnet mask of 255.255.255.0 sends a piece of data to system 192.198.45.10, the sending system first needs to determine whether the target computer exists on the same network or not. It does this by comparing the network IDs (see Table 4-2); if the network IDs are the same, then both systems exist on the same network and one system can send to the other without the use of a router. If the systems exist on different networks, the data will need to be passed to the router so that the router can send the data to the other network.

	Octet 1	Octet 2	Octet 3	Octet 4
IP address 1	192	168	1	15
Subnet mask	255	255	255	0
IP address 2	192	198	45	10

Table 4-2 Identifying Two Systems on Different Networks Using the Subnet Masks

Exercise 4-1: Identifying Remote Systems

In this exercise, you will determine whether two systems exist on the same network or on separate networks by filling in the following table:

ComputerA (IP address)	ComputerA (Subnet mask)	ComputerB (IP address)	Same Network?
12.45.8.34	255.0.0.0	14.34.212.5	
131.107.4.78	255.255.0.0	131.108.45.112	
198.45.23.2	255.255.255.0	198.45.23.14	
26.45.78.5	255.0.0.0	28.45.78.15	
176.34.56.12	255.255.0.0	176.34.12.10	

Default Gateway

When your system wants to send data to another system on the network, it looks at its own network ID and compares that to the destination system's network ID. If it appears that both have the same network ID, the data is sent directly from your system to the destination system. If the two systems are on different networks, your system must pass the data to the router so that the router can send the data to the destination system's router. How does your system know where the router is? The default gateway is the IP address of the router that will be used to send data from your network to another network.

NOTE In short, to communicate on the Internet, your system will need to be configured with an IP address, a subnet mask, and a default gateway. If you need to communicate only with other systems on your network, you will need only an IP address and a subnet mask.

TCP/IP Addressing

This section introduces you to the binary representation of an IP address and ensures that before you move on to Chapter 5, you feel comfortable with converting binary values to decimal and address classes. You'll also learn about types of addresses, address schemes, and TCP/IP ports.

Bit	8	7	6	5	4	3	2	1
Value	128	64	32	16	8	4	2	1

Table 4-3   Values Associated with Each Bit in an Octet

Understanding Binary

You know from the previous discussion that the IP address is a 32-bit address divided into four 8-bit octets. The four octets are normally displayed as decimal values, but they also have a binary representation that looks like this:

```
11000000 10101000 00000001 00001111
```

Notice that there are four sets of 8 bits (1 or 0), which make up the 32 bits (8 × 4 sets) of an IP address. Let's take a look at how you can determine the binary representation of an octet.

The values of the 8 bits within each octet are shown in Table 4-3. You can see that the first bit in an octet (far right) has a decimal value of 1, the second bit has a decimal value of 2, the third bit has a decimal value of 4, and the values keep doubling with each additional bit. You can also see that the eighth bit has a decimal value of 128.

NOTE   The first bit is known as the least significant bit, or low-order bit, while the eighth bit is known as the most significant bit, or high-order bit.

To calculate the binary value of an octet with a decimal number such as 192, for example, you need to enable, or turn on, the bits that will add up to the number 192, as shown in Table 4-4.

In the table, notice that bit 8 and bit 7 are turned on to provide a value of 128 + 64, which equals 192. The remaining bits will take an "off" state, which means they are not included in the calculation. A bit that has an on state takes a "1," and an off state takes a "0." So the combination of 8 bits to make the number 192 would be 11000000.

Now that you know how to convert a decimal value to binary and a binary value to decimal, try out Exercise 4-2 and Exercise 4-3 before moving on to the section on address classes.

Bit	8	7	6	5	4	3	2	1
Value	128	64	32	16	8	4	2	1
State	On	On						

Table 4-4   Calculating the Decimal Value of 192 in Binary

Exercise 4-2: Converting Decimal to Binary

In this exercise, you will practice converting decimal values to binary by filling out the following table:

Decimal	Binary
127	
131	
198	
224	
96	
192.168.1.100	
216.83.11.78	
202.14.45.0	

Exercise 4-3: Converting Binary to Decimal

In this exercise, you will practice converting binary values to decimal values by filling out the following table:

Binary	Decimal
10110101	
11000011	
10000111	
11111111	
10101011	
11000001.10000001.00001011.10100001	
00000111.10101001.00110101.10110101	
11000000.10100001.00000111.11111111	

Address Classes

Every IP address belongs to a distinct *address class*. The Internet community defined these classes to accommodate networks of various sizes. The class to which the IP address belongs initially determines the network ID and host ID portions of the address, along with the number of hosts that are supported on that network. The different class addresses are class A, class B, class C, class D, and class E.

	First Octet Value	Subnet Mask	# of Hosts per Network
Class A	1–127	255.0.0.0	16,777,214
Class B	128–191	255.255.0.0	65,534
Class C	192–223	255.255.255.0	254

Table 4-5 Important Aspects of Address Classes

Table 4-5 summarizes the important aspects of the address classes you should know for the exams. The following sections offer more details about each class.

Class A Addresses

A class A address has a default subnet mask of 255.0.0.0, which means that the first octet is the network ID and the last three octets represent the host ID portion of the address. Each octet can contain 256 possible values (0–255), so a class A address supports 16,777,216 hosts on the network (256 × 256 × 256). Actually, there are only 16,777,214 valid addresses to use on systems, because there are two addresses on each IP network you are not allowed to assign to systems because they are reserved. These are the addresses with all host bits set to 0s (the network ID) and all host bits set to 1s (the broadcast address). So with a class A address, you will not be able to assign *n*.0.0.0 or *n*.255.255.255 (where *n* is your network ID) to any hosts on the network.

 EXAM TIP You'll need to know how to identify class A addresses for your exam. Class A addresses have an IP address in which the first octet is between 1 and 127. Class A addresses also have a default subnet mask of 255.0.0.0. You can always identify a class A address because the value of the first octet falls between the numbers 1 and 127. Although an address that starts with 127 is technically a class A address, you are not allowed to use any address that starts with 127 because it is reserved for the loopback address (more on the loopback address later). An example of a class A address is the IP address 12.56.87.34: the first octet is 12, which falls in the range of 1–127.

Class B Addresses

Class B addresses have a default subnet mask of 255.255.0.0, which means that the first two octets are the network ID and the last two octets are the host ID portion of the address. This means that we can have 65,536 hosts (256 × 256) on the network. Oh, but wait! Don't forget to take off the two reserved addresses, so that gives us 65,534 addresses that can be assigned to hosts on the network. You can identify a class B address because the first octet starts with a number that falls between 128 and 191. Because of the number of hosts that are supported on a class B address, medium-sized companies use class B address.

EXAM TIP You'll need to know how to identify class B addresses for your exam. Class B addresses have an IP address in which the value of the first octet is between 128 and 191. Remember that class B addresses have a default subnet mask of 255.255.0.0.

Class C Addresses

Class C addresses have a subnet mask of 255.255.255.0, which means that the first three octets are the network ID and the last octet is the host ID. Having only one octet as the host ID means that a class C address can support only 254 hosts (256 − 2) on the network.

A class C address has a value for the first octet that ranges between 192 and 223. For example, an IP address of 202.45.8.6 is a class C address, because 202 falls between 192 and 223. You also know that this system has a subnet mask of 255.255.255.0 because it is a class C address.

EXAM TIP You'll need to know how to identify class C addresses for your exam. Class C addresses have an IP address in which the value of the first octet is between 192 and 223. In addition, remember that class C addresses have a default subnet mask of 255.255.255.0.

Class D Addresses

Class D addresses are used for special types of applications on the network—*multicasting applications*. Multicasting applications send data to a number of systems at the same time by sending data to the multicast address, and any system that has registered with that address will receive the data. Because class D addresses are used for multicast addresses, you will not be assigning them specifically to hosts on the network for normal network communication.

Class D addresses have a value on the first octet that ranges from 224 to 239. With that many ranges, class D has the potential for 268,435,456 unique multicast groups that users can subscribe to from a multicast application.

Class E Addresses

The funny thing about class E addresses is that they were designed for experimental purposes only, so you will never see a class E address on a network. Class E addresses have a first octet with a value between 240 and 247.

EXAM TIP It's guaranteed that you will see questions on identifying class A, B, and C addresses on both exams. Be sure to know the characteristics of each class such as the range of addresses in that class, the number of host supported, and the default subnet mask.

Exercise 4-4: Identifying Address Classes

In this exercise, you will practice identifying address classes for different IP addresses and their associated subnet masks. Fill in the following table:

IP Address	Subnet Mask	Address Class
27.56.89.234		
196.79.123.56		
130.49.34.23		
109.189.109.200		
189.90.23.100		
126.34.100.12		
14.198.120.100		

Rules for Defining Classes

I am often asked how the designers of IPv4 came up with the address ranges for each class. The designers determined the classes by having the boundaries of each class defined with the following rules:

- *Class A addresses always begin with a* 0. This gives binary values of **0**0000001 to **0**1111111, or 1 to 127 when converted to decimal. Note that you cannot have an address of 00000000, so this range starts at 1.

- *Class B addresses always begin with* 10. This gives binary values of **10**000000 to **10**111111, or 128 to 191 when converted to decimal.

- *Class C addresses always begin with* 110. This gives binary values of **110**00000 to **110**11111, or 192 to 223 when converted to decimal.

- *Class D addresses always begin with* 1110. This gives binary values of **1110**000 to **1110**1111, or 224 to 239 when converted to decimal.

- *Class E addresses always begin with* 11110. This gives binary values of **11110**000 to **11110**111, which is 240 to 247 when converted to decimal.

Loopback Address

You have learned that you are not allowed to have a host assigned an IP address that has a value of 127 in the first octet. This is because the class A address range of 127 has been reserved for the loopback address.

The loopback address is used to refer to the local system, also known as the *localhost*. If you want to verify that the TCP/IP software has initialized on the local system even though you may not have an IP address, you can ping the loopback address, which is typically referred to as 127.0.0.1.

NOTE You can test your own local system from a command line by typing **ping 127.0.0.1**, **ping localhost**, or **ping loopback** to verify that the TCP/IP protocol stack is functioning on your system.

Private Addresses

Another type of address you need to be aware of is a *private address*. A private address can be assigned to a system but cannot be used for any kind of Internet connectivity. Private addresses are *nonroutable* on the Internet, so any system using them will not be able to route data across the Internet. The following three address ranges are private:

- 10.0.0.0–10.255.255.255
- 172.16.0.0–172.31.255.255
- 192.168.0.0–192.168.255.255

Due to the growth of the Internet, it became impossible for every device that needed Internet access to use a public IP address as we were running out of addresses. So private addresses are used inside networks because they are not seen by other systems on the Internet; we use a Network Address Translation (NAT) device to translate the private address to a public address.

EXAM TIP Remember for the CCT/CCNA exams that one of the major design considerations with networks today is to use private addresses internally and use a NAT device to translate the private address, which is nonroutable on the Internet, to a public address that is routable on the Internet. This essentially enables a large number of computers running private addresses to share the public address of the NAT device to gain Internet access.

APIPA

Systems today support the *Automatic Private IP Addressing* (APIPA) feature. When a client boots up and cannot contact a DHCP server, the client will configure itself automatically with a 169.254.*x.y* address. If there is something wrong with the DHCP server and none of the systems on the network can obtain an address, all of the clients will assign themselves an address within the 169.254 address range and will then be able to communicate with one another (because they are all on the same network).

(continued)

APIPA does not assign a default gateway, so you will be unable to access resources on a remote network and the Internet—but you can still communicate with systems on your network. When troubleshooting to determine why a machine cannot communicate on the network, watch for systems that have the 169.254.*x.y* address range, because this indicates that they could not find a DHCP server.

Invalid IP Addresses for Hosts

A few IP addresses cannot be assigned to hosts on the network. You may wonder, for example, why a class C address can have only 254 hosts and not 256, as would seem more likely, since an 8-bit number can have 256 possible values. The reason for this seeming discrepancy is that two of the addresses are lost from the available host pool. The first is an address that has all bits set to 0s in the host ID, which signifies the network ID of the network. The second is an address that has all bits set to 1s in the host ID, which signifies the broadcast address for the network. So, for example, in the class C network 200.158.157.*x*, the addresses 200.158.157.0 (the network ID) and 200.158.157.255 (the broadcast address) are not available to assign to hosts on the network, reducing the available number of hosts from 256 to 254.

Another illegal address is any system that has the first octet of 127; remember that this is reserved as the loopback address, and you will not be able to assign the address to any host. The following summarizes illegal addresses:

- **Any address starting with 127** An IP address that starts with 127 is reserved for the loopback address and cannot be assigned to a system. An example of this illegal address is 127.50.10.23.

- **All host bits set to 0** You are not allowed to assign a system an IP address that has all of the bits in the host ID portion set to 0 because this is the network ID. An example of this illegal address is 131.107.0.0.

- **All host bits set to 1** You are not allowed to assign a system an IP address that has all the host bits set to 1 because this corresponds to the broadcast address of the network. An example of this type of illegal address is 131.107.255.255.

- **A duplicate address** You are not allowed to assign a system an address that another system is using because this results in a duplicate IP address error.

Not being able to route data across the Internet when using these addresses will not pose a problem, because, realistically, these private addresses will be sitting behind a NAT server that will translate the private address to a public address that can be routed on the Internet. Chapter 13 offers more information on NAT.

Exercise 4-5: Understanding Valid Addresses

In this exercise, you will practice identifying valid addresses by recording whether each of the following addresses is valid. A valid address can be assigned to a system on the network. If an address is invalid, specify why.

Address	Valid?
10.0.40.10	
127.54.67.89	
131.107.34.0	
45.12.0.0	
216.83.11.255	
63.256.4.78	
200.67.34.0	
131.107.23.255	

Addressing Schemes

On a network, data can be sent to the destination in several different ways: data can be sent to a unicast address, a broadcast address, or a multicast address. The following outlines the difference between unicast, broadcast, and multicast:

- **Unicast** Sends information to one system. With IP, this is accomplished by sending data to the IP address of the intended destination system.
- **Broadcast** Sends information to all systems on the network. Data that is destined for all systems is sent by using the broadcast address for the network. An example of a broadcast address for a network is 192.168.2.255. The broadcast address is determined by setting all host bits to 1 and then converting the octet to a decimal number. There is also an internetwork broadcast address of 255.255.255.255, which is for data that is to be sent to all networks.
- **Multicast** Sends information to a selected group of systems. Typically, this is accomplished by having the systems subscribe to a multicast address. Any data that is sent to the multicast address is then received by all systems subscribed to the address. Most multicast addresses start with 224.*x.y.z* and are considered class D addresses.

TCP/IP Ports

An application or process uses a TCP/IP port as an identifier for that application/process running on a system. When you send data from one computer to another, you send data to the port used by that application. For example, when you type the IP address of a web site in your web browser, the web browser connects to the web server (or web application) running at that system by sending data to port 80 (shown in Figure 4-1), which is the

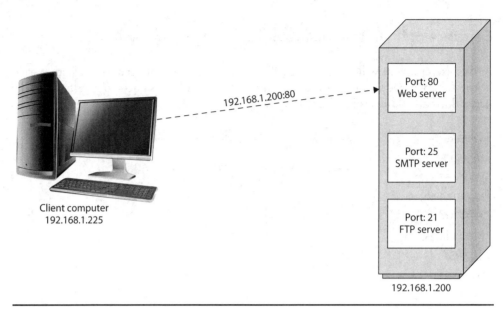

Figure 4-1 Sending data to a web server on port 80

default port of a web server. When the web server answers your request by sending the web page to your browser, because the browser is running on a particular port as well, the web server sends the page to the port of the web browser.

   EXAM TIP For the exam, remember that both the TCP and UDP protocols use port numbers.

Server applications typically use low port numbers under 1024, whereas client applications usually run on port numbers greater than 1024. There are three types of ports:

- **Well-known ports** These port numbers are used by servers and range from 0 to 1023.

- **Registered ports** These ports are assigned to certain applications or protocols. Registered ports range from 1024 to 49151.

- **Dynamic ports** These ports are used by applications temporarily and range from 49152 to 65535. They are called dynamic ports because many times, a port is selected at runtime by the application and is different each time the program runs. For example, when you start Internet Explorer, it may use a different port number each time the program is started, whereas a web server uses the same port each time (port 80).

Table 4-6 lists well-known port numbers that are used by different types of applications or protocols. Be sure to know these for the CCNA exams.

Another term that you will hear a lot is *socket*, which is the endpoint of communication and is made up of three components: the IP address of the system, the port number

Port Number	Process	Description
20	FTP-DATA	File Transfer Protocol—used to transfer data from one machine to another
21	FTP	File Transfer Protocol—used for control messages of the FTP session
22	SSH	Secure Shell—used to create a secure connection to manage a device such as a server, switch, or router
23	Telnet	Telnet—used by telnet to connect remotely to a system such as a server, switch, or router
25	SMTP	Simple Mail Transfer Protocol—used to send e-mail across the Internet
53	DNS	Domain Name System—used to query DNS servers for the IP address of a remote system
67 or 68	DHCP	Used by Domain Host Configuration Protocol (DHCP) clients and servers to configure clients automatically
69	TFTP	Trival File Transfer Protocol—a fast UDP-based file transfer protocol that does not require authentication
80	HTTP	Hypertext Transfer Protocol—used to deliver web pages from a web server to the web client
110	POP3	Post Office Protocol, version 3—used for reading e-mail over the Internet
119	NNTP	Network News Transfer Protocol—used to read news articles from a news server
123	NTP	Network Time Protocol—used to synchronize the time on systems
137–139	NetBIOS	Used by Windows systems for NetBIOS sessions
143	IMAP4	Internet Message Application Protocol, version 4—another Internet protocol for reading e-mail
443	HTTPS	Secure Hypertext Transfer Protocol—used to encrypt web traffic between a client and a server
445	SMB	Server Message Block—the Microsoft file-sharing protocol
1720	H.323	An older protocol used to deliver audio and video data over a computer network
2427/2727	MGCP	Media Gateway Control Protocol—a VoIP protocol used for controlling media gateways
3389	RDP	Remote Desktop Protocol—used to remotely connect to and administer a system
5004/5005	RTP	Real-time Transport Protocol—used to send voice data between phones with VoIP communication
5060/5061	SIP	Session Initiation Protocol—used to set up a voice over IP (VoIP) call

Table 4-6 Ports Used by Popular Internet Applications

of the application, and the protocol that is being used, either TCP or UDP. The socket is how data is sent from one system to another, or more accurately, from one application to another. The following formula defines what a socket is:

Socket = IP address + Port number + Protocol (TCP or UDP)

Configuring IP Address Settings

The new CCNA exam expects you to know how to configure and verify the IP address on host systems including Windows, Linux, and macOS systems. The following sections demonstrate how to configure and verify the TCP/IP settings on these systems.

Manual Configuration vs. DHCP

When configuring IP address settings on your workstations or network devices such as routers and switches, you can either manually configure the setting or dynamically assign addresses via DHCP.

Manual Configuration

Manual configuration of a workstation or device such as a router involves going into the configuration of the network interfaces and manually inputting the IP address, subnet mask, and default gateway setting. Manual configuration can be labor intensive, so we normally manual configure only servers, routers, and switches. The clients on the network obtain their IP address dynamically from the DHCP server.

Dynamic Configuration

Configuring IP addressing on a large TCP/IP-based network can be a nightmare, especially if machines are moved frequently from one network to another. DHCP can help with the workload of configuring systems on a network by assigning addresses to systems automatically on bootup.

The process of dynamically assigning IP addresses is managed via a DHCP server. The DHCP server can be a separate device, a service running on a server, or a service loaded on your Cisco router. The DHCP service is configured with a set of usable IP addresses, called a *scope*. The scope can also include the subnet mask, IP addresses of the default gateway, DNS servers, and other necessary addresses. When a PC powers on and is configured to use a DHCP server, it uses the following steps to obtain an address:

1. **DHCP Discover** The client sends out a DHCP Discover message, which is a broadcast request packet, looking for any DHCP services on the network.
2. **DHCP Offer** The DHCP server responds with a DHCP Offer message containing an IP address that the client can lease.
3. **DHCP Request** The client then accepts the offer by sending a DHCP Request message to the DHCP server for that address.
4. **DHCP Acknowledgment** The DHCP server responds by sending a DHCP ACK message to the client confirming the client is leasing the address. The DHCP ACK message also contains additional TCP/IP settings such as the lease time. The DHCP server marks the IP address in its database as being in use so that it is not assigned again.

NOTE   You will learn how to configure DHCP services on a Cisco router in Chapter 13.

Configuring TCP/IP on Systems

You can modify the TCP/IP configuration settings on your system. The steps are different depending on the operating system you are running, but the following sections show the general steps to configure Windows, Linux, and macOS systems.

Windows 10

To change the TCP/IP settings on your Windows system use these steps:

1. Click the Start button, and then type **control**. In the Best Match section of the Start button you will see Control Panel.

2. Choose Control Panel | Network and Internet | Network and Sharing Center.

3. Click the Change Adapter Settings link on the left.

4. Right-click Ethernet and choose Properties.

5. Select Internet Protocol Version 4 (TCP/IPv4) and choose Properties.

6. In the Properties dialog box, notice that, by default, the radio button Obtain An IP Address Automatically is selected, which means that the system is configured as a DHCP client:

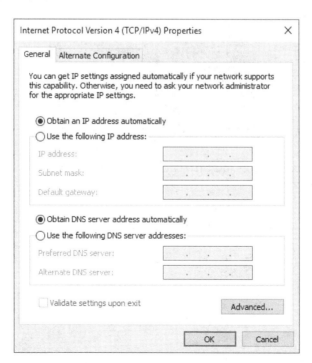

7. To configure the IP address statically, choose Use The Following IP Address: and then enter the IP address, subnet mask, and default gateway setting for the system.

8. To configure the system to use a specific DNS server, choose the Use The Following DNS Server Addresses and then enter the IP address of the DNS server you want to use.

9. Choose OK and close all windows.

Linux

There are a few different ways you can use to modify your IP address on Linux systems depending on the distribution. For years, administrators used the **ifconfig** command to change their IP address with the following syntax:

```
ifconfig  eth0 12.0.0.11 netmask 255.0.0.0
```

Where:

Eth0 is the interface or network card you are modifying.

12.0.0.11 is the IP address you want to use.

netmask 255.0.0.0 is the subnet mask.

You can also change your IP address in Linux using the graphical interface. To do this, follow these steps:

1. On your Linux system, in the top right corner, you will see a network icon. Right-click the network icon and choose Edit Connections:

2. Select your connection and then choose the Settings icon at the bottom (looks like a gear icon).

3. Choose the IPv4 Settings tab.

4. In the Method drop-down list, choose Manual.

5. Click the Add button to add the IP address, subnet mask, and default gateway you want to use.

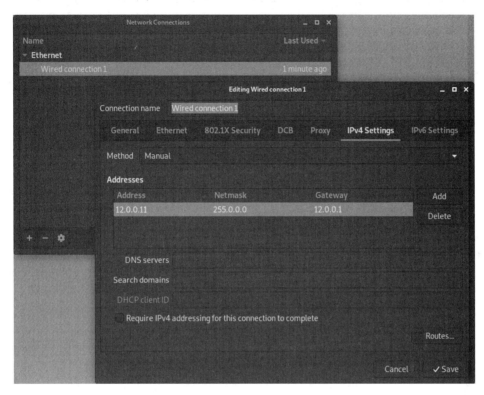

6. Enter the IP address of the DNS Servers and then click Save.

7. Close all windows.

macOS

Modify your macOS IP address using the following steps:

1. From the Apple menu, choose System Preferences.

2. Choose Network.

3. Select your network interface on the left.

4. Click the Advanced button in the bottom right corner.

5. Choose the TCP/IP tab.

6. To configure an IP address manually, from the Configure IPv4 drop-down list, choose Manually. Then enter your IP address, subnet mask, and router address (default gateway).

Verify IP Address Settings

Once you have configured your TCP/IP settings, it is a good idea to verify that the IP address settings have taken effect. You can do this in each of the operating systems with a quick command.

- **Windows**   Open a command prompt and type **ipconfig** to view basic TCP/IP settings such as the IP address, subnet mask, and default gateway. If you want to view all your TCP/IP settings including DHCP lease times and DNS server settings, use the **ipconfig /all** command.
- **Linux**   Depending on the version of Linux you are running, you can either use the **ifconfig** command to view your TCP/IP settings or use the Network Manager command **nmcli** to check out your IP settings.
- **macOS**   Use the **ifconfig** command to verify your TCP/IP settings.

Understanding the Pathway of Communication

Before we finish up on the basics of TCP/IP, you should understand the communication pathway of communication between two systems on a TCP/IP network. The following illustration shows the steps that occur when ComputerB sends data to ComputerD:

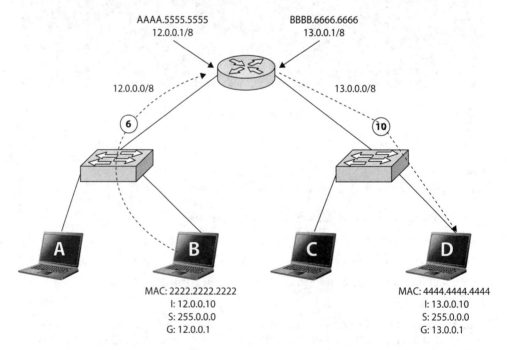

1. The command **ping 13.0.0.10** is entered at ComputerB to invoke communication.

2. ComputerB compares its IP address and subnet mask against the IP address that is being pinged to determine whether the system is on the same network. Because the network IDs are different, IP determines the systems are on different networks (note this is actually done at the binary level with a process called ANDing), as shown here:

```
12.0.0.10
255.0.0.0
13.0.0.10
```

3. ComputerB retrieves the default gateway settings from the TCP/IP settings, as that is the address it needs to send the data to in order to send data to a different network.

4. ComputerB then ARPs the IP address of the default gateway to obtain the MAC address of the default gateway.

5. The ARP reply message is returned to ComputerB with the MAC address of the default gateway.

6. ComputerB sends the data to the router with the following header information:

```
Layer 2 Header:
      Source MAC: 2222.2222.2222
   Destination MAC: AAAA.5555.5555
Layer 3 Header:
      Source IP: 12.0.0.10
   Destination IP: 13.0.0.10
```

7. The router receives the layer 2 frame and then reads the layer 3 header to determine where the packet is headed. The router sees that the packet is destined for 13.0.0.10, so it checks to see if it has a route in the routing table. It does, and it realizes it just needs to send data out the 13.0.0.1 interface to reach the destination.

8. To send the data, the router needs to know the MAC address of 13.0.0.10, so it sends out an ARP request message.

9. The router receives the ARP reply containing the MAC address of ComputerD.

10. The router sends the data to ComputerD with the following header information:

```
Layer 2 Header:
      Source MAC: BBBB.6666.6666
   Destination MAC: 4444.4444.4444
Layer 3 Header:
      Source IP: 12.0.0.10
   Destination IP: 13.0.0.10
```

The important point here is to notice that the layer 2 header is modified each step along the way to move the frame to the next step. But the layer 3 header is never modified, because it contains the network address to route the data to the correct network.

Exercise 4-6: Analyzing the Pathway to Communication

In this exercise, you will analyze the following network diagram and identify characteristics of the packet as it travels from ComputerA to ComputerD.

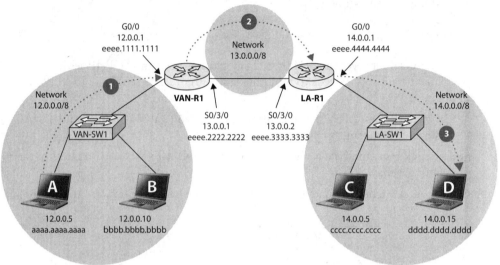

1. Looking at the diagram, record the layer 2 and layer 3 header information that the packet will have at the point circled with a 1.
   Layer 2 Source Address: _____
   Layer 2 Destination Address: _____
   Layer 3 Source Address: _____
   Layer 3 Destination Address: _____

2. Looking at the diagram, record the layer 2 and layer 3 header information that the packet will have at the point circled with a 2.
   Layer 2 Source Address: _____
   Layer 2 Destination Address: _____
   Layer 3 Source Address: _____
   Layer 3 Destination Address: _____

3. Looking at the diagram, record the layer 2 and layer 3 header information that the packet will have at the point circled with a 3.
   Layer 2 Source Address: _____
   Layer 2 Destination Address: _____
   Layer 3 Source Address: _____
   Layer 3 Destination Address: _____

Chapter Review

In this chapter you learned about the fundamentals of TCP/IP and what makes this protocol so common in today's networking market. The following list summarizes what you learned:

- The IP address and subnet mask are the most important configuration settings and must be specified correctly in order to communicate on a TCP/IP-based network. Next in importance is the default gateway, which specifies where to route packets if you are communicating outside the local network.

- The Dynamic Host Configuration Protocol (DHCP) automatically configures a workstation with the correct TCP/IP settings, relieving you of the burden of manually configuring every workstation.

- TCP/IP addressing involves a strong knowledge of the IP address, subnet mask, network classes, and special reserved addresses. (You should memorize each network class for the exam.)

- The most important portions of TCP/IP as it relates to your CCT and CCNA exams are the TCP/IP configuration concepts. You need these to configure workstations with TCP/IP. The concepts include the IP address, the subnet mask, and the default gateway.

With a strong understanding of the material presented in this chapter, you will have no problems with any TCP/IP-related questions on your exam. Not only is the material presented here important for each exam, but it will also be important after you ace the exam and continue on to a career as a networking professional.

Quick Review

TCP/IP Fundamentals

- TCP/IP addresses are 32-bit addresses.
- The IP address is a unique value assigned to the system that identifies the system on the network.
- The subnet mask is used to determine the network ID portion of an IP address.
- The network ID is used to determine whether or not the destination system exists on the same network. If the two systems have the same network ID, then they are on the same network.
- The host ID identifies the system within the network.
- The default gateway refers to the IP address of the router and is used to send data from the local network.

TCP/IP Addressing

- Class A addresses have a first octet ranging from 0 to 127 and have a default subnet mask of 255.0.0.0.

- Class B addresses have a first octet ranging from 128 to 191 and have a default subnet mask of 255.255.0.0.

- Class C addresses have a first octet ranging from 192 to 223 and have a default subnet mask of 255.255.255.0.

- Class D addresses are used for multicasting.

- An application or process uses a TCP/IP port to communicate between client and server computers.

- The most popular, and therefore most likely, exam choices to remember are the FTP ports (20 and 21), SMTP port (25), HTTP port (80), and HTTPS port (443).

- You have two options for configuring TCP/IP: configure it manually or use a DHCP server.

- DHCP is responsible for assigning IP addresses to systems and devices automatically and reduces the network administration load.

Configuring IP Address Settings

- You can use the **ipconfig** command in Windows to verify your TCP/IP settings.

- You can use the **ifconfig** command or the **nmcli** command to verify your TCP/IP settings in Linux, depending on the distribution and version of Linux.

- You can use the **ifconfig** command on a macOS to verify your TCP/IP address.

Understanding the Pathway of Communication

- Remember that the source and destination MAC addresses change with each step in the communication process.

- Remember that the source and destination IP addresses stay the same for the entire process of the packet being delivered to its destination.

Questions

The following questions will help you measure your understanding of the material presented in this chapter. Read all the choices carefully, as there may be more than one correct answer. Choose the correct answer(s) for each question.

1. One of the users on your network calls you over to his desk because he does not have Internet access. You use the **ipconfig** command to verify his settings and notice that the IP address is 169.254.34.10. What is most likely the reason why the user does not have Internet access?

    A. There is most likely a problem with DNS.

    B. There is no subnet mask configured.

    C. The router is down.

    D. There is most likely a problem with DHCP.

2. How many bits are in an IP address?

   A. 8 bits

   B. 32 bits

   C. 48 bits

   D. 96 bits

3. Which address class always begins with the first 3 bits of 110?

   A. Class A

   B. Class B

   C. Class C

   D. Class D

4. A computer with a subnet mask of 255.255.255.0 has how many octets for the network ID?

   A. 1

   B. 2

   C. 3

   D. 4

5. A computer with the IP address of 134.67.89.12 and a subnet mask of 255.255.0.0 is on the same network with which of the following systems?

   A. 134.76.89.11

   B. 134.67.112.23

   C. 13.4.67.34

   D. 109.67.45.10

6. Which network address class supports 65,534 hosts?

   A. Class A

   B. Class B

   C. Class C

   D. Class D

7. What is the default subnet mask for a class C network?

   A. 255.0.0.0

   B. 225.225.0.0

   C. 255.255.255.0

   D. 225.255.255.255

8. Which address is reserved for internal loopback functions?

   A. 0.0.0.0

   B. 1.0.0.1

   C. 121.0.0.1

   D. 127.0.0.1

9. What is the well-known port number for the HTTP service?

   A. 20

   B. 21

   C. 80

   D. 25

10. Which of the following addresses is/are a private IP address? (Select all that apply.)

    A. 10.0.0.34

    B. 191.167.34.5

    C. 172.16.7.99

    D. 12.108.56.7

11. Which port is used by SMTP?

    A. 23

    B. 25

    C. 443

    D. 110

12. What is the default subnet mask for 171.103.2.30?

    A. 255.0.0.0

    B. 255.255.0.0

    C. 255.255.255.0

    D. 255.255.255.255

13. Which network service is responsible for assigning IP addresses to systems on the network when they boot up?

    A. DNS

    B. WINS

    C. DHCP

    D. Server

Performance-based Questions

Performance-based questions are interactive questions that you will find on the Cisco exams where you must drag an object from one area of the screen to the other. The following are sample performance-based questions based on content found in this chapter.

1. Draw a line from the address on the left side of exhibit and connect it to the matching address type on the right side of the following exhibit.

127.0.0.1	An APIPA Address
200.45.67.100	A Private Address
169.254.65.78	Loopback Address
172.28.35.10	Class A Address
100.95.87.23	Class C Address

2. Using the port numbers on the left, write the correct port numbers in the appropriate box displaying the associated protocol. On the real exam, you would drag and drop the port number into the appropriate box.

TCP 22

TCP 3389

TCP 23

TCP 80

UDP 53

TCP 21

DNS	SSH
HTTP	Telnet
FTP	RDP

Answers

1. **D.** When troubleshooting TCP/IP communication issues, if you notice that a system is using an IP address of 169.254.*x.y*, you can assume that there is an issue communicating with the DHCP server. Addresses that start with 169.254.*x.y* are APIPA addresses and are self-configured when a DHCP server cannot be found.

2. **B.** An IP address, specifically an IPv4 address which is what was discussed in this chapter, is a 32-bit address.

3. **C.** Class C addresses always have the first 3 bits in the address set to 110. This gives binary values of **110**00000 to **110**11111, which is 192 to 223 when converted to decimal.

4. **C.** A subnet mask of 255.255.255.0 means that the first three octets are part of the network ID and the last octet is the host ID portion of the address.

5. B. Because the subnet mask is 255.255.0.0, any system that uses the same first two octets is on the same network. The network ID of the IP address is 134.67.*x.y*.

6. B. Class B networks support 65,534 hosts, because the last two octets are the host ID and each octet supports 256 possible values. 256 × 256 = 65,536—but don't forget that 2 addresses are unusable (reserved for the network ID and the broadcast address).

7. C. The default subnet mask of a class C network is 255.255.255.0; the first three octets represent the network ID and the last octet is the host ID.

8. D. The loopback address is typically known as the 127.0.0.1 address, but it could be any address starting with 127.*x.y.z*.

9. C. The port used by HTTP is port 80.

10. A, C. 10.0.0.34 and 172.16.7.99 are examples of addresses that fall into the private IP address ranges, which are not routable on the Internet.

11. B. Port 25 is used by SMTP to send e-mail over a TCP/IP network.

12. B. 171.103.2.30 is a class B address, so it has a subnet mask of 255.255.0.0.

13. C. DHCP is responsible for assigning IP addresses to systems automatically so that the network administrator does not have to perform that job manually.

Performance-based Answers

1. The following exhibit identifies the address with the correct address type.

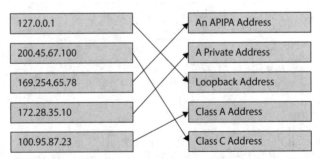

2. The following exhibit show the correct protocol with its associated port number.

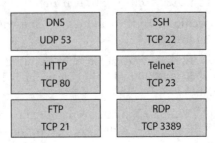

Subnetting and VLSM

In this chapter, you will

- Learn about subnetting networks
- Learn some subnetting shortcuts
- Understand the difference between classful and classless addressing
- Learn about Variable Length Subnet Masks (VLSMs)

In Chapter 4 you learned the basics of TCP/IP addressing. In this chapter, you'll learn how to divide one network address range into multiple network ranges, or *subnets*, so that you can assign each address range to a separate network (subnet) in your internetwork (network made up of multiple networks).

You may need to use multiple networks as a result of your business operating in several different physical locations, for example. Or, if you're working in one location, you may want to cut down on broadcast traffic being sent across the entire network by segmenting your network into multiple segments, placing a router in between each network segment.

Each segment will need its own network address range so that the router can route (send) the data from one network to another. If, for example, you had two physical networks but kept the single IP range without subnetting, the router would "logically" think that all systems were on the same network and would never try to route data from one side to the other.

 CAUTION If you do not subnet a network range that is divided into multiple physical network segments, the Internet Protocol (IP) will logically decide that all systems are on the same network, and it will not try to route the data across the router separating the network segments. As a result, you will be able to communicate with hosts on your segment, but not with the other segments.

Understanding Subnetting

You subnet a network ID to break the single logical network address into multiple logical network addresses so that you can assign a logical network ID and related addresses to each physical network segment on your network. In order to do this, you have to manipulate the subnet mask at the bit level and essentially take host bits away and convert them to subnet bits.

121

In this section, you will walk through how to subnet class A, class B, and class C network addresses. If you are new to subnetting, the best way to learn it is to perform each calculation on a blank piece of paper as we walk through it.

NOTE Subnetting is one of those topics that most IT professionals tend to avoid because of how tedious it is to sit down and calculate the required information to configure newly created subnets.

Subnetting Class A Networks

In this section, you will walk through subnetting a class A network address. In this example, you have an address range of 10.0.0.0 and you will divide the network into four subnetworks, or *subnets*. The physical network structure is shown in Figure 5-1. Subnetting involves taking some of the host bits from the subnet mask and using them as additional network bits, which will give you more networks. With subnetting, you are taking additional host bits and "masking" them (flagging them as network bits) by setting the bits to a 1 state so that they are no longer representing the host ID portion of the subnet mask. This creates additional networks, but it results in fewer hosts on each of the networks.

To begin, you need to know how many host bits are required to make the desired number of networks. To calculate how many bits are needed to subnet into four networks (subnets), you use the formula:

$$2^{masked\ bits} = number\ of\ subnets$$

For example, if you are looking for four subnets, the formula would be $2^2 = 4$ networks, or subnets. So you would steal, or mask, two of the host bits in the subnet mask and make them network bits—these are called *subnet bits*.

Now that you know that two bits must be masked to create the four subnets, the next step is to look at your IP range of 10.0.0.0 and ask yourself, "What is the default subnet mask of this address?" You should come up with 255.0.0.0 because it is a class A address.

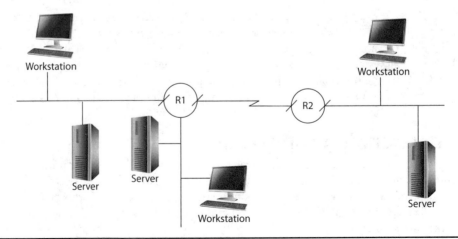

Figure 5-1 Subnetting to match this physical network structure

Once you know the default subnet mask, your next step is to break the subnet mask down into binary. A default class A decimal subnet mask in binary looks like the following:

Decimal	255	0	0	0
Binary	11111111	00000000	00000000	00000000

Once you've written out the subnet mask in binary in your work area, you can begin to calculate the new addresses of the four subnets. The first thing you need to do is steal, or "mask," two bits from the host ID portion of the subnet mask and make them subnet bits by setting them to a 1 state. Remember that you're taking two bits because of your earlier calculation. Because the last three octets of this subnet mask represent the host bits of a class A address, work from left to right and mask two additional bits to get the new binary table that follows:

Decimal	255	0	0	0
Binary	11111111	**11**000000	00000000	00000000

Notice that the two bits that are now enabled are in the second octet. Also notice that you always work from left to right in the subnet mask.

Calculate the New Subnet Mask

Now you can calculate the new subnet masks for all four networks. To do this, you convert the new binary value in the preceding table of 11111111.11000000.00000000.000 00000 to its decimal notation—you should get 255.192.0.0 as the new subnet mask of your four new subnets. Write that number down, because you'll need it later.

The next step is to calculate the IP ranges for the four different networks, but before that, you need to know five pieces of information about each of the new subnets you are designing before this walkthrough is complete:

- **New subnet mask**   After subnetting a network, you will have a new subnet mask that is used by all subnets you have created.

- **Network ID**   To calculate the network ID for each network, all host bits are set to 0.

- **First valid address**   To calculate the first valid address, you set the least significant host bit to 1; all other host bits are 0.

- **Broadcast address**   To calculate the broadcast address for each subnet, you set all host bits to 1.

- **Last valid address**   To calculate the last valid address, you set the least significant host bit to 0; all other host bits are 1.

You know that the new subnet mask is 255.192.0.0, so you can start by calculating the network ID of each of the four subnets.

Calculate the Network ID

To calculate the network IDs for each of the subnets, you need to determine all of the on/off states of the number of bits that you have converted from host bits to subnet bits. For example, two bits were used as subnet bits to create more networks, so there are four possible on/off states with two bits: 00, 01, 10, and 11. These are listed out in your binary work area and should look like the following table:

	First Octet (Decimal)	Second Octet (Binary)	Third Octet (Binary)	Fourth Octet (Binary)
Original IP	10	0	0	0
	10	**00**000000	00000000	00000000
	10	**01**000000	00000000	00000000
	10	**10**000000	00000000	00000000
	10	**11**000000	00000000	00000000

Next, you add in the remaining 0s to the bits that represent the host ID portion. Remember that the original network ID was 10.0.0.0, so the first octet will start with 10, no matter what you change in the binary, because you are starting your work with the second octet.

The next step is to bring the 10 down to the first octet; each network ID will start with 10 because that is what it was originally. After bringing the 10 down in the first octet, you then calculate the network ID of each of the two networks by leaving all host bits set to 0 (the nonbolded bits), as shown in the following table:

	First Octet (Decimal)	Second Octet (Binary)	Third Octet (Binary)	Fourth Octet (Binary)	Calculation
Original IP	10	0	0	0	
Subnet #1	10	**00**000000	00000000	00000000	10.0.0.0
Subnet #2	10	**01**000000	00000000	00000000	10.64.0.0
Subnet #3	10	**10**000000	00000000	00000000	10.128.0.0
Subnet #4	10	**11**000000	00000000	00000000	10.192.0.0

In this example, because the two subnet bits are being manipulated, and because all host bits are set to 0, the four new network IDs are created: 10.0.0.0, 10.64.0.0, 10.128.0.0, and 10.192.0.0. To calculate this, you simply convert all binary to decimal after listing out the on/off states that the two subnet bits can have.

Calculate the First Valid Address

Now that you have calculated the network ID of each subnet, the next number to calculate is the first valid address that can be assigned to a host on each of these networks. To calculate the first valid address, you simply enable the least significant bit, which will be the bit on the far right side of the network ID. Once you enable the least significant bit, you then convert all octets to decimal to figure out the first valid IP address of each network. The work area is shown in the following table, and you can see that with the four subnets, you have a first valid address for each network of 10.0.0.1, 10.64.0.1, 10.128.0.1, and 10.192.0.1:

	First Octet (Decimal)	Second Octet (Binary)	Third Octet (Binary)	Fourth Octet (Binary)	Calculation
Original IP	10	0	0	0	
Subnet #1	10	**00**000000	00000000	00000001	10.0.0.1
Subnet #2	10	**01**000000	00000000	00000001	10.64.0.1
Subnet #3	10	**10**000000	00000000	00000001	10.128.0.1
Subnet #4	10	**11**000000	00000000	00000001	10.192.0.1

Calculate the Broadcast Address

Now that you have calculated the first valid address for each of the four networks, you will need to calculate the broadcast address. The broadcast address is the address that any system will send data to in order to ensure that each system on the network receives the data. To calculate the broadcast address, you will enable all of the host bits (set them to 1), and then convert each octet from binary to decimal. You get the outcome in the following table:

	First Octet (Decimal)	Second Octet (Binary)	Third Octet (Binary)	Fourth Octet (Binary)	Calculation
Original IP	10	0	0	0	
Subnet #1	10	**00**111111	11111111	11111111	10.63.255.255
Subnet #2	10	**01**111111	11111111	11111111	10.127.255.255
Subnet #3	10	**10**111111	11111111	11111111	10.191.255.255
Subnet #4	10	**11**111111	11111111	11111111	10.255.255.255

As you can see, with all of the host bits enabled, if you convert that to decimal, you get 10.63.255.255, 10.127.255.255, 10.191.255.255, and 10.255.255.255 for the broadcast addresses of your four networks. Notice that the first two bits from the left in the second octet have not been changed in this entire process, but they are used in the conversion of that octet from binary to decimal. They have not changed because they are not host bits—they are subnet bits.

 EXAM TIP   For the exams, remember that a host address that has all host bits set to 0 (which is reserved for the network ID) or all host bits set to 1 (which is reserved for the broadcast address) is considered an invalid address to use on a system or device.

Calculate the Last Valid Address

Now that you have calculated the new subnet mask, the network ID, the first valid address, and the broadcast address for your four new subnets, the only additional information you need is the last valid address that may be assigned to hosts on each subnet.

To calculate the last valid host address of each subnet, simply subtract 1 from the broadcast address by disabling the least significant bit (the far-right host bit). To view the binary and decimal representations for our last valid address of each network, take a look at the following table:

	First Octet (Decimal)	Second Octet (Binary)	Third Octet (Binary)	Fourth Octet (Binary)	Calculation
Original IP	10	0	0	0	
Subnet #1	10	00111111	11111111	11111110	10.63.255.254
Subnet #2	10	01111111	11111111	11111110	10.127.255.254
Subnet #3	10	10111111	11111111	11111110	10.191.255.254
Subnet #4	10	11111111	11111111	11111110	10.255.255.254

You have now calculated all of the information required to configure the four physical network segments that you have created. The following table summarizes the configuration for each of the four network segments, and Figure 5-2 displays how these four network segments will be configured.

	Network ID	First Valid Address	Last Valid Address	Broadcast Address	Subnet Mask
Subnet 1	10.0.0.0	10.0.0.1	10.63.255.254	10.63.255.255	255.192.0.0
Subnet 2	10.64.0.0	10.64.0.1	10.127.255.254	10.127.255.255	255.192.0.0
Subnet 3	10.128.0.0	10.128.0.1	10.191.255.254	10.191.255.255	255.192.0.0
Subnet 4	10.192.0.0	10.192.0.1	10.255.255.254	10.255.255.255	255.192.0.0

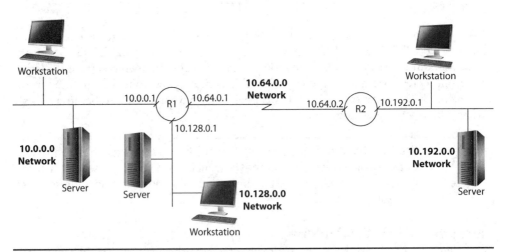

Figure 5-2 Subnetting a Class A network into four network segments

Verify the Network Size

On exam day, you will be given scenarios that say you need a certain number of subnets that can handle a certain number of hosts per subnet. You can verify that you have the correct numbers by performing some simple math:

- **Number of subnets**   To verify the number of subnets, use the formula $2^{subnet\ bits}$ = *number of subnets*. In our example, we have 2^2 = 4 subnets.

- **Number of hosts per subnet**   To verify that you are supporting the correct number of hosts per subnet, use the formula $2^{host\ bits} - 2$ = *number of hosts per subnet*. In our example, we have 2^{22} = 4,194,304 − 2 = 4,194,302 hosts per subnet.

Subnetting Class B Networks

Now let's take a look at subnetting a class B network address. Let's assume you have the network ID of 190.45.0.0. Remember that the default subnet mask for a class B network is 255.255.0.0. Assume that the scenario requires you to divide the address range into six subnets, because you have divided your network into six subnetworks.

Set Up the Work Area

The first step is to set up your work area on paper. You should write down what you know already:

```
            IP Range: 190.45.0.0
        Subnet mask: 255.255.0.0
Subnet mask (binary): 11111111.11111111.00000000.00000000
```

How Many Bits to Make Subnets?

Your next step is to decide how many bits from the host ID portion of the subnet masks you want to convert into subnet bits. Remember this formula:

$2^{masked\ bits}$ = *number of subnets*

So, 2^2 = four subnets, which is not enough, because you need six subnets. If you try 2^3, you get eight subnets, which is too many, but you must use it, because using 2^2 will not give you enough. Eight subnets meet your goal, with two additional subnets for future growth. Now that you have determined you want to convert three bits from host bits to subnet bits in the subnet masks, you get this:

```
            IP Range: 190.45.0.0
Subnet mask (binary): 11111111.11111111.11100000.00000000
```

You now know the new subnet mask for each of the six subnets (actually it is eight subnets, but you only require six of them). After making the change to the subnet mask in binary, if you convert it back to decimal, you will get a new subnet mask for each of the subnets, which is 255.255.224.0.

List the Combinations

The next step is to list all of the possible on/off states that the three subnet bits can make. You should come up with the same number of combinations as the number of subnets the three bits would create (which is eight):

```
000
001
010
011
100
101
110
111
```

Each of these combinations is then placed in the position of the three subnet bits and each creates a network ID. Because these three bits are starting out your third octet, fill in the first two octets with the original IP addresses so that you remember what you started with. Here is what you should have—notice that the subnet bits have been boldfaced so they stand out:

```
Subnet 1: 190.45.00000000.00000000
Subnet 2: 190.45.00100000.00000000
Subnet 3: 190.45.01000000.00000000
Subnet 4: 190.45.01100000.00000000
Subnet 5: 190.45.10000000.00000000
Subnet 6: 190.45.10100000.00000000
Subnet 7: 190.45.11000000.00000000
Subnet 8: 190.45.11100000.00000000
```

Calculate the Network ID

To calculate the network ID for each subnet, you should remember that all host bits must be set to 0 (which they are in the subnets just shown). If you convert all of the binary values to decimal, you will have the network ID for each of the subnets:

```
Subnet 1: 190.45.0.0
Subnet 2: 190.45.32.0
Subnet 3: 190.45.64.0
Subnet 4: 190.45.96.0
Subnet 5: 190.45.128.0
Subnet 6: 190.45.160.0
Subnet 7: 190.45.192.0
Subnet 8: 190.45.224.0
```

Calculate the First Valid Address

Next, you need to calculate the first valid address for each of those subnets. You should always do this in binary, and then convert to decimal. The rule for the first valid address of a subnet is this: take the least significant host bit and turn it on; then convert all the binary to decimal to get the following:

```
Subnet 1: 190.45.00000000.00000001 = 190.45.0.1
Subnet 2: 190.45.00100000.00000001 = 190.45.32.1
Subnet 3: 190.45.01000000.00000001 = 190.45.64.1
```

```
Subnet 4: 190.45.01100000.00000001 = 190.45.96.1
Subnet 5: 190.45.10000000.00000001 = 190.45.128.1
Subnet 6: 190.45.10100000.00000001 = 190.45.160.1
Subnet 7: 190.45.11000000.00000001 = 190.45.192.1
Subnet 8: 190.45.11100000.00000001 = 190.45.224.1
```

Calculate the Broadcast Address

The broadcast address is used to send messages to all systems on the network. The broadcast address is not to be assigned to a system on the network, but it is an address you should be familiar with. To calculate the broadcast address, you set all host bits (the bits to the right of the subnet bits) to 1 and then convert the entire address to decimal:

```
Subnet 1: 190.45.00011111.11111111 = 190.45.31.255
Subnet 2: 190.45.00111111.11111111 = 190.45.63.255
Subnet 3: 190.45.01011111.11111111 = 190.45.95.255
Subnet 4: 190.45.01111111.11111111 = 190.45.127.255
Subnet 5: 190.45.10011111.11111111 = 190.45.159.255
Subnet 6: 190.45.10111111.11111111 = 190.45.191.255
Subnet 7: 190.45.11011111.11111111 = 190.45.223.255
Subnet 8: 190.45.11111111.11111111 = 190.45.255.255
```

Calculate the Last Valid Address

To determine the last valid address of each subnet, you simply set all host bits to 1 except for the far-right host bit (known as the least significant bit). Then convert the binary to decimal to get your last valid address:

```
Subnet 1: 190.45.00011111.11111110 = 190.45.31.254
Subnet 2: 190.45.00111111.11111110 = 190.45.63.254
Subnet 3: 190.45.01011111.11111110 = 190.45.95.254
Subnet 4: 190.45.01111111.11111110 = 190.45.127.254
Subnet 5: 190.45.10011111.11111110 = 190.45.159.254
Subnet 6: 190.45.10111111.11111110 = 190.45.191.254
Subnet 7: 190.45.11011111.11111110 = 190.45.223.254
Subnet 8: 190.45.11111111.11111110 = 190.45.255.254
```

Subnetting Class C Networks

When subnetting a class C network, you follow the same steps, but because you are doing all of your manipulation of bits in the last octet, you will see some different numbers for things like the network IDs and the broadcast address. With class A and class B, those addresses usually end in a 0 or a 255.

In this scenario, you have a class network address of 202.78.34.0 and you need to divide the network into 12 subnets.

Set Up the Work Area

The first step is to set up your work area on paper. Write down what you know already:

```
            IP Range: 202.78.34.0
         Subnet mask: 255.255.255.0
Subnet mask (binary): 11111111.11111111.11111111.00000000
```

How Many Bits to Make Subnets?

Your next step is to decide how many bits from the host ID portion of the subnet mask you want to convert into subnet bits. Remember this formula:

$$2^{masked\ bits} = number\ of\ subnets$$

So, $2^2 = 4$ subnets, which is not enough—you need 12 subnets. If you try 2^3, you get 8 subnets, which is not enough. Using 2^4 gives you 16 subnets, which meets your goal, but with 4 additional subnets for future growth. Now that you have determined you want to convert four bits from host bits to subnet bits in the subnet masks, you get this:

```
              IP Range: 202.78.34.0
Subnet mask (binary): 11111111.11111111.11111111.11110000
```

You now know the new subnet mask for each of the 12 subnets (16, but you only require 12 of them). After making the change to the subnet mask in binary, you then convert it back to decimal to get your new subnet mask for each of the subnets. The new subnet mask for all subnets is 255.255.240.0.

List the Combinations

The next step is to list all of the possible on/off states that the four subnet bits can make. You should come up with the same number of combinations as the number of subnets the four bits would create (which is 16).

```
0000
0001
0010
0011
0100
0101
0110
0111
1000
1001
1010
1011
1100
1101
1110
1111
```

Each of these combinations is then placed in the position of the four subnet bits and creates each of the network IDs. Because these four bits are starting out our fourth octet, fill in the first three octets with the original IP addresses so that you remember what you started with. Here is what you should have; note that the subnet bits are boldfaced so that you do not confuse those bits with the four host bits that follow them:

```
Subnet 1: 202.78.34.00000000
Subnet 2: 202.78.34.00010000
Subnet 3: 202.78.34.00100000
Subnet 4: 202.78.34.00110000
Subnet 5: 202.78.34.01000000
```

```
Subnet  6: 202.78.34.01010000
Subnet  7: 202.78.34.01100000
Subnet  8: 202.78.34.01110000
Subnet  9: 202.78.34.10000000
Subnet 10: 202.78.34.10010000
Subnet 11: 202.78.34.10100000
Subnet 12: 202.78.34.10110000
Subnet 13: 202.78.34.11000000
Subnet 14: 202.78.34.11010000
Subnet 15: 202.78.34.11100000
Subnet 16: 202.78.34.11110000
```

Calculate the Network ID

To calculate the network ID for each subnet, you should remember that all host bits must be set to 0 (which they are in the subnets just shown). If you convert all of the binary values to decimal, you will have the network ID for each of the subnets:

```
Subnet  1: 202.78.34.00000000 = 202.78.34.0
Subnet  2: 202.78.34.00010000 = 202.78.34.16
Subnet  3: 202.78.34.00100000 = 202.78.34.32
Subnet  4: 202.78.34.00110000 = 202.78.34.48
Subnet  5: 202.78.34.01000000 = 202.78.34.64
Subnet  6: 202.78.34.01010000 = 202.78.34.80
Subnet  7: 202.78.34.01100000 = 202.78.34.96
Subnet  8: 202.78.34.01110000 = 202.78.34.112
Subnet  9: 202.78.34.10000000 = 202.78.34.128
Subnet 10: 202.78.34.10010000 = 202.78.34.144
Subnet 11: 202.78.34.10100000 = 202.78.34.160
Subnet 12: 202.78.34.10110000 = 202.78.34.176
Subnet 13: 202.78.34.11000000 = 202.78.34.192
Subnet 14: 202.78.34.11010000 = 202.78.34.208
Subnet 15: 202.78.34.11100000 = 202.78.34.224
Subnet 16: 202.78.34.11110000 = 202.78.34.240
```

Calculate the First Valid Address

Next you need to calculate the first valid address for each of those subnets. The rule for the first valid address of a subnet is this: turn on the least significant host bit (which is the far-right bit). Then convert all the binary to decimal to get the following:

```
Subnet  1: 202.78.34.00000001 = 202.78.34.1
Subnet  2: 202.78.34.00010001 = 202.78.34.17
Subnet  3: 202.78.34.00100001 = 202.78.34.33
Subnet  4: 202.78.34.00110001 = 202.78.34.49
Subnet  5: 202.78.34.01000001 = 202.78.34.65
Subnet  6: 202.78.34.01010001 = 202.78.34.81
Subnet  7: 202.78.34.01100001 = 202.78.34.97
Subnet  8: 202.78.34.01110001 = 202.78.34.113
Subnet  9: 202.78.34.10000001 = 202.78.34.129
Subnet 10: 202.78.34.10010001 = 202.78.34.145
Subnet 11: 202.78.34.10100001 = 202.78.34.161
Subnet 12: 202.78.34.10110001 = 202.78.34.177
Subnet 13: 202.78.34.11000001 = 202.78.34.193
Subnet 14: 202.78.34.11010001 = 202.78.34.209
Subnet 15: 202.78.34.11100001 = 202.78.34.225
Subnet 16: 202.78.34.11110001 = 202.78.34.241
```

Calculate the Broadcast Address

The broadcast address is used to send messages to all systems on the network. The broadcast address is not to be assigned to a system on the network, but it is an address you should be familiar with. To calculate the broadcast address, you set all host bits (the bits to the right of the bolded subnet bits) to 1 and then convert the entire address to decimal, as shown here:

```
Subnet 1:  202.78.34.00001111 = 202.78.34.15
Subnet 2:  202.78.34.00011111 = 202.78.34.31
Subnet 3:  202.78.34.00101111 = 202.78.34.47
Subnet 4:  202.78.34.00111111 = 202.78.34.63
Subnet 5:  202.78.34.01001111 = 202.78.34.79
Subnet 6:  202.78.34.01011111 = 202.78.34.95
Subnet 7:  202.78.34.01101111 = 202.78.34.111
Subnet 8:  202.78.34.01111111 = 202.78.34.127
Subnet 9:  202.78.34.10001111 = 202.78.34.143
Subnet 10: 202.78.34.10011111 = 202.78.34.159
Subnet 11: 202.78.34.10101111 = 202.78.34.175
Subnet 12: 202.78.34.10111111 = 202.78.34.191
Subnet 13: 202.78.34.11001111 = 202.78.34.207
Subnet 14: 202.78.34.11011111 = 202.78.34.223
Subnet 15: 202.78.34.11101111 = 202.78.34.239
Subnet 16: 202.78.34.11111111 = 202.78.34.255
```

Calculate the Last Valid Address

To determine the last valid address of each subnet, you simply set all host bits to 1 except for the far-right host bit (the least significant bit). Then convert the binary to decimal to get your last valid address:

```
Subnet 1:  202.78.34.00001110 = 202.78.34.14
Subnet 2:  202.78.34.00011110 = 202.78.34.30
Subnet 3:  202.78.34.00101110 = 202.78.34.46
Subnet 4:  202.78.34.00111110 = 202.78.34.62
Subnet 5:  202.78.34.01001110 = 202.78.34.78
Subnet 6:  202.78.34.01011110 = 202.78.34.94
Subnet 7:  202.78.34.01101110 = 202.78.34.110
Subnet 8:  202.78.34.01111110 = 202.78.34.126
Subnet 9:  202.78.34.10001110 = 202.78.34.142
Subnet 10: 202.78.34.10011110 = 202.78.34.158
Subnet 11: 202.78.34.10101110 = 202.78.34.174
Subnet 12: 202.78.34.10111110 = 202.78.34.190
Subnet 13: 202.78.34.11001110 = 202.78.34.206
Subnet 14: 202.78.34.11011110 = 202.78.34.222
Subnet 15: 202.78.34.11101110 = 202.78.34.238
Subnet 16: 202.78.34.11111110 = 202.78.34.254
```

Exercise 5-1: Subnetting an IP Addresses

In this exercise, you will determine the five pieces of information needed for a class A network that is being divided into six network segments. You can find the answers to this lab in the lab answer document with the companion content for the book.

Task 1: Subnetting a Class A Address   The network ID of the class A address is 120.0.0.0. Take a few pieces of paper and calculate the new subnet mask, the network ID, the first valid address, the last valid address, and the broadcast address of the four subnets. Once you have calculated your answers, fill in the following table. Refer to the subnetting example in this chapter as a guide to help you calculate the answers for this exercise.

	Network ID	First Valid Address	Last Valid Address	Broadcast Address	Subnet Mask
Subnet 1					
Subnet 2					
Subnet 3					
Subnet 4					
Subnet 5					
Subnet 6					
Subnet 7					
Subnet 8					

Task 2: Subnetting a Class B Address   You are responsible for subnetting the network ID of 190.34.0.0 into four subnets. Take some paper and walk through your binary work of subnetting this class B network into four subnets. Once you have calculated the information on paper, fill in the following table:

	Network ID	First Valid Address	Last Valid Address	Broadcast Address	Subnet Mask
Subnet 1					
Subnet 2					
Subnet 3					
Subnet 4					

Task 3: Subnetting a Class C Address   Your manager has purchased a class C network range and asked you to subnet this class C network into two subnets for the two network segments that will be built. One network segment will host client machines used by customers for online ordering, and the other segment will host the corporate machines used by your employees.

The class C network ID that you have purchased is 216.83.11.0. Once again, take a piece of paper and start by writing out the default subnet mask of this class C address.

Then start manipulating the host bits to get the network ID, first valid host ID, last valid host ID, broadcast address, and new subnet mask. Once you have calculated all the required information, fill in the following table:

	Network ID	First Valid Address	Last Valid Address	Broadcast Address
Subnet 1				
Subnet 2				

The new subnet mask for both subnets is_____.

This section has introduced you to the concept of subnetting, which you will need to know very well for the CCT/CCNA exams. Make sure you are familiar with identifying the class addresses and have a solid understanding of how to break those down into multiple subnets!

 EXAM TIP When preparing for the CCT/CCNA exams, practice subnetting a lot. You will need to do it very quickly on the exam, or you may run out of time!

Subnetting Shortcuts

One of the major challenges you'll find with the CCT/CCNA exams is being able to do the subnetting fairly quickly so that you do not run out of time. To help you figure out subnetting fairly quickly, here's a shortcut called the *increment shortcut*.

Let's do the class B network example of 190.45.0.0 again, but this time we will use our shortcut. Remember we want to divide this network into six subnets. The first step is still the same: determine how many bits to convert from host bits to subnet bits, using this formula:

$$2^3 = 8 \text{ subnets (we require only 6 subnets)}$$

Then write out the subnet mask in binary and convert the first three host bits to subnet bits as follows:

```
            IP Range: 190.45.0.0
Subnet mask (binary): 11111111.11111111.11100000.00000000
```

Notice that the new subnet mask for all subnets is 255.255.224.0 when you convert the new binary subnet mask to decimal.

Here is where the shortcut kicks in. Look at the value of the last subnet bit (far-right subnet bit) and use that as the increment. In this example, the increment is 32, because the first subnet bit has a value of 128, the second subnet bit has a value of 64, and the third and final subnet bit has a value of 32. This increment becomes the network ID for each subnet.

Start by writing out the network ID you began with, and then in the octet where the subnet bits are, increment it by the increment value for the next network ID; then continue that process as follows:

```
Subnet 1: 190.45.0.0
Subnet 2: 190.45.32.0
Subnet 3: 190.45.64.0
Subnet 4: 190.45.96.0
Subnet 5: 190.45.128.0
Subnet 6: 190.45.160.0
Subnet 7: 190.45.192.0
Subnet 8: 190.45.224.0
```

Once you have the network IDs, you can calculate the first valid addresses for each subnet by adding 1 to each of the network IDs:

```
First valid address (Subnet 1): 190.45.0.1
First valid address (Subnet 2): 190.45.32.1
First valid address (Subnet 3): 190.45.64.1
First valid address (Subnet 4): 190.45.96.1
First valid address (Subnet 5): 190.45.128.1
First valid address (Subnet 6): 190.45.160.1
First valid address (Subnet 7): 190.45.192.1
First valid address (Subnet 8): 190.45.224.1
```

Next, you can figure out the broadcast address for each subnet. To do this, simply take one number away from the next network ID. For example, the network ID for the second subnet was 190.45.32.0. The broadcast address for the first subnet is one number less the network ID of the second subnet, which is 190.45.31.255. Remember that to figure out the broadcast address of a subnet, you are always looking at the network ID of the next subnet (determined two steps ago). Here are the broadcast addresses for each subnet:

```
Broadcast address (Subnet 1): 190.45.31.255
Broadcast address (Subnet 2): 190.45.63.255
Broadcast address (Subnet 3): 190.45.95.255
Broadcast address (Subnet 4): 190.45.127.255
Broadcast address (Subnet 5): 190.45.159.255
Broadcast address (Subnet 6): 190.45.191.255
Broadcast address (Subnet 7): 190.45.223.255
Broadcast address (Subnet 8): 190.45.255.255
```

The exception to this rule is the last subnet. Because there is no next network ID to work with, the last subnet always ends with what would have been the original network's broadcast address.

After you have figured out the broadcast address, you can figure out the last valid address by taking one number away from the broadcast address as follows:

```
Last valid address (Subnet 1): 190.45.31.254
Last valid address (Subnet 2): 190.45.63.254
Last valid address (Subnet 3): 190.45.95.254
Last valid address (Subnet 4): 190.45.127.254
Last valid address (Subnet 5): 190.45.159.254
Last valid address (Subnet 6): 190.45.191.254
Last valid address (Subnet 7): 190.45.223.254
Last valid address (Subnet 8): 190.45.255.254
```

Now that you have figured all required information, you can put the data in a chart to clearly identify the network IDs, first valid address, last valid address, and broadcast address of each subnet.

Definitely take some time to practice using the shortcut method of subnetting so that you can answer subnetting questions quickly. Exercise 5-2 is a practice exercise using the shortcut.

Exercise 5-2: Subnetting Using the Shortcut Method

In this exercise, you will subnet three different networks using the shortcut method.

Task 1: Subnetting a Class A Address   The network ID of the class A address is 37.0.0.0. You need to subnet this network into four subnets using the shortcut method.

	Network ID	First Valid Address	Last Valid Address	Broadcast Address
Subnet 1				
Subnet 2				
Subnet 3				
Subnet 4				

New Subnet Mask: _____

Task 2: Subnetting a Class B Address   The network ID of the class B address is 139.45.0.0. You need to subnet this network into eight subnets using the shortcut method.

	Network ID	First Valid Address	Last Valid Address	Broadcast Address
Subnet 1				
Subnet 2				
Subnet 3				
Subnet 4				
Subnet 5				
Subnet 6				
Subnet 7				
Subnet 8				

New Subnet Mask: _____

Task 3: Subnetting a Class C Address The network ID of the class B address is 222.100.10.0. You need to subnet this network into four subnets using the shortcut method.

	Network ID	First Valid Address	Last Valid Address	Broadcast Address
Subnet 1				
Subnet 2				
Subnet 3				
Subnet 4				

New Subnet Mask: _____

Classful vs. Classless Addressing

Chapter 4 introduced the different class IP addresses. Each IP address that you use on a system falls into one of the three primary classes: class A, class B, or class C. This is known as *classful addressing*. Table 5-1 summarizes the three major address classes. Note that in the Octet Setup column, N means network ID and H means host ID to identify the network ID and host ID portions of the address.

Everything that you have learned about the different address classes, including network IDs, host IDs, and default subnet masks, is based on classful addressing.

 EXAM TIP For the exams, you need to remember that classful IP addressing divides the network ID and host ID portions of an IP address at an octet. For example, a class B address uses the first two octets as the network ID and the last two octets as the host ID.

IP Subnet Zero

Another subnetting concept you should be familiar with for the Cisco CCT and CCNA exams is *IP subnet zero*. A number of years ago, some networking devices and protocols could not use the first and last subnets we created when we divided the network into multiple subnets. This was because some of the older routing protocols did not send the

Address Class	Value of First Octet	Octet Setup	Number of Hosts
Class A	1–127	N.H.H.H	16,777,214
Class B	128–191	N.N.H.H	65,534
Class C	192–223	N.N.N.H	254

Table 5-1   Reviewing Classful IP Addressing

subnet mask information along with the network ID when the router shared information about the network. This meant that if the network was subnetted, let's say into four subnets, when a router shared knowledge of the 192.168.1.0 network, the receiving router had no way to know if it was subnetted or the entire 192.168.1.0 network. Today's routing protocols send the subnet mask information with the route—something like 192.168.1.0/26—so there is no question that this is the first of four subnetted networks.

Cisco devices can use the first and last subnets when subnetting a network, because the **ip subnet-zero** command configured on the device indicates that we can use the first and last subnets. If the command was changed to **no ip subnet-zero**, we would not be allowed to use the first and last subnets on the router.

 NOTE You will learn about some Cisco IOS commands in Chapter 7.

Variable Length Subnet Masks

One of the problems with the subnetting technique we've covered to far is that each of the subnets we've created has the same number of IP addresses assigned to it. This sometimes can waste addresses, because there may not be a need for the same number of IP addresses within each subnet. As an example, in Figure 5-3, you can see a network with three subnets. Subnet 1 has 21 hosts, subnet 2 has 2 hosts, and subnet 3 has 56 hosts. Each host on each subnet will need an IP address within the subnet, and we want to subnet the network into three subnets while conserving addresses.

To accomplish this goal, look at your network ID (216.83.11.0), and first work with the larger subnet—in this case, subnet 3. Subnet 3 requires 56 hosts, so to calculate the

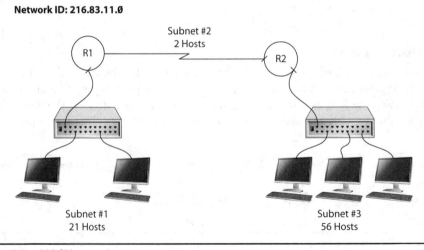

Figure 5-3 A VLSM scenario

subnet information, you need to determine how many *hosts bits* you need to create a subnet that supports 56 hosts. You can use the following formula:

$2^{host\ bits} - 2$ = *number of hosts supported*

Based on that formula we need 6 bits for host bits in order to support the 56 hosts on subnet 3 as follows:

2^6 = **64** – 2 = *62 hosts supported on subnet 3*

Keep in mind that using 6 bits for host bits gives you a few more host addresses than what you require, but you cannot go any lower, because five host bits would support only 30 (32 – 2) hosts. You subtract 2 because each subnet has two reserved addresses—the network ID and the broadcast address. Also note that although you are supporting 62 hosts with this subnet, the number of addresses is 64—this is known as the *block size* (or subnet size).

Keep in mind that if there are 6 bits for host bits (six 0s below in the fourth octet), that means the two remaining bits are subnet bits (highlighted in bold next). With this information, you can now document the subnet mask for subnet 3 as follows:

11111111.11111111.11111111.**11**000000 = 255.255.255.192

Now to show what address range this is, you can plot the network on a grid showing the different IP addresses used in the fourth octet. Note that subnet 3 will be using a block of 64 addresses, but you can use only 62 of them (2 are reserved). This means numbers 0–63 are the addresses for subnet 3, as shown in Figure 5-4. Notice that this is documented as 216.83.11.0/26. The /26 indicates that 26 bits in the subnet mask have been enabled, and it controls how many addresses are used in this subnet (64).

Now look at the next highest number of hosts on a network, and you'll see that subnet 1 requires 21 hosts (or 21 IP addresses). To calculate the subnet block for this, use the following formula:

2^5 = **32** – 2 = *30 hosts supported on subnet 1*

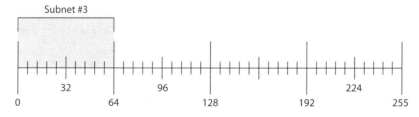

Figure 5-4 Plotting addresses for the largest VLSM subnet

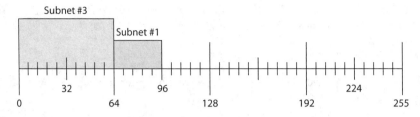

Figure 5-5 Plotting addresses for next VLSM subnet

The 30 hosts are a few more than the required 21, but this is okay, as described in previous examples. With this information, you can now document the subnet mask for subnet 1 as follows:

11111111.11111111.11111111.**111**00000 = 255.255.255.224

Now plot subnet 1 on the grid showing the different IPs in the fourth octet, as shown in Figure 5-5. Remember that subnet 1 will be using a block of 32 addresses, but two are unavailable. Because subnet 3 is using addresses 0–63, subnet 1 will start at 64 and go for 32 addresses, which will be to 95 (64 – 95 = 32 address block size).

This means numbers 64–95 are the addresses for subnet 1, as shown in Figure 5-5. Note that this is documented as 216.83.11.64/27. The /27 indicates that 27 bits in the subnet mask have been enabled, and it controls how many addresses are used in this subnet (32).

The last subnet to add to our planning grid is subnet 2. Because we need only two IP addresses on this subnet (one for each side of the WAN link), we need to use the following formula for two hosts:

2^2 = 4 – 2 = 2 hosts supported on subnet 2

This means we need to have only two host bits to support a subnet requiring only two IP addresses. This gives us the following IP configuration in binary:

11111111.11111111.11111111.**111111**00 = 255.255.255.252

Note that the block size is four (even though there are only two usable addresses). This means we will use the next addresses of 96–99 as the addresses in the fourth octet for this subnet (see Figure 5-6).

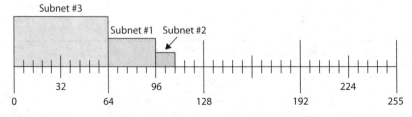

Figure 5-6 Plotting VLSM addresses for WAN link

Note that this is documented as 216.83.11.96/30. The /30 indicates that 30 bits in the subnet mask have been enabled, and it controls how many addresses are used in this subnet, which in this case is four (the block size).

The great news is that we have planned our IP address scheme for three subnets, and look at all of the addresses that are still available for future network changes! Addresses 100–255 are still available! Now that is conserving IP addresses and still getting the job done!

 TIP   I have specified the blocks as contiguous addresses for visual purposes. In the real world, you may want to spread them out a bit so that you can accommodate growth without needing to change all the address blocks.

Exercise 5-3: Using VLSM on a Network

In this exercise, you will calculate the VLSM for each different network segment based on the network diagram shown in Figure 5-7. The network address you have to subnet is 200.45.6.0.

Record your subnet information for each network segment:

Subnet #1: _____

Subnet #2: _____

Subnet #3: _____

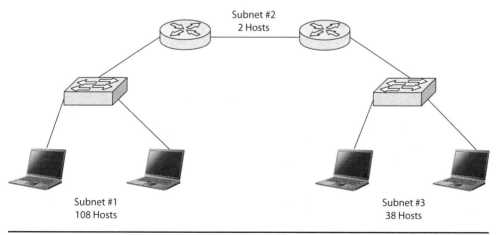

Figure 5-7   Network diagram for VLSM exercise

Route Summarization

Route summarization is the ability to take a bunch of contiguous network numbers in your routing table and advertise these contiguous routes as a single summarized or aggregated route. Route summarization enables you to summarize subnetted routes back to the class boundary. For instance, if you are using the network ID 192.168.1.0/24 and have subnetted it to 192.168.1.0/26, giving you four networks, you could summarize these subnets in your routing table and advertise them as the single class C network number 192.168.1.0/24, as shown in Figure 5-8. In this example, the routing entries are reduced from four to one in your routing updates. Notice in this example that the same class network, 192.168.1.0, has two masks associated with it: 255.255.255.192 (identified with /26) and 255.255.255.0 (identified with /24).

 NOTE This is not a complete discussion on route summarization. We still have yet to learn about routing, but I wanted to introduce the topics of route summarization and CIDR so that you are familiar with the terms. You will learn about routing in Chapters 11 and 12.

Advantages of Summarization

Summarization enables you to create a more efficient routing environment by providing the following advantages:

- It reduces the size of routing tables, requiring less memory and processing.
- It reduces the size of routing updates, requiring less bandwidth.
- It prevents routing table instability.

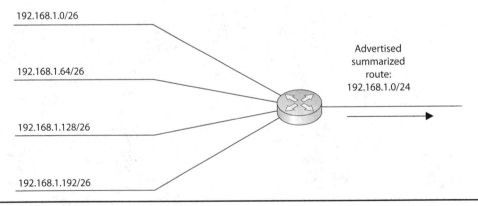

Figure 5-8   Simple route summarization example

There are a few disadvantages to route summarization as well:

- The summary route may contain subnets that are not in use, and the router may receive packets for routes that are not in use, although they do mathematically fall under the summary route. In this case the router will drop those packets.
- The router may choose a different pathway for the route because the pathway is more specific than that of the summary route.

Don't be too worried about these routing issues at this point. I bring them up only to provide a complete advantages/disadvantages discussion. This chapter is more about the design behind the numbers, so let's talk about how route summarization is performed.

To calculate the summary route, you first list out each of the network IDs and then convert them to their binary forms. Our four subnets can be listed as follows:

```
192.168.1.0/26      11000000.10101000.00000001.00000000
192.168.1.64/26     11000000.10101000.00000001.01000000
192.168.1.128/26    11000000.10101000.00000001.10000000
192.168.1.192/26    11000000.10101000.00000001.11000000
```

Next, you identify, from left to right, how many of the bits are the same with those four network IDs. That is your summary route:

```
192.168.1.0/26      11000000.10101000.00000001.00000000
192.168.1.64/26     11000000.10101000.00000001.01000000
192.168.1.128/26    11000000.10101000.00000001.10000000
192.168.1.192/26    11000000.10101000.00000001.11000000
```

Notice that in the first two bits of the fourth octet, the bits start to change for each subnet. All of the bits before that point are the common bits to create our summary route. When you convert the common bits back to decimal, you get a summary route of 192.168.1.0/24.

Classless Interdomain Routing (CIDR)

Classless Interdomain Routing (CIDR), specified in RFC 2050, is an extension to VLSM and route summarization. With VLSM, you can summarize subnets back to the class A, B, or C network boundary. Looking back at our example, if you have a class C network 192.168.1.0/24 and subnet it with a 26-bit mask, you have created four subnets. Using route summarization, you can summarize these four subnets back to 192.168.1.0/24. CIDR takes this one step further and enables you to summarize a block of contiguous class A, B, and/or C network numbers. This practice is commonly referred to as *supernetting*. Today's classless protocols support supernetting. However, it is most commonly configured by Internet service providers (ISPs) that use the Border Gateway Protocol (BGP) for routing.

Figure 5-9 shows an example of CIDR. In this example, a router is connected to four class C networks: 192.168.0.0/24, 192.168.1.0/24, 192.168.2.0/24, 192.168.3.0/24. It is summarizing those routes as 192.168.0.0/22.

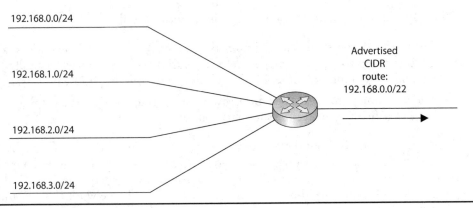

Figure 5-9 CIDR example

Let's break down how this is performed with CIDR. As I mentioned, CIDR is an extension of VLSM and route summarization so the technique to summarize those class C networks is the same as that with route summarization. Looking at the network addresses in binary, you identify the common bits to determine the summary network. Looking at the binary that follows, you can see that all the bits found in the first two octets of the four networks are the same. In the third octet, the first 6 bits are the same as well, totaling 22 bits that are common to all networks (so that is our summary route). Notice the subnet mask for this summarization: 255.255.252.0. This mask, along with the beginning network of 192.168.0.0, includes addresses from 192.168.0.0 to 192.168.3.255, which are behind this router.

```
192.168.1.0/24      11000000.10101000.00000001.00000000
192.168.2.0/24      11000000.10101000.00000010.01000000
192.168.3.0/24      11000000.10101000.00000011.10000000
192.168.4.0/24      11000000.10101000.00000100.11000000
```

 EXAM TIP For the exams remember that CIDR is similar to VLSM, in that CIDR enables you to summarize multiple contiguous class networks together, like multiple class C networks. This is also called supernetting.

Because there needed to be a standard method of indicating how many bits in the IP address were network bits, *CIDR notation* was created. With CIDR notation, you specify the IP address and a forward slash (/), followed by the number of bits that make up the network ID. For example, 10.0.0.0/8 specifies that the network ID is the first eight bits (which would mean the subnet mask is 255.0.0.0). Likewise, 131.107.64.0/18 indicates that this network ID is a result of subnetting a class B address.

It is important to note that the CIDR notation has become commonplace in many of the configuration dialog boxes and commands where you must input a network ID and a subnet mask.

Exercise 5-4: Additional Subnetting Practices

Because subnetting is such an important topic for the Cisco CCNA certification exam it is important to practice it as much as you can. In this additional exercise you will practice subnetting class A, B, and C addresses.

Task 1: Subnetting a Class B Network   You have a class B network ID of 150.87.0.0, and you need to divide this network into 16 subnets. Use some paper and calculate the network ID, first valid address, last valid address, and broadcast address of each of the *first six subnets of the 16.* Don't forget to determine the new subnet mask of these networks as well. Fill in the following table when you have completed your work on paper:

	Network ID	First Valid Address	Last Valid Address	Broadcast Address
Subnet 1				
Subnet 2				
Subnet 3				
Subnet 4				
Subnet 5				
Subnet 6				

New Subnet Mask: _____

Task 2: Subnetting a Class A Network   You have a class A network ID of 14.0.0.0, and you need to divide this network into eight subnets. Use some paper and calculate the network ID, first valid address, last valid address, and broadcast address of each of the eight subnets. Don't forget to determine the new subnet mask of these networks as well. Fill in the following table when you have completed your work on paper:

	Network ID	First Valid Address	Last Valid Address	Broadcast Address
Subnet 1				
Subnet 2				
Subnet 3				
Subnet 4				
Subnet 5				
Subnet 6				
Subnet 7				
Subnet 8				

New Subnet Mask: _____

Task 3: Subnetting a Class C Network   You have a class C network ID of 202.15.67.0, and you need to divide this network into four subnets. Use some paper and calculate the network ID, first valid address, last valid address, and broadcast address of each of the four subnets. Don't forget to determine the new subnet mask of these networks as well. Fill in the following table when you have completed your work on paper:

	Network ID	First Valid Address	Last Valid Address	Broadcast Address
Subnet 1				
Subnet 2				
Subnet 3				
Subnet 4				
New Subnet Mask: _____				

Chapter Review

In this chapter, you learned that from time to time you may need to divide a network range into multiple network blocks (subnets) to follow the physical structure of the network. Because the Cisco CCNA certification exam will have a number of questions that rely on your knowledge of subnetting, be sure to study this chapter well.

To subnet a network, you will need to know how many networks or hosts per network are required. You can then convert host bits in the subnet mask to become subnet bits, essentially altering your subnet mask and creating more networks while supporting less hosts per network.

The Variable Length Subnet Mask (VLSM) feature enables you to have a different subnet mask for each subnet on the network; this lets you make better use of addresses.

Quick Review

Understanding Subnetting

- The purpose of subnetting is to break one network ID into multiple subnetworks (subnets) so that you can follow the physical structure of the network.

- With subnetting, you take host bits from the subnet mask and turn them into network bits—thus creating more networks but fewer machines per network.

- To determine how many bits to take from the host ID portion of the subnet mask, use the formula $2^{masked\ bits} - 2 = number\ of\ networks$.

- For each subnet created, you must calculate the network ID, first valid address, last valid address, broadcast address, and new subnet mask.

Subnetting Shortcuts

- Look at the value of the last bit that was used to subnet and use that as your increment value.
- Using the increment value, list out all network IDs, and then add one to that to get the first valid address of each network.
- To determine the broadcast address of a subnet, use the number that is one less than the next network ID. The last valid address for a subnet will be one number less than the broadcast address.

Classful vs. Classless Addressing

- In classful addressing, the network ID falls into one of the default network IDs of a class A, class B, or class C address.
- In classless addressing, the network ID is altered from a normal classful address.

Variable Length Subnet Masks

- Creating subnets of the same size for each of your subnets is going to waste addresses when designing your network.
- VLSM enables you to use a different subnet mask for each subnet, so that you can make better use of your available addresses.

Questions

The following questions will help you measure your understanding of the material presented in this chapter. Read all the choices carefully, as there may be more than one correct answer. Choose the correct answer(s) for each question.

1. You have a network ID of 131.107.0.0 and you would like to subnet your network into six networks. What is your new subnet mask?

    A. 255.224.0.0

    B. 255.255.224.0

    C. 255.192.0.0

    D. 255.255.192.0

2. You want to divide your network into eight networks. How many bits will you need to take from the host ID portion of the subnet mask?

    A. 2

    B. 3

    C. 4

    D. 6

3. In binary, how do you calculate the broadcast address of a network range?

   A. All host bits set to 0

   B. All host bits set to 0, except for the low-order bit

   C. All host bits set to 1, except for the low-order bit

   D. All host bits set to 1

4. In binary, how do you calculate the network ID of a network range?

   A. All host bits set to 0

   B. All host bits set to 0, except for the low-order bit

   C. All host bits set to 1, except for the low-order bit

   D. All host bits set to 1

5. The last valid address of a subnet is always

   A. One more than the broadcast address

   B. One less than the broadcast address

   C. One more than the network ID

   D. One less than the network ID

6. You need to assign an IP address to the router that uses the fourth valid address of 200.56.88.96/27. Which address would you use?

   A. 200.56.88.68

   B. 200.56.88.104

   C. 200.56.88.97

   D. 200.56.88.100

7. Your system has an IP address of 138.97.25.10/20. Which of the following is a system on your network?

   A. 138.97.56.8

   B. 138.97.17.10

   C. 138.97.15.77

   D. 138.97.33.76

8. Which of the following is an example of CIDR notation?

   A. 16/10.34.56.78

   B. 10.34.56.78

   C. 10.34.56.0

   D. 10.34.56.78/16

9. Your router has an IP address of 216.83.11.65/27. You want to connect a new system on the network. Which of the following addresses would you assign to that new system?

   A. 216.83.11.45

   B. 216.83.11.87

   C. 216.83.11.95

   D. 216.83.11.96

10. You are configuring the gigabit interface on the Cisco router with the last valid IP address of the 131.107.48.0/20 network. What address would you use?

    A. 131.107.48.254

    B. 131.107.255.254

    C. 131.107.64.254

    D. 131.107.63.254

Performance-based Question

1. You are helping a junior administrator to understand the IP addressing scheme used on your network. You have subnetted your network to support 16 subnets with the address scheme of 200.15.36.0/28. Looking at the different addresses listed on the left side of the following exhibit, identify if the address is a broadcast address, network ID, or host address.

200.15.36.22
200.15.36.16
200.15.36.79
200.15.36.60
200.15.36.31
200.15.36.48

Broadcast Address

Network ID

Host Address

Answers

1. **B.** Given that you are dealing with a class B address, the default subnet mask is 255.255.0.0. Therefore, if you take three bits (needed for six networks) from the host ID, you will get a new subnet mask of 255.255.224.0.

2. **B.** You need to mask three bits to get a minimum of eight networks. The formula to calculate how many bits you need to take from the host ID portion of the subnet mask is $2^{masked\ bits}$ = *number of networks*. So, in this case, 2^3 = 8 networks.

3. **D.** The broadcast address is calculated by converting all host bits to 1.

4. A. The network ID is determined by setting all host bits to 0.

5. B. The last valid address is always one less than the broadcast address.

6. D. This is a tricky question. When answering these types of questions (and you will get them on the exam), you should first look at the address you were given—200.56.88.96/27. First focus on the /27; this indicates that 27 bits are enabled in the subnet mask. This is a class C address, which normally has only 24 bits enabled, so it tells you that this is a subnetted network. You know there are three extra bits that have been converted to subnet bits. Using the shortcut method, you know that the value of the last bit that was subnetted (the third extra bit) is 32. To answer the question, you should list out all the network IDs for the scenario on paper, using the increments: 200.56.88.0, 200.56.88.32, 200.56.88.64, 200.56.88.96, and so on. You can stop when you see the network that applies to this question—the 200.56.88.96 network (or subnet). Now you can answer the question about the fourth valid address of that subnet: 97 is the first valid address, 98 is second, 99 is third, and 100 is the fourth valid address.

7. B. Another tricky question, but you can answer it similar to question 6. Looking at the address, you can see that it starts with 138, which is a class B address. Class B addresses have a default subnet mask of 255.255.0.0, which means there are 16 bits enabled in the subnet mask—this is /16 in CIDR notation. Because the address given is using a /20 instead of a /16, you know that the question is a subnetted example. With the four extra bits, that means the increment is 16 (the value of the last enabled bit of the four subnetted bits), so you list out the subnets to determine what network you are dealing with. The subnets are 138.97.0.0, 138.97.16.0, 138.97.32.0, and so on. Note that the IP given in the question is 138.97.25.10, which is on the 138.97.16.0 network. To answer the question, you have to pick an address that falls between 138.97.16.0 and 138.97.32.0.

8. D. CIDR notation is used to identify how many bits make up the network ID in the IP address. With CIDR notation, you specify the number of bits that make up the network ID by placing a forward slash (/) after the IP address and then the number of bits that make up the network ID: for example, 10.34.56.78/16.

9. B. Because /27 is being used to identify the number of bits that make up the subnet mask, you know the network is subnetted (class C has a /24 by default). In this example, the network that the router is on is the 216.83.11.64 network, and 216.83.11.87 is the only valid address on that network listed here.

10. D. Because /20 is used to identify the number of bits that make up the subnet mask, you know the network is subnetted (class B has a /16 by default). Using the shortcut method, you known that /20 gives four additional bits to the subnet mask with 16 being the increment. The network range you are working with is 131.107.48.0, and you want to know the last valid address of that subnet. A quick way to determine this is to use the increment to determine the next network ID of 131.107.64.0 and then work backward from that, finding the last valid address. The address before 131.107.64.0 is 131.107.63.255, which is the broadcast address of the 131.107.48.0 network. The address before that, 131.107.63.154, is the last valid address.

Performance-based Answer

1. This is a tricky question, and you are sure to see similar questions to this on the Cisco exams where you need to identify network IDs, broadcast addresses, and host address. To answer this question, the first thing you do is focus on the address given of 200.15.36.0/28. This is a class C address with 4 subnet bits. Next, identify the value of the last bit of the 4 bits, which is the increment. In this case, it is 16. Then, write out on a piece of paper the different network IDs:

200.15.36.0
200.15.36.16
200.15.36.32
200.15.36.48
200.15.36.64
200.15.36.80

Now you know the different network IDs. The number before each of these network IDs would be the broadcast address of the previous network, and numbers in between are host addresses.

Broadcast Address	
200.15.36.79	200.15.36.31

Network ID	
200.15.36.16	200.15.36.48

Host Address	
200.15.36.22	200.15.36.60

Cisco Device Basics

In this chapter, you will
- Look at Cisco hardware and software
- Learn about memory types
- Connect to a Cisco device
- Start a Cisco device
- Learn about service-related tasks

Now that you understand networking concepts and TCP/IP addressing, let's dive into the world of working with Cisco devices. In this chapter you will learn more about the hardware aspects and startup process of Cisco devices. Then, Chapter 7 will focus on how to navigate through the operating system and perform administrative tasks.

Working with Cisco Devices and Software

Cisco provides several families of devices that provide different features and functionalities. For example, Catalyst products include a number of models of Cisco's layer 2 and layer 3 switches. In this section, you will learn about some of Cisco's different product lines that you may be working with.

Types of Cisco Devices

A number of different types of Cisco devices are currently on the market, with each device supporting specific features, hardware modules, and interfaces. The following is a quick rundown of some of the devices you may encounter.

Cisco Nexus Series Switches

Cisco's Nexus series switches are designed for data centers to improve performance with high availability features that enable all systems to access network and storage resources. Nexus series switches run the NX-OS network operating system.

- **Cisco Nexus 9000 Series** These switches provide speeds of 1, 10, 25, 50, 100, and 400 Gbps in the data center. A number of features help automate the network, including software-defined networking (SDN).

- **Nexus 7000 Series**   These modular switches offer performance of 10-, 40-, and 100-Gigabit networking. You can add 7000 series modules, such as the Cisco Network Analysis Module (NAM), which enables you to analyze packets and troubleshoot traffic issues.

- **Nexus 3000 Series**   These Nexus 3000 series switches are designed for general layer 2 and layer 3 switching with support for 1, 10, 25, 40, 100, and 400 Gbps. Some models in this series support programmability and network telemetry features.

Cisco Catalyst Series Switches

The Cisco Catalyst series switches are designed as LAN access switches and are used at the core and distribution layers.

- **Catalyst 9000 Series**   These switches are designed for campus deployments and can provide access to a network via wired and wireless functionalities.

- **Catalyst 6800 Series**   Designed as campus backbone switches, these devices offer a number of slots for inserting different hardware modules, and they support small form-factor pluggable (SFP) and SFP+ transceivers.

- **Catalyst 6500 E-Series**   These enhanced switches support 80 Gbps in each slot.

- **Catalyst 3850, 3650, 2960, and 1000 Series**   These switches are designed as access-layer switch models and support a number of different modules and configurations. For example, the 3650 modules support 1, 10, and 40 Gbps with SFP+ uplink ports to add an SFP+ transceiver of your choice.

Cisco ASR Series Routers

Cisco Aggregation Services Router (ASR) series routers are used in large enterprise networks or service providers. They are best suited for high-bandwidth application environments because they handle 100 Gbps. ASR series routers are powered by Cisco's IOS XR and IOS SE operating systems. Following are some popular ASR models:

- **Cisco 8000 Series**   These routers are designed for performance with up to 400GB throughput. They are cloud enhanced and able to integrate into management tools.

- **Cisco ASR 9000 Series**   These high-end routers are commonly used at the core layer or at the edge of the network. The ASR 9000 routers are powered by the IOS XR operating system.

- **Cisco ASR 1000 Series**   These routers are designed to be used at the edge of the network, and they are powered by the IOS XE operating system.

Cisco ISR Series Routers

The Integrated Services Router (ISR) series focuses on servicing small to midsize businesses with small to midsize networks. ISR routers are designed as edge routers to provide connectivity to branch offices. They are powered by the Cisco IOS operating system.

- **Cisco 4000 Series** These routers combine network, compute, and WAN services by supporting different connectivity options such as Gigabit Ethernet, T1/E1, and xDSL interfaces.

- **Cisco 1100 Series** These small, fanless routers provide connectivity and security features to connect branch offices to their main network.

- **Cisco 900 Series** These routers are designed for small offices and have four LAN ports as well as WAN ports and security services such as virtual private network (VPN), dynamic multipoint VPN (DMVPN), and a firewall.

- **Cisco 800 Series** These routers combine a switch and router together and add wireless capabilities.

Other Cisco Devices

The list of Cisco devices that exists continues with devices that are designed to operate in a cloud environment or devices that provide a large-scale platform for service providers. The following are some other Cisco devices you should be familiar with for the Cisco CCT exam:

- **MDS 9000 Series** The Cisco MDS 9000 series of switches are multilayer switches used for connectivity to storage environments. They are designed to offer network designers the capabilities to build highly available, secure, and scalable storage networks.

- **Meraki Switches** Meraki switches are the Cisco product line focused on management of the switches from the cloud. From a central dashboard that is accessed from across the web, administrators are able to manage all the switches in the organization.

- **NCS 5500 Series** The Cisco *Network Convergence System* (NCS) is designed for high-scale data center aggregation offering 100 Gbps architectures. It is a router product that uses the IOS XR operating system providing a number of services, such as application hosting for large enterprises or service providers.

- **NCS 5000 Series** An older model NCS routing solution, the NCS 5000 series is a routing platform designed for enterprise networks and service providers. These routing devices provide 10 Gbps throughput using the Cisco IOS XR software.

Identifying Device Model Numbers and Serial Numbers

You can identify the model and serial number of your Cisco device by looking at the stickers typically located on the back of the device chassis (though they are sometimes displayed on the front). In Figure 6-1, you can see that my device (the PID) is a WS-C3750G-24TS-S model. You can also see the serial number (SN): FDO1125Z6VQ.

Figure 6-1
Identifying serial
number and
model number

You can use other methods to identify the type of Cisco hardware you are working with. A Cisco router or switch device usually includes other markings, such as a logo displaying the device model number. You may also find markings that identify the model of the following devices:

- **Adapters**   These are network interface cards added to the Cisco device.
- **Modules**   Many different types of modules can be added to a slot on a Cisco device. A common example of a module is a WAN interface card (WIC) used to install a T1 interface or a serial port to the router.
- **Line card**   This is a circuit board that provides LAN or WAN ports to high-end routers that are designed to accept line cards.

Each of these devices may have markings that indicate the type of device or the model of the device. For example, if you look at the metal plate on a WIC module device, you will see the module type, such as WIC 1DSU/T1, which is a T1 WAN interface card.

You can also find the model number and serial number of your Cisco device by using the **show version** command. Looking at the following code example, I have highlighted some relevant sections that identify the model of the Cisco device, which you can see is a Cisco 1900 series device (at the top of the output), but farther down you can see that it is a Cisco 1921 router. The **show version** command also shows the serial number of the device in the "Processor board ID" field. The other great thing about the **show version** command, which you will learn later, is that it shows what interfaces exist in the device. You can see there are two Gigabit interfaces and a total of three serial interfaces (more on interfaces in a bit) on this device. The point here is that the **show version** command does not just show the version of the software but shows hardware-related information as well.

```
Router>enable
Router#show version
Cisco IOS Software, C1900 Software (C1900-UNIVERSALK9-M), Version 15.7(3)M2,
RELEASE SOFTWARE (fc2)
(output cut for briefness)
ROM: System Bootstrap, Version 15.0(1r)M12, RELEASE SOFTWARE (fc1)
Router uptime is 9 minutes
System returned to ROM by power-on
System image file is "usbflash0:c1900-universalk9-mz.SPA.157-3.M2.bin"
(output cut for briefness)
Cisco CISCO1921/K9 (revision 1.0) with 487424K/36864K bytes of memory.
Processor board ID FGL1551222Y
2 Gigabit Ethernet interfaces
1 Serial interface
2 Serial(sync/async) interfaces
(output cut for briefness)
```

Common Components on Cisco Devices

A number of components are commonly used on Cisco devices, such as ports, interfaces, modules, and transceivers. You will learn more about these components later in this chapter, and they are important to know for the Cisco CCT exam. Each model device is different with regard to the types of modules that it supports. When purchasing your Cisco device, be sure to review the capabilities of the device to ensure that it meets your needs.

Using Cisco Software

You need to be familiar with two aspects of the Cisco device: the software running on the device (the operation system) and the hardware components of the device. We'll take a look at the Cisco software in this section and discuss the hardware elements in the next section.

Types of Software

Each Cisco device is powered by a Cisco operating system that is responsible for providing the features of that device. You should be aware of the following operating systems for the Cisco CCT certification exam:

- **Cisco IOS**   The Cisco Internetwork Operating System (IOS) is one of the more common operation systems used with Cisco devices and is the one you need to know about for the exams. The IOS provides the networking functions, protocols, and security features of the device. The Cisco IOS runs directly on the hardware of the Cisco device.

- **Cisco IOS XE**   This operating system was originally released with the ASR 1000 and Catalyst 3850 Series routers. It differs from the IOS in that IOS XE is a Linux kernel that runs a version of the IOS on top of the kernel (which is why your IOS commands work with IOS XE). By running a Linux kernel as the foundation of the OS, you can run different applications on the device.

- **Cisco IOS XR**   This Unix-based OS is totally different from the Cisco IOS, but it uses many commands similar to those used on the Cisco IOS. Note, however, that all IOS commands may not necessarily work on the IOS XR. This OS is geared toward service providers and is used with devices such as Cisco XR 12000 Series routers.

- **Cisco NX-OS**   This operating system is for Cisco Nexus series switches. It is built on a Linux kernel and supports Python as a scripting language for automating changes to the device. Although it is different from the Cisco IOS, the commands used are very similar, which makes it easy for a technician to adapt to NX-OS.

Licensing Process

When you purchase your Cisco device, you must purchase licenses for the device, and if you replace a device with a newer device, you will need to obtain licenses for the new device. Each Cisco device includes a number of software features. For example,

Cisco firewall products include malware protection features and URL-filtering features. Each software feature, or *add-on*, requires that you acquire a software license to use it.

Part of licensing has to do with a support contract for the device and the features licensed for the device. The support contract enables you to receive technical support from Cisco if there is a hardware failure or a problem with the OS. There is also a support contract for the features being licensed, such as updates.

 NOTE You will learn how to install and view licenses on your Cisco device in Chapter 8.

You can purchase two types of support contracts with your Cisco device:

- **SMARTnet (SNT)**   This support agreement covers hardware and offers services such as next-business-day replacement of failed hardware. This agreement also enables you to receive updates on the device OS.
- **Software Support Service (SWSS)**   This support contract enables you to receive updates and support for any add-on features.

 NOTE Ensure that both support contracts are active at all times so that you can receive full support for your Cisco device and continued updates about its features. For example, if at renewal time you renew the SNT contract but do not renew SWSS, you will not receive updates regarding add-on features.

Bundle Mode and Install Mode
Cisco IOS XE switches, such as the 3850 and the 3650, support two operation modes: bundle mode and install mode. With bundle mode, the Cisco OS is stored as an image file in flash memory. The device loads that image into memory on bootup. (You will learn more about IOS image files and flash memory in Chapter 8.) Install mode is the default mode used on switches and includes the provisioning file packages.conf to boot the Cisco switch. The switch also contains a number of .pkg files in flash memory that are referenced by the packages.conf file. Install mode is most beneficial if you are using a large number of switches, because you can perform an upgrade on all the switches without needing to copy an image file.

Working with Ports on Cisco Devices
You will see a number of different types of ports on the back or front of a Cisco device. Figure 6-2 displays the back of the Cisco 1921 ISR router and identifies some common ports you'll see on many different Cisco devices.

Console Port
You connect your administrative workstation to the console port to administer the Cisco device locally—which means you are sitting at the device to perform administrative tasks. You would use a console cable (typically light blue in color), aka rollover cable, to

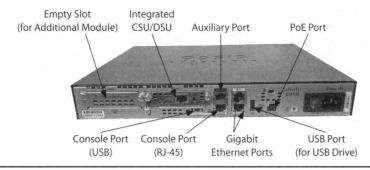

Empty Slot
(for Additional Module)   Integrated
CSU/DSU   Auxiliary Port   PoE Port

Console Port   Console Port   Gigabit   USB Port
(USB)   (RJ-45)   Ethernet Ports   (for USB Drive)

Figure 6-2   Identifying ports on a Cisco router

connect the serial port of your computer to the console port on the Cisco device. Then you would launch a terminal emulator program to administer the device from the command line interface (CLI).

 NOTE   You will learn more about how to launch the terminal emulator software later in the chapter in the section "Using Terminal Emulator Software."

You should know how to identify the console port on a Cisco device, which is usually labeled "Console" or "Con0." Figure 6-3 displays a close-up of the console port. Notice the USB port to the left of the console port; this is a *USB serial port*, a five-pin mini-USB type B port that you can use as the console connection instead of using the traditional console port (the RJ-45 type of console port). Also notice the LEDs labelled "EN," for "enabled". One LED lights up for whichever port you are using to console into the device.

Figure 6-3
Console port
used for local
administration

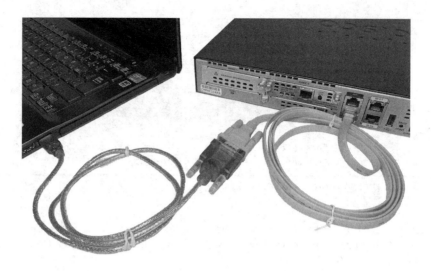

Figure 6-4   Using a USB-to-serial adapter to connect to a Cisco device

Many of today's desktops and laptops do not have a serial port for connecting the console cable to a laptop. You can, however, purchase a USB-to-serial adapter to connect to the USB port of your laptop, and then connect the adapter to the console cable that is connected to the Cisco device (shown in Figure 6-4).

Auxiliary Port

The auxiliary port, aka AUX port, is also used to connect to your Cisco router for administrative purposes, but it is designed to be an alternative method to administer your device remotely by connecting a modem to the AUX port, which then connects to the phone jack in your wall. Using this setup, you can dial into the router if it loses its Internet connection. Typically, you could remote into the device with telnet or Secure Shell (SSH) if the device had an Internet connection. Figure 6-5 displays a typical setup of the AUX port.

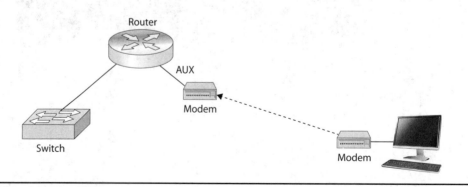

Figure 6-5   The AUX port connects a modem to a router.

Figure 6-6
Gigabit Ethernet
ports on a
Cisco router

 NOTE   Although the purpose of the AUX port is to connect a modem, you can still connect your console cable directly to the port and administer the device locally like you would if you were using the console port.

LAN Ports

Cisco devices also include some form of Ethernet ports to connect to the LAN—these are called interfaces. The type of Ethernet ports will depend on the age of the device. You may come across an older Cisco device with Ethernet ports, which Cisco uses as 10-Mbps ports. Fast Ethernet ports run at 100 Mbps, Gigabit ports run at 1000 Mbps (1 Gbps), and 10 Gigabit ports run at 10 Gbps. Figure 6-6 shows two Gigabit Ethernet ports on a Cisco router. Notice they are labeled GE0/0 and GE0/1 (Gigabit).

It is important that you know what type of Ethernet port you are working with, because the command to administer the port will be different depending on the type. For example, you reference a Fast Ethernet port as *FastEthernet0/0* and a Gigabit port as *GigabitEthernet0/0*. On an older device with a 10 Mbps Ethernet port, you would reference the port as *Ethernet0*. There are also abbreviations associated with each port type—for example, you could use *FE0/0* or *Gig0/0,* depending what port you were trying to reference.

Table 6-1 displays a listing of the different label identifiers for the different port types.

Another important point to make about interfaces is that in the past, they were referenced by identifiers that used the form *<TypeOfPort><Index#>*. For example, Ethernet0 would be the first Ethernet port on the router, while Ethernet1 would be the second Ethernet port. Over time, the identifier changed so that the index number started using the *0/0* type of syntax, because Cisco devices now have modules, which are cards that contain different types of ports that are added into the slots of a device. Each module

Port Type	Speed	Label Identifier Example
Ethernet	10 Mbps	Ethernet0 or Eth0
Fast Ethernet	100 Mbps	FastEthernet0/0 or FE0/0
Gigabit Ethernet	1000 Mbps / 1 Gbps	GigabitEthernet0/0 or Gig0/0
10 Gigabit Ethernet	10 Gbps	TenGigabitEthernet0/0

Table 6-1   LAN Port Speeds and Label Identifiers

Figure 6-7
Slots and
interfaces on a
Cisco device

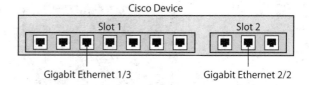

placed into a slot can have multiple interfaces. The *0/0* form of syntax references the slot number, then a slash, then the index number of the interface within the slot.

Looking at Figure 6-7 you can get an idea of how the slots and interface IDs on a Cisco switch would work. The LAN ports on a Cisco switch typically start with slot number 1 and an interface ID within the slot of 1, but on a router, ports typically start numbering at 0.

Note that with newer Cisco devices, the identifier is referenced as *<TypeOfPort> <DeviceIndex>/<Slot>/InterfaceID*—for example, *Gig0/1/0*. You still include the type of port—in this case it is a Gigabit interface—and then you include an index number referencing the device. Some devices can be stacked together to work as one unit; in this case, the first device would have device index 0, while the second device would be device index 1. After identifying the device, you include the slot and interface numbers as before.

WAN/Serial Ports

The different types of Ethernet ports are used to connect to your LAN environment, but a Cisco router also needs to connect to the WAN environment to send traffic from one network to another if a company has multiple locations. The serial interfaces on the Cisco router enable you to connect your Cisco router to other networks in two scenarios:

- **WAN link to service provider** Connect to your service provider, or ISP, network
- **Back-to-back serial connections** Create a point-to-point link directly between two routers. This link is typically used in test environments or in a study lab for your CCNA exam.

WAN Link to Service Provider To connect two office networks that are separated by some distance, you will subscribe to a monthly service such as a T1 or T3 link from your local telco or service provider. The telco provides the WAN network infrastructure to which your router's serial port connects to establish a link to the other location by way of the service provider's network.

Let's take a look at the example shown in Figure 6-8. On the left side of the figure are a router, a switch, and some client computers in the Vancouver office. The router has a serial interface with the identifier of s0/0/0 that is connected to an external channel service unit/data service unit (CSU/DSU). You also plug the WAN link that comes from your service provider into the CSU/DSU; this component is responsible for sending and receiving data from the service provider's network, essentially acting as a modem for your entire network. The CSU/DSU receives the data from the router and then converts it to a signal format that is used by the WAN infrastructure before sending the data to the service provider's network. The data then travels through the many different

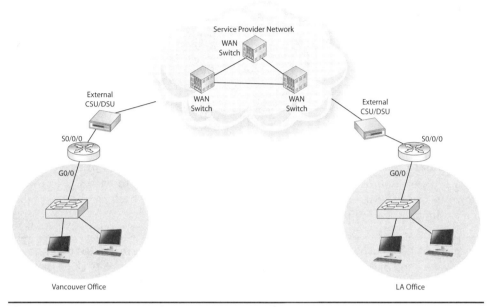

Figure 6-8   CSU/DSUs are used to connect routers to the WAN.

WAN switches before reaching the CSU/DSU in Los Angeles. The CSU/DSU in LA is responsible for converting the signal to user data that the router can receive on its serial port.

The router is considered a data terminal equipment (DTE) device, which sends or receives raw data that is converted to a signal for the WAN by the data communications equipment (DCE). In our example, the CSU/DSU is the DCE device, because it is responsible for converting the data or signal for the appropriate destination. Also in this example, the CSU/DSU is considered an external CSU/DSU because it is not integrated within the router. The external CSU/DSU connects to the serial port and normally sits on top or beside your router.

It is possible to install an internal CSU/DSU module into your router and then connect the WAN link into that module. Figure 6-9 displays an internal CSU/DSU module integrated directly into the router (note that the module is labeled as DSU/CSU).

Figure 6-9
An integrated
CSU/DSU

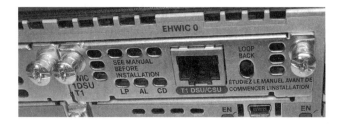

Figure 6-10
Back-to-back
serial cable

Back-to-Back Serial Connection   You can also use the serial ports to create a back-to-back connection between two routers, which requires a back-to-back serial cable, as shown in Figure 6-10. Connecting two routers using a back-to-back serial cable enables you to simulate a WAN link in a test environment.

NOTE   When you're using a back-to-back serial cable, make sure that one end of the cable is labeled "DTE" and the other end is labeled "DCE." The router that connects to the DCE end requires that an extra command be configured, as you will learn in Chapter 7.

Working with Cisco Hardware

The Cisco CCT certification exam expects you to understand the types of hardware components that you will encounter and how to work with them.

Understanding Transceiver Modules

Transceiver modules are an important feature of Cisco devices today. Instead of hard-wiring a Cisco device for a specific type of interface, Cisco installs transceiver ports in some of its devices so that you can purchase a transceiver module with the port type for the cabling you desire. For example, instead of requiring that you plug an RJ-45 port into a device for a gigabit interface, your Cisco device may include a transceiver port, so you can purchase a transceiver module that already contains an RJ-45 port on it. This gives you flexibility in that the Cisco device is not hard-coded for one specific type of interface. Then, later, if you decide that you need to connect a fiber-optic cable to the device, you simply purchase that transceiver type and insert it into the transceiver port on the Cisco device.

Figure 6-11 shows two transceiver modules for gigabit networking: a GLC-T module that connects to unshielded twisted pair (UTP) cabling using an RJ-45 connector (at left), and a GLC-SX-MM module that connects to fiber-optic cabling.

Installing a transceiver module is simple: slide the module into an SFP port on the Cisco device and lock it in place with the clamp, as shown in Figure 6-12.

Some example transceiver types, their transfer rates, and their media types (types of connector) they use are listed in Table 6-2.

Figure 6-11
GLC-T SFP
transceiver
module for UTP
(at left), and
GLC-SX-MM
fiber-optic
module

Figure 6-12
Installing
transceiver
into SFP slot

Table 6-2
Example
Transceiver
Modules

OEM Part Number	Transfer Rate	Media Type
GLC-T	1 Gbps	UTP
GLC-SX-MM	1 Gbps	Multimode fiber
GLC-LH-SM	1 Gbps	Single mode fiber
SFP-10G-SR-S	10 Gbps	Multimode fiber
SFP-10G-LR-S	10 Gbps	Single mode fiber
QSFP-40G-SR-S	40 Gbps	Multimode fiber
QSFP-40G-LR-W	40 Gbps	Single mode fiber

Installing and Replacing Hardware

After you purchase a Cisco device, you will need to install the device in a rack located in a server room or communications closet. Following are some common guidelines regarding installing your Cisco device:

- Ensure that the device is installed in the rack in a manner that enables you to see the front panel LEDs on the device and that you have access to all the ports.

- Ensure that the power cable can reach the device where it is being installed, and ensure that the network cabling is away from sources of electrical noise such as power lines and fluorescent lights.

- Ensure that there is adequate space around the Cisco device so that airflow through the vents is unrestricted.

- Ensure that cable lengths do not exceed the maximum distance based on their specification. For example, twisted pair cabling has a maximum distance of 100m (328 feet).

- Ensure that the temperature around the device does not exceed 113°F (45°C).

After you remove the device from the box, attach the mounting brackets so that the device can be secured into the communications rack. Using a Phillips screwdriver, screw the mounting brackets to the side of the device and then secure the device into the rack.

Installing and Replacing Modules

The Cisco CCT certification exam expects you to know how to install and replace modules on a Cisco router or switch. Following are some common examples of modules that you may install on a router (see Figure 6-13):

- **WIC-1T**   This WAN interface card with a DB-60 port provides a single serial port used to connect to the WAN environment.

- **WIC 1DSU/T1**   This WIC card with a single RJ-45 port is an internal CSU/DSU card that is used to connect to a T1 line.

- **WIC 2A/S**   This WIC module, with two V.35 serial connectors, enables connectivity to the WAN environment.

Remember that a label on the metal plate of each WIC card lists the card type. Each type of module is supported by specific devices and has minimum IOS versions that are required in order for the module to be recognized. For example, the WIC 1DSU/T1 module is not recognized in my Cisco 1921 router because my router needs an HWIC version of the module. The *High-Speed WAN Interface Card* (HWIC) is a newer version of the Cisco WIC card that supports higher speeds and better throughput.

Figure 6-13   Cisco WAN modules. WIC-1DSU-T1 (left), WIC-1T (middle), WIC 2A/S (right)

Here's how to install or replace a WIC or HWIC module:

1. Verify that the module is supported by your device and operating system version by searching the Cisco site for the model of the module.

2. Using a Philips screwdriver, unscrew the blanking plate, or existing module, to be removed from the slot. Then remove the blanking plate or existing module from the slot.

3. Slide the new module into the slot, ensuring that it is pushed all the way in.

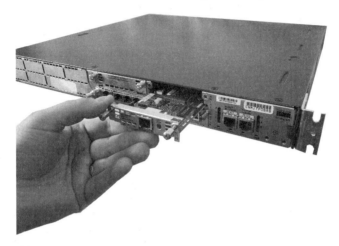

4. Screw in the module to secure it in place.

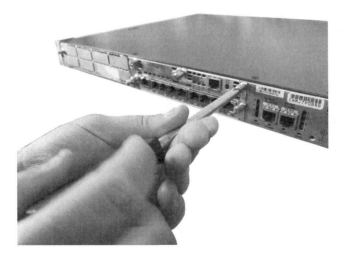

After installing your new hardware modules, power on your Cisco device and then verify the modules are detected by using the **show inventory** command. Looking at the following code example, we can gather some good details about the hardware. First, notice that the **show inventory** command displays the model of the Cisco device, which is again a Cisco 1921 series device. Also, notice that we can see the serial number of the device.

```
Router>enable
Router#show inventory
NAME: "CISCO1921/K9", DESCR: "CISCO1921/K9 chassis, Hw Serial#: FGL1551222Y,
Hw Revision: 1.0"
PID: CISCO1921/K9      , VID: V04 , SN: FGL1551222Y

NAME: "WAN Interface Card - HWIC CSU/DSU on Slot 0 SubSlot 0", DESCR: "WAN
Interface Card - HWIC CSU/DSU"
PID: HWIC-1DSU-T1      , VID: V02 , SN: FOC19092U9T

NAME: "WAN Interface Card - HWIC Serial 2T on Slot 0 SubSlot 1", DESCR: "WAN
Interface Card - HWIC Serial 2T"
PID: HWIC-2T           , VID: V02 , SN: FOC14226262
```

When looking at this output, you can also see information about the WIC cards, below the device information, that are installed in the slots of the device. Notice the first WIC card is an HWIC CSU/DSU in slot 0/0, with a model number of HWIC-1DSU-T1 and a serial number on the card of FOC19092U9T. Note the second card is a HWIC-2T that is in slot 0/1 with a serial number of FOC14226262.

If you run the **show inventory** command and you do not see your new hardware module. it could be because the hardware module is not supported by the device or you are not running the minimum IOS version. Always check the documentation for the card (hardware module) to ensure you know the supported devices and minimum IOS version.

 EXAM TIP Remember for the Cisco CCT exam that the **show version** command and the **show inventory** command can be used to view model information and serial numbers of hardware devices.

Loopback Plugs

A loopback plug can be connected to a port to verify that the port is able to send and receive a signal without the signal leaving the system. Loopback plugs are available for different types of interfaces such as an RJ-45 Ethernet interface, a T1 link, and a 56K link. The loopback plug is a specially designed connector that has the transmit pins of the connector (pins 1 and 2 for UTP cabling) connected to the bidirectional pins on the same connector (pins 4 and 5 for UTP cabling).

Let's look at an example of creating a loopback plug to use for a T1 interface. You will need a crimper, an RJ-45 connector, and a small piece of Ethernet cable (about 3 to 4 inches in length). Then follow these steps to make your own T1 loopback plug:

1. Cut a small section of Ethernet cable (about 3 or 4 inches).
2. Remove the outer jacket of the cable.
3. Position the RJ-45 connector clip away from you. The left side is pin 1 and the right side is pin 8 in the connector.

4. Using the orange wire color (it could be any wire), slide one end of the wire into pin 1 of the RJ-45 connector, and then bend the wire to connect the other end of the wire into pin 4 of the connector.

5. Using the blue wire color (it could be any wire), slide one end of the wire into pin 2 of the RJ-45 connector, and then bend the wire and connect the other end of the wire into pin 5 of the connector.

6. With the wires in place, put the RJ-45 connector into the crimper and squeeze to crimp the wire.

Once the loopback plug is created, you can connect it to the T1 port on your router and you should receive an indication of a link or loopback with an LED (depends on the interface).

Types of Cisco Device Cables

You should be familiar with several different types of cables for the Cisco CCT certification exam.

Console Cable

The console cable is typically a light-blue cable that has a serial port (RS-232) connector on one end and an RJ-45 connector on the opposite end. This cable is used to connect your computer to the Cisco device so you can locally configure the device. As mentioned earlier, if you do not have a serial port on your computer, as is the case with most laptops, you will need a USB-to-serial adapter so that you can connect the console cable to your USB port instead.

Ethernet Cable

You will use a straight-through Ethernet cable to connect the workstation to the switch or to connect the router to the switch. You may also need crossover cables to connect similar devices, such as two switches.

Serial Cable

Use a back-to-back serial cable to connect two routers using the routers' serial ports. There are a number of different types of serial ports, so make sure you have the correct types of cables for those ports. Figure 6-14 displays two different types of serial interfaces on a router and the appropriate cabling.

Figure 6-14
Serial cables to connect to the serial ports

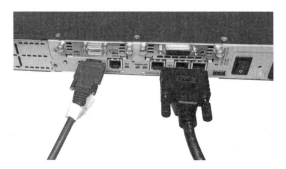

Figure 6-15
StackWise cable
to connect
switches in
a stack

Switch Stack Cable

Many of the enterprise-level switches support the StackWise feature, which enables you to connect the switches together as a manageable unit so you can centrally configure all switches from a single point. To connect the switches in a stack, you need to use a Stack-Wise cable, as shown in Figure 6-15.

Exercise 6-1: Identifying Cisco Device Components

In this exercise you will identify the components on a Cisco device by using the following diagram and locating the following parts (not all components are necessarily present):

Console port	Serial port
Ethernet ports	Auxiliary port
Integrated CSU/DSU	

Understanding Memory Types

Now let's take a look at the Cisco software components, starting with the different types of memory found on a Cisco device and the type of information that is stored in that memory. This is important stuff for the Cisco CCT exam, so be sure to study it well.

Read-Only Memory (ROM)

The software in ROM cannot be changed unless you actually swap out the ROM chip on your Cisco device. ROM is nonvolatile—meaning that when you turn off your device, the contents of ROM are not erased. ROM contains the firmware necessary to boot up your router and typically has the following three components:

- **Power-on self-test (POST)** Performs tests on the device's hardware components.
- **Bootstrap program** Brings the router up and determines how the IOS image and configuration files will be found and loaded.

- **ROM Monitor (ROMMON)**   A mini-OS that enables you to perform low-level testing and troubleshooting; for instance, ROMMON is used during the password recovery procedure. To abort the router's normal bootup procedure of loading IOS, press CTRL-BREAK to enter ROMMON mode. The prompt in ROMMON mode is either > or rommon>, depending on the router model.

EXAM TIP   POST performs self-tests on the hardware. The bootstrap program brings the router up and finds an IOS image. ROMMON contains a mini–operating system used for low-level testing and debugging. The Mini-IOS is a stripped-down version of the IOS used for emergency booting of a router and is referred to as RXBOOT mode. All of these components are stored in ROM.

Flash Memory

Flash is a form of nonvolatile memory, like ROM, meaning that when you turn the router off, the information stored in flash is not lost. Routers store their IOS image in flash, but other information can also be stored here, such as a secondary configuration file. Note that some lower-end Cisco routers actually run the IOS directly from flash (not RAM). Flash is slower than RAM, a fact that can create performance issues. Figure 6-16 displays flash memory being inserted into the compact flash slot.

Volatile RAM (VRAM)

Volatile RAM (VRAM) on a Cisco device is like RAM in your computer in the sense that it loses its contents when you shut the system down. On a router, volative RAM, sometimes just referred to as RAM, contains the running IOS image, the active configuration file (known as running config), any tables (including routing, ARP, and other tables), and internal buffers for temporarily storing information such as interface input and output buffers and logging messages. When you turn off your router, everything in RAM is erased, including the items mentioned, such as your running config.

Nonvolatile RAM (NVRAM)

NVRAM is like flash in that its contents are not erased when you turn off your router. It is slightly different, though, in that it uses a battery to maintain the information when the Cisco device is turned off. Routers (and switches) use NVRAM to store the configuration files, including the startup config, which is applied to the device during bootup after the IOS is loaded.

Figure 6-16
Flash memory on
a Cisco router

Exercise 6-2: Identifying Memory Types

In this exercise you will match the memory term with the description of what it does.

Term	Description
A. Flash memory	_____ Contains the startup configuration file
B. Volatile RAM	_____ Contains the running configuration file
C. ROM	_____ Contains the IOS image files
D. Nonvolatile RAM	_____ Contains bootstrap and ROMMON programs

Administering the Cisco Device

Once you have the device installed, you can boot up and configure the device. Before we get into the configuration (see Chapter 7), you should know that you can administer the device in several ways, discussed in this section.

Using the CLI

The first and most often used method of administrating a Cisco device is to use the command line interface (CLI). The CLI is a command environment similar to a Windows command prompt or Linux terminal where you must enter commands into the system to apply configuration changes. The Cisco CCT and CCNA certification exams expect you to know how to use the CLI to apply configuration changes.

You can use the CLI for local or remote administration. With local administration, you have connected your laptop to the console port of the device and will use the CLI to administer the device. The term "local" here means that you are in close physical proximity to the device and can connect to the console port. After the device has been configured and has an assigned IP address, you can remotely administer the device from a workstation connected to the network to telnet or SSH into the device from another part of the network.

Web-based Tools

With some Cisco devices, such as some switches and wireless access points, you can use a web interface to make configuration changes to the device. By using the web interface, you do not need to learn the commands to configure the device—you simply choose the appropriate options on the web pages.

The web interface is not a focus on the CCNA exam for two reasons:

- Not all configuration options are available through the web interface, so you will need to eventually use the CLI.

- Not all Cisco devices support a web interface.

Starting the Cisco Device

The Cisco CCT exam expects you to understand the bootup process for a Cisco device. In this section you will learn about what occurs when the Cisco device is started.

Boot Process

A router typically goes through six steps when booting up:

1. The router loads and runs POST (located in ROM), testing its hardware components, including memory and interfaces.

2. The bootstrap program is loaded and executed.

3. The configuration register is checked to determine how to boot up (where to find the IOS image and configuration file).

4. The bootstrap program finds and loads an IOS image. Possible locations of IOS images include flash or a TFTP server.

5. Once the IOS is loaded, the IOS attempts to find and load a configuration file, which is normally stored in NVRAM. If the IOS cannot find a configuration file, it starts up the System Configuration Dialog.

6. After the configuration is loaded, you are presented with the CLI (remember that the first mode you are placed into is user EXEC mode).

 EXAM TIP   Once POST completes and the bootstrap program is loaded, the configuration is checked to determine what to do next.

If you are connected to the console line, you'll see the following output as your router boots up:

```
System Bootstrap, Version 11.0(10c), SOFTWARE
Copyright (c) 1986-1996 by cisco Systems
2500 processor with 6144 Kbytes of main memory

F3: 5593060+79544+421160 at 0x3000060

Cisco Internetwork Operating System Software
IOS (tm) 2500 Software (C2500-I-L), Version 12.0(5)
Copyright (c) 1986-1999 by cisco Systems, Inc.
Compiled Tue 15-Jun-99 19:49 by phanguye Image text-base: 0x0302EC70, data-
base: 0x00001000 . . .
.

.
cisco 2504 (68030) processor (revision N) with
    6144K/2048K bytes of memory.
Processor board ID 18086269, with hardware revision
    00000003
Bridging software.
X.25 software, Version 3.0.0.
Basic Rate ISDN software, Version 1.1.
```

```
2 Ethernet/IEEE 802.3 interface(s)
2 Serial network interface(s)
32K bytes of non-volatile configuration memory.
16384K bytes of processor board System flash (Read ONLY)

00:00:22: %LINK-3-UPDOWN: Interface Ethernet0, changed
    state to up
00:00:22: %LINK-3-UPDOWN: Interface Ethernet1, changed
    state to up
.
.
.
Cisco Internetwork Operating System Software
IOS (tm) 2500 Software (C2500-I-L), Version 12.0(5)
Copyright (c) 1986-1999 by cisco Systems, Inc.
Compiled Tue 15-Jun-99 19:49 by phanguye

Press RETURN to get started!
```

 VIDEO 6.01. The digital resources that accompany this book contain a multimedia demonstration of booting up a Cisco router.

You should notice a few things about this output. First, notice that the router is loading the bootstrap program—"System Bootstrap, Version 11.0(10c)"—and then the IOS image—"IOS (tm) 2500 Software (C2500-I-L), Version 12.0(5)". During the bootup process, you cannot see the actual POST process (unlike Catalyst switches). However, you will see information about the interfaces going up and/or down—this is where IOS is loading the configuration and bringing up those interfaces that you previously activated. Sometimes, if the router has a lot of interfaces, the "Press RETURN to get started!" message is mixed in with the interface messages. Once the display stops, just press ENTER to access user EXEC mode. This completes the bootup process of the router.

 EXAM TIP For exam, remember this process: when a router boots up, it runs POST, loads the bootstrap program, finds and loads the IOS, and loads its configuration file—in that order.

Bootstrap Program

As you saw in the bootup code example, the bootstrap program found the IOS and loaded it. The bootstrap program goes through the following steps when trying to locate and load the IOS image:

1. It examines the configuration register value. This value is a set of four hexadecimal digits. The last digit affects the bootup process. If the last digit is between 0x2 and 0xF, the router proceeds to the next step. Otherwise, the router uses the values shown in Table 6-3 to determine how it should proceed.

2. It examines the configuration file in NVRAM for **boot system** commands, which tell the bootstrap program where to find the IOS. These commands are shown shortly.

3. If no **boot system** commands are found in the configuration file in NVRAM, it uses the first valid IOS image found in flash.

4. If no valid IOS images are in flash, it generates a TFTP local broadcast to locate a TFTP server (this is called a *netboot* and is not recommended, because it is very slow and not very reliable for large IOS images).

5. If no TFTP server is found, it loads the Mini-IOS in ROM (RXBOOT mode).

6. If there is a Mini-IOS in ROM, it loads the Mini-IOS and enters RXBOOT mode; otherwise, the router either retries to find an IOS image or loads ROMMON and goes into ROMMON mode.

Table 6-3 shows the three common configuration register values in the fourth hex character of the configuration register that are used to influence the bootup process. The values in the configuration register are represented in hexadecimal, the register being 16 bits long.

EXAM TIP   For the CCT and CCNA exams, know that the configuration register is used to influence how the IOS boots up. Remember the values in Table 6-3.

For step 2 of the bootup process, you can use the following **boot system** commands to influence the order that the bootstrap program should use when trying to locate the IOS image:

```
Router(config)# boot system flash name_of_IOS_file_in_flash
Router(config)# boot system tftp IOS_image_name
                    IP_address_of_server
Router(config)# boot system rom
```

NOTE   The order in which you enter the **boot system** commands is important, since the bootstrap program processes them in the order in which you configure them—once the program finds an IOS image, it does not process any more **boot system** commands in the configuration file. These commands are also supported on Catalyst IOS switches.

The **boot system flash** command tells the bootstrap program to load the specified IOS filename in flash when booting up. Note that, by default, the bootstrap program

Value in *Last* Digit	Bootup Process
0x0	Boot the router into ROMMON mode.
0x1	Boot the router using the first IOS image in flash or the Mini-IOS in ROM (RXBOOT mode), if the latter exists.
0x2–0xF	Boot the router using the default boot sequence.

Table 6-3   Fourth Hex Character Configuration Register Values

loads the *first* valid IOS image in flash. This command tells the bootstrap program to load an image that's different from the first one. This might be necessary if you perform an upgrade and you have two IOS images in flash—the old one and new one. By default, the old one still loads first (because it appears first in flash) unless you override this behavior with the **boot system flash** command or delete the old IOS flash image.

 VIDEO 6.02. The digital resources that accompany this book contain a multimedia demonstration of using **boot system** commands on a router.

You can also have the bootstrap program load the IOS from a TFTP server, but this is not recommended for large images, since the image is downloaded via the User Datagram Protocol (UDP), which is slow. And last, you can tell the bootstrap program to load the Mini-IOS in ROM with the **boot system rom** command. To remove any of these commands, just preface them with the **no** parameter.

 EXAM TIP The **boot system** commands can be used to modify the default behavior of where the bootstrap program should load the IOS. When the bootstrap program loads, it examines the configuration file stored in NVRAM for **boot system** commands. If they are found, the bootstrap program uses these commands to find the IOS. If no **boot system** commands are found, the router uses the default behavior in finding and loading the IOS image (first image in flash, a broadcast to a TFTP server, and then IOS in ROM, if it exists). When the router is booting and you see the message "boot: cannot open "flash:""; this indicates you misconfigured a **boot system** command and the corresponding IOS image filename in flash doesn't exist.

System Configuration Dialog

When a router boots up, runs its hardware diagnostics, and loads IOS software, the IOS then attempts to find a configuration file in NVRAM. If it can't find a configuration file to load, the IOS runs the System Configuration Dialog, commonly referred to as *Setup* mode, which is a script that prompts you for configuration information. The purpose of this script is to ask you questions that will enable you to set up a basic configuration on your router: It is not intended as a full-functioning configuration tool. In other words, the script doesn't have the ability to perform all the router's configuration tasks. Instead, it is used by novices who are not that comfortable with the IOS CLI. Once you become familiar with the CLI and many of the commands on the router, you'll probably never use this script again.

 EXAM TIP Remember that if no startup configuration can be found in NVRAM, the System Configuration Dialog script starts.

Running the System Configuration Dialog

One way to access the System Configuration Dialog is to boot up a router without a configuration in NVRAM. The second way is to use the **setup** privileged EXEC mode command, shown here:

```
Router# setup
           --- System Configuration Dialog ---
Continue with configuration dialog? [yes/no]: yes
At any point you may enter a question mark '?' for help.
Use ctrl-c to abort configuration dialog at any prompt.
Default settings are in square brackets '[]'.

Basic management setup configures only enough connectivity
for management of the system, extended setup will ask you
to configure each interface on the system

First, would you like to see the current interface summary? [yes]:
Interface IP-Address  OK? Method Status                 Protocol
Ethernet0 unassigned  YES unset  administratively down down
Ethernet1 unassigned  YES unset  administratively down down
Serial0   unassigned  YES unset  administratively down down

Would you like to enter basic management setup? [yes/no]: no
Configuring global parameters:
  Enter hostname [Router]:
  The enable secret is a password used to protect access to
  privileged EXEC and configuration modes. This password, after
  entered, becomes encrypted in the configuration.
  Enter enable secret: dealgroup1
  The enable password is used when you do not specify an
  enable secret password, with some older software versions,
  and some boot images.  Enter enable password: dealgroup2
  The virtual terminal password is used to protect
  access to the router over a network interface.
  Enter virtual terminal password: cisco
  Configure SNMP Network Management? [no]:
  Configure LAT? [yes]: no
  Configure AppleTalk? [no]:
  Configure DECnet? [no]:
  Configure IP? [yes]:
    Configure IGRP routing? [yes]: no
    Configure RIP routing? [no]:
.
.
.
Configuring interface parameters:
Do you want to configure Ethernet0  interface? [no]: yes
  Configure IP on this interface? [no]: yes
    IP address for this interface: 172.15.1.1
    Subnet mask for this interface [255.255.0.0] : 255.255.255.0
    Class B network is 172.15.0.0, 24 subnet bits; mask is /24
Do you want to configure Serial0  interface? [no]:
.
.
.
The following configuration command script was created:
hostname Router
enable secret 5 $1$/CCk$4r7zDwDNeqkxFO.kJxC3G0
enable password dealgroup2
```

```
line vty 0 4
 password cisco
 .
 .
 .
end

[0] Go to IOS command prompt without saving this config.
[1] Return back to the setup without saving this config.
[2] Save this configuration to nvram and exit.
Enter your selection [2]: 2
```

Information included in brackets ([ ]) indicates the default value—if you press ENTER, the value in the brackets is used. One problem with this script is that if you make a mistake, you can't go back to the preceding question. Instead, you must use the CTRL-C break sequence to abort the script and start over.

The following sections break down the different components of the script.

NOTE The questions that the script asks you may differ from router to router, depending on the hardware model, the interfaces installed in it, and the software running on it.

Status and Global Configuration Information

At the beginning of the script, you are asked whether or not you want to continue. If you answer *yes*, the script will continue; otherwise, if you answer *no*, the script is aborted and you are returned to privileged EXEC mode. Next you are asked whether you want to see the status of the router's interfaces. If you answer *yes*, you'll see all of the interfaces on the router, the interfaces' IP addresses, and the status of the interfaces.

After the status information, you be shown the actual configuration. The first part of the configuration deals with all configuration information for the router except for the interfaces, which is the second part. In this part of the configuration, you are asked for things such as the privileged EXEC password, virtual type terminal (VTY) password (telnet and SSH), which network protocols you want to activate globally, and other global configuration information.

NOTE Note that you are prompted for two privileged EXEC passwords in the script: **enable secret** and **enable password**. Even though you would normally configure only one, the script requires you to enter both and also requires that both passwords be different. You will need to enter privileged EXEC mode using the secret when the secret is set.

Protocol and Interface Configuration Information

After configuring the global information for the router, you are then led through questions about which interfaces you want to use and how they should be configured. The script is smart enough to ask configuration questions based on how you answered the

Option	Description
0	Discard the script's configuration and return to privileged EXEC mode.
1	Return to the beginning of the script.
2	Activate the script's configuration, save the configuration to NVRAM, and return to privileged EXEC mode.

Table 6-4 Options at the End of the System Configuration Dialog

global questions. As an example, if you activate IP, the script asks you for each activated interface, whether you want the interface to process IP, and, if yes, the IP addressing information for the interface.

EXAM TIP You should remember that the System Configuration Dialog script is started when the router boots up and there is no configuration in NVRAM, or you use the **setup** command from privileged EXEC mode. Also, know the three options at the end of the Setup dialog script. And remember that you can press CTRL-C to abort the script.

Exiting Setup Mode

After you answer all of the script's configuration questions, you are shown the router configuration the script created using your answers to the script's questions. Note that the IOS hasn't yet activated the configuration file. Examine the configuration closely and then make one of the three choices shown in Table 6-4. Also, if you enter **1** as your option, when the script starts over again, the information that you previously entered appears in brackets and will be the default values when you press the ENTER key on an empty line.

VIDEO 6.03. The digital resources that accompany this book contain a multimedia demonstration of using the System Configuration Dialog on a Cisco router.

Service-Related Tasks for Technicians

As a Cisco Certified Technician (CCT), you will be responsible for performing key administration tasks when answering a customer's service calls. In this section, you will learn how to perform common service-related tasks that you'll need to know for the exam.

Using a Text Editor

Although much of your administration is performed on a Cisco device, you should know how to launch a text editor in either Windows or Linux. You can use a text editor to prepare configuration commands and then paste them into the CLI to execute the command.

Launching Text Editor in Windows

To launch a text editor in Windows, follow these steps:

1. Click the Start button.
2. Type **notepad**.
3. In the Best Match section of the search results, choose Notepad.

Launching Text Editor in Linux

Depending on the distribution of Linux, you can use several different methods to launch a text editor. In Kali Linux, you can launch a text editor by following these steps:

1. Click the Applications button (the Kali Linux icon) in the top-left corner.
2. Choose Usual Applications.
3. Choose Text Editor.

Launching a Command Prompt

When troubleshooting connectivity problems, you may need to launch a command prompt and run a few of the troubleshooting commands from there. Here are some example troubleshooting commands:

- **ping** Use the **ping** *<ip_address>* command to verify that a device or system is up and running on the network.
- **traceroute** Use the **tracert** *<ip_address>* command in Windows or the **traceroute** *<ip_address>* command in Linux to verify the pathway that a packet takes to reach the destination.
- **nslookup** Use the **nslookup** *<dns_name>* command to send a query to DNS and find out the IP address of a *fully qualified domain name* (FQDN).
- **arp** Use the **arp -a** command on your laptop to view the ARP cache of the system.
- **pathping** The **pathping** command combines the **ping** and **tracert** commands like so: **pathping** *<dns_name>*—for example, **pathping www.dcatt.ca**.

Launching a Windows Command Prompt

To launch a command prompt in Windows and then execute a command, follow these steps:

1. Click the Start button.
2. Type **cmd** in the search box.
3. Choose Command Prompt from the Best Match section of the search results.

Launching a Linux Terminal Session

Linux administrators don't use the term "prompt" like Windows administrators do; instead a *terminal session* is used in Linux. To launch a terminal session in Kali Linux, follow these steps:

1. Right-click the desktop.
2. Choose Open Terminal Here.

Configuring NIC Settings

As a service technician, you may need to configure the TCP/IP settings on your technician laptop to gain access to the customer network when connecting the Ethernet port on your laptop to the Cisco equipment, typically a switch. To connect your laptop to the customer network, connect a straight-through Ethernet cable to the Ethernet port on your laptop to a port on the Cisco switch. You will then need to verify and possibly configure the TCP/IP settings to gain access to the network.

To verify your IP address settings, go to a command prompt and type the **ipconfig** command. If you need to change your TCP/IP settings in Windows 10, do the following:

1. Click the Start button.
2. Type **control** in the search box.
3. Choose Control Panel from the Best Match section of the search results.
4. Choose Network and Internet | Network and Sharing Center.
5. Choose Change Adapter Settings on the left.
6. Right-click the Ethernet adapter and choose Properties.
7. Select Internet Protocol Version 4 (TCP/IPv4) and then click the Properties button.
8. Type the IP address, subnet mask, and default gateway values.

Connecting to the Console Port

If you want to connect to the Cisco device locally without needing an IP address on your laptop, you can connect to the console port of the Cisco device using a console cable, also known as a rollover cable. To connect to the console port, you connect the console cable to the serial port on your laptop, or use a serial-to-USB adapter if you do not have a serial port on the laptop. Once you have connected the console cable to the Cisco device and your laptop, you are ready to launch terminal software to administer the device.

Using Terminal Emulator Software

When you're working with Cisco devices, a common service-related task is to use terminal emulator software to connect to the console port (local administration), to telnet into the device (nonsecure remote administration), or to SSH into the device (secure remote administration). There are a number of examples for terminal emulation software, but the Cisco CCT certification exam expects you to be familiar with PuTTY and Tera Term.

Connect Using PuTTY

After downloading and installing PuTTY on your technician laptop, follow these steps to connect to the console port using PuTTY:

1. Launch PuTTY to open the Configuration window:

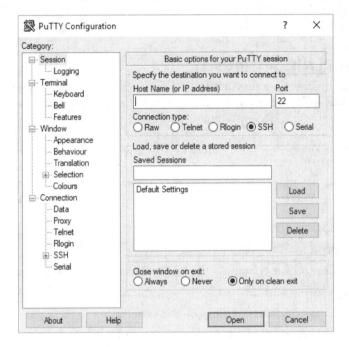

2. Under Connection Type, choose the Serial radio button to connect to the device using your serial port and the console cable.

3. After choosing the Serial option, the dialog box changes (the Host Name option becomes the Serial line option). In the Serial Line setting, you need to specify the COM port to use by specifying either COM1, COM2, COM3, or COM4, depending on your system. You can try each one individually until a connection is made.

4. After setting the COM number as your serial line, click Open

5. Click within the terminal window and press ENTER to open a prompt.

Connect Using Tera Term

After downloading and installing Tera Term on your technician laptop, follow these steps to connect to the console port using Tera Term:

1. Launch Tera Term. In the New Connection window, indicate how you would like to connect to the device. Note that under TCP/IP, you can choose remote access protocols, such as Telnet or SSH. You can also choose Serial to console directly into the device using your serial port.

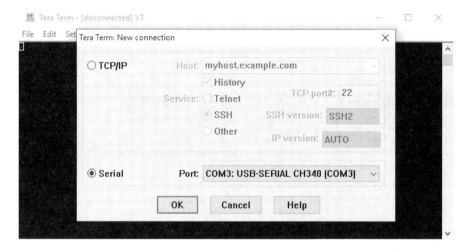

2. Select the Serial radio button in the bottom left to connect to the device using your serial port (and the console cable).

3. In the Port field, choose the serial port to use. Try each one individually until a connection is made.

4. After choosing the COM port number, click OK.

5. Click anywhere in the terminal window and press ENTER to open a prompt.

Copying and Pasting Configuration Settings

The Cisco CCT certification exam expects you to know how to copy and paste configuration to and from a router or switch using the terminal program of your choice.

To copy your router configuration to a file, follow these steps:

1. Open the PuTTY program and connect to your router.

2. Type **enable** and press ENTER.

3. Type **terminal length 0** and press ENTER. This command ensures that when the router shows you all the commands, it does not pause at full screens with a "--more--" prompt.

4. Right-click and choose Change Settings.

5. Choose Session | Logging | Log All Session Output. This will record the output of your commands to a file that you specify.

6. Choose the file you want to write to: choose Browse and then choose the location and filename.

7. Choose Apply.

8. Back on the Cisco device, type the command **show running-config** and press ENTER.

9. Locate the text file and open it to see the configuration commands.

Storing your running configuration in a text file is a great way to have a backup of your configuration. If you ever need to restore the configuration of your device back to what is in the configuration text file, you can copy and paste the contents of the text file into your terminal program at any time.

Connect and Verify the Status of the Device Interface

As we progress through the chapters that follow, you will learn how to configure the many different features of Cisco devices. To get started, I'll show you a few commands you can use to verify that the interfaces on the device are working. You will see these commands in more detail in Chapter 7.

In this scenario, you have connected a computer to interface 5 on the switch and you want to verify that the interface is working okay. Use the following commands to verify your interfaces are up and running:

- **show ip interface brief**   Use this great **show** command to get a list of all of the interfaces on the device and take a quick look at their statuses. You can determine whether the interface is up and running and view the IP address assigned to the interface.

- **show interfaces**   Use this command to view a list of all the interfaces and detailed specifications on the interfaces.

- **show interfaces g0/0**   Use this command to view the details of a specific interface.

- **show controllers s0/3/0**   Use the **show controllers** command on serial interfaces to view information such as the DCE and DTE details.

Chapter Review

In this chapter you learned about the many Cisco hardware and software features that are available with Cisco routers and switches. You learned about the different families of Cisco devices, such as the Cisco Nexus and Cisco Catalyst Series devices. You also learned how to identify the model of the Cisco device you are servicing and where to locate its serial number.

You also learned about the different types of ports included on a Cisco device, such as the console port, auxiliary port, Ethernet ports, and serial ports used for WAN connections. You learned about installing the Cisco device into a rack and using the SFP+ port to connect a transceiver of your choice.

You learned about the different types of memory that exist on a Cisco device such as ROM, VRAM, NVRAM, and flash memory. Finally, you learned about the boot process for a Cisco device when you power on the device.

Quick Review

Working with Cisco Devices and Software

- Cisco offers several product lines, such as Cisco Nexus Series switches and the Cisco Catalyst Series switches.

- The model and serial number are typically located on a sticker on the back of the Cisco device.

- The console port is used for local administration, while the auxiliary port is used to connect a modem to the router as a backup administration line.

- Each LAN port is identified by the type of port and an index number, such as FE0/0 for the first Fast Ethernet port in slot 0 or G0/3 as the third Gigabit port in slot 0.

Understanding Memory Types

- ROM memory stores the POST routines, the bootstrap program, and the ROMMON program used when troubleshooting boot issues.

- Flash memory stores the IOS images.

- Volatile RAM stores the running configuration and different tables in RAM, such as the routing table.

- Nonvolatile memory stores the startup config.

Administering the Cisco Device

- You can locally administer the Cisco device by connecting to the console port of the device using a console cable.

- You can remotely connect to the device over the network by using telnet or SSH to perform administration on a device.

- On some devices, such as wireless access points, you can use a web interface for administration.

Starting the Cisco Device

- When you boot the Cisco device, the POST runs first, and then the bootstrap program is loaded, which locates the IOS image to load. Finally, the startup configuration is applied after the IOS is loaded.

- If there is no startup configuration, the device will prompt you to run the System Configuration Dialog, which is a wizard-style interface that prompts you for the configuration information.

- Use the **boot system** command to specify which IOS image to boot from.

Service-Related Tasks for Technicians

- As a service technician, you must know how to connect to a Cisco device via the console port to perform local administration.
- Know how to use programs on your laptop, such as a text editor and terminal emulation software, to connect to the Cisco device.
- Know common troubleshooting commands such as **ping**, **ipconfig**, and **tracert** to troubleshoot communication issues.

Questions

The following questions will help you measure your understanding of the material presented in this chapter. Read all the choices carefully because there may be more than one correct answer. Choose the correct answer(s) for each question.

1. What type of memory on the Cisco devices stores the POST routines?
   A. NVRAM
   B. VRAM
   C. Flash
   D. ROM

2. You are reviewing the ports on a router with your customer, who asks what is the purpose of the AUX port. How would you respond?
   A. It's used to telnet into the router.
   B. It's used to connect a modem to the router.
   C. It's used to SSH into the router.
   D. It's used as an additional Ethernet connection.

3. You are administering a switch for a customer and need to reference the third Gigabit Ethernet port on the switch. What label identifier is used to reference the port?
   A. Eth1/3
   B. FE1/3
   C. Gig1/3
   D. Ethernet1/3

4. Where is the startup configuration file stored on the Cisco device?
   A. ROM
   B. VRAM
   C. NVRAM
   D. Flash

5. Your router has two serial ports used to connect to the WAN. You are connecting the external CSU/DSU to the second serial port. What is the label identifier to reference that port?

A. S0/1

B. S0/0

C. G0/0

D. G0/1

6. You need to make some changes to a customer's switch configuration. You have connected the console cable to the console port on the switch and the serial port on your laptop. What program would you use to administer the device? (Choose two.)

A. Notepad

B. PuTTY

C. Ping

D. Tracert

E. Tera Term

7. You have made a number of configuration changes to the Cisco device. What type of memory is used to store the running configuration?

A. ROM

B. Flash

C. NVRAM

D. VRAM

8. Your customer has called, indicating he is having trouble getting out to the Internet. You arrive at the customer's site and plug your laptop into the network. What command would you use to verify that the router is up and running?

A. ipconfig

B. ping

C. arp

D. netstat

9. What type of memory is used to store the IOS image file for the Cisco device?

A. Flash

B. VRAM

C. ROM

D. NVRAM

Performance-based Questions

1. Using the following exhibit, match the different commands with their definitions.

show inventory	Used to verify a system or device is up and running
nslookup	Used to view IOS and interface information
ping	Used to verify the pathway that a packet takes to reach its destination
traceroute	Used to view hardware components installed in the device
show version	Used to query the DNS server and find out an IP address of an FQDN

2. Place the steps that the Cisco device takes during the startup process in order by writing the step found on the left into the appropriate box on the right.

Steps

Startup config is applied

IOS is loaded from flash

Bootstrap program loaded and executed

Configuration register value read to determine location of IOS image and configuration file

Device loads and runs POST

1.

2.

3.

4.

5.

Answers

1. D. Read-only memory (ROM) is used to store the POST routines, bootstrap program, and the ROMMON program.

2. B. You can use the AUX port to connect a modem so that you can dial into the router if there are networking issues, such as the network interfaces are down.

3. C. The correct identifier is Gig1/3: Gigabit Ethernet interfaces are referenced beginning with *Gig*, *G*, or *GigabitEthernet*, followed by the index number of the slot, and then the index number of the interface.

4. C. The startup configuration is stored in nonvolatile RAM (NVRAM), which retains the configuration even when the device is powered off.

5. **A.** The serial port is referenced with *S* or *Serial*, followed by the slot and port numbers. Slot and port numbers on routers start at 0, so in this example, the second serial port would be S0/1.

6. **B, E.** You can use any terminal emulator, such as PuTTY or Tera Term. Both programs are available online as a free download.

7. **D.** The running configuration is lost when the device is powered down, so it is stored in volatile RAM (VRAM).

8. **B.** The **ping** command can be used to send test messages to a device by its IP address or DNS name and verify that the router is up and running.

9. **A.** The IOS image file is stored in flash memory.

Performance-based Answers

1. The following is the mapping of commands with their definition. Keep in mind that on the real exam you will need to drag items on the left side and drop them on the matching item on the right side.

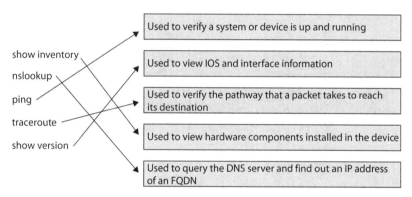

2. The following is the correct order of events when the Cisco device is started. Keep in mind that on the real exam you will need to drag items found on the left side and drop them into order on the right side.

Steps

1.	Device loads and runs POST
2.	Bootstrap program loaded and executed
3.	Configuration register value read to determine location of IOS image and configuration file
4.	IOS is loaded from flash
5.	Startup config is applied

Cisco IOS Basics

In this chapter, you will

- Learn about interacting with the command-line interface (CLI)
- Get familiar with the basics of IOS
- Learn about basic IOS configuration
- Learn about basic IOS security configuration
- Learn some IOS operation and verification commands

This book emphasizes the fundamental and important concepts of accessing, configuring, and managing Cisco routers and switches through the command-line interface (CLI) and the console port. You'll use commands and the console port connection to perform basic configuration of Cisco routers and switches.

These discussions assume that you have never configured a Cisco router or switch; we therefore begin with the basics—the operating system (OS) used by these devices, the advantages provided by Cisco's OS, and the use of commands to configure a Cisco device. The chapters that follow will continue the discussion by exploring configuration of Cisco switches, routing features, and security features.

Command-Line Interface

How you access IOS CLI on a Cisco device for the first time depends on the kind of device you are configuring. In almost every case, you will use the console interface initially to interact with the device; however, gaining access to the CLI from the console port can be different from one device to another. On a Cisco router, for instance, you are taken directly to IOS CLI when you log in from the console port. If IOS cannot find a configuration file for the router or switch, IOS takes you through Setup mode (via the System Configuration Dialog), which is a basic configuration script that prompts you for information about how you want to configure your IOS device (discussed in Chapter 6).

Once you have configured your Cisco device via the console port, you can then use other methods of accessing and changing its configuration, such as telnet or Secure Shell (SSH)—Cisco calls this *virtual type terminal* (VTY) access. Or you can use Trivial File Transfer Protocol (TFTP), File Transport Protocol (FTP), Simple Network Management

Protocol (SNMP), or a web-based solution (Cisco Configuration Professional, or CCP, for routers). A variety of Cisco management products can be used to configure and manage your Cisco device, such as the Cisco Security Manager (CSM); however, this book focuses primarily on IOS CLI.

IOS Differences

In this and subsequent chapters, you will see that even though both Cisco routers and switches run IOS, the commands used by these products are frequently different! In other words, how you configure a feature on a Cisco router may be different from how you configure the same feature on a Catalyst switch. However, how you access IOS and maneuver around IOS access levels, as well as how you use many of the management commands, is the same on *all* IOS products. This can be confusing to a Cisco novice—one command for a particular feature is the same on all Cisco products, but configuring another feature is different between a Cisco router and a Catalyst switch.

In addition to command differences between different products, such as routers and switches, command differences may exist within a product line, such as Cisco routers, for instance. For example, Cisco sells different flavors of its IOS software for routers, depending on the features that you need. Because of hardware differences, some commands work on some routers but not on others.

 NOTE Lately, the number of IOS implementations has greatly diminished. Each version of IOS may have had 5, 10, or even 15 or more different packages you'd need to download, based on what features you purchased. Today, the number of packages is smaller, typically 3 or fewer. Instead, Cisco bundles most features in an IOS package but requires you to purchase a license key to unlock those features. Licenses are discussed in Chapter 8.

Interacting with IOS

The CLI is a character- or text-based interface. To interact with the CLI, you simply need to type in commands, just as you would do when typing an essay in a text editor or a message in an e-mail program. You can even use functions such as copy-and-paste with IOS CLI: so, for example, you can copy the complete configuration from a router using a terminal emulator's copy function, paste this into a text editor, make changes to the configuration, select and copy the new configuration, and then paste all of these commands back into the CLI.

The CLI supports a command parser. Whenever you press the ENTER key, IOS parses the command and parameters that you entered and checks for correct syntax and options. When you paste multiple commands into the CLI, IOS still performs this process for each command that is included in the paste function. If you make a mistake with one command, the CLI parser will display an error message, but it will continue with the next command in the pasted list.

TIP Before making any configuration changes on your IOS device, you should first back it up! You'll learn how to do this across the network in Chapter 8, but you could easily do this by executing the **show running-config** command, copying the output configuration, and pasting it into a backup text file on your computer. The backup text file can then be referenced should something go wrong with a configuration change. You will learn more about backing up and restoring your configuration in Chapter 8.

CLI Access Modes

Each Cisco device supports several access modes. For CLI interaction, four modes are supported:

- **User EXEC**   Provides basic access to IOS with limited command availability (basically simple monitoring and troubleshooting commands)
- **Privileged EXEC**   Provides high-level management access to IOS, including all commands available at user EXEC mode
- **Global Configuration**   Enables configuration changes to be made to the device
- **ROM Monitor (ROMMON)**   Loads a bootstrap program that allows for low-level diagnostic testing of an IOS device, performing the password recovery procedure, and performing an emergency upgrade

Of the four modes, the first three apply to IOS. While in ROMMON mode, IOS has not loaded and therefore packets are not moved between interfaces of the device. Both EXEC modes can be password-protected, enabling you to limit who can access your device to perform management, configuration, and troubleshooting tasks. The next two sections introduce the two EXEC modes.

User EXEC Mode

Your initial access to the CLI is via the user EXEC mode, which has only a limited number of IOS commands you can execute. Depending on the Cisco device's configuration, you may be prompted for a password to access this mode. User EXEC mode is typically used for basic troubleshooting of networking problems. You can tell that you are in user EXEC mode by examining the prompt on the left side of the screen:

```
IOS>
```

If you see a > character at the end of the line, you know that you are in user EXEC mode. The information preceding the > is the name of the Cisco device. For instance, the default name of all Cisco routers is *Router*, whereas the 2960 switch's user EXEC prompt looks like this: **Switch>**. These device names can be changed with the **hostname** command, which is discussed later in this chapter. In the preceding example, I renamed the device *IOS*.

Privileged EXEC Mode

Once you have gained access to user EXEC mode, you can use the **enable** command to access privileged EXEC mode:

```
IOS> enable
IOS#
```

Once you enter the **enable** command, if a privileged EXEC password has been configured on the Cisco device, you will be prompted to enter it. Upon successfully authenticating, you will be in privileged EXEC mode. You can tell that you are in this mode by examining the CLI prompt—in the preceding code example, notice that the > changed to a #.

When you are in privileged EXEC mode, you have access to all of the user EXEC commands as well as many more advanced management and troubleshooting commands. These commands include extended ping and trace abilities, the ability to manage configuration files and IOS images, and the ability to perform detailed troubleshooting using **debug** commands. About the only thing that you can't do from this mode is change the configuration of the Cisco device—this can be done only from configuration mode.

To return to user EXEC mode from privileged EXEC mode, use the **disable** command:

```
IOS# disable
IOS>
```

Again, by examining the prompt, you can tell that you are now in user EXEC mode.

EXAM TIP   For the Cisco CCT certification exam, know the three different modes in IOS—user EXEC, privileged EXEC, and configuration modes— and what you can do in each mode. Also know that you use the **enable** command to go from user EXEC mode to privileged EXEC mode, use the **disable** command to go from privileged EXEC mode to user EXEC mode, and use the **exit** command to log out of the IOS device from either of these two modes.

Figure 7-1 displays a summary of how to navigate through the different modes. Once you get to the Global Configuration mode, you can then navigate to a number of sub-configuration modes (I added three as examples).

Logging Out of Your Device

You can log out of your Cisco device from either user EXEC mode or privileged EXEC mode by using the **logout** or **exit** command:

```
IOS# logout
   -or-
IOS# exit
```

VIDEO   7.01. The digital resources that accompany this book contain a multimedia demonstration of navigating through the configuration modes.

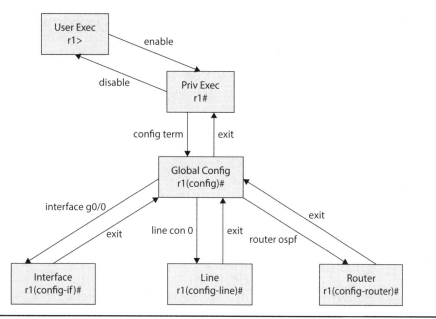

Figure 7-1 Navigating Cisco configuration modes

IOS Basics

The next few sections describe some of the features built into the CLI that will make your configuration and management tasks easier. These features include how to abbreviate commands, how to bring up detailed help on commands and their specific parameters, and how to decipher the output of commands, recall commands, and edit commands.

Command Abbreviation and Completion

The CLI of IOS enables you to abbreviate commands and parameters to their most unique characters. This feature is useful for those who are physically challenged at typing. As an example, you could type **en** instead of **enable** when you want to go from user EXEC mode to privileged EXEC mode, like this:

```
IOS> en
IOS#
```

The Cisco device, internally, completes the command for you. However, the characters that you enter must make the command unique. As an example, you couldn't type just the letter *e* for **enable**, since other commands being with the letter *e*, such as **exit**.

Context-Sensitive Help

One of the more powerful features of IOS is context-sensitive help. Context-sensitive help is supported at all modes within IOS, including user EXEC, privileged EXEC, and configuration modes. You can use this feature in a variety of ways. If you are not sure what command you need to execute, at the prompt, type either **help** or **?**. The Cisco device then displays a list of commands that can be executed at the level in which you are currently located, along with a brief description of each command. Here is an example from a router's CLI at user EXEC mode:

```
Router> ?
Exec commands:
  access-enable    Create a temporary Access-List entry
  cd               Change current device
  clear            Reset functions
  .
  .
  .
-- More --
```

 EXAM TIP   For the exam, remember that you can use the **help** command or the **?** to pull up context-sensitive help. Also, remember that you can abbreviate commands to their most unique characters.

If you see **-- More --** at the bottom of the screen, this indicates that more help information is available than can fit on the current screen. On a Cisco device, if you press the SPACEBAR, IOS pages down to the next screen of help information; if you press the ENTER key, help scrolls down one line at a time. Any other keystroke breaks out of the help text.

For more detailed help, you can follow a command or parameter with a space and a **?**. This causes the CLI to list the available options or parameters that are included for the command. For instance, you could type **erase** followed by a space and a **?** to see all of the parameters available for the **erase** command:

```
Router# erase ?
  /all             Erase all files(in NVRAM)
  flash:           Filesystem to be erased
  nvram:           Filesystem to be erased
  pram:            Filesystem to be erased
  slot0:           Filesystem to be erased
  slot1:           Filesystem to be erased
  startup-config   Erase contents of configuration memory
Router# erase
```

In this example, you can see at least the first parameter necessary after the **erase** command. Note that additional parameters may appear after the first one, depending on the next parameter that you enter.

If you're not sure how to spell a command, you can enter the first few characters and immediately follow these characters with a **?**. Typing **e?**, for instance, lists all the commands that begin with *e* at the current mode:

```
Router# e?
enable  erase  exit
Router# e
```

This example shows that three commands begin with the letter *e* in privileged EXEC mode.

VIDEO   7.02. The digital resources that accompany this book contain a multimedia demonstration of using the help within the IOS.

Error Messages

Errors inevitably creep in when you enter commands. If you mistype a command, IOS will tell you that it has encountered a problem after it tries to execute the command. For instance, this message indicates a CLI input error:

```
% Invalid input detected at '^'.
```

You should examine the line between the command that you typed in and the error message. Somewhere in this line, you'll see a ^ character. This is used by IOS to indicate that an error exists in the command line at that spot.

Here is another CLI error message:

```
% Incomplete command.
```

This error indicates that you have not entered all the necessary parameters for the command. The syntax of the command is correct, but more parameters are necessary. In this case, you can use the context-sensitive help feature to help you figure out what parameter or parameters you forgot.

You'll see an error message similar to the following if you do not type in enough characters to make a command or parameter unique:

```
% Ambiguous command: "show i"
```

In this example, apparently, more than one parameter for the **show** command begins with the letter *i*. Again, you can use context-sensitive help to figure out what parameter to use:

```
Router# show i?
idb  interfaces  ip  ipv6
Router# show i
```

If you enter a command that IOS does not understand, you'll see this error message:

```
% Unknown command or computer name, or unable to find computer address
```

If you see this, use the context-sensitive help to figure out the correct command to enter.

 EXAM TIP   Don't be afraid to take advantage of the context-sensitive help feature during the simulation and simlet questions in the exam. This feature can be used for help with entering commands, and it is available in the router and switch simulation and simlet questions in the exam; use it.

Entering Commands

Four key features included in IOS relate to entering commands:

- Symbolic translation
- Command prompting
- Syntax checking
- Command recall

Whenever you enter a command in the CLI, the command-line parser dissects the command, making sure that it is a valid command with valid parameters. In the case of Cisco IOS, if the CLI parser cannot find the actual command, IOS assumes that you are trying to telnet to a machine by that name and attempts a Domain Name System (DNS) resolution of the name to an IP address. This process, called *symbolic translation*, can be annoying at times. But it does make telnetting to a remote machine easier, since you have to type only the name or IP address of the machine instead of using the **telnet** command, as discussed in Chapter 8.

 TIP   Use the **no ip domain-lookup** configuration mode command to disable DNS lookups on your IOS device. This is typically one of the first commands I configure on a router. By doing this, any time you type an invalid command, IOS won't do a DNS lookup, but will return an invalid command message. The downside of this command is that IOS device will no longer do DNS lookups of any kind, but this is typically not an issue in most situations.

You have already been presented with the *command prompting* feature—this is most commonly seen when using the context-sensitive help, such as the following:

```
Router# show ?
  aaa                    Show AAA values
  aal2                   Show commands for AAL2
  access-expression      List access expression
  access-lists           List access lists
  accounting             Accounting data for active sessions
  .
  .
  .
Router# show
```

In this example, after you use the context-sensitive help with the **show** command, the command **show** remains on the command line after the displayed output. IOS is assuming that you are entering one of the parameters of this command and thus re-enters the command on the CLI. This can be annoying if you forget that the router is performing this function and re-enter the command, like this:

```
Router# show show
```

The CLI always parses your commands and checks their validity by using the *syntax checking* feature. Any nonexistent commands or improperly entered commands cause IOS to generate an error message with an appropriate error description.

TIP Whenever you enter a command correctly, rarely will you see any output from IOS, unless the command you typed somehow changes the state of the router or one of its components, such as an interface coming up or going down. Therefore, you should be concerned primarily after you enter a command and IOS displays a message—you should assume that a problem may exist.

Of course, when you are configuring an IOS device, you will sometimes make typing mistakes or enter invalid commands. If you typed in a 20-parameter command and made a mistake in the very last character, it would be sadistic on Cisco's part to make you type the complete command again. The *command recall* feature is extremely useful because it enables you to recall and edit previously executed commands. The next two sections discuss how to recall and edit previous (or current) commands.

Command-Line History

On any IOS device, you can use the **show history** command to see your previously entered commands:

```
IOS# show history
  enable
  show interface
  show version
  show history
IOS#
```

By default, an IOS device stores the last 10 commands that you executed. You can recall these commands by pressing either CTRL-P or the UP ARROW key. If you accidentally go past the command that you want to edit or re-execute, press CTRL-N or the DOWN ARROW key.

You can increase the size of the history buffer from 10 commands up to 256 by using the **terminal history size** command:

```
IOS# terminal history size #_of_commands
```

Editing the Command Line

Table 7-1 shows the control or command sequences that you can use to edit information on the command line.

EXAM TIP Remember the basic editing control sequences for editing commands in the CLI. By default, IOS stores the last 10 executed commands. You can use the TAB key to autocomplete commands.

Control Sequence	Description
CTRL-A	Moves the cursor to the beginning of the line
CTRL-E	Moves the cursor to the end of the line
ESC-B	Moves the cursor back one word at a time
ESC-F	Moves the cursor forward one word at a time
CTRL-B or LEFT ARROW	Moves the cursor back one character at a time
CTRL-F or RIGHT ARROW	Moves the cursor forward one character at a time
CTRL-P or UP ARROW	Recalls the last command
CTRL-N or DOWN ARROW	Recalls the most recently executed command
CTRL-D	Deletes the character the cursor is under
BACKSPACE	Deletes the character preceding the cursor
CTRL-R	Redisplays the current line
CTRL-U	Erases the line completely
CTRL-W	Erases the word the cursor is under
CTRL-Z	Takes you from configuration mode back to privileged EXEC mode
TAB	After you enter characters and press TAB, the IOS device completes the word, assuming that you typed in enough characters to make the command or parameter unique
$	At the beginning of a command line, this indicates that there are more characters to the right of the $

Table 7-1   Editing Control Sequences for IOS Devices

IOS Feature Example

This example uses the **clock** command to illustrate the helpfulness of some of IOS's command-line features. This command is used on a router to set the current date and time. As an example, let's assume that English isn't your native language and that you are not sure how to spell *clock*, but you do know that it begins with the letters *c* and *l*. Here's the example:

```
IOS# cl?
clear    clock
IOS# cl
```

Notice two things about the output in this example. First, two commands begin with **cl**: **clear** and **clock**. Second, notice the CLI after the help output—IOS kept the **cl** on the command line. Some administrators like this feature and some hate it. I'm in the latter camp, since I commonly forget that the IOS device is doing this and I start typing from the beginning, like this:

```
IOS# clclock
Translating "clclock"
% Unknown command or computer name, or unable to find computer address
IOS#
```

If you haven't already guessed, this is an invalid command.

Now that you know how to spell *clock*, if you don't know what parameter(s) to type after the **clock** command, you can use context-sensitive help:

```
IOS# clock ?
  set  Set the time and date
IOS# clock
```

The first column is the name of the parameter, and the second column is its description. In this case, IOS wants the word *set*:

```
IOS# clock set ?
  hh:mm:ss  Current Time
IOS# clock set
```

The next parameter wants the current time. This is based on UTC (unless you've changed the device's time zone) and is in a 24-hour format. For example, 3 P.M. would be 15:00:00. Again, use context-sensitive help to figure out if more parameters are required:

```
IOS# clock set 15:00:00 ?
  <1-31>  Day of the month
  MONTH   Month of the year
IOS# clock set 15:00:00
```

Whenever you see a range of numbers inside angle brackets, you must choose a value in this range. If you see a parameter in all caps, such as **MONTH**, you must supply a *name*. In this clocking example, IOS wants the number of the day or name of the month, such as *May*—with this command, the router isn't picky about in which order either of these parameters is entered, but in many cases the order does matter. Again, using context-sensitive help, indicate the number of the year following the name of the month:

```
IOS# clock set 15:00:00 23 May ?
  <1993-2035>  Year
IOS# clock set 15:00:00 23 May
```

Again, use context-sensitive help to see what's next:

```
IOS# clock set 15:00:00 23 May 2004 ?
  <cr>
IOS# clock set 15:00:00 23 May 2004
IOS#
```

The **<cr>** means that you can press the ENTER key and the IOS device will accept the command. On an IOS router, use the **show clock** command to see your current time and date:

```
IOS# show clock
15:00:02.187 UTC Fri May 23 2003
IOS#
```

Basic IOS Configuration

Here you'll learn the basics of accessing IOS software and creating a simple configuration on your IOS device. Many of the configuration commands are the same on Cisco routers and switches, simplifying a basic setup of these devices; however, as you'll see in subsequent chapters, certain features are specific to each product type, and thus each product has unique configuration commands.

Accessing Configuration Mode

All system/operating changes in IOS must occur within configuration mode. To access this mode, you must first be at privileged EXEC mode and use this command:

```
IOS# configure terminal
IOS(config)#
```

EXAM TIP When preparing for the exam, note which commands are configured directly from Global Configuration mode.

Notice that the prompt changed from # to **(config)#**, indicating the change in modes. This mode is commonly referred to as configuration mode or Global Configuration mode. You can abbreviate **configure terminal** to **conf t**. In configuration mode, you can execute commands that change your router's or switch's configuration; however, you cannot actually view the changes from within this mode, as this is done from privileged EXEC mode. To exit configuration mode and return to privileged EXEC mode, either type **end** or press CTRL-Z.

Device Identification

One of your first tasks is to change the name of your IOS device. This name has only local significance and is used for management purposes. For instance, the Cisco Discovery Protocol (CDP) uses the device name. (CDP is discussed in Chapter 8.) On both routers and switches, you use the **hostname** command to change the name of the device. Here is a simple example of changing the name *Router* to the name *Perimeter*:

```
Router(config)# hostname Perimeter
Perimeter(config)#
```

First, notice that the new name of the device (*Perimeter*) is placed after the **hostname** command. As soon as you press ENTER, the new CLI prompt is immediately changed—it contains the device's new name.

To undo changes or negate a command on a Cisco device, you can precede the command with the **no** parameter. As an example, to change the hostname back to the factory default, use this command:

```
Perimeter(config)# no hostname Perimeter
Router(config)#
```

In certain cases, you don't have to include the parameters of the command when negating it. In the preceding example, you could easily have typed in **no hostname** to accomplish the change, but in other cases, you must type in **no** and follow it with the entire configuration command.

EXAM TIP For the Cisco CCT certification, remember that the **hostname** command assigns a locally significant identifier to IOS device. In some of the exam simulation questions, you may be required to configure the hostname as part of your configuration. On the exam, the name will be case-sensitive!

VIDEO 7.03. The digital resources that accompany this book contain a multimedia demonstration of configuring a hostname on your Cisco device.

Subconfiguration Modes

Certain configuration commands on IOS devices take you into a specific subconfiguration mode, commonly referred to as a *subcommand mode*. Table 7-2 shows a few subconfiguration modes that you may see on IOS devices.

NOTE Not all subconfiguration modes are supported on all IOS devices. When you are working in a subconfiguration mode, the commands you enter affect only a specific component of the router or switch.

To leave a subconfiguration mode and return to Global Configuration mode, use the **exit** command. Using the **end** command or pressing CTRL-Z will always take you back to privileged EXEC mode no matter what configuration mode you are currently working in. Here is an example of going from a subconfiguration mode to Global Configuration mode:

```
IOS(config)# line con 0
IOS(config-line)# exit
IOS(config)#
```

In many cases, when you are working in a subconfiguration mode and type in a Global Configuration mode command, IOS executes it and the mode changes to Global Configuration mode, like this:

```
IOS(config)# line con 0
IOS(config-line)# hostname 2960
2960(config)#
```

Table 7-2	IOS Prompt	Subconfiguration Mode
Subconfiguration Modes on IOS Devices	**(config-if)#**	Interface subconfiguration mode
	(config-subif)#	Subinterface subconfiguration mode
	(config-line)#	Line subconfiguration mode
	(config-controller)#	Controller subconfiguration mode
	(config-router)#	IP routing protocol subconfiguration mode

EXAM TIP Remember that many Global Configuration mode commands affect the IOS device as a whole, such as the **hostname** command: you enter the command once and it affects the entire device. Subconfiguration mode commands affect only one specific component of an IOS device, such as an interface, a line, or a routing protocol, to name a few. Use the **exit** command to go back one configuration level. Use the **end** command or press CTRL-Z to exit configuration mode.

Notice that when the **hostname** command was executed in line subconfiguration mode, the switch changed its name as well as the mode. Sometimes, you'll get an invalid command response from the router; in that case you'll have to exit out of subconfiguration mode before executing the command in global configuration.

Line Configuration

Lines on IOS devices provide access to an EXEC shell; sometimes this is called *character mode access*, since it deals with a CLI. Table 7-3 shows the supported line types. The **line** command is used to reference a line in configuration mode. You must specify the type of line you want to configure as well as the line number, where line numbers begin at *0* and work their way up. Note that the console and auxiliary lines have only one line number: *0*. When configuring VTYs and TTYs, you can specify a range of numbers. Executing the **line** command takes you into subconfiguration mode, where the commands you enter affect that particular line or possibly multiple lines with VTYs and teletype terminals (TTYs).

Line Type	Description	Command Nomenclature
Console	Physical port that provides the initial CLI access; used for troubleshooting when remote access to IOS device isn't functioning. Only one is supported on a device.	**line con 0**
Auxiliary	Backup physical port typically used for dialup into IOS device; not all devices have an auxiliary port, and only one is supported per device.	**line aux 0**
VTY	Logical port that allows for remote access connections such as telnet and SSH to gain access to the CLI. Many VTYs are supported on an IOS device, and the number is dependent on the device, model, and software version.	**line vty 0 4**
TTY	Physical port used for connecting to a modem for a terminal service or for access to the console ports of other devices. These ports are found only on routers, and the number supported depends on the router model and asynchronous card installed.	**line tty 0 31**

Table 7-3 IOS Line Types

Changing the Inactivity Timeout

By default, an IOS device automatically logs you off after 10 minutes of inactivity. You can change this using the **exec-timeout** line subconfiguration mode command:

```
IOS(config)# line line_type line_#
IOS(config-line)# exec-timeout minutes seconds
```

Remember that this changes the configuration only for the line (or lines) you've specified—other lines will still use the default idle time. If you don't want a particular line to time out ever, you can set the minutes and seconds values to **0**, like this:

```
IOS(config)# line console 0
IOS(config-line)# exec-timeout 0 0
```

CAUTION   Disabling the timeout for a line is not recommended in a production environment, since it creates security issues. However, for training purposes, such as studying for the CCNA exam, this is okay.

If you want to disable the use of a line completely, use this configuration:

```
IOS(config)# line line_type line_#
IOS(config-line)# no exec
```

To verify your line configuration, use the **show line** command:

```
IOS# show line con 0
 Tty Typ   Tx/Rx A Modem Roty AccO AccI Uses Noise Overruns
*  0 CTY           -    -     -    -     -     0     0     0/0

Line 0, Location: "", Type: ""
Length: 24 lines, Width: 80 columns
Status: Ready, Active
Capabilities: none
Modem state: Ready
Special Chars: Escape Hold Stop Start Disconnect Activation
                ^^x   none   -     -      none
Timeouts: Idle EXEC   Idle Session  Modem Answer  Session  Dispatch
          never       never                       none     not set
Session limit is not set.
Time since activation: 0:04:49
Editing is enabled.
History is enabled, history size is 10.
Full user help is disabled
Allowed transports are pad telnet mop.  Preferred is telnet.
No output characters are padded
No special data dispatching characters
```

In this example, notice that the timeout value is set to **never**.

TIP   Notice that the **show** command is not entered from configuration mode. To enter user and privileged EXEC mode commands in configuration mode, preface the commands with the word **do**, like so: **do show line con 0**. This saves you from always having to exit back to use a **show** command and view the effects of your change. A huge time-saver!

Restricting VTY Protocol Access

By default, all methods of access are allowed for the VTYs, including telnet and SSH (using telnet and SSH is discussed in Chapter 8). Controlling the type of connection allowed on the VTYs is done with the **transport input** (what protocol can be used to connect to the router) and **transport output** (what protocol can be used to connect from the router) commands:

```
IOS(config)# line vty line_# [line_#]
IOS(config-line)# transport input {all | telnet | ssh}
IOS(config-line)# transport output {all | telnet | ssh}
```

By default, all protocols are allowed.

In the following example, only the SSH protocol is allowed on the VTYs (to or from the router):

```
Router(config)# line vty 0 15
Router(config-line)# transport input ssh
Router(config-line)# transport output ssh
```

Setting up telnet and SSH is discussed in more depth in Chapter 8.

 EXAM TIP   For the CCNA exam, be familiar with restricting protocol access to the VTYs.

CLI Output

One nice feature of an IOS device is that when certain types of events occur, such as an interface going down or up, an administrator making a configuration change, or an output of **debug** commands, the IOS device, by default, prints an informational message on the console line. It won't, however, display the same messages if you happen to have logged into the IOS device via telnet or SSH or accessed the device via the auxiliary or TTY lines.

If the latter is the case, you can have IOS display these messages on your screen by executing the privileged EXEC **terminal monitor** command, as shown here:

```
IOS# terminal monitor
```

You must execute this command after you have logged into IOS from the VTY, TTY, or auxiliary lines. Once you log out, however, this command does not apply to anyone else logging into IOS device on the same line; each individual line session must re-execute this command.

One annoying problem with the information messages displayed on your CLI screen is that if you are typing in an IOS command, when the device displays the message, it starts printing it right where the cursor is, making it difficult to figure out where you left off typing. If you remember, just keep typing your command, or press CTRL-C to abort the command. A better approach, though, is to set up IOS so that after the message prints in your window, IOS redisplays what you have already entered on a new CLI prompt. The **logging synchronous** command accomplishes this:

```
IOS(config)# line line_type line_#
IOS(config-line)# logging synchronous
```

Notice that this command is executed under the line subconfiguration mode. If you want to implement this feature, you'll need to set it up under all the lines from which you'll be accessing your IOS device, including your VTYs and console port. You can also press CTRL-R to refresh the screen.

Interface Configuration

The Cisco CCT certification exam expects you to understand how to configure an Ethernet interface and a serial interface as well as troubleshoot layer 1 and layer 2 issues with the interfaces. In this section you will learn to configure common settings on Ethernet and serial interfaces such as enabling and disabling the interfaces, as well as configuring the speed and duplex settings. Later in this chapter you will learn the **show** commands used to troubleshoot layer 1 and layer 2 issues with the interfaces.

To configure an interface, you must first enter interface subconfiguration mode:

```
IOS(config)# interface type [slot_#/]port_#
IOS(config-if)#
```

You must specify two components to the **interface** command: the *type* and the *location*. When you enter the complete **interface** command, notice that the prompt changes, signifying that you are in interface subconfiguration mode for the specified interface—**(config-if)#** in this example.

TIP You can't determine what interface you are working in by examining the prompt. If you aren't sure, use the command recall feature to recall the **interface** command and re-execute it.

When specifying the interface, you can use any of the following nomenclatures:

```
IOS(config)# interface GigabitEthernet 0/1
IOS(config)# interface GigabitEthernet0/1
IOS(config)# int g 0/1
IOS(config)# int g0/1
IOS(config)# int gig 0/1
IOS(config)# int gig0/1
```

NOTE You can separate the type and location with a space, or concatenate the two together. Likewise, you can abbreviate the commands and parameters.

Assign IP Address

After navigating to the interface, you can execute a number of commands to modify the characteristics of the interface. On a Cisco router, for example, you may want to assign an IP address to an interface with the following commands:

```
IOS>enable
IOS#config term
Enter configuration commands, one per line.  End with CNTL/Z.
IOS(config)#interface G0/0
IOS(config-if)#ip address 14.0.0.1 255.0.0.0
```

In this example, I first navigate to the Gigabit Ethernet interface I would like to configure and then assign an IP address and subnet mask to the interface.

You can also configure the interface for a dynamic IP address (receive the IP address from a DHCP server) by using the following command:

```
IOS(config-if)#ip address dhcp
```

Enable and Disable the Interface

On the Catalyst switches, the interfaces are *enabled* by default; on Cisco routers, the interfaces are *disabled* by default. You can disable interfaces with the **shutdown** command while at the interface subconfiguration prompt:

```
IOS(config)# interface type slot_#/port_#
IOS(config-if)# shutdown
```

To enable the interface, use the **no shutdown** command. Usually after assigning an IP address to the interface, I try to make it a habit to enable the interface.

 EXAM TIP   For the Cisco CCT and CCNA exam, remember that IOS switch interfaces are enabled by default, but router interfaces are disabled by default. Also remember how to enable and disable an interface on an IOS device: **no shutdown** and **shutdown**, respectively.

Whenever the interface changes status, IOS prints a message on the screen telling you so. Here is an example in which an interface on a router is being activated:

```
IOS(config)# interface gigabitethernet0/1
IOS(config-if)# no shutdown
1w0d: %LINK-3-UPDOWN: Interface GigabitEthernet0/1, changed state to up
1w0d: %LINEPROTO-5-UPDOWN: Line protocol on Interface
      GigabitEthernet0/1, changed state to up
IOS(config-if)#
```

In this example, the first information line indicates that the physical layer is activated. The second information line indicates that the data link layer protocol is enabled, which in this case is Ethernet—for a WAN port, the layer 2 protocol is High-Level Data Link Control (HDLC) or Point-to-Point Protocol (PPP).

NOTE   When copying and pasting a configuration file into the router, and the router interface is disabled with the **shutdown** command, the pasted configuration file must contain the **no shutdown** command in order to active the interface. This is a common problem when copying and pasting a configuration file from an old router to a new router, where the interfaces on the new router are disabled by default.

Description

You can add a description to any interface by using the **description** command:

```
IOS(config)# interface type [slot_#/]port_#
IOS(config-if)# description interface_description
```

The **description** command supplies a one-line description of the device to which the interface is connected, or whatever description you want to assign. This description appears in the output of the **show interfaces** command, discussed later in the chapter.

Speed and Duplexing for Ethernet Interfaces

To set the speed and duplexing speeds of Ethernet-based interfaces, use the following configuration:

```
IOS(config)# interface ethernet_type [slot_#/]port_#
IOS(config-if)# speed 10|100|1000|auto
IOS(config-if)# duplex full|half|auto
```

NOTE   For 10/100/1000 Ethernet ports, it is no longer recommended that you hard-code the speed and duplexing with the **speed** and **duplex** commands; instead, let the interface autosense these settings from the directly connected device. The commands to change the speed and duplex settings are there for troubleshooting situations where autonegotiate is not working and you need to force a speed or duplex setting.

It is important to note that if you set the duplex setting incorrectly or the speed incorrectly, this could cause communication problems. This is a reason to change the **duplex** and **speed** settings; if they were originally set incorrectly, you may need to change them to match the network environment.

VIDEO   7.04. The digital resources that accompany this book contain a multimedia demonstration of configuring a Gigabit interface on the router.

Serial Interfaces on Routers

Things are a little different when configuring serial interfaces, because you need to configure not only an IP address, but you must also specify a layer 2 protocol to use.

First let's assign an IP address and description to the serial interface with the following commands:

```
IOS(config)#interface s0/3/0
IOS(config-if)#ip address 13.0.0.2 255.0.0.0
IOS(config-if)#description LINK-TO-ISP
```

After the IP address is assigned to the serial interface, you can choose the layer 2 protocol you want to use to carry traffic across the serial link. On the LAN, the layer 2 protocol is Ethernet, but that is not used on our serial lines. We need to specify what type of layer 2 frame we want to put the IP packet inside before sending data out the serial port.

Two main serial link protocols are used on Cisco routers:

- **HDLC**   This protocol is a Cisco proprietary protocol that is used to send data across a serial link. The great thing about HDLC is that it requires no configuration and is the default encapsulation protocol if you do not specify one.

- **PPP**   This industry standard protocol is supported by many different vendors and products and should be used if you have a mix of Cisco devices and non-Cisco devices on the network.

For this discussion we will choose to use HDLC as the encapsulation protocol. Remember that you can always use the **help** command if you want to see what encapsulation protocols are supported by the serial interface:

```
IOS(config-if)#encapsulation ?
  hdlc          Serial HDLC synchronous
  ppp           Point-to-Point protocol
IOS(config-if)#encapsulation hdlc
```

If you want to configure the serial interface to use PPP as the encapsulation protocol, you would use the following command.

```
IOS(config-if)#encapsulation ppp
```

NOTE   In order for the serial interface to function properly, you must have the same encapsulation protocol configured on both ends of the link.

One of the benefits of PPP is that you can configure authentication—which means that in order to send data over the serial link, other routers must know the password on the serial link. To configure authentication with PPP:

- Set the hostname on each router.

- Create a username and password on each of the routers that matches the name of the other router.

- Enable authentication with the authentication protocol of PAP or CHAP. CHAP is preferred because PAP sends the username and password in clear text.

The following shows the commands for each of these steps:

```
VAN-R1#config term

VAN-R1(config)#username LA-R1 password wanpass

VAN-R1(config)#interface s0/3/0

VAN-R1(config-if)#encapsulation ppp

VAN-R1(config-if)#ppp authentication chap
```

Looking at the preceding code you can see I am configuring the VAN-R1 router for the username of the LA-R1 router. I then enable the encapsulation protocol of PPP, and then finally configure the PPP authentication protocol to CHAP. You would then configure the LA-R1 router in a similar way.

Now that we have configured the IP address and encapsulation protocol on the serial interface, all we need to do is make sure that the interface is receiving the clocking speed, or timing, of the link. Setting the clocking speed is the responsibility of the data communications equipment (DCE). When connecting the router to the ISP, the ISP is the DCE end of the link, and as such the ISP sets the clocking speed of the link. In the ISP example, your router is the data terminal equipment (DTE), so you are not allowed to set the clock speed of the link.

Why am I mentioning this if it is set by the ISP? Well, if you are connecting two routers together over their serial ports with a back-to-back serial cable, one end of the cable is typically labeled "DCE" and the other end of the cable is labeled "DTE." On the router that has the DCE end of the cable, you will need to set the clock rate with the following command:

```
IOS(config-if)#clock rate 64000
```

If you try to execute the **clock rate** command when you are configuring the DTE device, you will get a message that the command is performed on DCE devices only. No harm in trying, though.

The last command you configure on the serial interface is to enable the interface by using the **no shutdown** command (whether you are the DCE or DTE device):

```
IOS(config-if)#no shutdown
```

 VIDEO 7.05. The digital resources that accompany this book contain a multimedia demonstration of configuring a serial interface on the router.

If you are not sure which router has the DTE end of the cable and which has the DCE end, you can determine this with the **show controllers** command:

```
Router> show controllers serial [slot_#/]port_#
```

This is one of the few commands in which you *cannot* concatenate the type and the port number—you must separate them by a space. Here is an example of the use of this command:

```
Router> show controllers serial 0/3/0
HD unit 0, idb = 0x121C04, driver structure at 0x127078
buffer size 1524 HD unit 0, DTE V.35 serial cable attached
.
.
.
```

Notice that the second line of this example holds two important pieces of information: the connection type (DTE) and the type of cable (V.35).

Here is an example of an interface connected to the end of a DCE cable:

```
Router> show controllers serial 0/3/0
HD unit 0, idb = 0x1BA16C, driver structure at 0x1C04E0
buffer size 1524  HD unit 0, V.35 DCE cable, clockrate 64000
.
.
.
```

In this example, the clocking has already been configured: 64,000 bps.

 EXAM TIP   For the exam, remember that you can use the **show controllers** command to determine DTE and DCE connections and use the **clock rate** command to configure the speed for DCE connections.

Exercise 7-1: Basic Router Configuration

In this exercise you will need two Cisco routers and two Cisco switches or a network simulator that enables you to create a diagram with two routers and two switches. Figure 7-2 shows the network you will configure in this example. This exercise is focused on the configuration of the two routers; we will focus on the switches in the switching chapters.

1. Ensure that you have all physical components such as routers and switches connected as per Figure 7-2, and then power them on.

2. Connect your workstation to the console port of the router that will become VAN-R1. Then launch PuTTY, choose Serial connection, set the correct COM port, and choose Open.

3. Press ENTER in the PuTTY window to get a prompt on your Cisco device.

4. Set the name of the Cisco router to VAN-R1 with the following command:

```
Router>enable
Router#config term
Router(config)#hostname VAN-R1
```

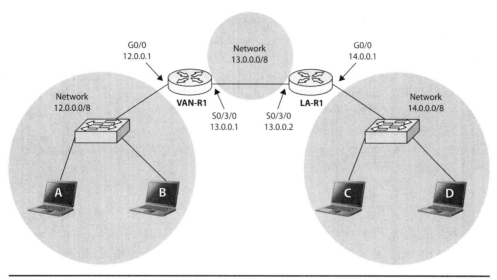

Figure 7-2   Network topology for exercise

5. Configure the IP address on the Gigabit Ethernet 0/0 interface with the following commands:

```
VAN-R1(config)#interface g0/0
VAN-R1(config-if)#ip address 12.0.0.1 255.0.0.0
VAN-R1(config-if)#no shutdown
```

Notice that the g0/0 interface changes to a state of up (it is not up and running).

6. Configure the serial 0/3/0 interface on the router with the following commands:

```
VAN-R1(config-if)#interface s0/3/0
VAN-R1(config-if)#ip address 13.0.0.1 255.0.0.0
VAN-R1(config-if)#encapsulation hdlc
VAN-R1(config-if)#clock rate 64000
VAN-R1(config-if)#no shutdown
```

Notice that the serial interface status message indicates that it is still down, even though it is fully configured. This is because the other end of the serial link (the LA-R1 router) must be configured before the link comes up.

7. It is important to remember that you must save these changes to NVRAM by entering the following commands:

```
VAN-R1(config-if)#exit
VAN-R1(config)#exit
VAN-R1#copy running-config startup-config
Destination filename [startup-config]?
Building configuration...
[OK]
```

8. Connect to the console port of the router that will be LA-R1 and then press ENTER in the PuTTY screen to refresh the screen. You should be connected to the second router now.

9. Set the hostname on the second router to LA-R1.

10. Configure the IP address on the Gigabit Ethernet 0/0 interface to 14.0.0.1 and ensure that the interface is enabled.

11. Configure the serial 0/3/0 interface on the router for the IP address of 13.0.0.2 and set the encapsulation protocol; note that if this is the DTE end of the connection, you do not need to set the clock rate.

12. Save the new changes to NVRAM.

13. To verify that LA-R1 can ping the IP address of VAN-R1, type the following commands:

```
LA-R1#ping 13.0.0.1
Type escape sequence to abort.
Sending 5, 100-byte ICMP Echos to 13.0.0.1, timeout is 2 seconds:
!!!!!
Success rate is 100 percent (5/5), round-trip min/avg/max = 1/1/2 ms
```

14. On LA-R1, use the following commands to review your configuration (take a few minutes and look at the output of each):

```
LA-R1#show interfaces
LA-R1#show interfaces g0/0
LA-R1#show ip interface brief
```

15. On VAN-R1, use the following commands to review your configuration (take a few minutes and look at the output of each):

```
VAN-R1#show interfaces
VAN-R1#show interfaces g0/0
VAN-R1#show ip interface brief
```

16. Leave the routers up and running for the next exercise.

Basic IOS Security Configuration

The Computer Security Institute (CSI) is an organization that provides education and training on network security fundamentals. It periodically performs market research studies on security issues with companies. In one study, more than 70 percent of all the companies polled reported experiencing some kind of security breach. Knowing this information, as a network administrator, one of your roles will be to ensure that access to your networking devices is strictly controlled. The following sections will introduce you to securing your IOS device.

 NOTE The information introduced in this chapter includes only a few of the security features you'll set up on your IOS devices; many more of these features are discussed throughout the book, such as port security on the switches in Chapter 9 and access control lists (ACLs) in Chapter 17, to name a couple.

Physical and Environmental Threats

Many network administrators forget that the first line of defense in securing their network devices includes protecting against physical and environmental threats, including the following:

- **Hardware**   Restricting physical access to the router via physical measures, such as locked doors, key cards, video cameras, and so on
- **Electrical**   Ensuring that equipment is protected from power surges/spikes, brownouts, and loss of power
- **Environmental**   Protecting equipment from temperatures that are too cold or too hot, or from too much humidity
- **Maintenance**   Ensuring that you follow electrostatic discharge procedures when handling sensitive electronic parts, have spares on hand for critical parts, and properly label equipment and cables

An in-depth discussion of these issues is beyond the scope of this book; they are covered in a bit more depth in Cisco's CCNA and CCNP Security courses.

Passwords

The most common way of restricting physical access to IOS devices is to use some type of user authentication. For example, you can configure passwords to restrict access to the lines on IOS devices (user EXEC mode) as well as access to privileged EXEC mode. Configuring passwords on Catalyst IOS switches, such as the 2950s and 2960s, is the same as configuring passwords on IOS routers. The following sections discuss the configuration of passwords on IOS devices.

User EXEC Password Protection

Controlling access to user EXEC mode on an IOS device is accomplished on a line-by-line basis: console, auxiliary, TTYs, and VTYs. Remember that not all devices support auxiliary ports, only routers support TTYs, and the number of VTYs an IOS device supports is product-dependent, ranging from five VTYs (0–4) to almost a thousand.

To secure the console port, you must first go into the console's line subconfiguration mode with the **line console 0** command to configure the line password:

```
IOS(config)# line console 0
IOS(config-line)# password console_password
IOS(config-line)# login
```

The **0** in the first command specifies the console port. Lines and interfaces are numbered from *0* upward. Even though IOS devices have only a single console port, it is designated as *0* (this is true of most, but not all, Cisco products). Next, notice that the prompt on the second line changed. Once you are in line subconfiguration mode, you can use the **password** command to assign the console password. The final command of **login** is needed as an indication that you want the Cisco device to force people to authenticate using that password if they connect to the console 0 port. Passwords on IOS devices are *case-sensitive*. Remember that the **password** command, when executed under **line console 0**, sets the user EXEC password for someone trying to access the IOS device from the console port only.

The auxiliary port is typically used as a remote access port with a modem attached to it, which enables you to dial into the router if something has happened to the Internet connection and you cannot remote in via telnet or SSH. The following code shows the syntax for setting up password authentication on the auxiliary port:

```
Router(config)# line aux 0
Router(config-line)# password aux_password
Router(config-line)# login
```

Again, the **login** command is required; if you forget it, you will have set a password on the port and will not have asked the Cisco device to prompt for that password when someone connects to the port.

To set up a telnet password for your VTYs, use this configuration:

```
IOS(config)# line vty 0 15
IOS(config-line)# password telnet_password
IOS(config-line)# login
```

The **vty** parameter in this command refers to *virtual terminal*, a fancy name for telnet or SSH access. Cisco devices support multiple simultaneous VTY (telnet) sessions, where each connection is internally tracked by a number: 0–15. Depending on the router model and IOS software version, this number may range from 5 (0–4) on up to almost 1000. You could assign a different password to each VTY, but then you wouldn't know which password to use when telnetting into the IOS device. However, IOS enables you to specify multiple VTYs ports with the **line** command, simplifying your configuration, as in the preceding configuration: **line vty 0 15**. You need to specify the beginning and ending VTY numbers on the same line.

Once you are in line subconfiguration mode, use the **password** command to set your password. You also need to enter the **login** command to force authentication on those ports, essentially telling the device to prompt for the password if someone tries to connect via telnet.

 EXAM TIP Remember for the CCNA exam that if you telnet into a Cisco device, and you see the message "Password required but none set," then you have not configured a password on the line with the **password** command and won't be able to log in until you configure one. Remember that you should secure your VTYs with a password and login process. Another security option to secure your VTY ports is to apply an ACL. ACLs are discussed in Chapter 17.

If you specify only one number when configuring your VTYs, such as the following, then you are configuring *only that* VTY:

```
IOS(config)# line vty 0
IOS(config-line)# password cisco123
IOS(config-line)# login
```

In this example, only the VTY 0 line is assigned a password, and authentication is enforced by requiring someone to log into the port. If this was the only item you configured for your VTYs on a factory-default IOS device, then only one person could remotely access the IOS device using telnet or SSH via VTY 0.

 VIDEO   7.06. The digital resources that accompany this book contain a multimedia demonstration of configuring passwords on your line ports.

Creating Usernames and Passwords

Other ways of validating access are available, such as a local username database or an external authentication server. A local username database on the router enables you to specify both a username and a password to restrict access to the lines on an IOS device. Using usernames and passwords is recommended over using only passwords on lines: the advantage of this approach is that each user can have his or her own password instead of sharing a password, providing for more accountability. The following commands illustrate the setup of a local username database and its use on VTYs:

```
IOS(config)# username name {secret | password} password
IOS(config)# line vty 0 15
IOS(config-line)# login local
```

The **username** command specifies the name and password for the user. The main difference between the **secret** and **password** parameters is that the **secret** parameter tells IOS to encrypt the password with an MD5 hash, and the **password** parameter doesn't (the password is stored in clear text). This is true of the line subconfiguration mode **password** command: it also is stored in clear text.

 NOTE   The **login local** command can be used on any of the lines on Cisco device to tell the device to perform authentication using the local username and password database. You can use this on console, auxiliary, and VTY ports to force the Cisco device to require a username *and* password when someone connects.

Privileged EXEC Password Protection

Along with protecting access to the lines on an IOS device, you can also control access to privileged EXEC mode by assigning a password to it. Two configuration options are shown here:

```
Switch(config)# enable password Privilege_EXEC_password
```

or

```
Switch(config)# enable secret Privilege_EXEC_password
```

Both of these commands configure the privileged EXEC password. The main difference between the two, as with the **username** command, is that the **secret** parameter encrypts the privileged EXEC password and the **password** parameter doesn't. If you configure both of these commands, the password configured with the **enable secret** command always takes precedence over the password configured with the **enable password** command. The **enable password** command is still supported by Cisco for backward-compatibility purposes.

 EXAM TIP For the exam, you'll need to remember that without user EXEC *and* privileged EXEC authentication (passwords), you will not be able to access IOS device remotely via telnet or SSH, by default.

Password Encryption

Passwords that are not encrypted can be encrypted by using the **service password-encryption** Global Configuration mode command. However, the **enable secret** command's encryption is *much* stronger than using the **service password-encryption** command to do the encryption.

 EXAM TIP Remember for the CCT and CCNA exam that you use the **enable password** or **enable secret** command to secure privileged EXEC access. Remember that the **enable secret** command creates an encrypted secret value that takes precedence over the password if both are configured. With VTY access, you should also configure a password on the VTY ports and you must also specify the **login** command to have the device prompt for the password. Use the **service password-encryption** command to encrypt all clear-text passwords within your configuration: this includes the **password** command for the VTYs and other lines, the **enable password** command, and other commands that have a clear-text password.

Exercise 7-2: Configuring Passwords

In this exercise you will continue with the configuration of the previous exercise and add passwords to the two routers. You will configure a console password, an auxiliary password (if you have an aux port), and VTY port passwords. See Figure 7-3.

1. Ensure you are consoled into VAN-R1.

2. To configure a console password of *conpass* on VAN-R1, enter the following commands:

```
VAN-R1>enable
VAN-R1#config term
VAN-R1(config)#line con 0
VAN-R1(config-line)#password conpass
VAN-R1(config-line)#login
```

3. To configure an aux password of *auxpass* on VAN-R1, enter the following commands:

```
VAN-R1(config-line)#line aux 0
VAN-R1(config-line)#password auxpass
VAN-R1(config-line)#login
```

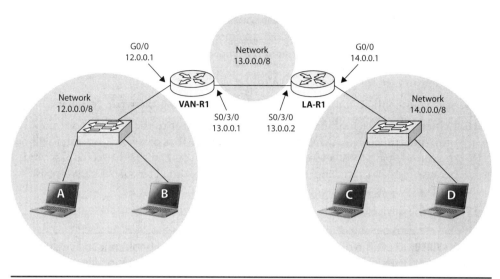

Figure 7-3 Network topology for exercise

4. To configure telnet passwords of *telnetpass* by configuring the VTY ports, enter the following commands:

```
VAN-R1(config-line)#line vty 0 4
VAN-R1(config-line)#password telnetpass
VAN-R1(config-line)#login
```

5. Create an enable password of *enablepass*:

```
VAN-R1(config-line)#exit
VAN-R1(config)#enable password enablepass
```

6. Create an enable secret of *enablesecret*:

```
VAN-R1(config)#enable secret enablesecret
VAN-R1(config)#exit
VAN-R1#
```

7. Save the configuration changes to NVRAM by entering the following command:

```
VAN-R1# copy running-config startup-config
```

Note that you could have also used the **write** command, which does not prompt you to confirm the destination of the save operation.

8. Exit out and verify each of the passwords as you connect to the console port; then move into privileged EXEC mode. Note that the first password you enter will be the console password, and the second password you enter is the secret password, because it takes precedence over the enable password. The enable password is used only if the enable secret is not set.

9. Now configure the passwords on router LA-R1. Ensure you are consoled into LA-R1.

10. Configure a console password of *LAconpass* on LA-R1.

11. Configure an aux password of *LAauxpass* on LA-R1.

12. Configure VTY passwords of *LAtelnetpass* on LA-R1.

13. Create an enable password of *LAenablepass*.

14. Create an enable secret of *LAenablesecret*.

15. Save your configuration changes to NVRAM by using the **write** command.

16. Exit and verify each of the passwords as you connect to the console port; then move into privileged EXEC mode. Note that the first password you enter will be the console password, and the second password you enter is the secret password, because it takes precedence over the enable password. The enable password is used only if the enable secret is not set.

17. Keep the devices up and running for the next exercise.

 VIDEO   7.07. The digital resources that accompany this book contain a multimedia demonstration of encrypting passwords within the configuration file.

Configuring Banners

Banners provide a way for you to display messages to administrators when they connect to your Cisco device. There are different types of banners, such as message-of-the-day (MOTD) and login banners, which differ in the timing of when they appear. The following is a list of some of the common types of banners that can be set:

- **MOTD banner**   The MOTD banner appears before the administrator is asked to log in and is used to display a temporary message that may change from day to day.

- **Login banner**   The login banner displays before the administrator logs in, but after the MOTD banner appears, and is used to display a more permanent message to the administrator.

- **Exec banner**   The exec banner is used to display a message after the administrator authenticates to the system and after he enters user EXEC mode.

To see a list of banners supported on your Cisco device, use the help feature on the **banner** command:

```
Switch(config)#banner ?
  LINE            c banner-text c, where 'c' is a delimiting character
  exec            Set EXEC process creation banner
  incoming        Set incoming terminal line banner
  login           Set login banner
  motd            Set Message of the Day banner
  prompt-timeout  Set Message for login authentication timeout
  slip-ppp        Set Message for SLIP/PPP
```

The setup of each of the banners is similar, so let's take a look at setting a few of the common ones.

MOTD Banner

You can set up a MOTD banner on your IOS device that will display a message *before* the administrator is asked to log in to the device (before the console, aux, or VTY passwords). Use the **banner motd** command to create the MOTD banner:

```
IOS(config)# banner motd delimiting_char your_banner end_with_delimiting_char
IOS(config)#
```

After the **banner motd** command, you must enter the delimiting character, which is used to signify the beginning and ending of the banner—it cannot appear in the actual banner. After you enter the delimiting character, when the IOS parser sees this character later in your message text, IOS terminates the banner and returns you to the CLI prompt. One nice feature of the banner is that when you press the ENTER key, it doesn't terminate the banner, so you can have banners that span multiple lines of text. Whenever you have completed your banner, type the delimiting character to end the command.

Here is an example of setting up a MOTD banner:

```
IOS(config)# banner motd $
Long weekend upcoming.  We will be performing maintenance.
Back up all your configuration.
$
IOS(config)#
```

In this example, the banner spans multiple lines and the delimiting character is the dollar sign ($). A banner doesn't have to span multiple lines, but it can be placed on a single line, as in this example:

```
IOS(config)# banner motd 'Keep Out!'
IOS(config)#
```

In this example, the single quote (') is the delimiting character. Once you have created a MOTD banner, test it by disconnecting from the device and connecting back in. You should see your MOTD banner appear *before* being asked for the password of the device.

EXAM TIP   You'll be expected to know that the **banner motd** command displays a banner before the administrator authenticates to the device.

Login Banner

You can also create a login banner. Like the MOTD banner, the *login banner* also appears before the administrator logs in, but it appears *after* the MOTD banner text appears. The login banner is designed to be more of a permanent message that would not change very often. To create the login banner, replace the **motd** parameter in the **banner motd** command with **login**. The following is an example of setting up a login banner:

```
IOS(config)# banner login $
This is a private system and only authorized individuals
          are allowed!
All others will be prosecuted to the fullest extent of the law!
$
IOS(config)#
```

 CAUTION You should not use such words as *welcome* or any type of welcoming salutation in your banner; using such words can be misconstrued and may enable attackers to defend their actions by citing the welcome salutation in your login banner.

Exec Banner

Use the exec banner to display a message *after* the administrator has authenticated to the device with her console or aux password, but before she enters user EXEC mode. You configure the exec banner password with the **exec** keyword:

```
IOS(config)# banner exec $
Remember to save your changes with the write command.
Please ensure all changes are authorized by your team lead.
$
IOS(config)#
```

Exercise 7-3: Setting Banners

In this exercise you will continue with the configuration of the previous exercise and add banners to the two routers. You will configure a MOTD banner, a login banner, and an exec banner. See Figure 7-4.

1. Ensure that you are consoled into VAN-R1.

2. To configure a MOTD banner on VAN-R1, enter the following commands:
```
VAN-R1>enable
VAN-R1#config term
VAN-R1(config)# banner motd $
Long weekend upcoming.  We will be performing maintenance.
Back up all your configuration.
$
VAN-R1(config)#
```

3. To configure a login banner on VAN-R1, enter the following commands:
```
VAN-R1(config)# banner login $
This is a private system and only authorized individuals
          are allowed!
All others will be prosecuted to the fullest extent of the law!
$
VAN-R1(config)#
```

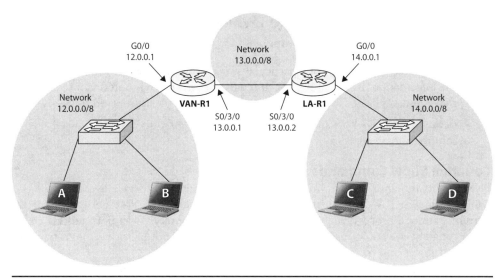

Figure 7-4 Network topology for exercise

4. To configure an exec banner on VAN-R1, enter the following commands:

```
VAN-R1(config)# banner exec $
Remember to save your changes with the write command.
$
VAN-R1(config)#
```

5. Save your changes with the **write** command.

6. To test the banners, exit out, and disconnect from the device. Reconnect again and watch the timing of when the banners appear.

7. Connect to LA-R1 and configure the three banners on LA-R1.

8. Save the changes on LA-R1 to NVRAM by using the **write** command.

9. Disconnect from LA-R1 and reconnect to it to test the banners.

10. Keep the routers running for the next exercise.

 VIDEO 7.08. The digital resources that accompany this book contain a multimedia demonstration of configuring a MOTD banner.

IOS Operation and Verification

Once you have configured your IOS device, many commands are available to use to examine and troubleshoot your configuration. This section covers some of the basic **show** commands that are available to help you verify and troubleshoot configuration of your Cisco device. Subsequent chapters will discuss additional commands you can use to help troubleshoot more complex problems.

Show and Debug Command Overview

You can use two basic commands to troubleshoot problems on an IOS device:

- **show** Takes a snapshot of a particular process and displays information about it; the information displayed is static and will not refresh itself unless you re-execute the command (you can use the command-line history feature to do this).

- **debug** Displays how a particular process is currently operating, showing information as it basically happens, in real time.

Common Show Commands

Use **show** commands to get a quick idea about how an IOS device is configured (the configuration in RAM, a routing protocol, or Spanning Tree Protocol [STP]) or the current state of a process (such as an interface, a routing table, or a port address table). Unfortunately, in certain instances, **show** commands may not provide enough information to diagnose and fix a problem correctly.

Some common **show** commands that you should experiment with are listed here:

- **show ip interface brief** Lists of all of the interfaces on the device and offers a quick look at their statuses; indicates whether an interface is up and running and the IP address assigned to the interface

- **show interfaces** Lists all the interfaces and detailed specifications on the interfaces

- **show interfaces g0/0** Lists the details of a specific interface

- **show controllers s0/3/0** Lists information such as the DCE and DTE details on serial interfaces

---

 VIDEO 7.09. The digital resources that accompany this book contain a multimedia demonstration of common **show** commands you should know for the Cisco exams.

Common Debug Commands

The **debug** commands, on the other hand, display how a process is currently running or behaving, such as the contents of a routing update received by a neighboring router, and are therefore typically more useful in troubleshooting difficult problems. The main disadvantage of **debug** commands is that they are process-intensive on IOS devices and should be used with care.

Running and Startup Configuration

When you configure a Cisco device, the configuration settings are stored in a configuration file. By default, two configurations are possible on Cisco devices:

- **running-config** This file contains the actual configuration running in the RAM of an IOS device (the settings that the device is currently using).

- **startup-config** This file contains the saved configuration settings in nonvolatile RAM (NVRAM) of a Cisco device and are applied at bootup.

Configuration files can reside in many locations, including RAM, NVRAM, or a Trivial File Transfer Protocol (TFTP) or FTP server, among other places. Whenever you make changes to an IOS's configuration by typing in commands from configuration mode, these changes are made in RAM (running-config). These changes can then be saved to NVRAM (startup-config), which is a *static* form of memory; when the Cisco device is turned off, the contents of NVRAM are not erased and are available upon a power-up. IOS devices do *not* automatically save the configuration file from RAM to NVRAM; this must be done *manually*. Configuration changes can also be saved to an external server using TFTP, FTP, and Secure Copy Protocol (SCP)—this, however, requires that you configure IP addressing and possibly a default gateway address on your IOS device. (These topics are discussed in Chapter 8.)

The following sections discuss how you view your IOS device's configuration files as well as how to back up and restore your configuration files locally on your IOS device.

Viewing Configurations

To examine the active or running configuration on an IOS device, use the **show running-config** command. You must be in privileged EXEC mode to execute this command. Here is an example of this command on a Cisco router:

```
Router# show running-config
Building configuration...
Current configuration:
!
version 12.0
no service udp-small-servers
no service tcp-small-servers
!
hostname Router
.
.
.
```

Notice the references to **Building configuration...** and **Current configuration** in this example. Both of these refer to the configuration in RAM.

Saving Your Changes

The startup configuration file is stored in NVRAM for both switches and routers. When an IOS device boots up, IOS loads the configuration from NVRAM and places it in RAM. After booting the device, you can make configuration changes, which are stored in RAM (running-config). To have that configuration retained during reboots of the device, you will need to save the new changes to NVRAM (startup-config). To save the active configuration to NVRAM, you must execute the **copy running-config startup-config** command from privileged EXEC mode. Upon executing this command, the IOS device takes the active configuration in RAM and saves it to NVRAM. In this process, the old configuration file in NVRAM is overwritten.

Here is an example of this command:

```
IOS# copy running-config startup-config
Destination filename [startup-config]?
Building configuration...
[OK]
IOS#
```

When executing this command, you are asked for a filename for the configuration file—the default is *startup-config*. This is the filename IOS looks for when booting up. You can change the name for backup revisioning purposes (different versions of the backed-up configuration), but make sure that your most current configuration is saved as startup-config. On the IOS device, you can view the saved configuration in NVRAM with the **show startup-config** privileged EXEC mode command.

 TIP   A shortcut to save IOS's configuration to NVRAM is the **write memory** command: you can abbreviate this to just **write**. I use **write** all the time to save my changes quickly to the startup configuration. Note that **write memory** is a deprecated command, so although it currently works, it will eventually be removed as a command in future versions of IOS.

To see the configuration file stored in NVRAM, use this command:

```
Router# show startup-config
Using 4224 out of 65536 bytes
!
version 11.3
no service udp-small-servers
no service tcp-small-servers
!
hostname Router
.
.
.
```

One difference between this output and that from the **show running-config** command is the first line of output: **Using 4224 out of 65536 bytes** refers to the amount of NVRAM currently used by the saved configuration file.

 EXAM TIP   You should know that IOS devices do not automatically save configuration changes. You must manually enter the **copy running-config startup-config** command or the **write** command. This command backs up your configuration to NVRAM. Also remember that any time you want to examine or manipulate a configuration, you must be in privileged EXEC mode. If you make configuration changes to a Cisco router and forget to save the configuration to NVRAM, you will lose those changes when you reboot the device.

Reverting Your Configuration

To revert your configuration from NVRAM to RAM, use the **copy startup-config running-config** command from privileged EXEC mode:

```
IOS# copy startup-config running-config
Destination filename [running-config]?
947 bytes copied in 0.320 secs (2959 bytes/sec)
IOS#
```

One important thing to note is that when you take a configuration file from any location and copy it to RAM, IOS uses a merge process to load in the configuration file from the source, overwriting matching commands in RAM and adding new commands that don't exist in RAM, but not deleting commands that don't exist in NVRAM but do exist in RAM.

Device Version Information

If you want to see general information about your IOS device—its model number, the types of interfaces, the different kinds and amounts of memory, its software version, where IOS is located and loaded and its configuration file, as well as the configuration settings—you can use the **show version** command.

Here is an example of this command on a Cisco router:

```
Router> show version
Cisco Internetwork Operating System Software
IOS (tm) 3600 Software (C3640-JS-M), Version 12.0(3c), RELEASE SOFTWARE (fc1)
Copyright (c) 1986-1999 by cisco Systems, Inc.
Compiled Tue 13-Apr-99 07:39 by phanguye
Image text-base: 0x60008918, data-base: 0x60BDC000

ROM: System Bootstrap, Version 11.1(20)AA2, EARLY DEPLOYMENT
RELEASE SOFTWARE (fc1)

Router uptime is 2 days, 11 hours, 40 minutes
System restarted by power-on
System image file is "flash:c3640-js-mz.120-3c.bin"

cisco 3640 (R4700) processor (revision 0x00) with 49152K/16384K
bytes of memory.
.
.
.
1 FastEthernet/IEEE 802.3 interface(s)
8 Low-speed serial(sync/async) network interface(s)
1 Channelized T1/PRI port(s)
DRAM configuration is 64 bits wide with parity disabled.
125K bytes of non-volatile configuration memory.
32768K bytes of processor board System flash (Read/Write)

Configuration register is 0x2102
```

In the middle of the output is **System restarted** followed by how the IOS device was last started. In this example, the device had its power turned on. The last line of this output is the configuration register value. This value determines how the router will boot up, including how it will find its IOS and its configuration file. The bootup process of the router is discussed in more depth in Chapter 6.

 EXAM TIP   Be familiar with the output of the **show version** command, including what is displayed, such as IOS version; the uptime; the amount of RAM, NVRAM, and flash; the type and number of interfaces; and the configuration register value. You can also view the last method used to boot up the IOS device, such as someone executing the **reload** command or power-cycling the device.

Interface Information

The CCT certification objectives include objective 4.11, which is to identify and correct common network problems at layer 1 and layer 2. Layer 1 problems would be related to identifying physical connection issues such as an unconnected device cable. Layer 2 issues would be related to the layer 2 protocol configuration such as a serial link having HDLC or PPP configured properly on the serial interfaces.

In this section you will learn a number of commands that you can use to identify layer 1 and layer 2 problems, to determine whether an interface is configured for full or half duplex, and to verify the speed of the interface.

You typically will notice any problems with an interface when you enable it, because a status message states whether the interface is up (enabled with no problems) or down (unable to enable due to configuration errors). In Ethernet, a status message could be issued if the wrong cable type (crossover versus straight-through) is used, there is a mismatch in the speed or duplex settings, or a bad cable is used. This section will discuss how to diagnose these problems with the **show interfaces** command.

Viewing Interface Information

One of the most common commands that you will use on an IOS device is the **show interfaces** command. This command enables you to see the status and configuration of your interfaces, as well as some statistical information. Here is the syntax:

```
IOS> show interfaces [type [slot_#/]port_#]
```

If you don't specify a specific interface, the IOS device displays all of its interfaces—those enabled as well as those disabled. Here is an example of the output of this command on a router:

```
LA-R1>show interfaces g0/0
GigabitEthernet0/0 is up, line protocol is up (connected)
  Hardware is CN Gigabit Ethernet, address is 0004.9ab9.5601 (bia
0004.9ab9.5601)
  Internet address is 14.0.0.1/8
  MTU 1500 bytes, BW 1000000 Kbit, DLY 10 usec,
     reliability 255/255, txload 1/255, rxload 1/255
  Encapsulation ARPA, loopback not set
  Keepalive set (10 sec)
  Full-duplex, 100Mb/s, media type is RJ45
  output flow-control is unsupported, input flow-control is unsupported
  ARP type: ARPA, ARP Timeout 04:00:00,
  Last input 00:00:08, output 00:00:05, output hang never
  Last clearing of "show interface" counters never
  Input queue: 0/75/0 (size/max/drops); Total output drops: 0
  Queueing strategy: fifo
  Output queue :0/40 (size/max)
  5 minute input rate 0 bits/sec, 0 packets/sec
  5 minute output rate 0 bits/sec, 0 packets/sec
     0 packets input, 0 bytes, 0 no buffer
     Received 0 broadcasts, 0 runts, 0 giants, 0 throttles
     0 input errors, 0 CRC, 0 frame, 0 overrun, 0 ignored, 0 abort
     0 watchdog, 1017 multicast, 0 pause input
     0 input packets with dribble condition detected
     0 packets output, 0 bytes, 0 underruns
     0 output errors, 0 collisions, 1 interface resets
```

```
0 unknown protocol drops
0 babbles, 0 late collision, 0 deferred
0 lost carrier, 0 no carrier
0 output buffer failures, 0 output buffers swapped out
```

In the output, notice the information about the interface, such as the MAC address (layer 2 address), the IP address (layer 3 address), the maximum transmission unit (MTU), the encapsulation protocol (ARPA means Ethernet), and the duplex setting and speed on the interface.

Troubleshooting Interface Problems

One of the first things that you want to examine in this display is the status of the interface: **GigabitEthernet0/0 is up, line protocol is up (connected)**. The first **up** refers to the status of the physical layer, and the second **up** refers to the status of the data link layer.

Here are the possible values for the physical layer status:

- **Up**   The device is sensing a physical layer signal on the interface.

- **Down**   The device is not sensing a physical layer signal on the interface, a condition that can arise if the attached device is turned off, no cable is attached, or the wrong type of cable is being used.

- **Administratively down**   Use the **shutdown** command to disable the interface.

Here are the possible values for the data link layer status:

- **Up**   The data link layer is operational.

- **Down**   The data link layer is not operational, a condition that can be caused by missed keepalives on a serial link, no clocking, an incorrect encapsulation type, or a disabled physical layer.

NOTE   If the interface status is "up and up," the interface is operational. If the status is "up and down," this indicates a problem with the data link layer (layer 2) protocol such as a configuration error on the layer 2 protocol. If the status shows as "down and down," a physical layer problem (layer 1) exists, because the part indicating the layer 2 status will never show as up if the layer 1 part of the status is down. If the status is "administratively down and down," the interface was disabled with the **shutdown** command by one of the administrators. The "Hardware is" refers to the physical (layer 1) properties of the interface and the "Encapsulation" refers to the data link (layer 2) properties of the interface.

The second line of output from the **show interfaces** command shows the hardware interface type (in this example, it's a Gigabit Ethernet controller). This is followed by the MAC address on the interface. The third line shows the IP address and subnet mask configured on the interface (you won't see this on a layer 2 switch's interface). The fourth line shows the MTU Ethernet frame size as well as the routing protocol metrics. Notice the **BW** parameter in this line. Referred to as the *bandwidth* of the link, this is used by some routing protocols, such as Open Shortest Path First (OSPF) and Enhanced Interior Gateway Routing Protocol (EIGRP), when making routing decisions. For Gigabit Ethernet, this is 1,000,000 Kbps. The line after this refers to the layer 2 encapsulation (frame) type used; with Ethernet, this can be ARPA, but on a WAN interface you may see serial link protocols such as HDLC or PPP.

Table 7-4 explains some of the elements that you may see with the **show interfaces** command. Note that depending on the kind of IOS device and type of interface, the output displayed in the **show interfaces** command may differ slightly.

Element	Description
Address	The MAC address of the interface; BIA (burnt-in address) is the MAC address burnt into the Ethernet controller—this can be overridden with the Interface **mac-address** command.
Last input/output	The last time a packet was received on or sent out of the interface—can be used to determine whether the interface is operating or not.
Last clearing	The last time the **clear counters** command was executed on the interface.
Output queue	The number of packets waiting to be sent out the interface—the number after the slash (/) is the maximum size of the queue, followed by the number of packets dropped because the queue was full.
Input queue	The number of packets received on the interface and waiting to be processed—the number after the slash (/) is the maximum size of the queue, followed by the number of packets dropped because the queue was full.
No buffers (input)	The number of received packets dropped because the input buffer was full.
Runts (input)	Number of packets received that were less than the minimum for the encapsulation type (64 bytes for Ethernet).
Giants (input)	The number of packets received that were greater than the maximum allowed size (1518 bytes for Ethernet).
Input errors	The total number of input errors received on the interface.
CRC (input)	The number of packets received that had checksum errors.
Frame (input)	The number of packets received that had both CRC errors and cases where the length of the frame was not on a byte boundary.
Overruns (input)	The number of times the inbound packet rate exceeded the capabilities of the interface to process the traffic.
Ignored (input)	The number of inbound packets that were dropped because of the lack of input buffer space.
Aborts (input)	The number of received packets that were aborted.
Collisions (output)	The number of times the interface tried transmitting a packet, but a collision occurred—this should be less than 0.1 percent of total traffic leaving the interface.
Interface resets (output)	The number of times the interface changed state by going down and then coming back up.
Restarts (output)	The number of times the controller was reset because of errors—use the **show controllers** command to troubleshoot this problem.

Table 7-4 Explanation of the Elements in the **show interfaces** Command

EXAM TIP Be familiar with the output of the **show interfaces** command. The MTU size indicates the maximum packet size (not frame or segment).

In the following example, notice that there are a lot of input and CRC errors for the fa0/0 switchport:

```
Switch# show interfaces fa0/0
FastEthernet 0/1 is up, line protocol is up (connected)
  Hardware is MCI Ethernet, address is 0000.0c00.1234
  MTU 1500 bytes, BW 10000 Kbit, DLY 100000 usec, rely 255/255,
                  load 1/255
  Encapsulation ARPA, loopback not set, keepalive set (10 sec)
  Full-duplex, 100Mbps, media type is 10/100BaseTx
  input flow-control is off, output flow-control is unsupported
  Last input 0:00:00, output 0:00:00, output hang never
  Last clearing of "show interface" counters 0:00:00
  Output queue 0/40, 0 drops; input queue 0/75, 0 drops
  Five minute input rate 354000 bits/sec, 335 packets/sec
  Five minute output rate 357000 bits/sec, 328 packets/sec
     12375 packets input, 1900414 bytes, 0 no buffer
     Received 1133 broadcasts (0 multicasts)
     0 runts, 0 giants, 0 throttles
     735 input errors, 731 CRC, 0 frame, 0 overrun, 0 ignored, 0 abort
  .
  .
  .
```

Notice that the fa0/0 interface is configured for full-duplex 100 Mbps. If autosensing of the speed/duplex was used (which is the default), then the word *auto* would appear in the duplexing line. The culprit is probably a duplex mismatch on the other end.

 EXAM TIP Remember that if devices connected to a subnet can ping each other, but devices cannot ping the router connected to the same subnet, you can use the **show interfaces** command to verify that the interface is operational and that the router has the correct IP address configured on it.

WAN Serial Loopback Test

When troubleshooting connectivity over the WAN, you may need to perform a loopback test on the serial port of the Cisco device. A loopback test is a way to verify where the problem occurs with the WAN link: Is it on your side or is it with the service provider?

It is a great idea to start testing connectivity to the channel service unit/data service unit (CSU/DSU) by performing a CSU/DSU loopback test to verify your T1 link or your 56K link. If that is successful, you can then verify connectivity from the CSU/DSU to the service provider by performing a telco-assisted loopback test with the service provider.

Two types of loopback testing can be performed on the CSU/DSU:

- **Software** Use Cisco IOS commands to test functionality from the router to the CSU/DSU.
- **Hardware** Connect a loopback plug/cable to the CSU/DSU to perform the loopback test.

Let's walk through some commands you can use to troubleshoot the WAN interface and perform a software loopback test. First, you can see the hardware that exists in your device by using the **show inventory** command as follows:

```
Router>enable
Router#show inventory
NAME: "2811 chassis", DESCR: "2811 chassis, Hw Serial#: FTX1022A1ZJ, Hw
Revision: 52.57"
PID: CISCO2811        , VID: V02 , SN: FTX1022A1ZJ

NAME: "c2811 Motherboard with 2FE and integrated VPN", DESCR: "c2811
Motherboard with 2FE and integrated VPN"
PID: CISCO2811        , VID: V02 , SN: FOC1020257J

NAME: "9 Port FE Switch", DESCR: "9 Port FE Switch"
PID: HWIC-D-9ESW      , VID: VN/A, SN: FOC100131K6

NAME: "WAN Interface Card - DSU/CSU T1 Fractional (V2)", DESCR: "WAN
Interface Card - DSU/CSU T1 Fractional (V2)"
PID:                  , VID: 1.2, SN: FOC10174ES5
```

Notice in the **show inventory** command output that this is a 2800 series router that contains nine Fast Ethernet ports. You can also see that there is a WAN interface card—an internal CSU/DSU device. To see if there is a serial port created by the card, use the **show ip interface brief** command as follows:

```
Router#show ip interface brief
Interface              IP-Address      OK? Method Status        Protocol
(output cut for briefness)
Serial0/2/0            13.0.0.1        YES manual up            up
Vlan1                  unassigned      YES NVRAM  up            down
```

Notice the serial interface of S0/2/0. If you want to view details of that interface, use the **show interface s0/2/0** command:

```
Router#show interface s0/2/0
Serial0/2/0 is up, line protocol is up
  Hardware is GT96K with integrated T1 CSU/DSU
  MTU 1500 bytes, BW 1544 Kbit, DLY 20000 usec,
     reliability 255/255, txload 1/255, rxload 1/255
  Encapsulation HDLC, loopback not set
  Keepalive set (10 sec)
 (output cut for briefness)
```

In this output you can see that the layer 1 and layer 2 components are fine (they are up). The serial port exists due to an integrated CSU/DSU, and the encapsulation protocol is HDLC. The final point to notice is that the loopback is not set. To perform the loopback test on this interface, you need to enable loopback. To do that, use these commands:

```
Router#config term
Router(config)#interface s0/2/0
Router(config-if)#loopback ?
  dte     Loopback on the router side of the CSU/DSU
  line    Loopback on the line side of the CSU/DSU
  remote  Loopback on the remote side of the CSU/DSU
```

To enable loopback, you navigate to the interface first. Then you can use the **loopback** command and specify what you want to perform the loopback test on. Notice that if you use the **dte** parameter, you are testing the router side of the CSU/DSU, but if you set the **line** parameter, you are testing the provider's side of the CSU/DSU. If you set the parameter to **remote**, you are testing connectivity to the other end of the WAN link. For this discussion, we are testing from the router (the DTE device) to the CSU/DSU:

```
Router(config-if)#loopback dte
Loopback in progress
```

To verify that loopback is enabled, use the **show interface** command again on the serial port. You should see the message "loopback is set" instead of "loopback not set."

Now you can use the extended ping feature of the Cisco device to test connectivity. The extended ping is a special ping feature that gives you control over the ping messages that are sent by your Cisco device and gives you a number of advanced options. To use the extended ping, go into privileged EXEC mode and use the **ping** command with no parameters. The Cisco device will prompt you for a number of settings, such as giving you a chance to set the source and destination addresses for the ping messages, the number of ping messages to send, and the size of the messages:

```
Router#ping
Protocol [ip]:
Target IP address: 13.0.0.1
Repeat count [5]: 50
Datagram size [100]: 1500
Timeout in seconds [2]:
Extended commands [n]: y
Source address or interface: 13.0.0.1
Type of service [0]:
Set DF bit in IP header? [no]:
Validate reply data? [no]:
Data pattern [0xABCD]:
Loose, Strict, Record, Timestamp, Verbose[none]:
Sweep range of sizes [n]:
Type escape sequence to abort.
Sending 50, 1500-byte ICMP Echos to 13.0.0.1, timeout is 2 seconds:
Packet sent with a source address of 13.0.0.1
!!!!!!!!!!!!!!!!!!!!!!!!!!!!!!!!!!!!!!!!!!!!!!!!!!!
Success rate is 100 percent (50/50), round-trip min/avg/max = 31/39/47 ms
Router#
```

Note that the loopback testing is intrusive to your WAN link, so you should turn it off after testing by navigating to the interface and using the **no loopback dte** command.

Exercise 7-4: Viewing Your Configuration

In this exercise you will continue with the configuration of the previous exercises and verify the configuration by using a number of **show** commands. See Figure 7-5.

1. Ensure that you are consoled into VAN-R1.

2. To view the configuration of the interfaces and their statuses, use the **show ip interface brief** command. Review the output.

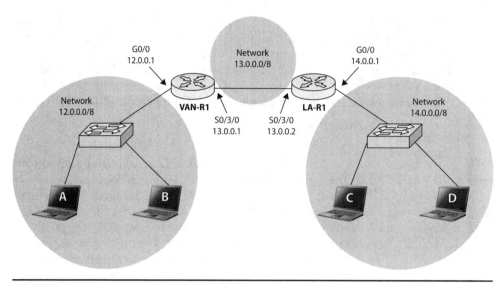

Figure 7-5   Network topology for exercise

3. To view the status of the g0/0 interface including its IP address and whether it is functioning at layer 1 and layer 2, use the **show interfaces g0/0** command. Review the output.

4. To view whether your serial port is a DCE or DTE device, use the **show controllers s0/3/0** command. Review the output.

5. Change the hostname of the router to *VAN-TEMP*.

6. To view your current configuration in RAM, use the **show running-config** command. Review the output. You should see the hostname VAN-TEMP line.

7. To view the configuration of NVRAM, use the **show startup-config** command. Review the output. You should see that this configuration still has the hostname of VAN-R1. This is because you have not saved your changes to NVRAM.

8. Save your changes to NVRAM with the **write** command.

9. Look at your running configuration and your startup configuration again. They should both have the hostname of VAN-TEMP.

10. Change your hostname back to *VAN-R1*.

11. Save your changes to NVRAM with the **write** command.

 VIDEO   7.10. The digital resources that accompany this book contain a multimedia demonstration of using ping on your Cisco device.

Chapter Review

This chapter introduced you to the IOS CLI and how to make basic configurations on Cisco's switches and routers. Your terminal emulator on your PC will need to be configured for 9600 bps, 8 data bits, 1 stop bit, no parity, and no flow control for a console connection.

The nomenclature of a switch interface is this: *type slot_#/port_#*. The type of interface is the media type, such as **Ethernet, FastEthernet,** or **GigabitEthernet**. Following this is the slot number. For all fixed interfaces on the 2960 switches, the slot number is always *0*. All switch port numbers start at *1* and work their way up. The nomenclature of a router interface is either **type** *slot_#/port_#* or **type** *port_#*. The type of interface is the media type, such as **Ethernet**, **FastEthernet**, **GigabitEthernet**, and **Serial**, as well as many others. Following this is the slot number for modular routers. The slot numbers start at *0* and work their way up. All port router numbers within a slot and type start at *0* and work their way up, which is different from the Catalyst switches.

IOS provides a CLI with many features, including context-sensitive help accessed by using **help** or **?**, command-line history, and advanced editing features, which are available at all modes, including the user EXEC, privileged EXEC, and configuration modes. Within configuration mode are subconfiguration modes. To access privileged EXEC mode, use the **enable** command, and to access configuration mode, use **configure terminal**.

You can protect access to your Cisco device by assigning user EXEC and privileged EXEC passwords. Use the line subconfiguration mode **password** command and the **enable secret** or **enable password** command for the two respective levels. The **service password-encryption** command encrypts clear-text passwords on the IOS device. The **banner motd** command displays a login banner before any username or password prompt.

To view the active configuration, use the **show running-config** command. On IOS devices, you must manually save your configuration to NVRAM with the **copy running-config startup-config** command.

Switch interfaces are enabled by default, but router interfaces need to be enabled using the **no shutdown** command. For DCE serial interfaces, routers need a clock rate applied with the **clock rate** command. Use the **show interfaces** command to view the status and configuration of your interfaces.

Quick Review

- In your terminal emulation package, set the speed to 9600 bps, data bits to 8, stop bits to 1, parity to none, and flow control to none.
- Interfaces have a name, possibly a slot number, and a port number. The slot number of the 2960 is *0*; port numbers start at *1*. Router slot numbers begin with *0*; port numbers start at *0* and restart with each type within each slot.

Command-Line Interface (CLI)

- Four CLI access modes exist: user EXEC (**IOS>**), privileged EXEC (**IOS#**), configuration (**IOS(config)#**), and ROMMON mode (**>**).

- The **enable** command moves you from user EXEC to privileged EXEC mode. The **exit** command logs you out of an IOS device.

IOS Basics

- Use the **?** to display context-sensitive help in any mode of a router; it lists available commands and their valid parameters.

- If you execute a command and see the resulting output of the command, be sure to examine the output to ensure that no error is present in the command you entered.

- You can use the arrow keys on your keyboard to recall and edit commands.

- Use the TAB key to autocomplete a command.

Basic IOS Configuration

- Use the privileged EXEC **configure terminal** command to enter configuration mode.

- The **hostname** command assigns a locally significant name to the router. The **no** parameter negates/undoes a configuration change.

- The **no shutdown** command enables an interface; interfaces on switches are enabled by default, but router interfaces are disabled. The **clock rate** command specifies the speed of a DCE serial interface on a router and is required when connecting two serial interfaces, back-to-back, without using external clocking devices such as CSU/DSUs. Use the **show controller** command to verify whether or not the serial interface is a DTE or DCE.

Basic IOS Security Configuration

- Lines (access to user EXEC mode) can be secured with the **password** command. Access to privileged EXEC mode can be secured with either the **enable password** or **enable secret** command; the former is unencrypted and the latter is strongly encrypted.

- Clear-text passwords can be encrypted with the **service password-encryption** command.

- You can display a login banner before a username/password prompt with the **banner motd** command; after the authentication takes place and before the user sees an EXEC prompt, you can display a banner with the **banner exec** command.

IOS Operation and Verification

- You must be at privileged EXEC mode to manipulate configuration files. The **show running-config** command displays the running configuration in RAM. The **show startup-config** command displays the backed-up configuration in NVRAM.

- IOS devices do not automatically save their configurations from RAM to NVRAM; use the **copy running-config startup-config** command to do this.

- Use the **show version** command to see the IOS version of the device as well as its hardware characteristics.

- The **show interfaces** command is used to see the operational status of the physical and data link layers of an IOS device's interface.

Questions

The following questions will help you measure your understanding of the material presented in this chapter. Read all the choices carefully, as there may be more than one correct answer. Choose the correct answer(s) for each question.

1. A _____ cable is used to connect to the console port of your IOS device.

2. Match the device modes with the appropriate command or task.

Device Mode	Command or Task
A. User EXEC	_____ **show running-config**
B. Privileged EXEC	_____ **enable**
C. Global configuration	_____ Password recovery
D. ROMMON	_____ **line vty 0 4**

3. Which of the following enable you to use context-sensitive help? (Choose two.)

   A. **help**

   B. **show**

   C. **?**

   D. **verify**

4. Which control sequence takes you to the beginning of the CLI?

   A. CTRL-E

   B. CTRL-A

   C. ESC-B

   D. CTRL-B

5. Enter the IOS command that will change the device name to *Perimeter*: _____.

6. Match the following commands to their description.

Command	Description
A. shutdown	____ Shows if an interface is DTE/DCE
B. show controller	____ Specifies the use of an IOS database for authentication
C. login local	____ Specifies the speed of a serial interface
D. clock rate	____ Disables an interface

7. You execute the **line console 0** command from configuration mode. What will the router's prompt be?

   A. **Router(config)#**

   B. **Router(config-line)#**

   C. **Router(config-interface)#**

   D. **Router#(config-if)**

8. Enter the IOS command that will encrypt all unencrypted passwords: _____.

9. Which IOS command would display a message of "This is Router5" after a user logs in?

   A. **banner motd $**

   B. **login exec $**

   C. **banner exec $**

   D. **login motd $**

10. You examine your interfaces, and the GigabitEthernet 0/0 interface status says "GigabitEthernet 0 is up, line protocol is down." What does this indicate?

   A. A physical layer problem

   B. A data link layer problem

   C. A network layer problem

   D. No problem

11. What IOS command saves the active configuration to NVRAM?

   A. **copy nvram startup-config**

   B. **copy startup-config running-config**

   C. **copy running-config nvram**

   D. **copy running-config startup-config**

Performance-based Questions

The Cisco exams include performance-based questions that require you to drag a box from the left side of the screen to its proper place on the right side of the screen to answer the question. The following are some sample performance-based questions related to this chapter.

1. Using the following exhibit, draw a line from the description to the appropriate command for that description. Not all descriptions are used.

Description

Manually assigns an IP address to an interface

Configures the interface to receive an IP address from the DHCP server

Configured on the DEC end of a point-to-point serial link

Restricts the VTY ports to accept only SSH traffic

Configures a DHCP server

Configures the console to timeout after 5 minutes of inactivity

Command

Router(config-line)# exec-timeout 5.0

Router(config-line)# transport input ssh

Router(config-if)#ip address 14.0.0.1 255.0.0.0

Router(config-if)#ip address dhcp

Router(config-if)#clock rate 64000

2. Using the following exhibit, write each of the commands found on the left at the top of the box that identifies the output for that command.

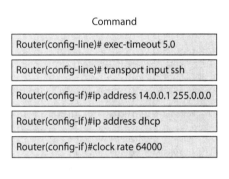

```
Interface Serial0/3/0
Hardware is PowerQUICC MPC860
DCE V.35, clock rate 64000
idb at 0x81081AC4, driver data structure at 0x81084AC0
SCC Registers:
General [GSMR]=0x2:0x00000000, Protocol-specific [PSMR]=0x8
Events [SCCE]=0x0000, Mask [SCCM]=0x0000. Status [SCCS]=0x00
Transmit on Demand [TODR]=0x0, Data Sync [DSR]=0x7E7E
```

```
Building configuration...

Current configuration : 959 bytes
!
version 15.1
no service timestamps log datetime msec
no service timestamps debug datetime msec
no service password-encryption
!
hostname VAN-R1
!
```

VAN-R1# show running-config

VAN-R1#show interface g0/0

VAN-R1#show ip interface brief

VAN-R1# show controllers s0/3/0

```
Interface        IP-Address      OK? Method Status                  Protocol
GigabitEthernet0/0   12.0.0.1    YES manual up                      up
Serial0/3/0          13.0.0.1    YES manual up                      up
Serial0/3/1          unassigned  YES unset  administratively down   down
Vlan1                unassigned  YES unset  administratively down   down
```

```
GigabitEthernet0/0 is up, line protocol is up (connected)
  Hardware is CN Gigabit Ethernet, address is 0009.7c04.ab01 (bia 0009.7c04.ab01)
  Internet address is 12.0.0.1/8
  MTU 1500 bytes, BW 1000000 Kbit, DLY 10 usec,
     reliability 255/255, txload 1/255, rxload 1/255
  Encapsulation ARPA, loopback not set
  Keepalive set (10 sec)
  Full-duplex, 100Mb/s, media type is RJ45
  output flow-control is unsupported, input flow-control is unsupported
```

Answers

1. A *rollover* cable is used to connect to the console port of your IOS device. It provides your initial access to an IOS device via the console port/line.

2. The following shows the matchup of mode with the command or task:

Device Mode	Command or Task
A. User EXEC	**B** show running-config
B. Privileged EXEC	**A** enable
C. Global configuration	**D** Password recovery
D. ROMMON	**C** line vty 0 4

3. **A** and **C.** The **?** and **help** commands enable you to use the context-sensitive help feature.

4. **B.** Pressing CTRL-A takes you to the beginning of the CLI.

5. The **hostname Perimeter** command will change the device name to *Perimeter*.

6. The **show controller** command shows whether an interface is DTE/DCE; **shutdown** disables an interface; **login local** specifies the use of an IOS database for authentication; **clock rate** specifies the speed of a serial interface. The following shows the correct command with its definition:

Command	Description
A. shutdown	**B** Shows if an interface is DTE/DCE
B. show controller	**C** Specifies the use of an IOS database for authentication
C. login local	**D** Specifies the speed of a serial interface
D. clock rate	**A** Disables an interface

7. **B.** When you execute the **line console 0** command, your prompt changes to **Router(config-line)#**.

8. The **service password-encryption** command will encrypt unencrypted passwords.

9. **C.** The **banner exec** command displays a banner after the user authenticates, but before the EXEC prompt is displayed.

10. **B.** The "…line protocol is down" message refers to a problem in the data link layer.

11. **D.** Use the **copy running-config startup-config** command to back up your configuration from RAM to NVRAM.

Performance-based Answers

The following are the answers to the performance-based questions for this chapter. Note that on the real Cisco exams it is common to drag the items from the left side of the screen to the matching items on the right side of the screen.

1. The following shows the matching commands for each description.

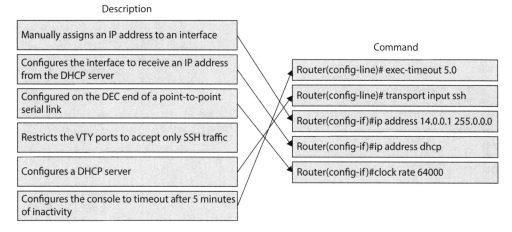

2. The following shows the command associated with each of the boxes showing command output.

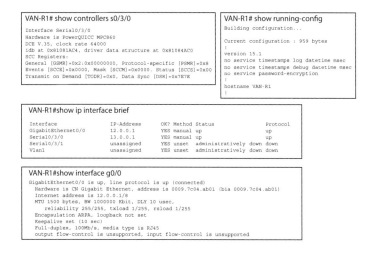

Cisco Device Management

In this chapter, you will

- Learn about router configuration files
- Learn how to make changes in your network
- Get familiar with IOS image files
- Learn how to gain remote access to your Cisco device
- Learn how to perform configuration register changes and password recovery
- Learn how to troubleshoot and debug
- Learn about licensing management

This chapter covers important IOS features that you can use to manage your IOS device. Many of these features are supported across all IOS devices, but some are supported on only certain devices. This chapter offers an in-depth discussion of configuration files. It also discusses how to upgrade your IOS device and remotely access it via Secure Shell (SSH). You can use many tools on your IOS device for troubleshooting connection problems, including the Cisco Discovery Protocol (CDP), ping, traceroute, telnet, and debug. These tools are discussed toward the end of the chapter.

Router Configuration Files

You had a basic introduction to configuration files in Chapter 7. Remember that a configuration file contains the commands used to configure an IOS device. Configuration files are typically located in one of three places: RAM, NVRAM, and/or an external server, such as a TFTP, FTP, HTTP, or Secure Copy Protocol (SCP) server. The configuration that the router is currently using is in RAM. You can back up or save this configuration either to NVRAM or to an external server.

As you may recall from Chapter 7, the commands *related* to configuration files, even **show** commands, require you to be working in privileged EXEC mode. Also, the running configuration of an IOS device is not automatically saved to NVRAM—you must manually do this by issuing the **copy running-config startup-config** command. The following sections show you how to manipulate your configuration files.

Saving Configuration Files

Chapter 7 explained how to save your configuration from RAM to NVRAM with the **copy running-config startup-config** command. When you execute this command, whatever filename (the default is *startup-config*) you are copying to in NVRAM is completely overwritten. If you want to keep an old copy *and* a newer one in NVRAM, you'll need to specify a name other than startup-config. Note that the **copy** command has two parameters: the first parameter refers to where the source information is (where you want to copy from) and the second parameter refers to where the destination is (where you want to copy to).

You can copy your running-config or startup-config configuration file to flash, like this:

```
IOS# copy running-config flash:file_name
IOS# copy startup-config flash:file_name
```

This enables you to have multiple configuration files stored locally on your IOS device; by default, when booting up, your IOS device will use the startup-config file in NVRAM to load its configuration.

 TIP   It is not a common practice to copy configuration files to flash, and for exam purposes, this is not where you back up configuration files. However, I commonly do this when an FTP or TFTP server currently isn't available.

You can also back up your configuration to an external server. You must have the server software on a server or PC and IP configured correctly on your IOS device to access the server. The syntax looks like this on your IOS device:

```
IOS# copy running-config URL_location
```

So, for example, to back up your configuration file to a TFTP server, the configuration would look like this:

```
IOS# copy running-config tftp://192.168.1.10/mybackupfile.txt
```

The configuration is backed up to an ASCII text file. If you don't supply the full URL, just the protocol information, you'll be prompted for the additional information:

```
IOS# copy running-config tftp
Address or name of remote host []? 192.168.1.10
Destination filename [router-confg]? mybackupfile.cfg
!!
781 bytes copied in 5.8 secs (156 bytes/sec)
IOS#
```

If the filename already exists on the server, the server *overwrites* the old file. After entering this information, you should see bang symbols (!) indicating the successful transfer of

UDP segments to the TFTP server. If you see periods (.), this indicates an unsuccessful transfer. Plus, upon a successful transfer, you should also see how many bytes were copied to the server.

 VIDEO 8.01. The digital resources that accompany this book contain a multimedia demonstration of backing up your router configuration to a TFTP server.

Restoring Configuration Files

There may be situations in which you have misconfigured your router or switch and want to reload a saved configuration file into your Cisco device. You can do this by reversing the source and destination information in the **copy** command:

```
IOS# copy URL_location running-config
IOS# copy URL_location startup-config
```

You can use three variations of the **copy** command to restore your configuration. A TFTP server is used in this example for the first two options. In the first example, the configuration file is copied from a TFTP server to NVRAM (the startup-config file); if the file already exists in NVRAM, it will be overwritten:

```
IOS# copy tftp startup-config
Address or name of remote host []? 192.168.1.10
Source filename []? mybackupfile.cfg
Destination filename [startup-config]?
Accessing tftp://192.168.1.10/mybackupfile.cfg...
Loading mybackupfile.cfg from 192.168.1.10 (via Ethernet0): !
[OK - 781/1024 bytes]
[OK]
781 bytes copied in 11.216 secs (71 bytes/sec)
```

 VIDEO 8.02. The digital resources that accompany this book contain a multimedia demonstration of restoring your router configuration.

You can also restore your configuration from a TFTP server to active memory:

```
IOS# copy tftp running-config
```

There is one main difference between moving the configuration from TFTP to NVRAM and moving it from TFTP to RAM. With the former method, the file in NVRAM is replaced with the one being copied; with the latter method, a *merge* process is used. During a merge process, IOS updates commands that are common to both places—the new file and in RAM. IOS also executes any new commands it finds in the uploaded configuration file and adds them to running-config. However, IOS does not delete any commands in RAM that it does not find in the uploaded configuration file. In other words, this is *not* a replacement process. As an example, assume that you have a configuration file on a TFTP server that has *Setting1* and *Setting2* in it, but your RAM configuration has *Setting2* and *Setting3*. In this example, the router updates the *Setting2*, adds the *Setting1*, but leaves *Setting3* commands as they are.

This process is also true if you want to restore your configuration from NVRAM to RAM with this command (the third restore option):

```
IOS# copy startup-config running-config
```

If your backed-up configuration is in flash, use this syntax to restore it:

```
IOS# copy flash:file_name running-config|startup-config
```

 EXAM TIP   For the Cisco CCT exam, remember that the **copy** command is used to save your configuration and backup and restore configuration files. Use **copy running-config startup-config** to save your configuration changes to NVRAM, and use **copy running-config tftp** to back up your configuration to a TFTP server. The **copy startup-config running-config** and **copy tftp running-config** or **copy tftp startup-config** commands restore the configuration file. The **erase startup-config** command deletes the configuration file.

Creating and Deleting Configuration Files

Along with knowing how to back up and restore configuration files, you also need to know how to create and delete them. Actually, you already know how to create a basic configuration file by going into configuration mode with the privileged EXEC **configure terminal** command. When you are executing commands within this mode (whether by typing them or pasting them in), IOS is using a merge process (unless you use the **no** parameter for a command to delete or negate it).

You can also delete your configuration file in the startup-config file in NVRAM by using the following command:

```
IOS# erase startup-config
IOS# erase nvram
```

You can also use the **write erase** command to delete your startup configuration.

To verify the erasure, use the **show startup-config** command. If the startup-config was erased, you will get the following message when you try to show the startup-config:

```
IOS# show startup-config
%% Non-volatile configuration memory is not present
```

Configuration File Nomenclature

Starting with IOS 12.0 and later, Cisco introduced command and naming nomenclatures that follow Cisco IOS File System (IFS) guidelines (what you are used to when entering a URL in a web browser address text box). Therefore, instead of entering a command and having a router prompt you for additional information, such as the IP address of a TFTP server and the filename, you can now put all of this information on a single command line. Commands that reference configuration files and IOS images contain prefixes in front of the file type, as shown in Table 8-1.

Let's take a look at an example. Suppose you want to back up your router's configuration from RAM to NVRAM. With the new syntax, you could use the following:

```
IOS# copy system:running-config nvram:startup-config
```

You don't always have to include the type; for instance, instead of the preceding example, you could have used this:

```
IOS# copy running-config startup-config
```

In many cases, IOS knows, based on the name of the file, which location you're referring to. For example, when you use running-config, IOS assumes you're referring to RAM, or system:, as the location.

To view the active configuration, you can use this command:

```
IOS# more system:running-config
```

If you want to delete a file in flash, such as a backed-up configuration file, use the following command:

```
IOS# delete flash:file_name
```

Location	Description
bootflash	Bootflash memory
flash	Flash memory on the motherboard
flh	Flash load helper log files
ftp	FTP server
nvram	Nonvolatile RAM (NVRAM)
rcp	Remote Copy Protocol (RCP) server
scp	Secure Copy (SCP) server – uses RCP through an SSH tunnel
slot0	PCMCIA slot 0
slot1	PCMCIA slot 1
system	RAM
tftp	TFTP server

Table 8-1   File Locations

Location (From)	Location (To)	Command	IOS Process
RAM	NVRAM	**copy running-config startup-config**	Overwrite
RAM	TFTP	**copy running-config tftp**	Overwrite
NVRAM	RAM	**copy startup-config running-config**	Merge
NVRAM	TFTP	**copy startup-config tftp**	Overwrite
TFTP	RAM	**copy tftp running-config**	Merge
TFTP	NVRAM	**copy tftp startup-config**	Overwrite
CLI	RAM	**configure terminal**	Merge

Table 8-2   Overview of IOS Process When Dealing with Configuration Files

You'll be asked to verify whether you want to delete the file. You can also use this command to delete any file in flash.

NOTE   The older style of entering configuration and IOS commands is still supported along with the new one. One command that I constantly use in production environments is the **write memory** command, which can be abbreviated as **wr**. This performs the equivalent of the **copy running-config startup-config** command, but it requires only two keystrokes to perform! Please note, however, that the older command syntax is not supported on Cisco exams!

Review of Configuration Files

It is important that you understand what action IOS will take when it is either backing up or restoring a configuration file to a particular location. Table 8-2 summarizes this information for the routers.

EXAM TIP   Here is a quick way of remembering whether IOS is using a merge or overwrite process. Anything copied into RAM uses a merge process, whereas any other copy operation uses an overwrite process. Be familiar with the commands listed in Table 8-2 and what they do for the Cisco CCT exam.

Exercise 8-1: Manipulating Your Router's Configuration Files

In this exercise you will work with the configuration files of your Cisco device. You will first look at your configuration files, make a change to your configuration, and then save the change to NVRAM. Here's the diagram of our lab environment:

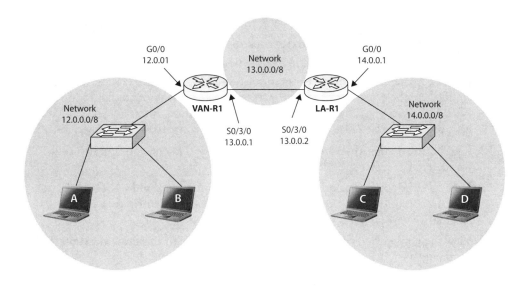

1. Ensure that all physical components such as routers and switches are connected as per the network diagram, and then power on the devices.

2. Connect your workstation to the console port of the router that will become VAN-R1. Then launch PuTTY, choose Serial connection, set the correct COM port, and choose Open.

3. Press ENTER in the PuTTY window to open a prompt on your Cisco device.

4. Access VAN-R1's Privileged EXEC mode and view the running configuration by using the following commands:

```
VAN-R1>enable
VAN-R1#show running-config
```

Notice the hostname in running-config.

5. View the contents of NVRAM by using the **show startup-config** command.

Notice that the hostname in startup-config is the same as the hostname setting in running-config.

6. Change the hostname to *Test* with the following commands:

```
VAN-R1#config term
Enter configuration commands, one per line.  End with CNTL/Z.
VAN-R1(config)#hostname Test
Test(config)#
```

7. Compare the contents of NVRAM and the running-config again and notice that the change was made in running-config, but not startup-config.

Hostname in running config: _____

Hostname in startup config: _____

8. Save your router's active configuration to NVRAM by using the **copy running-config startup-config** command. Alternatively, you could use the **write** command.

9. Verify that the setting is saved to NVRAM by using **show startup-config**.

10. Change the hostname on the router back to VAN-R1. This is changed in running-config, but not startup-config, until you use the **copy** command again.

11. Before copying the running-config to startup-config, practice erasing startup-config. Use the **erase startup-config** command to erase your configuration in NVRAM. Press ENTER when asked to confirm the erase. Alternatively, you could have used the **write erase** command to delete the contents of NVRAM.

12. Use the **show startup-config** command to verify that the configuration file was deleted.

13. Now save the configuration file from RAM (running-config) to NVRAM (startup-config) with the **copy running-config startup-config** command. Alternatively, you could use the **write** command.

14. View the newly saved configuration file in NVRAM with the **show startup-config** command.

Saving the configuration to startup-config (NVRAM) means that when you restart your device, the configuration settings are retained.

Changes in Your Network

When you decide to make changes to your network, including the addition or deletion of devices, you should always do some preparation work *before* you make the changes. Making changes can cause things to malfunction or not function at all, so you should always prepare beforehand. The following two sections cover the basics of handling changes.

 TIP Remember that it is much easier to restore a backup copy than it is to re-create something from scratch. Also, whenever you make changes, always test the change to ensure that your Cisco device is performing as expected.

Adding Devices

Before you add an IOS device to your network, gather the following information and perform the following tasks:

1. Decide which IP address you'll assign to the device for management purposes.

2. Configure the ports of the device, including the console and virtual type terminal (VTY) ports.

3. Set up your passwords for User and Privileged EXEC access.

4. Assign the appropriate IP addresses to the device's interface(s).

5. Create a basic configuration on the device so that it can perform its job.

Changing Devices

You will constantly be making configuration changes to your network to enhance performance and security. *Before* you make any changes to your network, you should *always* back up your configuration files. Likewise, before you perform a software upgrade on your Cisco device, you should always back up the old IOS image.

You should check a few things before loading the new image on your IOS device. Ask yourself the following before proceeding to load the new image: First, does the new image contain all of the features that your previous image had? Or does it contain at least the features you need? Also, does your IOS device have enough flash *and* RAM to store and load the IOS image?

At times, you may need to upgrade hardware or add a new module to your Cisco device. Some devices require that you turn them off before doing the upgrade, while other devices can stay powered on.

 CAUTION   It is extremely important that you read the installation manual that comes with the hardware before performing an installation. If you install a hardware component into a device that requires that the device be turned off, and the device is running, you could damage your new component or, worse, electrocute yourself.

IOS Image Files

The default location of IOS images is in flash. On some IOS devices, flash is built into the motherboard, some use PCMCIA cards for storage, and some use a combination of both. At times, you will have to deal with the device's flash when you want to perform an upgrade, for instance.

To view your files in flash, use the **show flash** command:

```
IOS# show flash
-#- --length-- -----date/time------ path
1              0 Sep 18 2007 15:42:20 +00:00 .Trashes
2           4096 Sep 18 2007 15:42:20 +00:00 ._.Trashes
3          12292 Sep 18 2007 15:55:12 +00:00 .DS_Store
4           1159 Sep 9 2007 18:01:42 +00:00 udp.phdf
5        4787200 Oct 3 2007 14:33:50 +00:00 sdm.tar
6           2679 Sep 9 2007 18:01:28 +00:00 ip.phdf
7         113152 Oct 3 2007 14:34:02 +00:00 home.tar
8           2227 Dec 4 2007 16:02:28 +00:00 pre_autosec.cfg
.
.
.
16      23787192 Sep 9 2007 17:45:30 +00:00
                        c1841-advipservicesk9-mz.124-6.T7.bin
.
.
.
31946752 bytes available (31922176 bytes used)
```

In this example, you can see that a router's flash holds many files. Below the list of files, you can see how much flash is used (about 32MB), how much is available (about 32MB), and the total amount of flash on the router (64MB). You can also see how much flash you have installed on your IOS device with the **show version** command.

 EXAM TIP For the Cisco CCT exam, remember you can use the **show flash**, **show version**, or **dir** command to see how much flash memory is installed on your IOS device. You should also know how to verify the amount of free space in flash.

In addition to using the **show flash** command, you can also use the **dir** command to see how much flash memory is available on your IOS device:

```
IOS# dir
Directory of flash:/
    1  drw-          0  Sep 18 2007 15:42:20 +00:00  .Trashes
    2  -rw-       4096  Sep 18 2007 15:42:20 +00:00  ._.Trashes
.
.
.
16  -rw-   23787192  Sep 9 2007 17:45:30 +00:00
                              c1841-advipservicesk9-mz.124-6.T7.bin
63868928 bytes total (31946752 bytes free)
```

In this example, the amount of available flash is 31,946,752 bytes—you need to ensure that there is enough flash available before adding files to flash.

 VIDEO 8.03. The digital resources that accompany this book contain a multimedia demonstration of viewing the contents of flash memory.

Naming Conventions for IOS Images

Cisco has implemented a naming convention for its IOS images, which enables you to see the platform, software version, and features included in the image just by looking at the image filename. As an example, consider the image name from the preceding **show flash** command, c1841-advipservicesk9-mz.124-6.T7.bin, which is from a router. Here's an explanation of the nomenclature that Cisco uses for IOS image filenames:

- **c1841** Refers to the name of the platform on which the image will run. This is important, because different router models have different processors, and an image compiled for one processor or router model will typically *not* run on a different model. Therefore, it is very important that you load the appropriate image on your device.

- **advipservicesk9** Refers to the features included in this IOS version, commonly referred to as the *feature set*. In this example, IOS is the advanced IP services and *k9* refers to the inclusion of encryption support.

- **mz or z**   Means that the image is compressed and must be uncompressed before loading/running. If you see *l* (the letter *l*, not the number *1*) here, this indicates where the IOS image is run from. The *l* indicates that it is a relocatable image and that the image can be run from RAM. Remember that some images can run directly from flash, depending on the router model.

- **124-6.T7**   Indicates the software version number of IOS. In this instance, the version is 12.4(6)T7. Image filenames with *T* indicate new features, and those without *T* indicate the mainline (only bug fixes are made to it).

- **.bin**   At the end of the filename, indicates that this is a binary image.

 NOTE   The naming nomenclature discussed here applies to IOS images that are either included on your IOS device when you buy it from Cisco or applied when you download them from Cisco's web site. However, the name, in and of itself, has no bearing on the actual operation of IOS when it is loaded on your IOS device. For instance, you can download an image from Cisco and rename it myciscoos.bin, and this will have no impact on the IOS device's performance.

Before Upgrading the IOS Image

This section and the next discuss how to upgrade and back up the IOS software (not the config) on your router. Before you upgrade the IOS on your device, you should first back up the existing image to an external server, for two reasons: First, your flash may not be large enough to support two images—the old one and the new. If you load the new one and you experience problems with it, you'll probably want to load the old image back onto your device. Second, Cisco doesn't keep every software version available on its web site. Older versions of IOS are hard to locate, so if you are upgrading from an old version of IOS, I would highly recommend backing it up first.

You can back up your Cisco IOS (and configuration files) to a TFTP server or to an FTP server. Although both are File Transfer Protocols, they do differ in their underlining use. TFTP uses UDP port 69 and does not require authentication (a username and password) to connect to the TFTP server. FTP uses TCP port 21 (command channel) and TCP port 20 (data channel) and does use authentication by having the person connecting supply a username and password that is configured on the server.

 EXAM TIP   For the Cisco exams remember that TFTP uses UDP port 69 and does not require authentication, while FTP uses TCP port 21/20 and does require authentication.

Creating the TFTP Server

Before backing up your IOS or configuration files to a TFTP server, you must first install a TFTP server! The great news is that you can download and install free TFTP server software on a desktop computer or a laptop (you don't actually need a physical server).

Figure 8-1
SolarWinds TFTP
Server software
message

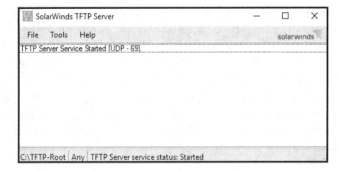

There are many free versions of TFTP server software out there, but I like to use Solar-Winds TFTP server software that you can download from this URL:

https://www.solarwinds.com/free-tools/free-tftp-server

You will need to register when downloading by filling out the form, but once you do that, you'll see the link to download the software.

Here are the steps to install the TFTP server software:

1. Download the TFTP server software.

2. Install the TFTP server software.

3. Configure the host-based firewall on the TFTP server to allow UDP port 69 traffic through to the system (that is the port used by TFTP which your firewall may block by default).

4. Verify that the TFTP software is running.

After downloading the software, you can install it on a system such as a server, desktop, or laptop—wherever you would like to store a backup of the configuration files and the Cisco IOS. After installing the software, you should ensure that you configure your host-based firewall to allow UDP port 69 traffic through to the system.

Before trying to back up the configuration of a device, or the IOS, to the newly installed TFTP server, verify that the server software is running. You can launch the SolarWinds TFTP server software by clicking the Start button and then typing **TFTP**. You should see the program called TFTP Server. Choose the program to launch it. The TFTP server displays notifications throughout the process. You can see that the server is running by the message in the status bar of the window shown in Figure 8-1.

Verifying Server Information

Before you back up your IOS image to an external server, ask the following questions to determine whether you're ready to go:

- Is the server reachable (test with the **ping** command)?

- Are you able to connect to the port? For example, with TFTP it would be UDP port 69.

- Is there enough disk space on the server to hold the IOS image?
- Does the server support the file nomenclature that you want to use?

Once you have performed these checks, you are ready to continue with the backup process.

Exercise 8-2: Installing TFTP Software

In this exercise you will download the SolarWinds TFTP software and install it on a Windows 10 system to back up your configuration and later back up your Cisco IOS. You will install the TFTP server on a Windows 10 system with the IP address of 12.0.0.100, as shown in the following network diagram:

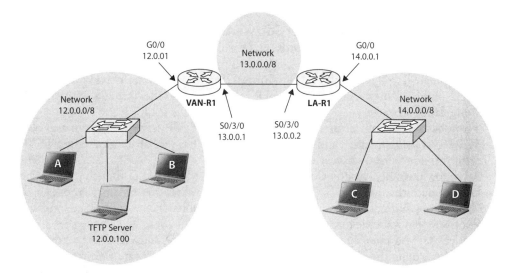

1. Ensure that you have added a Windows 10 system to the Vancouver office network with the IP address of 12.0.0.100.

2. On your Windows 10 system, navigate to https://www.solarwinds.com/free-tools/ free-tftp-server and download SolarWinds free TFTP server software.

3. Install the TFTP Server software on your Windows 10 system.

4. Create a firewall rule on your Windows firewall to open UDP port 69.

5. Launch the TFTP server software and ensure that it says that it is Started in the status bar.

6. Note in the status bar that the folder for the TFTP server is c:\TFTP-Root. This is the folder that uploaded IOS images and configuration files will be saved to.

Figure 8-2
Tftpd64 server software interface

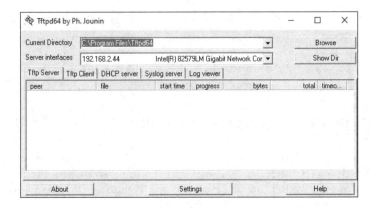

Using TFTPD32/TFTPD64 Server Software

Although I like to use the SolarWinds TFTP software, the Cisco CCT exam objectives specifically make reference to using the Tftpd32 or the Tftpd64 software. You can download Tftpd32/Tftpd64 from https://tftpd32.jounin.net/tftpd32.html. The Tftpd32 is the 32-bit version of the TFTP software, while the Tftpd64 is the 64-bit version of the software.

Tftpd has some cool features. First, it is not only a TFTP server, but it can also be a DHCP server, a DNS server, and a syslog server. It also has the capabilities to be a TFTP client if you don't already have a TFTP client.

After downloading Tftpd64 (I recommend using the 64-bit edition), you can run the installer to perform a very quick installation of the software. After the installation, you'll see an icon on your desktop for TFTP that you can double-click to launch the software. The software has a simple interface, as you can see in Figure 8-2.

Notice that you can change the directory that the Tftpd64 software uses to store files that you back up to the service, and you can select which network card from your system you want the software to use. If you click the Settings button, you can change settings for each of the services, such as the port used by the TFTP service, the address pool to use if you wanted to use the DHCP service, and other settings related to all of the services it provides.

Once you have selected the interface, note the IP address beside the interface, because that is the IP address you will use from your Cisco device to back up the configuration files or the IOS image.

Installing FTP Server Software

Although you can use any FTP server software to back up your Cisco configuration or IOS image files, the Cisco CCT certification objectives reference FileZilla as the example software to use. FileZilla has FTP server software that you can download and install from https://filezilla-project.org/. Note that FileZilla also has FTP client software, but we are interested in the server software, so we can copy our Cisco IOS to the FTP server.

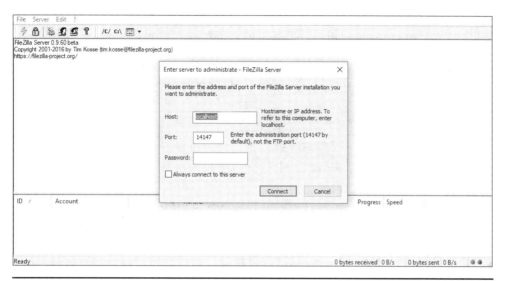

Figure 8-3   FileZilla FTP server software installation

(The Cisco IOS has FTP client software built in, which enables us to talk to the FTP server software.) When performing the installation of the FileZilla FTP server software, accept all the defaults during installation.

Once the product is installed, the administration interface is launched automatically (see Figure 8-3). Enter the IP address of the FTP service (localhost by default), the port of the administration site (14147 by default), and the password (which has not been configured yet), and then click Connect.

Once the software is launched, you can modify the configuration of the server software by choosing Edit | Settings. Within the settings, you can configure the port that FTP is using (TCP port 21 by default), and information such as the maximum number of users that can connect at a time and the welcome message will displayed after a connection.

You can also manage a list of usernames and passwords that are authorized to connect to the FTP server by choosing Edit | Users.

After you have installed the TFTP server or the FTP server software, you are ready to connect to it from your Cisco device and back up the configuration files or the IOS image files.

Backing Up an IOS Image

There are multiple ways to back up your Cisco IOS and then eventually restore the IOS to a device if the IOS goes corrupt or needs replacing. For example, you can back up to a TFTP server, an FTP server, or a USB drive, or use Xmodem to perform backups and restores of the IOS. Let's take a look at methods to back up the IOS.

The great thing about backing up the configuration of the device or the IOS is that it is all part of the **copy** command; you just change your source and destination. If you want to back up the IOS to the TFTP server, you use **copy flash tftp**; if you want to back it up to an FTP server, you use **copy flash ftp**. Use help from the **copy** command (**copy ?**) to find out what your options are for the source (what you want to copy):

```
R1#copy ?
  flash:           Copy from flash: file system
  ftp:             Copy from ftp: file system
  running-config   Copy from current system configuration
  scp:             Copy from scp: file system
  startup-config   Copy from startup configuration
  tftp:            Copy from tftp: file system
```

After you choose the location of the data that you want to copy (such as **flash:**), you can again use help (**copy flash: ?**) to see what your options are for the destination:

```
R1#copy flash: ?
  ftp:             Copy to ftp: file system
  running-config   Update (merge with) current system configuration
  scp:             Copy to scp: file system
  startup-config   Copy to startup configuration
  tftp:            Copy to tftp: file system
```

Using a TFTP Server

To back up your IOS image, you'll use the **copy flash *URL*** command. Optionally, you can specify the filename of the IOS in the command line. The *URL* specifies a URL-style syntax and includes the protocol such as TFTP, the IP address of the server, possibly the directory to put it in, and the name the image will be called on the server. Optionally, you can just specify the protocol in the URL, and you'll be prompted for the rest of the information, like this:

```
Router# copy flash tftp
Source filename []? c3640-js-mz.120-11
Address or name of remote host []? 192.168.1.10
Destination filename [c3640-js-mz.120-11]?
!!!!!!!!!!!!!!!!!!!!!!!!!!!!!!!!!!!!!!!!!!!!!!!!!!!!!!!!!!!!!!!
.
.
.
6754416 bytes copied in 64.452 secs (105537 bytes/sec)
```

As the image is backed up to the TFTP server (see Figure 8-4), you should see a bunch of exclamation points filling up your screen. This indicates the successful copy of a packet. If you see a sequence of periods instead, this indicates a failure. After a successful copy operation, you should see the number of bytes copied as well as how long it took. Compare the number of bytes copied to the file length in flash to verify that the copy was actually successful.

 VIDEO 8.04. The digital resources that accompany this book contain a multimedia demonstration of backing up your IOS image file to a TFTP server.

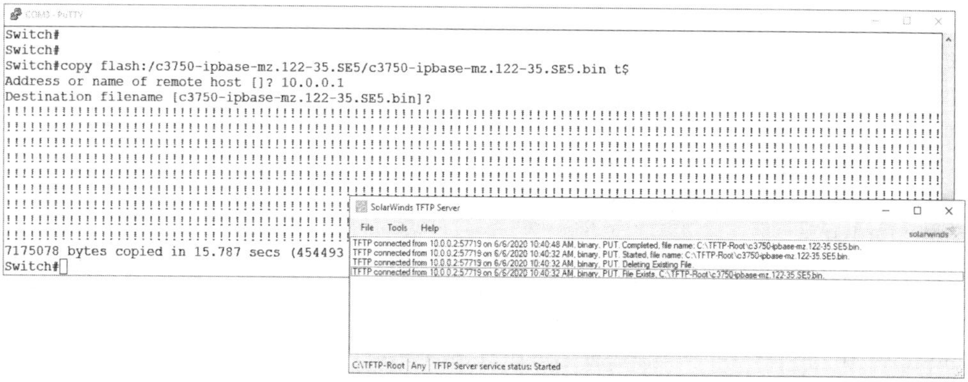

Figure 8-4 Backing up the IOS to a TFTP server

Using FTP

If you have an FTP server available, you can use that to back up your configuration files for your Cisco IOS. The first step is to configure the Cisco device for the FTP username and password needed to authenticate to the target FTP server. Use the following commands to do that:

```
R1#config terminal
R1(config)#ip ftp username ftpuser
R1(config)#ip ftp password ftppass
R1(config)#end
R1#
```

Next, use the **copy** command and specify **ftp:** as the source or destination, depending on whether you are copying from the FTP server or copying to the FTP server, respectively. It is important to note that you can also copy the configuration of the device, or the Cisco IOS, when using the **copy** command. Here is an example of backing up the configuration of the device to the FTP server:

```
R1#copy running-config ftp:
Address or name of remote host []? 192.168.2.25
Destination filename []? R1_backup_config
Writing R1_backup_config !
1015 bytes copied in 3.554 secs (244 bytes/sec)
R1#
```

As with TFTP, once the configuration is saved to the FTP server, you can restore the configuration to a replacement device at any time. First, make sure you configure the FTP username and password as shown in the earlier code example. Then you can copy the configuration to the new device by using the following commands:

```
NewRouter#copy ftp: running-config
Address or name of remote host []? 192.168.2.25
Source filename []? R1_backup_config
Destination filename [running-config]?
```

```
Accessing ftp://192.168.2.25/R1_backup_config...
Loading R1_backup_config !
[OK - 1030/4096 bytes]
1015 bytes copied in 10.222 secs (67 bytes/sec)
R1#
```

These code examples are backing up the configuration to the FTP server, but if you wanted to back up the Cisco IOS to the FTP server, you would use the **copy flash: ftp:** command.

Keep in mind that you will be prompted for the relevant information such as the IOS file to copy from flash and the IP address of the FTP server, so it is a good idea to get a listing of flash with the **dir flash:** command before using the **copy** command. For example, the following commands could be used to configure the FTP username and password on your device and get a listing of the contents of flash memory. Then you can use the **copy** command to copy the IOS file to the FTP server:

```
R1>enable
R1#config term
R1(config)#ip ftp username ftpuser
R1(config)#ip ftp password ftppass
R1(config)#exit
```

As I said, it is nice to have the contents of flash in front of you before you use the **copy** command. I like to use the **dir flash:** command to do this:

```
R1#dir flash:
Directory of flash0:/
    3  -rw-    33591768         <no date>  c2900-universalk9-mz.SPA.151-4.M4.bin
    2  -rw-       28282         <no date>  sigdef-category.xml
    1  -rw-      227537         <no date>  sigdef-default.xml
255744000 bytes total (221896413 bytes free)
R1#copy flash: ftp:
Source filename []? c2900-universalk9-mz.SPA.151-4.M4.bin
Address or name of remote host []? 12.0.0.100
Destination filename [c2900-universalk9-mz.SPA.151-4.M4.bin]?
Writing c2900-universalk9-mz.SPA.151-4.M4.bin...
[OK - 33591768 bytes]
33591768 bytes copied in 56.293 secs (596000 bytes/sec)
R1#
```

NOTE You can use the **dir flash:** command or the **show flash** command to display the contents of flash memory.

Using USB Storage

If your Cisco device has USB ports, you can back up the configuration or the Cisco IOS to the USB drive. First connect the USB drive to the USB port on the Cisco device. You should see a message on the console stating that a USB device was connected. The drive is assigned an identifier such as usbflash0:, where 0 is an index number representing the drive.

To back up your Cisco configuration to the USB drive, use the **copy current-config usbflash0:** command. You could then copy the configuration settings to a Cisco device at a later time by reversing the parameters, but again before doing this, I recommend using the **dir** command to get a listing of files on the flash drive. The following commands could be used to copy from the USB flash to the Cisco device:

```
R1# dir usbflash0:
R1# copy usbflash0:R1_config current-config
```

If you want to copy your IOS to the USB drive, you can use the **copy** command as well:

```
R1# copy flash:c2900-universalk9-mz.SPA.151-4.M4.bin usbflash0:
```

Again, it is useful to use the **dir flash:** or the **show flash** command first so that you can see a list of filenames that exists in flash memory.

Upgrading an IOS Image

Before you upgrade IOS on your Cisco device, you first need to verify that your device meets the minimal hardware requirements by asking these questions:

- Does your router have the minimal amount of required RAM?
- Does your router have the minimal amount of required flash memory?

You can see the amount of installed RAM and flash with the **show version** command (see Chapter 6). Also remember to verify that your IOS device has enough free flash memory to add the additional device (**show flash** or **dir** command); if not, you'll need to delete unneeded files to make room for the new image.

 TIP Before upgrading IOS on a Cisco device, you should verify the flash and RAM requirements of the new IOS: does your IOS device support the new image's requirements? You can verify the amount of RAM and flash installed on your IOS device with the **show version** command. You can verify the amount of free flash memory with the **show flash** or **dir** command.

If you want to upgrade your IOS or load a previously saved IOS image, you'll need to place the IOS image on an external server (such as TFTP or FTP) and use the **copy URL flash** command. You'll be prompted for the same information you needed when you used the **copy flash tftp** command; however, the process that takes place after you enter your information is different. After you enter your information, IOS first verifies that the image exists on the TFTP server. If the file exists on the server, IOS then asks you if you want to erase flash. Answer **y** if you don't have enough space in flash for the older image(s) as well as the new one. If you answer **y**, flash is erased and reprogrammed; as this step proceeds, you will see a line of *e*'s on the screen.

After flash is initialized, your router pulls the IOS image from the TFTP server. Just as in the copy operations with configuration files, a bunch of exclamation marks indicates successful copies, while periods indicate unsuccessful copies.

Here is an example of loading an IOS image into your router:

```
Router# copy tftp flash
Address or name of remote host []? 192.168.1.10
Source filename []? c3640-js-mz.120-7
Destination filename [c3640-js-mz.120-7]?
%Warning:There is a file already existing with this name
Do you want to over write? [confirm] y
Accessing tftp://192.168.1.1/c3640-js-mz.120-7...
Erase flash: before copying? [confirm] y
Erasing the flash filesystem will remove all files! Continue?
[confirm] y
Erasing device... eeeeeeeeeeeeeeeeeeeeeeeeeeeeeeee ...erased
Erase of flash: complete
Loading c3640-js-mz.120-7 from 192.168.1.1 (via FastEthernet0/0):
!!!!!!!!!!!!!!!!!!!!!!!!!!!!!!!!!!!!!!!!!!!!!!!!!!!!!!!!!!!!!!!!!!
.
.
.
[OK - 6754416/13508608 bytes]

Verifying checksum...  OK (0xCAF2)
6754416 bytes copied in 66.968 secs (102339 bytes/sec)
Router#
```

In this example, the router noticed that the name of the image that exists on the TFTP server is the same name that is in flash and verifies that you want to overwrite it. Also notice that the router prompts you to erase flash—this is the default with IOS and will delete *all* files. Answer **n** if you don't want to completely erase flash.

 NOTE When copying files into flash, remember that the default is to erase flash before the copy is performed.

After the router copies the IOS image to flash, you must reboot your router in order for it to use the new image. However, by default, the Cisco device loads the first valid IOS image in flash. To use a different one, you need to define this in your configuration with the **boot system** command and save this as part of the startup configuration file. The **boot system** commands are processed in order in the startup configuration file—if there is one there that is no longer needed, you should remove it with the corresponding **no boot system** command, followed by the old IOS image name.

You can reboot your router in two ways: do a hard reboot by turning the router off and back on, or do a soft reboot by using the privileged EXEC **reload** command. The following command tells the Cisco device to boot off the IOS image c2900-universalk9-mz.SPA.151-4.M4.bin that is located in flash memory:

```
boot system flash c2900-universalk9-mz.SPA.151-4.M4.bin
```

If you want, you can also boot your system from an IOS that is located on a TFTP server by using the **boot system tftp <IOS_filename>** command. Keep in mind that the boot process will be much slower as the device has to read the IOS from across the network.

If you place an incorrect image on your router—for instance, a 3600 series image on a 2800 series router—the router will not boot up. You'll need to break into ROM Monitor (ROMMON) mode and either do a TFTP boot or boot from the Mini IOS in ROM (if this exists).

 NOTE   To copy from TFTP, use the **copy flash tftp://***URL* command to back up the IOS image, and use the **copy tftp://***URL* **flash** command to restore or upgrade the IOS. The **reload** command reboots the router. When doing an upgrade, if either the server is not reachable or you have misconfigured the IP address or filename, you'll get an error message within the CLI.

If you encounter a problem with accessing a remote server when performing the upgrade, you'll get an error message. This could be because you configured the wrong IP address of the server in the **copy** command or you entered a nonexistent IOS image name. Here's an example illustrating this problem:

```
Router# copy tftp://192.168.101.66/iosimage.bin flash
Destination filename [iosimage.bin]?
Accessing tftp://192.168.101.66/iosimage.bin...
%Error opening tftp://192.168.101.66/iosimage.bin (Timed out)
```

Using tftpdnld

You can use the **tftpdnld** command option to load an IOS onto a Cisco device if an IOS is missing or corrupt. This is used if an IOS is not booted and you have entered ROM-MON mode. To use **tftpdnld** you will need to have ROMMON loaded and you will need network connectivity to load an IOS via **tftpdnld**. It is important to note two key points about the **tftpdnld** command option in ROMMON mode:

- It erases all files that exist in flash memory before downloading the IOS image specified.
- The transfer happens over the first port on the device.

After booting to ROMMON mode, before you use the **tftpdnld** option, you must first configure a few of the environment variables that are used to perform the copy:

```
rommon 1> IP_ADDRESS=12.0.0.50
rommon 2> IP_SUBNET_MASK=255.0.0.0
rommon 3> DEFAULT_GATEWAY=12.0.0.1
rommon 4> TFTP_SERVER=12.0.0.100
rommon 5> TFTP_FILE=c2900-universalk9-mz.SPA.151-4.M4.bin
```

Once you have set the environment variables, you can then use the **tftpdnld** command from ROMMON to start the IOS download from the TFTP server:

```
rommon 6 > tftpdnld
         IP_ADDRESS: 12.0.0.50
     IP_SUBNET_MASK: 255.0.0.0
    DEFAULT_GATEWAY: 12.0.0.1
        TFTP_SERVER: 12.0.0.100
          TFTP_FILE: c2900-universalk9-mz.SPA.155-3.M4a.bin
```

```
Invoke this command for disaster recovery only.
WARNING: all existing data in all partitions on flash will be lost!
Do you wish to continue? y/n:  [n]:  y
```

After the download is complete, you will see a ROMMON prompt. You can then use the **reset** command to reboot the Cisco device.

Using xmodem

To use the ROMMON **tftpdnld** command, you must have network connectivity, but what if your Cisco device is not loading an IOS and does not have network connectivity? What you could do is boot to the ROMMON prompt and then use the **xmodem** command, which will copy the Cisco IOS from the computer connected to the console port to your Cisco device using the console port. This is a huge convenience if you do not have network connectivity, but it is also a very slow technique for copying the Cisco IOS using the COM port on the computer.

To use the **xmodem** command, you'll need to have a terminal program that allows you to send a file via Xmodem, such as Tera Term. You can use this open source terminal emulator to connect to your Cisco device to manage it.

Follow these steps to use the **xmodem** command on a Cisco switch:

1. Boot your switch to ROMMON mode by unplugging the switch, holding down the mode button, and then plugging the power back into the switch. Hold the mode button until the device boots to the **switch:** prompt.

2. Launch Tera Term and choose to connect via Serial connection. Use the serial connection to connect to the COM port that is connected to the console port on your Cisco device.

3. If you are working on a Cisco switch, you may need to initialize flash memory by using the following command:
   ```
   switch: flash_init
   ```

4. Once flash memory has been initialized, you can copy from the computer (using Xmodem) to flash memory (using the case-sensitive filename of your IOS stored on the computer):
   ```
   switch: copy xmodem: flash:c3750-ipbase-mz.122-35.SE5.bin
   ```
   You will see a prompt stating to begin the Xmodem transfer.

5. In Tera Term, choose File | Transfer | Xmodem | Send to send a file via Xmodem.

6. When you are prompted for the filename, browse to the folder on your computer and choose the file. The transfer will then begin (see Figure 8-5).

7. After the transfer has completed you can test the loading of the new IOS by typing:
   ```
   switch: boot flash:c3750-ipbase-mz.122-35.SE5.bin
   ```

TIP The default baud rate within Xmodem is 9600, but you can increase the baud rate within ROMMON or Tera Term before starting the file transfer to speed up the copy operation. The ROMMON command to increase the baud rate is **set BAUD 57600**.

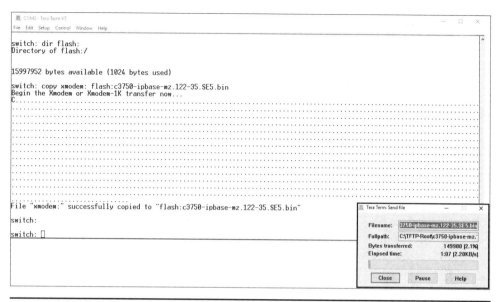

Figure 8-5   Using Xmodem to restore an IOS image

Exercise 8-3: Backing Up and Restoring Device Configuration and IOS

In this exercise, you will back up VAN-R1's device configuration to the TFTP server and then restore it from the TFTP server. You will then back up the IOS to the TFTP server so that it can be restored at a later time.

1. Ensure that you performed Exercise 8-2, and have a TFTP server available at the IP address 12.0.0.100.

2. To back up the running configuration of VAN-R1 to the TFTP server, enter the following commands:

```
VAN-R1>enable
VAN-R1#copy running-config tftp
Address or name of remote host []? 12.0.0.100
Destination filename [VAN-R1-confg]? VAN-R1-config
Writing running-config....!!
[OK - 882 bytes]
882 bytes copied in 3.015 secs (292 bytes/sec)
```

3. Before restoring the configuration, make a change to your device, such as changing the hostname:

```
VAN-R1#config term
Enter configuration commands, one per line. End with CNTL/Z.
VAN-R1(config)#hostname Test
Test(config)#
```

4. Now restore your configuration from the TFTP server to the running-config to verify that the old hostname is restored:

```
Test(config)#exit
Test#copy tftp running-config
Address or name of remote host []? 12.0.0.100
Source filename []? VAN-R1-config
Destination filename [running-config]? <<ENTER>>
Accessing tftp://12.0.0.100/VAN-R1-config...
Loading VAN-R1-config from 12.0.0.100: !
[OK - 882 bytes]
882 bytes copied in 0.001 secs (882000 bytes/sec)
VAN-R1#
```

Notice that the hostname of VAN-R1 was restored.

5. Now use the same strategy to back up the Cisco IOS in case it becomes corrupted and needs to be restored. To look at the contents of your flash memory, use the following command:

```
AN-R1#show flash
System flash directory:
File  Length    Name/status
   3  33591768  c2900-universalk9-mz.SPA.151-4.M4.bin
   2  28282     sigdef-category.xml
   1  227537    sigdef-default.xml
[33847587 bytes used, 221896413 available, 255744000 total]
249856K bytes of processor board System flash (Read/Write)
```

6. To back up the Cisco IOS file to the TFTP server, use the following commands:

```
VAN-R1#copy flash: tftp:
Source filename []? c2900-universalk9-mz.SPA.151-4.M4.bin
Address or name of remote host []? 12.0.0.100
Destination filename [c2900-universalk9-mz.SPA.151-4.M4.bin]? <<ENTER>>
Writing c2900-universalk9-mz.SPA.151-4.M4.bin...!!!!!!!!!!!!!!!!!!!!!!!!!!
!!!!!!!!!!!!!!!!!!!!!!!!!!!!!!!!!!!!!!!!!!!!!!!!!!!!!!!!!!!!!!!!!!!!!!!!!!!!!
!!!!!!!!!!!!!!!!!!!!!!!!!!!!!!!!!!!!!!!!!!!!!!!!!!!!!!!!!!!!!!!!!!!!!!!!!!!!!!
!!!!!!!!!!!!!!!!!!!!!!!!!!!!!!!!!!!!!!!!!!!!!!!!!!!!!!!!!!!!!!!!!!!!!!!!!!!!!!
!!!!!!!!!!!!!!!!!!!!!!!!!!!!!!!!!!!!!!!!!!!!!!!!!!!!!!!!!!!!!!!!!!!!!!!!!!!!!!
!!!!!!!!!!!!!!!!!!!!!!!!!!!!!!!!!!!!!!!!!!!!!!!!!!!!!!!!!!!!!!!!!!!!!!!!!!!!!!
!!!!!!!!!!!!!!!!!!!!!!!!!!!!!!!!!!!!!!!!!!!!!!!!!!!!!!!!!!!!!!!!!!!!!!!!!!!!!!
!!!!!!!!!!!!!!!!!!!!!!!!!!!!!!!!!!!!!!!!!!!!!!!!!!!!!!!!!!!!!!!!!!!!!!!!!!!!!!
!!!!!!!!!!!!!!!!!!!!!!!!!!!!!!!!!!!!!!!!!!!!!!!!!!!!!!!!!!!!!!!!!
[OK - 33591768 bytes]

33591768 bytes copied in 1.061 secs (3324219 bytes/sec)
VAN-R1#
```

If you ever needed to restore the IOS from the TFTP server to flash memory, you could use the **copy tftp: flash:** command and follow the prompts.

Remote Access to Your Cisco Device

In many instances, it may not be possible to be physically in front of your IOS device to manage it. You can optionally manage it remotely by accessing its CLI via telnet or SSH, or you can manage it with a GUI with a web browser. To access your IOS device's CLI remotely, you must first set up its VTYs (discussed in Chapter 7). If you're accessing a layer 2 IOS switch, you'll need to assign an IP address to a VLAN interface (discussed in Chapter 9); if you're accessing a router, you'll need to assign an IP address to one of its interfaces and enable it (discussed in Chapter 7). By default, only telnet is enabled on the router; this section will discuss how you enable SSH.

SSH vs. Telnet Access

One of the most common tools used by network administrators to manage their devices remotely is the telnet application. Telnet enables you access to the CLI of a device. The problem with telnet, however, is that all information sent between you and the Cisco device is sent in clear text, including your username and/or password. Since you don't want someone eavesdropping on your connection and seeing everything you do—logging in, viewing the operation of the device, and configuring the device—you need to protect yourself by encrypting the traffic.

The easiest way to accomplish this is to replace the use of telnet with SSH (Secure Shell). SSH uses RSA as an encryption algorithm to encrypt any data sent between you and your networking device. SSH is actually disabled by default on your IOS device.

 EXAM TIP   The exam will expect you to know the basics of telnet versus SSH. Telnet sends traffic in clear text, including authentication traffic, making it susceptible to an eavesdropping attack. To secure remote access to your IOS device and prevent eavesdropping on the commands you're entering and the configurations you're viewing, use SSH as your remote-access terminal connection. SSH encrypts all traffic, including authentication traffic. To prevent an access attack against your IOS device, you should combine SSH with filtering of management access to your device by using access control lists (which indicate what IP addresses can manage it).

Let's start by looking at how to configure your device for remote administration via telnet, and then we'll look at how to configure SSH on your Cisco device to support more secure remote administration.

Telnet Configuration

In this section, you will learn how to configure telnet on a Cisco device. Then you'll learn how to use telnet to make a connection to a Cisco device after it has been configured.

Configuring Telnet

Before you can remote connect to the router using telnet, you need to ensure that an IP address is assigned to the device. On a Cisco router, this will be an IP address on the interface, but for a Cisco switch, you will assign an IP address to the management VLAN (typically VLAN 1). Note that if you are going to telnet into a switch from another network, you will need to set the default gateway setting on the switch so that the switch can send data off the network.

After configuring an IP address, you'll then configure VTY passwords and a password (or secret value) to enter privileged EXEC mode. On a Cisco device, you cannot telnet into the device if those passwords are not set. Use the following commands to configure a password on VTY ports:

```
VAN-R1>enable
VAN-R1#config term
Enter configuration commands, one per line.  End with CNTL/Z.
VAN-R1(config)#line VTY 0 15
VAN-R1(config-line)#password telnetpass
VAN-R1(config-line)#login
```

 VIDEO   8.05. The digital resources that accompany this book contain a multimedia demonstration of configuring telnet on your Cisco router.

Using Telnet

If you've configured your Cisco devices correctly (with IP addressing and routing information and the appropriate commands on the VTYs), you should be able to telnet to them successfully. However, if you followed the advice mentioned later in the "SSH Configuration" section, you may need to test connectivity with SSH instead. Cisco routers and switches support both incoming and outgoing telnet and SSH. This assumes you have set up the VTYs and configured your IP addressing correctly.

 NOTE   Here I am demonstrating how to telnet into a Cisco device from another Cisco device, but you can also telnet into a Cisco device from a laptop or desktop computer if you have a telnet client running on the system. Examples of telnet client software are PuTTY and Tera Term.

To open up a telnet session from your IOS device, you can use any of the following three methods:

```
IOS# name_of_the_destination | destination_IP_address
```

or

```
IOS# telnet name_of_the_destination | destination_IP_address
```

or

```
IOS# connect name_of_the_destination | destination_IP_address
```

All three of these methods work in the same manner: they all have IOS attempt to telnet to the specified destination.

 TIP   If you mistype a command name from the CLI, the IOS assumes you're trying to telnet into a system with that name and attempts to resolve the name to an IP address using the local host table, or a DNS server query. This freezes up the CLI until the query attempt times out. To stop this behavior, use the **no ip domain-lookup** command.

Suspending Telnet Sessions

If you are using an IOS device and telnet to a remote destination, you may want to go back to your IOS device. One way of doing this is to exit the remote device; however, you may just want to go back to your source Cisco device, make a quick adjustment, and then return to the remote device. Logging off and back on to the remote device is a hassle in this instance.

Cisco, however, has solved this problem by allowing you to *suspend* a telnet session, return to your original router or switch, do what you need to do, and then jump right back into your remote device—all without your having to log off and back on to the remote device. To suspend a telnet session, press CTRL-SHIFT-6, x (hold down the CTRL, SHIFT, and 6 keys simultaneously, let go, and then press the x key).

On your source IOS, if you want to see the open telnet sessions that are currently suspended, use the **show sessions** command:

```
IOS# show sessions
Conn Host        Address      Byte   Idle   Conn Name
   1 10.1.1.1    10.1.1.1        0      1    10.1.1.1
*  2 10.1.1.2    10.1.1.2        0      2    10.1.1.2
```

This example shows two open telnet sessions. The one with the asterisk (*) preceding it is the default (last accessed) session. To resume the last session, all you have to do is press ENTER on an empty command line.

To resume a specific session, use this command:

```
Router# resume connection_#
```

The connection number to enter is the number in the Conn column of the **show sessions** command. As a shortcut, you can just list the connection number without including **resume**; this will accomplish the same thing. If you are on the source router or switch and want to terminate a suspended telnet session without having to resume and then log out of the telnet session, you can use this command:

```
Router# disconnect connection_#
```

Verifying and Clearing Connections

If you are logged into an IOS device, you can view other users who are also logged in with this command:

```
Router# show users
    Line         User      Host(s)    Idle    Location
    0    con 0                        idle
    2    vty 0              idle          0    10.1.1.1
*   3    vty 1              idle          0    10.1.1.2
```

The asterisk in the first column indicates the current session.

If you want to terminate someone's session, use the privileged EXEC **clear line** command:

```
Router# clear line line_#
```

The line number that you enter here should match the appropriate number in the Line column of the output of the **show users** command.

EXAM TIP For the exam, you'll need to remember how to suspend, resume, and disconnect telnet sessions. Use the CTRL-SHIFT-6, X control sequence to suspend a telnet session. Pressing ENTER on a blank command line resumes the last suspended telnet session. Use the **resume** command to resume a suspended telnet connection. Use the **show sessions** command to see your suspended telnet sessions. Use the **disconnect** command to disconnect a suspended telnet session.

Exercise 8-4: Configuring Telnet on the Cisco Device

In this exercise you will configure the VAN-R1 router so that you can telnet into it and perform remote administration. This exercise assumes the same network configuration as the previous exercises in this chapter.

1. Before you can administer the Cisco device remotely, passwords must be configured for privileged EXEC mode:

```
VAN-R1>enable
VAN-R1#config term
Enter configuration commands, one per line.  End with CNTL/Z.
VAN-R1(config)#enable password enablepass
VAN-R1(config)#enable secret secretpass
```

2. Next, configure passwords on the VTY lines (telnet ports):

```
VAN-R1(config)#line vty 0 15
VAN-R1(config-line)#password telnetpass
VAN-R1(config-line)#login
```

3. Console into router LA-R1 and then enter **ping 12.0.0.1**. You should receive replies of exclamation marks (!), which verifies that you can communicate with VAN-R1. Note that your prompt is LA-R1 because that is the router you are connected to right now.

4. To telnet into VAN-R1, enter **telnet 12.0.0.1**. You should receive a prompt asking for the password. Keep in mind that this is the password for the VTY ports.

5. Enter **telnetpass** as the password and press ENTER.

6. You should now have a connection to VAN-R1 (notice that your prompt has changed). You can now enter any commands you want to administer the VAN-R1 device.

7. To disconnect temporarily from the session and go back to LA-R1, press CTRL-SHIFT-6, X. You should see that you are now on LA-R1 and can administer LA-R1.

8. If you want to see the telnet sessions that are open, use the **show sessions** command:

```
LA-R1>show sessions
Conn Host               Address          Byte  Idle Conn Name
*  1 12.0.0.1           12.0.0.1            0     2 12.0.0.1
```

9. In this example, there is only one session with the ID of 1, connected to 12.0.0.1. To connect to that session, use the **resume 1** command and press ENTER twice. You will return to the VAN-R1 device.

10. To disconnect permanently from the telnet session, type **exit** and press ENTER.

 VIDEO 8.05. The digital resources that accompany this book contain a multimedia demonstration of using the telnet command to remotely connect from one device to another.

SSH Configuration

To set up SSH on your Cisco device so that you can use an SSH client to access it, you'll need to configure the following:

- **A local username and password** SSH requires both a username and password configured on the device (the **username** command configures both).

- **A hostname and a domain name** Hostname and domain name are required to label the RSA key pair on the IOS device (**hostname** and **ip domain-name** commands).

- **The SSH version to use** You should configure the specific SSH version you want to use. The default is version 1, but the recommended version to use is 2 (**ip ssh version** command).

- **RSA public and private keys** You will need to generate the encryption keys. These are used to encrypt and decrypt data that travels through the remote-access connection (**crypto key generate rsa** command).

- **Restricting VTY access** Finally, you will ensure that remote access can be achieved only through SSH and not telnet, because telnet does not encrypt communication. By default, telnet is allowed on the VTYs—you should ensure that only SSH access is allowed (**login local** and **transport input** line subconfiguration commands).

Here is an example configuration for setting up SSH:

```
IOS(config)# username glen secret mypassword
IOS(config)# hostname R1
R1(config)# ip domain-name gleneclarke.com
R1(config)# ip ssh version 2
Please create RSA keys to enable SSH. R1(config)# crypto key generate rsa
The name for the keys will be: R1.gleneclarke.com
Choose the size of the key modulus in the range of 360 to 2048 for
    your General Purpose Keys. Choosing a key modulus greater than 512
    may take a few minutes. How many bits in the modulus [512]: 1024
% Generating 1024 bit RSA keys, keys will be non-exportable...[OK]
*Oct  5 16:48:23.455: %SSH-5-ENABLED: SSH 2.0 has been enabled
R1(config)# line vty 0 15
R1(config-line)# login local
R1(config-line)# transport input ssh
R1(config-line)# exit
```

NOTE The **transport input** command on a line restricts remote-access connectivity to the device by the protocol you specify.

Notice in this example that when you execute the **crypto key generate rsa** command, you are prompted for the length of the RSA keys. The longer the keys, the more secure your connection will be, with 2048-bit keys being the strongest. Choosing a higher value, however, will take longer for the IOS device to generate. On IOS devices shipped today, this shouldn't take that long: it took me about 30 seconds to generate 2048-bit keys on an 1841 router.

 VIDEO 8.06. The digital resources that accompany this book contain a multimedia demonstration of configuring SSH on your Cisco router.

Another item to point out about this configuration is the two commands on the VTYs. The **login local** command specifies the use of the local database (**username** command) for authentication; this causes the IOS device to prompt for both a username *and* password for authentication. Without the **local** parameter, the IOS device prompts only for a password, using the **password** command on the line to do the authentication (this process was discussed in Chapter 7). SSH requires the use of both usernames and passwords. The **transport input ssh** command restricts access to the VTYs to SSH use only; by default, all forms of remote access, including telnet, are allowed.

 TIP If you will be using SSH to access your IOS device, you must use either a local username database, as described here, for your VTYs, or an authentication server (AAA). Also, I commonly use PuTTY as a console access program, telnet client, and SSH client. It's a great little program that does all these things, and it's free!

Configuration Registers and Password Recovery

One of the common tasks that you will be required to perform in the real world, and on the Cisco exams, is password recovery. You'll use password recovery procedures when you forget the password to your Cisco device and need to bypass the password so you can administer the device and reset the password. In this section, you will learn about configuration registers, which are a key concept to password recovery.

Configuration Registers

The *configuration register* setting is used by the bootstrap program to determine the location from which the IOS image and configuration file should be loaded. The configuration register is a 16-bit field (shown in Figure 8-6) that is stored in NVRAM and can be modified to control how your device boots. For example, if you forgot your password on

	Boot Fields
Value	**Description**
0	Boot to ROMMON
1	Boot RX-boot
2 to F	Load file from flash

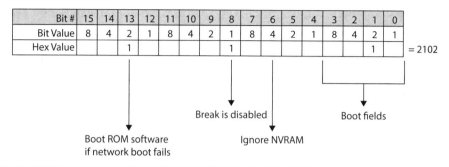

Figure 8-6 Calculating the configuration register

your Cisco device, you can modify the configuration register not to load the startup configuration at bootup in order to bypass the password. You will learn how to implement password recovery in the next section.

The 16 bits are divided into four, 4-bit blocks, with each 4-bit chunk known as a *nibble*. Remember that 8 bits make a byte? Well, having only 4 bits makes a nibble (half a byte).

Note that the values of the 4 bits in a nibble start on the right side as 1, then 2, then 4, and finally 8. Those values repeat for each of the four nibbles that exist in the 16-bit register fields.

Turning on one of the bits in the configuration registers is a method to enable a feature during bootup. For example, if bit number 6 is turned on, the contents of NVRAM are ignored and not applied during bootup. Table 8-3 outlines the meaning of some of the common bits in the configuration registers.

For example, if you wanted to boot the device and have it load the IOS and the startup configuration, you would set the configuration register value to 2102 (the default setting).

Bit Number	Explanation
0–3	Known as the boot fields discussed in next section
6	Ignore the contents of NVRAM
7	Disable the display of boot messages
8	Break is disabled
10	IP broadcast with all zeros
13	Loads the default ROM software if network boot fails

Table 8-3 Configuration Register Fields

But if you wanted to restart the Cisco device and have it load the IOS, but not the startup configuration, you would set the configuration register to 2142 (which enables bit 13, bit 8, bit 6, and bit 1).

Boot Fields

The first 4-bit nibble on the right side is known as the *boot field*, which controls how the Cisco device boots up. If the boot field equals a specific decimal value, then the bootup of the device happens a specific way. Following is a breakdown of the result of the boot field:

- **0**   If the boot field equals 0 (no bits enabled), the Cisco device will boot to ROMMON mode. This boot mode is typically used when troubleshooting startup issues or needing to download or install a new IOS image file. When booted to ROMMON mode, the **rommon>** prompt is displayed. To boot to ROMMON mode, the configuration register value would be 2100.

- **1**   If the boot field has a decimal value of 1, the device boots to a Mini IOS that is located on ROM and known as RXBOOT. When a device is booted into RXBOOT, the prompt is **router (boot)>**. The configuration register in this case would be set to 2101.

- **2 to F**   Having the boot field set to a value from 2 to F indicates the IOS image that should be loaded from flash memory. To boot an IOS image from flash memory, the configuration register would have a value of 2102 through to 210F.

Looking at the Configuration Register Value

Once the router is booted up, you can view the current configuration register value with the **show version** command:

```
Router> show version
Cisco IOS Software, 1841 Software (C1841-ADVIPSERVICESK9-M),
      Version 12.4(6)T7, RELEASE SOFTWARE (fc5)
Technical Support: http://www.cisco.com/techsupport
Copyright (c) 1986-2007 by Cisco Systems, Inc.
Compiled Thu 29-Mar-07 03:28 by khuie

ROM: System Bootstrap, Version 12.4(13r)T, RELEASE SOFTWARE (fc1)

Router1 uptime is 3 days, 22 hours, 5 minutes
System returned to ROM by reload at 19:06:33 UTC Fri Dec 7 2007
System image file is "flash:c1841-advipservicesk9-mz.124-6.T7.bin"
.
.
.
125K bytes of non-volatile configuration memory.
32768K bytes of processor board System flash (Read/Write)
Configuration register is 0x2102
```

At the very bottom of the **show version** output, the current value of the configuration register is shown—in this case it is *0x2102*.

EXAM TIP For the Cisco exams, remember that you can see the system image the router used upon bootup with the **show version** command. Also know that if you misconfigured the **boot system** command, the router may not be able to find and load an IOS image.

Changing the Configuration Register from Configuration Mode

You can change the configuration register value from configuration mode or from ROM-MON mode. If you already have privileged EXEC access to the router and want to change the register value, use this command:

```
Router(config)# config-register 0xhexadecimal_value
```

TIP If you configured your router, rebooted it, and it came up with the System Configuration dialog prompt, then you either forgot to save your running configuration before rebooting or misconfigured the configuration register.

The register value is four hexadecimal digits, or 16 bits, in length. Each bit position in the register, though, indicates a function that the bootstrap program should take. Therefore, you should be very careful when configuring this value on your router.

When entering the register value, you must always precede it with *0x*, indicating that this is a hexadecimal value. If you don't do this, the router assumes the value is decimal and *converts* it to hexadecimal. On Cisco routers, the default configuration register value is *0x2102*, which causes the router to use the default bootup process in finding and locating IOS images and configuration files. If you change this to *0x2142*, this tells the bootstrap program that, upon the next reboot, it should locate IOS using the default behavior, but it should *not* load the configuration file in NVRAM; instead, you are taken directly into the System Configuration dialog. This is the value that you will use to perform the password recovery procedure.

EXAM TIP Remember for the Cisco CCT exam that the default configuration register value is *0x2102*, which causes a router to boot up using its default bootup process. (Look for **boot system** commands in the startup configuration, and if none are found, load the first IOS in flash, and then load the default startup configuration file.) You can see the configuration register value with the **show version** command. If you've changed this value, you will see the existing value and the value the router will use upon rebooting. If the router boots up and doesn't have a configuration, but one exists in NVRAM, check the router's configuration register to see if it is set to *0x2142*: this register setting causes IOS to ignore any configuration file in NVRAM when booting.

Changing the Configuration Register from ROM Monitor

Of course, one problem with the configuration mode method of changing the register value is that you must gain access to Privileged EXEC mode first. This can be a problem if you don't know the passwords on the router. A second method, though, enables you to change the register value without having to log into the router. To use this method, you'll need console access to the router—you can't do this from the auxiliary line or from a VTY session. Next, you'll turn off the router and then turn it back on. As the router starts booting, you'll break into ROMMON mode with the router's break sequence. To break into the router, once you see the bootstrap program has loaded, you can, in most cases, use the CTRL-BREAK control sequence to break into ROMMON mode. Note that this control sequence may differ, depending on the terminal emulation program you are using on your PC.

Once you're in ROMMON mode, you can begin the process of changing the register value using one of two methods, depending on the router model that you have. Cisco devices typically use the **confreg** command to modify the configuration register from ROMMON. You can use the command by following it with the value you want to change the configuration register to, as shown here:

```
rommon 4 > confreg 0x2142
```

Or you can use it in script mode, where it prompts you about how you want to set the setting. This script asks you basic questions about the function and bootup process of the router. What's nice about the script is that you don't need to know the hexadecimal values for the configuration register, since the router will create them for you as you answer these questions. Here is an example of using this script:

```
rommon 5 > confreg
    Configuration Summary
enabled are:
load rom after netboot fails
console baud: 9600
boot: image specified by the boot system commands
      or default to: cisco2-C3600

do you wish to change the configuration? y/n  [n]:  y
enable  "diagnostic mode"? y/n  [n]:
enable  "use net in IP bcast address"? y/n  [n]:
disable "load rom after netboot fails"? y/n  [n]:
enable  "use all zero broadcast"? y/n  [n]:
enable  "break/abort has effect"? y/n  [n]:
enable  "ignore system config info"? y/n  [n]:
change console baud rate? y/n  [n]:
change the boot characteristics? y/n  [n]:

    Configuration Summary enabled are:
load rom after netboot fails
console baud: 9600
boot: image specified by the boot system commands
      or default to: cisco2-C3600
do you wish to change the configuration? y/n  [n]:  n
rommon 6 >
```

TIP As a shortcut, you could also execute the **confreg 0x2142** command in ROMMON mode.

Just as in the System Configuration dialog, any information in brackets ([ ]) represents default values. The first question you're asked is whether you want to change the configuration, which means change the register: answer **y** to continue. If you answer **y** to Ignore System Config Info?, the third hexadecimal digit becomes 4, making a router's register value appear as *0x2142*. This option is used when you want to perform the password recovery procedure. For the next-to-last question, Change The Boot Characteristics?, if you answer **y**, it will repeat the questions again. Answer **n** to exit the script. If you make any changes, you are asked to save them (Do You Wish To Change The Configuration?)—answer **y** to save your new register value. Once you are done changing the register, reboot the router. On many routers, just type **i** or **b** in ROMMON mode to boot it up.

Password Recovery

One of the times you may want to manipulate the configuration registers is when you have forgotten the password for your Cisco device and need to bypass the password to be able to administer the device. The passwords are stored in your startup configuration, which is stored in NVRAM. To bypass the password you need to modify the configuration registers so that your device boots without loading the startup configuration (ignore NVRAM). Once the device has booted without your startup configuration, you will be able to gain access without a password and can then set the password to a new value.

To configure your Cisco device to ignore NVRAM, you will need to enable bit 6, which has a value of 4, resulting in the configuration register value of *0x2142* instead of the default *0x2102*.

Following are the steps to recover the password on your Cisco device:

1. Use the **show version** command to view the current configuration register value. It is most likely *0x2102*.

2. When you power on the Cisco router, press CTRL-BREAK to disrupt the boot process and go into ROMMON mode. You should see the **rommon>** prompt.

3. Type the following command to configure the device to skip startup config when booting:

```
rommon>confreg 0x2142
```

4. Reboot the router with the **reset** command.

5. When the router reboots, it will not load the startup configuration and ask if you want to use the System Configuration dialog. Type **No** and press ENTER.

6. At the **router>** prompt, enter the **enable** command to get into privileged EXEC mode. Notice you are not asked for a password:

```
Router>enable
Router#
```

7. Use the **copy startup-config running-config** command to copy the startup configuration that was not read during bootup to be your current configuration. This is so you do not lose any settings.

8. View the configuration with the **show running-config** command.

9. Change the password by using the **enable password <newpass>** or **enable secret <newsecret>** command within global configuration mode. You can also remove the password by using the **no enable password** or **no enable secret** command.

10. Copy that from your current configuration to your startup configuration by using the **copy running-config startup-config** command (or use the **write** command).

11. Use the **config-register 0x2102** command to change the configuration registers back to the default value of *0x2102* so that NVRAM is read during bootup.

12. Reboot the router with the **reload** command.

 EXAM TIP Remember for the CCT exam how to perform password recovery procedures. You need to break into ROMMON mode, change the configuration register value to *0x2142*, and reboot the router.

Exercise 8-5: Using the Password Recovery Procedure

In this exercise you will pretend that you forget the password for the VAN-R1 router. Note that the enable password is configured as *enablepass*, and the secret is set as *secretpass* from the last exercise. This exercise assumes the same network configuration as the previous exercises in this chapter.

1. Console into VAN-R1 and navigate to privileged EXEC mode.

2. Use the **show version** command to view the current configuration register value. Record it here: _____.

3. Power off the Cisco router.

4. Power on the Cisco router, press CTRL-BREAK to disrupt the boot process, and go into ROMMON mode. You should see the **rommon>** prompt.

5. Type the following command to configure the device to skip startup config when booting:

```
rommon>confreg 0x2142
```

6. Reboot the router with the **reset** command.

7. When the router reboots, it will not load the startup configuration and ask you to use the System Configuration dialog. Type **No** and press ENTER.

8. At the **router>** prompt, enter the **enable** command to get into privileged EXEC mode. Notice you are not asked for a password:

```
Router>enable
Router#
```

9. Use the **copy startup-config running-config** command to copy the startup configuration that was not read during bootup to be your current configuration. This is so you do not lose any settings.

10. View the configuration with the **show running-config** command.

11. Change the enable password by using the **enable password labpass** global configuration command.

12. Change the secret by using the **enable secret labsecret** global configuration command.

13. Copy the password and secret from your current configuration to your startup configuration by using the **copy running-config startup-config** command (or use the **write** command).

14. Use the **config-register 0x2102** command to change the configuration registers back to the default value of *0x2102* so that NVRAM is read during bootup.

15. Reboot the router with the **reload** command.

16. When the router reboots, use the password **labsecret** to enter privileged EXEC mode.

Troubleshooting and Debugging

This section focuses on troubleshooting tools that you can use on your routers and switches. One of your first troubleshooting tasks is to determine in which layer of the OSI reference model things are not working. By narrowing down the problem to a specific layer, you can greatly reduce the amount of time you'll need to fix the problem or problems.

When you're troubleshooting problems from a user desktop, Cisco always recommends that you start at the lowest layer and work your way up. Follow these steps:

1. Verify the Ethernet cable connection.

2. Verify the operation of the NIC (**ipconfig**).

3. Verify the IP configuration of the NIC (**ipconfig**).

4. Verify the application information.

 EXAM TIP Be familiar with these steps for the exams. Of course, many administrators perform the verification steps in the reverse order (4 to 1); however, the exam tests you on Cisco's troubleshooting preference.

Cisco offers a wide variety of troubleshooting tools that you can also use. Table 8-4 shows common IOS commands and identifies at which layer of the OSI model each can be used in troubleshooting. The sections that follow cover most of these commands in depth.

OSI Reference Model Layer	Command
Layer 2	**show ip arp**
Layer 2	**show interfaces** (covered in Chapter 9)
Layer 2	**show cdp neighbors**
Layer 3	**ping**
Layer 3	**traceroute**
Layer 7	**telnet**
Layers 2–7	**debug**

Table 8-4 IOS Troubleshooting Commands

 EXAM TIP For the exam, you'll need to remember at which layer of the OSI model the commands shown in Table 8-4 operate.

Local ARP Table

Recall from Chapter 3 that the Address Resolution Protocol (ARP) is used to resolve layer 3 IP addresses to layer 2 MAC addresses. When a LAN device in a subnet needs to access resources beyond the subnet, it must forward its frames to the MAC address of the default gateway (router) and use ARP for the resolution. The router builds a local ARP table when it receives traffic on an interface, keeping track of the IP-to-MAC address mappings. You can view the mappings using the **show arp** or **show ip arp** command:

```
IOS# show ip arp
Protocol  Address    Age (min)  Hardware Addr   Type   Interface
Internet  10.0.6.2        -      0007.0e46.4070  ARPA   FastEthernet0/0
Internet  172.30.6.2      -      0007.0e46.4071  ARPA   FastEthernet0/1
Internet  172.30.6.7      0      0050.5480.7e01  ARPA   FastEthernet0/1
```

A dash (–) in the (min) column means the address is local to the router; a time value indicates that the router learned the IP/MAC addressing mapping dynamically. The last entry in this example was dynamically learned within the last minute. If a particular MAC address isn't shown for a period of time, it is aged out of the ARP table. Likewise, when a frame matches an existing entry in the table, its aging time is reset to 0 in the table. The Type column denotes the Ethernet encapsulation type (ARPA, SNAP, or SAP) used in the frame: TCP/IP uses ARPA for Ethernet.

 VIDEO 8.07. The digital resources that accompany this book contain a multimedia demonstration of using the **show ip arp** command.

The **show ip arp** command is important, because if you see at least the router's own mappings in the table for its interfaces, and you see that entries are being learned and updated in the table, then you know you have layer 2 connectivity on those interfaces.

Cisco Discovery Protocol

Cisco Discovery Protocol (CDP) is a Cisco proprietary data link layer protocol that was made available in version 10.3 of the router IOS. Many, but not all, Cisco devices support CDP, including Cisco routers and Catalyst switches. For those devices that support CDP, it is enabled by default. CDP messages received from one Cisco device, by default, are not forwarded to any other devices behind it. In other words, you can see CDP information about *only* other Cisco devices directly connected to your device. Most people misunderstand this, since CDP uses multicasts to disseminate its information. You would think that a Cisco switch would flood this kind of traffic; however, CDP is an exception to the rule in a network of Cisco devices.

 EXAM TIP   About CDP, you should remember that if you are receiving CDP frames from a directly connected Cisco neighbor, then at least the data link layer is functioning correctly. CDP information is not propagated to other Cisco devices behind your directly connected neighboring Cisco devices.

CDP Information

CDP, as mentioned, works at the data link layer. However, since CDP uses a Subnetwork Access Protocol (SNAP) frame type, not every data link layer media type is supported. The media types that are supported are Ethernet, Token Ring, Fiber Distributed Data Interface (FDDI), Point-to-Point Protocol (PPP), High-Level Data Link Control (HDLC), Asynchronous Transfer Mode (ATM), and Frame Relay.

The information shared in a CDP packet about a Cisco device includes the following:

- Name of the device configured with the **hostname** command
- IOS software version
- Hardware capabilities, such as routing, switching, and/or bridging
- Hardware platform of your device
- The layer 3 address(es) of the device
- The interface on which the CDP update was generated

CDP Configuration

As mentioned in the last section, CDP is enabled on all Cisco CDP–capable devices when you receive your product from Cisco. On Cisco routers and switches, you can globally disable or enable CDP with this command:

```
IOS(config)# [no] cdp run
```

You can also enable or disable CDP on an interface-by-interface basis:

```
IOS(config)# interface type [slot_#/]port_#
IOS(config-if)# [no] cdp enable
```

Since CDP doesn't use many IOS resources (a small frame is generated once a minute), it is recommended that you keep it enabled unless your router is connected to the Internet or untrusted devices; then you should at least disable CDP on these interfaces. At a minimum, the information is only 80 bytes in length. Other, optional commands are related to CDP, such as changing the update and hold-down timers, but these commands are beyond the scope of this book.

EXAM TIP For the Cisco CCNA exam, you should know how to disable CDP globally on the device with the **no cdp run** command, and on a specific interface with the **no cdp enable** command.

CDP Status

To see the status of CDP on your Cisco device, use this command:

```
IOS# show cdp
Global CDP information:
Sending CDP packets every 60 seconds
Sending a holdtime value of 180 seconds
Sending CDPv2 advertisements is  enabled
```

As you can see from this output, CDP is enabled and generating updates every 60 seconds. The hold-down timer is set to 180 seconds. This timer determines how long a CDP neighbor's information is kept in the local CDP table without seeing a CDP update from that neighbor. These are the default timers for CDP.

VIDEO 8.08. The digital resources that accompany this book contain a multimedia demonstration of using the **show cdp** commands.

You can also see the CDP configuration on an interface-by-interface basis by adding the **interface** parameter to the **show cdp** command:

```
Router# show cdp interface
Serial0 is up, line protocol is up, encapsulation is HDLC
  Sending CDP packets every 60 seconds
  Holdtime is 180 seconds
Ethernet0 is up, line protocol is up, encapsulation is ARPA
  Sending CDP packets every 60 seconds
  Holdtime is 180 seconds
```

CDP Neighbors

To see a summarized list of the CDP neighbors to which your Cisco device is connected, use the **show cdp neighbors** command:

```
IOS# show cdp neighbors
Capability Codes: R - Router, T - Trans Bridge, B - Source Route
                  Bridge S - Switch, H - Host, I - IGMP,
                  r - Repeater

Device ID   Local Intrfce  Holdtme  Capability  Platform  Port ID
Router-A    Eth 0/0          176       R          2621      Fas 0/1
```

In this example, one device is connected with a device ID of *Router-A*, which is a 2621 router. If you see a MAC address for the device ID, this indicates that the connected Cisco device wasn't assigned a name with the **hostname** command. This update was received on ethernet0/0 on this device 4 seconds ago (hold-down time of 176 seconds subtracted from the hold-down time of 180 seconds). The Port ID refers to the port at the remote side from which the device advertised the CDP message.

You can add the optional **detail** parameter to the preceding command to see the details concerning the connected Cisco device. You can also use the **show cdp entry** * command. Here is an example of a CDP detailed listing:

```
Router# show cdp neighbor detail
-------------------------
Device ID: Router-A
Entry address(es):
  IP address: 192.168.1.1
Platform: cisco 2621,  Capabilities: Router
Interface: Ethernet0/0,  Port ID (outgoing port): FastEthernet0/1
Holdtime : 127 sec

Version :
Cisco Internetwork Operating System Software
IOS (tm) C2600 Software (C2600-IK9O3S3-M), Version 12.2(15)T9,
        RELEASE SOFTWARE (fc2)
TAC Support: http://www.cisco.com/tac Copyright (c) 1986-2003 by cisco Systems, Inc.
Compiled Sat 01-Nov-03 04:43 by ccai

advertisement version: 2
Duplex: half
```

In this example, you can see that the connected device is a 2621 series router running IOS 12.2(15)T9 and has an IP address of 192.168.1.1 configured on the connected interface.

To list the details of a specific neighbor, use this command:

```
Router# show cdp entry neighbor's_name
```

The advantage of this approach over the approach in the preceding example is that this command lists only the specified neighbor's information. You can use an asterisk (*) as a wildcard to display all the neighbors. Here's an example of this command:

```
Router1# show cdp entry Router2
-------------------------------
Device ID: Router2
Entry address(es):
  IP address: 10.1.2.1
Platform: Cisco 2610, Capabilities: Router
Interface Serial0/0, Port ID (outgoing port): Serial0/1
Holdtime: 125 sec
```

In this example, Router2 has an IP address of 10.1.2.1 and Router1's serial0/1 interface is connected to Router2's serial0/0 interface.

IOS devices support one additional CDP command, which enables you to view CDP traffic statistics:

```
IOS# show cdp traffic
Total packets output: 350, Input: 223
Hdr syntax: 0, Chksum error: 0, Encaps failed: 0
No memory: 0, Invalid: 0, Fragmented: 0
```

If you are receiving CDP traffic (the **Input** parameter is incrementing with each execution of the command every minute), then the data link layer is functioning correctly.

 EXAM TIP Remember that CDP is enabled, by default, on all Cisco devices. CDP updates are generated as multicasts every 60 seconds with a hold-down period of 180 seconds for a missing neighbor. The **no cdp run** command globally disables CDP, while the **no cdp enable** command disables CDP on an interface (you should do this on a device's interface connected to the Internet or untrusted devices). Use **show cdp neighbors** to list your directly connected Cisco neighboring devices. Adding the **detail** parameter will display the layer 3 addressing, device model, software version, and other information configured on the neighbor. Be familiar with the output of the **show cdp** commands for the exams.

Using LLDP

One of the drawbacks of CDP is that it is a Cisco proprietary protocol. If you had a mixed environment of Cisco devices and non-Cisco devices, CDP would not be able to discover the non-Cisco devices for you. The IEEE has created an industry-standard protocol for device discovery, the Link Layer Discover Protocol (LLDP), which is known as the IEEE 802.1ab standard.

With LLDP running on your Cisco devices, you can use it to discover any other devices running LLDP, much like CDP. LLDP is not enabled on Cisco devices by default, but it can be enabled with the following command:

```
Router(config)#lldp run
```

Once enabled, LLDP is enabled for all interfaces. You can disable LLDP with the **no lldp run** global configuration command. If you wanted to disable LLDP on a specific interface, you can navigate to the interface and disable transmitting and receiving of LLDP on the interface:

```
Router(config-if)#no lldp transmit
Router(config-if)#no lldp receive
```

Of course, you can enable LLDP communication on the interface by using the **lldp transmit** command and the **lldp receive** command. But remember, LLDP traffic is enabled for both transmit and receive on all interfaces by default after you enable LLDP with the **lldp run** command.

You can verify that LLDP is running on your Cisco device by using the **show lldp** command, shown in the following example. Notice that you can see that LLDP is active and that advertisement messages are sent out every 30 seconds by default.

```
Router#show lldp
Global LLDP Information:
    Status: ACTIVE
    LLDP advertisements are sent every 30 seconds
    LLDP hold time advertised is 120 seconds
    LLDP interface reinitialisation delay is 2 seconds
```

 EXAM TIP For the CCNA exam, remember that LLDP is an industry standard discovery protocol used in a multivendor environment, while CDP is a Cisco proprietary protocol used in environments that just have Cisco devices.

Layer 3 Connectivity Testing

CDP can be very useful in determining whether the data link layer is working correctly with another directly connected Cisco device, or it is commonly used to create a network map by discovering the different devices on the network. You can even see the layer 3 address(es) configured on your neighboring device and use this for testing layer 3 connectivity. In addition to using CDP, you could also use the **show interfaces** command for data link layer testing (see Chapter 9).

The main limitation of these two tools, however, is that they don't test layer 3 problems, though Cisco does offer tools for testing layer 3 connectivity. This section focuses on two of these commands: **ping** and **traceroute**. Both commands come in two versions: one for user EXEC mode and one for privileged EXEC mode. The privileged EXEC version provides additional options and parameters that can assist you in your troubleshooting process. The following sections cover these tools in more depth.

Using Ping

Ping (Packet Internet Groper) is a command utility that you can use to verify layer 3 connectivity on a Cisco device. Ping uses ICMP as the status reporting protocol to identify whether or not a system is up and running. You can use the **ping** command on your Cisco device by typing **ping <ip_address>**.

Users can use the **ping** command from their Windows desktop to check for connectivity as well. Here are a couple of messages that indicate problems and possible reasons:

- **Destination host unreachable**   The router connected to the remote host cannot contact that host on the connected segment.
- **Destination network unreachable**   A router between the source and destination doesn't have a routing table entry that determines how to reach the destination.

 EXAM TIP Remember for the Cisco CCT and CCNA exams that both the Cisco IOS **ping** and **traceroute** commands test layer 3 connectivity.

When using the **ping** command to perform the communication test, if the destination is reachable, the destination responds with an echo reply message for each echo sent by the source. If the destination is not reachable, an intermediate router, if it exists, will respond with a destination network unreachable message, indicating where the problem begins. If a router is connected to the remote segment where the destination host is connected, and that router can't reach the destination host, this will cause a "destination host unreachable" message. Also note that you may not receive a reply if ICMP is being blocked by a firewall.

Simple ping Command   To execute a simple **ping** from either user EXEC mode or privileged EXEC mode, enter the **ping** command on the CLI and follow it with the IP address or hostname of the destination:

```
IOS> ping destination_IP_address_or_host_name
```

Here is a simple example of using this command:

```
IOS> ping 192.168.1.10
Type escape sequence to abort.
Sending 5, 100-byte ICMP Echos to 192.168.1.10,
    timeout is 2 seconds:
!!!!!
Success rate is 100 percent (5/5),
    round-trip min/avg/max = 2/4/6 ms.
```

In this example, five test packets were sent to the destination and the destination responded to all five, as is shown by the exclamation marks (!). The default timeout to receive a response from the destination is 2 seconds—if a response is not received from the destination for a packet within this time period, a period (.) is displayed.

Table 8-5 shows examples of ping messages that you may see in displayed output. The bottom of the output shows the success rate—how many replies were received and the minimum, average, and maximum round-trip times for the ping packets sent (in milliseconds). You can use this information to detect whether a delay exists between you and the destination.

EXAM TIP   Be familiar with the output descriptors used by the **ping** command in Table 8-4 for both the Cisco CCT and CCNA exams.

NOTE   You might see a period (.) in the output for a couple of reasons: either a response was received after the timeout period, or no response was received at all. If a response was received after the timeout period, this might be because an ARP had to take place to learn the MAC address of a connected device or because of congestion—and this process could have occurred on multiple segments. Consider two examples: .!!!! and !!..!. If devices have to perform ARPs to get the MAC address of the next-hop device, you'll typically see .!!!! in your output. However, if your output is !!..! you're probably experiencing congestion or performance problems.

Ping Output	Explanation
.	A response was not received before the timeout period expired.
!	A response was received within the timeout period.
U	A remote router responded that the destination is unreachable—the network segment is reachable, but not the host.
N	A remote router responded that the network is unreachable—the network cannot be found in the routing table.
P	A remote device responded that the protocol is not supported.
Q	The source quench tells the source to slow its output.
M	The ping packet needed to be fragmented, but a remote router couldn't perform fragmentation.
A	The ping packet was filtered by a device with an access control list (administratively prohibited).
?	The ping packet type is not understood by a remote device.
&	The ping exceeded the maximum number of hops supported by the routing protocol.

Table 8-5   Output Codes for the **ping** Commands

Extended ping Command   IOS devices support an extended **ping** command, which can be executed only at Privileged EXEC mode.

To execute this command, just type **ping** by itself on the command line:

```
Router# ping
 Protocol [ip]:
 Target IP address: 192.168.1.10
 Repeat count [5]:
 Datagram size [100]:
 Timeout in seconds [2]:
 Extended commands [n]: y
 Source address:
 Type of service [0]:
 Set DF bit in IP header? [no]:
 Data pattern [0xABCD]:
 Loose, Strict, Record, Timestamp, Verbose[none]:
 Number of hops [9]:
 Loose, Strict, Record, Timestamp, Verbose[RV]:
 Sweep range of sizes [n]:
Type escape sequence to abort.
Sending 5, 100-byte ICMP Echos to 192.168.1.10,
     timeout is 2 seconds:
 .
 .
 .
```

Following is an explanation of the parameters that may be required when you execute this command:

- **Protocol**   The protocol to use for the ping (defaults to IP).
- **Target IP address**   The IP address or hostname of the destination to test.

- **Repeat count**   How many echo requests should be generated for the test (defaults to 5).

- **Datagram size**   The size, in bytes, of the ping packet (defaults to 100).

- **Timeout in seconds**   The amount of time to wait before indicating a timeout for the echo (defaults to 2 seconds). When seeing a mix of periods and explanation points (!) in the displayed output, increasing this value can help determine whether you are experiencing congestion problems with a slow response time between your IOS device and the destination.

- **Extended commands**   Whether or not the remaining questions should also be asked (defaults to no).

- **Source address**   The IP address that should appear as the source address in the IP header (defaults to the IP address of the interface the ping will use to exit the IOS device).

- **Type of service**   The IP level for QoS (defaults to 0).

- **Set DF bit in IP header?**   Whether or not the ping can be fragmented when it reaches a segment that supports a smaller MTU size (the default is no—don't set this bit). Sometimes a misconfigured MTU can cause performance problems. You can use this parameter to pinpoint the problem, since a device with a smaller MTU size will not be able to handle the larger packet.

- **Data pattern**   The data pattern that is placed in the ping. It is a hexadecimal four-digit (16-bit) number (defaults to 0xABCD) and is used to solve cable problems and crosstalk on cables.

- **Loose, Strict, Record, Timestamp, Verbose**   IP header options (defaults to none of these). The record parameter records the route that the ping took—this is somewhat similar to traceroute. If you choose record, you will be asked for the maximum number of hops that are allowed to be recorded by the ping (defaults to 9, and can range from 1 to 9).

- **Sweep range of sizes**   Send pings that vary in size. This is helpful when trying to troubleshoot a problem related to a segment that has a small MTU size (and you don't know what that number is). This defaults to *n* for no.

 EXAM TIP   The Cisco CCT and CCNA exams expect you to know how to troubleshoot communication issues with the computer as well. When troubleshooting PC problems, first determine whether the user can ping the loopback address of their PC: **ping 127.0.0.1**. If this fails, you know something is wrong with the TCP/IP protocol stack installation on the PC. Next, have the user try to ping the configured IP address. If this fails, you know that something is wrong with their IP address configuration. Next, have the user ping the default gateway. If this fails, either something is wrong with the configured default gateway address, the default gateway itself, the subnet mask value configured on the user's PC, or the layer 2 switch connecting them together (perhaps a mismatch in the VLAN on the router and PC interfaces of the switch).

Using Traceroute

One limitation of **ping** is that it will not tell you where, between you and the destination, layer 3 connectivity is broken. The **traceroute** command, on the other hand, will list each router along the way, including the final destination. Therefore, if a layer 3 connection problem exists, **traceroute** will tell you at least where the problem begins. Like the `ping` command, `traceroute` has two versions: one for user EXEC mode and one for privileged EXEC mode. The following two sections cover the two different versions.

Simple traceroute Command   The simple **traceroute** command, which works at both user and privileged EXEC modes, has the following syntax:

```
Router> traceroute destination_IP_address_or_host_name
```

Here is an example of this command:

```
Router> traceroute 65.32.13.33
Type escape sequence to abort.
Tracing the route to 65.32.13.33
  1 10.98.240.1 20 msec 24 msec 16 msec
  2 65.32.15.254 16 msec 16 msec 12 msec
  3 65.32.13.33 12 msec 12 msec 12 msec
```

In this example, the destination was three hops away—each hop is listed on a separate line. For each destination, three tests are performed, where the round-trip time is displayed for each test. If you don't see a round-trip time, typically indicated by an asterisk, this indicates a possible problem or timeout in the response (for example, if ICMP is blocked at the firewall).

Table 8-6 shows other values that you may see instead of the round-trip time.

Traceroute Output	Explanation
*	Either the wait timer expired while waiting for a response or the device did not respond at all potentially because of a firewall blocking ICMP traffic.
A	The trace packet was filtered by a remote device (administratively prohibited).
U	The port of the device is unreachable (the destination received the trace packet but discarded it).
H	The destination is unreachable (the destination segment was reachable, but not the host).
I	The user interrupted the traceroute process.
N	The network is unreachable (the destination segment was not reachable).
P	The protocol is unreachable (the device doesn't support traceroute).
Q	The source quench tells the source to slow its output.
T	The trace packet exceeded the configured timeout value.
?	The device couldn't identify the specific trace types in the trace packet.

Table 8-6   Traceroute Messages

VIDEO 8.08. The digital resources that accompany this book contain a multimedia demonstration of using the **ping** and **traceroute** commands on your Cisco device.

In certain cases, for a specific destination, you might see three asterisks (***) in the output. Don't be alarmed if you see this, since it can occur for a variety of reasons: for instance, there may be an inconsistency in how the source and destination devices have implemented traceroute, or the destination may be configured not to reply to these messages. However, if you continually find the same destination repeated in the output with these reply messages, this indicates a layer 3 problem starting with either this device or the device preceding it.

TIP If you have DNS lookups enabled on your IOS device (this is the **ip domain-lookup** command), IOS will attempt to resolve the IP address to a domain name before printing the output line for that device. If your traces seem to take a long time, DNS lookups is usually the culprit. You can disable DNS lookups on your IOS device with the **no ip domain-lookup** command.

Extended traceroute Command   The extended **traceroute** command is similar to the extended **ping** command and requires privileged EXEC mode access to execute it:

```
Router# traceroute
Protocol [ip]:
Target IP address: IP_address_of_the_destination
Source address:
Numeric display [n]:
Timeout in seconds [3]:
Probe count [3]:
Minimum Time to Live [1]:
Maximum Time to Live [30]:
Port number [33434]:
Loose, Strict, Record, Timestamp, Verbose [none]:
.
.
.
```

Some of these options are the same ones used by **ping**.
   Here is an explanation of the other options:

- **Numeric display**   Turns off a DNS lookup for the names of the routers and the destination
- **Time to Live**   Specifies how many hops the trace is allowed to take
- **Loose**   Tells the router that the hops you specify must appear in the trace path, but other routers can appear as well
- **Strict**   Restricts the trace path only to those routers that you specify
- **Record**   Specifies the number of hops to leave room for in the trace packet

- **Timestamp**   Enables you to specify the amount of space to leave room for in the trace packet for timing information
- **Verbose**   Automatically selected whenever you choose any of the options from this question; prints the entire contents of the trace packet

One important item to point out about the **traceroute** command is that if more than one path exists to reach the destination, this command will test *each* path, which can take the trace process longer. And like the extended **ping** command, instead of using the script to perform the test, you can enter the command and all of its parameters on a single command line.

EXAM TIP   For the exam, remember that the **ping** command uses ICMP to test layer 3 connectivity to a device. The **traceroute** command lists each routing device along the way to the destination (a list of the layer 3 hops) and is typically used to troubleshoot routing problems. Windows devices can perform a traceroute by using the **tracert** command.

Layer 7 Connectivity Testing

The **ping** and **traceroute** commands can test only layer 3 connectivity. If you can reach a destination with either of these two commands, this indicates that layer 3 and below are functioning correctly. You can use other tools, such as telnet, to test the application layer. If you can telnet to a destination, then all seven layers of the OSI model are functioning correctly. As an example, if you can telnet to a machine but can't send an e-mail to it, then the problem is *not* a networking problem, but an application problem (with the e-mail program). Of course, if you are filtering traffic with an access control list (discussed in Chapter 17), this could also be the culprit.

EXAM TIP   The CCT certification exam expects you to know how to use telnet. The **telnet** command can be used to test layer 7 (application layer) connectivity. To test telnet, the remote destination must have telnet configured and enabled. If the remote device is an IOS device, you must minimally configure the **login** and **password** commands on the VTYs.

Debug Overview

One problem with using **show** commands is that they display only what is currently stored somewhere in the router's RAM, and this display is *static*. You have to re-execute the command to get a refreshed update. And **show** commands, unfortunately, do not always display detailed troubleshooting information. For example, perhaps you want the router to tell you when a particular event occurs and display some of the packet contents of that event. The **show** commands cannot do this; however, **debug** commands can. One of the most powerful troubleshooting tools of IOS is the **debug** command, which enables you to view events and problems, in real time, on your Cisco device.

The **debug** commands, however, have a drawback: Since the router has to examine and display many different things when this feature is enabled, the performance of IOS will suffer. As an example, if you want to see every IP packet that travels through a router, the router has to examine each packet, determine whether it is an IP packet, and then display the packet or partial packet contents on the screen. On a very busy router, this debug process can cause serious performance degradation. Therefore, you should be very careful about enabling a debug process on your router; you may want to wait till after hours or periods of lesser activity before using this tool.

 CAUTION You should never use the **debug all** command—this enables debugging for every process related to IOS features enabled on your router. In this situation, you'll see pages and pages of output messages on all kinds of things and, on a busy IOS device, probably crash it.

Typically, you will use **debug** commands for detailed troubleshooting. For instance, you may have tried using **show** commands to discover the cause of a particular problem, but without any success. You should then turn to using a particular **debug** command to uncover the source of the problem. This command has many, many options and parameters—use context-sensitive help to view them. Many of the remaining chapters in this book will cover specific **debug** commands and their uses. To enable **debug**, you must be at privileged EXEC mode. If you are not on the console when enabling **debug**, you'll also need to execute the privileged EXEC **terminal monitor** command to see the **debug** output on your non-console line.

Once you've fixed your problem or no longer need to see the **debug** output, you should always disable the **debug** process. You can disable it either by prefacing the **debug** command with the **no** parameter or executing one of the following two commands:

```
IOS# no debug all
```

or

```
IOS# undebug all
```

These two commands disable all running **debug** commands on your router. You can first use the **show debug** command to see which events or processes you have enabled.

 EXAM TIP For the exam, remember that you can use the **undebug all** or **no debug all** command to disable all debug functions.

If you want to see timestamps displayed in your debug output, enter the following command:

```
Router(config)# service timestamps debug datetime msec
```

The **datetime** parameter displays the current date and time, and the **msec** parameter displays an additional timing parameter: milliseconds.

TIP If you think your **debug** commands are causing performance problems, use the **show processes cpu** command to check your CPU utilization for the device's various processes, including **debug**.

Exercise 8-6: Using the Router's Troubleshooting Tools

In this exercise you will practice using some of the troubleshooting tools available in the Cisco IOS. Note that this exercise is using the same network topology used in the last exercise.

1. Console into router VAN-R1 and use the **show cdp neighbors** command to see what neighboring devices are connected to VAN-R1. Record them here:

   Device ID: _____
   Local Interface: _____
   Platform: _____
   Capability: _____
   Remote Port: _____

   Note that you cannot see the IP address of the neighboring device.

2. To see the IP address of the neighboring device with CDP, use the **show cdp neighbors detail** command. Record the information here:

   Device ID: _____
   IP Address: _____
   IOS Version: _____

3. Now that you know the IP address of the neighboring device, you could telnet into it and then discover other devices from that device (if telnet was configured and you had the password). This is how you can document the network topology using CDP.

Licensing Cisco Devices

Licensing Cisco ISR G2 routers has become more and more common across many of Cisco platforms; even Cisco's switches are starting to support licensing of features and use. Prior to Cisco IOS version 15 on Cisco routers, Cisco had up to 12 different image types for a particular device model and software version. To simplify this, Cisco now has only four image types:

- IP Base
- Data (MPLS and ATM)
- Unified Communications (VoIP and IP telephony)
- Security (firewall, IPS, and VPNs)

You can use the **show license feature** command to view the technology package licenses and the feature licenses supported by your router. Here's an example of the use of this command:

```
Router# show license feature
Feature name    Enforcement Evaluation Subscription Enabled RightToUse
ipbasek9        no          no         no           yes     no
securityk9      yes         yes        no           yes     yes
uck9            yes         yes        no           yes     yes
datak9          yes         yes        no           no      yes
LI              yes         no         no           no      no
ios-ips-update  yes         yes        yes          no      yes
```

Licensing is enforced starting with Cisco ISR G2 routers (1900, 2900, and 3900 series). Licensing unlocks features in IOS code. Licenses come in two types:

- **Evaluation**   This license is a temporary license that is valid for a particular period of time, such as 60 days or one year.
- **Permanent**   This license is valid for the life of the product.

Licenses are associated with two values from a Cisco ISR G2 router, referred to as a universal device identifier (UDI):

- Product ID (platform type)
- Serial number (located in ROM on the motherboard)

The importance of the UDI is that the license you obtain from Cisco is tied to this value. In other words, you can't take a license from one router and copy it to another router: the license is tied to the UDI value of your Cisco ISR G2 router. Here's an example of viewing the UDI information for license purposes on a 3925 ISR G2 router:

```
Router# show license udi
Device#  PID              SN            UDI
-------------------------------------------------------------------
*0       C3900-SPE100/K9  FHH13030044   C3900-SPE100/K9:FHH13030044
```

Use the **show license feature** command to view the package and feature licenses installed on your router.

Installing Licenses

Your router comes with an evaluation license, also known as a temporary license, for most packages and features supported on your router. If you want to try a new software package or feature, you can activate the evaluation license for that package or feature.

To install a permanent license, use the following privileged EXEC command:

```
Router# license install URL-location
```

The license file is an XML file that you download from Cisco. Typically you would place this in flash on the router, but you could pull it from a remote server via TFTP or FTP. Here's an example of installing a license on a 3950 router:

```
Router# license install flash0:uck9-C3900-SPE150_K9-FHH12250057.xml
Installing licenses from "uck9-C3900-SPE150_K9-FHH12250057.xml"
Installing...Feature:uck9...Successful: Supported
1/1 licenses were successfully installed
0/1 licenses were existing licenses
0/1 licenses were failed to install
```

Once you've installed a license, it is not used until the router is rebooted. You can execute the **reload** command to reboot the router.

To activate an evaluation license to try out technology packages, use this command:

```
Router(config)# license boot module module_name
                technology-package package_name
```

The *module_name* is the product model, such as **c3900** for a 3950 router. The technology *package_name* is one of the four packages. For example, the Security package parameter is **securityk9**. As with a permanent license, you must reboot the router for the license to take effect.

Licensing Verification

One of the first commands you can use to verify your licensing is the **show version** command (introduced in Chapter 6). Here's an example based on the previous license installation example:

```
Router# show version
Cisco IOS Software, C3900 Software (C3900-UNIVERSALK9-M), Version 12.4(24.6)
PI11k PI11 ENGINEERING WEEKLY BUILD, synced to V124_24_6_T9
.
.
.
Cisco C3945 (revision 1.0) with 2025472K/71680K bytes of memory.
Processor board ID FHH1226P01E
3 Gigabit Ethernet interfaces
4 Serial(sync/async) interfaces
2 ISDN Basic Rate interfaces
1 ATM interface
25 terminal lines
1 Virtual Private Network (VPN) Module
DRAM configuration is 72 bits wide with parity enabled.
255K bytes of non-volatile configuration memory.
2000880K bytes of ATA System CompactFlash 0 (Read/Write)
License Info:
License UDI:
-------------------------------------------------
Device#    PID                 SN
-------------------------------------------------
*0         C3900-SPE150/K9     FHH12250057
```

```
Technology Package License Information for Module:'c3900'
------------------------------------------------------------------
Technology       Technology-package          Technology-package
                 Current      Type           Next reboot
------------------------------------------------------------------
ipbase           ipbasek9     Permanent      ipbasek9
security         None         None           None
uc               uck9         Permanent      uck9
data             None         None           None
```

Notice that in this example, the router has both an IP Base and Unified Communications (UC) permanent license installed.

You can also use the **show license** command to view the installed license, as shown in this example:

```
Router# show license
Index 1 Feature: ipbasek9
        Period left: Life time
        License Type: Permanent
        License State: Active, In Use
        License Count: Non-Counted
        License Priority: Medium
Index 2 Feature: securityk9
        Period left: 8 weeks, 3 days
        Period Used: 15  minute 38 second
        License Type: EvalRightToUse
        License State: Active, In Use
        License Count: Non-Counted
        License Priority: Low
Index 3 Feature: uck9
        Period left: Not Activated
        Period Used: 0  minute  0  second
        License Type: EvalRightToUse
        License State: Not in Use, EULA not accepted
        License Count: Non-Counted
        License Priority: None
    .
    .
    .
```

In this example, the IP Base package has a permanent license installed, the Security package has an activated evaluation license installed, and the Unified Communications package doesn't have a license installed.

Managing Licenses

This section will cover how to back up your license as well as how to uninstall a license. To back up a license, use the **license save** command:

```
Router# license save URL
```

You can save the license file to the local file system or a remote server. Here's an example of the use of this command:

```
Router# license save flash:/licenses.lic
license lines saved......to flash:licenses.lic
```

To uninstall (remove) a license from a router, you need to perform two actions:

1. Disable the technology package.

2. Clear the license.

To disable the technology package, use the **license boot module** command. Here's an example of disabling the Unified Communications package on a 3900 series router:

```
Router(config)# license boot module c3900 technology-package
                 uck9 disable
Router(config)# exit
Router# copy running-config startup-config
Router# reload
```

Once the router has rebooted, you need to clear the license with the **license clear** command. Here's an example:

```
Router# license clear uck9
*Jul  7 00:34:23.691: %SYS-5-CONFIG_I: Configured from console by console
clear uck9
Feature: uck9
    1   License Type: Permanent
        License State: Active, Not in Use
        License Addition: Exclusive
        License Count: Non-Counted
        Comment:
        Store Index: 15
        Store Name: Primary License Storage
Are you sure you want to clear? (yes/[no]): yes
*Jul  7 00:34:31.223: %LICENSE-6-REMOVE: Feature uck9 1.0 was removed
from this device.
UDI=C3900-SPE150/K9:FHH12250057; StoreIndex=15:Primary License Storage
```

Once done, you can re-enable the technology package:

```
Router(config)# no license boot module c3900 technology uck9 disable
Router(config)# exit
Router# reload
```

Upon rebooting, use the **show version** command to verify the license change.

Chapter Review

Use the **copy** commands to manipulate files, including configuration files and IOS images. Any time you copy something into RAM, IOS uses a merge process. For any other location, IOS uses an overwrite process. On IOS devices, use the **erase startup-config** command to delete the startup-config file in NVRAM. SSH should be used instead of telnet for remote terminal (CLI) access to the router since SSH encrypts traffic between your desktop and an IOS device.

CDP is a Cisco-proprietary protocol that functions at the data link layer. Every 60 seconds, a Cisco device generates a multicast on each of its interfaces, containing basic information about itself, including the device type, the version of software it's running, and its IP address(es). To disable CDP globally, use the **no cdp run** command. To see a list of your neighbors, use the **show cdp neighbors** command.

The **ping** and **traceroute** commands support an extended version at privileged EXEC mode. If you want to suspend an active telnet session, use the CTRL-SHIFT-6, X control sequence. Pressing ENTER on a blank command line resumes the last suspended telnet session. Use the **resume** command to resume a telnet connection. Use the **show sessions** command to see your open telnet session. Use the **disconnect** command to disconnect a suspended telnet session. To disable debug on your IOS device, use **undebug all** or **no debug all**. Debug functions only at privileged EXEC mode.

Starting in IOS version 15.0, the ISR G2 routers now require licenses to operate legally. Licenses are of two types: evaluation and permanent. To install a permanent license, use the **license install** command. To verify the licensing on your router, use the **show version** and **show license** commands.

Quick Review

Router Configuration Files

- These commands perform a merge process: **copy startup-config running-config**, **copy tftp running-config**, and **configure terminal**. These commands perform an overwrite process: **copy running-config startup-config** and **copy running-config tftp**.

- IOS devices do not automatically save their configuration in RAM: you must execute the **copy running-config startup-config** command to save the active configuration file to NVRAM.

Changes in Your Network

- Always back up your configuration before making any changes to it—preferably to a remote server using SCP, which encrypts it.

IOS Image Files

- When upgrading your IOS, make sure you download the version of IOS from Cisco that contains the features that you purchased, and verify that your router has enough flash and RAM for the new image.

- Use the **copy tftp: flash:** command to copy the IOS image file from the TFTP server to the flash memory on your device.

- Use the **tftpdnld** command to download an IOS image file from the TFTP server when in ROMMON mode.

- Use the **xmodem** command to copy the IOS image file from a computer to the Cisco device using the console cable when there are no networking capabilities.

- Use the **reload** command to reboot your router.

Remote Access to Your Cisco Device

- To telnet into a device, you must have VTY ports configured with passwords and there must be a password on privileged EXEC mode.

- Use SSH for an encrypted remote-access terminal session to your router. Use the **transport input** command to limit what management protocols are allowed on the VTYs.

Troubleshooting and Debugging

- For layer 2 troubleshooting, use the **show interfaces** command and **show cdp** command. For layer 3 troubleshooting, use **ping** and **traceroute**. For layer 7 troubleshooting, use **telnet**. For detailed troubleshooting, use **debug**.

- CDP is a Cisco proprietary protocol that is used to learn basic information about directly connected Cisco devices. It generates a multicast every 60 seconds and is enabled by default on Cisco devices.

- The *Link Layer Discovery Protocol* (LLDP) is an IEEE standard protocol used to discover devices on the network.

- To execute an extended **ping** or **traceroute**, you must be at privileged EXEC mode. The **ping** command tests only if the destination is reachable, while **traceroute** lists each layer 3 device along the way to the destination.

- To suspend a telnet session, use the CTRL-SHIFT-6, X.

- The **debug** commands require privileged EXEC access. To disable all **debug** commands, use **no debug all** or **undebug all**.

Licensing Cisco Devices

Use the **license install** command to install a new license. Use the **show version** and **show licenses** command to view installed licenses.

Questions

The following questions will help you measure your understanding of the material presented in this chapter. Read all the choices carefully, as there may be more than one correct answer. Choose the correct answer(s) for each question.

1. Which router commands perform an overwrite process? (Choose two.)

   A. **copy running-config startup-config**

   B. **copy startup-config running-config**

   C. **copy tftp running-config**

   D. **copy running-config tftp**

2. Enter the router command to delete your configuration file in NVRAM:

   _____.

3. You have executed the **show startup-config** command and see the following message: "%%Non-volatile configuration memory is not present." Which of the following answers are correct about these two things? (Choose two.)

   A. This command displays the running configuration in NVRAM.

   B. This command displays the saved configuration in NVRAM.

   C. This command displays the saved configuration in flash.

   D. The message indicates that flash needs to be reformatted.

   E. This message indicates that NVRAM needs to be reformatted.

   F. This message indicates that there is nothing stored in this memory location.

4. When backing up your IOS image from flash, which of the following will the **copy flash tftp** command prompt you for? (Choose three.)

   A. TFTP server IP address

   B. Verification to copy

   C. Source filename

   D. Destination filename

5. What IOS command will display the version of software your device is running?

   A. **show startup-config**

   B. **show flash**

   C. **show version**

   D. **dir and show version**

6. Enter the IOS configuration on the first five VTYs to allow only SSH access and to prompt for both a username and password for line authentication: _____.

7. Enter the IOS command that will create RSA public and private keys to encrypt and decrypt traffic for an SSH session: _____.

8. Which of the following is true of CDP?

   A. The **show cdp neighbor** command displays what version of software the neighbor is running.

   B. The **no cdp run** command disables CDP on an interface.

   C. CDP sends out broadcasts every 60 seconds.

   D. CDP can be used to validate layer 2 connectivity.

9. Which router command would you use to test only layer 3 connectivity?

   A. **telnet**

   B. **show cdp traffic**

   C. **show interfaces**

   D. **traceroute**

10. How would you suspend a telnet session?

    A. CTRL-SHIFT-X, 6

    B. CTRL-SHIFT-6, X

    C. CTRL-ALT-INS

    D. CTRL-C

11. What IOS command is used to verify the installed licenses on a Cisco router?

    A. show installed-licenses

    B. show flash:licenses

    C. license view

    D. show version

12. What command was used to generate the following output?

```
Capability Codes: R - Router, T - Trans Bridge, B - Source Route Bridge
                  S - Switch, H - Host, I - IGMP, r - Repeater, P - Phone
Device ID    Local Intrfce   Holdtme   Capability   Platform   Port ID
LA-R1        Ser 0/3/0       155            R        C2900      Ser 0/3/0
```

    A. Show cdp neighbor detail

    B. Show interfaces

    C. show cdp neighbor

    D. show ip interface brief

13. What command was used to generate the following output?

```
Device ID: LA-R1
Entry address(es):
  IP address : 13.0.0.2
Platform: cisco C2900, Capabilities: Router
Interface: Serial0/3/0, Port ID (outgoing port): Serial0/3/0
(output cut for briefness)
```

    A. Show cdp neighbor detail

    B. Show interfaces

    C. show cdp neighbor

    D. show ip interface brief

14. As the network administrator for your company you need to create a network diagram containing all of the network devices that include Cisco devices, Juniper devices, and devices from other vendors. What command would you use on your Cisco devices?

    A. cdp run

    B. lldp run

    C. show cdp neighbor

    D. cdp enable

Performance-based Questions

The Cisco exams have performance-based questions where you must drag an item from the left side of the screen to its proper place on the right side of the screen to answer the question. Following are some sample performance-based questions related to security.

1. You have configured an extended access list with the following rules:

```
access-list 120 deny tcp 145.13.45.100 0.0.7.255 any eq 23
access-list 120 deny tcp 145.13.45.100 0.0.7.255 any eq http
access-list 120 permit ip any any
```

Using the following exhibit, identify which packets would be denied and which packets would be permitted by writing the packet information in the boxes on the right. On the real exam, you would need to drag the box representing the packet to the appropriate category on the right.

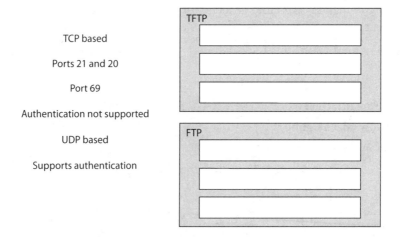

2. Draw a line from the command on the left side to the appropriate description on the right side. Not all descriptions are used.

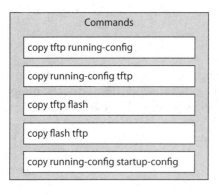
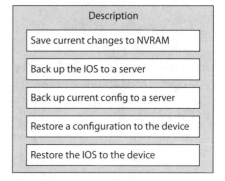

Answers

1. **A** and **D.** Use the router commands **copy running-config startup-config** and **copy running-config tftp** to perform an overwrite. Copying to any place other than RAM (*running-config*) causes an overwrite.

2. Use the **erase startup-config** command to delete your configuration file in NVRAM.

3. **B** and **F.** The **show startup-config** command displays the saved configuration found in NVRAM. If no configuration is stored in this memory location, you see the "%%Non-volatile configuration memory is not present" message.

4. **A, C,** and **D.** When you use the **copy flash tftp** command, you are prompted for the TFTP server's IP address, the source filename of IOS in flash, and the name you want to call the IOS image on the TFTP server.

5. **C.** The **show version** command will display the current software version your IOS device is running.

6. `line vty 0 4`
   `    transport input ssh`
   `    login local`

7. **crypto key generate rsa**

8. **D.** CDP can be used to validate that you have layer 2 connectivity with a connected device.

9. **D.** The **traceroute** command tests layer 3.

10. **B.** Use CTRL-SHIFT-6, x to suspend a telnet session.

11. **D.** Use the **show version** or **show licenses** command to display the licenses activated on an IOS device.

12. **C.** The **show cdp neighbor** command is used to display a list of neighboring devices detected with CDP and characteristics such as the ports used to connect to that device and the capabilities of the device.

13. **A.** The **show cdp neighbor detail** command is used to list out the characteristics of neighboring devices including the IP address of the device, the platform, capabilities, and the IOS version.

14. **B.** LLDP is an industry standard discovery protocol that is supported by many vendors of network devices (CDP is only for Cisco devices). To use LLDP on your Cisco device to discover other devices, you must enable LLDP first with the **lldp run** global configuration command.

Performance-based Answers

1. The following illustration shows the correct characteristics placed with either FTP and TFTP:

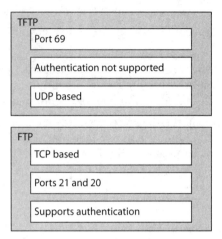

2. The following illustration shows the correct matching of the **copy** command with the description of what the command is designed to achieve.

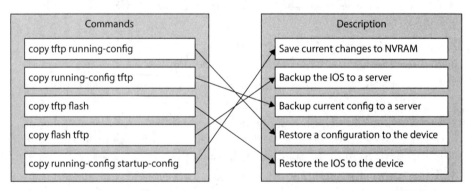

Switching Basics

In this chapter, you will

- Learn about switch features
- Get familiar with switch components
- Learn how to configure settings on a switch
- Understand interface configuration settings
- Learn about working with VLANs

The Cisco CCT and CCNA certification exam will expect you to have a basic understanding of switch operations and how to configure the basic settings on a Cisco switch. In this chapter, you will learn about the core features of a switch, the basic configuration settings on the switch, and how to configure features on the interfaces of the switch.

Understanding Switch Features

In Chapter 1, you were introduced to switches. As a quick review, a *switch* is a central connectivity device to which all systems connect in order to communicate with one another. In Chapter 1, you also learned that switches have replaced hubs, because switches offer more advanced capabilities, such as being able to filter traffic by sending data only to the destination port (while the hub always sends data to all ports). A switch also supports other features, such as full-duplex communication, which means that devices can send and receive at the same time; back in the hub days, communication devices were only half-duplex (devices can send and receive, but not at the same time). Switches also have the benefit of being able to be divided into multiple virtual local area networks (VLANs). You will learn about VLANs later in this chapter.

After you unbox the switch, you'll appreciate that it does not require any configuration to perform its job role, which is to act as a connectivity point for all devices on the network. The switch is ready to perform that job out of the box; simply give it power and then connect the systems to the switch, and it will forward traffic to each of the connected devices as needed. Unlike a router, a switch, by default, doesn't require that you apply configuration settings. There are, however, a number of features that you can configure on the switch that enable you to tweak how the switch operates and to use advanced features that are not configured by default.

Switch Functions

Switches are layer 2 devices—that is, they operate at the data link layer of the Open Systems Interconnection (OSI) model. Although a switch has many capabilities, they do have core functions: they learn, forward, and avoid loops (more on those three functions in a bit). Switches make all of their switching decisions based on the destination Media Access Control (MAC) address in the header of the frame that is received, and all of the processing is performed in hardware by using application-specific integrated circuits (ASICs). ASICs are specialized processors built to perform very few specific tasks. Because they do only a few things, ASICs are much more cost-effective than generic processors, such as the one in your PC. Cisco, like most networking vendors, extensively uses ASICs throughout its switching products.

A switch has the following three main functions:

- **Address learning/MAC learning** When a computer sends a frame to another computer and that frame reaches the switch, the switch records the sending MAC address and the port that system is connected to in the MAC table of the switch. Any time the switch receives a frame, it checks the MAC table to see what port the destination system is connected to.

- **Filtering/forwarding** Switches filter traffic by forwarding the frame only to the port of the destination system—again, drawing on information the switch has recorded in its MAC table.

- **Loop avoidance** Switches prevent layer 2 loops on the network by using a loop prevention protocol such as the Spanning Tree Protocol (STP).

Address Learning/MAC Learning

One of the three functions of a switch is to learn which devices are connected to which ports of the switch. The switch uses this information to forward frames intelligently. When a switch receives a frame, it reads the source MAC address in the frame and compares it to a local MAC address table, called a *MAC address table* or *content addressable memory* (CAM) table. If the address is not already in this table, the switch adds the address and the port number on which the frame was received. For example, in Figure 9-1, you can see that ComputerB with the MAC address bbbb.bbbb.2222 is sending data. When the switch receives this data it will record that the address bbbb.bbbb.2222 is located at port 2 on the switch.

If the address is already in the CAM table, the switch compares the incoming port with the port already in the table. If the two are different, the switch updates the CAM table with the new port information. This is important, because you may have moved the device from one port to another, and you want the switch to determine the new location. If the port has not been changed, the switch resets the age timer for the entry. Because this MAC address table is stored in memory on the switch and is generated dynamically based on traffic (by default), entries will age out after 300 seconds by default if the entry is not updated by the system sending traffic.

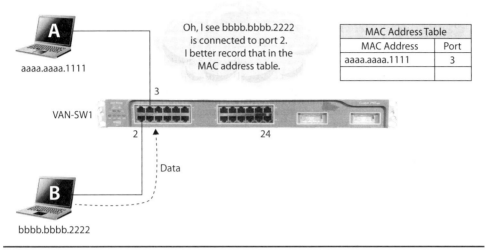

Oh, I see bbbb.bbbb.2222 is connected to port 2. I better record that in the MAC address table.

MAC Address Table	
MAC Address	Port
aaaa.aaaa.1111	3

VAN-SW1

3

2

24

Data

aaaa.aaaa.1111

bbbb.bbbb.2222

Figure 9-1 Switches learn MAC address by the sending system.

The CAM table can be built statically or dynamically. By default, when you turn on a switch, the CAM table is empty unless you have configured static entries in it. As traffic flows through the switch, the switch will begin learning address locations based on the source MAC address of the frame and will build its CAM table. This dynamic building process is a very nice feature, because the other method of having addresses appear in the MAC address table is to build them manually using static addresses. With static entries, you must manually add each device's MAC address and the port to which it is connected into the CAM table yourself.

EXAM TIP   For the Cisco CCNA exam, remember that switches learn the ports that devices are connected to by analyzing the *source MAC address* of a frame and placing it in the CAM table along with the port that the frame was received on.

Filtering and Forwarding

The second function of a switch is known as *frame switching*, or filtering and forwarding, where the switch forwards traffic intelligently. To do this, the switch uses the MAC address table to help it find where destinations are located. When a frame is received on a port, the switch examines the destination MAC address in the frame header and looks for a corresponding entry in the MAC address table. If the switch finds a matching entry, it forwards the frame out of the specified port. If the port is the same port on which the frame was received (the source and destination are connected to the same port), the switch drops the frame. If the switch doesn't find the entry in the MAC address table, the switch *floods* the frame out all of the remaining ports.

EXAM TIP For the Cisco CCNA exam, remember that if a switch does not know where to send a frame, it will flood the frame to all ports on the switch; this is known as *frame flooding*. This is not a broadcast message, however. The difference between frame flooding and a broadcast is that the flooded frame has a specific destination MAC address in the header of the frame, whereas a frame being broadcast has a destination MAC address of FF-FF-FF-FF-FF-FF.

Loop Avoidance

The third function of a switch is to avoid layer 2 loops. Having layer 2 loops on the network can cause serious problems with the network and even bring the network down. We want to have multiple links between switches so there is a fault-tolerant pathway between the switches. Having a layer 2 loop can cause many problems, including instability in the MAC address table that confuses the switch and eventually causes the switch to distrust its MAC address table and flood all frames (essentially acting as a hub). For an example of how a loop can cause confusion, see Figure 9-2. In the figure, ComputerA is sending data to ComputerB (destination MAC address bbbb.bbbb.2222). When the data leaves ComputerA, it is sent to the VAN-SW1 switch on port 3. The VAN-SW1 checks to see if it has the destination MAC address of bbbb.bbbb.2222 in its MAC address table and finds that it does not, so it then floods the frame to all ports. This causes the frame to go

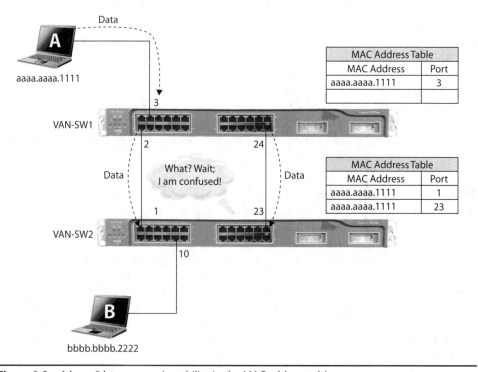

Figure 9-2 A layer 2 loop causes instability in the MAC address table.

out ports 2 and 24 toward VAN-SW2. When VAN-SW2 receives the frame, it records in the MAC address table that the sending ComputerA can be reached via port 1 and port 23 of the VAN-SW2 switch. This is where one of the issues with layer 2 loops occurs: the switch will get confused about whether it can trust the data in the MAC address table, because the same system appears to be reached by two different ports.

To correct this problem, Cisco switches use STP, a loop prevention protocol that places one of the ports causing the loop in a blocking state. If a port is in a blocking state, it cannot send or receive any data until it is placed back in a forwarding state. STP will automatically detect when the other link goes down and will change the state to forwarding on the link that was originally blocked. You will learn more about STP in Chapter 10.

Exercise 9-1: Verifying the Loop Avoidance Feature

In this exercise, you will connect two switches together with redundant links. After connecting with redundant links, you will witness the switch placing one of the links in a blocking state. The following illustration represents the network diagram for this scenario:

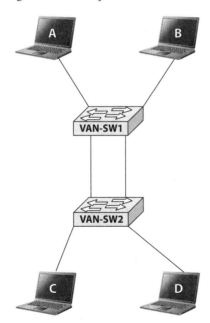

1. Connect port 1 on VAN-SW1 to port 1 on VAN-SW2 using a crossover cable.

2. To create a fault-tolerant link between the two switches, connect port 24 on VAN-SW1 to port 24 on VAN-SW2 using a crossover cable.
   This will create the fault-tolerant link, but it also creates a loop on the network. The loop is bad, so you will notice that after a minute or so, one link will be green and the other stays amber as it is placed in a blocking state.

3. After one minute, notice which port was placed in the blocking state by entering a Yes or No value beside each port (you can tell by the placement of the amber-colored link light):

VAN-SW1 – Port 1: _____

VAN-SW2 – Port 1: _____

VAN-SW1 – Port 24: _____

VAN-SW2 – Port 24: _____

4. Now disconnect the crossover cable that has a green link light at both ends to see if the other link becomes fully active. Wait 30 seconds to see if both link lights become green. Do they? _____

Your answer should be yes. This is proof that the switch is automatically preventing layer 2 loops on the network.

Operation Modes

The switching method used affects how a layer 2 device receives, processes, and forwards a frame. Bridges support only one switching method, store-and-forward, while switches may support one, two, or three different switching methods. The following three switching methods are supported by layer 2 devices:

- Store-and-forward
- Cut-through
- Fragment-free

Store-and-Forward Switching

Store-and-forward switching is the most basic form of switching. With store-and-forward switching, the layer 2 device must receive the entire frame into the buffer of the inbound port and will check the frame for errors (the FCS checksum field on the frame) before the switch will perform any additional processing of the frame. When checking the FCS, commonly called a *cyclic redundancy check* (CRC), the switch will calculate a CRC value, just as the source device did, and compare this value to what was included in the FCS of the frame. If they are the same, the frame is considered good, and the switch can forward the frame out the correct destination port of the switch. If the FCS value in the frame and computed CRC value are different, the switch will drop the frame.

The advantage of store-and-forward is that the switch can check the frame for errors before forwarding it on. The downfall is the wait time for the switch to read the entire frame, which is longer than that of the other methods.

Cut-Through Switching

Cut-through switches were designed to improve the performance of a switch as it relates to processing frames. With cut-through switching, the switch only waits to read the destination MAC address before it begins forwarding the frame. Cut-through switching is faster than store-and-forward switching. Its biggest problem, though, is that the switch may be forwarding bad frames—though the header may be legible, the rest of the frame could be corrupted from a late collision.

Fragment-Free Switching

Fragment-free switching is a modified form of cut-through switching. Whereas cut-through switching reads up to the destination MAC address field in the frame before making a switching decision, fragment-free switching makes sure that the frame is at least 64 bytes long before switching it (64 bytes is the minimum legal size of an Ethernet frame). The goal of fragment-free switching is to reduce the number of Ethernet *runt frames* (frames smaller than 64 bytes) that are being switched. Fragment-free switching is sometimes called *modified cut-through* or *runtless* switching. With fragment-free switching, a switch could still be switching corrupt frames, because the switch is checking only the first 64 bytes.

 EXAM TIP For the CCNA exam remember the key points about the switch operation modes. Store-and-forward switching reads the whole frame, checks the FCS, and then forwards the frame. This increases latency for switching but reduces the number of bad frames on the network. Cut-through switching switches a frame as soon as it sees the destination MAC address in the frame. Fragment-free switching will start forwarding a frame after the switch sees at least 64 bytes, which prevents the forwarding of runt frames.

Identifying Switch Components

Before you begin connecting any cables to your Cisco switches, you should become familiar with the different LEDs on the switch and their meanings, along with the different ports and interfaces on the switch.

Chassis and Physical Ports

Every switch model will be a little bit different with regard to the type of interface that exists. Older switches may have only Fast Ethernet (FE) interfaces, some may have mostly FE with Gigabit Ethernet (GE) interfaces to use as uplink ports, or current switches will have all GE interfaces at least.

Figure 9-3 shows a switch that contains the display status LEDs on the left side (covered in the next section). To the right of the display status LEDs are the switch (Ethernet) ports or interfaces used to connect devices to the switch. (In this example, the

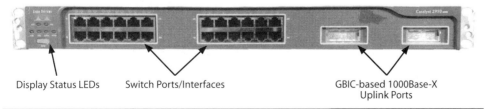

Display Status LEDs   Switch Ports/Interfaces   GBIC-based 1000Base-X
                                                            Uplink Ports

Figure 9-3 The displays and ports on the front of a switch

switch has 24 ports, but other switches may have 8 ports, 12 ports, 24 ports, or 48 ports.) To the right of the switch ports are two fixed gigabit interface converter (GBIC)–based ports that are used to insert GBIC modules to use as uplink ports. The benefit of the GBIC-based port is that it can accept any type of module you want to insert into the port, such as an RJ-45 port to connect UTP cabling, or you could insert a GBIC module that enables you to use fiber-optic cabling.

The back side of the switch will have a place to connect the power cable and the console port to enable you to administer the device. Note that on some switches, the console port is on the front of the switch instead of on the back.

LEDs and Display Modes

The front sides of many of the Cisco switches have display mode LEDs you can use to monitor a switch's activity and performance. Figure 9-4 takes a look at the LEDs on a Cisco switch.

As shown in the figure, at the top-left of the switch are the System and RPS (redundant power supply) LEDs. When you power on the switch, the System and RPS LEDs light up to indicate the following: the System LED indicates the overall health status of the switch, while the RPS LED indicates the status of the RPS. The colors displayed by these LEDs and their meanings are shown in Table 9-1.

EXAM TIP When preparing for the Cisco CCNA exam, remember that if the System LED is amber, the switch is experiencing a malfunction.

Mode Button

The meaning of the LED above each port on the front of the switch depends on the display mode setting. You can change the display mode by pressing the Mode button (see Figure 9-4). Just above the Mode button are four port-mode LEDs: STAT (status mode), UTIL (utilization mode), DUPLX (duplex mode), and SPEED (speed mode).

Figure 9-4
The LEDs on a Cisco Catalyst switch

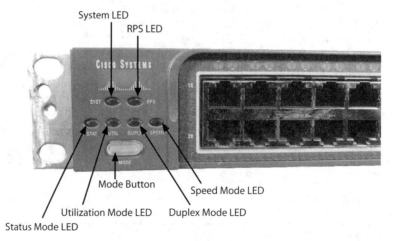

LED	Color	Description
System	Green	The system is powered on and operational.
	Amber	The system experienced a malfunction.
	Off	The system is powered down.
RPS	Green	The RPS is attached and operational.
	Amber	The RPS is installed but is not operational. Check the RPS to ensure that it hasn't failed.
	Flashing amber	Both the internal power supply and the external RPS are installed, but the RPS is providing power.
	Off	The RPS is not installed.

Table 9-1 System and RPS LEDs on a Cisco Switch

By default, the STAT LED is lit, indicating that the LEDs above the Ethernet ports refer to the status of the port. The following outlines the meaning of each LED color while in STAT mode:

- **Green** A physical layer connection exists with a device attached to the port.
- **Flashing green** Traffic is entering and/or leaving the port.
- **Amber** The port has been disabled manually (shut down) by the administrator, placed in a blocking state due to STP, or disabled because of port security.
- **Off** No physical connection exists on the port.

If you push the Mode button, the STAT mode LED turns off and the UTIL LED lights up. This means that each of the LEDs above the ports is showing information about the utilization on each port.

Let's look at an example that shows how all of the LEDs on the ports work together to show you a bandwidth utilization level on the switch. For this model switch, the LEDs in utilization mode work as follows:

- If all ports have a green LED, the bandwidth utilization is above 50 percent.
- If all ports except the last port are green, the bandwidth utilization of the switch is between 25 and 49 percent.
- If all ports except the last two are green, the bandwidth utilization of the switch is less than 25 percent.

If you press the Mode button once, the display mode LED will change from STAT to DUPLX. After changing to the DUPLX mode, the LEDs above each of the ports will reflect the duplex setting of the associated port. The following outlines the duplex LEDs:

- **Off** If the LED above the port is off, the port is set to half duplex.
- **Green** If the LED is green, the port is set to full duplex.

Press the Mode button again, and the display mode LED will change from DUPLX to SPEED. When the display mode is set to SPEED, the LEDs above the port refer to the speed at which the port is operating:

- **Off**   If the LED is off, the port is operating at 10 Mbps.
- **Green**   If the LED is solid green, the port is operating at 100 Mbps.
- **Blinking Green**   If the LED is blinking green, the port is running at 1 Gbps.

If you press the Mode button again, the STAT LED will light. As you can see, you can use the Mode button to cycle through the different display modes to get information about each of the ports. If the display mode LED is either DUPLX or SPEED, it will automatically change back to STAT after 1 minute.

TIP   If you don't have connectivity through the switch and the switch port LEDs are all off, make sure the switch is powered on. Reseat the cable connectors in their ports. Also check the cables to make sure they are the correct type: straight through versus cross-over.

Basic Switch Configuration

In this section, you will learn about making basic configuration settings on a switch. The concepts you learned with Cisco routers, as far as configuration modes and passwords go, apply to switches as well. This section will demonstrate some of the commands that are unique to switches.

Initial Configuration Dialog

If no configuration has occurred before the switch boots up, the Internetwork Operating System (IOS) will run the setup script, commonly called the initial configuration dialog. This script asks you questions to help create a basic configuration on the switch. When posing questions, the setup script uses brackets ([ ]) to indicate default values. Leaving an answer blank (that is, not supplying an answer) results in the script accepting the value indicated in brackets for the configuration component. In the script, you can configure the switch's hostname, set up a privileged EXEC password, assign a password for the virtual type terminals (VTYs), and set up an IP address for a VLAN interface to manage the switch remotely.

NOTE   If a switch boots up without a configuration in Non-Volatile RAM (NVRAM), the setup script, or initial configuration dialog, will be presented to the administrator.

Here's an example of this script, with answers in boldface:

```
Would you like to enter the initial configuration dialog? [yes/no]: yes
At any point you may enter a question mark '?' for help.
Use ctrl-c to abort configuration dialog at any prompt.
Default settings are in square brackets '[]'.

Basic management setup configures only enough connectivity
for management of the system, extended setup will ask you
to configure each interface on the system

Would you like to enter basic management setup? [yes/no]: yes
Configuring global parameters:
  Enter host name [Switch]:
  The enable secret is a password used to protect access to
  privileged EXEC and configuration modes. This password, after
  entered, becomes encrypted in the configuration.
  Enter enable secret: cisco
  The enable password is used when you do not specify an
  enable secret password, with some older software versions, and
  some boot images.
  Enter enable password: enable
  The virtual terminal password is used to protect
  access to the router over a network interface.
  Enter virtual terminal password: remotepass
  Configure SNMP Network Management? [no]:

Current interface summary
Interface            IP-Address      OK? Method Status          Protocol
Vlan1                unassigned      YES unset  up              down
FastEthernet0/1      unassigned      YES unset  down            down
FastEthernet0/2      unassigned      YES unset  down            down
.
.
.
GigabitEthernet0/1   unassigned      YES unset  down            down
GigabitEthernet0/2   unassigned      YES unset  down            down

Enter interface name used to connect to the
management network from the above interface summary: vlan1

Configuring interface Vlan1:
  Configure IP on this interface? [no]: yes
    IP address for this interface: 12.0.0.2
    Subnet mask for this interface [255.0.0.0] :
    Class A network is 12.0.0.0, 8 subnet bits; mask is /8
Would you like to enable as a cluster command switch? [yes/no]: no
```

```
The following configuration command script was created:

hostname Switch
enable secret 5 $1$.N.L$t4q9Jw5DTffPTPE.KkKNX/
enable password enable
line vty 0 15
 password remotepass
no snmp-server

interface Vlan1
 no shutdown
 ip address 12.0.0.2 255.0.0.0
!
interface FastEthernet0/1
.

.

.
interface GigabitEthernet0/1
!
interface GigabitEthernet0/2
end
[0] Go to IOS command prompt without saving this config.
[1] Return back to the setup without saving this config.
[2] Save this configuration to nvram and exit.
Enter your selection [2]: 2
```

At the end of the script, enter **2** to accept and activate your changes, as well as save the configuration to NVRAM. (Entering 0 aborts the script, and entering 1 starts the script over, remembering what you just entered as the defaults for the questions you were just asked.)

TIP   One problem with this script is that once you answer a question—correctly or incorrectly—there is no way of going back to the question. To abort the script, press CTRL-C and start over. To run the script from the command line interface (CLI) without rebooting the switch, go to privileged EXEC mode and execute the **setup** command.

Basic Settings

You can change the configuration settings of your Cisco switch at any time using IOS commands. In this section, you will learn how to change the device name and set an IP address and default gateway on the switch.

Naming the Device

The first configuration change I typically make with a switch is to change the hostname. If you change the hostname, the prompt within the CLI changes to the hostname, making it easy to know which device you are configuring. Use the hostname global configuration command to modify the name of your device, as shown here:

```
Switch>enable
Switch#config term
Enter configuration commands, one per line.  End with CNTL/Z.
Switch(config)#hostname VAN-SW1
VAN-SW1(config)#
```

Assigning an IP Address

After you change the hostname, you may want to assign an IP address to your switch. Note that a switch is a layer 2 device and does not need an IP address to perform its job of learning and forwarding frames on the network. By assigning an IP address to a switch, however, you can remotely connect to the switch using HTTP, telnet, or SSH. You can remotely manage it instead of depending on connecting through a local console port.

Switches work a bit differently from routers in the sense that you do not assign IP addresses to the ports of the switch. The devices that are connected to the ports, such as computers or IP phones, have their IP addresses assigned. To assign an IP address to a switch, you first navigate to a special VLAN interface and then assign the IP to the VLAN of the switch, as shown here:

```
VAN-SW1>enable
VAN-SW1#config term
Enter configuration commands, one per line.  End with CNTL/Z.
VAN-SW1(config)#interface vlan1
VAN-SW1(config-if)#ip address 12.0.0.2 255.0.0.0
VAN-SW1(config-if)#no shutdown
%LINK-5-CHANGED: Interface Vlan1, changed state to up
%LINEPROTO-5-UPDOWN: Line protocol on Interface Vlan1, changed state to up
VAN-SW1(config-if)#
```

Notice in this code example that from global configuration mode, you navigate to the vlan1 (default VLAN) by using the **interface** command. Once at the interface prompt, you use the IP address command to assign an IP address and subnet mask to the switch. You then must enable the interface by using the **no shutdown** command. You will learn more about VLANs in the next chapter.

Setting Up a Default Gateway

Once you've assigned the IP address and subnet mask, you can remotely administer the switch as long as you are on the same network as the switch. If you want to administer the switch from a different network, you must configure a default gateway so that the switch knows how to send data off the network. To configure a default gateway on the switch, use the following commands:

```
VAN-SW1>enable
VAN-SW1#config term
Enter configuration commands, one per line.  End with CNTL/Z.
VAN-SW1(config)#ip default-gateway 12.0.0.1
```

Notice that we navigated to global configuration mode and then used the **ip default-gateway** command to set the default gateway.

Exercise 9-2: Configuring a Switch

In this exercise, you will apply basic configuration settings to the VAN-SW1 and LA-SW1, which are located in the Vancouver office and the Los Angeles office, respectively. The network diagram for this exercise and the remaining exercises is shown in the following illustration. Notice that this is a basic network topology, with three networks—the 12.0.0.0, 13.0.0.0, and 14.0.0.0 networks that we use for most of the exercises. Because we are using public IP addresses, it is a good practice to ensure that your lab environment is not connected to any production network and is isolated.

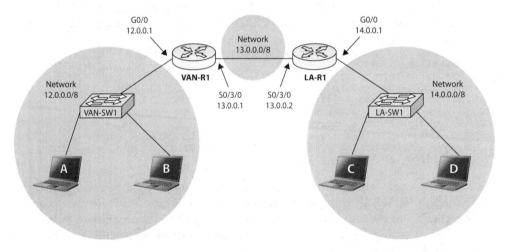

Note that ComputerA is connected to port 5 of VAN-SW1, while ComputerB is connected to port 15 of VAN-SW1. ComputerC is connected to port 5 of LA-SW1, while ComputerD is connected to port 15 on LA-SW1.

1. Ensure all routers and switches are booted up.

Configuring VAN-SW1

2. Connect to the console port of VAN-SW1 with PuTTY.

3. Change the name of the switch with the following commands:

```
Switch>enable
Switch#config term
Enter configuration commands, one per line.  End with CNTL/Z.
Switch(config)#hostname VAN-SW1
VAN-SW1(config)#
```

4. Assign an IP address to the switch with the following commands:

```
VAN-SW1(config)#interface vlan1
VAN-SW1(config-if)#ip address 12.0.0.2 255.0.0.0
VAN-SW1(config-if)#no shutdown
```

5. Assign a default gateway setting to the switch with the following commands:

```
VAN-SW1(config-if)#exit
VAN-SW1(config)#ip default-gateway 12.0.0.1
```

6. Verify that the IP address has been configured by viewing the status on the VLAN1 interface:

```
VAN-SW1(config)#exit
%SYS-5-CONFIG_I: Configured from console by console
VAN-SW1#show interface vlan1
Vlan1 is up, line protocol is up
  Hardware is CPU Interface, address is 00d0.ff58.9cde (bia 00d0.ff58.9cde)
  Internet address is 12.0.0.2/8
  MTU 1500 bytes, BW 100000 Kbit, DLY 1000000 usec,
     reliability 255/255, txload 1/255, rxload 1/255
  Encapsulation ARPA, loopback not set
(output cut for briefness)
VAN-SW1#
```

Configuring LA-SW1

Using the commands you entered for VAN-SW1 as a guide, configure the LA-SW1 switch by following these steps:

7. Connect to the console port on LA-SW1 and press ENTER in PuTTY to refresh the prompt.

8. Change the name of the switch to LA-SW1.

9. Assign the IP address of 14.0.0.2 to the switch.

10. Assign a default gateway setting of 14.0.0.1 to the switch.

11. Verify that the IP address has been configured by viewing the status on the VLAN1 interface.

MAC Address Table

You'll recall that one of the three main functions of a switch is to learn which devices—that is, MAC addresses—are associated with which interfaces or ports on the switch. You also learned that this information is stored in the MAC address table, or CAM table. On newer switches, you can view the MAC address table by using the **show mac address-table** command:

```
VAN-SW1>enable
VAN-SW1#show mac address-table
          Mac Address Table
-------------------------------------------
Vlan    Mac Address       Type       Ports
----    -----------       --------   -----
   1    0050.0fdd.d03a    DYNAMIC    Gig1/0/1
   1    0090.0c9e.76a8    DYNAMIC    Gig1/0/5
```

In this example, you can see that two MAC addresses are stored in the CAM table: one associated with Fa0/1 and the other, Fa0/5. Remember that these entries are automatically created based on the switch receiving traffic through these ports.

 EXAM TIP Some exam questions require you to be familiar with the output of the **show mac address-table** command. Also remember that if a destination MAC address is not in the table (unknown), the switch will flood the frame to all ports on the switch.

To clear dynamically learned entries from the CAM table, use the **clear mac address-table** command from privileged EXEC mode.

 NOTE On older Cisco switches, such as the 2960, use the **show mac-address-table** and **clear mac-address-table** commands.

Static MAC Addresses

In addition to having the switches learn MAC addresses dynamically, you can manually create static entries. The benefit of static entries is that they are part of your switch configuration, so they are retained even if the switch is rebooted (whereas dynamic entries are lost after a reboot and must be learned again).

To add a static entry in the MAC address table, use the following syntax:

```
Switch(config)# mac address-table static MAC_address
                  vlan VLAN_#
                  interface type module/port_#
```

For example, you could add a static entry for port 8 with the following command:

```
Switch(config)# mac address-table static 0000.1111.2222 vlan 1 int g1/0/8
```

In addition to specifying the MAC address of the device and the interface where the device is located, you must also specify the VLAN in which the device is located (see Chapter 10 for more on VLANs). Use the **show mac-address-table** command to view your new entries. To remove a static entry from the CAM table, preface the command with the **no** parameter: **no show mac-address-table**.

 NOTE Statically configuring MAC addresses on the switch is not commonly done today. If configured, static entries are typically used for network devices, such as servers and routers. If you are concerned about controlling what device is connected to a specific port on the switch, use the port security feature.

Exercise 9-3: Working with the MAC Address Table

In this exercise you will have a look at the MAC address table, also known as a CAM table, on a Cisco switch and add a static MAC address to the MAC address table.

1. Connect to the console port on VAN-SW1 and press ENTER in PuTTY to refresh the prompt.

2. To view the MAC address table that contains a list of all the addresses that the switch has learned, enter the following commands:

```
VAN-SW1>enable
VAN-SW1#show mac address-table
```

Note that only an address is learned for port 1 on the switch (the one connected to the router). To verify that the switch will learn a MAC address dynamically, ping the router from ComputerA and then check the MAC address table again.

3. Open the command prompt on ComputerA, and enter **ping 12.0.0.1** to ping the router. You should get replies.

4. Go back to the console window of the VAN-SW1 switch.

5. Execute the **show mac address-table** command again. Notice the MAC address of the device that is connected to port 5 on the switch. Also note that both entries are dynamic entries, because they were learned based on network traffic.

6. To create a static entry and associate it with port 3, enter the following commands:

```
VAN-SW1#config term
VAN-SW1(config)# mac address-table static 0000.1111.2222 vlan 1 int g1/0/3
```

7. View the MAC address table to verify that the static address has been added.

Interface Configuration

Now that we have covered the basic configuration settings of the switch, let's move into configuring the ports on the switch. In the following sections, you will learn to configure basic settings on a port, and then you'll learn how to limit which systems can connect to a port with the port security feature.

Configuring Ports

You'll use several common commands to configure ports on a switch. Here you'll learn about commands to add a port description, configure the switch speed, configure the duplex setting, enable and disable a port, and verify port settings.

Adding a Port Description

From time to time, you may want to add a description to the port that specifies what the port is used for. For example, if a web server is connected to a port, you may want to add a "Web Server" description label. The following code example labels the port "UpLink Port," because it connects to another switch:

```
VAN-SW1>enable
VAN-SW1#config term
Enter configuration commands, one per line.  End with CNTL/Z.
VAN-SW1(config)#interface GigabitEthernet1/0/1
VAN-SW1(config-if)#description UpLink Port
```

Once you have added a description to a port, you will see that label when you view the status of the interface with the **show interface g1/0/1** command.

Configuring Switch Speed

Most switches today have ports that support 10 Mbps (Ethernet), 100 Mbps (Fast Ethernet), and 1000 Mbps (Gigabit Ethernet). The switch will detect the speed of the device that is connected to it and run the port at that speed. For example, if you were to connect a computer with a network interface card (NIC) that supports 100 Mbps, the switch would detect this and configure the port for 100 Mbps. This *autodetect feature* sets the speed of the port. To configure the speed on the port manually, you can navigate to the port using the interface global configuration command:

```
VAN-SW1>enable
VAN-SW1#config term
Enter configuration commands, one per line.  End with CNTL/Z.
VAN-SW1(config)#interface g1/0/1
```

If you are not sure what speeds are supported by the interface, you can use the help feature on the **speed** command as follows:

```
VAN-SW1(config-if)#speed ?
  10    Force 10 Mbps operation
  100   Force 100 Mbps operation
```

```
1000  Force 1000 Mbps operation
auto  Enable AUTO speed configuration
```

Notice that the speeds of 10/100/1000 are supported, and you can set the speed to auto if you want to the switch to autodetect the speed (the default). So, to configure the port to run at 1000 Mbps, you'd use the following command:

```
VAN-SW1(config-if)#speed 1000
```

To configure any of these settings on multiple ports at one time, use the **interface range** command to select multiple ports and then change the setting. In this example, I set the speed of all 24Gb ports:

```
VAN-SW1(config)#interface range g1/0/1 - 24
VAN-SW1(config-if-range)#speed 1000
```

Configuring Duplex Setting

You can configure the duplex setting on your ports by using the **duplex** command on the interface. This setting also has an autodetect feature that detects the duplex setting of the device connected and then sets the duplex setting on the port to match it. Note that you can set the duplex setting to **full** to send and receive data on the port at the same time, or set it to **half** to send and receive data, but not at the same time:

```
VAN-SW1>enable
VAN-SW1#config term
Enter configuration commands, one per line.  End with CNTL/Z.
VAN-SW1(config)#interface g0/1
VAN-SW1(config-if)#duplex ?
  auto  Enable AUTO duplex configuration
  full  Force full duplex operation
  half  Force half-duplex operation
VAN-SW1(config-if)#duplex full
```

Enabling and Disabling Ports

You will want to disable or enable a port on the switch from time to time. For example, you may decide to disable a port for security reasons, so that no one can use the port until you enable it. This section shows you how to disable and enable a port on a switch.

Disable Interfaces   To disable a port, navigate to the interface of the port you want to disable and then use the **shutdown** command. After executing this command, you'll receive feedback that the state of the port has been changed to "administratively down." This means that the administrator has disabled the port; when the port shows a status of "down," it means that the port is not working because of a configuration or protocol error. Here's an example:

```
VAN-SW1>enable
VAN-SW1#config term
```

```
Enter configuration commands, one per line.  End with CNTL/Z.
VAN-SW1(config)#interface g1/0/1
VAN-SW1(config-if)#shutdown
%LINK-5-CHANGED: Interface GigabitEthernet1/0/1, changed state to
administratively down
```

Again, don't forget that you can use the **interface range** command to configure multiple ports at one time. In this example, I want to disable Gigabit ports 1 and 2 on the switch, so I can use the **interface range** command to select them first, and then use the **shutdown** command:

```
VAN-SW1(config-if)#interface range g1/0/1 - 2
VAN-SW1(config-if-range)#shutdown
%LINK-5-CHANGED: Interface GigabitEthernet1/0/1, changed state to
administratively down
%LINK-5-CHANGED: Interface GigabitEthernet1/0/2, changed state to
administratively down
```

Enable Interfaces   If a port has been disabled (administratively down), you can enable it with the **no shutdown** command. Remember that with Cisco switches, you typically reverse something by placing the word **no** in front of the command:

```
VAN-SW1(config-if)#interface g1/0/1
VAN-SW1(config-if)#no shutdown
```

Again, to enable multiple interfaces, you can use the **interface range** command to select the interfaces and then use the **no shutdown** command:

```
VAN-SW1(config-if)#interface range g1/0/1 - 2
VAN-SW1(config-if-range)#no shutdown
%LINK-5-CHANGED: Interface GigabitEthernet1/0/1, changed state to up
%LINK-5-CHANGED: Interface GigabitEthernet1/0/2, changed state to up
```

Verifying Port Settings

Once you have configured the settings you want on the interface, you must verify that the settings are correct. When troubleshooting communication issues, you typically want to check the status on the interface by using the **show interfaces** command and then specifying the interface you want to check (otherwise, you get a list of all the interfaces and their settings). Here's an example:

```
VAN-SW2#show interfaces g1/0/1
GigabitEthernet1/0/1 is administratively down, line protocol is down (disabled)
  Hardware is Lance, address is 0002.1653.0701 (bia 0002.1653.0701)
  Description: UpLink Port
  MTU 1500 bytes, BW 1000000 Kbit, DLY 1000 usec,
     reliability 255/255, txload 1/255, rxload 1/255
```

```
Encapsulation ARPA, loopback not set
 Keepalive set (10 sec)
 Full-duplex, 1000Mb/s
(output cut for briefness)
```

In this code, notice that the interface is administratively down, meaning you disabled it. Notice the description, full-duplex, and that 1000 Mbps has been configured. And notice the Encapsulation ARPA—this is the layer 2 protocol being used. In this case it means that Ethernet is the layer 2 protocol.

Exercise 9-4: Configuring Interfaces on a Switch

In this exercise, you will practice configuring interfaces on a switch by changing the description, speed, and duplex settings.

1. Ensure that all routers and switches for the lab environment are booted up.

2. Connect to the console port of VAN-SW1 with PuTTY.

3. Navigate to port 8 on the switch:

```
VAN-SW1>enable
VAN-SW1#config term
Enter configuration commands, one per line.  End with CNTL/Z.
VAN-SW1(config)#interface g1/0/8
VAN-SW1(config-if)#
```

4. To view a list of supported speeds, type the **speed ?** command and press ENTER.

5. Set the speed of the interface to 100 Mbps by entering **speed 100**. Then press ENTER.

6. To set the description on this port to "Web Server," type **description Web Server** and then press ENTER.

7. To disable the port, type **shutdown** and press ENTER.

8. Enter the following commands to view the status on port 8:

```
VAN-SW1(config-if)#exit
VAN-SW1(config)#exit
VAN-SW1#show interface g1/0/8
GigabitEthernet1/0/8 is administratively down, line protocol is down (disabled)
  Hardware is Lance, address is 00d0.ba2a.9508 (bia 00d0.ba2a.9508)
  Description: Web Server
  MTU 1500 bytes, BW 100000 Kbit, DLY 1000 usec,
     reliability 255/255, txload 1/255, rxload 1/255
  Encapsulation ARPA, loopback not set
  Keepalive set (10 sec)
  Half-duplex, 100Mb/s
(output cut for briefness)
```

Notice that the interface is administratively down, has a description assigned to it, has a speed of 100 Mbps, and is half duplex.

9. Navigate back to the interface and set its speed to 1000.

10. Enable the interface by using the **no shutdown** command.

Understanding Port Security

Port security is a switch feature that enables you to lock down switch ports based on the MAC address or addresses associated with the interface; this prevents unauthorized access to a LAN. For example, you could configure port security on port g0/5 for the MAC address of aaaa.aaaa.1111, specifying that the system with that MAC address is the only authorized device for that port. If any other system connects to that port, a security violation results. As an administrator, you control what should happen when a violation occurs, be it generating a notification about the issue, dropping traffic for the MAC address that caused the violation, or completely disabling the port where the violation occurred.

EXAM TIP Remember for the CCNA exam that port security is a feature that can be used to lock down ports on a switch, preventing unauthorized access to your LAN.

The port security feature will not work on trunk ports, Switch Port Analyzer (SPAN) ports, and EtherChannel ports. However, it is compatible with 802.1X and voice VLANs. You will learn more about these topics in Chapter 10.

Port Security Configuration

The port security feature is configured per interface with a number of **switchport** commands. The following **switchport** commands are used to configure port security on an interface:

```
switch(config)# interface fastethernet|gigabit 0/port_#
switch(config-if)# switchport mode access
switch(config-if)# switchport port-security
switch(config-if)# switchport port-security maximum value
switch(config-if)# switchport port-security violation
                   protect|restrict|shutdown
switch(config-if)# switchport port-security mac-address MAC_address
```

EXAM TIP For the exam, be familiar with configuring port security with the **switchport port-security** commands (enabling it, limiting the MAC addresses, setting violation mode). You will be asked questions about port security on the CCNA exam.

Let's review the commands. First, you must enter the appropriate interface where you want to set up port security. The second command, **switchport mode access**, places the interface in access mode, which is used by a host instead of as a trunk port. (Trunking is explained in Chapter 10.) The third command on the interface, **switchport port-security**, enables port security (it is disabled by default). The fourth command, **switch-port port-security maximum**, specifies the maximum number of devices that can be associated with the interface. This defaults to 1 and can range from 1 to 132.

 TIP   When configuring port security, set the maximum parameter to 1 address for an interface so that only one MAC address is associated with the port. As a result no other addresses are learned when a different system is connected to the port.

The fifth command on the interface specifies what should occur if a security violation occurs—a different MAC address is connected to the port. Three options are possible:

- **Protect command**   This command sends an alert to the administrator when an unauthorized device is connected to the port.

- **Restrict command**   The **restrict** setting results in the port being able to forward frames for the authorized device only. If an unauthorized device connects to the port, the switch will drop those frames.

- **Shutdown command**   With this command, the port is disabled the second an authorized device connects to the port. The port is disabled until the administrator issues the **no shutdown** command. This is the default violation mode if you don't specify the mode.

The last command lets you specify the exact MAC address that is allowed to be associated with this interface—this is statically defining the MAC addresses allowed off of the port. The following is a complete code example of configuring port security on port 4:

```
switch(config)# interface g1/0/4
switch(config-if)# switchport mode access
switch(config-if)# switchport port-security
switch(config-if)# switchport port-security maximum 1
switch(config-if)# switchport port-security violation shutdown
switch(config-if)# switchport port-security mac-address cccc.cccc.3333
```

Sticky Learning

Port security is a great feature and very common on networks to prevent unauthorized devices from connecting an enabled port on the switch. The problem is, however, that it poses a huge administrative burden to set up, because you have to specify the MAC address of authorized devices on each port. There is a solution to cut down on the administrative burden: use the **sticky** option instead of a MAC address. When you use the **sticky** option, the switch will dynamically learn the MAC address of the system already connected to the port and then configure the port security feature using that MAC address. This is very useful when you're looking at configuring multiple ports at one time for port security by using the **interface range** command to select the interfaces. The following example shows how to use the **sticky** option:

```
switch(config)# interface gigabitethernet0/4
switch(config-if)# switchport mode access
switch(config-if)# switchport port-security
switch(config-if)# switchport port-security maximum 1
switch(config-if)# switchport port-security violation shutdown
switch(config-if)# switchport port-security mac-address sticky
```

 EXAM TIP For the exam, make sure you are familiar with how to use the **sticky** option with port security.

Port Security Verification

To check which ports you have configured port security on and also view the security action and violation count, use the **show port-security** command as follows:

```
Switch#show port-security
Secure Port MaxSecureAddr CurrentAddr SecurityViolation Security Action
            (Count)       (Count)      (Count)
-----------------------------------------------------------------------
    Gig1/0/4       1           1              0           Shutdown
-----------------------------------------------------------------------
Switch#
```

To see the MAC addresses that are statically defined or dynamically learned with port security, use the **show port-security address** command:

```
Switch#show port-security address
                 Secure Mac Address Table
-----------------------------------------------------------------------
Vlan  Mac Address     Type            Ports               Remaining Age
                                                          (mins)
----  -----------     ----            -----               -------------
1     CCCC.CCCC.3333  SecureConfigured GigabitEthernet1/0/4     -
-----------------------------------------------------------------------
Total Addresses in System (excluding one mac per port)     : 0
Max Addresses limit in System (excluding one mac per port) : 1024
Switch#
```

In this example, notice that port G1/0/4 has a MAC address associated with it.

If you want to see a bit more port security detail on a specific port, use the **show port-security interface** command as follows:

```
Switch#show port-security interface g1/0/4
Port Security               : Enabled
Port Status                 : Secure-down
Violation Mode              : Shutdown
Aging Time                  : 0 mins
Aging Type                  : Absolute
SecureStatic Address Aging  : Disabled
Maximum MAC Addresses       : 1
Total MAC Addresses         : 1
Configured MAC Addresses    : 1
Sticky MAC Addresses        : 0
Last Source Address:Vlan    : 0000.0000.0000:0
Security Violation Count    : 0
```

In this example, you can see that port security is enabled, the violation mode is shutdown, the maximum number of MAC addresses that can be connected to the port is 1, and one MAC address has to be statically configured for the port. At the bottom of the output, notice that no security violations have occurred on the port.

 EXAM TIP Be familiar with the **show port-security interface** command for the exam. Remember that if the Port Security value is set to **Disabled**, you must execute the **switchport port-security** command on the interface to enable it. Also, you'll be expected to be able to determine the number of MAC addresses configured (allowed).

Exercise 9-5: Configuring Port Security on a Cisco Switch

In this exercise, you will practice configuring port security on a Cisco switch. Then you'll verify that port security is working.

1. Ensure that all routers and switches are running.

2. On ComputerA, launch a command prompt.

3. To verify that ComputerA can communicate on the network, type **ping 12.0.0.1** and press ENTER.

   You should receive four ping replies. This proves that ComputerA can communicate on the network.

   You will next configure port security with a bogus MAC address on port 5 of the switch, which is not the MAC address of ComputerA. This will cause port 5 to shut down and no longer allow ComputerA to communicate on the network.

4. Connect to the console port of VAN-SW1 with PuTTY.

5. Navigate to port 5 on the switch:

```
VAN-SW1>enable
VAN-SW1#config term
Enter configuration commands, one per line.  End with CNTL/Z.
VAN-SW1(config)#interface g1/0/5
VAN-SW1(config-if)#
```

6. To place the port in access mode and then enable the port security feature on port 5, use the following commands:

```
switch(config-if)# switchport mode access
switch(config-if)# switchport port-security
```

7. To specify that a maximum of 1 MAC address can be associated with the port, use this command:

```
switch(config-if)# switchport port-security maximum 1
```

8. To shut down the port until an administrator enables it if an unauthorized device tries to use the port, enter the following:

```
switch(config-if)# switchport port-security violation shutdown
```

9. To specify the MAC address of the device that is authorized to connect to the port, type the following:

```
switch(config-if)# switchport port-security mac-address cccc.cccc.3333
```

10. Switch back to the command prompt on ComputerA and try to ping 12.0.0.1. Notice that you can no longer ping. This is because the port has been configured to allow only the device with the MAC address of cccc.cccc.3333 to use the port. The port should now be disabled and cannot be used until the administrator enables it.

11. Change back to the VAN-SW1 switch and type the following command:

```
VAN-SW1#show port-security
Secure Port MaxSecureAddr CurrentAddr SecurityViolation Security Action
                (Count)       (Count)        (Count)
--------------------------------------------------------------------------
    Gig1/0/5         1             1              1              Shutdown
--------------------------------------------------------------------------
VAN-SW1#
```

Notice that port 5 has one security violation and that the security action was shut down.

12. To view the port security details on the port, type the following:

```
VAN-SW1#show port-security interface g1/0/5
Port Security                 : Enabled
Port Status                   : Secure-shutdown
Violation Mode                : Shutdown
```

```
Aging Time                      : 0 mins
Aging Type                      : Absolute
SecureStatic Address Aging      : Disabled
Maximum MAC Addresses           : 1
Total MAC Addresses             : 1
Configured MAC Addresses        : 1
Sticky MAC Addresses            : 0
Last Source Address:Vlan        : 0030.F2E8.4203:1
Security Violation Count        : 1
```

Notice that the port status is Secure-shutdown, meaning that the port is shut down because of a security violation.

13. Use the **show interfaces g1/0/5** command to view the interface stats on the port. Note the err-disabled on the first line, stating that this port was disabled due to error.

14. To enable the port once again, use the following commands:

```
VAN-SW1#config term
VAN-SW1(config)#interface g1/0/5
VAN-SW1(config-if)#shutdown
%LINK-5-CHANGED: Interface GigabitEthernet1/0/5, changed state to
administratively down
VAN-SW1(config-if)#no shutdown
%LINK-5-CHANGED: Interface GigabitEthernet1/0/5, changed state to up
```

15. Use the **show interface g1/0/5** command to see that the interface is up. Note that you cannot use the port from ComputerA, because the port security is still configured, so the port will get disabled again.

Working with VLANs

A *virtual LAN* (VLAN) is a logical grouping of network devices in the same broadcast domain that can span across multiple switches. The top part of Figure 9-5 shows an example of a simple VLAN, where every device is in both the same collision and broadcast domains. In this example, a hub is providing the connectivity, which represents, to the devices connected to it, that the segment is a logical segment.

The bottom part of Figure 9-5 shows an example of a switch with four PCs connected to it. One major difference between the switch and the hub is that all devices connected to the hub are in the same collision domain, whereas in the switch example, each port of the switch is a separate collision domain. By default, all ports on a switch are in the same broadcast domain. In this example, however, the configuration of the switch places PC-E and PC-F in one broadcast domain (VLAN) and PC-G and PC-H in another broadcast domain.

Switches are used to create VLANs, or separate broadcast domains. VLANs are not restricted to any physical boundary in the switched network, assuming that all the devices are interconnected via switches and that there are no intervening layer 3 devices.

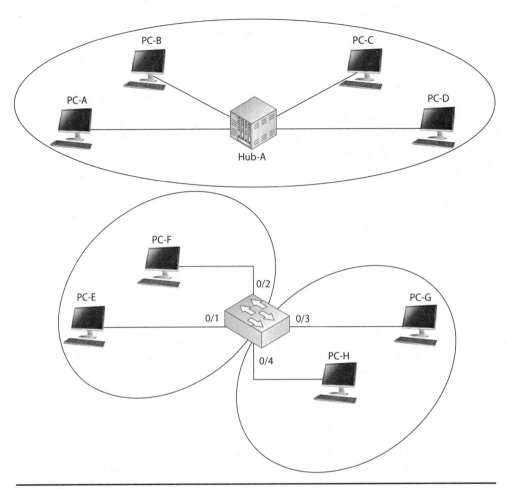

Figure 9-5   VLAN examples

For example, a VLAN could be spread across multiple switches, or it could be contained in the same switch, as shown in Figure 9-6. This example shows three VLANs. Notice that VLANs are not tied to any physical location: PC-A, PC-B, PC-E, and PC-F are in the same VLAN but are connected to different ports of different switches. However, a VLAN could be contained to one switch, as PC-C and PC-D are connected to SwitchA.

The switches in your network maintain the integrity of your VLANs. For example, if PC-A generates a broadcast, SwitchA and SwitchB will make sure that only other devices in that VLAN (PC-B, PC-E, and PC-F) will see the broadcast, and that other devices will not, and that holds true even across switches, as is the case in Figure 9-6.

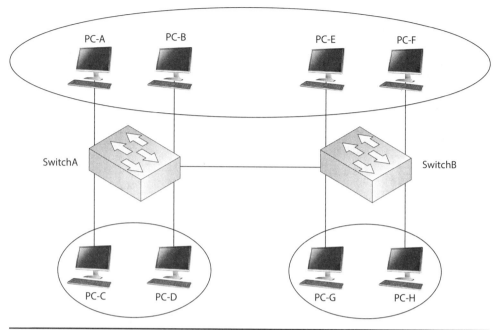

Figure 9-6 Physical switched topology using VLANs

 EXAM TIP Remember for the CCNA exam that a VLAN is a group of devices in the same broadcast domain or subnet. VLANs are good at logically separating/ segmenting traffic between different groups of users. VLANs contain/isolate broadcast traffic, where you need a router to move traffic between VLANs. VLANs create separate broadcast domains; they increase the number of broadcast domains but decrease the size of the broadcast domains.

Subnets and VLANs

Logically speaking, VLANs are also subnets. A subnet, or a network, is a contained broadcast domain. A broadcast that occurs in one subnet will not be forwarded, by default, to another subnet. Routers, or layer 3 devices, provide this boundary function. Each of these subnets requires a unique network number. And to move from one network number to another, you need a router. In the case of broadcast domains and switches, each of these separate broadcast domains is a separate VLAN; therefore, you still need a routing function to move traffic between different VLANs.

From the user's perspective, the physical topology shown in Figure 9-6 would actually look like Figure 9-7. And from the user's perspective, the devices know that to reach another VLAN (subnet), they must forward their traffic to the default gateway address in their VLAN—the IP address on their router's interface.

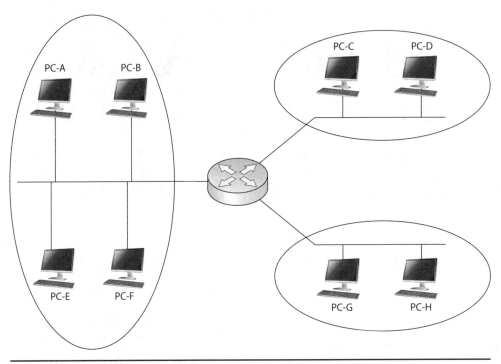

Figure 9-7   Logical topology using VLANs

 EXAM TIP   Some exam questions will require that you remember that each VLAN must be associated with a unique subnet or network number.

Remember two important things about VLANs and switches: First, a switch can handle multiple VLANs on a single port, and a router can route between these VLANs on the same single port if that port is designated as a *trunk* port (more on trunk ports later in this chapter). Second, remember that a VLAN is a broadcast domain, so if you want to optimize traffic, it is recommended that a VLAN not exceed 500 devices.

Scalability

Through segmentation of broadcast domains, VLANs increase your network's scalability. Because VLANs are a logical construct, a user can be located anywhere in the switched network and still belong to the same broadcast domain. If you move a user from one switch to another switch in the same switched network, you can still keep the user in his or her original VLAN. This includes a move from one floor of a building to another floor or from one part of the campus to another. The limitation is that the user, when moved, must still be connected to the same layer 2 network.

NOTE   VLANs provide for location independence in a switched network: many logical networks can use the same network infrastructure. This flexibility makes adding, changing, and moving of networking devices a simple process. It also enables you to group people together, perhaps according to their job function, which makes implementing your security policies easier. Logically separating people using VLANs provides additional security, since traffic must traverse a layer 3 device to go from one VLAN to another, where you can use an access control list to filter traffic.

VLANs and Traffic Types

Many network administrators use VLANs not only to separate different types of user traffic (commonly separated by job function), but also to separate based on the type of traffic, placing network management, multicast, and voice over IP (VoIP) traffic into their own distinctive VLANs.

Network management traffic is traffic generated by the different protocols and features of network devices in order to help discover, monitor, and maintain devices on the network. Some examples of network management traffic may be SNMP traffic, NTP traffic, CDP traffic, and syslog traffic. Network management traffic may also involve device configuration backups and network upgrade traffic. As a network designer you may decide to have some of this traffic on its own segment.

Multicast traffic is commonly used by video applications to transmit video streams intelligently from a server to one or more clients interested in seeing it, where UDP is used as a transport for the video stream. An example of a video solution that uses multicasts is Cisco's IP/TV server. Video traffic is delay sensitive—too much delay can be noticeable by the end user, because the actual video picture looks jumpy and jagged. By separating this traffic from other types through VLANs, and by setting up the necessary quality of service (QoS) for this VLAN traffic, you can help minimize or prevent delay issues.

VoIP traffic includes two kinds of traffic: signaling information sent from the VoIP phones to the VoIP gateway products, such as Cisco Unified Communications Manager (formerly called Cisco CallManager), and the actual voice conversations, which use UDP as a transport between VoIP phones and/or digital phones connected to VoIP PBXs. One issue with VoIP traffic is that it is delay-sensitive, so mixing this kind of traffic with other data types can cause performance issues that are very noticeable on voice connections. Therefore, separating this traffic in its own VLAN and using QoS to ensure that this kind of traffic is given higher priority than other types is an important design consideration. Some Cisco Catalyst switches support a special type of VLAN, called a *voice VLAN*. With the voice VLAN feature, switches will automatically place a Cisco VoIP phone into the voice VLAN once the VoIP phone is plugged into the switch. The advantage of this approach is that when a VoIP phone is added to the network, you, as an administrator, no longer have to worry about configuring the switch to place the phone into the correct VLAN.

TIP Different types of traffic, such as delay-sensitive voice or video traffic (multicast), network management traffic, and data application traffic, should be separated into different VLANs via connected switches to prevent problems of one traffic type affecting the performance of other types of traffic. QoS can be used to prioritize traffic types such as VoIP and video to ensure that they receive the necessary bandwidth and are prioritized over other types of data traffic.

VLAN Membership

A device's membership in a VLAN can be determined by one of three methods: static, dynamic, or voice. These methods affect how a switch will associate a port in its chassis with a particular VLAN. When you are dealing with static VLANs, you must manually assign a port on a switch to a VLAN using an *interface subconfiguration* mode command. VLANs configured in this way are typically called *port-based* VLANs.

With dynamic VLANs, the switch automatically assigns the port to a VLAN using information from the user device, such as its MAC address, IP address, or even directory information (a user or group name, for instance). The switch then consults a policy server, called a *VLAN membership policy server* (VMPS), which is proprietary to Cisco and contains a mapping of device information to VLANs. One of the switches in your network must be configured as this server. Low-end Cisco switches cannot serve as VMPS server switches, but other switches, such as the Catalyst 6500, can. In this situation, the low-end switches act as clients and use the 6500 to store the dynamic VLAN membership information.

Another option is to use 802.1X authentication, which is used to authenticate a device's access to a switch or wireless access point. The authentication credentials are stored on an authentication server. One policy you can assign to the user account (associated with the authenticating device) on the authentication server is the VLAN to which the device belongs—the server can pass this to the layer 2 device, which, in turn, can associate the VLAN to the port with which the authenticated device is associated.

Dynamic VLANs have one main advantage over static VLANs: they support plug-and-play movability. For instance, if you move a PC from a port on one switch to a port on another switch and you are using dynamic VLANs, the new switch port will automatically be configured for the VLAN to which the user belongs. About the only time that you have to configure information with dynamic VLANs is if you hire an employee and the employee leaves the company or changes job functions.

If you are using static VLANs, not only will you have to configure the switch port manually with this updated information, but, if you move the user from one switch to another, you will also have to perform this manual configuration to reflect the user's new port. One advantage, though, that static VLANs have over dynamic VLANs is that the configuration process is easy and straightforward. Dynamic VLANs require a lot of initial preparation involving matching users to VLANs. (This book focuses exclusively on static VLANs, as dynamic VLANs are beyond its scope.)

Voice VLANs are unique. They are associated to ports that have VoIP phones attached. Some VoIP phones may have a multiport switch attached to them to enable other devices to connect to the switch via the phone. In this instance, the phone may tag frames to indicate which device is sending the traffic—phone or computer—so that the switch can then deal with the traffic correctly.

VLAN Connections

When dealing with VLANs, switches support two types of switch ports: access ports and trunk ports. When setting up your switches, you will need to know what type of connection an interface should use and then configure it appropriately. As you will see, the configuration process for each type of interface is different. This section discusses the two types of connections.

Access Ports

An *access port* provides a connection to a device that has a standardized Ethernet NIC that understands only standardized Ethernet frames—in other words, a normal NIC that understands IEEE 802.3 and Ethernet II frames. Access port connections can be associated only with a single VLAN (voice VLAN ports are an exception to this). This means that any device or devices connected to this port will be in the same broadcast domain.

For example, if ten users are connected to a hub, and you plug the hub into an access port interface on a switch, then all of these users will belong to the same VLAN that is associated with the switch port. If you wanted five users on the hub to belong to one VLAN and the other five to a different VLAN, you would need to purchase an additional hub and plug each hub into a different switch port. Then, on the switch, you would need to configure each of these ports with the correct VLAN identifier.

 EXAM TIP   Remember for the exam that an access port is used to connect an end-point device, such as a server, a workstation, or a laptop, to the network via that port. An access port is typically associated with a single VLAN.

Trunk Ports for Interswitch Connectivity

Unlike access ports, *trunk* ports are capable of carrying traffic for multiple VLANs and are configured on ports that are connecting to other switches. To support trunking, the original Ethernet frame must be modified to carry VLAN information, commonly called a *VLAN identifier* or number. This ensures that the broadcast integrity is maintained. For instance, if a device from VLAN 1 has generated a broadcast and the connected switch has received it, when this switch forwards it to other switches, these switches need to know the VLAN origin so that they can forward this frame out only VLAN 1 ports and not other VLAN ports.

Cisco supports two Ethernet trunking methods:

- Cisco's proprietary InterSwitch Link (ISL) protocol for Ethernet
- IEEE 802.1Q, commonly referred to as *dot1q* for Ethernet

EXAM TIP For the exam, remember that a trunk modifies the original frame to carry VLAN information, including a VLAN identifier in the frame. IEEE 802.1Q defines a standard method of VLAN trunking. A trunk connection between two switches enables the same VLANs on the two switches to intercommunicate (like VLAN 2 devices on both switches).

Cisco's high-end switches, such as the Catalyst 6500s, support both methods; however, Cisco's low-end switches support only 802.1Q: ISL is being phased out by Cisco. This book focuses on the use of the latter trunk method, dot1q.

Trunk Tagging

Trunking methods create the illusion that instead of a single physical connection between the two trunking devices, a separate logical connection exists for each VLAN between them. When trunking, the switch adds the source port's VLAN identifier to the frame so that the device (typically a switch) at the other end of the trunk understands what VLAN originated this frame and the destination switch can make intelligent forwarding decisions on not just the destination MAC address, but also the source VLAN identifier.

Since information is added to the original Ethernet frame, normal NICs will not understand this information and will typically drop the frame. Therefore, you need to ensure that when you set up a trunk connection on a switch's interface, the device at the other end also supports the same trunking protocol and has it configured. If the device at the other end doesn't understand these modified frames or is not set up for trunking, it will, in most situations, drop them.

The modification of these frames, commonly called *tagging*, is done in hardware by application-specific integrated circuits (ASICs). ASICs are specialized processors. Since the tagging is done in hardware at faster than wire speeds, no latency is involved in the actual tagging process. And to ensure compatibility with access port devices, switches will strip off the tagging information and forward the original Ethernet frame to the device or devices connected to access port connections. From the user's perspective, the source generates a normal Ethernet frame and the destination receives this frame, which is an Ethernet 802.3 or II frame coming in and the same going out. In reality, this frame is tagged as it enters the switched infrastructure and sheds the tag as it exits the infrastructure; the process of tagging and untagging the frame is hidden from the users connected to access ports.

Trunk-Capable Devices

Trunk links are common between certain types of devices, including switch-to-switch, switch-to-router, and switch-to-file server connections. Using a trunk link on a router is a great way of reducing your layer 3 infrastructure costs. For instance, in the old days of bridging, in order to route between different broadcast domains, you needed a *separate* physical router interface for each broadcast domain. So if you had two broadcast domains, you needed two router ports; if you had 20 broadcast domains, you needed 20 router ports. As you can see, the more broadcast domains you had with bridges, the more expensive the router would become.

Today, with the advent of VLANs and trunk connections, you can use a single port on a router to route between your multiple broadcast domains. Whether you have 2 or 20 broadcast domains, you can use just one port on the router to accomplish the routing between these different subnets. Of course, you need a router and an interface that support trunking. Not every Cisco router supports trunking; you need at least a Cisco 1751 or better router with the correct type of Ethernet interface. If your router doesn't support trunking, you would need a separate router interface for each VLAN you created to route between the VLANs. Therefore, if you have a lot of VLANs, it makes sense to economize and buy a router and the correct type of interface that supports trunking.

TIP   Routing between VLANs is a great use of layer 3 switches (switches that have routing functionality as well). You could have a layer 3 core switch, with all the VLANs configured, performing the job of routing internally.

You can also purchase specialized NICs for PCs or servers, such as file servers or virtualization servers, that support trunking. For instance, suppose you want multiple VLANs to access a file server. You could use a normal NIC and set it up with an access port connection to a switch. Because this is an access port connection, the server could belong only to one VLAN. The users in the same VLAN, when accessing the server, would have all their traffic switched via layer 2 devices to reach it. Users in other VLANs, however, would require that their traffic be routed to this server via a router, since the file server is in a different broadcast domain.

TIP   If the same VLANs are on two connected switches, use a trunk connection between the switches to enable the associated VLANs on each side to communicate with each other. Trunk connections are commonly used on routers so that routers, via subinterfaces, can route between the VLANs. The trunking encapsulation, however, must match between the two trunking devices (such as using 802.1Q on both sides, or Cisco's proprietary ISL on both sides).

If throughput is a big concern, you may want to buy a trunk NIC for the file server. Configuring this NIC is different from configuring a normal NIC on a file server. For each VLAN in which you want the file server to participate, you would create a virtual NIC, assign your VLAN identifier and layer 3 addressing to the virtual NIC for the specific VLAN, and then associate it with the physical NIC. Once you have created all of these logical NICs on your file server, you need to set up a trunk connection on the switch to the server. And once you have done this, members of VLANs in the switched network will be able to access the file server directly without going through a router. These trunk-capable NICs are common enough today that you may even see them in certain PCs, since the NICs are commonly used to support virtualization.

TIP A good example of a device that may need a trunk-capable NIC is a DHCP server, because it may need to assign IP addresses to users across multiple VLANs. If you don't have a trunk-capable NIC, but users are spread across multiple VLANs, you could use the IP helper feature on a Cisco router connected to the users' VLANs and have the router forward the DHCP broadcasts to the DHCP server located in a different VLAN. Another example of a device that may need a trunk-capable NIC is a server in a data center: this is commonly necessary to support the many virtual machines (VMs) running on the server.

Trunking Example

Figure 9-8 shows an example of a trunk connection between SwitchA and SwitchB in a network that has three VLANs. In this example, PC-A, PC-F, and PC-H belong to one VLAN; PC-B and PC-G belong to a second VLAN; and PC-C, PC-D, and PC-E belong to a third VLAN. The trunk between the two switches is also tagging VLAN information so that the remote switch understands the source VLAN of the originator.

Let's take a look at an example of the use of VLANs and the two different types of connections by using the network shown in Figure 9-9. In this example, PC-C generates a local broadcast. When SwitchA receives the broadcast, it examines the incoming port and knows that the source device is from the gray VLAN (the access port connections are marked with dots). Seeing this, the switch knows to forward this frame only out of

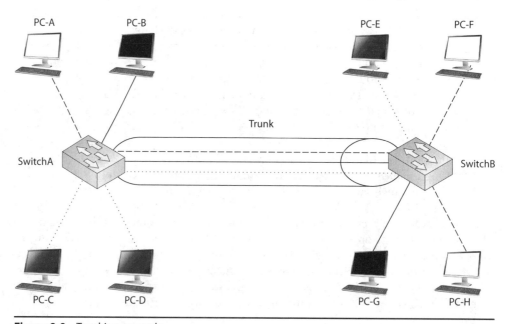

Figure 9-8 Trunking example

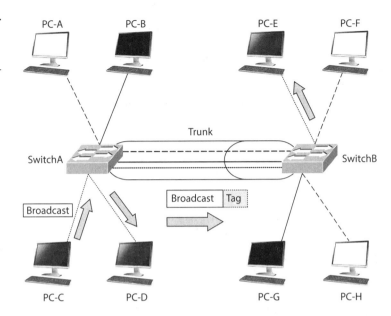

Figure 9-9
Broadcast traffic example

ports that belong to the same VLAN: this includes access port connections with the same VLAN identifier and trunk connections. On this switch, one access port connection belongs to the same VLAN, PC-D, so the switch forwards the frame directly out this interface.

The trunk connection between SwitchA and SwitchB handles traffic for multiple VLANs. A VLAN tagging mechanism is required to differentiate the source of traffic when moving it between the switches. For instance, assume that no tagging mechanism took place between the switches. PC-C generates a broadcast frame, and SwitchA forwards it unaltered to PC-D and then SwitchB across the trunk. The problem with this process is that when SwitchB receives the original Ethernet frame, it has no idea what port or ports to forward the broadcast to, since it doesn't know the origin VLAN.

As shown in Figure 9-9, SwitchA tags the broadcast frame, adding the source VLAN to the original Ethernet frame (the broadcast frame is tagged). When SwitchB receives the frame, it examines the tag and knows that this is meant only for the VLAN to which PC-E belongs. Of course, since PC-E is connected via an access port connection, SwitchB first strips off the tagging and then forwards the original Ethernet frame to PC-E. This is necessary because PC-E has a standard NIC and doesn't understand VLAN tagging. Through this process, both switches maintain the integrity of the broadcast domain.

IEEE 802.1Q

InterSwitch Link (ISL), a Cisco proprietary protocol, is being phased out in Cisco's products and being replaced with the IEEE 802.1Q trunking standard, which was introduced in 1998. One of the advantages provided by the IEEE standard is that it allows trunks between different vendors' devices, whereas ISL is supported only on certain Cisco devices.

Therefore, by using 802.1Q you should be able to implement a multivendor trunking solution without having to worry about whether or not a specific type of trunk connection is or is not supported. The 2960 and better switches, along with Cisco's higher-end switches such as the 6500 series, support 802.1Q. Actually, the new switch models support *only* 802.1Q trunking—they don't support ISL at all. 802.1Q trunking is supported on switch ports that are capable of either Fast Ethernet or Gigabit Ethernet speeds.

802.1Q trunks support two types of frames: tagged and untagged. An untagged frame does not carry any VLAN identification information in it—basically, this is a standard, unaltered Ethernet frame. The VLAN membership for the frame is determined by the switch's port configuration: if the port is configured in VLAN 1, the untagged frame belongs to VLAN 1. This VLAN is commonly called a *native* VLAN. A tagged frame contains VLAN information, and only other 802.1Q-aware devices on the trunk will be able to process this frame.

One of the unique aspects of 802.1Q trunking is that you can have *both* tagged and untagged frames on a trunk connection, such as that shown in Figure 9-10. In this example, the white VLAN (PC-A, PC-B, PC-E, and PC-F) uses tagged frames on the trunk between SwitchA and SwitchB. Any other device that is connected on this trunk line would need to have 802.1Q trunking enabled to see the tag inside the frame to determine the source VLAN of the frame. In this network, a third device is connected to the trunk connection: PC-G. This example assumes that a hub connects the two switches and the PC together.

PC-G has a normal Ethernet NIC and obviously wouldn't understand the tagging and would drop these frames. However, this presents a problem: PC-G belongs to the dark

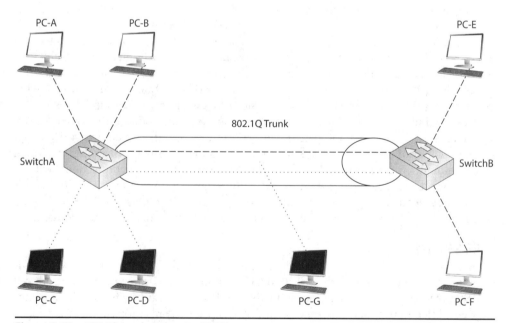

Figure 9-10   802.1Q trunk and native VLAN

VLAN, where PC-C and PC-D are also members. Therefore, in order for frames to be forwarded among these three members, the trunk must also support untagged frames so that PC-G can process them. To set this up, you would configure the switch-to-switch connection as an 802.1Q trunk but set the native VLAN as the dark one, so that frames from this VLAN would go untagged across it and would allow PC-G to process them.

One restriction placed on an 802.1Q trunk configuration is that it must be the *same* on both sides. In other words, if the dark VLAN is the native VLAN on one switch, the switch at the other end must have the native VLAN set to the dark VLAN. Likewise, if the white VLAN is having its frames tagged on one switch, the other switch must also be tagging the white VLAN frames with 802.1Q information.

With the 802.1Q tagging method, the original Ethernet frame is modified. A 4-byte *tag* field is *inserted* into the header of the original Ethernet frame, and the original frame's FCS (checksum) is recomputed on the basis of this change. The first 2 bytes of the tag are the protocol identifier. For instance, an Ethernet type frame has a protocol identifier value of 0x8100, indicating that this is an Ethernet tagged frame. The next 3 bits are used to prioritize the frame, which is defined in the IEEE 802.1p standard. The fourth bit indicates if this is an encapsulated Token Ring frame (Cisco no longer sells Token Ring products), and the last 12 bits are used for the VLAN identifier (number).

Figure 9-11 shows the process that occurs when tagging an Ethernet frame by inserting the 802.1Q field into the Ethernet frame header. As you can see in this figure, step 1 is the normal, untagged Ethernet frame. Step 2 inserts the tag and recomputes a new FCS value. Below step 2 is a blowup of the actual TAG field. As you can see in the figure, the tag is inserted directly after the source and destination MAC addresses in the Ethernet header.

NOTE 802.1Q is a standardized trunking method that inserts a 4-byte field into the original Ethernet frame and recalculates the FCS. Newer Cisco switches support only 802.1Q trunking and not the older ISL protocol. The native VLAN contains untagged frames, even on trunk connections.

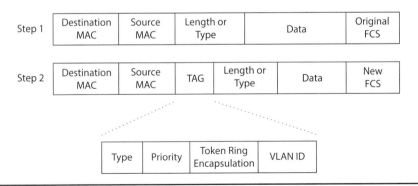

Figure 9-11 802.1Q framing process

One advantage of using this tagging mechanism is that, since you are adding only 4 bytes, your frame size will not exceed 1518 bytes, and thus you could actually forward 802.1Q frames through the access port connections of switches, since these switches would forward the frame as a normal Ethernet frame.

Configuring Trunks

This section covers the setup of trunk ports on your switches using the 802.1Q trunking protocol. Configuring a port as a trunk port enables it to carry VLAN traffic from one switch to another across the trunk port. Before we get into the configuration, however, you should first be familiar with a protocol that is used to form a trunk between two devices: the Dynamic Trunk Protocol.

Dynamic Trunking Protocol

Cisco's proprietary *Dynamic Trunking Protocol* (DTP) is used to form and verify a trunk connection dynamically between two Cisco switches using a trunk connection. It supports five trunking modes, shown in Table 9-2.

If the trunk mode is set to *on* or *trunk* for an interface, it causes the interface to generate DTP messages on the interface and to tag frames on the interface, based on the trunk type (802.1Q). When set to *on*, the trunk interface always assumes the connection is a trunk, even if the remote end does not support trunking. Most newer Cisco switches use the term *trunk* instead of *on*.

If the trunk mode is set to *desirable*, the interface will generate DTP messages on the interface, but it will make the assumption that the other side is not trunk-capable and will wait for a DTP reply message from the remote side. In this state, the interface starts as an access port connection. If the remote side sends a DTP message, and this message indicates that trunking is compatible between the two switches, a trunk will be formed and the switch will start tagging frames on the interface. If the other side does not support trunking, the interface will remain as an access port connection.

If the trunk mode is set to *auto*, the interface passively listens for DTP messages from the remote side and leaves the interface as an access port connection. If the interface receives a DTP message, and the message matches trunking capabilities of the interface, then the interface will change from an access port connection to a trunk connection and

DTP Mode	Generate DTP Messages	Default Frame Tagging
On or trunk	Yes	Yes
Desirable	Yes	No
Auto	No	No
No-negotiate	No	Yes
Off	No	No

Table 9-2 DTP Modes and Operation

	Your Switch	Remote Switch
Table 9-3 Forming Trunks	On	On, desirable, auto
	Desirable	On, desirable, auto
	Auto	On, desirable
	No-negotiate	No-negotiate

start tagging frames. This is the default DTP mode for a Cisco switch interface that is trunk-capable.

If an interface is set to *no-negotiate*, the interface is set as a trunk connection and will automatically tag frames with VLAN information; however, the interface will not generate DTP messages: DTP is disabled. This mode is typically used when connecting trunk connections to non-Cisco devices that don't understand Cisco's proprietary trunking protocol and thus won't understand the contents of these messages.

If an interface is set to *off*, the interface is configured as an access port. No DTP messages are generated in this mode, nor are frames tagged.

Table 9-3 shows when switch connections will form a trunk. In this table, one side needs to be configured as either *on* or *desirable* and the other side as *on*, *desirable*, or *auto*, or both switches need to be configured as *no-negotiate*. Note that if you use the no-negotiate mode, trunking is formed but DTP is not used, whereas if you use on, desirable, or auto, DTP is used. One advantage that DTP has over no-negotiate is that DTP checks for the trunk's characteristics: if they don't match on the two sides (for instance, as to the type of trunk or a mismatch with the native VLAN), then the trunk will not come up and the interfaces will remain as an access port connection. With no-negotiate, if the trunking characteristics don't match on the two sides, the trunk connection will probably fail.

 EXAM TIP Remember the DTP information in Tables 9-2 and 9-3 for the exam. The result of a successful DTP completion is the formation of an 802.1Q trunk. When you're using DTP autosensing, if the native VLAN doesn't match, a native VLAN mismatch error will occur.

Switch Trunk Configuration

Setting up a trunk on a Cisco switch involves navigating to the interface, configuring the trunking protocol on that interface, enabling trunking, and then specifying the native VLAN:

```
switch(config)# interface type slot_#/port_#
switch(config-if)# switchport trunk encapsulation dot1q
switch(config-if)# switchport mode trunk|dynamic desirable|
                   dynamic auto|nonegotiate
switch(config-if)# switchport trunk native vlan VLAN_#
```

For example, I can use the following commands to configure port 24 on a Cisco 3650 switch as a trunk port:

```
VAN-SW1(config-if)#interface g1/0/24
VAN-SW1(config-if)#switchport trunk encapsulation dot1q
VAN-SW1(config-if)#switchport mode trunk
```

Remember that newer Cisco switches support only 802.1Q trunking (and not the older ISL trunking protocol), so you must set up a trunk connection only to other 802.1Q trunking devices. If you want a trunk to be in an *on* state, use the **trunk** parameter. For a *desirable* DTP state, use **dynamic desirable**, and for an *auto* state, use **dynamic auto**. The default mode is auto. If you don't want to use DTP but still want to perform trunking, use the **nonegotiate** parameter. For 802.1Q trunks, the native VLAN is VLAN 1. You can change this with the **switchport trunk native vlan** command, but then you'll need to match up the native VLAN on all switches in the layer 2 network. If two interconnected switches have a different native VLAN on the connecting trunks, then traffic from one VLAN on one switch will end up in a different VLAN on the remote switch, which can create all kinds of problems.

 EXAM TIP   For the Cisco CCNA exam, remember to use the **switchport mode** command to enable trunking on a switch. Use the **switchport trunk native vlan** command to designate the untagged traffic. By default, this is VLAN 1. Also remember that mismatched native VLANs between switches can create connectivity problems.

After you have configured your trunk connection, you can use this command to verify it:

```
switch# show interfaces type 0/port_# switchport|trunk
```

Here's an example using the **switchport** parameter:

```
switch# show interfaces fastEthernet0/1 switchport
Name: Fa0/1
Switchport: Enabled
Administrative mode: trunk
Operational Mode: trunk
Administrative Trunking Encapsulation: dot1q
Operational Trunking Encapsulation: dot1q
Negotiation of Trunking: Disabled
Access Mode VLAN: 0 ((Inactive))
Trunking Native Mode VLAN: 1 (default)
Trunking VLANs Enabled: ALL
Trunking VLANs Active: 1,2
Pruning VLANs Enabled: 2-1001
Priority for untagged frames: 0
Override vlan tag priority: FALSE
Voice VLAN: none
```

In this example, FA0/1's trunking mode is set to **trunk** (on), with the native VLAN set to 1. Here's an example using the **trunk** parameter:

```
switch# show interfaces trunk
Port    Mode        Encapsulation  Status     Native vlan
Fa0/1   on          802.1q         trunking   1
Port    Vlans allowed on trunk
Fa0/1   1-4094
Port    Vlans allowed and active in management domain
Fa0/1   1-2
Port    Vlans in spanning tree forwarding state and not pruned
Fa0/1   1-2
```

EXAM TIP   For the CCNA exam, remember to use the **show interfaces switchport|trunk** command to verify trunking. Be familiar with the output of this command.

In this example, one interface is trunking—fa0/1: the trunking mode is on, the trunking protocol is 802.1Q, and the native VLAN is 1.

NOTE   When executing the **show mac address-table** command, if you see multiple MAC addresses associated with a single interface, this can indicate that the interface is a trunk connection or that the interface is an access port connection to another switch or hub.

Creating VLANs

This section covers how you can create VLANs on your switches and then statically assign interfaces to your newly created VLANs. Here are some guidelines to remember when creating VLANs:

- The number of VLANs you can create is dependent on the switch model and IOS software.
- Some VLANs are preconfigured on every switch, including VLAN 1 and 1002–1005 (1002–1005 are used in Token Ring and FDDI networks only). These VLANs cannot be deleted!
- To add or delete VLANs, your switch must use either VTP server or transparent mode.
- VLAN names can be changed, but VLAN numbers can't; you must delete a VLAN and re-add it in order to renumber it.

- All interfaces, by default, belong to VLAN 1.
- CDP, DTP, and VTP advertisements are sent in the native VLAN, which is VLAN 1, by default.
- Before you delete a VLAN, reassign any ports from the current VLAN to another; if you don't, any ports from the deleted VLAN will be inoperable.
- Unknown destination MAC addresses are flooded only in the VLAN in which the source MAC address resides.

 EXAM TIP Remember the bulleted items for the exam.

You can create VLANs with the **vlan** command in global configuration mode, like this:

```
switch(config)# vlan VLAN_#
switch(config-vlan)# name VLAN_name
```

When you execute the **vlan** command, you have access to the VLAN subconfiguration mode, where you can enter your configuration parameters for the VLAN, such as its name. Use the **no** parameter in front of the **vlan** command to delete the VLAN at any time.

 EXAM TIP Remember for the CCNA exam that your switch must be a VTP server or transparent switch to create or delete VLANs on it. Also, before you delete a VLAN, move all ports in the VLAN to a different one; otherwise, ports associated with a deleted VLAN will not be able to communicate with other ports until you either re-add the VLAN number back or move the ports to an existing VLAN. When this happens, the port LED(s) will be solid amber.

Once you have created a VLAN, you need to assign the interfaces you want be part of that VLAN. To assign a port to a VLAN, navigate to the port, ensure that it is running as an access port, and then assign it to a VLAN:

```
switch(config)# interface type 0/port_#
switch(config-if)# switchport mode access
switch(config-if)# switchport access vlan VLAN_#
switch(config-if)# switchport voice vlan VLAN_#
```

Notice in this code example that after I navigate to the interface, I configure the port as an access port with the **switchport mode access** command. The **switchport access vlan** command assigns the port to a VLAN, while the **switchport voice vlan** command is used to specify the VLAN to be used for VoIP devices connected to the port.

This configuration enables you to connect a VoIP phone to the port and then have a computer connected to the phone—all sending data through the same port on the switch, but with different types of traffic going to different ports. Note that the voice VLAN line of code is optional; if you just want to assign the port to a data VLAN, you need only the first three lines of code in the preceding code listing.

NOTE If you associate a nonexistent VLAN to a switch port with the **switchport access vlan** command, IOS will automatically create the VLAN.

Once you have created and assigned your VLANs, you can use various **show** commands to review and verify your configuration. The **show vlan** command displays the list of VLANs and which ports are assigned to them:

```
switch# show vlan
VLAN Name        Status      Ports
---- --------------- --------- ------------------------------
1    default         active    Fa0/1, Fa0/2, Fa0/3, Fa0/4
                               Fa0/5, Fa0/6, Fa0/7, Fa0/8
                               Fa0/9, Fa0/10, Fa0/11, Fa0/12
                               Fa0/13, Fa0/14, Fa0/15, Fa0/16
                               Fa0/17, Fa0/18, Fa0/19, Fa0/20
                               Fa0/21, Fa0/22, Fa0/23, Fa0/24
                               Gi0/1, Gi0/2
1002 fddi-default              act/unsup
 .
 .
 .
```

In this example, all the ports are assigned to VLAN 1. Add the **brief** parameter to this command, and it will not display the details for each VLAN at the bottom of the display. You can also use the **show interface switchport** command to see a specific interface's VLAN membership information. This command was shown earlier in the chapter in the "Switch Trunk Configuration" section.

EXAM TIP For the CCNA exam, remember that you can use the **vlan** command to create a VLAN. Use the **switchport mode access** and **switchport access vlan** commands to assign a VLAN to an interface. Also remember that if an interface is configured as an access port, it cannot form a trunk. The **show vlan** command displays VLAN information: if the same interface is displayed for multiple VLANs, this interface is probably a trunk port.

Basic Troubleshooting of VLANs and Trunks

Now that you know how to set up a VLAN-based network, you will probably eventually run into a problem that is related to your VLAN configuration. Basically, you should check the following, in order, to determine the cause of the problem:

1. Check the status of your interface to determine whether it is a physical layer problem.

2. Check your switches' and routers' configurations to make sure nothing was added or changed.

3. Verify that your trunks are operational.

4. Verify that your VLANs are configured correctly and that the STP is functioning correctly.

The following sections cover some of the basic things that you should check whenever you experience switching problems.

Performance Problems

If you are experiencing slow performance or intermittent connection problems, you should first check the statistics on the interfaces of your switch with the **show interfaces** command. Are you seeing a high number of errors, such as collisions?

A few things can cause these problems. The most common is a mismatch in either the duplexing or the speed on a connection. Examine the settings on both sides of the connection. Also make sure that you are using the correct cabling type: straight for a DTE-to-DCE connection and crossover for a DTE-to-DTE or DCE-to-DCE connection (as covered in Chapter 1). And make sure that the cable does not exceed the maximum legal limit. Also, make sure that the connected IC is not experiencing a hardware problem or failure.

Local Connection Problems

If you are attempting to access the console port of a switch or router, and all you see is garbage in your terminal session, this could indicate an incorrect terminal setting. Usually the culprit is an incorrect baud rate. Some devices allow you to perform an operating system upgrade via the console port, and an administrator might change it to the highest possible value but forget to change it back to 9600 bps. If you suspect this, keep on changing your baud rate until you find the right speed.

If you are having problems accessing devices in the switched network, you can look at a few options. First, is the device you are trying to reach in the same VLAN? If so, make sure that you are using the correct IP addressing scheme in the VLAN and that the two devices trying to share information have their ports in the same VLAN. If the two devices are Cisco devices, you can use CDP to elicit some of this information, for instance the IP address, by using the **show cdp** command (discussed in Chapter 8). Is the switch learning about the devices in your network? You may want to examine your CAM tables and make sure that a port security violation is not causing your connectivity problem.

For VLAN information, use the **show** commands on your switches to check your VLAN configuration. Also check the VLAN configuration on each switch and make sure the VLANs are configured with the same parameters by using the **show vlan** command. If the port LED is solid amber, your problem could be that the port's VLAN was deleted and the port wasn't reassigned. Other problems can also cause the port LED to turn amber, such as STP placing the port in a blocking state or port security disabling the port because of a security violation. Actually, if you see that a lot of port LEDs are amber, a deleted VLAN is probably the problem. Use the **show interface switchport** command to determine whether a deleted VLAN is the problem: if you see that the VLAN assigned to the port is inactive, like this, then you've identified the culprit:

```
switch# show interface fastEthernet0/1 switchport
Name: Fa0/1
Switchport: Enabled
Administrative mode: static access
Operational Mode: static access
Administrative Trunking Encapsulation: dot1q
Operational Trunking Encapsulation: native
Negotiation of Trunking: Off
Access Mode VLAN: 5 (Inactive)
Trunking Native Mode VLAN: 1 (default)
.
.
.
```

Notice in this example that VLAN 5 is inactive, indicating that the interface is assigned to the VLAN, but the VLAN was deleted, making the interface inoperable.

If you are using trunks between the switches, make sure that the trunks are configured correctly: **show interface trunk**. Make sure that the native VLAN number matches on both ends of the trunk: if they are mismatched, a trunk will not form.

Also check VTP (if you are using it) by executing the **show vtp** command. Make sure you have trunk connections between your switches, since VTP messages only traverse trunks. When using a server/client implementation, make sure that the domain name and, if using the password option, the password match among the VTP switches. Also, all switches must be running the same VTP version (by default this is version 1).

Inter-VLAN Connection Problems

If you are having problems reaching devices in other VLANs, make sure that, first, you can ping the default gateway (router) that is your exit point from the VLAN. A common misconfiguration on a user's PC is a misconfigured default gateway. If you *can't* ping the default gateway, then go back to the preceding section and check local VLAN connectivity issues. If you *can* ping the gateway, check the router's configuration and its interface. Also make sure that the router has a route to the destination VLAN (**show ip route**). If you do have a route to the destination, make sure the destination VLAN is configured correctly and that the default gateway in that VLAN can reach the destination device.

Exercise 9-6: Configuring VLANs

In this exercise you will practice configuring VLANs across two Cisco switches. After creating the VLANs, you will need to create the trunk ports so that VLAN traffic can travel between the two switches. For this exercise, two switches in the Vancouver office are configured as shown here:

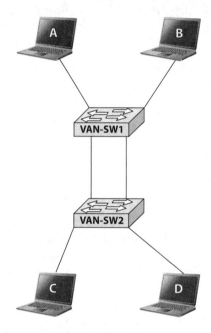

Note that ComputerA is connected to port 5 of VAN-SW1, while ComputerB is connected to port 15 of VAN-SW1. ComputerC is connected to port 5 of VAN-SW2, while ComputerD is connected to port 15 on VAN-SW2.

1. Ensure that both switches are powered up.

2. Ensure that ComputerA and ComputerD have IP addresses of 12.0.0.5 and 12.0.0.15, respectively, and that ComputerB and ComputerC have IP addresses of 14.0.0.5 and 14.0.0.15, respectively.

3. Connect port 1 on VAN-SW1 to port 1 of VAN-SW2 using a crossover cable.

4. Connect port 24 on VAN-SW1 to port 24 of VAN-SW2 using a crossover cable. Wait a minute for the green link lights to show. Notice that one link light will stay amber due to loop prevention features of the switch (more on that in the next chapter).

5. On VAN-SW1, create a MKT VLAN with VLAN ID 2, and a SALES VLAN with VLAN ID 3. Use the following commands as a guide:

```
VAN-SW1>enable
VAN-SW1#config term
Enter configuration commands, one per line.  End with CNTL/Z.
VAN-SW1(config)#vlan 2
VAN-SW1(config-vlan)#name MKT
VAN-SW1(config-vlan)#vlan 3
VAN-SW1(config-vlan)#name SALES
VAN-SW1(config-vlan)#exit
VAN-SW1(config)#exit
VAN-SW1#
```

6. View the list of VLANs with the **show vlan** command. Note that VLAN 2 and VLAN 3 now exist, but there are no ports assigned to the VLANs.

7. Place ComputerA (port 5) into the MKT VLAN using the following commands:

```
VAN-SW1#config term
Enter configuration commands, one per line.  End with CNTL/Z.
VAN-SW1(config)#interface g1/0/5
VAN-SW1(config-if)#switchport mode access
VAN-SW1(config-if)#switchport access vlan 2
```

8. Place ComputerB (port 15) into the SALES VLAN using the following commands:

```
VAN-SW1(config-if)#interface g1/0/15
VAN-SW1(config-if)#switchport mode access
VAN-SW1(config-if)#switchport access vlan 3
VAN-SW1(config-if)#exit
VAN-SW1(config)#exit
VAN-SW1#
```

9. View the list of VLANs and note that VLAN 2 and VLAN 3 now have ports in them.

10. Connect to the console port of VAN-SW2 and press ENTER in PuTTY to refresh the screen.

11. On VAN-SW2, perform the same tasks. Create a MKT VLAN with VLAN ID 2 and create a SALES VLAN with VLAN ID 3.

12. On VAN-SW2, place port 15 in the MKT VLAN and port 5 in the SALES VLAN.

13. View the VLANs and ensure that port 15 is in the MKT VLAN and port 5 is in the SALES VLAN.

14. Go to the command prompt on ComputerA. Can you ping 12.0.0.15 (ComputerD)? _____
You should *not* be able to ping ComputerD, because you need to set up the links between the two switches as trunk ports so that they carry all VLAN traffic between the two switches.

15. On VAN-SW1, configure port 1 as a trunk port using the following commands:

```
VAN-SW1>enable
VAN-SW1#config term
Enter configuration commands, one per line. End with CNTL/Z.
VAN-SW1(config)#interface g1/0/1
VAN-SW1(config-if)#switchport trunk encapsulation dot1q
VAN-SW1(config-if)#switchport mode trunk
```

16. On VAN-SW1, configure port 24 as a trunk port as well:

```
VAN-SW1(config-if)#interface g1/0/24
VAN-SW1(config-if)#switchport trunk encapsulation dot1q
VAN-SW1(config-if)#switchport mode trunk
```

17. To view the status of the trunk ports, use the **show interfaces trunk** command and answer the following questions:

What is the status of port 1 and port 24? _____

What VLAN traffic is allowed to travel through the trunk ports? _____

18. Close the VAN-SW1 tab.

19. Go to ComputerA and ping 12.0.0.15 (ComputerD). Are you able to ping?
_____

The VLAN traffic is now allowed to cross the trunk port so the ping message should go to ComputerD on the other switch.

20. From ComputerA, are you able to ping 14.0.0.15 (ComputerB)? _____
Note that ComputerB is on the same switch, but you are not able to ping it because it exists in a different VLAN. A VLAN is a communication boundary.

Chapter Review

This chapter focused on basic configuration tasks specific to Cisco switches. The physical characteristics of switches were reviewed, including the meanings of the LEDs and the use of the Mode button.

You learned about the core functions of the switch and the switch operation modes. You then learned about basic configuration settings on a switch, such a changing the name of the switch and configuring an IP address and default gateway on the switch. That was followed by configuration of ports on the switch.

You then learned about the port security feature, which is a way to prevent unauthorized devices from connecting to the network. You learned about the different port violation modes and the commands to configure port security.

As a final topic in this chapter, you were introduced to VLANs as a method to create broadcast domains and communication boundaries between devices. You learned that VLANs may span across connected switches and that you need to configure a trunk port to carry VLAN traffic between switches.

Quick Review

Understanding Switch Features

- The switch has three core functions: address learning, filtering/forwarding, and loop avoidance.
- Layer 2 switches have three operation modes: store-and-forward, cut-through, and fragment-free. Cisco switches use fragment-free.

Identifying Switch Components

- The System LED will be amber if the switch experiences a malfunction during startup.
- Use the Mode button to change between display modes on the switch.
- While in STAT display mode, if a port LED is amber, the port has been disabled because of a shutdown, STP blocking, or port security violation. If the port is green, it means there is a connection to a device, and if it is flashing green, it means there is network activity on that port.
- When in DUPLX display mode, if a port LED is showing a solid green light, then the port is running in full duplex. If the port LED is off, it means the port is in half-duplex mode.

Basic Switch Configuration

- An IP address can be assigned to a VLAN interface on a switch to access it remotely via telnet or SSH.
- The **ip default-gateway** command assigns a router address the switch should use to access other subnets.
- The **show mac address-table** command displays the MAC address table of the switch and any addresses that have been learned.

Interface Configuration

- Port security is used to prevent unauthorized access to a LAN on access interfaces (non-trunk connections).
- The **switchport port-security** commands are used to configure port security.
- The defaults for port security are learning one MAC address on the interface with a violation mode of shutdown.
- Sticky learning enables a switch to dynamically learn which MAC addresses are connected to an interface and then configure those as the port security addresses that are authorized to access the port.

Working with VLANs

- A VLAN is a group of devices, in the same broadcast domain, that have the same network or subnet number. VLANs are not restricted to physical locations, so users can be physically located anywhere in the switched network.

- Static, or port-based, VLAN membership is manually assigned by the administrator. Dynamic VLAN membership is determined by information from the user device, such as its MAC address or 802.1x authentication credentials.

- An access port is a connection to another device that supports standard Ethernet frames and supports only a single VLAN. A trunk port is a connection that tags frames and allows multiple VLANs. Trunking is supported only on ports that are trunk-capable; not all Ethernet ports support trunking.

- IEEE 802.1Q is a standardized trunking method. Newer Cisco switches support only this trunking protocol. The 802.1Q method inserts a VLAN tag in the middle of the frame and recomputes the frame's checksum. It supports a native VLAN—this is a VLAN that is not tagged on the trunk link. On Cisco switches, this defaults to VLAN 1.

- DTP is a Cisco-proprietary protocol that determines whether two connected interfaces can become a trunk link. There are five modes: on, desirable, auto-negotiate, off, and no-negotiate. If one side's mode is on, desirable, or auto, and the other side's mode is on or desirable, a trunk will form. No-negotiate mode enables trunking but disables DTP.

- To enable trunking on a switch interface, use the **switchport trunk encapsulation dot1q** command and then **switchport mode trunk**. To verify trunking, use the **show interfaces switchport|trunk** command.

- All ports on a switch are automatically placed in VLAN 1. To add a VLAN on a switch, use the **vlan** command. To assign an interface to a VLAN, use **switchport mode access** and **switchport access vlan**. To view your VLANs and the ports assigned to them, use **show vlan**.

Questions

The following questions will help you measure your understanding of the material presented in this chapter. Read all the choices carefully, as there may be more than one correct answer. Choose the correct answer(s) for each question.

1. The System LED will be _____ if the switch has experienced a malfunction during startup.

    A. green

    B. off

    C. amber

    D. red

2. You use the Mode button to switch to the Duplex display mode. You notice that all of the ports except for one are showing a green LED. What does the green LED mean?

   A. The port is running half duplex.

   B. Full duplex is disabled.

   C. The port is running simplex.

   D. The port is running full duplex.

3. Which of the following is *not* asked for during the System Configuration Dialog script?

   A. Enabling interfaces

   B. Default gateway address

   C. VLAN interface to use for management functions

   D. Enable secret password

4. In which configuration mode is the default gateway address configured for a switch?

   A. Interface

   B. Line

   C. Global

   D. Port

5. By default, an IP address is not assigned to a switch. Under what circumstances may you want to assign an IP address to a switch?

   A. In order for the switch to forward frames

   B. To remotely administer the switch remotely

   C. In order for the switch to flood frames

   D. In order for the switch to route IP packets

6. Enter the switch command that enables you to see the contents of the CAM table:

   _____.

7. Examine the following MAC address table on a switch. What will happen if a switch sees a frame with a destination MAC address of 0000.1111.DDDD?

```
Switch> show mac address-table
Vlan    Mac Address       Type      Ports
----    -----------       ----      -----
   1    0000.1111.AAAA    DYNAMIC   Gig0/1
   1    0000.1111.CCCC    DYNAMIC   Gig0/2
   1    0000.1111.BBBB    DYNAMIC   Gig0/3
```

   A. Flood to all ports

   B. Drop the frame

   C. Forward it out Gig0/1

   D. Forward it out Gig0/1 and Gig0/2

8. Which switch feature is used to prevent unauthorized access to a LAN?

   A. Port security

   B. Port security and 802.1Q

   C. VTY passwords

   D. Enable password

9. You are configuring port security on interface Gig0/6. You would like the switch to configure port security for whichever MAC address is currently using the port. What command would you use?

   A. port-security mac-address dynamic

   B. switchport port-security mac-address cccc.cccc.3333

   C. switchport port-security mac-address sticky

   D. switchport port-security violation shutdown

10. You arrive to work on Monday morning and receive a complaint from a user who says she no longer has access to the network. You view the status on the interface her workstation is connected to using the following command. What is the problem?

```
VAN-SW2#show int g0/9
GigabitEthernet0/9 is administratively down, line protocol is down (disabled)
  Hardware is Lance, address is 0002.1653.0701 (bia 0002.1653.0701)
  Description:
  MTU 1500 bytes, BW 1000000 Kbit, DLY 1000 usec,
     reliability 255/255, txload 1/255, rxload 1/255
  Encapsulation ARPA, loopback not set
  Keepalive set (10 sec)
  Full-duplex, 1000Mb/s
```

   A. The port has been disabled due to a security violation.

   B. The line protocol is bad.

   C. The port is missing a description.

   D. The port has been disabled by an administrator.

11. What Cisco switch command would you use to enable trunking on an interface?

   A. switchport mode trunk

   B. trunking on

   C. trunking enable

   D. switchport trunk on

12. What Cisco switch command would you use to assign port 10 to VLAN ID 5?

   A. **vlan-membership static 10**

   B. **vlan 5**

   C. **switchport access vlan 5**

   D. **switchport mode access**

Performance-based Questions

The Cisco exams have performance-based questions where you must drag an item from the left side of the screen to its proper place on the right side of the screen in order to answer the question. The following are some sample performance-based questions related to this chapter.

   1. You are responsible for configuring the LA-SW1 switch in the LA office so that it can be remotely administered from the other networks. Drag the appropriate set of commands into the switch configuration section that you would use to configure the switch.

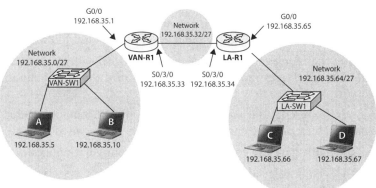

```
VAN-SW1(config)#interface vlan1
VAN-SW1(config-if)#ip address 192.168.35.98 255.255.255.224
VAN-SW1(config-if)#no shutdown
VAN-SW1(config-if)#exit
VAN-SW1(config)#ip default-gateway 192.168.35.65
```

```
VAN-SW1(config)#interface vlan1
VAN-SW1(config-if)#ip address 192.168.35.92 255.255.255.224
VAN-SW1(config-if)#no shutdown
VAN-SW1(config-if)#exit
VAN-SW1(config)#ip default-gateway 192.168.35.65
```

```
VAN-SW1(config)#interface g0/0
VAN-SW1(config-if)#ip address 192.168.35.92 255.255.255.224
VAN-SW1(config-if)#no shutdown
VAN-SW1(config-if)#exit
VAN-SW1(config)#ip default-gateway 192.168.35.65
```

```
VAN-SW1(config)#interface vlan1
VAN-SW1(config-if)#ip address 192.168.35.98 255.255.255.224
VAN-SW1(config)#ip default-gateway 192.168.35.65
```

LA-SW1 Configuration Commands

2. Looking at the command on the left side of the following exhibit, draw a line to connect it to the description of what that command does.

Command		Description
hostname VAN-SW1		Displays the MAC addresses associated with each port.
no shutdown		Configures port security to learn only one MAC address for a port.
ip default-gateway 12.0.0.1		Sets the device name.
show mac address-table		Configures port security for the MAC address of the currently connected device.
switchport port-security mac-address sticky		Enables an interface.
switchport port-security maximum 1		Sets the default gateway on the device.

Answers

1. **C.** The System LED will be amber if the switch has experienced a malfunction during startup. If the system boots without error, the System LED will display green.

2. **D.** When in the Duplex display mode, each port LED will display green if it is running in full-duplex mode, but the LED is off if the port is running in half duplex.

3. **A.** Enabling the interfaces is *not* asked for during the System Configuration Dialog script. Interfaces are enabled by default on Cisco switches.

4. **C.** The **ip default-gateway** command is a global configuration mode command.

5. **B.** An IP address is assigned to the switch so that you can use telnet or SSH to administer the switch remotely.

6. To view the CAM table, also known as the MAC address table, you would use the **show mac address-table** command.

7. **A.** If the switch receives a frame that contains a destination address that is not located in the MAC address table, the switch will flood the frame to all ports on the switch.

8. **A.** Port security is used to prevent unauthorized access to a LAN.

9. **C.** When configuring port security, you can configure the port security feature to authorize the MAC address of the system using the port by using the sticky option (**switchport port-security mac-address sticky**). This prevents you from having to input each MAC address on each port.

10. D. The port states that it is administratively down; this means that the port was disabled by an administrator.

11. A. The **switchport mode trunk** command enables trunking on a Cisco switch. Keep in mind that you would run this command after setting the encapsulation mode with **switchport trunk encapsulation dot1q**.

12. C. The **switchport access vlan** command assigns an interface to a VLAN. You would run this command after placing the interface in access mode.

Performance-based Answers

The following are the answers to the performance-based questions in this chapter.

1. This question is tricky as it is two questions in one. First, it is testing your knowledge of assigning an IP address to the switch, and the default gateway. Second, it is an IP subnetting questions because you also need to ensure the commands you use are using an IP address in the correct IP range.

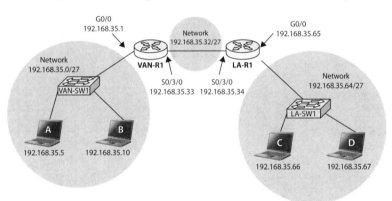

```
VAN-SW1(config)#interface vlan1
VAN-SW1(config-if)#ip address 192.168.35.98 255.255.255.224
VAN-SW1(config-if)#no shutdown
VAN-SW1(config-if)#exit
VAN-SW1(config)#ip default-gateway 192.168.35.65
```

LA-SW1 Configuration Commands

```
VAN-SW1(config)#interface vlan1
VAN-SW1(config-if)#ip address 192.168.35.92 255.255.255.224
VAN-SW1(config-if)#no shutdown
VAN-SW1(config-if)#exit
VAN-SW1(config)#ip default-gateway 192.168.35.65
```

```
VAN-SW1(config)#interface g0/0
VAN-SW1(config-if)#ip address 192.168.35.92 255.255.255.224
VAN-SW1(config-if)#no shutdown
VAN-SW1(config-if)#exit
VAN-SW1(config)#ip default-gateway 192.168.35.65
```

```
VAN-SW1(config)#interface vlan1
VAN-SW1(config-if)#ip address 192.168.35.98 255.255.255.224
VAN-SW1(config)#ip default-gateway 192.168.35.65
```

2. On the real Cisco exams, you will need to drag an item on the left side and drop it onto the matching item on the right side. In this question you need to match the switch command with its description. The following is the correct answer for this performance question.

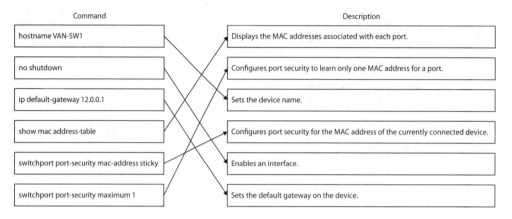

Command	Description
hostname VAN-SW1	Displays the MAC addresses associated with each port.
no shutdown	Configures port security to learn only one MAC address for a port.
ip default-gateway 12.0.0.1	Sets the device name.
show mac address-table	Configures port security for the MAC address of the currently connected device.
switchport port-security mac-address sticky	Enables an interface.
switchport port-security maximum 1	Sets the default gateway on the device.

Advanced Switching Features

In this chapter, you will

- Learn how to set up and manage the VLAN Trunking Protocol
- Learn about the Spanning Tree Protocol
- Learn about the Rapid Spanning Tree Protocol
- Learn how to manage EtherChannels

This chapter is the last chapter on layer 2 functions. Most larger networks implement redundancy to protect data in case of failures; redundancy can involve multiple wide area network (WAN) connections, multiple paths in your layer 3 network, and/or multiple paths in your layer 2 network. This chapter focuses on layer 2 redundancy and the issues involved with layer 2 loops, including two features that are commonly used to solve these problems: the Spanning Tree Protocol and EtherChannels.

VLAN Trunking Protocol

The VLAN Trunking Protocol (VTP) is a proprietary Cisco protocol used to share virtual local area network (VLAN) configuration information between Cisco switches on trunk connections. VTP enables switches to share and synchronize their VLAN information, which ensures that your network has a consistent VLAN configuration.

Assume, for instance, that your network has two switches, and you need to add a new VLAN. You could easily accomplish this by adding the VLAN manually on both switches. However, this process becomes more difficult and tedious if you have 30 switches to deal with. In this situation, you could make a mistake in configuring the new VLAN on one of the switches, such as giving it the wrong VLAN identifier, or you might forget to add the new VLAN to one of the 30 switches. VTP can take care of these issues. With VTP, you can add the VLAN on one switch and have this switch propagate the new VLAN, via VTP messages, to all of the other switches in your layer 2 network, causing them to add the new VLAN also.

This is also true if you modify a VLAN's configuration or delete a VLAN—VTP can verify that your VLAN configuration is consistent across all of your switches. VTP can even perform consistency checks with your VLANs to make sure that all the VLANs are configured identically. Components of a VLAN can include a VLAN number, name, and type. So, for example, if you have a VLAN number of 1 and a name of "admin" on one switch, but the name "administrator" is used on a second switch for the same VLAN 1, VTP checks for and fixes the configuration mismatches.

VTP messages will propagate *only* across *trunk* connections, so you will need to set up trunking between your switches in order to share VLAN information via VTP. VTP messages are propagated as layer 2 multicast frames by layer 2 devices. Therefore, if a router separates two of your switches, the router will *not* forward the VTP messages from one of its interfaces to another because it is a layer 3 device.

For VTP to function correctly, you must associate your switch with a *VTP domain*. A domain is a group of switches that have the same VLAN information applied to them. Basically, a VTP domain is similar to an autonomous system, which is used by some routing protocols (autonomous systems and routing protocols are introduced in Chapter 11). A switch can belong only to a single VTP domain. VTP domains are given names, and when switches generate VTP messages, they include the VTP domain name in their messages. When a VTP message is received by a switch, the VTP message is only processed if the VTP domain in the message is the same as the VTP domain name configured on the switch. In other words, a switch in one VTP domain will ignore VTP messages from switches in other VTP domains. The following sections cover the components and messages that VTP uses, as well as some of the advantages that it provides, such as pruning.

TIP VTP is a Cisco-proprietary protocol that traverses trunks. It is used to create a consistent VLAN configuration across all switches in the same domain. A VLAN can be added on one switch and propagated to other switches; however, switches will ignore VTP messages from other VTP domains.

VTP Modes

When you are setting up VTP, you can choose from three different modes for your switch's configuration:

- Client
- Server
- Transparent

Table 10-1 shows the differences between these VTP modes.

EXAM TIP The new CCNA exam does not have VTP as an exam topic, but you may encounter VTP on existing networks. For that reason, this chapter is introducing VTP to you.

A switch configured in either VTP server or transparent mode can add, modify, and delete VLANs. The main difference between these two modes is that the configuration

Description	Server	Client	Transparent
Can add, modify, and delete VLANs	Yes	No	Yes
Can generate VTP messages	Yes	No	No
Can propagate VTP messages	Yes	Yes	Yes
Can accept changes in a VTP message	Yes	Yes	No
Default VTP mode	Yes	No	No
Saves VLANs to NVRAM	Yes	No	Yes

Table 10-1   Description of VTP Modes

changes made to a transparent switch affect only *that* switch and no other switch in the network. A VTP server switch, however, will make the change and then propagate a VTP message concerning the change to all of its trunk ports. If a server switch receives a VTP message, it will incorporate the update and forward the message out its remaining trunk ports. A transparent switch, on the other hand, ignores VTP messages—it will accept them on trunk ports and forward them out its remaining trunk ports, but it will not incorporate the changes in the VTP message in its local VLAN configuration. In this sense, transparent switches are like little islands, where changes on a transparent switch affect no one else but the transparent switch itself, and changes to other switches do not affect transparent switches.

A VTP client switch cannot make changes to its VLAN configuration itself—it requires a server switch to tell it about the VLAN changes. When a client switch receives a VTP message from a server switch, it incorporates the changes and then floods the VTP message out its remaining trunk ports.

Normally, you would set up one switch in server mode and all other switches in client mode. Then you would control who could make changes on the server switch. However, you should keep in mind that if you make a VLAN configuration mistake on the server switch, this mistake is *automatically propagated* to all the client switches in your network. Imagine the outcome if you accidentally deleted a VLAN on your server switch, and this VLAN had 500 devices in it. If this occurred, all the switches would remove the VLAN from their configurations.

Given this and similar problems, some administrators don't like to use VTP server and client modes; they prefer to configure all of their switches in transparent mode. The problem with transparent mode, however, is that it isn't very scalable; if you need to add a VLAN to your network and your network has 20 switches, you would have to add the VLAN manually to each individual switch, which is a time-consuming process. Of course, the advantage of this approach is that if you make a mistake on a transparent switch, the problem is *not* propagated to other switches: it's localized.

You could also set up all of your switches in server mode, which is the default setting for VTP. You could even mix and match these options—set up a couple of server switches, and have the remaining switches as clients, or set your switches initially as servers and clients, add all your VLANs on the server switch, allow the clients to acquire this information, and then change all the switches to transparent mode. This process allows you to populate your switches' configurations easily with a consistent VLAN configuration during the setup process. Note that if you don't specify the VTP mode for your switch, it will default to *server*. As you can see, a wide range of VTP configuration options is available.

VTP Messages

If you use a client/server configuration for VTP, these switches can generate three types of VTP messages:

- Advertisement request
- Subset advertisement
- Summary advertisement

An *advertisement request* message is a VTP message a client generates to acquire VLAN information, to which a server will respond. When the server responds to a client's request, it generates a *subset advertisement*. This subset advertisement contains detailed VLAN configuration information, including the VLAN numbers, names, types, and other information. The client will then configure itself appropriately.

A *summary advertisement* is also generated by a switch in VTP server mode. Summary advertisements are generated every 5 minutes (300 seconds) by default, or when a configuration change takes place on the server switch. Unlike a subset advertisement, a summary advertisement contains only summarized VLAN information.

When a server switch generates a VTP advertisement, it can include the following information:

- The number and name of the VLAN
- The maximum transmission unit (MTU) size used by the VLAN
- The frame format used by the VLAN
- The Security Association identifier (SAID) value for the VLAN (needed if it is an 802.10 VLAN, which is implemented in networks using Fiber Distributed Data Interface [FDDI])
- The configuration revision number
- The name of the VTP domain

This list includes a couple of important items that need further discussion. Switches in either server or client mode will process VTP messages if they are in the same VTP domain; however, some restrictions are placed on whether the switch should incorporate the changes or not. For instance, one function of the VTP summary advertisements is to ensure that all of the switches have the most current changes. If you didn't make a change on a server switch in the five-minute update interval, when the countdown timer expires, the server switch still sends out a summary advertisement with the same exact summary information.

It makes no sense to have other switches, which have the most up-to-date information, incorporate the same information in their configuration.

To make this process more efficient, the *configuration revision number* is used to keep track of what server switch has the most recent changes. Initially this number is set to zero (0). If you make a change on a server switch, it increments its revision number and advertises this to the other switches across its trunk links. When a client or server switch receives this information, it compares the revision number in the message to the last message it received. If the newly arrived message has a higher number, this server switch must have made changes. If the necessary VLAN information isn't in the VTP summary advertisement, all client and server switches will generate an advertisement request and the server will respond with the details in a subset advertisement.

NOTE VTP servers generate VTP multicasts every five minutes. The configuration reversion number is used to determine which server has the most up-to-date VLAN information: the highest number is the most current. Remember that when connecting an existing server switch to an existing server/client VTP network, whichever server switch has the highest revision number will win out and its VLANs will be used. The VLANs from the other switch(es) will be deleted.

If a server switch receives a VTP message from another server, and the advertising server has a lower revision number, the receiving server switch will respond to the advertising server with a VTP message with its current configuration revision number. This will tell the advertising server switch that it doesn't have the most up-to-date VLAN information and should request it from the server that does. In this sense, the revision number used in a VTP message is somewhat similar to the sequence number used in TCP. Also, remember that transparent switches are not processing these VTP advertisements—they simply passively forward these messages to other switches on their trunk ports.

VTP Pruning

VTP pruning is a Cisco feature that enables your switches to delete or add VLANs to a trunk dynamically, creating a more efficient switching network. By default, all VLANs are associated with a trunk connection. This means that if a device in *any* VLAN generates a broadcast, a multicast, or an unknown unicast, the switch will flood this frame out all ports associated with the source VLAN port, including trunks. In many situations, this flooding is necessary, especially if the VLAN spans multiple switches. However, it doesn't make sense to flood a frame to a neighboring switch if that switch doesn't have any active ports in the source VLAN.

Trunking Without Pruning

In the example shown in Figure 10-1, VTP pruning is not enabled. PC-A, PC-B, PC-E, and PC-F are in the same VLAN. If PC-A generates a broadcast, SwitchA will forward this to the access link to which PC-B is connected as well as the trunk (since a trunk is a member of all VLANs, by default). This makes sense, since PC-E and PC-F, connected to SwitchB, are in the same VLAN.

Figure 10-1 shows a second VLAN with two members: PC-C and PC-D. If PC-C generates a local broadcast, SwitchA will obviously send to this to PC-D's port. What doesn't make sense is that SwitchA will flood this broadcast out its trunk port to SwitchB, considering that no devices on SwitchB are in this VLAN. This is an example of wasting bandwidth and resources. A single broadcast isn't a big problem in this example; however, if a video multicast stream at 5 Mbps was coming from PC-A, the network could experience throughput problems on the trunk, since a switch treats a multicast just like a broadcast—it floods it out all ports associated with the source port's VLAN.

You could use one of two methods to fix this problem: static VLAN pruning or dynamic VLAN pruning. With a static configuration, you would manually prune the inactive VLAN off the trunk on both switches, as shown in Figure 10-2. Notice that in this figure, the dark VLAN (indicated by dotted lines) has been pruned from the trunk. The problem with manual pruning is that if you add a dark VLAN member to SwitchB, you will have to log into both switches and manually add the pruned VLAN back to the trunk. This can become very confusing in a multiswitched network with multiple VLANs, where every VLAN is not necessarily active on every switch. It would be easy to prune a VLAN accidentally from a trunk that shouldn't have been pruned, thus creating connectivity problems.

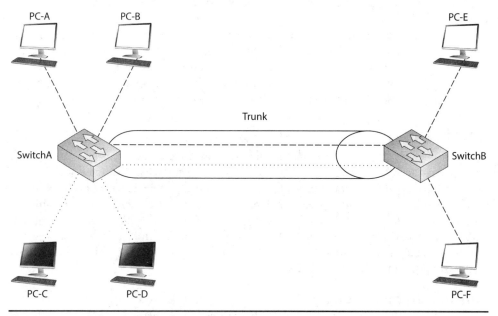

Figure 10-1   Trunking without VTP pruning

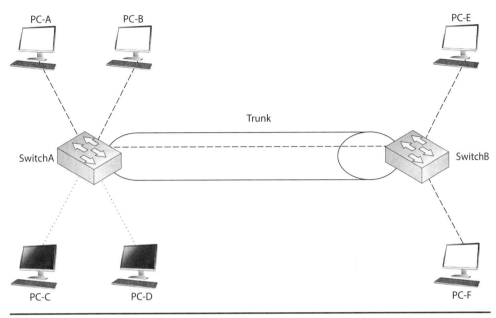

Figure 10-2 VLAN pruning

Trunking with Pruning

The VTP pruning feature enables the switches to share additional VLAN information and to prune inactive VLANs dynamically from trunk connections. In this instance, the switches share which VLANs are active. For example, SwitchA tells SwitchB that it has two active VLANs (the white one and the dark one). SwitchB, on the other hand, has only one active VLAN, and it shares this fact with SwitchA. Given the shared information, both SwitchA and SwitchB realize that the dark VLAN is inactive across their trunk connection, and therefore the dark VLAN should be dynamically removed from the trunk's configuration.

The nice thing about this feature is that if you happen to activate the dark VLAN on SwitchB by connecting a device to a port on the switch and assigning that port to the dark VLAN, SwitchB will notify SwitchA about the newly active VLAN, and both switches will dynamically add the VLAN back to the trunk's configuration. This will enable PC-C, PC-D, and the new device to send frames to each other, as is shown in Figure 10-3.

NOTE By default, all VLANs can traverse a trunk. VTP pruning is used on trunk connections dynamically to remove VLANs not active between the two switches. It must be enabled on a VTP server switch, and the other switches must be either servers or clients.

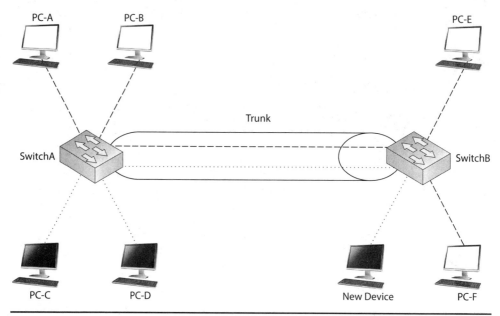

Figure 10-3 VTP pruning activating a VLAN on a trunk

Only a VTP switch in *server* mode can enable VTP pruning, and the remaining switches in the domain must be either in VTP server or client mode. If you have transparent mode switches, you'll have to prune VLANs off their trunk links manually.

Management VLAN

Unlike Cisco routers, every Cisco switch comes with a default configuration. For instance, some preconfigured VLANs are already on the switch, including VLAN 1. During the configuration, all VLAN commands refer to the VLAN number, even though you can configure an optional name for the VLAN. Every port on your switch, by default, is associated with VLAN 1. And all communications from the switch itself—VTP messages, Cisco Discovery Protocol (CDP) multicasts, and other traffic the switch originates— occur in VLAN 1. Recall from Chapter 9 that the Cisco switch's IP configuration is based on the VLAN interface for which you configure your IP address.

VLAN 1 is sometimes called the *management VLAN*, even though you can use a different VLAN. It is a common practice to put all of your management devices—switches and management stations—in their own VLAN. If you decide to put your switch in a different VLAN than VLAN 1, it is recommended that you change this configuration on all your management devices so that you can more easily secure them, since other VLANs would have to go through a layer 3 device to access them; and on this layer 3 device, you can set up access control lists to filter unwanted traffic.

It's important that all your switches are in the same management VLAN, since many of the switches' management protocols, such as CDP, VTP, and the Dynamic Trunk Protocol (DTP), occur within the switch's management VLAN. If one switch has its management VLAN set to 1 and another connected switch has its management VLAN set to 2, the two switches would lose a lot of interswitch functionality.

Configuring VTP

If troubleshooting an existing network setup or configuring VTP yourself, it is important to understand the common VTP parameters and their values. Table 10-2 shows the default VTP configuration for Cisco switches. The following sections cover the configuration of these VTP parameters.

You configure VTP from Global Configuration mode on the Cisco switch:

```
switch(config)# vtp domain VTP_domain_name
switch(config)# vtp mode server|client|transparent
switch(config)# vtp password VTP_password
switch(config)# vtp pruning
```

The **vtp domain** command defines the domain name for your switch. Remember that in order for switches to share VTP information, they must be in the same domain. Messages received from other domains are ignored. If you don't configure a domain name, the switch will learn this from a server advertisement.

The rest of the commands in the configuration are optional. The second **vtp** command defines the VTP mode of the switch. If you don't configure this command, the default mode is server mode. You can configure a VTP MD5 password for your switches, which must match the password configured on every switch in the domain. Switches will use this password to verify VTP messages from other switches; if the created hashed values placed in VTP messages (generated by running the VTP message and password through MD5 to create the hash signature) can't be verified, the switches ignore the VTP messages. On most switches, pruning is disabled by default, but you can disable or enable it with the **vtp pruning** command. It is important to note that if pruning is enabled on a server switch, the server switch will propagate this to all other server and client switches in the same domain.

Table 10-2
VTP Default
Configuration
Values

VTP Component	VTP Default Value
Domain name	None
Mode	Server
Password	None
Pruning	Disabled
Version	1

Once you are done configuring VTP, use the **show vtp status** command to check your configuration:

```
switch# show vtp status
VTP Version : 1
Configuration Revision : 17
Maximum VLANs supported locally : 255
Number of existing VLANs : 7
VTP Operating Mode : Server
VTP Domain Name : dealgroup
VTP Pruning Mode : Enabled
VTP V2 Mode : Disabled
VTP Traps Generation : Disabled
MD5 digest : 0x95 0xAB 0x29 0x44 0x32 0xA1 0x2C 0x31
Configuration last modified by 0.0.0.0 at 3-1-03 15:18:37
Local updater ID is 192.168.1.4 on interface Vl1
    (lowest numbered VLAN interface found)
```

In this example, 17 configuration changes have occurred (see the Configuration Revision field). The switch is operating in server mode in the dealgroup domain.

NOTE The **vtp password** command is used to authenticate VTP messages between switches. The **show vtp status** command will display the VTP mode in which the switch is operating, the configuration revision number, and the VTP domain to which the switch belongs.

Use the **show vtp counters** command to display VTP statistics concerning VTP messages sent and received:

```
switch # show vtp counters
VTP statistics:
  Summary advertisements received : 12
  Subset advertisements received : 0
  Request advertisements received : 0
  Summary advertisements transmitted : 7
  Subset advertisements transmitted : 0
  Request advertisements transmitted : 0
  Number of config revision errors : 0
  Number of config digest errors : 0
  Number of V1 summary errors : 0
```

In this example, you can see that the switch has sent and received VTP summary advertisements.

Exercise 10-1: Working with VTP

In this exercise, you will use VTP to send a list of VLANs from one switch to another so that there is a consistent list of VLAN across all your switches. Use the following network diagram to represent the two switches in the Vancouver office:

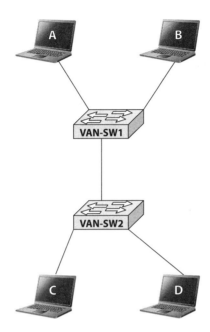

1. Power on both switches.

2. Ensure that a crossover cable is connecting the two switches using port 1 on both switches.

3. Console into VAN-SW1 and configure port 1 as a trunk port using the following commands:

```
VAN-SW1>enable
VAN-SW1#config term
Enter configuration commands, one per line.  End with CNTL/Z.
VAN-SW1(config)#interface g1/0/1
VAN-SW1(config-if)#switchport trunk encapsulation dot1q
VAN-SW1(config-if)#switchport mode trunk
```

4. To configure VAN-SW1 as a VTP server, enter the following commands:

```
VAN-SW1(config-if)#exit
VAN-SW1(config)#vtp domain Lab101
Changing VTP domain name from NULL to Lab101
VAN-SW1(config)#vtp mode server
Device mode already VTP SERVER.
VAN-SW1(config)#vtp password vtppass
Setting device VLAN database password to vtppass
```

5. To verify the VTP settings, type the following commands:

```
VAN-SW1(config)#exit
VAN-SW1#show vtp status
```

Note the VTP version, the VTP domain name, and the VTP operating mode.

6. Use the **show vlan** command to display the list of VLANs. Note that there are only default VLANs.

7. Use the following commands to create two VLANs:

```
VAN-SW1#config term
Enter configuration commands, one per line.  End with CNTL/Z.
VAN-SW1(config)#vlan 2
VAN-SW1(config-vlan)#name Sales
VAN-SW1(config-vlan)#vlan 3
VAN-SW1(config-vlan)#name Mkt
VAN-SW1(config-vlan)#exit
```

8. Use the **do show vlan** command to display the list of VLANs. Note the two additional VLANs.

9. Console into VAN-SW2.

10. Use the **show vlan** command to display the VLANs. Note there are only default VLANs and there is no Sales or Mkt VLAN.

11. Use the **show vtp status** command to display VTP information. Note that the VTP domain is set, but the mode is server. You need to change this to client so that VLANs are not configured on this switch but can be received from the server (VAN-SW1).

12. Configure VAN-SW2 in VTP client mode so it can receive the list of VLANs from VAN-SW1 with the following commands:

```
VAN-SW2#config term
VAN-SW2(config)#vtp mode client
VAN-SW2(config)#vtp password vtppass
```

13. Use the **show vtp status** command to verify that the mode was changed to client.

14. Use the **show vlan** command to verify that the list of VLANs was received from the VAN-SW1 switch.

15. You can now place different interfaces into the Sales and Mkt VLANs on VAN-SW2.

 VIDEO　10.01. The digital resources that accompany this book contain a multimedia demonstration of configuring VTP on two switches.

Spanning Tree Protocol

The main function of STP is to remove layer 2 loops from your topology, logically speaking. Digital Equipment Corporation (DEC), now a part of Hewlett-Packard (HP), originally developed STP. The Institute of Electrical and Electronics Engineers (IEEE) enhanced the initial implementation of STP, giving us the IEEE 802.1d standard. Because the two different implementations of STP, DEC STP and 802.1d, are not compatible with each other, you need to make sure that all of your devices support either one or the other. Additions were made to 802.1d, including Rapid STP (RSTP) and Multiple STP (MSTP). Based on these inclusions, the IEEE implementation today is referred to as 802.1D. All of Cisco's switches support the IEEE 802.1D protocol, which is enabled by default on their switches when sending out untagged frames (the native VLAN). If you have a mixed-vendor environment where some devices are running 802.1D and others are running DEC's STP, you may run into layer 2 looping problems.

NOTE Typically IEEE uses a lowercase letter, such as d, to indicate a draft or ongoing development state and uses an uppercase letter, such as D, to indicate a finalized standard. In this book, when 802.1d is mentioned, this specifies the original implementation of STP by IEEE, which excludes RSTP and MSTP. RSTP is covered later in the chapter, but MSTP is beyond the scope of this book.

Bridge Protocol Data Units

For STP to function, the switches need to share information about themselves and their connections. What they share are Bridge Protocol Data Units (BPDUs), which are sent out as *multicast* frames to which only other layer 2 switches or bridges are listening. Switches will use BPDUs to learn the topology of the network: what switch is connected to other switches, and whether any layer 2 loops are based on this topology.

To prevent loops on the network, the switches will logically disable a port or ports in the topology to ensure that there are no loops. Note that the switches don't actually shut down the port(s), but they place the port(s) in a special disabled state for user traffic, as discussed later in the chapter in the "Port States" section. When the port is placed in this special disabled state, the loop on the network is prevented and data can only travel one pathway between the switches. If any changes occur on the layer 2 network—a link goes down, a new link is added, a new switch is added, or a switch fails—the switches will share this information, causing the STP algorithm to be re-executed, and a new loop-free topology is then created.

By default, BPDUs are sent out every two seconds. This helps speed up convergence. *Convergence* is a term used in networking to describe the amount of time it takes to deal with changes and get the network back up and running. The shorter the time period to find and fix problems, the quicker your network is back online. Setting the BPDU advertisement time to two seconds enables changes to be quickly shared with all the other switches in the network, reducing the amount of time any disruption would create.

BPDUs contain a lot of information to help the switches determine the topology and any loops that result from that topology. For instance, each bridge has a unique identifier, called a *bridge* or *switch ID*. This is typically the priority of the switch and the MAC address of the switch itself. When a switch advertises a BPDU, it places its switch ID in the BPDU so that a receiving switch can tell from which switch it is receiving topology information. The following sections cover the steps that occur while STP is being executed in a layer 2 network.

EXAM TIP Remember that STP is a layer 2 protocol that is used to prevent loops on the network. STP implements the IEEE 802.1d standard, which involves having switches exchange BPDUs to help detect loops on the network. *Bridge Protocol Data Unit* (BPDU) messages are special frames sent between switches to share information that is necessary to configure and maintain a loop-free network with spanning tree. BPDU messages are sent out as multicasts every two seconds. The BPDU contains information about ports and switches on the network.

Root Switch

As you know, STP is used to find and remove loops from a layer 2 network. The STP algorithm works in a way that's similar to how link state routing protocols, such as Open Shortest Path First (OSPF), ensure that no layer 3 loops are created; of course, STP deals only with layer 2 loops.

A spanning tree is created first. Basically, a spanning tree is an inverted tree. At the top of the tree is the root, or what is referred to in STP as the *root switch* or *bridge.* From the root switch, branches (physical Ethernet connections) extend and connect to other switches, then branches from these switches connect to other switches, and so on.

Take a look at the physical topology of a network, shown in Figure 10-4, which demonstrates a spanning tree. When STP is run, a logical tree structure is built, similar to that shown in Figure 10-5. As you can see in Figure 10-5, Switch-A is the root switch and is at the top of the tree. Underneath it are two branches connecting to Switch-B and Switch-C. These two switches are connected to Switch-E, creating a loop. Switch-B is also connected to Switch-D. At this point, STP is still running, and a loop still exists. As STP runs, the switches will determine, out of the four switches—Switch-A, Switch-B, Switch-C, and Switch-E—which port on these switches will be logically disabled in order to remove the loop. This ensures that from one device to any other device in the network, only one path will be used to connect the devices.

Actually, the very first step in STP is to elect the root switch. BPDUs are used for the election process. As mentioned earlier, when a device advertises a BPDU, the switch puts

Figure 10-4
Physical layer 2
looped topology

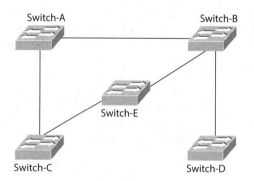

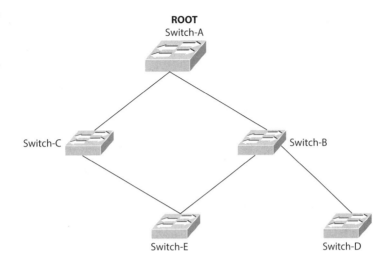

Figure 10-5
Logical layer 2
STP topology

its switch ID in the BPDU. The switch ID is used to elect the root switch. The switch with the *lowest* switch ID is chosen as root. The switch ID is made up of two components:

- The switch's priority, which defaults to 32,768 on Cisco switches (2 bytes in length)
- The switch's MAC address (6 bytes in length)

With Cisco switches, the default priority is 32,768, which is defined by IEEE 802.1d. Assuming that all your switches are Cisco switches and you don't change the default priority, the switch with the *lowest* MAC address will be chosen as the root switch. You can override the election process by changing the priority value assigned to a switch. If you want one switch to be the root, assign it a priority value that is lower than 32,768. Through the sharing of the BPDUs, the switches will figure out which switch has the lowest switch ID, and that switch is chosen as the root switch. Note that this election process is taking place almost simultaneously on each switch, where each switch will come up with the same result.

For Cisco Catalyst switches that implement VLANs (discussed in Chapter 9), the switches will have a different switch ID *per* VLAN and a *separate* instance of STP *per* VLAN. Each VLAN has its own root switch (which can be the same switch for all VLANs, or different switches for each VLAN). And within each VLAN, STP will run and remove loops in that particular VLAN. Cisco calls this concept *per-VLAN STP* (PVST). This topic is discussed later in the "Per-VLAN Spanning Tree+ (PVST+)" section.

EXAM TIP   Exam questions will require that you remember that the switch with the lowest switch (bridge) ID is chosen as the root switch.

The election process of the root switch takes place each time a topology change occurs in the network, such as the failure of a root switch or the addition of a new switch. All the other switches in the layer 2 topology expect to see BPDUs from the root switch within the *maximum age time*, which defaults to 20 seconds. If the switches don't see a BPDU message from the root within this period, they assume that the root switch has failed and will begin a new election process to choose a new root switch.

Root Port

After the root switch is elected, every other switch in the network needs to choose a single port on itself that it will use to reach the root. This port on each switch is called the *root port*. For some switches, such as Switch-D in Figure 10-4, this is very easy—it has only one port it can use to access the switched topology. However, each of the other switches, such as Switch-B, Switch-C, or Switch-E in Figure 10-4, may have two or more ports it can use to reach the root switch. If multiple port choices are available, an intelligent method needs to be used to choose the best port. With STP, a few factors are taken into consideration when choosing a root port. It is important to note that the root switch itself will never have a root port—it's the root, so it doesn't need a port to reach itself!

Port Costs and Priorities

First, each port is assigned a *port cost*. The lower the cost, the more preferable the port, as shown in the 802.1d's cost list in Table 10-3. The cost is an inverse reflection of the bandwidth of the port. Switches always prefer lower cost ports over higher cost ones. Each port also has a priority assigned to it, called a *port priority* value, which defaults to 32. Again, switches will prefer a lower priority value over a higher one.

Path Costs

Path costs are calculated from the root switch. A path cost is basically the accumulated port costs from the root switch to other switches in the topology. When the root advertises BPDUs out its interfaces, the default path cost value in the BPDU frame is 0. When a connected switch receives this BPDU, it increments the path cost by the cost of its local incoming port. If the port was a Fast Ethernet port, then the path cost would be figured like this: 0 (the root's path cost) + 19 (the switch's port cost) = 19. This switch, when it advertises BPDUs to switches behind it, will include the updated path cost. As the BPDUs propagate farther and farther from the root switch, the accumulated path cost values become higher and higher.

 EXAM TIP   Remember that path costs are incremented as a BPDU comes into a port, not when a BPDU is advertised out of a port.

Table 10-3	Connection Type	New Cost Value
Port Costs for STP	10 Gbps	2
	1 Gbps	4
	100 Mbps	19
	10 Mbps	100

Root Port Selection

If a switch has two or more choices of paths to reach the root, it needs to choose one path and thus have one root port. A switch will go through the following STP steps when choosing a root port:

1. Choose the path with the *lowest* accumulated path cost to the root when it has a choice between two or more paths to reach the root.

2. If multiple paths to the root are available with the same accumulated path cost, the switch will choose the neighboring switch (that the switch would go through to reach the root) with the *lowest* switch ID value.

3. If multiple paths all go through the same neighboring switch, it will choose the local port with the lowest priority value.

4. If the priority values are the same between the ports, the switch will choose the physically lowest numbered port on the switch. For example, on a 2960, that would be FastEthernet 0/1 or Gigabit 0/1.

After going through this selection process, the switch will have one, and only one, port that will become its root port.

EXAM TIP You'll be quizzed on the four steps used to choose a root port on a switch.

Designated Port

You now know that each switch has a single root port that it uses to reach the root switch. In addition to each switch having a root port, each segment also has a single port that it uses to reach the root, and this port is called a *designated port*. Imagine, for example, that a segment has two switches connected to it. Either one or the other switch will forward traffic from this segment to the rest of the network.

The third step in running STP is to elect a designated port on a single switch for each segment in the network. The switch (and its port) that is chosen should have the best path to the root switch. Here are the steps taken by switches in determining which port on which switch will be chosen as the designated port for a particular LAN segment:

1. The connected switch on the segment with the lowest accumulated path cost to the root switch will be used.

2. If there is a tie in accumulated path costs between two switches, the switch with the lowest switch ID will be chosen.

3. If it happens that it is the same switch, but with two separate connections to the LAN segment, the switch port with the lowest priority is chosen.

4. If there is still a tie (the priorities of the ports on this switch are the same), the physically lowest numbered port on the switch is chosen.

After going through these steps for each segment, each segment will have a single designated port on a connected switch that it will use to reach the root switch. Sometimes the switch that contains the designated port is called a *designated switch*. This term is misleading, though, since it is a port on the switch that is responsible for forwarding traffic. A switch may be connected to two segments, but it may be the designated switch for only one of those segments; another switch may provide the designated port for the second segment.

 EXAM TIP Remember the four steps for choosing a designated port for a segment for the CCNA exam.

Interestingly enough, *every* active port on the root switch is a designated port. This makes sense, because the cost of the attached network segments to reach the root is 0, the lowest accumulated cost value. In other words, each of these LAN segments is directly attached to the root switch, so in reality, it costs nothing for the segment to reach the root switch itself.

Port States

A port can be in one of five states when it is participating in STP:

- Blocking
- Listening
- Learning
- Forwarding
- Disabled

Of the five states, only the first four are used when the algorithm is running. The following sections cover these port states for STP.

 VIDEO 10.02. The digital resources that accompany this book contain a multimedia demonstration of how STP is used to prevent a layer 2 loop.

Blocking State

Ports will go into a *blocking* state under one of three conditions:

- During election of a root switch (for instance, when you turn on all the switches in a network)
- When a switch receives a BPDU on a port that indicates a better path to the root switch than the port which the switch is currently using to reach the root
- If a port is not a root port or a designated port

A port in a blocking state will remain there for 20 seconds by default (the maximum age timer). During this state, the port is listening to and processing only BPDUs on its interfaces. Any other frames that the switch receives on a blocked port are dropped. In a blocking state, the switch is attempting to figure out which port is going to be the root port, which ports on the switch need to be designated ports, and which ports will remain in a blocking state to break up any loops.

Listening State

After the 20-second timer expires, a root port or a designated port will move to a *listening* state. Any other port will remain in a blocking state. During the listening state, the port is still listening for BPDUs and double-checking the layer 2 topology. Again, the only traffic that is being processed on a port in this state consists of BPDUs; all other traffic is dropped. A port will stay in this state for the length of the *forward delay timer*. The default for this value is 15 seconds.

Learning State

From a listening state, a root and designated ports move into a *learning* state. During the learning state, the port is still listening for and processing BPDUs on the port; however, unlike while in the listening state, the port begins to process user frames. When processing user frames, the switch is examining the source addresses in the frames and updating its MAC or port address table, but the switch is still not forwarding these frames out destination ports. Ports stay in this state for the length of the forward delay time (which defaults to 15 seconds).

Forwarding State

Finally, after the forward delay timer expires, ports that were in a learning state are placed in a *forwarding* state. In a forwarding state, the port will process BPDUs, update its MAC address table with frames that it receives, *and* forward user traffic through the port.

Disabled State

The *disabled* state is a special port state. A port in a disabled state is not participating in STP. This could be because the port has been manually shut down by an administrator, manually removed from STP, disabled because of security issues, or rendered nonfunctional because of a lack of a physical layer signal (such as the patch cable being unplugged).

 EXAM TIP   Remember the four major port states used in STP (802.1d): blocking (20 seconds), listening (15 seconds), learning (15 seconds), and forwarding. It can take 30 to 50 seconds for STP convergence to take place. STP must recalculate if a new root is discovered or a topology change occurs in the network (a new switch added or a change in the state of a port on a switch occurs). Also remember some of the following about these states: In blocking and listening states, only BPDUs are processed. In a learning state, the MAC address table is being built. In a forwarding state, user frames are moved between ports. STP leaves ports in a blocking state to remove loops.

Layer 2 Convergence

As you should have noticed in the last section, STP goes through a staged process, which *slows down* convergence. For switches, convergence occurs once STP has completed: a root switch is elected, root and designated ports have been chosen, the root and designated ports have been placed in a forwarding state, and all other ports have been placed in a blocking state.

If a port has to go through all four states, convergence takes 50 seconds: 20 seconds in blocking, 15 seconds in listening, and 15 seconds in learning. If a port doesn't have to go through the blocking state but starts at a listening state, convergence takes only 30 seconds. This typically occurs when the root port is still valid but another topology change has occurred. Remember that during this time period (until the port reaches a forwarding state), no user traffic is forwarded through the port. So, if a user was performing a telnet session, and STP was being recalculated, the telnet session, from the user's perspective, would appear stalled or the connection would appear lost. Obviously, a user will notice this type of disruption.

EXAM TIP Remember for the CCNA exam that STP convergence has occurred when all root and designated ports are in a forwarding state and all other ports are in a blocking state.

PortFast Overview

The faster that convergence takes place, the less disruption it will cause for your users. You can reduce the two timers to speed up your convergence time, but this can create more problems if you aren't aware of what you are doing when you change them. For user ports, you can use the *PortFast* feature to speed up convergence. PortFast should be used only on ports that will not create layer 2 loops, such as ports connected to PCs, servers, and routers (sometimes referred to as user, or edge, ports).

A port with PortFast enabled is always placed in a forwarding state—this is true even when STP is running and the root and designated ports are going through their different states. So, when STP is running, PortFast ports on the same switch can still forward traffic among themselves, limiting your STP disruption somewhat. However, if these devices wanted to talk to devices connected to other switches, they would have to wait until STP completed and the root and designated ports had moved into a forwarding state.

PortFast is a great option to configure when you want to use Preboot Execution Environment (PXE) boot with your workstations, where the device booting is trying to contact a DHCP server right away at bootup. If you are not using PortFast in this scenario, the workstation will not be able to contact the DHCP server before the 50-second timers of STP have expired. PortFast is the solution!

CAUTION Ports connected to non-switch devices should be configured with PortFast, such as PCs, servers, and routers. However, make sure that you don't enable PortFast on a port connected to another layer 2 switch, because you may inadvertently be creating a layer 2 loop, which can bring down the network.

PortFast Configuration

PortFast works with all versions of STP supported by Cisco switches. Configuring the PortFast feature is simple, and you can enable it globally or on an interface-by-interface basis. To enable it globally, use this command:

```
Switch(config)# spanning-tree portfast default
```

This command enables PortFast on all non-trunking ports on the switch.

To enable PortFast on an interface, use this configuration:

```
Switch(config)# interface type [slot_#/]port_#
Switch(config-if)# spanning-tree portfast [trunk]
```

The optional **trunk** parameter enables PortFast on trunk connections to non-switch devices, such as a router or server with a trunk card.

BPDU Guard Feature

BPDU Guard is used on ports configured with the PortFast feature. In this instance, if a PortFast port receives a BPDU, the switch immediately disables the port. Remember that PortFast is used on non-switch ports to keep them in a forwarding state; the assumption is that a PortFast port is not connected to a switch and therefore shouldn't be receiving BPDUs.

To enable BPDU Guard, use the following Global Configuration command:

```
Switch(config)# spanning-tree portfast bpduguard
```

Use the **show spanning-tree summary totals** command to verify your configuration:

```
Switch# show spanning-tree summary totals
Root bridge for: none.
PortFast BPDU Guard is enabled
UplinkFast is disabled
BackboneFast is disabled
Spanning tree default pathcost method used is short

Name                 Blocking Listening Learning Forwarding STP Active
-------------------- -------- --------- -------- ---------- ----------
  1 VLAN                    0         0        0          1          1
```

At the reception of BPDUs, the BPDU Guard operation disables the port that has PortFast configured. The BPDU Guard transitions the port into an errdisable (error disabled) state, and a message appears on the console. Here is an example of this message:

```
2001 May 23 18:13:12 %SPANTREE-2-RX_PORTFAST:Received BPDU on PortFast enable
port. Disabling 1/0/4
```

When a port has been placed in an error disabled state, use the **errdisable recovery cause bpduguard** command to remove the error disabled state:

```
Switch(config)# errdisable recovery cause bpduguard
```

Notice that you are in Global Configuration mode when executing this command.

Optionally, you can have the switch periodically do this by configuring the command with an interval, specified in seconds:

```
Switch(config)# errdisable recovery interval seconds
```

This automatically clears all errdisable states, including BPDU violations, on all ports every *x* seconds. However, if a BPDU violation occurs again, the port is placed back into an errdisable state.

 EXAM TIP For the CCNA exam, know that BPDU Guard immediately disables a port by placing it in an error disabled state when a BPDU is received on a port configured for PortFast.

Per-VLAN Spanning Tree+ (PVST+)

STP doesn't guarantee an optimized, loop-free network. For instance, take a look at the network shown in Figure 10-6, an example of a network that is poorly designed. In this example, the network has two VLANs, and the root switch is Switch-8. The Xs are ports placed in a blocked state to remove any loops. If you look at this configuration for VLAN 2, it definitely isn't optimized. For instance, VLAN 2 devices on Switch-1, if they want to access VLAN 2 devices on Switch-4, have to go to Switches-2, 3, 6, 9, 8, and then 4. Likewise, VLAN 1 devices on either Switch-5 or Switch-7 that want to access VLAN 1 devices on Switch-4 must forward their traffic first to Switch-8 and then to Switch-4.

When one instance of STP is running, this is referred to as a *Common Spanning Tree* (CST). Cisco also supports a process called *Per-VLAN Spanning Tree Plus* (PVST+). With PVST+, *each* VLAN has its own instance of STP, with its own root switch, its own set of priorities, and its own set of BPDUs. In this scenario, the BPDUs have an

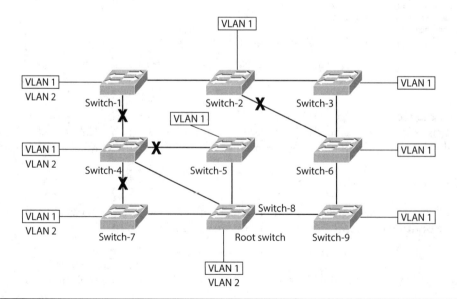

Figure 10-6 STP and VLANs

additional field that is a component of the switch or bridge ID with these three sub-fields: switch priority, extended system ID, and the switch's MAC address. The extended system ID is a new field and carries the VLAN ID (VID) for the instance of STP.

With the addition of this field, it is possible to have different priorities on switches in different VLANs; thus you have the capability of having multiple root switches—one per VLAN. Each VLAN in PVST+, by default, will develop its own loop-free topology. Of course, PVST+, just like CST, doesn't create an optimized, loop-free network; however, you can make STP changes in *each* VLAN to optimize traffic patterns for each separate VLAN. It is highly recommended that you tune STP for each VLAN to optimize it. Another advantage that PVST+ has is that if STP changes are occurring in one VLAN, they do not affect other instances of STP for other VLANs, making for a more stable topology. Given this, it is highly recommended that you implement VTP pruning to prune off VLANs from trunks of switches that are not using those VLANs. Pruning was discussed earlier in this chapter in the section "VTP Pruning."

The downside of PVST+ is that because each VLAN has its own instance of STP, more overhead is involved: more BPDUs and STP tables are required on each switch. Plus, it makes no sense to use PVST+ unless you tune it for your network, which means more work and monitoring on your part.

EXAM TIP   Remember for the CCNA exam that PVST+ supports one instance of STP per VLAN, enabling you to tune for the most optimal paths for each VLAN. CST supports one instance of STP for *all* VLANs.

Simple STP Example

To help you get more familiar with the workings of 802.1d STP, let's take a look at an example of STP in action. Use the network shown in Figure 10-7 as a starting point and assume that these switches do not support Rapid STP (RSTP), discussed later in the chapter, but only 802.1d STP. I'll also assume that there is only one VLAN. The ports on each switch are labeled with a letter and a number. The letter is the port designator, and the number is the cost of the port as a BPDU enters the port.

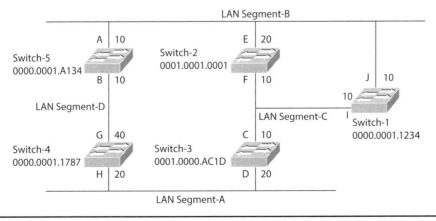

Figure 10-7   STP example network

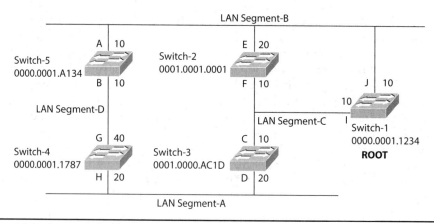

Figure 10-8 Root switch election

Electing the Root Switch

The first thing that occurs once all these switches are booted up is the election of the root switch. The switches share BPDUs with one another to elect the root. In this example, all of the switches are using the default priority (32,768). Remember that the switch with the lowest switch ID is elected as root. Since all of the switches have the same priority, the switch with the lowest MAC address, which is Switch-1, is chosen as the root switch. Based on the election process, the new network topology looks like that shown in Figure 10-8.

Choosing Root Ports for Each Switch

After the root switch is elected, each non-root switch must choose a root port that it will use to reach the root. Let's take this one switch at a time so that you can see the decision process in detail. With Switch-1, which is the root switch, there are no root ports—if you recall, all ports on the root switch are designated ports.

Switch-2 has two ports to use to reach the root: E and F. When Switch-1 generates its BPDUs on ports I and J, the original path cost is set to 0. As these BPDUs are received by other switches, the receiving switch increments the path cost by the cost of the port on which the BPDU was received. As the BPDU comes into port E, Switch-2 increments the path cost to 20, and for port F, a cost of 10. The first check that Switch-2 makes is to compare the path costs. Port F has the best path cost and therefore is chosen as the root port, which is shown as *RP* in Figure 10-9. Switch-3 also has two paths to reach the root: via ports C and D. Port C's accumulated path cost is 10, while D's cost is 70. Therefore, port C is chosen as the root port. Switch-4 also has two ports to use to access the root: H and G. Port H has an accumulated path cost of 30, while G has a cost of 50, causing Switch-4 to choose port H as the root port. Switch-5's two ports, A and B, have accumulated path costs of 10 and 40, respectively, causing Switch-5 to choose port A as the root port. Note that all the switches in the network are simultaneously running STP and figuring out for themselves where the root switch is and which of their own ports should be the root port. This is also true for choosing a designated port on a segment, discussed in the next section.

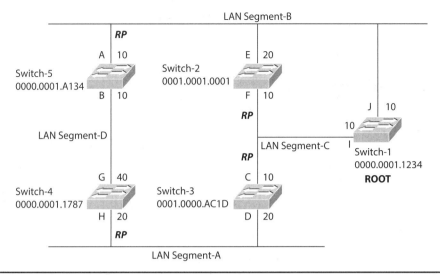

Figure 10-9 Root ports

Choosing Designated Ports for Each Segment

After the root ports are chosen, each switch will figure out, on a segment-by-segment basis, whether its connected port to the segment should be a designated port or not. Remember that the designated port on a segment is responsible for moving traffic back and forth between the segment and the rest of the layer 2 network. The segments themselves, of course, are completely unaware of this process of choosing a designated port—the switches are figuring this out.

When choosing a designated port, the first thing that is examined is the accumulated path cost for the switch (connected to the segment) to reach the root. For two switches connected to the same segment, the switch with the lowest accumulated path cost will be the designated switch for that segment, and its port connected to that segment becomes a designated port.

Going back to our network example, let's start with the easiest segments: B and C. For Switch-1, the accumulated path cost for LAN Segment-B is 0, Switch-2 is 20, and Switch-5 is 10. Since the root switch (Switch-1) has the lowest accumulated path cost, its local port (J) becomes the designated port for LAN Segment-B. This process is also true for LAN Segment-C—the root switch has the lowest accumulated path cost (0), making port I on Switch-1 the designated port for LAN Segment-C.

LAN Segment-A has two choices: Switch-3's port D and Switch-4's port H. Switch-3 has the lower accumulated path cost: 10 versus Switch-4's 50. Therefore, Switch-3's port D becomes the designated port for LAN Segment-A.

LAN Segment-D also has two choices for a designated port: Switch-5's port B and Switch-4's port G. Switch-5 has an accumulated path cost of 10, and Switch-4 has a cost of 30. Therefore Switch-5's port B becomes the designated port for LAN Segment-D.

Figure 10-10 shows the updated STP topology for our network, where *DP* represents the designated ports for the LAN segments.

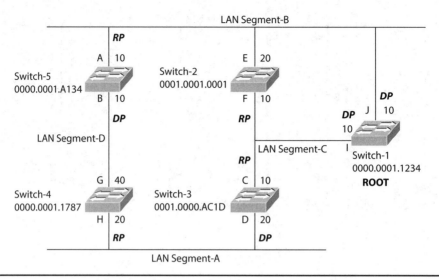

Figure 10-10 Root and designated ports

Changing Port States

After the designated ports are chosen, the switches will move their root and designated ports through the various states—blocking, listening, learning, and forwarding—whereas any other ports will remain in a blocking state. Figure 10-11 shows the ports in a blocking state designated by an X. Remember that on Switch-2, only port F (the root port) is in a forwarding state: port E will remain in a blocking state. In this example, two ports are left in a blocking state: Switch-2's port E and Switch-4's port G.

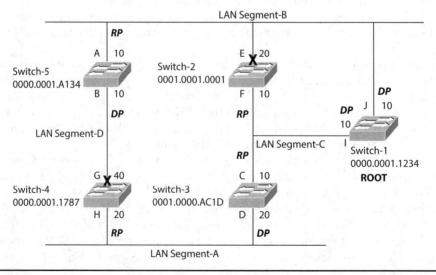

Figure 10-11 Ports in a blocking state

NOTE STP guarantees only a layer 2 loop-free topology—it does not guarantee an optimal topology! For example, in the network shown in Figure 10-10, networking devices on LAN Segment-A would have to go through Switches-3, 1, and 5 in order to reach LAN Segment-D, since Switch-4's port G is in a blocking state.

Rapid Spanning Tree Protocol

The 802.1d standard was designed back when waiting for 30 to 50 seconds for layer 2 convergence wasn't a problem. However, in today's networks, this can cause serious performance problems for networks that use real-time applications, such as voice over IP (VoIP) or video. To overcome these issues, Cisco developed proprietary bridging features called PortFast (discussed earlier), UplinkFast, and BackboneFast. The problem with these features, however, is that they are proprietary to Cisco.

RSTP is an IEEE standard, defined in 802.1w, which is interoperable with 802.1d and an extension to it. With RSTP, there are only three port states:

- Discarding
- Learning
- Forwarding

A port in a discarding state is basically the grouping of 802.1d's blocking, listening, and disabled states. The following sections cover some of the enhancements included in RSTP.

NOTE RSTP is backward compatible with 802.1d.

Additional Port Roles

With RSTP, there is still a root switch and there are still root and designated ports, performing the same roles as those in 802.1d. However, RSTP adds two additional port types: *alternate* ports and *backup* ports. These two ports are similar to the ports in a blocking state in 802.1d. An alternate port has an alternative path or paths to the root but is currently in a discarding state. A backup port is on a segment that could be used to reach the root switch, but an active port is already designated for the segment. The best way to think about this is that an alternate port is a secondary, unused root port, and a backup port is a secondary, unused designated port. The third port role change in RSTP is that there is no longer a blocking state; this has been replaced by a *discarding* state. All ports are either in a forwarding or a discarding state: the root ports and designated ports are in a forwarding state—all other ports are in a discarding state.

Given these new port roles, RSTP calculates the final spanning tree topology the same way as 802.1d. Some of the nomenclature was changed and extended, and this is used to enhance convergence times, as you will see later in the "RSTP Convergence Features" section.

 EXAM TIP For the CCNA exam, know the new port states introduced in RSTP include alternate, backup, and discarding ports. All active ports in RSTP are either in a forwarding, learning, or discarding state. Once all ports are in a forwarding or discarding (blocking) state, RSTP has converged.

RSTP BPDUs

The 802.1w standard introduced a change with BPDUs. Some additional flags were added to the BPDUs, so that switches could share information about the role of the port the BPDU is exiting or leaving. This can help a neighboring switch converge faster when changes occur in the network.

In 802.1d, if a switch didn't see a root BPDU within the maximum age time (20 seconds), STP would run, a new root switch would be elected, and a new loop-free topology would be created. This is a time-consuming process. With 802.1w, if a BPDU is not received in three expected hello periods (6 seconds), STP information can be aged out instantly and the switch considers that its neighbor is lost and actions should be taken. This is different from 802.1d, where the switch had to miss the BPDUs from the root. In 802.1w, if the switch misses three consecutive hellos from a neighbor, actions are immediately taken.

RSTP Convergence Features

The 802.1w standard includes new convergence features that are very similar to Cisco's proprietary UplinkFast and BackboneFast features. The first feature, which is similar to Cisco's BackboneFast feature, allows a switch to accept *inferior BPDUs.*

Look at Figure 10-12 to understand the inferior BPDU feature. In this example, the root bridge is Switch-A. Both of the ports on Switch-B and Switch-C directly connected to the root are root ports. For the segment between Switch-B and Switch-C, Switch-B provides the designated port and Switch-C provides a backup port (a secondary way of reaching the root for the segment). Switch-B also knows that its designated port is an alternative port (a secondary way for the switch to reach the root), via Switch-C from Switch-C's BPDUs.

Following the example in Figure 10-12, the link between the root and Switch-B fails. Switch-B can detect this by either missing three hellos from the root port or detecting a physical layer failure. If you were running 802.1d, Switch-B would see an inferior root BPDU (worse cost value) coming via Switch-C, and therefore all ports would have to go through blocking, listening, and learning states, which would take 50 seconds, by default, to converge. With the inferior BPDU feature, assuming that Switch-B knows that Switch-C has an alternate port for their directly connected segment, Switch-B can notify Switch-C to take its alternate port and change it to a designated port, and Switch-B will change its designated port to a root port. This process takes only a few seconds, if even that.

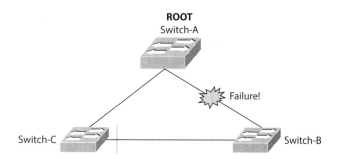

Figure 10-12
Accepting
inferior BPDUs

The second convergence feature introduced in 802.1w is *rapid transition*. Rapid transition includes two new components: edge ports and link types. An edge port is a port connected to a non–layer 2 device, such as a PC, server, or router. RSTP with rapid transition of edge ports to a forwarding state is the same as Cisco's proprietary PortFast. Changes in the state of these ports do not affect RSTP to cause a recalculation, and changes in other port types will keep these ports in a forwarding state.

Rapid transition can take place in RSTP only for edge ports and links that are point-to-point (P2P). The link type is automatically determined in terms of the duplexing of the connection. Switches make the assumption that if the port is configured for full duplex between the two switches, the port can rapidly transition to a different state without having to wait for any timers to expire. If they are half duplex, this feature won't work by default, but you can manually enable it for P2P half-duplex switch links.

Let's take a look at an example of rapid transition of P2P links by using the topology in Figure 10-13. The topology in Figure 10-13 is the same as that shown in Figure 10-12, except the link between Switch-A (the root) and Switch-C fails in Figure 10-13. When this happens, Switch-C can no longer reach Switch-A on its root port. However, looking at the BPDUs it has been receiving from Switch-A and Switch-B, Switch-C knows that the root is reachable via Switch-B and that Switch-B provides the designated port (which is in a forwarding state) for the segment between Switch-B and Switch-C. Switch-C, knowing this, changes the state of the backup port to a root port and places it immediately into a forwarding state, notifying Switch-B of the change. This update typically takes less than a second, assuming that the failure of the segment between the root and Switch-C is a physical link failure, instead of three missed consecutive hello BPDUs.

Figure 10-13
Rapid transition
example

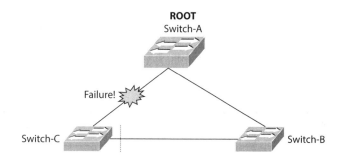

EXAM TIP Remember for the CCNA exam that RSTP converges much more rapidly than the original IEEE STP (802.1d) on point-to-point (P2P) links.

RSTP Configuration

Cisco switches support three types of STP, as displayed in Table 10-4. The default configuration on Cisco switches is a separate instance of STP per VLAN, one root switch for all the VLANs, and no load sharing.

This book focuses only on PVRST+, and briefly at that. To enable PVRST+, use the following command:

```
Switch(config)# spanning-tree mode rapid-pvst
```

EXAM TIP Know for the CCNA exam that the **spanning-tree mode rapid-pvst** command enables RSTP on an IOS switch.

Once enabled, you can view the STP on a per-VLAN basis with this command:

```
Switch# show spanning-tree vlan VLAN_# [detail]
```

Here's an example of this command:

```
Switch# show spanning-tree vlan 10
VLAN0010
Spanning tree enabled protocol rstp
Root ID Priority 32768
This bridge is root
Hello Time 2 sec Max Age 20 sec Forward Delay 15 sec
Bridge ID Priority 32768 (priority 32768 sys-id-ext 10)
Address 0000.01c1.1111
Hello Time 2 sec Mag Age 20 sec Forward Delay 15 sec
Aging Time 300
Interface  Role  Sts  Cost  Pior.Nbr  Type
---------  ----  ---  ----  --------  ----
Fa0/1      Desg  FWD  19    128.1     P2p
Fa0/2      Desg  FWD  19    128.2     P2p
Fa0/3      Desg  FWD  19    128.3     P2p
.
.
.
```

STP	Description
PVST+	802.1d per VLAN with Cisco-proprietary extensions (PortFast, UplinkFast, BackboneFast)
PVRST+	802.1w (RSTP) per VLAN
Multiservice Transport Platform (MSTP)	802.1s, referred to as multiple STP, combines Cisco's PVST+ with IEEE standards

Table 10-4 STP Types

In this example, the switch is the root for VLAN 10 and RSTP is being used. Notice that all of its ports are designated ports (Desg) and are in a forwarding state (FWD)—if this were true for all active ports, then this switch would be the root switch, which indeed is the case here, as indicated by the fourth line of output (This bridge is root).

 EXAM TIP Be familiar with the output of the **show spanning-tree vlan** and **show spanning-tree interface** commands for the exam.

You can also verify STP on a per-port basis with the **show spanning-tree interface** command. Here's an example:

```
Switch# show spanning-tree interface fastethernet 1/0/5
Vlan      Role Sts Cost Prio.Nbr Type
--------- ---- --- ---- -------- ----
VLAN0001 Root FWD 19    128.1    P2P
VLAN0002 Altn DIS 19    128.2    P2P
VLAN0003 Root FWD 19    128.2    P2P
```

In this example, F1/0/5 is an alternate port in VLAN 2 either because it has a higher path cost to the root bridge or because there is a tie and this neighbor has a higher bridge ID.

 TIP To troubleshoot problems with PVRST+, use the **debug spanning-tree pvst+** command; to troubleshoot problems with ports changing state within STP, use **debug spanning-tree switch state**.

PVST+ and RSTP Optimization

To understand the advantages offered by PVST+ and RSTP, examine Figure 10-14. This example shows two VLANs, numbered 1 and 2. The default behavior with Cisco's switches is that a single root switch is used for all VLANs, based on the switch with the lowest switch ID. In this instance, this is Switch-A. Notice that based on RSTP's

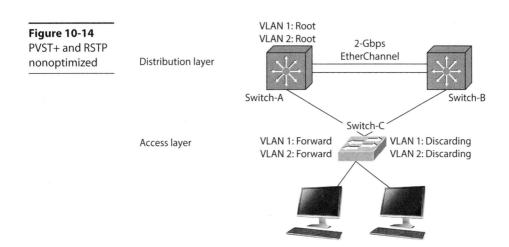

Figure 10-14
PVST+ and RSTP
nonoptimized

calculation, Switch-C disabled its port to Switch-B for both its VLANs. The downside of this design is that of the two connections to the distribution layer, only one is being utilized on the access switch.

A better design is shown in Figure 10-14. To obtain this kind of topology, however, you must tune your network, making sure that Switch-A is the root for VLAN 1 and Switch-B is the root for VLAN 2. With this kind of design, you can actually utilize both of your uplink connections on your access layer switch up to the distribution layer switches. In Figure 10-15, VLAN 1 will use the left-hand uplink connection and VLAN 2 the right-hand uplink connection.

 NOTE Based on the design in Figure 10-15, you should make sure the default gateway for VLAN 1 is Switch-A (assuming it's a layer 3 switch) and for VLAN 2 is Switch-B (assuming it's a layer 3 switch). If you don't configure it this way, but you have the default gateway associated with Switch-A, VLAN 2's traffic will have to go from the access layer switch to Switch-B, and then across the EtherChannel to Switch-A before leaving the subnet. You can learn more about this in Cisco's CCNP Switching course.

Remember that the topology in Figure 10-15 is created by you: you must manually change each switch's priority to create the desired topology. The commands to accomplish this include the following:

```
Switch(config)# spanning-tree vlan VLAN_# root primary
Switch(config)# spanning-tree vlan VLAN_# root secondary
Switch(config)# spanning-tree vlan VLAN_# priority priority_#
```

Remember that the default priority for a switch is 32,768. The first command changes the switch's priority to 4096 for the specified VLAN. The second command changes the switch's priority to 8192 for the specified VLAN. The third enables you to customize the priority for the specified VLAN.

Figure 10-15
PVST+ and RSTP
optimized

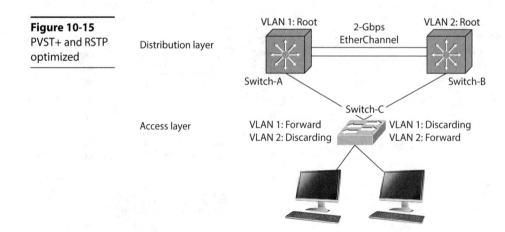

Based on the example in Figure 10-15, Switch-A's configuration would look like this:

```
Switch-A(config)# spanning-tree mode rapid-pvst
Switch-A(config)# spanning-tree vlan 1 root primary
Switch-A(config)# spanning-tree vlan 2 root secondary
```

Switch-B's configuration would look like this:

```
Switch-B(config)# spanning-tree mode rapid-pvst
Switch-B(config)# spanning-tree vlan 2 root primary
Switch-B(config)# spanning-tree vlan 1 root secondary
```

The only difference between these two configurations is that the priorities for the primary and secondary are switched on the two VLANs to allow for the use of both uplinks from Switch-C, the access layer switch.

 NOTE Any STP configuration changes you make on your switches are affected immediately, which means that layer 2 will have to reconverge, causing a brief disruption in your layer 2 network.

STP Troubleshooting

Troubleshooting problems created by loops can be a difficult task. This section covers some simple steps you can take to identify and fix layer 2 loop problems.

Before we look at the different layer 2 loop problems, I want to define a *broadcast storm*. Switches send broadcast messages to all ports on the switch (except the port it was received on). If you have a layer 2 loop, that means there are multiple pathways between the switches, and the broadcast message would be rebroadcasted from one switch to another, using up bandwidth and processing power on the switches—this is a broadcast storm. Broadcast storms are bad, because they will eventually bring the network down.

Loop Identification

One indication of a broadcast storm is very high CPU and port utilization on your switches. As mentioned at the beginning of the chapter, you can examine a switch's or several switches' CPU utilization with the **show processes** and **show process cpu** commands. A constantly high CPU utilization could indicate a loop. To verify that a layer 2 loop is causing the problem, capture and analyze traffic with a protocol analyzer to determine whether the same packet appears multiple times. This is typically done by connecting your protocol analyzer to a switch and using the Switch Port Analyzer (SPAN) feature on your switch, which copies frames from an interface or VLAN to the SPAN port. A good protocol analyzer should be able to see that a loop exists and notify you of this problem.

Once a loop is identified, to restore connectivity quickly, you should start disabling ports that are part of the loop; then diagnose the problem to determine whether a configuration issue on your part or the addition of a new layer 2 device is causing the problem. If you are having problems identifying what is causing the loop, turn on debug for STP (**debug spanning-tree events**).

Configuration Remedies

To simplify your troubleshooting process, disable as many features as necessary. For example, if you have EtherChannels enabled, disabling the channel will help determine whether the channel itself is not functioning correctly and possibly creating the layer 2 loop.

If you are not certain which switch is the root switch, log into the switch that logically should be the root and force it to become the root by changing its priority to 1 with the **spanning-tree vlan** *VLAN_#* **priority** command.

 TIP A good step on your part should be to include the MAC addresses of each switch in your network topology diagram. Then, when troubleshooting loop problems, you'll find it much easier to determine whether a rogue switch was introduced into the topology that may be creating the loop.

Make sure that all your switches are running either 802.1d or 802.1w (RSTP), preferably the latter. Use the **show spanning-tree** command to verify this as well as whether or not the switch is playing the role of root for a VLAN.

Exercise 10-2: Monitoring STP

In this exercise, you will connect two switches together and verify that a port was placed in a blocking state with STP. You will use the network configuration of the previous exercise in this chapter.

1. Ensure that both switches are powered on.

2. Ensure that each port 1 on both switches is connected to the other with a crossover cable.

3. Wait a minute, and notice that both ends of the link turn green.

4. Create a link between VAN-SW1 and VAN-SW2 using port 24 on each switch with a crossover cable. Wait a minute, and notice that one of the links will stay amber as it is placed in a blocking state to prevent the loop.

5. Console into VAN-SW1 and run the **show spanning-tree vlan 1** command to view the spanning tree setup. Note the bridge ID priority and address and compare it to the Root ID at the top of the output. If the values are the same, you know this is the root switch; if they are not the same, you know this switch is not the root switch. Remember that the root switch will have all ports involved in the loop in a forwarding state.

6. Record the following information about VAN-SW1:

    Root ID Priority: _____
    Root ID Address: _____
    Bridge ID Priority: _____
    Bridge ID Address: _____

7. Is VAN-SW1 the root bridge (the previous values recorded are the same if it is)? _____

8. Look at the status of the interfaces at the bottom of the output and record the role of each:

   VAN-SW1 – Port 1: _____
   VAN-SW1 – Port 24: _____

9. Console into VAN-SW2 and run the **show spanning-tree vlan 1** command.

10. Record the following information about VAN-SW2:

    Root ID Priority: _____
    Root ID Address: _____
    Bridge ID Priority: _____
    Bridge ID Address: _____

11. Is VAN-SW2 the root bridge (the previous values recorded are the same if it is)? _____

12. Look at the status of the interfaces at the bottom of the output and record the role of each:

    VAN-SW2 – Port 1: _____
    VAN-SW2 – Port 24: _____

13. Look at the LEDs on each of the connected interfaces on both switches. The interface you recorded that is in the blocking state should have an amber light, indicating it is in a blocking state.

14. Console into the switch that has the port in a blocking state. You are going to force this switch to be the root bridge by changing the priority (this will cause all ports on this switch to be in a forwarding state while the blocking state port will move to the other switch). To change the priority of the switch, enter the following commands (I am assuming it is VAN-SW1 in this code example, but you may experience it as VAN-SW2):

```
VAN-SW1>enable
VAN-SW1#config term
VAN-SW1(config)#spanning-tree vlan 1 root primary
VAN-SW1(config)#exit
VAN-SW1#show spanning-tree vlan 1
```

15. View the spanning tree status on the other switch to verify that the blocking port has moved to the other switch.

EtherChannels

It is common to need higher bandwidth speeds for certain kinds of connections in your network, such as connections from the access layer to the distribution layer, between distribution layer switches, between distribution and core layer switches, and between certain servers or routers and their connected switches. For example, looking back at Figure 10-15, you can see dual layer 2 connections between the two distribution layer switches as well as between the distribution and core layer switches. The problem with this type of design, however, is that it creates layer 2 loops; and with STP running, STP will ensure that only one path is active between two devices, limiting you to the bandwidth of one of possibly multiple connections.

EtherChannel Overview

An EtherChannel is a layer 2 solution that enables you to aggregate multiple layer 2 Ethernet-based connections between directly connected devices. Basically, an EtherChannel bundles together multiple Ethernet ports between devices, providing what appears to be a single logical interface. From STP's perspective, it sees the EtherChannel as a single logical connection between the connected devices, which means that you can actually use all of the individual connections, simultaneously, in the channel you've created.

EtherChannels provide these advantages:

- **Redundancy** If one connection in the channel fails, you can use other connections in the channel.
- **More bandwidth** Each connection can be used simultaneously to send frames.
- **Simplified management** Configuration is done on the logical interface, not on each individual connection in the channel.

EtherChannel Restrictions

Interfaces in an EtherChannel must be configured identically: speed, duplexing, and VLAN settings (in the same VLAN if they are access ports, or the same trunk properties) must be the same. When setting up EtherChannels, you can use up to eight interfaces bundled together:

- Up to eight Fast Ethernet connections, providing up to 800 Mbps
- Up to eight Gigabit Ethernet connections, providing up to 8 Gbps
- Up to eight 10-Gigabit Ethernet connections, providing up to 80 Gbps

Typically you can have a total of six EtherChannels on a switch, but this is larger on the higher-end IOS switches.

 EXAM TIP Remember for the CCNA exam that when forming an EtherChannel, all ports must be configured for the same speed, trunk encapsulation type (access, 802.1Q, or ISL), and duplex setting.

EtherChannel Operations

Channels can be formed dynamically between devices by using one of two protocols: Port Aggregation Protocol (PAgP) or Link Aggregation Control Protocol (LACP), compared in Table 10-5. Remember that ports participating in a channel must be configured identically.

Once a channel is formed, load balancing can be used by the connected devices to utilize all the ports in the channel. Load balancing is performed by reducing part of the binary addressing in the frame or packet to a numeric value and then associating the

Protocols	Description
PAgP	Proprietary to Cisco. It enables connected devices to group similarly configured ports dynamically into a single channel.
LACP	Defined in the IEEE 802.3ad standard. Like PAgP, it learns from a connected device which ports between the two are identically configured and dynamically forms a channel between them.

Table 10-5   EtherChannel Protocols

numeric value to one of the ports in the channel. Load balancing can use MAC or IP addresses, source or destination addresses, or both source and destination address pairs. With load balancing, you are guaranteed that all links in the channel will be utilized; however, you are not guaranteed that all the ports will be utilized the same.

For example, if you are load balancing based on source addresses, you are guaranteed that different source MAC addresses will use different ports in the channel. All traffic from a single-source MAC address, however, will always use the same port in the channel. Given this situation, if one device is generating a lot of traffic, that link will possibly be utilized more than other links in the channel. In such a situation, you may want to load balance based on the destination address or both the source and destination addresses.

 NOTE   To configure load balancing properly for a channel, you must understand the traffic patterns in your network. Once you understand your traffic patterns, you can get the most utilization out of your channel by choosing the correct load balancing type.

EtherChannel Configuration

As mentioned, you should make sure that all interfaces in the channel are configured identically (configuring interface properties was discussed in Chapter 9); otherwise, a channel may not form. Here is the configuration to set up an EtherChannel:

```
Switch(config)# interface type [slot_#/]port_#
Switch(config-if)# channel-group group_# mode mode
Switch(config-if)# port-channel load-balance {dst-ip | dst-mac |
                        src-dst-ip | src-dst-mac | src-ip | src-mac}
```

The *group_#* specifies the channel group to which the interface belongs, which can be from 1 to 6 (remember that you can have up to six EtherChannels on your switch). The *mode* can be one of those listed in Table 10-6. When using PAgP, one side needs to be configured as desirable and the other side as desirable or auto; or you can configure both sides to be on. When using LACP, one side needs to be active and the other side can be active or passive.

 NOTE   If you want to treat this as a layer 3 interface, on a router for example, and assign an IP address to it, the port channel must be designated as **interface port-channel** *group_#*.

Mode	Protocol	Description
auto	PAgP	Passively listens for PAgP queries from a Cisco device configured with either desirable or on. By default, the interface is not part of a channel.
desirable	PAgP	Generates PAgP queries to form a channel, but by default is not part of a channel.
on	PAgP	Generates PAgP queries and assumes the port is part of a channel.
active	LACP	Enables a channel if the other side responds to its LACP messages.
passive	LACP	Passively listens for LACP messages to form a channel from an active port.

Table 10-6 EtherChannel Modes

Use the **port-channel load-balance** command to configure the type of load balancing you want to use on the channel. If you omit this command, it defaults to load balancing based on source MAC addresses (**src-mac**).

 EXAM TIP Remember for the CCNA exam that if one side of a PAgP EtherChannel is set to auto for the mode, the other needs to be set to either on or desirable. The active and passive modes are used only to establish an EtherChannel using LACP.

Here's a configuration of SwitchA forming an EtherChannel to SwitchB using PAgP:

```
SwitchA(config)# interface g1/0/1
SwitchA(config-if)# channel-group 1 mode auto
SwitchA(config-if)# exit
SwitchA(config)# interface g1/0/2
SwitchA(config-if)# channel-group 1 mode auto
SwitchA(config-if)# exit
```

Because the auto mode is used on SwitchA for PAgP, SwitchB must use either a mode of on or desirable, like this:

```
SwitchB(config)# interface g1/0/4
SwitchB(config-if)# channel-group 1 mode on
SwitchB(config-if)# exit
SwitchB(config)# interface g1/0/5
SwitchB(config-if)# channel-group 1 mode on
SwitchB(config-if)# exit
```

Exercise 10-3: Working with EtherChannel

In this exercise, you will configure an EtherChannel connection between the VAN-SW1 and VAN-SW2 switches in the Vancouver office.

1. Ensure that both switches are powered on.

2. If the crossover cables are still connected from the previous exercise, remove them.

3. Use crossover cables to connect ports 1 and 2 between the two switches.

4. Console into VAN-SW1 and enter the following commands:

```
VAN-SW1>enable
VAN-SW1#config term
Enter configuration commands, one per line.  End with CNTL/Z.
VAN-SW1(config)#interface g1/0/1
VAN-SW1(config-if)#channel-group 1 mode auto

VAN-SW1(config-if)#interface g1/0/2
VAN-SW1(config-if)#channel-group 1 mode auto
```

5. View the EtherChannel summary information by running the **show etherchannel summary** command. Record the following information:

Group: _____

Protocol: _____

Ports: _____

6. View the status of the port-channel 1 interface with the **show interfaces port-channel 1** command. Note that the command could also be abbreviated as **show interfaces po1**.

7. Switch to VAN-SW2 and enter the following commands to place interfaces 1 and 2 in an EtherChannel:

```
VAN-SW2>enable
VAN-SW2#config term
VAN-SW2(config)#interface g1/0/1
VAN-SW2(config-if)#channel-group 1 mode on

VAN-SW2(config-if)#interface g1/0/2
VAN-SW2(config-if)#channel-group 1 mode on
```

8. View the EtherChannel summary information by running the **show etherchannel summary** command. Record the following information:

Group: _____

Protocol: _____

Ports: _____

9. View the status of the port-channel 1 interface with the **show interfaces port-channel 1** command.

 VIDEO 10.03. The digital resources that accompany this book contain a multimedia demonstration of configuring EtherChannel on your switch.

Chapter Review

VTP is a Cisco-proprietary protocol that transmits VLAN information across trunk ports. Switches must be in the same domain to share messages. There are three modes for VTP: client, server, and transparent. Server and transparent switches can add, change, and delete VLANs, but server switches advertise these changes. Clients can accept updates only from server switches. There are three VTP messages: advertisement request, subset advertisement, and summary advertisement. Servers generate summary advertisements every five minutes on trunk connections. The configuration revision number is used to determine which server switch has the most current VLAN information. VTP pruning is used to prune off VLANs that are not active between two switches, but it requires switches to be in server and/or client mode.

On the Cisco switch, use the **vtp domain** command and **vtp server|client|transparent** commands to configure VTP. The default mode is server. To configure a VTP password, use the **vtp password** command.

BPDUs are used by STP to learn about other neighboring switches. These are generated every two seconds as multicasts. When running STP, a root switch is elected—the one with the lowest switch or bridge ID. The switch ID is composed of a priority and the switch's MAC address. Each switch chooses a root port to reach the root switch—the one with the lowest accumulated path cost. Each segment has one port on one switch that becomes a designated port, which is used to forward traffic to and from the segment. This is typically the port on the switch with the lowest accumulated path cost. There are five port states: blocking (20 seconds), listening (15 seconds), learning (15 seconds), forwarding, and disabled. PortFast puts a port immediately into forwarding mode and should be used only on non-switch ports. PVST+ has an instance of STP running per VLAN—this is proprietary to Cisco but standardized by IEEE with MSTP.

RSTP reduces convergence to a few seconds by having switches determine valid alternate root ports and backup designated ports that they can use when topology changes take place. PVST+ with RSTP is enabled with the **spanning-tree mode rapid-pvst** command.

EtherChannels bundle layer 2 connections between devices, creating a single logical port from STP's perspective. Load balancing can then be performed on the ports in the channel. PAgP or LACP is used to form the channel. No more than eight interfaces can be part of a channel.

If your CPU and/or port utilization is high, you may have a layer 2 loop. Typically you should use a protocol analyzer and look for multiple copies of the same frame in your frame captures.

Quick Review

VLAN Trunking Protocol

- VTP is used to share VLAN information to ensure that switches have a consistent VLAN configuration.
- VTP has three modes: server (can make and accept changes and propagates changes), transparent (can make changes, ignores VTP messages), and client (accepts changes from servers and doesn't store them in NVRAM). The default mode is server.

- VTP messages are propagated only across trunks. For a switch to accept a VTP message, the domain name and optional password must match. There are three VTP messages: advertisement request (client or server request), subset advertisement (server response to an advertisement), and summary advertisement (server sends out every five minutes). The configuration revision number is used in the VTP message to determine whether it should be processed or not.

- VTP pruning allows for the dynamic addition and removal of VLANs on a trunk based on whether or not there are any active VLANs on a switch. Requires switches to be in server and/or client mode.

Spanning Tree Protocol

- STP is defined in 802.1d. It removes loops from your network.

- The switch with the lowest switch ID (priority + MAC address) is elected as the root.

- Each switch chooses the best path to the root, and this port is called a root port. Each segment needs a switch port to access the rest of the network—this port is called a designated port.

- BPDUs are used to elect root switches and to share topology information. BPDUs are multicasts that are advertised every two seconds.

- There are five STP port states: blocking (only processing BPDUs—20 seconds), listening (only processing BPDUs—15 seconds), learning (processing BPDUs and building the CAM table—15 seconds), forwarding (processing BPDUs, building the CAM table, and forwarding user traffic), and disabled (the port is not enabled). Root and designated ports will eventually move into a forwarding state, which can take between 30 and 50 seconds.

- PortFast keeps a port in a forwarding state when STP is recalculating; it should *not* be used on switch-to-switch connections because it could lead to inadvertent loops.

- PVST+ is proprietary to Cisco and allows for a separate STP instance per VLAN.

Rapid Spanning Tree Protocol

- RSTP has three port states: discarding, learning, and forwarding.

- RSTP supports two additional port types: alternate (secondary to a root port) and backup (secondary to a designated port).

EtherChannels

- From STP's perspective, an EtherChannel, which is a grouping of layer 2 physical connections between devices, is seen as a single logical connection.

- Ports must be configured identically in an EtherChannel. PAgP or LACP can be used to form a channel.

Questions

The following questions will help you measure your understanding of the material presented in this chapter. Read all the choices carefully, as there may be more than one correct answer. Choose the correct answer(s) for each question.

1. Which VTP mode(s) can create and delete VLANs?

    A. Client and server

    B. Server

    C. Client and transparent

    D. Transparent

    E. Server and transparent

2. The root switch is the one elected with the _____.

    A. lowest MAC address

    B. highest MAC address

    C. lowest switch ID

    D. highest switch ID

3. The switch port that is chosen to forward traffic for a segment is called a(n) _____.

    A. root port

    B. alternate port

    C. backup port

    D. designated port

4. With STP, which of the following is true concerning a port that is in a listening state? (Choose two.)

    A. It remains there for 15 seconds.

    B. It forwards BPDUs and builds the CAM table.

    C. It remains there for 20 seconds.

    D. It forwards BPDUs.

5. How many port states are there in RSTP?

    A. 3

    B. 4

    C. 5

    D. 6

6. What port role will be assigned to a port that has the second-best path to the root switch?

    A. Root

    B. Designated

C. Alternate

D. Backup

7. Which command enables RSTP with PVRST+ on a Cisco switch?

A. **spanning-tree mode rapid-pvst**

B. **spanning-tree state rapid-pvst**

C. **stp state rapid-pvst**

D. **spanning-tree mode rstp**

8. Which of the following is/are true concerning EtherChannels?

A. You can have up to six ports in a channel.

B. You can have up to eight channels on a switch.

C. Ports must be configured identically to form a channel.

D. RSTP dynamically groups ports into a channel.

9. What symptom should you look for to determine whether you have a layer 2 loop?

A. High number of broadcast and/or multicast frames

B. High port utilization

C. User switch interfaces dropping and reconnecting

D. Port address tables not being updated

10. What tool would you use to determine whether you had a broadcast storm caused by a layer 2 loop?

A. **show interface** command

B. Protocol analyzer

C. **debug broadcast** command

D. **traceroute** command

11. You have two switches with VTP configured that are not connected together. The first switch is running in server mode with VLANs Accounting, HR, and Executives and a configuration revision value of 55. The second switch is also running in server mode with VLANs Engineering, Sales, and Marketing and a configuration revision value of 57. You connect the two switches together with a crossover cable. What will happen? (Choose two.)

A. If the domain names don't match, nothing occurs.

B. If the domain names don't match, the VLANs on the higher revision switch are used and the other ones are deleted.

C. If the domain names match, the Engineering, Sales, and Marketing VLANs are deleted.

D. If the domain names match, the Accounting, HR, and Executives VLANs are deleted.

Performance-based Question

The Cisco exams have performance-based questions where you must drag an item from the left side of the screen to its proper place on the right side of the screen in order to answer the question. The following is a sample performance-based question related to this chapter.

1. Using the following exhibit, identify characteristics of STP and EtherChannel by placing the description on the left side of the diagram into the appropriate category on the right side of the diagram. Not all descriptions found on the left will necessarily be used.

STP

| Combines bandwidth of multiple Fast Ethernet of Gigabit Ethernet Ports |

| Designed to prevent layer 2 loops |

| Allows redundancy on the links |

EtherChannel

| Places redundant links in a blocking state |

| Designed to prevent layer 3 loops |

Answers

1. **E.** Switches operating in VTP modes of server mode or transparent mode can manage VLANs. Server mode switches will send the VLAN updates to other switches, while transparent mode switches do not send their VLAN updates to other switches.

2. **C.** The switch with the lowest switch ID is elected as the root switch. The switch ID is based on the switch's priority and MAC address.

3. **D.** The switch port that is chosen to forward traffic for a segment is called a designated port.

4. **A, D.** With STP, a port that is running in a listening state will process and forward BPDUs. A port stays in the listening state for 15 seconds.

5. **A.** There are three port states in RSTP: discarding, learning, and forwarding.

6. **C.** An alternate port has the second-best path to the root switch.

7. **A.** The **spanning-tree mode rapid-pvst** command enables RSTP with PVST+ on a Cisco switch.

8. **C.** Ports must be configured identically before they can form a channel. For example, ports should be configured with the same speed and duplex setting.

9. **B.** If you have a layer 2 loop, the switch's CPU and/or port utilization will be very high.

10. **B.** When using a protocol analyzer to troubleshoot layer 2 loop problems, look for the same frame being repeated constantly.

11. **A, D.** If the domain names don't match, they ignore each other's VTP messages. If the domain names match, the configuration of the switch with the highest revision number is used; the switch with the lowest revision number will have its VLANs deleted.

Performance-based Answer

The following is the answer to the performance-based questions in this chapter.

1. On the real Cisco exams, you will need to drag the boxes on the left to the appropriate category on the right. The following identifies the characteristics of STP and EtherChannel.

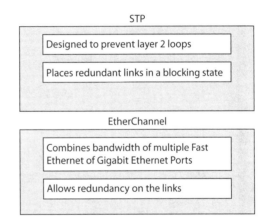

STP

Designed to prevent layer 2 loops

Places redundant links in a blocking state

EtherChannel

Combines bandwidth of multiple Fast Ethernet of Gigabit Ethernet Ports

Allows redundancy on the links

Designed to prevent layer 3 loops

CHAPTER 11

Introduction to Routing

In this chapter, you will

- Learn some routing basics
- Learn about dynamic routing
- Read about the routing process
- Learn some routing troubleshooting commands
- Learn how to set up and use a router-on-a-stick
- Read about router high availability

In this chapter you are introduced to routing and the routing process. You will learn about the steps a router takes to select a route to a destination, including the important concept of *administrative distance*, a feature that routers use to rank and select the best route to take; this is very important to know for the CCNA exam.

You will also learn how to add a static route to the routing table and the purpose of dynamic routing protocols. For the exam, you need to know about Open Shortest Path First (OSPF) only as one of several routing protocols; you should also be familiar with the fact that other routing protocols exist, and you need to know the administrative distance for each of those.

This chapter introduces the concepts of routing, static routes, dynamic routing, and floating static routes, which are super important for the Cisco CCNA exam, but this chapter only provides examples of routing with IPv4. In Chapter 14, you will learn the commands to configure static routes and dynamic routing with IPv6. The concepts are the same, but you'll use a different type of address with IPv6.

Understanding Routing

Routing is the process of sending data from one network to another along a chosen path. After we have divided a network into segments, it is up to the routers to move the data from one network segment to another, as shown in Figure 11-1.

The router is responsible for routing information to the destination network, and it does this by using information stored in a *routing table*. A routing table is a list of destination networks that resides in memory on the router; the router uses this information to identify where to send data to reach a destination. If a destination is not included in the routing table, the router will not be able to send the information to the destination.

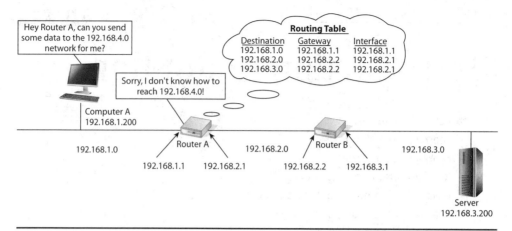

Figure 11-1   A router depends on its routing table for knowledge of destination networks.

In Figure 11-1, Computer A is trying to send data off the network by first sending it to Router A. Router A looks in its routing table to see whether the destination of 192.168.4.0 is listed, and as you can see in the figure, the router does not know how to reach that destination, so it returns an error.

Look at the third entry in the routing table: you can see that Router A includes the 192.168.3.0 network destination in its routing table. Therefore, if any systems on the 192.168.1.0 network send data to the 192.168.3.0 network, the router will send the information to the next *hop value* for that entry (shown as the "Gateway" column in the table). The hop value determines where the router needs to send the data to reach a particular destination. In this case, it will send the data to the 192.168.2.2 hop value, and it will get to 192.168.2.2 by sending the data out the interface of 192.168.2.1 on Router A, as shown in the "Interface" column. This column is important, because it lets the router know how a gateway can be reached from Router A.

Routing Concepts

Before we look at how to configure routing on a router, let's go over some routing concepts and terminology. Following are some key routing terms you should be familiar with for the CCNA certification exam:

- **Loopback interface**   Routers have network interface cards installed that provide network connections so that data can be sent (routed) from one network to another. The router can also include a loopback interface, which is a virtual network interface card configured on the router. You might configure a loopback interface for testing purposes or because a router feature may require the use of a loopback interface—for example, the routing protocol OSPF uses the IP address of the loopback interface as its router ID. To control the router ID, you can configure a loopback interface and then assign an IP address to it.

- **Routing loops**   A routing loop occurs when two routers send a packet back and forth because each believes the packet belongs to the other router's network (because of the destination IP of the packet and the route on the router). Routers use the Time-To-Live (TTL) field as a method to prevent infinite routing loops by decreasing the TTL every time a packet reaches a router. Once the TTL reaches 0, the packet is removed from the network.

- **Routing tables**   The routing table is a list of destinations the router is aware of (destinations stored in the router's memory). It indicates the route by which data should travel in order to reach a destination. The router compares the destination IP address of the packet against the destination networks in its routing table. If there is a match, the router sends the packet to the IP address specified with that entry in the routing table. If the destination network is not included in the routing table, the router sends an error message.

- **Static vs. dynamic routes**   Routes are either manually added to a routing table by the network administrator (*static routes*), or they are automatically learned from other routers (*dynamic routes*) using a routing protocol. You will learn more about static routes and dynamic routes as the chapter progresses.

When discussing network traffic, properties of network traffic, or even routing of network traffic, network professionals typically use the following terms:

- **PDU**   A *protocol data unit* is a single unit of data communication being delivered and typically contains control information such as addressing information or data from an application. The PDU for layer 1 is known as a *bit*, the PDU for layer 2 is a *frame*, the PDU for layer 3 is a *packet*, and the PDU for layer 4 is a *segment*.

- **MTU**   The *maximum transmission unit* is the maximum size of a packet on the network. With Ethernet networks, the MTU is typically 1514 bytes.

Interface Configuration

Routers are used to connect networks and route data between these networks. A router connects to different networks via network cards, which are *interfaces* built into the router. Each interface is assigned an IP address and is connected to a network (as shown in Figure 11-1).

Refer back to Figure 11-1. Let's assume that Router A and Router B are Cisco routers. Assume that on Router A, the interface assigned the IP address of 192.168.1.1 is an Ethernet interface (which connects to an Ethernet network). Assume that the interface on Router A that is assigned the IP address of 192.168.2.1 is a serial interface. Serial interfaces are used either to connect to your wide area network (WAN) or to serve as a point-to-point link (a direct connection between two routers).

Configuring an Ethernet Interface

Let's review a few Cisco router commands. To assign an IP address to the Ethernet interface on Router A (ROUTERA in the following code example), you type the following commands (excluding what appears before > or #—those are the prompts):

```
ROUTERA> enable
ROUTERA# configure terminal
ROUTERA(config)# interface fastethernet0/0
ROUTERA(config-if)# ip address 192.168.1.1 255.255.255.0
ROUTERA(config-if)# no shutdown
```

Let's take a look at what each of these commands does.

1. The first command, **enable**, is used to move from user EXEC mode of the router to privileged EXEC mode. In user EXEC mode, you are unable to make changes; privileged EXEC mode is required to make changes.

2. To change the settings of the Ethernet interface, you start at the interface prompt, which is in Global Configuration mode, where most changes are made. To move to Global Configuration mode, type **configure terminal**. Then, to move to the interface prompt, type **interface fastethernet0/0**. Here, **fastethernet0/0** is the first Fast Ethernet interface on the router. (If you had a second Ethernet interface, it would be **fastethernet0/1**.)

3. Once at the Ethernet interface prompt, you assign the IP address using the **ip address** command.

4. The last command, **no shutdown**, enables the interface. (You can also disable the interface at any time using the **shutdown** command.)

 VIDEO   11.01. The digital resources that accompany this book contain a multimedia demonstration of configuring an Ethernet interface on the router.

Configuring a Serial Interface

To assign the IP address to the Serial 0 port on ROUTERA, you type the following commands:

```
ROUTERA> enable
ROUTERA# configure terminal
ROUTERA(config)# interface serial0
ROUTERA(config-if)# ip address 192.168.2.1 255.255.255.0
ROUTERA(config-if)# encapsulation hdlc
ROUTERA(config-if)# no shutdown
```

Notice that the commands here are basically the same as those used to configure the Ethernet interface, except that we navigate to the serial0 interface instead of the fastethernet0/0 interface. After you assign the IP address with the **ip address** command, you then set the encapsulation protocol for the serial link. Popular encapsulation protocols over a serial link are *High-level Data Link Control* (HDLC) and *Point-to-Point Protocol* (PPP). You need to ensure that you are using the same protocol that is used on the other end of the serial link.

 VIDEO   11.02. The digital resources that accompany this book contain a multimedia demonstration of configuring a serial interface on the router.

Configuring the Bandwidth Parameter

Each interface has a *bandwidth* value assigned to it. A bandwidth value is used by certain routing protocols, such as OSPF and Enhanced Interior Gateway Routing Protocol (EIGRP), when making routing decisions. (You will learn about OSPF in Chapter 12.)

For LAN-based interfaces, the speed of the interface becomes the bandwidth value, where the bandwidth is measured in kilobits per second (Kbps). However, for serial interfaces, the bandwidth defaults to 1554 Kbps, or the speed of a T1 link. This is true no matter what the physical clock rate is on the interface (which you learned about in Chapter 7). To change the bandwidth value for an interface, use the **bandwidth** command:

```
Router(config)# interface serial [slot_#/port_#]
Router(config-if)# bandwidth rate_in_Kbps
```

Here's an example in which a serial interface clocked at 56,000 bps should have its bandwidth value changed to 56 Kbps:

```
Router(config)# interface serial 0
Router(config-if)# bandwidth 56
```

 EXAM TIP   Remember for the exam that the **bandwidth** command does not change the clock rate on an interface; the **clock rate** command does this. The **bandwidth** command affects only routing protocols that use bandwidth as a metric.

Viewing the Routing Table

Once you have assigned the IP addresses to each interface, you will need to ensure that routing is enabled on the router by typing the following commands:

```
ROUTERA> enable
ROUTERA# configure terminal
ROUTERA(config)# ip routing
```

 NOTE   The **ip routing** command enables routing. To disable routing, you would type **no ip routing**.

Figure 11-2
Looking at the routing table of a Cisco router

```
ROUTERA>show ip route
Codes: C - connected, S - static, I - IGRP, R - RIP, M - mobile, B - BGP
       D - EIGRP, EX - EIGRP external, O - OSPF, IA - OSPF inter area
       N1 - OSPF NSSA external type 1, N2 - OSPF NSSA external type 2
       E1 - OSPF external type 1, E2 - OSPF external type 2, E - EGP
       i - IS-IS, L1 - IS-IS level-1, L2 - IS-IS level-2, ia - IS-IS inter area
       * - candidate default, U - per-user static route, o - ODR
       P - periodic downloaded static route

Gateway of last resort is not set

C    192.168.1.0/24 is directly connected, Ethernet0
C    192.168.2.0/24 is directly connected, Serial0
ROUTERA>_
```

Once routing has been enabled, the router will automatically add a route for each of the networks it is directly connected to. To view the routing table and verify that the routes are added, use the following:

`ROUTERA> `**`show ip route`**

In Figure 11-2, notice that the **show ip route** command was typed and the routing table is displayed. Notice that the routes to the 192.168.1.0 and 192.168.2.0 networks are automatically added because the router is connected to those networks. Also notice the letter *C* to the left of each route entry; this means that the route is included because the router is directly connected to the network.

VIDEO   11.03. The digital resources that accompany this book contain a multimedia demonstration of using the **show ip route** command to view the routing table.

Configuring Static Routing

When administering a Cisco router, you will need to add any required routes that do not already exist in the routing table. For example, looking back to Figure 11-1, Router A knows about the 192.168.1.0 and 192.168.2.0 networks by default, but not the 192.168.3.0 network. If you want to configure Router A so that it knows about the 192.168.3.0 network, you need to add the route manually by creating a static route or using a dynamic routing protocol. The following command adds the static route to the 192.168.3.0 network:

```
ROUTERA> enable
ROUTERA# configure terminal
ROUTERA(config)# ip route 192.168.3.0 255.255.255.0 192.168.2.2
```

In this code listing, the command **ip route** (also shown in Figure 11-3) adds a route to the routing table. The 192.168.3.0 is the address of the destination network you are adding, and its subnet mask, 192.168.2.2, is the *next hop*—the address to which Router A will send data to reach the 192.168.3.0 network. Notice that 192.168.2.2 is the address of an interface on Router B that Router A can communicate directly with.

Figure 11-3

Adding a static route to a Cisco router

```
ROUTERA>enable
ROUTERA#config term
Enter configuration commands, one per line.  End with CNTL/Z.
ROUTERA(config)#ip route 192.168.3.0 255.255.255.0 192.168.2.2
ROUTERA(config)#
```

The idea here is that in order for Router A to send data to the 192.168.3.0 network, it will pass the data to Router B via the interface at 192.168.2.2, which will then send the data on to the 192.168.3.0 network.

 EXAM TIP For the exam, know that the **ip route** command is used to add a static route on a Cisco router and that the **show ip route** command is used to display the router's routing table.

If you view the routing table by using the **show ip route** command, you will notice that certain routes in the routing table are included because the router is connected to that network, as indicated with a letter *C*. Figure 11-4 displays the new routing table with the static route added, indicated with a letter *S*.

 VIDEO 11.04. The digital resources that accompany this book contain a multimedia demonstration of how to add a static route.

Deleting a Static Route on a Cisco Router

It was pretty easy to add a route to the Cisco router's routing table with the **ip route** command, and it is just as easy to delete a route with the **no ip route** command. To delete a route from the routing table, use the following syntax:

```
ROUTERA> enable
ROUTERA# configure terminal
ROUTERA(config)# no ip route 192.168.3.0 255.255.255.0
```

 VIDEO 11.05. The digital resources that accompany this book contain a multimedia demonstration of how to delete a static route.

Figure 11-4

Displaying the routing table after the static route has been added

```
ROUTERA>show ip route
Codes: C - connected, S - static, I - IGRP, R - RIP, M - mobile, B - BGP
       D - EIGRP, EX - EIGRP external, O - OSPF, IA - OSPF inter area
       N1 - OSPF NSSA external type 1, N2 - OSPF NSSA external type 2
       E1 - OSPF external type 1, E2 - OSPF external type 2, E - EGP
       i - IS-IS, L1 - IS-IS level-1, L2 - IS-IS level-2, ia - IS-IS inter area
       * - candidate default, U - per-user static route, o - ODR
       P - periodic downloaded static route

Gateway of last resort is not set

C    192.168.1.0/24 is directly connected, Ethernet0
C    192.168.2.0/24 is directly connected, Serial0
S    192.168.3.0/24 [1/0] via 192.168.2.2
ROUTERA>
```

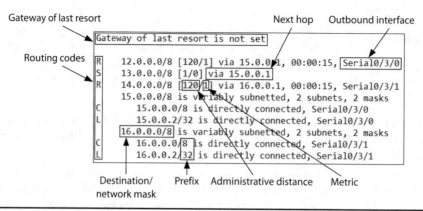

Figure 11-5   Components of the routing table

Components of the Routing Table

Figure 11-5 shows a different example and identifies the key components you need to identify when looking at the routing table.

 EXAM TIP   The Cisco CCNA certification exam expects you to understand the components of the routing table; you are sure to receive questions testing you on the output of **show ip route**.

You will learn more about these components as we progress through the chapter, but I wanted to call out these components of the routing table before moving on. You should be able to identify the following components of a routing table:

- **Routing code**   The routing code, or routing protocol code, indicates how knowledge of the route occurred—a locally connected route, a static route, or a route learned through a routing protocol such as RIP (R) or OSPF (O). (RIP is the Routing Information Protocol.)

- **Prefix**   The network prefix indicates the number of bits that make up the network ID.

- **Destination/network mask**   This identifies the network ID in the destination network.

- **Next hop**   This identifies where data is to be sent in order to reach that particular network destination. For example, in Figure 11-5, you can see a static route (*S*) to the destination network of 13.0.0.0/8. So if a packet arrives destined for the 13.0.0.0/8 network, the router will forward the packet to 15.0.0.1 (the next hop).

- **Administrative distance**   The administrative distance identifies how the route was learned—directly connected, through RIP, through OSPF, or a static route. Each type of route has a different administrative distance, which indicates how trustworthy the knowledge of the route is. The lower the administrative distance number, the more trustworthy the information is. You will learn more about administrative distance throughout this chapter; it is a very important concept that you need to understand for CCNA certification.

- **Metric**   When multiple routes are available to the same destination, with the same administrative distance, the router will choose a route based on a *metric*. The metric value indicates which routes are more efficient than others. For example, in Figure 11-5, the RIP route (*R*) for the 14.0.0.0 network has a metric of 1. With RIP, this would be a hop count. If there were another RIP route to the 14.0.0.0 network with a hop count (metric) of 5, the router would use the route with the lowest metric pathway. Note the metric is not always based on hops; it could also be based on bandwidth of the route. The type of metric that is used is dependent on the type of route it is. (This is discussed later in the chapter in the section "Types of Routes.")

- **Gateway of last resort (GWLR)**   The GWLR references an IP address where the router is to send all traffic for which it does not have a route. Essentially, this feature is similar to the default gateway setting on your Windows computer. In the Figure 11-5 example, the GWLR is not set.

- **Outbound interface**   The outbound interface is the local interface on the router that the router sends the data out in order to reach the destination.

Exercise 11-1: Configuring Cisco Routers

In this exercise you will configure the IP addresses on the interfaces of two Cisco routers shown in the following network diagram:

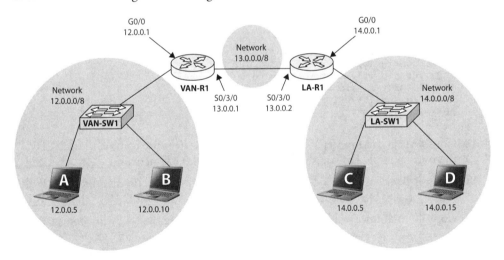

1. Ensure that all physical components, such as routers and switches, are connected as per the network diagram. Then power on the devices.

2. Connect your workstation to the console port of VAN-R1. Then launch PuTTY, choose Serial Connection, set the correct COM port, and click Open.

3. Press ENTER in the PuTTY window to open a prompt on your Cisco device.

4. Access VAN-R1's privileged EXEC mode and assign the IP address of 12.0.0.1 to the Gigabit Ethernet interface connected to the LAN; then enable the interface:

```
VAN-R1>enable
VAN-R1#config term
VAN-R1(config)#interface g0/0
VAN-R1(config-if)#ip address 12.0.0.1 255.0.0.0
VAN-R1(config-if)#no shutdown
```

5. To configure the serial interface, assign the IP address of 13.0.0.1 to the serial interface connected to the LA-R1 router:

```
VAN-R1(config-if)#interface s0/3/0
VAN-R1(config-if)#ip address 13.0.0.1 255.0.0.0
```

6. Set the encapsulation protocol on the serial interface to HDLC:

```
VAN-R1(config-if)#encapsulation hdlc
```

7. If the serial interface on VAN-R1 is the data communications equipment (DCE) device, set the clock rate to 64000:

```
VAN-R1(config-if)#clock rate 64000
VAN-R1(config-if)#no shutdown
```

8. Console into router LA-R1 and configure the G0/0 interface for the IP address of 14.0.0.1/8; then enable the interface:

```
LA-R1>enable
LA-R1#config term
Enter configuration commands, one per line.  End with CNTL/Z.
LA-R1(config)#interface g0/0
LA-R1(config-if)#ip address 14.0.0.1 255.0.0.0
LA-R1(config-if)#no shutdown
```

9. On LA-R1, configure the s0/3/0 interface for the IP address of 13.0.0.2/8, encapsulation protocol of hdlc; then enable the interface:

```
LA-R1(config-if)#interface s0/3/0
LA-R1(config-if)#ip address 13.0.0.2 255.0.0.0
LA-R1(config-if)#encapsulation hdlc
LA-R1(config-if)#no shutdown
LA-R1(config-if)#exit
LA-R1(config)#exit
LA-R1#
```

10. Console back into router VAN-R1. Use the **show ip route** command to display the routing table. Do you see a route for the 14.0.0.0/8 network? _____

11. Console back into router LA-R1. Use the **show ip route** command to display the routing table. Do you see a route for the 12.0.0.0/8 network? _____

12. Console back into VAN-R1. To add a static route, use the following command:

```
VAN-R1#config term
Enter configuration commands, one per line.  End with CNTL/Z.
VAN-R1(config)#ip route 14.0.0.0 255.0.0.0 13.0.0.2
```

13. To view the route in the routing table, use the **show ip route** command. You should see the newly added route:

```
VAN-R1(config)#do show ip route
```

14. Console into LA-R1 and add a static route to the 12.0.0.0/8 network. Then view the routing table to verify that the static route was added:

```
LA-R1#config term
LA-R1(config)#ip route 12.0.0.0 255.0.0.0 13.0.0.1
LA-R1(config)#do show ip route
```

15. On the VAN-R1 router, verify that you can ping the 14.0.0.1 IP address.

Understanding Dynamic Routing

Dynamic routing protocols are used to share routes between routers so that administrators do not need to add the routes manually. For the CCNA exam, you are required to know about OSPF, but you also need to know the administrative distances associated with different routing protocols. For that reason, I am going to introduce you to a few other routing protocols here.

Managing the entries in routing tables on a large internetwork could be a time-consuming task. To help administrators with this, *dynamic* routing protocols are enabled. These protocols enable the routers to share information contained within their routing tables with one another. As a result, routes that are known by one router will be shared with the other routers, thus saving the administrator from having to add all the routes manually! *Convergence*, also known as steady state, occurs when all routing tables (routes) have been shared with all other routers and all routers have updated their routing tables with that new information.

There are two major categories of routing protocols:

- **Interior gateway protocols (IGPs)** An IGP shares routing table information with other routers located inside your network, known as an *autonomous system* (AS). An example of an IGP is the Routing Information Protocol (RIP) or the Enhanced Interior Gateway Routing Protocol (EIGRP).

- **Exterior gateway protocols (EGPs)** An EGP that is loaded on a router will share routing table information to other routers outside your network. An example of an EGP is the Border Gateway Protocol (BGP).

 EXAM TIP The CCNA exam expects you to be familiar with the term *convergence*. Convergence, also known as steady state, occurs when all routing tables (routes) have been shared with all other routers and all routers have updated their routing tables with that new information.

Routing Metrics

A routing protocol decides on the best route to a network by analyzing the routing table and choosing the route with the lowest metric value. Determining the "best route" metric value can involve different things, depending on the routing protocol. Following are common values used to measure the metric value of a route:

- **Hop count** Some routing protocols use hop count as a metric value, which means that the best route is determined based on how many hops away the network is. Every router that data must pass through is considered a hop, and the lowest hop count is the best route to take with this metric.

- **MTU or bandwidth** Some routing protocols determine the best route to take based on the MTU or bandwidth of the link. Routes with more bandwidth would be preferred over lower bandwidth routes.

- **Costs** Some routing protocols choose the best route based on the lowest cost. A cost value is considered a preference value on the link, and the link with the lowest cost value will be selected as the route to the destination. For example, a link to a destination with a cost of three is chosen over a different link to the same destination with a cost value of five.

- **Latency** Some routing protocols use the latency of the link as the metric value. Latency refers to how long it takes a packet to travel from one place to another. Lower latency routes are preferred over higher latency routes with this metric criterion.

- **Administrative distance** The administrative distance is the "trustworthiness" of the route that is in the routing table. Each different method of adding a route to a routing table has an administrative distance value—if the router was to learn about a route two or more different ways, then the route with the lower administrative distance is the one the router would use. For example, a static route has an administrative distance of 0, while a route learned via RIP has an administrative distance of 120. In this case, if the routes were for the same destination network, the router would use the static route, because it is considered to be more trustworthy.

It is important to note that some routing protocols combine some of these different metric values to determine the best route possible.

When discussing the different routing protocols, it is important to note that there are two major classes: *distance vector* and *link state*. Each routing protocol is either a distance vector protocol or a link state protocol.

Configuring a Routing Protocol

Before we talk about how to configure a dynamic routing protocol such as RIP, let's consider some basic configuration tasks that are required no matter what dynamic routing protocol you are running. You need to perform two basic steps when setting up IP routing on your router:

- Enable the routing protocol.
- Assign IP addresses to your router's interfaces.

Note that the order of these tasks is not important. You already know how to configure an IP address on the router's interface: this was discussed in Chapter 7. The following sections cover the first bullet point in more depth.

The router Command

Enabling an IP routing protocol is a two-step process. First, you must go into router sub-configuration mode. This mode determines the routing protocol that you'll be running. Within this mode, you'll configure the characteristics of the routing protocol. To enter the routing protocol's configuration mode, use the following command:

```
Router(config)# router name_of_the_IP_routing_protocol
Router(config-router)#
```

The **router** command is used to access the routing protocol that you want to configure; it doesn't enable it. If you are not sure of the name of the routing protocol that you want to enable, use the context-sensitive help feature:

```
Router(config)# router ?
  bgp                Border Gateway Protocol (BGP)
  eigrp              Enhanced Interior Gateway Routing
                       Protocol (EIGRP)
  isis               ISO IS-IS
  iso-igrp           IGRP for OSI networks
  mobile             Mobile routes
  odr                On Demand stub Routes
  ospf               Open Shortest Path First (OSPF)
  rip                Routing Information Protocol (RIP)
Router(config)#
```

As you can see from the context-sensitive help output, you have a lot of IP routing protocols at your disposal.

The network Command

Once you have enabled the routing protocol, you need to specify what interfaces are to participate in the routing process. By default, no interfaces participate in the routing process. To specify which interfaces will participate, use the **network** mode command:

```
Router(config-router)# network IP_network_#
```

As soon as you enter a network number, the routing process becomes *active*.

Distance Vector Protocols

Distance vector routing protocols measure the best route to use based on the lowest hop count. The hop count is increased by 1 for every router between the source and the destination. With distance vector routing protocols, the route with the lowest hop count is typically selected as the destination path for the data.

 EXAM TIP Remember that distance vector routing protocols include RIP and IGRP.

RIP/RIPv2

RIP is a distance vector protocol that is responsible for sharing its routing table information with neighboring routers by broadcasting the information over User Datagram Protocol (UDP) every 30 seconds. This broadcasting, or *advertising*, of routing table information with neighboring routers exempts the network administrator from having to add the routes manually.

RIP is an industry-standard routing protocol, which means that it is supported by many different vendors, so you could use it as a routing protocol to share routing table information between routers from different manufacturers. RIP will choose the route with the lowest hop count, but if two different routes have the same hop count, RIP will load-balance the traffic over those two routes. Be aware that RIP is limited to 15 hops, so it is used only on small networks.

RIPv1 works only with classful addresses because it doesn't send subnet mask information with the routing table. RIPv2 is an update to RIPv1 and does support classless addressing and variable-length subnet masks, because it sends the subnet mask information with the routing table.

Let's go back in Figure 11-1 for another example. Assume you are the administrator for Router A. Router A will have routes to the 192.168.1.0 and 192.168.2.0 networks by default. If you wanted to configure RIP on Router A to advertise knowledge of those two networks, you would type the following commands on Router A:

```
ROUTERA> enable
ROUTERA# configure terminal
ROUTERA(config)# router rip
ROUTERA(config-router)# version 2
ROUTERA(config-router)# network 192.168.1.0
ROUTERA(config-router)# network 192.168.2.0
```

Once RIP, or any other routing protocol, has been enabled on both Router A and Router B, the two routers will share knowledge of any networks they know about. Router A receives knowledge of the 192.168.3.0 network and builds the new network into its routing table; this is called *convergence*. Figure 11-6 displays the routing table on Router A after RIP has been enabled on both routers. Notice the letter *R* beside the 192.168.3.0 route, meaning that the route was learned about through RIP.

 VIDEO 11.06. The digital resources that accompany this book contain a multimedia demonstration of how to configure RIP.

Figure 11-6

The routing table displays the new route learned through RIP.

```
ROUTERA>show ip route
Codes: C - connected, S - static, I - IGRP, R - RIP, M - mobile, B - BGP
       D - EIGRP, EX - EIGRP external, O - OSPF, IA - OSPF inter area
       N1 - OSPF NSSA external type 1, N2 - OSPF NSSA external type 2
       E1 - OSPF external type 1, E2 - OSPF external type 2, E - EGP
       i - IS-IS, L1 - IS-IS level-1, L2 - IS-IS level-2, ia - IS-IS inter area
       * - candidate default, U - per-user static route, o - ODR
       P - periodic downloaded static route

Gateway of last resort is not set

C    192.168.1.0/24 is directly connected, Ethernet0
C    192.168.2.0/24 is directly connected, Serial0
R    192.168.3.0/24 [120/1] via 192.168.2.2, 00:00:14, Serial0
ROUTERA>_
```

IGRP

IGRP is a classful routing protocol that was built by Cisco, so you will use it only on networks where you have only Cisco routers. IGRP was designed to improve on RIP limitations; it has a maximum hop count of 255 and uses the concepts of an *autonomous system* (AS). An autonomous system is a grouping of routers that share routing table information. Routers using IGRP will share the routes only with other routers in the AS. Another improvement is that the full routing table is advertised every 90 seconds instead of 30 seconds, as is the case with RIP.

To enable IGRP on your Cisco router, type the following commands:

```
ROUTERA> enable
ROUTERA# configure terminal
ROUTERA(config)# router igrp 10
ROUTERA(config-router)# network 192.168.1.0
ROUTERA(config-router)# network 192.168.2.0
```

In this code listing, notice that enabling IGRP on a Cisco router is similar to enabling RIP. The difference, however, is that when you enable IGRP, you specify the AS number for the router. In this case, I have used 10 for the AS number, so any other router with an AS number of 10 will receive routing information for the 192.168.1.0 and 192.168.2.0 networks.

Link State Protocols

Link state routing protocols are a little more advanced than distance vector routing protocols in the sense that a link state routing protocol knows about the entire network topology. A link state protocol is responsible for monitoring the state of the link between the routers. This link state information is then used to determine the optimal route to a destination network. Although protocols such as RIP have knowledge of neighboring routers, link state protocols have knowledge of the entire network topology and multicast the routing table information to the entire network.

One of the benefits of the link state routing protocols is that if a link is down, that information is stored in the routing table and that pathway will not be used. Because a distance vector routing protocol does not store link state information, it is possible that it will not know that a link is unavailable for some time and could still send traffic through that pathway.

OSPF

Open Shortest Path First (OSPF) is an example of a link state protocol. OSPF is an industry-standard protocol, which means that it is available to routers built by different manufacturers, and you can use it to share routing information between dissimilar routers.

Like IGRP, OSPF uses autonomous systems, but it also has the capability of dividing the AS into logical groups, called *areas*. OSPF supports Variable Length Subnet Masks (VLSMs) and has an unlimited hop count.

 NOTE Because OSPF is the important routing protocol to know for the CCNA exam, all of Chapter 12 has been dedicated to it.

IS-IS

The *Intermediate System-Intermediate System (IS-IS)* routing protocol competes with OSPF by being a link state routing protocol for inside the network (interior gateway). IS-IS was developed by Digital Equipment Corporation (DEC) and has become an industry-standard protocol, although it's not as popular as OSPF. Like OSPF, IS-IS uses a link state algorithm to maintain status information on all the links and routes on the network so that each router running the IS-IS protocol will have knowledge of the entire network topology.

Hybrid Protocols

Hybrid routing protocols combine the features of distance vector and link state. Cisco uses two hybrid protocols: EIGRP and BGP.

 EXAM TIP For the Cisco CCNA exam, you only need to know "about" the different routing protocols. You should, however, know the difference between distance vector and link state protocols, and you do need to know the details of OSPF, which is covered in the next chapter. Also, remember that EIGRP is an example of a hybrid routing protocol.

EIGRP

As a popular hybrid routing protocol that was built by Cisco, EIGRP improves upon IGRP by being a *classless* routing protocol that supports VLSM and both IPv4 and IPv6. EIGRP also has a maximum hop count of 255 hops.

To configure EIGRP on your Cisco router, use the following commands:

```
ROUTERA> enable
ROUTERA# configure terminal
ROUTERA(config)# router eigrp 10
ROUTERA(config-router)# network 192.168.1.0
ROUTERA(config-router)# network 192.168.2.0
```

VIDEO 11.07. The digital resources that accompany this book contain a multimedia demonstration of how to configure EIGRP.

BGP

BGP is an EGP that is responsible for sharing routing table information with routers *outside* your autonomous system. The protocols discussed previously such as RIP, EIGRP, and OSPF are known as interior gateway protocols, which are responsible for sharing routing tables *within* your autonomous system (or network).

BGP is designed to send changes made to the routing table when they occur, versus at a regular interval as RIP does. BGP sends only the change, while other routing protocols such as RIP send the entire table. BGP is also a classless routing protocol that supports Classless Interdomain Routing (CIDR).

 NOTE BGP is a newer version of the EGP.

The Routing Process

Several different types of routes can exist on a Cisco router. Determining the best route involves consideration of a number of criteria.

Types of Routes

A number of different types of routes can exist in the routing table of a Cisco router. For the CCNA exam, you need to be familiar with static routes, network routes, default routes, host routes, and floating static routes. This chapter focuses on IPv4, but the CCNA exam expects you to know these concepts for both IPv4 and IPv6. Know that the knowledge you learn here applies to IPv6, but it's the same information you'll need to know when working with an IPv4 address. (You will learn about IPv6 in Chapter 14.) The type of address you work with does not change the purpose of such things as static routes, floating static routes, or dynamic routes. Let's take a look at several routing concepts for IPv4.

Network Route

A network route points to the network ID of a network or subnet. For example, in order for the router to send data to a server with an IP address of 14.0.0.10, the router would look in its routing table for a route to the 14.0.0.0/8 network. A network route may appear in the routing table because the network is connected to the router—a connected route—or because the administrator added it manually—a static route.

Connected Route   To determine a *connected* or *directly connected* route, a router will look at its active interfaces, examine the addresses configured on the interfaces and determine the corresponding network numbers, and populate the routing table with this information.

Static Route A *static route* is a manually configured route on your router. Static routes are typically used in smaller networks and when few networks or subnets exist, or with WAN links that have little available bandwidth. With a network that has hundreds of routes, static routes are not scalable, since you would have to configure each route and any redundant paths for each route on each router. This section covers the configuration of static routes and some of the issues associated with them.

To configure a static route for IP, use one of these two commands:

```
Router(config)# ip route destination_network_# [subnet_mask]
                IP_address_of_next_hop_neighbor
                [administrative_distance] [permanent]
```

or

```
Router(config)# ip route destination_network_# [subnet_mask]
                exit_interface_name
                [administrative_distance] [permanent]
```

The first parameter that you must specify is the destination network number. If you omit the subnet mask for the network number, it defaults to the Class A (255.0.0.0), B (255.255.0.0), or C (255.255.255.0) default subnet mask, depending on the network number of the destination.

After the subnet mask parameter, you can specify how to reach the destination network in one of two ways: you can tell the router the next-hop neighbor's IP address, or indicate the interface the router should exit to reach the destination network. Use the former method for a multi-access link (the link has more than two devices on it—three routers, for instance). Use the latter method for a point-to-point link. In this instance, you must specify the *name* of the interface on the router, like so: **serial0**.

Optionally, you can change the administrative distance of a static route. If you omit this value, it will use one of two default values, depending on the configuration of the previous parameter: If you specified the next-hop neighbor's IP address, the administrative distance defaults to 1. If you specified the interface on the router it should use to reach the destination, the router treats the route as a connected route and assigns it an administrative distance of 0.

Note that you can create multiple static routes to the *same* destination. For instance, you may have primary and backup paths to the destination. For the primary path, you could use the default administrative distance value. For the backup path, you could use a number higher than this, such as 2. Once you have configured a backup path, the router will use the primary path, and if the interface on the router fails for the primary path, the router will use the backup route.

The **permanent** parameter will keep the static route in the routing table even when the interface the router uses for the static route fails. If you omit this parameter, and the interface used by the static route fails, the router will remove this route from its routing table and attempt to find an alternative path to place in the routing table. You may want to use the **permanent** parameter if you never want packets to use another path to a destination, perhaps because of security reasons.

EXAM TIP   Remember the syntax for creating a static IP route with the **ip route** command, where you can specify a next-hop address or a local interface to use to reach a remote destination. And remember that if you omit the administrative distance, it defaults to 0 or 1, depending on how you configured the static route.

Default Route

One special type of static route is a *default route*, commonly called the *gateway of last resort* (GWLR). If the specified destination is not listed in the routing table, the default route can be used to route the packet. A default route has an IP address of 0.0.0.0 and a subnet mask of 0.0.0.0, often represented as 0.0.0.0/0. Default routes are commonly used in small networks on a perimeter router pointing to the directly connected ISP router.

To set up a default route, use the following syntax for a static route:

```
Router(config)# ip route 0.0.0.0 0.0.0.0
                IP_address_of_next_hop_neighbor
                [administrative_distance] [permanent]
```

or

```
Router(config)# ip route 0.0.0.0 0.0.0.0
                exit_interface_name
                [administrative_distance] [permanent]
```

 VIDEO   11.08. The digital resources that accompany this book contain a multimedia demonstration of how to configure a default route.

Default Network Configuration   An alternative way to configure a default route is to define a default network. When you configure the **ip default-network** command, the router considers routes to that network for installation as the GWLR on the router. This command is used when no other route exists in the routing table (connected, static, or dynamic). Use the **show ip route** command to verify that the default route has been set:

```
Router# show ip route
Codes: C - connected, S - static, I - IGRP, R - RIP, M - mobile,
       B - BGP, D - EIGRP, EX - EIGRP external, O - OSPF,
       IA - OSPF inter area, N1 - OSPF NSSA external type 1,
       N2 - OSPF NSSA external type 2, E1 - OSPF external type 1,
       E2 - OSPF external type 2, E - EGP, i - IS-IS, su - IS-IS summary,
       L1 - IS-IS level-1, L2 - IS-IS level-2, ia - IS-IS inter area,
       * - candidate default, U - per-user static route, o - ODR,
       P - periodic downloaded static route
Gateway of last resort is not set
     161.44.0.0/24 is subnetted, 1 subnets
C       161.44.192.0 is directly connected, Ethernet0
     131.108.0.0/24 is subnetted, 1 subnets
C       131.108.99.0 is directly connected, Serial0
S    198.10.1.0/24 [1/0] via 161.44.192.2
```

Between the code table at the top of the output and the routes at the bottom is the line "Gateway of last resort is not set." This is the default configuration. To define a GWLR, use this command:

```
Router(config)# ip default-network network_number_to_use
```

The network number you define is the network the router should access as a last resort. Note that your routing table will need an entry indicating how to reach this default network, such as a next-hop address. This is typically done via a static route.

EXAM TIP Use an address and subnet mask of 0.0.0.0 0.0.0.0 when creating a default route when no other specific route is available to a destination within the routing table. The GWLR is defined with the **ip default-network** command.

Host Route

A host route references the full IP address of a computer on the network. You may see an entry that appears in the routing table with a */32*, meaning that all bits are network bits—you should treat the entire address as a network ID.

Floating Static Route

A floating static route is a backup route to a destination to which you have a primary route. The floating static route will not appear in the routing table until the primary route fails, and then the floating static route will appear. You configure a floating static route by creating a static route with an administrative distance that is higher than the route you are trying to back up (whether it be another static route or a route learned via a dynamic routing protocol). The following example adds a floating static route by setting the administrative distance to 10:

```
VAN-R1#config term
VAN-R1(config)#ip route 14.0.0.0 255.0.0.0 12.0.0.100 10
```

VIDEO 11.09. The digital resources that accompany this book contain a multimedia demonstration of configuring a floating static route.

Selecting a Route

When the Cisco device selects a route to use for a particular destination, it uses a number of criteria: it first checks for a longest matching network prefix, then it selects a route based on the administrative distance, and finally it may look at the metric value if the network prefix and administrative distance are equal on multiple routes. Let's take a look at each of these criteria.

Longest Match

The first routing criteria used by a router is the longest matching prefix. It essentially chooses the route to a destination network with the longest network or subnet ID. This ensures that if the network is subnetted, the more specific route is being used.

Administrative Distance

Each router needs to choose a *best* path to a destination. This process can become somewhat complicated if the router is receiving routing update information for a single network from multiple sources, such as connected, static, and IGP routing protocols, and must choose *one* of these sources as the best and place this choice in the router's routing table. After choosing routes based on network ID matching, the router looks at the administrative distance to determine a trustworthiness for the knowledge of a route—the lower the administrative distance, the more trustworthy the route. For example, suppose a connected route has an administrative distance of 0, while a static route has an administrative distance of 1. If you added a static route for a network ID that already existed because the router was connected to that network, the router would use the connected route over your static route. (From a trust point of view, you could have a typo in your static route so the router trusts what it is connected to over what the administrator typed.)

As another example, the RIP has an administrative distance of 120, so if RIP is sharing a network ID, and you have configured a static route to the same destination, the router will choose your static route over the route learned through RIP, because static routes have a lower administrative distance value (1).

 EXAM TIP On the exam, you will see questions that offer a scenario in which the router is learning of the network 10.0.0.0/8 destination from both RIP and EIGRP, and you need to know which route will get added to the routing table. Since RIP has an administrative distance value of 120, and EIGRP has a value of 90, the router will use the EIGRP route.

Table 11-1 displays some of the default administrative distances Cisco has assigned to the different types of routes that you need to know for the CCNA exam.

Administrative Distance	Route Type
0	Connected interface route
1	Static route
90	Internal EIGRP route (within the same AS)
110	OSPF route
120	RIPv1 and v2 route
170	External EIGRP (from another AS)
255	Unknown route (considered an invalid route and will not be used)

Table 11-1 Administrative Distance Values

Metric	Routing Protocols	Description
Bandwidth	EIGRP	The capacity of the links in Kbps (T1 = 1554)
Cost	OSPF	Measurement in the inverse of the bandwidth of the links
Delay	EIGRP	Time it takes to reach the destination
Hop count	RIP	How many layer 3 hops away from the destination
Load	EIGRP	The path with the least utilization
MTU	EIGRP	The path that supports the largest frame sizes
Reliability	EIGRP	The path with the least amount of errors or downtime

Table 11-2   Routing Protocol Metrics

 EXAM TIP   You need to know these administrative distances (ADs) for the exam: remember that connected routes have an AD of 0, static routes have an AD of 1, EIGRP has an AD of 90, OSPF has an AD of 110, and RIP has an AD of 120. The route with a lower administrative distance is preferred over a route with a higher administrative distance.

Routing Protocol Metric

The route selection process so far chooses a route based on the network destination ID first, and then the administrative distance. But what if there are multiple routes with the same administrative distance—let's say two routes being shared to your router via OSPF? If a situation arises where two paths to the destination network exist, and the *same* routing protocol is being used to share that knowledge to your router, the router will use a measurement called a *metric* to determine which path is the best path to place in the routing table.

Table 11-2 lists some common metrics, the routing protocols that use them, and brief descriptions of the metrics. As you can see, some routing protocols use only a single metric. For instance, RIP uses hop count as a metric and OSPF uses cost. Other routing protocols use multiple metric values to choose a best path to a destination. For instance, EIGRP can use bandwidth, delay, reliability, load, and MTU when choosing a best path to a destination.

Routing Troubleshooting Commands

Once you have configured your routing protocol, you can use a variety of commands to verify and troubleshoot the routing configuration and operation. Here are some example commands:

- **clear ip route**
- **show ip protocols**
- **show ip route**
- **debug ip rip**

The clear ip route Command

The **clear ip route** * command is a privileged EXEC mode command. This command clears and rebuilds the IP routing table. Any time you make a change to a routing protocol, you should clear and rebuild the routing table with this command. You can replace the asterisk (*) with a specific network number; if you choose to do so, this will clear only the specified route from the routing table. Note that the **clear** command clears only routes learned from a routing protocol (dynamic routes); static and directly connected routes cannot be cleared from the routing table using the **clear** command. Static routes must be cleared manually using the **no ip route** command, and directly connected routes are persistent and cannot be removed from the routing table unless the interface they are associated with is not operational.

The show ip protocols Command

The **show ip protocols** command displays all the IP routing protocols, including RIP, which you have configured and are running on your router. Here's an example of this command:

```
Router# show ip protocols
Routing Protocol is "rip"
  Sending updates every 30 seconds, next due in 5 seconds
  Invalid after 180 seconds, hold down 180, flushed after 240
  Outgoing update filter list for all interfaces is not set
  Incoming update filter list for all interfaces is not set
  Redistributing: rip
  Default version control: send version 2, receive version 2
    Interface        Send  Recv  Triggered RIP Key-chain
    Ethernet0         2     2
    Ethernet1         2     2
  Automatic network summarization is in effect
  Maximum path: 4     Routing for Networks:
    192.168.1.0
    192.168.2.0    Routing Information Sources:
    Gateway          Distance      Last Update
    192.168.2.2          120       00:00:22
    192.168.3.2          120       00:03:30
  Distance: (default is 120)
```

In this example, RIPv2 is running on the router. The routing update interval is 30 seconds, with the next update being sent in 5 seconds. You can see that two interfaces are participating: Ethernet0 and Ethernet1. RIPv2 is being used to generate and receive updates on these two interfaces. You can see the two networks specified with the **network** commands: 192.168.1.0 and 192.168.2.0. In this example, this router received an update 22 seconds ago from a neighboring router: 192.168.2.2. For the second gateway, 192.168.3.2, the router hasn't seen an update from it in 210 seconds. Given that the flush timer is 240 seconds, if the local router doesn't receive an update from 192.168.3.2 within 30 seconds, 192.168.3.2 and its associated routes are removed from the local router (flushed). And last, the default administrative distance of RIP is 120.

 VIDEO   11.10. The digital resources that accompany this book contain a multimedia demonstration of the **show ip protocols** command for RIP on a router.

The show ip route Command

To view the routing table, use the **show ip route** command. Here's an example of a routing table that has two RIP routes:

```
Router# show ip route
Codes: C - connected, S - static, I - IGRP, R - RIP,
       M - mobile, B - BGP, D - EIGRP, EX - EIGRP external,
       O - OSPF, IA - OSPF inter area, N1 - OSPF NSSA
       external type 1, N2 - OSPF NSSA external type 2,
       E1 - OSPF external type 1, E2 - OSPF external type 2,
       E - EGP, i - IS-IS, L1 - IS-IS level-1,
       L2 - IS-IS level-2, * - candidate default,
       U - per-user static route, o - ODR,
       T - traffic engineered route

Gateway of last resort is not set
     172.16.0.0/24 is subnetted, 2 subnets
C       172.16.1.0 is directly connected, Ethernet0
R       172.16.2.0 [120/1] via 172.16.1.2, 00:00:21, Ethernet0
     192.168.1.0/24 is subnetted, 2 subnets
C       192.168.1.0 is directly connected, Serial0
R     192.168.2.0/24 [120/2] via 192.168.1.2, 00:00:02, Serial2
```

 EXAM TIP For the CCNA exam you need to be very familiar with the output of the **show ip route** command, especially identifying the administrative distance and metric values.

In this example, you can see that two types of routes are in the routing table: *R* is for RIP and *C* is for a directly connected route. For the RIP entries, you can see two numbers in brackets: the administrative distance of the route and the metric. For instance, 172.16.2.0 has an administrative distance of 120 and a hop count of 1 (the metric in this example). Following this information is the neighboring RIP router that advertised the route (172.16.1.2), how long ago an update for this route was received from the neighbor (21 seconds), and on which interface this update was learned (Ethernet0).

 VIDEO 11.11. The digital resources that accompany this book contain a multimedia demonstration of the **show ip route** command for RIP on a router.

The debug ip <*protocol*> Command

Remember that the **show** commands show a static display of what the router knows, and they sometimes don't display enough information concerning a specific issue or problem. For instance, you might be looking at your routing table with the **show ip route** command and expect a certain RIP route to appear from a connected neighbor, but this network is not shown. Unfortunately, the **show ip route** command won't tell you why a route is or isn't in the routing table. However, you can resort to **debug** commands to assist you in your troubleshooting. We will use the command to troubleshoot RIP (since you learn about OSPF in the next chapter).

For more detailed information about the events and packets being sent or received with a routing protocol that can be used to troubleshoot routing protocol problems, you can use the **debug ip <*protocol*>** command, where <*protocol*> can be RIP, EIGRP, or OSPF. Here's a RIP example:

```
Router# debug ip rip
RIP protocol debugging is on
Router#
00:12:16: RIP: received v1 update from 192.168.1.2 on Serial0
00:12:16:      192.168.2.0 in 1 hops
00:12:25: RIP: sending v1 update to 255.255.255.255 via Ethernet0
172.16.1.1)
00:12:26:      network 192.168.1.0, metric 0
00:12:26:      network 192.168.2.0, metric 1
```

This command displays the routing updates sent and received on the router's interfaces. In this code example, the router received a V1 update from 192.168.1.2 on Serial0. This update contained one network, 192.168.2.0, indicating that this network is reachable from this and the advertising routers. After this update, you can see that your router generated a RIP update (local broadcast—255.255.255.255) on its Ethernet0 interface. This update contains two networks: 192.168.1.0 and 192.168.2.0. Also notice the metrics associated with these routes: 192.168.1.0 is connected to this router, while 192.168.2.0 is one hop away. When the neighboring router connected to Ethernet0 receives this update, it will increment the hop count by 1 for each route in the update.

 TIP   When using **debug** commands, you must be in privileged EXEC mode. To disable a specific **debug** command, negate it with the **no** parameter. To turn off debugging for all **debug** commands, use either the **undebug all** or the **no debug all** command.

Router-on-a-Stick

You learned about switches in Chapters 9 and 10 and the fact that VLANs can be used to configure communication boundaries on the network. To enable communication between VLANs, you can either connect a router interface to each VLAN or use the router-on-a-stick method.

Typically, we think of routing as traffic entering one physical interface and leaving another physical interface. As you learned in Chapter 10, however, trunks can be used to support multiple VLANs, where each VLAN has a unique layer 3 network or subnet number. Certain router models and interface combinations, such as the 1800 series, support trunk connections. A *router-on-a-stick* is a router that has a single trunk connection to a switch and routes between the VLANs on this trunk connection. You could easily do this without a trunk (access-link connection), but each VLAN would require a separate access-link (physical) interface on the router, and this would increase the price of the router solution.

For instance, if you had five VLANs and your router didn't support trunking, you would need five physical LAN interfaces on your router, and on your switch, to route between the five VLANs. However, with a trunk connection, you can route between all five VLANs on a *single* interface. Because of cost and scalability, most administrators prefer using a router-on-a-stick approach to solve their routing problems in switched networks.

 NOTE A router-on-a-stick is a router that has a single trunk connection to a switch and routes between multiple VLANs on this trunk. Subinterfaces are used on the router to designate the VLAN with which they are associated. Each VLAN needs a different IP subnet configuration.

Subinterface Configuration

To set up a router-on-a-stick, you need to break up your router's physical interface into multiple logical interfaces, or *subinterfaces*. Cisco supports up to 1000 interfaces on a router, including both physical and logical interfaces. Once you create a subinterface, a router will treat this logical interface just like a physical interface: you can assign layer 3 addressing to it, enable, it, disable it, and do many other things.

To create a subinterface, use the following command:

```
Router(config)# interface type port_#.subinterface_#
                       [point|multipoint]
Router(config-subif)#
```

After entering the physical interface type and port identifier, follow this with a dot (.) and a subinterface number. The subinterface number can range from 0 to 4,294,967,295. The number that you use for the subinterface number is only for reference purposes within IOS, and the only requirement is that when creating a subinterface, you use a unique subinterface number. Many administrators prefer to use the VLAN number that the subinterface will handle for the subinterface number; however, this is not a requirement and the two numbers are not related in any way.

At the end of the statement, you must specify the type of connection *if* the interface is of type serial; otherwise, you can omit it. The **point** parameter is used for point-to-point serial connections, and **multipoint** is used for multipoint connections (many devices connected to the interface). The **multipoint** parameter is used for connections that have more than one device connected to them (physically or logically). For a router-on-a-stick configuration, you can omit the connection type, since the default is **multipoint** for LAN interfaces.

Interface Encapsulation

Once you create a subinterface, you'll notice that your CLI prompt has changed and that you are now in subinterface configuration mode. If you are routing between VLANs, you'll need an interface that supports trunking. Some things are configured on the major interface, and some things are configured on the subinterface. Configurations such as duplexing and speed are done on the major (or physical) interface. Most other tasks are done on the subinterface (the logical interface), including to which VLAN the subinterface belongs and its IP addressing information.

When setting up your subinterface for a router-on-a-stick, you must configure the type of trunking—InterSwitch Link (ISL) or 802.1Q—and the VLAN with which the subinterface is associated, like this:

```
Router(config)# interface type port_#.subinterface_#
Router(config-subif)# encapsulation isl|dot1q VLAN_#
```

Use the **encapsulation** command to specify the trunk type and the VLAN associated with the subinterface. The VLAN number you specify here *must* correspond to the correct VLAN number in your switched network. You must also set up a trunk connection on the switch for the port to which the router is connected. Once you do this, the switch will send tagged frames to the router, and the router, using your encapsulation, will understand how to read the tags. The router will be able to see from which VLAN the frame came and match it up with the appropriate subinterface that will process it. Remember that only a few of Cisco's switches today support ISL: all of them support 802.1Q, which is denoted with the **dot1q** parameter.

EXAM TIP   Be familiar with how to create a subinterface with the **interface** command. The router and switch must be using the same VLAN encapsulation type: 802.1Q or ISL.

Router-on-a-Stick Example Configuration

Let's look at an example to see how a router-on-a-stick is configured. Figure 11-7 shows this configuration. Assume that the Fast Ethernet interface on the router is the first interface in the first slot and that the switch is using 802.1Q trunking on the connected interface.

Figure 11-7
Router-on-a-stick
example

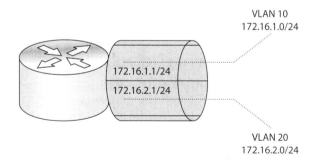

VLAN 10
172.16.1.0/24

172.16.1.1/24

172.16.2.1/24

VLAN 20
172.16.2.0/24

Here's the code example for this router:

```
Router(config)# interface fastethernet0/0
Router(config-if)# duplex full
Router(config-if)# no shutdown
Router(config-if)# exit
Router(config)# interface fastethernet0/0.1
Router(config-subif)# encapsulation dot1q 10
Router(config-subif)# ip address 172.16.1.1 255.255.255.0
Router(config-subif)# exit
Router(config)# interface fastethernet0/0.2
Router(config-subif)# encapsulation dot1q 20
Router(config-subif)# ip address 172.16.2.1 255.255.255.0
Router(config-subif)# exit
```

Notice in this example that the subinterface numbers in the **interface** command (1 and 2) do not match the VLAN numbers in the **encapsulation** command (10 and 20); remember that the subinterface numbers are used by IOS only to reference the particular subinterface and do not have to match any configuration on the subinterface.

 TIP If you are configuring static routes and want to route traffic out of a particular subinterface, specify the major interface along with the subinterface number, such as fastethernet0/0.2.

Router High Availability

The remainder of this chapter focuses on layer 3 redundancy issues. With layer 3 redundancy, you're normally dealing with having multiple paths to a destination and using a dynamic routing protocol to find the best or an alternative path. This section, however, deals with another type of layer 3 redundancy: default gateways and server load balancing. These are issues typically found at the access and distribution layers (see Chapter 1). I'll begin by talking about some of the issues of default gateway redundancy and some of the solutions that are available but that don't work very well. The main part of this section deals with Cisco's Hot Standby Router Protocol (HSRP) as well as other solutions, such as the Virtual Router Redundancy Protocol (VRRP) and Gateway Load Balancing Protocol (GLBP).

Problems of Traditional Default
Gateway Redundancy Solutions

You can easily place two routing devices at the distribution layer of each switch block to provide redundancy for end stations to leave their VLAN. However, this may not provide a true fault-tolerant solution. This is especially true for situations in which end stations do not support a router discovery protocol to learn which routers they can use or which routers can't be configured to use more than one default gateway address.

Proxy ARP Issues

Some end stations can use Proxy ARP to discover the IP address of the default gateway. In this situation, the end station dynamically acquires the IP address and MAC address of the default gateway and sends all of its inter-VLAN traffic to this routing device. To begin, the end station doesn't know how to reach the destination and generates an ARP request for the destination. Obviously, if the destination is not in the same VLAN, no one responds and the end station assumes that the destination is not reachable. However, a Cisco router can proxy this ARP by sending back its own MAC address to the end station, and the end station can then use the router to send traffic out of the subnet. From the end station's perspective, it thinks it's sending traffic directly to the destination, but it's actually being relayed by the router. On Cisco IOS devices with routing enabled, Proxy ARP is enabled, by default, on the routing interfaces.

A problem arises, however, when the default gateway fails. In this situation, the end station still sends its information to the failed default gateway, where the traffic is dropped. Sometimes a client re-performs the ARP after a lengthy period of time to verify the destination's (default gateway's) existence. (At this point, it will have discovered that the default gateway has failed, and then another routing device can perform the proxy.) However, in most implementations of ARP, the end station continues to use the same failed default gateway MAC address unless it is rebooted.

ICMP Router Discovery Protocol Issues

The Internet Control Message Protocol Router Discovery Protocol (IRDP) is not a routing protocol like OSPF or RIP; instead, it is an extension to ICMP that enables an end station to automatically discover the default gateways connected to the same VLAN. IRDP is covered in RFC 1256. In this environment, the routing devices periodically generate special multicast packets that announce the router's existence to the clients. This time period is usually between 5 and 10 minutes. Learned information usually has a maximum lifetime of 30 minutes on the client if no more IRDP messages are received from the advertising routing device. The multicast packet includes the routing device's address and a lifetime value.

With IRDP, end stations can dynamically discover other routing devices when their primary default gateway fails. However, this may take up to 30 minutes, based on the lifetime value in the original multicast packet from the routing device. And even if you may consider using IRDP with your access layer devices, most end-station IP stacks do not support IRDP.

Routing Protocol Issues

To overcome these two previous problems, you may be able to run a routing protocol on the end station—if the client supports this type of function. With IP, the only routing protocol that most end stations *might* support is RIP or OSPF. In RIP or OSPF, the end station could make intelligent decisions about which layer 3 routing device to use to access other subnets. However, the issue with RIP is that its convergence is very slow—it could take up to 180 seconds before an alternative routing device is chosen when the current primary routing device fails. With TCP sessions, this would cause a timeout.

Because of this, as well as all the additional overhead that RIP creates, this solution is not very desirable for your end stations—and this assumes that your end stations and other network devices support a routing protocol such as RIP.

User Device Issues

In most campus environments, end stations are assigned a single IP address for the default gateway (which is usually done via DHCP). In this environment, if the routing device (default gateway) were to fail, the end station would lose its capability to access other networking devices outside of its VLAN. Unfortunately, there is no redundancy in this implementation, because an end station can have only one default gateway address configured (whether it is assigned via DHCP or statically configured).

Hot Standby Router Protocol

HSRP is a Cisco-proprietary protocol that provides a single definition of a default gateway on the end station and provides layer 3 redundancy for overcoming the issues of IRDP, Proxy ARP, and end-station routing protocols. Unlike the four previous solutions, HSRP is completely transparent to the end stations—you do not have to perform any additional configuration on the end stations themselves. HSRP enables Cisco routing devices to monitor one another's status, which provides a very quick failover when a primary default gateway fails. This is done by establishing HSRP groups.

With HSRP, a group of routing devices represents a single virtual default gateway. This virtual default gateway has a virtual IP address and a virtual MAC address. If the primary routing device fails, another routing device in the HSRP group takes over and processes the frames sent by the end stations to the virtual MAC address.

An advantage of HSRP groups is that different subnets (VLANs) can have different default gateways, thus providing load balancing. Also, within each HSRP group is a primary default gateway and the capability to use multiple routers to perform a backup function. You can have up to 256 standby groups per routing device, providing up to 255 default gateways. Routing devices can provide backup for multiple primary default gateways. Each standby group keeps track of the primary routing device that's currently forwarding traffic sent to the virtual MAC address. Note that only one routing device is actually forwarding traffic with HSRP.

Another nice feature of HSRP is that you can customize it based on the size of your network. For instance, if you have a VLAN with 1000 devices in it, you can set up two HSRP groups: one group for 500 devices and another group for the other 500 devices. You can then assign routing devices to each group. For example, if you had only two routing devices, you could have the first routing device be the active routing device for group 1 but the standby for group 2, and vice versa for the second routing device. Through this process, you can have both of your routing devices forwarding traffic while still providing redundancy—if the active routing device in either group fails, the other routing device promotes itself to an active state.

HSRP Operation

As mentioned in the previous section, only one routing device actually forwards traffic for an HSRP group. Using a priority scheme, one routing device is elected as the forwarding router and the others perform as backups for a group. Each routing device has a default priority of 100, which you can manipulate. The routing device with the highest priority in the group is elected as the active router, and the other routing devices are placed in standby mode. The active routing device responds to any ARP packets from end stations and replies with the virtual MAC address of the group.

Each HSRP group must have a unique virtual IP address and a virtual MAC address, which means these addresses must be unique across different groups. This MAC address is 0000.0c07.ac*XX*. The 0000.0c is Cisco's vendor code. The 07-ac is HSRP's well-known address. The *XX* is the group number (in hexadecimal) for the HSRP group. Therefore, each HSRP group must have a unique address to ensure that the MAC address is unique in a VLAN.

 EXAM TIP   For the exam, you'll be expected to know that the HSRP virtual MAC address begins with 0000.0c07.ac*XX*, where the last two digits represent the HSRP group number, in hexadecimal. The active/master routing device for the VLAN is responsible for processing traffic sent to the virtual MAC and virtual IP addresses in the subnet/VLAN.

With HSRP, the end stations would perform an ARP with the virtual IP address, requesting the virtual MAC address of the default gateway routing device. Note that in this setting, the end stations are completely unaware of the actual routing devices handling traffic destined for a virtual router. Even when the primary fails and the standby routing device starts handling traffic for the broadcast domain, the end stations still think they're talking to the same routing device.

Types of Routing Devices   Every HSRP group contains the following types of routing devices that perform certain roles:

- Virtual routing device
- Active routing device
- Standby routing device
- Other HSRP routing devices

The role of the virtual routing device is to provide a single RP that's always available to the end stations. It is not a real RP because the IP and MAC addresses of the virtual RP are not physically assigned to any one interface on any of the routing devices in the broadcast domain.

The role of the active and standby routing devices is based on the priority of the routing devices in the HSRP group. The routing device with the *highest* priority is elected as the active routing device, and the one with the second highest priority is elected as the standby routing device. If the priorities are the same, the IP address of the routing device is used as a tiebreaker. In this situation, the routing device with the *higher* IP address is elected for the role.

The active routing device is responsible for forwarding all traffic destined to the virtual routing device's MAC address, and the standby routing device keeps tabs on the active routing device by looking for HSRP multicast messages, called *HSRP hellos*. The active routing device generates a hello every 3 seconds. If the standby routing device does not see any hellos for 10 seconds from the active routing device, the standby device promotes itself and begins performing the functions of the active device. Like the active device, the standby device also announces itself every 3 seconds so that if it fails, one of the other HSRP routers in the standby group can assume the standby routing device role.

The other routing devices in the HSRP group, if any exist, listen for the hello multicasts from the standby and active routing devices to ensure that they are performing their respective roles. When the active routing device fails, the view from the end stations' perspective is the same—they're still forwarding their frames to the virtual MAC address. When this happens, the standby routing device starts processing the frames sent to the virtual MAC address, and one of the other HSRP routers in the group is elected to the standby role.

NOTE   If any end station uses a real MAC address of one of the routing devices in the broadcast domain, that specific routing device—whether it is active, standby, or another routing device—processes and forwards the frame.

HSRP Multicast Messages   To declare which routing devices will become the active and standby routing devices, all the routing devices in the HSRP group initially send out HSRP multicast messages. These UDP messages, using port number 1985, are addressed to the all-router multicast address (224.0.0.2) with a Time-To-Live (TTL) value of 1. A TTL of 1 ensures that any multicast routing protocol that's running will not forward the message to a different subnet. The HSRP message contains the following information:

- HSRP version number
- Operation code (opcode) message type:
  - **Hello messages**   Used by the routing devices for the election process and by the active and standby routing devices when they have been elected
  - **Resign messages**   Used by an RP when it wants to stop performing the function of the active RP
  - **Coup messages**   Used by an RP that wants to become the active RP
- Current HSRP state (see the next section)
- Hello time interval of HSRP messages (defaults to 3 seconds)—that is, how often HSRP messages are generated
- Hold-down time interval (defaults to 10 seconds)—the length of time that a hello message is considered valid
- Priority of the RP—used to elect the active and standby routing devices
- Standby group number (0–255)
- Authentication password, if configured
- Virtual IP address of the HSRP group—the default gateway IP address that your end stations should use

HSRP States   HSRP supports six different states. A routing device may go through all these states or only a few of them, depending on whether it becomes an active or standby routing device:

- Initial
- Learn
- Listen
- Speak
- Standby
- Active

When the routing devices are enabled, they start in an *initial state*. Note that they have not begun the HSRP process in an initial state—only the routing devices themselves and their associated interfaces have been activated. In a *learn state*, a routing device listens for an active routing device. The routing device initially has no knowledge of any other HSRP routers. In this state, its purpose is to discover the current active and standby routing devices and the virtual IP address for the group.

After the routing device sees a multicast from the active/standby routing device, it learns about the virtual IP address. This is called the *listen state*. In this state, the routing device is neither the active nor the standby routing device. If there's already a standby and active routing device, the listening routing device remains in this state and does not proceed to any of the next three states. The exception to this is if you've configured *preemption*. With preemption, a new routing device with a higher priority can usurp an existing active or standby routing device.

If the routing device enters the *speak state*, the device propagates multicast messages so that it can participate in the election process for the standby or active role. These hellos are sent out periodically so that other routing devices in the group know about everyone's existence. Note that for a routing device to enter this state, it must have the virtual IP address configured on it.

Based on the routing device's priority, it becomes either a *standby* or *active* routing device. In a standby state, the routing device is the next in line to assume the role of the active routing device if the active routing device fails. In an active state, the routing device is responsible for forwarding all traffic sent to the virtual MAC address of the broadcast domain. There can be only one active and one standby routing device. Both of these routing devices generate periodic hellos to other routing devices in the group to guarantee that end stations always have a default gateway that can forward their traffic if either of them fails.

It's important to point out that if you don't configure preemption, the first routing device that comes up takes on the active role and the second routing device takes on the standby role. Therefore, if you're setting up load balancing between routing devices so that certain routing devices handle traffic for certain VLANs and other routing devices handle traffic for other VLANs, you'll want to use preemption so that whenever a failed routing device comes back online, it resumes its former role.

HSRP Configuration

The configuration of HSRP is a simple process. The following sections discuss its configuration as well as how to optimize it for larger networks.

Basic Configuration   Only one command, **standby**, is necessary to enable HSRP. Execute one of the following **standby** commands on the routing device's interface. Use a subinterface for a trunk port and a VLAN interface for an internal routing device, such as a layer 3 switch.

```
Router(config)# interface type [slot_#/]port_#
Router(config-if)# standby [group_#] ip IP_address
```

or

```
Switch(config)# interface vlan VLAN_#
Switch(config-if)# standby [group_#] ip IP_address
```

Each interface supports 256 HSRP groups. After you execute the **standby** command on an active interface, the routing device enters the learning state. In this command, *group_#* is optional. If you omit it, it defaults to 0. Note that *group_#* is required if you have multiple standby groups. Remember that the IP address you specify in the **standby** command is not the actual IP address that's on the interface, but rather the virtual IP address. You need to take the virtual IP address and either hard-code it as the default gateway address on end stations or put it in your DHCP server configuration.

To ensure that the end stations do not discover the real MAC address of the routing device's LAN interface, enabling HSRP disables ICMP redirects. You'll see the **no ip redirects** command on the routing device's interface.

Load Balancing   To influence which routing devices perform the active and standby roles, you can increase the routing device priorities. To do so, execute the following **standby** command on the routing device's interface:

```
IOS(config-if)# standby [group-number] priority new_priority
```

Remember that the higher the priority, the more likely it is that the routing device will become a standby or active routing device. The priority defaults to 100 but can be set to a value from 0 to 255. To configure a routing device so that it can preempt the current standby or active routing device, use the **preempt** parameter:

```
Switch(config-if)# standby [group-number] preempt [delay delay_value]
```

The default delay is 0 seconds, which causes the routing device to begin the preemption process immediately. You can delay this by putting in a delay value of 0 to 3600 seconds (1 hour). The one problem with preemption, however, is that it causes a slight disruption in traffic, because the currently active routing device demotes itself and the new routing device promotes itself.

To modify the hello and hold-down times, execute the following **standby** command:

```
Switch(config-if)# standby [group_#] timers hello_time holddown_time
```

Here, **hello_time** defaults to 3 seconds and can range from 0 to 255 seconds, and **holddown_time** defaults to 10 seconds and has the same range of valid values. Note that the **holddown_time** value should be at least three times greater than the **hello_time** value to ensure proper functioning of HSRP.

 TIP It is a common practice to adjust these timers to smaller values to speed up HSRP convergence. If you do this, however, you must be careful not to set these values too small, which may cause inadvertent switchovers.

If you want to configure authentication, execute the following **standby** command on the interface:

```
Router(config-if)# standby [group-number] authentication password
```

The password can be up to eight characters; if omitted, the password defaults to *cisco*. The password needs to match on all HSRP routers in the same group.

Interface Tracking   In certain cases, it may be necessary for the active routing device to step down from its role and let another routing device assume the role. Consider the example shown in Figure 11-8. In this example, RP-B is the active RP for VLAN 20. If RP-B fails, RP-A notices this after missing the hello messages from RP-B. Then RP-A promotes itself and starts forwarding frames that are destined to the virtual MAC address.

Let's assume, however, that RP-B does not fail but instead its interface vlan40 fails (connected to the core), as shown in Figure 11-9. Without HSRP running, RP-B would detect the failure and generate an ICMP redirect message to RP-A. This would enable

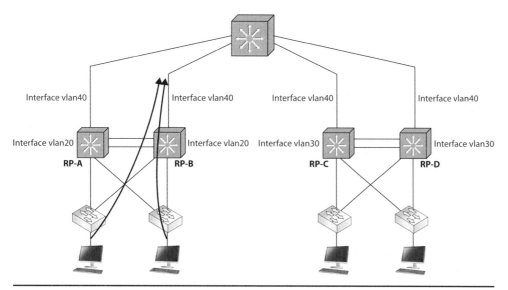

Figure 11-8   HSRP example

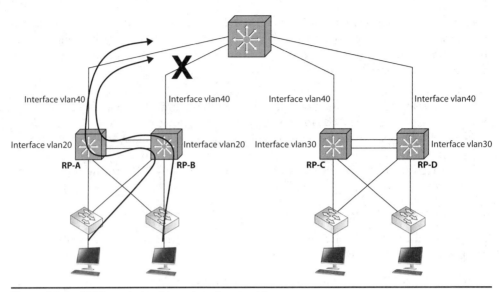

Figure 11-9   HSRP example without interface tracking

RP-A to handle the redirected traffic. However, if RP-A and RP-B are participating in an HSRP group, ICMP redirects are disabled. This means that RP-B still functions as the active routing device and handles all traffic sent to the virtual MAC address. The problem, however, is that after the layer 3 routing protocol has converged, the traffic still reaches its destination. But to reach the destination, the traffic must pass through both RP-B *and* RP-A, thus introducing unnecessary latency.

To overcome this problem and still be able to deploy HSRP, you can employ the HSRP interface tracking feature. Interface tracking enables the active routing device to lower its priority when one of the interfaces that it's tracking fails. This would enable another RP to assume the active role. In the example shown in Figure 11-9, RP-B, with interface tracking configured, would lower its priority—essentially telling the other routing devices that it no longer wants to serve as the active routing device. When RP-A sees that RP-B is advertising a lower priority than itself, RP-A promotes itself and handles all traffic destined for the virtual MAC address. The advantage of this approach is that the traffic from the user will traverse only one RP: RP-A.

To configure interface tracking, execute the following command on the HSRP group interface:

```
Switch(config-if)# standby [group_#] track interface_type interface_#
                          [decrement_value]
```

The **track** parameter is used to enter the interface that you want the HSRP RP to track. If this interface fails, for whatever reason, the active routing device decrements its HSRP priority by the configured value. Note that *decrement_value* is optional and, if omitted, defaults to a decrement of 10 for the priority.

HSRP Verification

To verify the overall operation of HSRP, use the **show standby** command on the RP:

```
Switch# show standby
Vlan 1 - Group 1
  Local state is Active, priority 110, may preempt
  Hellotime 3 holdtime 10
  Next hello sent in 0:00:01
  Hot standby IP address is 172.16.10.1 configured
  Active router is local
  Standby router is 172.16.10.2 expires in 0:00:07
  Standby virtual mac address is 0000.0c07.ac01
Tracking interface states for 3 interfaces, 3 up:
  Up  Vlan1 Priority decrement: 10
```

In the output, you can see that the active routing device is 172.16.10.1 and the standby RP is 172.16.10.2.

For a shorter description, add the **brief** parameter to the preceding command:

```
Router# show standby brief
                             Active      Standby Group
Interface  Grp Prio P State  addr        addr    addr
Vlan1       1   100    Standby 172.17.10.2 local  172.16.10.254
```

In this example, the router for VLAN1 is in a standby state and the virtual IP address for the standby group is 172.16.10.254.

For additional troubleshooting, you can use the **debug standby** command from privileged EXEC mode. This command displays all HSRP messages that have been sent and received by the RP.

Other Protocols

You can use two other protocols instead of HSRP:

- Virtual Router Redundancy Protocol (VRRP)
- Gateway Load Balancing Protocol (GLBP)

VRRP

VRRP performs a similar function as Cisco's proprietary HSRP. The one major downside to HSRP is that it is a proprietary protocol. VRRP, however, is an open standard and is defined in IETF RFC 2338. Like HSRP, VRRP has end stations that use a virtual router for a default gateway. VRRP is supported for Ethernet media types as well as in VLANs and multiprotocol label switching (MPLS) VPNs.

NOTE   HSRP and VRRP are very similar and accomplish the same goal: default gateway redundancy. HSRP is proprietary to Cisco and VRRP is an open standard.

VRRP and HSRP are very similar protocols. One main difference between VRRP and HSRP, however, is that HSRP uses a virtual IP address for the default gateway, whereas VRRP can use either a virtual IP address or the interface address of the master router.

If a virtual IP address is used, an election process takes place to choose a master router. The router with the highest priority is chosen as the master. All other routers are backup routers. If a real IP address is used, the router that has that address assigned to its interface must be the master router.

VRRP is an IP protocol and has an IP protocol number of 112. The VRRP master router is responsible for generating VRRP multicast messages. It sends these messages to a multicast address of 224.0.0.18. The master typically generates these messages every second. If the master VRRP router fails, a backup VRRP router seamlessly processes the traffic sent to the master router's IP address. This process is referred to as *object tracking*: it ensures that the best VRRP router is selected as the master of the group based on priority and interface tracking. VRRP supports preemption so that a failed master, after it has been repaired, can resume its role as master.

 NOTE   The configuration of VRRP is beyond the scope of this book.

GLBP

GLBP is a Cisco-proprietary protocol, like HSRP. One of the limitations of HSRP and VRRP is that only one router in the HSRP group is active and can forward traffic for the group—the rest of the routers sit idle. This is not an efficient process, because one or more routing devices are not processing any traffic and you are not taking advantage of the bandwidth of the connections that these other routing devices are connected to.

Cisco designed GLBP to rectify this issue. GLBP enables the dynamic assignment of a *group* of virtual addresses to end stations. With GLBP, up to four routing devices in the group can participate in the forwarding of traffic. Plus, if a GLBP routing device fails, fault detection occurs automatically and another GLBP routing device picks up the forwarding of packets for the failed routing device.

Here are some of the benefits of GLBP:

- Like HSRP, GLBP supports clear-text and MD5 password authentication between GLBP routing devices.
- GLBP supports up to 1024 virtual routers on a routing device.
- GLBP can load balance traffic via four forwarding routing devices in a subnet or VLAN.

GLBP Operation   In GLBP, there are two types of routers: active virtual gateways (AVGs) and active virtual forwarders (AVFs). The AVG is the master gateway device and is responsible for assigning virtual MAC addresses to end stations when the end stations perform an ARP for the GLBP default gateway address. Basically, the AVG is responsible for address management in the GLBP group. An AVF is a routing device that forwards traffic for a GLBP group. The AVG is also an AVF. Basically, up to four routing devices configured in the same GLBP group are AVFs.

Figure 11-10
GLBP operation

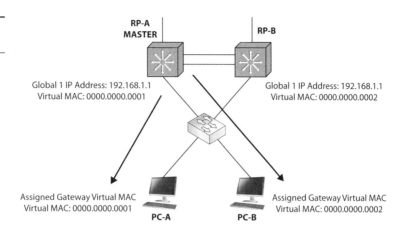

Figure 11-10 shows a basic illustration of how GLBP works. In this example, RP-A is the master (AVG). When PC-A sends an ARP request for the default gateway MAC address, the AVG is responsible for responding with a virtual MAC address to the end station. In this example, it responds with its own virtual MAC address. PC-B then ARPs for the same gateway address. RP-A responds with a virtual MAC address. Based on the load-balancing algorithm (discussed in the next section) used by GLBP, RP-A responds with a different virtual MAC address (RP-B's address). As you can see from this example, both RP-A and RP-B are forwarding traffic for the same VLAN.

GLBP also supports interface tracking. With interface tracking, if a tracked interface on an AVF fails, the AVF demotes itself and has another AVF pick up the processing associated with this failed interface. This process is similar to HSRP's interface tracking feature.

Load Balancing with GLBP   Multiple RPs can be used to forward traffic with GLBP to perform load balancing. GLBP supports three methods of load balancing:

- Round-robin
- Weighted
- Host-dependent

The default method of load balancing is round-robin, in which the AVG assigns a different AVF default gateway address to each client. If you have two routing devices and six clients, three clients will use the AVG and three will use the AVF.

With weighted load balancing, a weighting factor is used to determine which AVF's address the AVG routing device assigns to an end station. This enables you to tune GLBP so that a certain amount of hosts use one routing device rather than another if there is a difference in processing power between the routing devices.

With host-based load balancing, a host is assigned the same virtual gateway address each time. However, if the routing device associated with this address fails, another routing device within GLBP can pick up the processing so that redundancy is provided.

Chapter Review

In this chapter you learned about important concepts related to the routing process with Cisco routers. You learned about core routing concepts, such as how configured interfaces add connected routes to the routing table. You will need to add additional routes manually or use a dynamic routing protocol to learn of additional routes.

For the exam, be familiar with when static routes are used versus a dynamic routing protocol. Understand the syntax of the **ip route** command and the default values, if omitted. Know how to configure a default route. Be able to find misconfigured static routes in a router's configuration. Know how to read the output of the **show ip route** command and to find the administrative distance and metric values of dynamic routing protocols in this output.

You learned about the routing process and the fact that when a packet is received by the router, it first looks for a matching network ID in the routing table. If it finds multiple routes with matching network IDs, the router will use the route with the lowest administrative distance. If there are multiple routes with the same network ID and the same administrative distance, the router will select a route based on the metric value. Remember this for the exam!

You learned about troubleshooting commands you can use with the router such as the **show ip route**, the **show ip protocols**, and the **debug ip <protocol>** commands. Review the output of these commands; you should be very comfortable with them.

You learned how to configure a router-on-a-stick, how subinterfaces are created, and how the **encapsulation** command associates a VLAN to the subinterface. Remember that the trunking protocol must match between the switch and the router: either 802.1Q or ISL. The IP address on the subinterface is the default gateway address for devices associated with that VLAN.

The HSRP active/master routing device for the VLAN is responsible for processing traffic sent to the virtual MAC and virtual IP addresses in the subnet/VLAN. The HSRP virtual MAC address begins with 0000.0c07.ac*XX*, where the last two digits represent the HSRP group number, in hexadecimal. The default hello timer is 3 seconds, and the dead interval timer is 10 seconds. Up to 255 HSRP groups are supported per interface.

Quick Review

Understanding Routing

- There are different types of routes: With a *connected* route, the router establishes a direct connection to the network. You must manually configure a *static* route.
- Use the **ip route** command to configure a static route.
- Use the **show ip route** command to view the routing table.

Understanding Dynamic Routing

- There are two major types of routing protocols: *distance vector* and *link state*.
- Distance vector routing protocols share routing information with neighboring routers and measure the best route according to the number of hops required to reach a destination.
- Link state routing protocols share routing information with all routers on the network and include information on the state of the link.
- RIP and IGRP are examples of distance vector routing protocols.
- OSPF and IS-IS are examples of link state routing protocols.
- Use the **router** and **network** commands to set up dynamic routing protocols.

The Routing Process

- A floating static route is used as a backup to a primary route.
- You configure a floating static route by creating a static route with an administrative distance higher than the primary route.
- Routes are first selected based on the network ID with the longest network prefix. For example, 10.0.0.0/24 would be selected over 10.0.0.0/8.
- After the router selects the routes that match the destination network with the longest prefix, if there are still multiple routes to the destination, the router will select the one with the lowest administrative distance value.
- If there are multiple routes because they have the same administrative distance value, the router will select the route based on the metric value.

Routing Troubleshooting Commands

- Use the **clear ip route** command to rebuild the routing table.
- Use the **show ip route** command to view the routing table.
- Use the **show ip protocols** command to view details about the dynamic routing protocol being used.

Router-on-a-Stick

- A router-on-a-stick is a router with a single trunk connection to a switch; a router routes between the VLANs on this trunk connection.
- To route between VLANs with a router-on-a-stick, use subinterfaces and specify the VLAN with the **encapsulation isl|dot1q** command on the subinterface.

Router High Availability

- To enable HSRP, use the **standby ip** command on a routing device's interface.
- HSRP is proprietary and VRRP is an open standard. Both accomplish the same thing: default gateway redundancy within a VLAN.

- HSRP uses a virtual address as the default gateway address; VRRP supports the use of a physical or virtual address.
- GLBP, which is proprietary to Cisco and based on HSRP, enables more than one active routing device in a subnet.

Questions

The following questions will help you measure your understanding of the material presented in this chapter. Read all the choices carefully, as there may be more than one correct answer. Choose the correct answer(s) for each question.

1. What is the first technique used by the router in the routing selection process to select a route for a packet?

   A. Administrative distance

   B. Dynamic routing protocol used

   C. Routing protocol metric

   D. Longest matching prefix

2. What command is used to add the gateway of last resort of 192.168.9.1 to the router?

   A. **ip route 192.168.9.1 0.0.0.0 0.0.0.0**

   B. **ip route 0.0.0.0 0.0.0.0 192.168.9.1**

   C. **network route 0.0.0.0 0.0.0.0 192.168.9.1**

   D. **default route 192.168.9.1**

3. Your router is running RIP and OSPF, and both routing protocols are learning 192.168.1.0/24. Which routing protocol will your router use for this route?

   A. Both

   B. RIP

   C. OSPF

   D. Neither

4. Which of the following is a valid virtual MAC address for an HSRP group?

   A. 0000.6e00.0014

   B. 0000.0c07.ac18

   C. 0000.ac07.0c0a

   D. 0000.0cac.0c0f

5. What is the administrative distance of RIP?

   A. 120

   B. 110

   C. 1

   D. 90

6. How do you create a floating static route?

   A. Add a static route with a smaller AD.

   B. Add a dynamic route with a smaller AD.

   C. Add RIP with an AD of 1.

   D. Add a static route with a larger AD.

7. What is the administrative distance value for OSPF?

   A. 120

   B. 110

   C. 1

   D. 90

8. Which router-on-a-stick command defines the VLAN for the interface?

   A. vlan

   B. encapsulation

   C. trunk

   D. frame-type

9. Looking at the following network diagram, what is the command to add a static route on VAN-R1 to reach network 14.0.0.0/8?

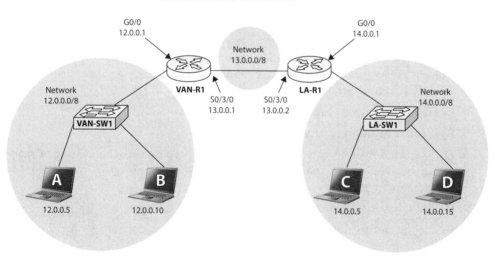

   A. route add 14.0.0.0 255.0.0.0 13.0.0.1

   B. ip route 14.0.0.0 13.0.0.1

   C. ip route 14.0.0.0 255.0.0.0 13.0.0.2

   D. ip route 14.0.0.0 13.0.0.2

Performance-based Question

1. Identify the components of the routing table by writing each of the labels in the box at the bottom beside the appropriate number on the left.

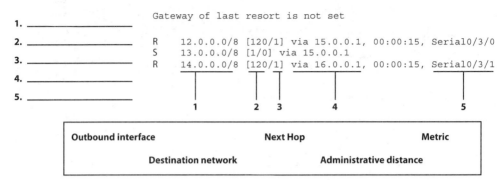

1. _____
2. _____
3. _____
4. _____
5. _____

```
Gateway of last resort is not set

R    12.0.0.0/8 [120/1] via 15.0.0.1, 00:00:15, Serial0/3/0
S    13.0.0.0/8 [1/0] via 15.0.0.1
R    14.0.0.0/8 [120/1] via 16.0.0.1, 00:00:15, Serial0/3/1
```

| Outbound interface | | Next Hop | | Metric |
| Destination network | | | Administrative distance | |

Answers

1. **D.** The router chooses the best route by first matching the packet to the route with the longest matching network prefix.

2. **B.** The correct command is **ip route 0.0.0.0 0.0.0.0 192.168.9.1**. You can configure the gateway of last resort (GWLR) by adding a static route to the address of 0.0.0.0 with a subnet mask of 0.0.0.0. The GWLR is the route used if there is no matching destination network in the routing table for a packet.

3. **C.** Your router would select the route using OSPF, because it has a lower administrative distance than RIP. OSPF uses an administrative distance of 110, while RIP has an administrative distance of 120.

4. **B.** HSRP virtual MAC addresses begin with 0000.0c07.ac

5. **A.** RIP has an administrative distance of 120.

6. **D.** To create a floating static route, which is a backup route for an existing primary route, you simply add a static route but increase the administrative distance so it is higher than the primary route.

7. **B.** OSPF has an administrative distance of 110.

8. **B.** Use the **encapsulation** command to specify the trunking, encapsulation, and VLAN number for the subinterface.

9. **C.** The command **ip route 14.0.0.0 255.0.0.0 13.0.0.2** is correct. You use the **ip route** command and specify the destination network, the subnet mask, and the IP address of where to send the data to reach that network.

Performance-based Answer

1. The following illustration identifies the components of the routing table. Be sure to know these for the CCNA exam. On the real exam, you will need to drag and drop the labels to the appropriate locations.

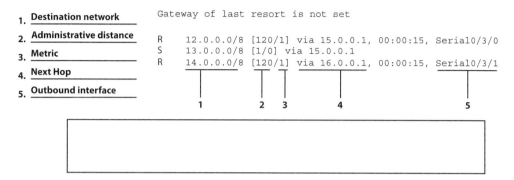

1. **Destination network** _____

2. **Administrative distance** _____

3. **Metric** _____

4. **Next Hop** _____

5. **Outbound interface** _____

CHAPTER 12

OSPF Routing

In this chapter, you will

- Learn the basics about the Open Shortest Path First protocol
- Learn how OSPF operates
- Learn how to configure OSPF
- Learn about troubleshooting OSPF

The Open Shortest Path First (OSPF) protocol is a link state protocol that handles routing for IP traffic. OSPF version 2, which is described in RFC 2328, is an open standard, as are versions 1 and 2 of the Routing Information Protocol (RIP), which is also a routing protocol. Chapter 11 offered a brief introduction to link state protocols. As you will see in this chapter, OSPF draws heavily on the concepts described in Chapter 11, but OSPF also has some unique features, which are described here. In addition to covering the characteristics of OSPF, this chapter presents information that will enable you to undertake a basic routing configuration using OSPF.

NOTE An excellent resource for OSPF, the "OSPF Design Guide," can be viewed and downloaded free from Cisco's web site: www.cisco.com/c/en/us/support/docs/ip/open-shortest-path-first-ospf/7039-1.html. It covers both single- and multi-area designs in much depth.

OSPF Overview

OSPF was created in the mid-1980s to overcome many of the deficiencies and scalability problems of RIP in large enterprise networks. Because it is based on an open standard, OSPF is very popular in many corporate networks today and has many advantages, including these:

- It will run on most routers, since it is based on an open standard.
- It uses the SPF algorithm, developed by Edsger Dijkstra, to provide a loop-free topology.
- It provides fast convergence with triggered, incremental updates via link state advertisements (LSAs).

- It is a classless protocol and allows for a hierarchical design with Variable Length Subnet Masking (VLSM) and route summarization, thus reducing routing overhead.

- It contains a two-layer hierarchy to contain problems within an area and to reduce routing overhead.

- It has an intelligent metric (cost), which is the inverse of the bandwidth of an interface.

- It enables you to control routing update information extensively through summarization and filtering.

Given its advantages, OSPF does have its share of disadvantages:

- It requires more memory to hold the adjacency (list of OSPF neighbors), topology (a link state database containing all of the routers and their routes/links), and routing tables.

- It requires extra CPU processing to run the SPF algorithm, which is especially true when you first turn on your routers and they are initially building the adjacency and topology tables.

- For large networks, it requires careful design to break up the network into an appropriate hierarchical design by separating routers into different areas.

- It is more complex to configure and more difficult to troubleshoot than distance vector protocols.

 EXAM TIP Remember the advantages and disadvantages of OSPF for the exam.

Knowing the advantages and disadvantages of any routing protocol is useful when it comes to picking a protocol. Typically, OSPF is used in large enterprise networks that have either a mixed-routing–vendor environment or a policy that requires an open standard for a routing protocol, which gives a company flexibility when it needs to replace any of its existing routers.

 TIP Typically, when you have more than 50 routers, Cisco recommends that you use a more advanced routing protocol such as Open Shortest Path First (OSPF) or Enhanced Interior Gateway Routing Protocol (EIGRP). In a mixed-vendor environment, there is basically one choice between these two: OSPF.

Hierarchical Design: Areas

To provide scalability for very large networks, OSPF supports two important concepts: autonomous systems and areas. *Autonomous systems* (ASs) were introduced in Chapter 11. Within an AS, *areas* are used to provide hierarchical routing. An area is a group of contiguous networks. Basically, areas are used to control when and how much routing information is shared across your network. In flat network designs, such as those that use IP RIP, if a change occurs on one router (perhaps a flapping route problem), it affects *every* router in the entire network. With a correctly designed hierarchical network, these changes can be contained within a single area.

EXAM TIP   Remember that OSPF supports a two-layer hierarchy: the backbone (area 0 or 0.0.0.0) and areas connected to the backbone.

OSPF implements a two-layer hierarchy: the backbone and areas off the backbone, as shown in Figure 12-1. This network includes a backbone and three areas connected to the backbone. Each area is given a unique number that is 32 bits in length. The area number can be represented by a single decimal number, such as 1, or in a dotted-decimal format, such as 0.0.0.1. Area 0 is a special area and represents the top-level hierarchy of the OSPF network, commonly called the *backbone*. Through a correct IP addressing design, you should be able to summarize routing information between areas. By summarizing your routing information, perhaps one summarized route for each area, you are reducing the amount of information that routers need to know about. For instance, each area in Figure 12-1 is assigned a separate Class B network number. Through summarization on the border routers between areas, other areas would not need to see all the Class B subnets—only the summarized network numbers for each respective area (the Class B network numbers themselves).

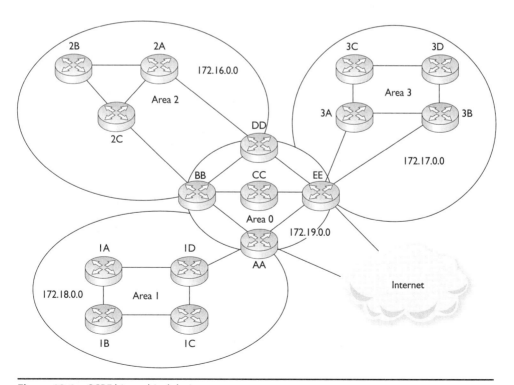

Figure 12-1   OSPF hierarchical design

NOTE The backbone (area 0) in OSPF is required and non-0 areas (such as areas 1, 2, 3, and so on) must be connected to the backbone. The preferred connection is a physical connection; however, OSPF supports a feature called *virtual links* that enables an area to be logically connected to the backbone. A discussion of virtual links is beyond the scope of this book.

Area 2, for instance, doesn't need to see all of the subnets of Area 1's 172.18.0.0 network number, since only two paths exist out of Area 2 to the backbone. Area 2, however, needs to see all of its internal subnets to create optimized routing tables to reach its own internal networks within Area 2. Therefore, in a correctly designed OSPF network, each area should contain specific routes only for its own areas and summarized routes to reach other areas. By performing this summarization, the routers have a smaller topology database (they know only about links in their own area and the summarized routes) and their routing tables are smaller (they know only about their own area's routes and the summarized routes). Through a correct hierarchical design, you can scale OSPF to very large sizes. Chapter 5 discussed route summarization.

EXAM TIP Note that the CCNA exam focuses on only single-area designs, and the material throughout the rest of the sections of this chapter covers only single-area concepts. The CCNP-level material, however, spends a lot of time on both single- *and* multi-area designs. Designing a multi-area OSPF network can become very complicated and requires a lot of networking knowledge and skill.

Metric Structure

Unlike RIP, which uses hop count as a metric, OSPF uses cost. Cost is actually the inverse of the bandwidth of a link: the faster the speed of the connection, the lower the cost. The most preferred path is the one with the lowest accumulated cost value. By using cost as a metric, OSPF will choose more intelligent paths than RIP. (Metrics are discussed in more depth in the "OSPF Metric Values" section later in the chapter.)

Remember that on synchronous serial links, no matter what the clock rate of the physical link is, the bandwidth always defaults to 1544 Kbps. You'll want to code this correctly with the **bandwidth** interface subconfiguration mode command (discussed in Chapter 11). This is important if you have multiple synchronous serial paths to a destination, especially if they have different clock rates. OSPF supports load balancing of up to 16 equal-cost paths to a single destination; however, only 4 equal-cost paths are used by default. Remember that if you don't configure the bandwidth metric correctly on your serial interfaces, your router may accidentally include paths with different clock rates, which can cause load-balancing issues.

For example, if you have one serial connection clocked at 1544 Kbps and another clocked at 256 Kbps and you don't change the bandwidth values, OSPF will see *both* connections as 1544 Kbps and attempt to use 1544 Kbps when reaching a single destination across these links. This is because the default bandwidth on a serial link is 1544, no matter what the clock speed of the interface is. This can create throughput problems when the router is performing load balancing—half of the connections will go down one link and half down the other, creating congestion problems for the 256-Kbps connection. Therefore, remember that you should change bandwidth of the interface with the **bandwidth** command.

OSPF Operation

As mentioned, OSPF is a link state protocol similar to what was generically described in Chapter 11. However, each link state protocol, such as OSPF and Intermediate System-Intermediate System (IS-IS), has its own unique features and characteristics. This section introduces you to how OSPF operates in a single-area design.

Router Identities

Each router in an OSPF network needs a unique ID—this must be unique not just within an area, but within the entire OSPF network. The ID is used to provide a unique identity to the OSPF router. The ID is included in any OSPF messages the router generates that other OSPF routers will process. The router ID is chosen according to one of the following criteria:

- The highest IP address on the router's active loopback interfaces is used (this is a logical interface on a router).
- If no loopback interface exists with an IP address, the highest IP address on its active interfaces is used when the router boots up.

NOTE Loopbacks typically have a host mask (/32). Cisco supports other masks for loopback interfaces, but many vendors restrict you to a /32 mask.

The router ID is used by the router to announce itself to the other OSPF routers in the network. This ID must be unique. If no loopback interfaces are configured, the router will use the highest IP address from one of its active physical interfaces. Optionally, you can manually define the router ID, always ensuring how it will be defined no matter what interfaces exist on the router.

EXAM TIP Remember for the CCNA exam how a router acquires its router ID for OSPF: the active loopback with the highest IP address or the active physical interface with the highest IP address.

If no active interface exists, the OSPF process will not start, and therefore you will not have any OSPF routes in your routing table. It is highly recommended, therefore, that you use a loopback interface, because it is always up and thus the router can obtain a router ID and start OSPF.

Finding Neighbors

Whereas RIP accepts routing updates from just about any other RIP router (unless RIPv2 with authentication is configured), OSPF has some rules concerning if and how routing information should be shared. First, before a router will accept any routing information from another OSPF router, the routers must build an *adjacency* between them, on their connected interfaces. When this adjacency is built, the two routers (on the connected interfaces) are called *neighbors*, indicating a special relationship between the two.

An OSPF router learns about its OSPF neighbors and builds its adjacency and topology tables by sharing link state advertisements (LSAs), which exist in different types. When learning about the neighbors to which a router is connected, as well as keeping tabs on known neighbors, OSPF routers will generate LSA hello messages every 10 seconds. When a neighbor is discovered and an adjacency is formed with the neighbor, a router expects to see hello messages from the neighbor. If a neighbor's hello is not seen within the dead interval time, which defaults to 40 seconds, the neighbor is declared dead. When this occurs, the router will advertise this information, via an LSA message, to other neighboring OSPF routers.

In order for two routers to become neighbors, the following items must match on each router:

- The area number
- The hello and dead interval timers on their connected interfaces
- The OSPF password (optional), if it is configured
- The area stub flag, indicating the type of area (a stub is used to contain OSPF messages and routing information, which is beyond the scope of this book)
- Maximum transmission unit (MTU) sizes on the connected interfaces

If these items do not match, the routers will not form an adjacency and will ignore each other's routing information.

 EXAM TIP   For the Cisco CCNA exam, remember that the hello process is used to discover and maintain a neighbor relationship with other OSPF routers. In order to form a neighbor relationship, two OSPF routers on the same segment must be in the same area, must have matching hello and dead interval timers, must have the same password if authentication is configured, must be of the same type (stub, not-so-stubby, or no stub), and must have the same MTU size configured on their interfaces.

Let's assume that you turned on all your routers simultaneously on a segment. In this case, the OSPF routers will go through three states, called the *exchange process*, in determining whether they will become neighbors:

1. **Down state**   The routers have not exchanged any OSPF information with any other router.

2. **Init state**   A destination router receives a new router's hello and adds it to its neighbor list (assuming that values in the preceding bullet points match). Note that communication is only unidirectional at this point.

3. **Two-way state**   The new router receives a unidirectional reply (from the destination router) to its initial hello packet and adds the destination router to its neighbor database.

Once the routers have entered a *two-way* state, they are considered neighbors. At this point, an election process takes place to elect the designated router (DR) and the backup designated router (BDR) on the segment.

Designated and Backup Designated Routers

An OSPF router will not form adjacencies to just any router. Instead, a client/server design is implemented in OSPF on *each* broadcast segment. For each multi-access broadcast segment, such as Ethernet, there is a DR and a BDR as well as other OSPF routers, called *DROTHERs*. As an example, if you have ten VLANs in your switched area, you'll have ten DRs and ten BDRs. The one exception of a segment not having these two routers is on a WAN point-to-point link.

When an OSPF router comes up, it forms adjacencies with the DR and the BDR on each multi-access segment to which it is connected; if it is connected to three segments, it will form three sets of adjacencies. Any exchange of routing information is between these DR/BDR routers and the other OSPF neighbors on a segment (and vice versa). An OSPF router talks to a DR using the IP multicast address 224.0.0.6. The DR and the BDR talk to all OSPF routers using the 224.0.0.5 multicast IP address.

 EXAM TIP   Remember for the CCNA exam that OSPF routers use link state advertisements (LSAs) to communicate with each other. One type of LSA is a hello, which is used to form neighbor relationships and as a keepalive function. Hellos are generated every 10 seconds. When sharing link information (directly connected routes), links are sent to the DR (224.0.0.6) and the DR disseminates link information to everyone else (224.0.0.5) on the segment. On point-to-point links, since no DR/BDR is used, all OSPF packets are addressed to 224.0.0.5.

The OSPF router with the highest priority becomes the DR for the segment. If there is a tie, the router with the highest *router ID* (not IP address on the segment) will become the DR. By default, all routers have a priority of 1 (priorities can range from 0 to 255—it's an 8-bit value). If the DR fails, the BDR is promoted to DR and another router is elected as the BDR. Figure 12-2 shows an example of the election process, where router E is elected as the DR and router B is elected as the BDR. Note that in this example, each router has the default priority, 1; therefore, router E is chosen as the DR since it has the highest router ID, and router B is chosen as the BDR because it has the second-highest router ID. If a router has a priority of 0, it will never become the DR or BDR.

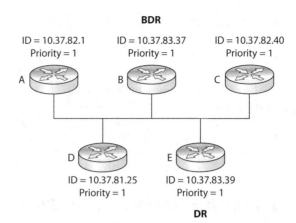

Figure 12-2
DR and BDR
election process

The DR and BDR priority is changed on an interface-by-interface basis and is configured with the **ip ospf priority** command within the interface subconfiguration mode. Once the DR and BDR are elected, they maintain these roles even if other routers form adjacencies with them that have higher priorities: an election or re-election will occur only if no DR or BDR exists.

 EXAM TIP An important topic to understand for the CCNA exam is how a router becomes the DR. The router with the highest priority (or highest router ID) becomes the DR—note that it is not the highest IP address on the link. This process is true for multi-access segments, but not point-to-point links, where DRs/BDRs are not used. Setting the priority to 0 means the router will never become the DR or BDR.

Sharing Routing Information

After electing the DR/BDR pair, the routers continue to generate hellos to maintain communication. This is considered an *exstart* state, in which the OSPF routers are ready to share link state information. The process the routers go through is called an *exchange protocol*, and is outlined here:

1. **Exstart state** The DR and BDR form adjacencies with the other OSPF routers on the segment. Then, within each adjacency, the router with the highest router ID becomes the master and starts the exchange process first (shares its link state information). Note that the DR is not necessarily the master for the exchange process. The remaining router in the adjacency will be the slave.

2. **Exchange state** The master starts sharing link state information first with the slave. These are called *database description packets* (DBDs, sometimes DDPs). The DBDs contain the link state type, the ID of the advertising router, the cost of the advertised link, and the sequence number of the link. The slave responds back with an LSACK—an acknowledgment to the DBD from the master. The slave then compares the DBD's information with its own.

3. **Loading state**   If the master has more up-to-date information than the slave, the slave will respond to the master's original DBD with a link state request (LSR). The master will then send a link state update (LSU) with the detailed information of the links to the slave. The slave will then incorporate this into its local link state database. Again, the slave will generate an LSACK to the master to acknowledge the fact that it received the LSU. If a slave has more up-to-date information, it will repeat the exchange and loading states.

4. **Full state**   Once the master and the slave are synchronized, they are considered to be in a full state.

To summarize these four steps, OSPF routers share a type of LSA message in order to disclose information about available routes; basically, an LSA update message contains a link and a state, as well as other information. A *link* is the router interface on which the update was generated (a connected route). The *state* is a description of this interface, including the IP address configured on it and the relationship this router has with its neighboring router. However, OSPF routers will not share this information with just any OSPF router—it is shared between the OSPF routers and the DR/BDR on a segment.

EXAM TIP   Be familiar with the four steps a router will go through to share routes with a DR/BDR. Also remember that OSPF routers share information about their connected routes with the DR/BDR, which includes the link state type, the ID of the advertising router, the cost of the advertised link, and the sequence number of the link.

OSPF uses incremental updates after entering a full state. This means that whenever a change takes place, only the change is shared with the DR, which will then share this information with other routers on the segment. Figure 12-3 shows an example of this. In this example, Network Z, connected to router C, goes down. Router C sends a multicast to the DR and the BDR (with a destination multicast address of 224.0.0.6), telling them about this change. Once the DR and the BDR incorporate the change internally, the DR then tells the other routers on the segment (via a multicast message sent to 224.0.0.5, which is all OSPF routers) about the change concerning Network Z. Any router receiving the update will then share this update to the DRs of other segments to which they are connected.

Note that the communications between OSPF routers is connection-oriented, even though multicasts are used. For example, if a router tells a DR about a change, the DR acknowledges this new piece of information with the source of the communication. Likewise, when the DR shares this information with the other routers on the segment, the DR expects acknowledgments from each of these neighbors. Remember that when an OSPF router exchanges updates with another, the process requires an acknowledgment: this ensures that a router or routers have received the update.

The exception to the incremental update process is that the DR floods its database every 30 minutes to ensure that all of the routers on the segment have the most up-to-date link state information. It does this with a destination address of 224.0.0.5 (all OSPF routers on the segment).

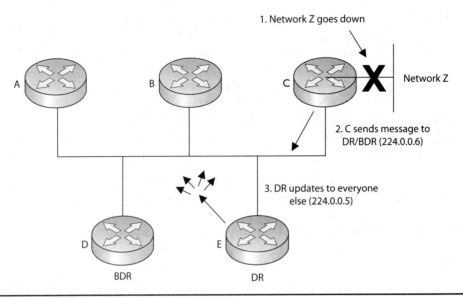

Figure 12-3 LSA update process

Each LSA message has a type associated with it. This book focuses on the following three, which are all found within a single area:

- **LSA Type 1 (Router LSA)** These are generated by every router for each link that belongs to an area. They are flooded only inside of the area to which they belong. The Link ID of this LSA is the Router ID of the router that generated it.

- **LSA Type 2 (Network LSA)** These are generated by the DR and describe the routers that are connected to that segment. They are sent inside the area for which the network segment belongs. The Link ID is the interface IP address of the designated router, which describes that particular segment.

- **LSA Type 5 (External LSA)** Autonomous system external LSAs are generated by autonomous system boundary routers (ASBRs) and contain routes to networks that are external to the current AS. The Link ID is a network number advertised in the LSA.

In summary, the first two LSA types represent links within the local area and the last LSA type represents links from a different autonomous system. These LSA types are placed in a local database on the routing device. Other LSA types exist, but they are beyond the scope of this book.

When building the routing table using link state information, an OSPF router can keep up to 16 paths to a single destination in its routing table. The only restriction is that the paths must have the same accumulated cost metric.

EXAM TIP For the CCNA exam remember that a two-way state indicates that two OSPF routers are neighbors. A full state indicates the completion of sharing of links between routers. In order to build and maintain the OSPF database, hello (establish neighbors) and LSA (routing information) messages are used.

OSPF Configuration

Configuring OSPF is slightly different from configuring routing protocols such as RIP. When configuring OSPF, use the following syntax:

```
Router(config)# router ospf process_ID
Router(config-router)# network IP_address wildcard_mask
                       area area_#
```

The **process_ID** is locally significant and is used to differentiate between OSPF processes running on the same router. It can be any number from 1 to 65,535. Your router might be a boundary router between two OSPF autonomous systems, and to differentiate them on your router, you'll give them unique process IDs. Note that these ID numbers do *not* need to match between different routers and they have nothing to do with autonomous system numbers. You would need to use different process numbers if your routing device was connected to two different OSPF networks: you would need a different, locally unique process number for each OSPF network. Each OSPF process will have its own OSPF database identified by the process ID.

EXAM TIP Remember for the Cisco CCNA exam that when configuring the OSPF routing process, you must specify a process ID (identifier). This uniquely identifies an instance of the OSPF database on the router and is only locally significant: it doesn't have to match on each router in the AS. It can be any number from 1 to 65,535.

When configuring OSPF, you specify what interfaces go into an OSPF area by using the **network** command. Different process ID numbers are used to identify different OSPF networks a routing device is connected to. Therefore, for example, the **network 0.0.0.0 255.255.255.255 area 0** command will include all interfaces in area 0. Each OSPF process will have its own OSPF database identified by the process ID.

As you can see in the command for configuring OSPF, the syntax of this command is different from that of RIP's configuration, where you specify only a class address. OSPF is classless. With this configuration command, you can be very specific about what interface belongs to a particular area. The syntax of this command lists an IP address or network number, followed by a *wildcard mask*, which is different from a subnet mask. A wildcard mask tells the router the interesting component of the address—in other words, what part of the address it should match on. This mask is also used with access lists, which are discussed thoroughly in Chapter 17.

A wildcard mask is 32 bits in length. A 0 in a bit position means there must be a match, and a 1 in a bit position means the router doesn't care. Actually, a wildcard mask is an *inverted* subnet mask, with the 1s and 0s switched. Using a wildcard mask, you can be very specific about which interfaces belong to which areas. The last part of the configuration command tells the router to which area these addresses on the router belong.

 EXAM TIP Unlike in RIP, the **network** statement enables you to specify an IP address and a wildcard mask, which is an inverted subnet mask. You must also specify to which area this address or addresses will belong: **network network_# wildcard_mask area area_#**. A trick of converting a subnet mask to a wildcard mask is to subtract the subnet mask from 255.255.255.255; the result will be the corresponding wildcard mask. (You will learn more about access list and how wildcard masks in Chapter 17.) For the exam, you'll need to be able to look at a wildcard mask in an OSPF **network** command and determine which interface or interfaces it includes.

Let's look at some code examples to see how the wildcard mask works. Use the router shown in Figure 12-4 as an illustration.

```
Router(config)# router ospf 1
Router(config-router)# network 10.1.1.1 0.0.0.0 area 0
Router(config-router)# network 10.1.2.1 0.0.0.0 area 0
Router(config-router)# network 172.16.1.1 0.0.0.0 area 0
Router(config-router)# network 172.16.2.1 0.0.0.0 area 0
```

In this example, the interfaces with addresses of 10.1.1.1, 10.1.2.1, 172.16.1.1, and 172.16.2.1 all are associated with area 0. A wildcard mask of 0.0.0.0 says that there must be an exact match against the address on the router's interface in order to place it in area 0.

Here's another example that accomplishes the same thing:

```
Router(config)# router ospf 1
Router(config-router)# network 10.0.0.0 0.255.255.255 area 0
Router(config-router)# network 172.16.0.0 0.0.255.255 area 0
```

In this example, interfaces beginning with an address of 10 or 172.16 are to be included in area 0.

Figure 12-4
OSPF network configuration example

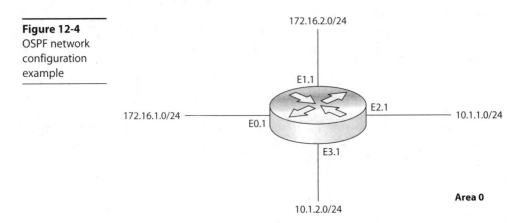

Or, if all the interfaces on your router belonged to the same area, you could use this configuration:

```
Router(config)# router ospf 1
Router(config-router)# network 0.0.0.0 255.255.255.255 area 0
```

In this example, all interfaces are placed in area 0.

As you can see, OSPF is very flexible in enabling you to specify which interface or interfaces will participate in OSPF and to which area they will belong.

VIDEO   12.01. The digital resources that accompany this book contain a multimedia demonstration of configuring OSPF on your routers.

Loopback Interfaces

A *loopback interface* is a logical, virtual interface on a router. By default, the router doesn't have any loopback interfaces, but they can be easily created. All IOS platforms support loopback interfaces, and you can create as many of these interfaces as you need. These interfaces are treated as physical interfaces on a router: you can assign addressing information to them, include their network numbers in routing updates, and even terminate IP connections on them, such as telnet and SSH.

EXAM TIP   For the Cisco CCNA exam, remember the value of a loopback interface. A loopback interface is a logical interface that always remains up. Use the **interface loopback** command to create it.

Here are some reasons you may want to create a loopback interface:

- To assign a router ID to an OSPF router
- To use for testing purposes, since this interface is always up
- To terminate special connections, such as GRE tunnels or IPsec connections, since this interface is always up

TIP   The router ID for OSPF is chosen when the OSPF routing process is started. This occurs when you execute the **router ospf** command manually or when the router's configuration is loaded when booting up. Therefore, if you create a loopback interface *after* enabling OSPF, the loopback won't be used as the router ID; however, if you reboot the router, the loopback interface will be used, by default. Therefore, I recommend that you create your loopback interface and assign an IP address to it first and then enable OSPF to eliminate any confusion about what your router's router ID is.

To create a loopback interface, use the following command:

```
Router(config)# interface loopback port_#
Router(config-if)# ip address IP_address subnet_mask
```

As you can see, creating a loopback interface is easy. You can specify port numbers from 0 to 2147483647. The number you use is only locally significant. Once you enter the loopback interface, you can execute almost any interface command on it; for instance, you can assign it an IP address with the **ip address** command.

Default Route Propagation

On your perimeter OSPF router connected to the ISP, you typically have a default route pointing to the ISP. To take this route and redistribute it into your OSPF process, basically making your perimeter router an ASBR, use the following configuration:

```
Router(config)# ip route 0.0.0.0 0.0.0.0
                         ISP_interface_or_IP_address
Router(config)# router ospf process_ID
Router(config-router)# default-information originate
```

TIP Make sure your default route doesn't point to your internal network, but your ISP's network; otherwise, you'll be creating a routing loop.

OSPF Metric Values

You can affect the cost metric that OSPF uses in picking the best-cost routes for the routing table in two ways. First, remember that the cost metric is the inverse of the accumulated bandwidth values of routers' interfaces. The default measurement that Cisco uses in calculating the cost metric is: cost = 10^8 / (interface bandwidth); 10^8 represents 100 Mbps. You can also affect the value of the cost by changing the 10^8 value with the **auto-cost reference-bandwidth** command.

EXAM TIP For the exam, you'll need to remember the OSPF interface costs in Table 12-1, especially for serial connections.

Table 12-1 contains some default costs for different interface types.

Table 12-1 Default OSPF Costs for Different IOS Interfaces	Cost Value	Interface Type
	1785	56-Kbps serial line
	1652	64-Kbps serial line
	64	T1
	10	Ethernet (10 Mbps)
	1	Fast Ethernet (100 Mbps)
	1	Gigabit Ethernet (1000 Mbps/1 Gbps)
	1	10 Gigabit Ethernet (10 Gbps)
	1	100 Gigabit Ethernet (100 Gbps)

To change the cost of an interface manually, use the following configuration:

```
Router(config)# interface type [slot_#/]port_#
Router(config-if)# ip ospf cost cost_value
```

Notice that the cost is assigned within an interface. This value can range from 1 to 65,535. Note that each vendor might use a different calculation to come up with a cost value.

 CAUTION   It is very important that the costs for a link match for every router on a given segment. Mismatched cost values on a segment can cause routers to run the SPF algorithm continually, greatly affecting the routers' performance.

Normally, you won't be changing the default cost values on an interface. However, since OSPF uses the inverse of bandwidth as a metric, and serial interfaces default to a bandwidth of 1544 Kbps, you will definitely want to match the bandwidth metric on the serial interface to its real clock rate. To configure the bandwidth on your router's interfaces, use the following command:

```
Router(config) interface type [slot_#/]port_#
Router(config-if)# bandwidth speed_in_Kbps
```

As an example, if the clock rate were 64,000, you would use the **bandwidth 64** command to configure the bandwidth correctly. Note that the speed is in *Kbps* for the **bandwidth** command. For example, assume you configured the bandwidth with this: **bandwidth 64000**. The router would assume the bandwidth metric of the interface is 64 Mbps, not Kbps.

By default, the router will place up to 8 equal-cost OSPF paths to a destination in the router's routing table. This can be increased up to 16 equal-cost paths with the following configuration:

```
Router(config)# router ospf process_ID
Router(config-router)# maximum-paths #_of_max_paths
```

 EXAM TIP   For the CCNA remember that the **bandwidth** command should be used on synchronous serial interfaces to match the bandwidth metric to the clocked rate of the interface. Synchronous serial interfaces, no matter what they are clocked at, default to a bandwidth metric of 1544 Kbps. The default number of maximum paths is eight.

OSPF Authentication

OSPF supports authentication of neighbors and routing updates. This is used to prevent rogue OSPF routers from injecting bad or misleading routing information into your topological databases. Authentication can be done with a clear-text password or a digital signature created with the MD5 algorithm. Of the two, the latter is the more secure: clear-text passwords can be seen by an eavesdropper between two OSPF neighbors.

When using MD5, to prevent against a replay attack where the same information is always sent to a neighbor, such as a hello message, a non-decreasing sequence number is included in the message to ensure that the message and the signature are unique. The authentication information is placed in every LSA and validated before being accepted by an OSPF router. To become neighbors, the keying information—clear-text password or key for the MD5 algorithm—must match on the two peers.

 NOTE Remember that if the password/key values on two OSPF neighbors don't match, an adjacency will not occur. Of the two methods, using MD5 is definitely much more secure than a clear-text password.

Configuring authentication is a two-step process: specifying the password/key to use, and enabling authentication. The configuration of the key is done on an interface-by-interface basis, which means that every neighboring OSPF router off of the same interface must use the password/key. Here's the command to configure the password/key value:

```
Router(config)# interface type [slot_#/]port_#
Router(config-if)# ip ospf authentication-key password
```

Starting in Cisco IOS 12.4, any password greater than eight characters is truncated to eight characters by the router. The password is stored in clear text in the router's configuration. To encrypt it, use the **service password-encryption** command, which is discussed in Chapter 17.

Next, you must specify whether the password is sent in clear text or used by MD5 to create a digital signature. This can be done on the interface or on an area-by-area basis. To specify the interface method, use this configuration:

```
Router(config)# interface type [slot_#/]port_#
Router(config-if)# ip ospf authentication [message-digest]
```

If you omit the **message-digest** parameter, the key is sent as a clear-text password.

Your other option is to configure the use of the password/key for an area with which the router is associated:

```
Router(config)# router ospf process_ID
Router(config-router)# area area_# authentication
                        [message-digest]
```

Again, if you omit the **message-digest** parameter, the key is sent as a clear-text password.

Of the two approaches, the latter is the older method: the interface method (former method) was added in IOS 12.0 and is the preferred approach.

OSPF Troubleshooting

Once you have configured OSPF, the following commands are available to view and troubleshoot your OSPF configuration and operation:

- **show ip protocols**
- **show ip route**

- **show ip ospf**
- **show ip ospf database**
- **show ip ospf interface**
- **show ip ospf neighbor**
- **debug ip ospf adj**
- **debug ip ospf events**
- **debug ip ospf packet**

The following sections cover these commands.

The show ip protocols Command

The **show ip protocols** command displays all of the IP routing protocols that you have configured and that are running on your router. Here's an example of this command with OSPF:

```
Router# show ip protocols
Routing Protocol is "ospf 1"
  Outgoing update filter list for all interfaces is not set
 Incoming update filter list for all interfaces is not set
  Router ID 192.168.100.1
  Number of areas in this router is 1. 1 normal 0 stub 0 nssa
  Maximum path: 4
  Routing for Networks:
    0.0.0.0 255.255.255.255 area 0
  Routing Information Sources:
    Gateway          Distance        Last Update
    192.168.1.100        110         00:00:24
    192.168.100.1        110         00:00:24
  Distance: (default is 110)
```

In this example, the router's ID is 192.168.100.1. All interfaces are participating in OSPF (0.0.0.0 255.255.255.255) and are in area 0. There are two OSPF routers in this network: 192.168.1.100 (another router) and 192.168.100.1 (this router). Notice that the default administrative distance is 110.

EXAM TIP   The Cisco CCNA expects you to know the administrative distance of connected routes, static routes, RIP, EIGRP, and OSPF. Remember that the default administrative distance for a connected route is 0; a static route is 1; RIP routes have an administrative distance of 120; EIGRP routes have an administrative distance of 90; and OSPF routes have an administrative distance of 110. Review Chapter 11 for more information on administrative distance.

The show ip route Command

Your router keeps a list of the best IP paths to destinations in a routing table. To view the routing table, use the **show ip route** command:

```
Router# show ip route
Codes: C - connected, S - static, I - IGRP, R - RIP,
       M - mobile, B - BGP, D - EIGRP, EX - EIGRP external,
       O - OSPF, IA - OSPF inter area, N1 - OSPF NSSA
       external type 1, N2 - OSPF NSSA external type 2,
       E1 - OSPF external type 1, E2 - OSPF external type 2,
       E - EGP, i - IS-IS, L1 - IS-IS level-1,
       L2 - IS-IS level-2, * - candidate default,
       U - per-user static route, o - ODR,
       T - traffic engineered route
Gateway of last resort is not set
       10.0.0.0/24 is subnetted, 1 subnets
O        10.0.1.0 [110/65] via 192.168.1.100, 00:04:18, Serial0
C      192.168.1.0/24 is directly connected, Serial0
C      192.168.100.0/24 is directly connected, Ethernet0
```

In this example, there is one OSPF route (**O**): 10.0.1.0. This route has an administrative distance of 110, a metric cost of 65, and can be reached via neighbor 192.168.1.100.

 EXAM TIP   For the CCNA exam, remember that OSPF routes show up as an **O** in the output of the **show ip route** command. Remember the two numbers in brackets ([ ]): administrative distance and cost (when dealing with an OSPF route).

The show ip ospf Command

To view an overview of your router's OSPF configuration, use the **show ip ospf** command:

```
Router# show ip ospf
  Routing Process "ospf 1" with ID 10.1.1.1 and Domain ID 10.1.1.1
  Supports only single TOS(TOS0) routes
  Supports opaque LSA
  SPF schedule delay 5 secs, Hold time between two SPFs 10 secs
  Minimum LSA interval 5 secs. Minimum LSA arrival 1 secs
  LSA group pacing timer 100 secs
  Interface flood pacing timer 55 msecs
  Retransmission pacing timer 100 msecs
  Number of external LSA 0. Checksum Sum 0x0
  Number of opaque AS LSA 0. Checksum Sum 0x0
  Number of DCbitless external and opaque AS LSA 0
  Number of DoNotAge external and opaque AS LSA 0
  Number of areas in this router is 1. 1 normal 0 stub 0 nssa
  External flood list length 0
     Area BACKBONE(0)
         Number of interfaces in this area is 2
         Area has message digest authentication
```

```
SPF algorithm executed 4 times
Area ranges are
Number of LSA 4. Checksum Sum 0x29BEB
Number of opaque link LSA 0. Checksum Sum 0x0
Number of DCbitless LSA 3
Number of indication LSA 0
Number of DoNotAge LSA 0
Flood list length 0
```

This command shows the OSPF timer configurations and other statistics, including the number of times the SPF algorithm is run in an area.

VIDEO 12.02. The digital resources that accompany this book contain a multimedia demonstration of using the **show ip route** and the **show ip ospf** commands.

The show ip ospf database Command

To display lists of information related to the OSPF database for a specific routing device, including the collection of OSPF link states, use the **show ip ospf database** command. Here's an example:

```
Router# show ip ospf database
OSPF Router with ID(192.168.1.11) (Process ID 1)
              Router Link States(Area 0)
 Link ID         ADV Router      Age      Seq#        Checksum Link count
 192.168.1.8     192.168.1.8     1381     0x8000010D   0xEF60   2
 192.168.1.11    192.168.1.11    1460     0x800002FE   0xEB3D   4
 192.168.1.12    192.168.1.12    2027     0x80000090   0x875D   3
 192.168.1.27    192.168.1.27    1323     0x800001D6   0x12CC   3
              Net Link States(Area 0)
 Link ID         ADV Router      Age      Seq#        Checksum
172.16.1.27      192.168.1.27    1323     0x8000005B   0xA8EE
172.17.1.11      192.168.1.11    1461     0x8000005B   0x7AC
```

In the two sections, the Router Link States section indicates the LSA type 1 messages and the Net Link States section indicates the LSA type 2 messages. The Link ID column represents the router ID number. The ADV Router column represents the router ID of the advertising routing device. The Age column represents how old the link state information is. The Seq# column is used to detect old or duplicate LSAs from OSPF neighbors. The Checksum column is the checksum of the update to ensure reliability. The Link count column represents the number of interfaces detected for a routing device.

EXAM TIP For the CCNA exam, remember that the **show ip ospf database** command displays the collection of OSPF links learned from other OSPF routing devices.

The show ip ospf interface Command

On an interface-by-interface basis, your OSPF router keeps track of what area an interface belongs to and what neighbors, if any, are connected to the interface. To view this information, use the **show ip ospf interface** command:

```
Router# show ip ospf interface
Ethernet 1 is up, line protocol is up
Internet Address 172.16.255.1/24, Area 0
Process ID 100, Router ID 172.16.255.1, Network Type BROADCAST, Cost: 10
Transmit Delay is 1 sec, State DROTHER, Priority 1
Designated Router id 172.16.255.11, Interface address 172.16.255.11
Backup Designated router id 172.16.255.10, Interface addr 172.16.255.10
Timer intervals configured, Hello 10, Dead 40, Wait 40, Retransmit 5
Hello due in 0:00:03
Neighbor Count is 3, Adjacent neighbor count is 2
   Adjacent with neighbor 172.16.255.10  (Backup Designated Router)
   Adjacent with neighbor 172.16.255.11  (Designated Router)
```

In this example, the router ID is 172.16.255.1. Its state is DROTHER, which means that it is *not* the DR or BDR. Actually, the DR is 172.16.255.11 and the BDR is 172.16.255.10 (these are their router IDs). Also notice that the hello and dead interval timers are at their default values: 10 and 40 seconds, respectively. A total of three neighbors have two adjacencies—remember that adjacencies are built only between routers and the DR and BDR, not all routers on the segment.

EXAM TIP   The **show ip ospf interface** command displays your router's ID, the ID of the DR and BDR, the hello timer (10 seconds), the dead interval (40 seconds), the number of neighbors, and the number of adjacencies. Remember that the hello and dead interval time values must match to become a neighbor with another OSPF router. Be able to identify the output of this command for the CCNA exam.

The show ip ospf neighbor Command

To see all of your router's OSPF neighbors, use the **show ip ospf neighbor** command:

```
Router# show ip ospf neighbor
   ID            Pri   State         Dead Time   Address         Interface
172.16.255.11    1     FULL/DR        0:00:31     172.16.255.11   Ethernet0
172.16.255.10    1     FULL/BDR       0:00:33     172.16.255.10   Ethernet0
172.16.255.9     1     2WAY/DROTHER   0:00:35     172.16.255.9    Ethernet0
172.16.254.2     1     FULL/DR        0:00:39     172.16.254.2    Serial0.1
```

EXAM TIP   Remember for the CCNA exam that the **show ip ospf neighbor** command lists all of the router's OSPF neighbors, their OSPF states, their router IDs, and which interface the neighbors are connected to.

In this example, three routers are connected to Ethernet0: 172.16.255.11 is a DR, 172.16.255.10 is a BDR, and 172.16.255.9 is another OSPF router (DROTHER). Notice that for the DR and the BDR, the state is *full*, which is to be expected, since this router and the DR/BDR share routing information with each other. The DROTHER router is in a *two-way* state, which indicates that the router is a neighbor, but this router and the DROTHER router will not share routing information directly with each other since the other router is *not* a DR or BDR. Optionally, you can add the ID of the neighbor to the **show ip ospf neighbor** command to get more information about a particular neighbor.

 CAUTION   If the MTU sizes are different on the OSPF routers' interfaces, they will not become neighbors; verify the MTU size on each neighbor with the **show interfaces** or **show ip interfaces** command.

The debug ip ospf adj Command

For more detailed troubleshooting, you can use **debug** commands. If you want to view the adjacency process that a router builds to other routers, use the **debug ip ospf adj** command:

```
Router# debug ip ospf adj
172.16.255.11 on Ethernet0, state 2WAY
OSPF: end of Wait on interface Ethernet0
OSPF: DR/BDR election on Ethernet0
OSPF: Elect BDR 172.16.255.10
OSPF: Elect DR 172.16.255.11
      DR: 172.16.255.11 (Id) BDR: 172.16.255.10 (Id)
OSPF: Send DBD to 172.16.255.11 on Ethernet0
      seq 0x10DB opt 0x2 flag 0x7 len 32
OSPF: Build router LSA for area 0, router ID 172.16.255.11
```

In this example, you can see the election process for the DR and BDR and the sharing of links (DBDs) with the DR.

If two routers have misconfigured the authentication type for OSPF, such as clear-text passwords on one and MD5 on the other, you'll see the following with the previous **debug** command:

```
OSPF: Rcv pkt from 192.168.1.1, Serial1/0:
Mismatch Authentication type. Input packet specified
                     type 0, we use type 1
```

However, if you have mismatched the passwords (keys) on the two OSPF routers, you'll see something like this:

```
OSPF: Rcv pkt from 192.168.1.1, Serial1/0 :
Mismatch Authentication Key - Clear Text
```

The debug ip ospf events Command

If you want to view OSPF events on your router, use the **debug ip ospf events** command:

```
Router# debug ip ospf events
4d02h: OSPF: Rcv hello from 192.168.1.100 area 0 from Serial0 192.168.1.100
4d02h: OSPF: End of hello processing
```

Field Value	Explanation
Aid:	OSPF Area ID number
Auk:	OSPF authentication key used for neighbor authentication
Aut:	Type of OSPF authentication (0–none, 1–simple password, 2–MD5 hashing)
Keyid:	MD5 key value if this authentication mechanism is enabled
L:	Length of the packet
Rid:	OSPF router ID
Seq:	Sequence number
T:	OSPF packet type (1–hello, 2–data description, 3–link state request, 4–link state update, 5–link state acknowledgment)
V:	OSPF version number

Table 12-2 Debug Field Explanations for **debug ip ospf packet** Command

EXAM TIP Make sure you are familiar with these **debug** commands and the reasons that can cause two routers not to become neighbors.

In this example, the router received a hello packet from 192.168.1.00, which is connected to Serial0. You might see the following kinds of information as well:

- Hello intervals that do not match for routers on a segment
- Dead intervals that do not match for routers on a segment
- Mismatched subnet masks for OSPF routers on a segment

The debug ip ospf packet Command

If you want to view OSPF packet contents of LSAs, use the **debug ip ospf packet** command:

```
Router# debug ip ospf packet
4d02h: OSPF: rcv. v:2 t:1 l:48 rid:192.168.1.100
    aid:0.0.0.0 chk:15E4 aut:0 auk: from Serial0
```

Table 12-2 explains the values shown in this command.

Exercise 12-1: Configuring OSPF

The last few sections of this chapter dealt with configuring OSPF on a router. This exercise will help you reinforce your understanding of this material for setting up and troubleshooting OSPF. In this exercise, you'll set OSPF on the two routers (VAN-R1 and LA-R1). Your routers should be configured as shown in the following network diagram:

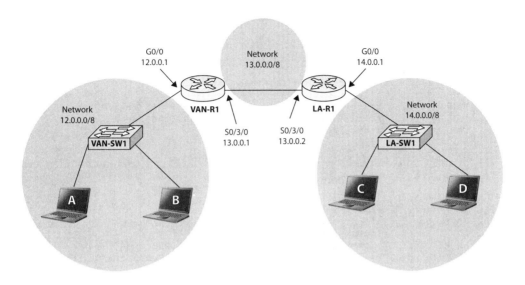

1. Ensure that all devices are connected as per the diagram and powered on, and that IP addresses have been assigned.

2. Go to the CLI of VAN-R1.

3. On the VAN-R1 router, verify that the Gig0/0 and Serial0/3/0 interfaces are up by viewing their statuses.

4. View the routing table on VAN-R1 with the **show ip route** command.

   You should have two connected networks: 12.0.0.0 connected to Gig0/0 and 13.0.0.0 connected to Serial0/3/0.

5. Switch to the CLI of LA-R1 and view the status of the interfaces Gig0/0 and Serial0/3/0. Note the IP addresses of each interface.

6. View the routing table of LA-R1 by using the **show ip route** command.

   You should have two connected networks: 14.0.0.0 connected to Gig0/0 and 13.0.0.0 connected to Serial0/3/0.

7. Test connectivity between ComputerA and VAN-R1 by launching a command prompt on ComputerA and using the **ping 12.0.0.1** command.

   The ping should be successful.

8. Test connectivity between ComputerC and the LA-R1 by launching a command prompt on ComputerC and using the **ping 14.0.0.1** command.

   The ping should be successful.

9. Test connectivity between ComputerA and ComputerC.

   From a command prompt on ComputerA, type **ping 14.0.0.5**. The ping should fail: there is no route from the VAN-R1 to the 14.0.0.0 network.

10. Enable OSPF on the VAN-R1 router, using a process ID of 1, and put all interfaces in area 0 by using the following commands:

```
VAN-R1>enable
VAN-R1#config term
Enter configuration commands, one per line.  End with CNTL/Z.
VAN-R1(config)#router ospf 1
VAN-R1(config-router)#network 12.0.0.0 0.255.255.255 area 0
VAN-R1(config-router)#network 13.0.0.0 0.255.255.255 area 0
VAN-R1(config-router)#end
VAN-R1#
```

11. Enable OSPF on the LA-R1 router, using a process ID of 1, and put all interfaces in area 0 by using the following commands:

```
LA-R1>enable
LA-R1#config term
Enter configuration commands, one per line.  End with CNTL/Z.
LA-R1(config)#router ospf 1
LA-R1(config-router)#network 13.0.0.0 0.255.255.255 area 0
00:17:53: %OSPF-5-ADJCHG: Process 1, Nbr 13.0.0.1 on Serial0/3/0 from
LOADING to FULL, Loading Done
LA-R1(config-router)#network 14.0.0.0 0.255.255.255 area 0
LA-R1(config-router)#end
LA-R1#
%SYS-5-CONFIG_I: Configured from console by console
```

12. On the LA-R1, verify the operation of OSPF by using the following commands:

- Use the **show ip protocols** command to make sure that OSPF is configured and running. Note the following:
  Routing protocol: _____
  Router ID: _____
  Routing for Networks: _____
  Last updates: _____
  Distance: _____

- Use the **show ip route** command and look for the 14.0.0.0 network as an OSPF (**O**) entry in the routing table.

- Use the **show ip ospf neighbor** command to view your neighboring router.

13. Is either router a DR or BDR on the WAN link?

14. On the VAN-R1 router, verify the operation of OSPF by using the following commands.

- Use the **show ip protocols** command to make sure that OSPF is configured and running.

- Use the **show ip route** command and look for the 14.0.0.0 network number as an OSPF (**O**) entry in the routing table.

- Use the **show ip ospf neighbor** command to view your neighboring router.

15. On ComputerA, can you ping ComputerC?

Chapter Review

OSPF is an open-standard routing protocol for IP, which uses cost as a metric. It uses the Dijkstra algorithm (SPF) to provide a loop-free routing topology and uses incremental updates with route summarization support. OSPF is hierarchical, supporting two layers: backbone (area 0) and areas connected to the backbone. Its downside is that OSPF requires more memory and CPU processes than distance vector protocols, and it is more difficult to configure and troubleshoot.

Each OSPF router has a router ID, which is either the highest IP address on a loopback interface or the highest IP address on an active interface. LSAs are used to develop neighbor relationships and are sent as multicasts every 10 seconds. For LAN segments, a DR and a BDR are elected (highest router ID) to disseminate routing information. Routers use 224.0.0.6 to send information to the DR/BDR. OSPF is connection-oriented in that any routing information sent to another router requires a responding ACK. When DRs share routing information to their neighbors, the multicast address used is 224.0.0.5.

Configuring OSPF requires you to specify a process ID, which is locally significant to the router. When configuring the **network** command, you specify an IP address or network number, a wildcard mask (inverted subnet mask), and a number for the area to which the address or network belongs. The **show ip ospf interface** command displays OSPF information about the router's ID, the DR and BDR, and timer information. The **show ip ospf neighbor** command displays your router's neighbors as well as their OSPF states.

Quick Review

OSPF Overview

- OSPF is an open-standard, link state protocol. It's classless and supports hierarchical routing and route summarization. It uses cost as a metric, which is the inverse of the bandwidth of a link.

- OSPF requires more memory and faster processors to handle its additional information.

OSPF Operation

- Each OSPF router has an ID, which is either the highest IP address on a loopback interface, if one exists, or the highest IP address on an active interface.

- Routers use link state advertisements (LSA) to learn the topology of the network. To share information with another router, the routers must be neighbors: their area numbers and types, timers, and passwords must match.

- Designated router (DR) and backup designated router (BDR) assist in sharing topology information. Traffic sent to a DR/BDR pair is multicast to 224.0.0.6. Traffic sent to all routers on a segment has a destination address of 224.0.0.5. Hello messages are sent out every 10 seconds, with a dead interval timer of 40 seconds. The DR sends a periodic update every 30 minutes.

OSPF Configuration

- You must give the OSPF routing process a process ID, which is locally significant to the router. You use a wildcard mask when specifying which interfaces are in which areas and are participating in OSPF: **network *IP_address wildcard_mask* area *area_#*.**

- Loopback interfaces are always active unless manually disabled and are used to give an OSPF router an ID.

- The **bandwidth** command is used to derive a cost value for an interface metric; it should be configured on serial interfaces since the bandwidth defaults to 1544 Kbps on these.

- By default, OSPF load-balances across four equal-cost paths to a destination.

OSPF Troubleshooting

- The administrative distance for OSPF is 110.

- The **show ip ospf interface**, **show ip ospf database**, **show ip ospf neighbor**, **debug ip ospf adj**, and **debug ip ospf events** commands can be used to troubleshoot neighbor relationship problems.

Questions

The following questions will help you measure your understanding of the material presented in this chapter. You are sure to see questions about OSPF on the CCNA certification exam, so read this chapter carefully, perform the exercises, and work through the following review questions.

1. Which of the following is false concerning OSPF?

   A. It provides a loop-free topology.

   B. It is a classful protocol and allows for a hierarchical design.

   C. It requires more memory and processing cycles than distance vector protocols.

   D. It is complex to configure and difficult to troubleshoot.

2. OSPF uses _____ as a metric.

   A. Bandwidth

   B. Delay

   C. Cost

   D. Hop count

3. An OSPF's router ID is based on _____.

   A. The lowest IP address on its loopback interface, if configured, or the lowest IP address on its active interfaces

   B. The highest IP address on its loopback interface, if configured, or the highest IP address on its active interfaces

   C. The highest IP address on its active interfaces, if configured, or the highest IP address on its loopback interfaces

   D. The lowest IP address on its active interfaces, if configured, or the lowest IP address on its loopback interfaces

4. OSPF hellos are sent every _____ seconds on a multi-access medium.

   A. 5

   B. 10

   C. 15

   D. 40

5. Looking at the output of the following command, what would be the OSPF router ID?

```
VAN-R1>show ip interface brief
Interface           IP-Address     OK? Method Status                 Protocol
GigabitEthernet0/0  12.0.0.1       YES manual up                     up
GigabitEthernet0/1  unassigned     YES unset  administratively down  down
GigabitEthernet0/2  unassigned     YES unset  administratively down  down
Serial0/3/0         13.0.0.1       YES manual up                     up
Serial0/3/1         unassigned     YES unset  administratively down  down
Vlan1               unassigned     YES unset  administratively down  down
Loopback1           172.16.0.1     YES manual
```

   A. 172.16.0.1

   B. 1.1.1.1

   C. 12.0.0.1

   D. 13.0.0.1

6. Which of the following is true concerning OSPF?

   A. Setting an interface priority to 0 causes a router to become a DR on that interface.

   B. If the dead interval timer doesn't match between two OSPF routers, they will not become neighbors.

   C. DRs are elected on broadcast, multi-access, and point-to-point segments.

   D. Routers use a multicast address of 224.0.0.5 to send LSAs to the DR/BDR.

7. The OSPF process ID is _____.

   A. Locally significant and is the router ID

   B. Globally significant and must match on every router

   C. Locally significant

   D. An AS number

8. You use the **show ip route** on your router. What does the value of 110 represent on the OSPF route entry?

```
Gateway of last resort is not set
O       12.0.0.0/8 [110/65] via 13.0.0.1, 00:02:07, Serial0/3/0
        13.0.0.0/8 is variably subnetted, 2 subnets, 2 masks
C          13.0.0.0/8 is directly connected, Serial0/3/0
L          13.0.0.2/32 is directly connected, Serial0/3/0
        14.0.0.0/8 is variably subnetted, 2 subnets, 2 masks
C          14.0.0.0/8 is directly connected, GigabitEthernet0/0
L          14.0.0.1/32 is directly connected, GigabitEthernet0/0
```

   A. The router ID

   B. The route cost

   C. The autonomous system number

   D. The administrative distance number

9. You want to change the OSPF priority number on a router's interface. What command would you use?

   A. **if-priority ospf 25**

   B. **ip ospf priority 25**

   C. **ospf priority 25**

   D. **priority 25**

10. Which of the following can you *not* see by issuing the **show ip ospf interface** command?

    A. Process and router ID of you and the neighboring OSPF routers

    B. Hello and dead interval timers

    C. Priority of your router

    D. Cost of the interface

11. Two OSPF routers cannot form a neighbor relationship. Which of the following would not cause this problem?

    A. Hello and dead intervals don't match.

    B. MTU sizes don't match.

    C. Subnet masks don't match.

    D. Router IDs don't match.

Performance-based Questions

1. One of your coworkers is configuring OSPFv2 neighbor adjacencies and is wondering which OSPF parameters must be the same for the neighbor adjacency to work. Place each item on the left into the appropriate category.

Parameters

Router ID

Area ID

Timers

Netmask

IP address

Must have unique value

Must have matching values

2. Looking at the following exhibit, match the command with the definition of what the command does.

Command	Definition
show ip ospf database	Displays all of the IP routing protocols that are configured.
show ip ospf neighbor	Displays the routes in the routing table.
show ip route	Displays the collection of OSPF links learned from other OSPF routing devices.
debug ip ospf packet	Displays the router ID, the ID of the DR and BDR, timer values, the number of neighbors and the number of adjacencies.
show ip ospf interface	Displays all of your router's OSPF neighbors.
show ip protocols	Displays the OSPF packets as they are sent or received.

Answers

1. B. OSPF is a classless, not a classful, protocol.

2. C. OSPF uses cost as a metric.

3. B. An OSPF's router ID is based on the highest IP address on its loopback interface, if configured, or the highest IP address on its active interfaces.

4. B. OSPF hellos are sent every 10 seconds.

5. **A.** The correct answer is 172.16.0.1. If the OSPF router ID has not been explicitly configured, the router ID will be the IP address of the loopback interface with the highest IP assigned. If there are no loopback adapters configured, the router ID will be the highest IP address assigned to an active interface.

6. **B.** The hello and dead interval timers, the area number, the OSPF router, the area type, and the MTU sizes must match on a segment for routers to form a neighbor relationship.

7. **C.** The OSPF process ID is locally significant.

8. **D.** When looking at the routing table after using the **show ip route** command, you will see the administrative distance of a route. OSPF uses an administrative distance of 110.

9. **B.** The OSPF designated router (DR) is determined by the router with the highest interface priority number. You can change the priority number of an interface with the **ip ospf priority <*num*>** command.

10. **A.** By issuing the **show ip ospf interface** command, you can see the router IDs of the other routers off an interface, but not their process IDs, which are locally significant.

11. **D.** Router IDs in an autonomous system (AS) must be unique and cannot match.

Performance-based Answers

1. With this performance-based question, you must identify which OSPF parameters must be unique between OSPF neighbors and which ones must be configured the same on both neighboring devices. Remember that the IP address and router ID must be unique to each device, while the OSPF area ID, timers, and network mask must be configured the same.

Parameters

Must have unique value

| IP address |
| Router ID |

Must have matching value

| Area ID |
| Timers |
| Netmask |

2. On the real exam, you may be asked to drag the command on the left side of the screen to the matching description on the right side of the screen. The following shows the correct answer that matches the command to its definition.

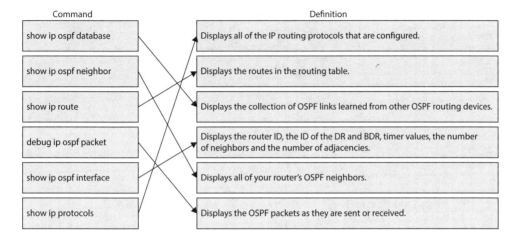

Command	Definition
show ip ospf database	Displays all of the IP routing protocols that are configured.
show ip ospf neighbor	Displays the routes in the routing table.
show ip route	Displays the collection of OSPF links learned from other OSPF routing devices.
debug ip ospf packet	Displays the router ID, the ID of the DR and BDR, timer values, the number of neighbors and the number of adjacencies.
show ip ospf interface	Displays all of your router's OSPF neighbors.
show ip protocols	Displays the OSPF packets as they are sent or received.

CHAPTER 13

IP Services

In this chapter, you will
- Learn how to configure common network services on your Cisco device
- Learn how to configure DHCP services
- Learn how to deploy network address translation on a Cisco router
- Learn how to configure logging and syslog
- Learn to use NetFlow on Cisco devices

Now that you understand how to configure and manage your Cisco routers and switches, it is time to discuss some common IP services that are used on networks and are available with your Cisco device. In this chapter you will learn about common network services such as Dynamic Host Control Protocol (DHCP), Network Address Translation (NAT), and name resolution techniques. You will also learn about monitoring tools such as logging and NetFlow.

Understanding Network Services

Several basic network services are used or provided by Cisco network devices. This section will introduce you to hostname resolution services, Network Time Protocol (NTP), Simple Network Management Protocol (SNMP), File Transfer Protocol (FTP), Trivial File Transfer Protocol (TFTP), telnet, and Secure Shell (SSH).

Hostname Resolution

When entering commands on your Cisco device, you will want to simplify by supplying friendly names to the commands instead of using device IP addresses. Friendly names can be resolved to an IP address in a couple of ways: you can create a hostname table that resolves the names locally on your device, or you can configure your device to query a Domain Name System (DNS) server.

Creating Hostname Tables

To reference the devices on the network by their names, you can create a hostname table of names and matching IP addresses that are local to the device. To create a hostname entry in the hostname table you use the **ip host** *<name>* *<ip_address>* command from Global Configuration mode. For example, if you are connected to VAN-R1 and want to reference LA-R1 by name using ping or telnet, you would use the following commands to configure LA-R1 as a resolvable name:

```
VAN-R1>enable
VAN-R1#config term
VAN-R1(config)#ip host LA-R1 13.0.0.2
```

You can create multiple entries by executing the **ip host** command multiple times with a different name and IP address each time. Once you have created the entries in the table, you can view the entries with the **show hosts** command:

```
VAN-R1(config)#exit
VAN-R1#show hosts
Default Domain is not set
Name/address lookup uses domain service
Name servers are 255.255.255.255
Codes: UN - unknown, EX - expired, OK - OK, ?? - revalidate
       temp - temporary, perm - permanent
       NA - Not Applicable None - Not defined
Host                     Port  Flags      Age Type   Address(es)
LA-R1                    None  (perm, OK)   0  IP        13.0.0.2
```

Notice the LA-R1 entry and the IP address of 13.0.0.2. Also notice that this is a permanent entry with an age of 0 (it will not time out).

After you've created the hostname entry, you can use that hostname with other commands, such as **ping**, **telnet**, or **traceroute**. The following **ping** command uses LA-R1 as a hostname. Notice that the name resolves to the IP address, and then the ping occurs:

```
VAN-R1#ping LA-R1
Type escape sequence to abort.
Sending 5, 100-byte ICMP Echos to 13.0.0.2, timeout is 2 seconds:
!!!!!
Success rate is 100 percent (5/5), round-trip min/avg/max = 1/1/1 ms
```

If you wanted to remove an entry from the hostname table, you would use the **no ip host** command. In our example, this would be **no ip host LA-R1**.

Understanding DNS

Domain Name System is a common network service that enables system names to be translated into their IP addresses; this enables us to communicate using friendly names. DNS is a hierarchy of servers that are designed to resolve *fully qualified domain names* (FQDNs) to IP addresses. For example, looking at Figure 13-1, if you try to connect to my web site at www.gleneclarke.com, your system first sends a query to the DNS server on your network asking for the IP address of www.gleneclarke.com. If your local DNS server does not know the IP address of the site, it then sends the query to the DNS root servers on the Internet. They then forward the request on to the .com name servers, and then on to my DNS server. My DNS server has the IP address of my web site in its database, so my server sends that back to your DNS server in your office. Your DNS server then sends the IP address to your client system that wants to visit the web site.

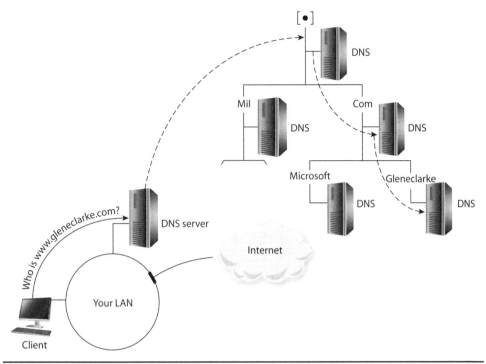

Figure 13-1 DNS resolves FQDNs to IP addresses.

Configure DNS Lookups If you want your Cisco device to perform DNS lookups on entries you type that are not commands, such as server1.gleneclarke.com, you can configure DNS lookups with the **ip domain-lookup** command. DNS lookup is actually enabled by default, but many administrators disable it using the **no ip domain-lookup** command, because if typos appear in a command, the device thinks it is a name and tries to resolve it (which takes extra time).

After ensuring that domain lookups are enabled, you then specify the DNS server where the lookup will be performed using the **ip name-server <*ip_dns_server*>** command. You can also configure the optional setting of the domain name if you like, which is then automatically appended to any hostnames that are used to create an FQDN. The following commands show how to configure DNS lookups:

```
VAN-R1>enable
VAN-R1#config term
VAN-R1(config)#ip domain-lookup
VAN-R1(config)#ip name-server 12.0.0.100
VAN-R1(config)#ip domain-name gleneclarke.com
```

If you want to verify that your device is configured to perform domain lookups, use the **show hosts** command:

```
VAN-R1#show hosts
Default Domain is gleneclarke.com
Name/address lookup uses domain service
Name servers are 12.0.0.100
Codes: UN - unknown, EX - expired, OK - OK, ?? - revalidate
       temp - temporary, perm - permanent
       NA - Not Applicable None - Not defined
Host                    Port  Flags     Age Type  Address(es)
LA-R1                   None  (perm, OK)  0   IP      13.0.0.2
```

Notice in the output that the default domain is applied, name lookups are using domain services, and the name server is 12.0.0.100.

 EXAM TIP For the CCNA exam, remember that you can verify whether DNS lookups are configured on your Cisco device by using the **show hosts** command.

Network Time Protocol

The date and time on your router are important for a multitude of reasons. The two most common ones are

- Logging of messages
- Using digital certificates for authentication

Obviously, having the correct timestamp on a log message will help you in forensics when examining logging messages regarding security. Digital certificates are used for authentication, and one of the components validated on a device's certificate is whether it is current: the certificate includes beginning and ending dates and times. A peer that receives the certificate will compare its current time and make sure that it falls between the beginning and ending dates and times on the certificate.

As you can see, the date and time on your router is also important. You can set the date and time on your device in two ways:

- Manually configure the date and time using the **clock set** command (see Chapter 7)
- Use NTP

NTP is an open standard that enables you to synchronize your router's time with a centralized time server, where your device periodically polls the NTP server for the current date and time. NTP uses the User Datagram Protocol (UDP) on port 123. NTP running on your device can get the correct time from an internal or external server. The reliability of the server refers to the stratum level of the clock source. The most accurate source is an atomic clock, but most networks typically don't need that kind of precision and instead obtain time from a global positioning system (GPS) source. You can also synchronize you devices' times by using global time servers available on the Internet, such as the Google public time service, to synchronize time with Google's atomic clocks. In this case, you can configure the NTP settings on your devices to refer to time.google.com.

NTP has three basic methods of delivering time messages between the time server and the NTP client:

- **Broadcast**   The NTP server periodically announces the time using a broadcast message. This method assumes that all clients are in a local subnet.

- **Multicast**   The NTP server periodically announces the time using a multicast message. In most cases, multicast routing must be set up to disseminate the time across the network. (Note that multicast routing is beyond the scope of this book.)

- **Unicast**   The NTP client periodically (commonly, every 10 minutes) queries the NTP server for the correct time.

 NOTE   Most administrators will implement a multicast solution, because it scales the best: the server sends out only one message, which, if multicast routing is configured correctly, will appear on all network segments that have NTP clients. The unicast approach is commonly used in smaller networks because it is easier to set up. This book will focus only on the NTP unicast method.

Cisco IOS devices support two versions of NTP:

- NTPv3/v4
- SNTP (Simple NTP)

NTPv3/v4 supports MD5 for authentication. A shared key is preconfigured on the time server and your networking device. This key is commonly referred to as a *pre-shared key* (PSK), because it must exist on both devices before it can be used for authentication purposes. The time server hashes the current date and time message with the PSK using MD5 and adds this signature to the time message. Your router repeats this process with the received date and time and its locally configured PSK, and it then compares the two hash values; this is commonly referred to as a *message digest* or *digital signature*, and it verifies that the message is valid (the same key was used).

SNTP, as its name implies, is a simpler method of acquiring time. Unlike NTPv3 or NTPv4, Cisco's IOS implementation of SNTP (as well as that of most vendors) doesn't support authentication of time messages. SNTP is not a focus of Cisco certification exams so we will focus on NTP here.

 NOTE   You should set up your own time server, called a *local master clock* (don't use one on the Internet, however, since it typically won't support authentication of messages), and implement MD5 authentication with NTP. SNTP is a simpler form of NTP that doesn't support any authentication and therefore is not recommended for use in a production network.

NTP is a critical component for network management on networking devices, including logging and authentication functions. NTP ensures that all your devices are synchronized with the same time source. However, NTP doesn't require authentication with a time source. Because of this, a hacker could send NTP packets to your devices, changing their time, and as a result affecting logging and authentication functions. There are three solutions to this problem:

- Use NTP or a virtual private network (VPN) to connect to the time source.
- Use access control lists (ACLs) (discussed in Chapter 17) to filter timing information from only valid time sources.
- Set up your own master time source instead of using an untrusted one on the Internet.

NTP Configuration

IOS devices can be configured as NTP servers and/or clients. They are typically configured as time servers to relay time from a reliable local master clock. This section covers the configuration of an NTP client on a Cisco device.

 NOTE You should not use an IOS device as a local master clock, because IOS doesn't support a method of connecting to an externally reliable time source, such as GPS. However, many operating systems, such as Windows and Linux, support NTP server applications that support external clock connections such as GPS.

Here is the router command to define NTP servers on an IOS device:

```
IOS(config)# ntp server IP_address [version number]
             [key keyid] [source interface] [prefer]
```

You first need to define the IP address of the remote NTP server. If you don't specify the version number for NTP, it defaults to 3 (NTPv3). The optional **key** parameter references authentication information to be used to verify the server's or peer's timing communications: this must match what the server is using when NTPv3 authentication is performed (the use of this parameter is covered in the next paragraph). The **source** parameter specifies what IP address on the IOS device to use as the source address in the IP packet header when sending communications to the remote NTP server (note that you identify the layer 3 interface on the IOS device to reference the IP address to use). If you omit this parameter, it defaults to the address of the outgoing layer 3 interface. When you are entering multiple NTP servers, you can use the **prefer** parameter, which specifies that this NTP server is preferred over other servers for synchronization purposes; otherwise, the first server configured is the first one that the IOS device will query.

You need to configure three commands to set up authentication:

```
IOS(config)# ntp authenticate
IOS(config)# ntp authentication-key key_# md5 key_value
IOS(config)# ntp trusted-key key_#
```

The **ntp authenticate** command enables NTP authentication. The **ntp authentication-key** command defines a reference number for the key (*key_#*) as well as the authentication key. (The same *key_#* and *key_value* must be configured on the remote NTP server.) Last, the **ntp trusted-key** command specifies which NTP devices should be trusted with authentication, which prevents an accidental synchronization to a system that is not trusted. Notice that a reference number is used. This reference number must match that used in the **ntp authentication-key** command. By using a key number, you can create multiple keys, enabling you to update keys more easily and to use different keys for different peers.

Once you have defined authentication, you need to reference the key number in the corresponding **ntp server** command, which tells the IOS device which key to use when sending messages to specific peers.

NTP Verification

Once you have configured NTP on your IOS device, you can use various **show** commands to examine your configuration and troubleshoot problems. To see the current time on the router's software clock, use the **show clock** command.

You'll use two basic commands to examine NTP information:

- **show ntp associations**
- **show ntp status**

The **show ntp associations** command displays associations with the NTP server(s). Here is an example of this command:

```
IOS> show ntp associations
  address        ref clock      st  when  poll  reach  delay  offset  disp
*~192.168.1.11  192.168.1.11   2   31    1024  377    4.1    -8.38   1.5
* master (synced), # master (unsynced), + selected, - candidate,
    ~ configured
```

The first set of leading characters displays synchronization information:

*	This router is synchronized to this peer.
#	This router is almost synchronized to this peer.
+	The peer has been selected for possible synchronization.
-	The peer is a candidate for synchronization.
~	The peer has been statically configured.

Each column contains the following information:

- **address**   Lists the addresses of the NTP peer devices
- **ref clock**   Lists the addresses of where peers in the address column are getting their time
- **st**   Indicates the stratum level of the peer
- **when**   Indicates the time since the last NTP message was received from this peer
- **poll**   Indicates the polling interval, in seconds, that this router is using to contact the specified peer
- **reach**   Indicates the peer's reachability, in octal
- **delay**   Displays the round-trip delay, in milliseconds, to the peer
- **offset**   Displays the relative time of the peer's clock to the local router's clock, in milliseconds
- **disp**   Dispersion is a value reported in seconds. It represents the maximum clock difference ever reported between the server and the local clock.

The **show ntp status** command displays the status of NTP on the router. Here is an example:

```
IOS# show ntp status
Clock is synchronized, stratum 2, reference is 192.168.1.11
nominal freq is 250.0000 Hz, actual freq is 249.9990 Hz, precision is 2**19
reference time is AFE2525E.70597C87 (00:10:39.511 EDT Thu Jan 1 2004)
clock offset is 6.21 msec, root delay is 83.98 msec
root dispersion is 81.96 msec, peer dispersion is 2.02 msec
```

In this example, IOS is synchronized to the NTP server at 192.168.1.11, which provides a stratum level 2 service.

NTP Configuration Example

Now that you have a basic understanding of NTP and its configuration, let's look at a simple example where a perimeter router needs to synchronize its time to an NTP server, shown in Figure 13-2. Here's the router's NTP client configuration:

```
Router(config)# ntp server 192.168.1.11 key 99 source ethernet0
Router(config)# ntp authenticate
Router(config)# ntp authentication-key 99 md5 55ab8972G
Router(config)# ntp trusted-key 99
Router(config)# interface ethernet1
Router(config-if)# ntp disable
Router(config)# interface ethernet2
Router(config-if)# ntp disable
```

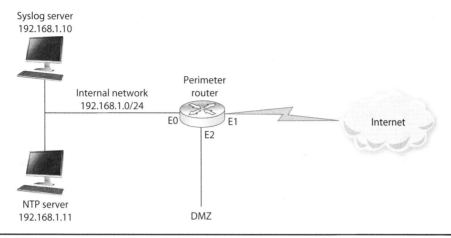

Figure 13-2 NTP configuration example

In this example, the NTP server is 192.168.1.11, which is specified in the first command. The next three commands set up authentication, and refer back to the first command with the key reference number of 99. Notice that the hash key is 55ab8972G, which must *also* be configured on the NTP server. Last, NTP is disabled on two interfaces that it doesn't expect to receive time messages from. As you can see, setting up NTP is straightforward.

 VIDEO   13.01. The digital resources that accompany this book contain a multimedia demonstration of configuring and verifying NTP on a Cisco router.

Simple Network Management Protocol

Some management of network devices requires the use of SNMP, which is commonly used to manage (configure and/or monitor) a remote networking device. The following sections briefly provide an overview of SNMP and its configuration.

SNMP Overview

SNMP comprises three components:

- **Network management station (NMS)**   This device accesses and manages agents and is sometimes referred to as the *manager*.
- **Agent**   This is a device managed by an NMS.
- **Management information base (MIB)**   This database defines how information (configuration, operational, and statistical) is stored on an agent.

The interaction is between the NMS and the agent, which can involve two types of connections:

- NMS sends **get** or **set** commands to the agent; **get** commands are used for retrieving MIB information, and **set** commands are used to change MIB information.
- The agent sends *traps*, or *informs*, to the NMS, which are a form of log message, indicating an important condition on the device.

Information stored on an agent is located in an MIB. Each MIB is uniquely identified with an object identifier (OID). Get, send, and trap messages are based on the MIB information identified by a particular OID.

EXAM TIP Be familiar with the three components of SNMP: manager, agent, and MIB. Understand what an SNMP trap/inform is: an alert generated by an agent.

SNMP Versions

There are three main versions of SNMP. SNMPv1 and v2 use community strings for security: read-only and read-write. The read-only community string is used to restrict the reading of MIB information, and the read-write community string is used to change MIB information. The main problem with community strings, however, is that they are sent in clear text and are thus susceptible to eavesdropping attacks. SNMPv2c also added the support of inform requests, which allows for acknowledged notifications, and get bulk requests, which enables a management station to access multiple MIBs in one request.

SNMPv3 is an enhancement of SNMPv2. In addition to supporting the same MIB structure and gets, sets, and traps, SNMPv3 supports authentication, message integrity, and payload encryption. Message integrity is used to ensure that SNMP messages have not been tampered with and are coming from a legitimate source; this is accomplished with the MD5 or Secure Hashing Algorithm v1 (SHA-1) hashed message authentication code (HMAC) functions. Payload encryption is used so that a man-in-the-middle (MITM) attack cannot examine the get, set, and trap command information. In an MITM attack, an attacker's device sees traffic flowing between the source and destination. Encryption can be used to defeat MITM attacks: the attacker can still see the packets, but the content is encrypted from eavesdropping. Encryption is accomplished with the Data Encryption Algorithm (DES), Triple DES (3DES), or Advanced Encryption Standard (AES) encryption algorithms. For more information on security and securing Cisco devices, check out Chapters 16 and 17.

EXAM TIP Be familiar with the differences between SNMPv2c and SNMPv3. SNMPv2c uses community strings and adds the use of the inform and get bulk requests. SNMPv3 adds message integrity, authentication, and encryption.

SNMP Version	Level	Authentication	Encryption	What Happens
1	**NoAuthNoPriv**	Community string	No	Authenticates with a community string match.
2c	**NoAuthNoPriv**	Community string	No	Authenticates with a community string match.
3	**NoAuthNoPriv**	Username	No	Authenticates with a username.
3	**AuthNoPriv**	MD5 or SHA	No	Provides MD5/SHA for authentication.
3	**AuthPriv**	MD5 or SHA	DES, 3DES, AES	Provides MD5/SHA for authentication and encryption via DES/3DES/AES.

Table 13-1   SNMP Security Models

Table 13-1 provides an overview of the security models and levels for the different SNMP versions.

SNMP Configuration

This section briefly introduces you to the configuration of SNMPv2c and SNMPv3 on IOS devices. Of the two, configuring SNMPv2c is simpler, but less secure. With either version, the following commands define the location and contact information of the SNMP device:

```
IOS(config)# snmp-server location location_information
IOS(config)# snmp-server contact contact_name
```

The first command identifies the location of the device, such as the building, floor, and wiring closet in which the Cisco device resides. The second command identifies the administrator contact information. Both of these can be pulled from the NMS.

SNMPv2c Configuration   Here are the basic commands to set up SNMPv2c communications:

```
IOS(config)# snmp-server community string ro
IOS(config)# snmp-server community string rw
IOS(config)# snmp-server host NMS_IP_address traps string
IOS(config)# snmp-server enable traps
```

The first command defines the community string used to enable read-only access. The second command defines the community string for read-write access. Note that the community string is sent, in clear text, in the SNMP packet to restrict access. The last two commands enable the sending of SNMP traps to an SNMP management station (you also have to match the community string on the IOS device to what the NMS has configured).

SNMPv3 Configuration   The configuration of SNMPv3 is much more complicated. Here's a list of commands involved in its setup:

```
IOS(config)# snmp-server view view_name oid_mib
             {included | excluded}
IOS(config)# snmp-server group group_name {v1 | v2c | v3}
             {auth | noauth | priv} [read read_view]
             [write write_view] [notify notify_view]
             [access-list ACL_ID]
IOS(config)# snmp-server user user_name group_name {v1 | v2c | v3}
             [auth {md5 | sha} auth_password] [priv {des |
             3des | aes {128 | 192 | 256}} encr_password]
             [access ACL_ID]
IOS(config)# snmp-server host host_name_or_IP [traps | informs]
             [version {1 | 2c | 3} [auth user_name]
IOS(config)# snmp-server enable traps
```

SNMP views (**snmp-server view**) control which OIDs can or can't be accessed. Using views is optional, but by default there's no restriction to accessing the OIDs if you have SNMP access to the IOS device.

Groups (**snmp-server group**) define the level of access. With groups, you can specify which version of SNMP is used, the required authentication type, which views can be accessed via gets, sets, and traps, and which NMS can access them (via an ACL, discussed in Chapter 17).

Users define the actual NMS. The authentication credentials define the HMAC signature function and key used to create signatures, and the privilege credentials define the encryption algorithm and key to use.

Here's a simple SNMPv3 configuration example:

```
IOS(config)# access-list 10 permit host 10.0.1.12
IOS(config)# snmp-server view myview interfaces included
IOS(config)# snmp-server group mygroup v3 priv read myview access 10
IOS(config)# snmp-server user myuser mygroup v3 auth sha a3fh95t11a
     priv aes 128 dkfjiewokd892a
IOS(config)# snmp-server host 10.0.1.12 traps version 3 auth myuser
IOS(config)# snmp-server enable traps
```

In this example, an SNMP view was created that includes the "interfaces" MIB/OID. An SNMP group for v3 was created, limiting the view to read access. The group references the view and the ACL to restrict SNMPv3 access. The SNMP user specifies the access credentials (protection) and references the group to use. The SNMP server is defined with traps being sent to the server, and the SNMP user configuration is referenced so the router knows the access method to enforce. Finally, SNMP traps are enabled so the router can send events to the SNMP management station.

Other Network Services

The Cisco CCNA exam expects you to be familiar with other network services, such as services used to transfer files and services used for remote administration. These topics were discussed in detail in Chapter 8, but let's review these network services now.

TFTP and FTP

Cisco administrators can use TFTP or FTP services to transfer files to and from their Cisco devices. Both TFTP and FTP are file transfer protocols with a few differences:

- TFTP does not support authentication, while FTP does.
- TFTP uses UDP, while FTP is TCP based.
- TFTP runs on UDP port 69 by default, while FTP uses TCP port 21 by default.

Cisco administrators typically use TFTP to back up their device configuration and their IOS. The **copy** command in Cisco supports TFTP as both a source and a destination, so you can copy to the TFTP server or copy from the TFTP server. For example, to back up your IOS to the TFTP server, you can use the **copy flash: tftp:** command and answer the questions, such as what is the filename to copy, what is the IP address of the remote host (the TFTP server), and what is the filename to be created at the destination.

You can also use FTP to back up files from the Cisco device. As you learned in Chapter 8, a bit more configuration is needed to use FTP, such as the username and password that needs to be configured before using the FTP feature.

NOTE Be sure to review the commands in Chapter 8 for FTP and TFTP.

Telnet and SSH

Cisco administrators will want to administer their devices remotely either by using telnet as the protocol or using SSH. Again, this was discussed in Chapter 8, but let's do a quick review.

Telnet has been a remote administration protocol for many years but has a major drawback in that it is a protocol that sends all data, including username and passwords, in clear text. This means anyone who can intercept the telnet traffic can see what you are doing and also discover your credentials to log on to the device.

This is where SSH comes in. SSH is a protocol that also enables remote administration of your devices, but it encrypts all the traffic from your administration computer to the device you are managing. This means that if someone intercepts the traffic, it is encrypted, so the attacker will not be able to view the details of what you are doing. It is important to note that SSH also encrypts the username and password that is used during logon.

NOTE Review Chapter 8 for more on telnet and SSH.

Exercise 13-1: Configuring Hostname Resolution

In this exercise you will configure hostname tables on VAN-R1 and LA-R1. You will also configure each system for DNS name resolution using a DNS server. The following is our network diagram for this exercise:

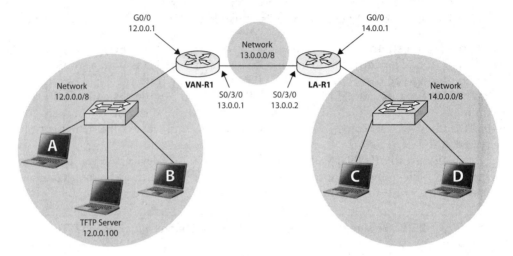

1. Ensure that all physical components such as routers and switches are connected as per the network diagram, and then power on the devices.

2. Connect your workstation to the console port of VAN-R1, then launch PuTTY, choose Serial Connection, and set the correct COM port. Then click Open.

3. In the PuTTY window, press ENTER to get a prompt on your Cisco device.

4. Access VAN-R1's privileged EXEC mode and configure a hostname entry for LA-R1 that references the 13.0.0.2 IP address:

```
VAN-R1>enable
VAN-R1#config term
VAN-R1(config)#ip host LA-R1 13.0.0.2
```

5. View the hostname table with the **show hosts** command.

6. Create a hostname for TFTPServer with the IP address 12.0.0.100.

7. View the hostname table with the **show hosts** command.

8. Ping both names to verify that the hostname table is working.

9. Configure the router for the domain name of exer13-1.loc, and point to the DNS server of 12.0.0.100 for name resolution (we will pretend the TFTP server is a DNS server as well).

```
VAN-R1(config)#ip domain-lookup
VAN-R1(config)#ip name-server 12.0.0.100
VAN-R1(config)#ip domain-name exer13-1.loc
```

10. Go to LA-R1 and create a hostname entry for 13.0.0.1 that refers to VAN-R1.

11. Verify the hostname creation by using the **show hosts** command.

12. Configure LA-R1 for DNS name resolution with the same settings that were applied to VAN-R1.

Configuring DHCP Services

DHCP enables devices to acquire their IP addressing information dynamically, without the administrator needing to configure IP address information on each host on the network. DHCP is built on a client/server model and defines two components:

- **Server**   Delivers IP configuration information to the DHCP client (hosts)
- **Client**   Requests and acquires host configuration information from the DHCP server

Using a DHCP server to assign addressing information provides these three networking advantages over manually configuring addressing information on devices:

- Reduces the amount of time it takes to address a network
- Reduces the likelihood of IP addressing errors on devices
- Provides mobility for employees to move around the network, connect, and obtain the correct IP addressing information based on their location

In this section you will learn to configure two DHCP features on IOS devices:

- DHCP server
- DHCP relay

Understanding DHCP

DHCP is an application-layer protocol that can automatically configure each system on the network with IP address information. Your first step to configuring a DHCP server on your Cisco router is to enable the service; then you can configure a pool. A *pool* is the range of IP addresses that DHCP gives out on the network, as well as any additional settings such as the router address (the *default gateway*), the DNS server, and how long the system is to have the IP address.

As shown in Figure 13-3, a DHCP client goes through four phases to obtain an IP address from the DHCP server:

- **DHCP Discover**   The DHCP discover message is sent by a client to all systems on the network using the destination broadcast address (FF-FF-FF-FF-FF-FF). This message is basically saying, "If you are a DHCP server, I need an IP address." Note that all phases use this broadcast address for communication because the client does not have an IP address yet.

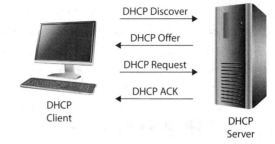

Figure 13-3
Looking at DHCP
phases

- **DHCP Offer**   Any DHCP servers on the network that receive the discover message will send an offer to the client basically stating, "I am a DHCP server and you can have this IP address." If a system is not a DHCP server, it discards the DHCP discover message when it receives it.

- **DHCP Request**   After receiving an offer, the client sends out a DHCP request message stating which offer (IP address) it wants to receive. Keep in mind that the client may receive many offers, so when the client sends out the DHCP request message confirming which offer it is taking, all other DHCP servers retract their offers.

- **DHCP Acknowledgment (ACK)**   After the DHCP server receives the DHCP request message from the client requesting to have the IP address that was offered, the DHCP server sends a final acknowledgment message indicating to the client that the address is now that server's address and indicating how long the server will have the address (*lease time*). The DHCP acknowledgment message also contains any additional IP address options for the client, such as the router address and the DNS server address.

When configuring DHCP, you will need to create a DHCP *scope*, which is a group of addresses, known as a *pool*, that the DHCP server is allowed to give out to clients. When configuring the scope, you also specify the DHCP *lease time*, or how long a client is to have the IP address assigned to it. Configuring shorter lease times such as one day means that more traffic is generated, because the client needs to renew the address sooner than it would if the lease time were set to seven days, for example.

 EXAM TIP   Make sure that you know the four phases of DHCP for the Cisco CCT and CCNA exams.

DHCP Server Configuration

The following shows the more common commands used to configure a DHCP server on a Cisco IOS device:

```
IOS(config)# service dhcp
IOS(config)# ip dhcp pool pool_name
IOS(dhcp-config)# network network_number [mask | /prefix-length]
IOS(dhcp-config)# domain-name domain
IOS(dhcp-config)# dns-server address [address2... address8]
```

```
IOS(dhcp-config)# default-router address
IOS(dhcp-config)# lease {days [hours] [minutes] | infinite}
IOS(dhcp-config)# exit
IOS(config)# ip dhcp excluded-address low-address [high-address]
```

In the example,

- **service dhcp** Enables the DHCP server and/or relay features on your IOS device. Without this command, the IOS device will not act as a server or relay agent. As of IOS 12.2, this command is enabled by default.

- **ip dhcp pool** Creates a name for the DHCP server address pool and places you in DHCP pool subcommand mode.

- **network** Specifies the subnet network number and mask of the DHCP address pool. Also, *prefix-length* specifies the number of bits that make up the address prefix. The prefix is an alternative way of specifying the network mask of the client. The prefix length must be preceded by a forward slash (/).

- **domain-name** Specifies the domain name to be assigned to the client.

- **dns-server** Specifies the IP address of a DNS server that is available to a DHCP client. One IP address is required; however, you can specify up to eight IP addresses in one command line.

- **default-router** Specifies the IP address of the default gateway to be assigned to the DHCP client.

- **lease** Specifies the duration of the lease. IP addresses are leased to hosts, typically on a temporary basis. When a client's address lease time reaches half the life of the lease, it will attempt to renew the existing addressing information it obtained previously. If unsuccessful in its renewal attempt, the device will continue to attempt renewal at periodic intervals. The default lease duration is one day, but other parameters can be configured for the pool, such as an TFTP server address for VoIP phones, but this is beyond the scope of this book. You can set the lease to infinite, which would mean the lease does not expire.

 EXAM TIP For the Cisco CCT and CCNA exams, know that a DHCP server assigns IP address settings to a requesting host. The CCNA exam expects you to know how to configure DHCP—on Cisco IOS DHCP servers, addresses are defined in a pool. If you are defining network numbers for your pool, be sure to exclude the network number and the directed broadcast address from the pool. IP addresses are leased to hosts, and when a client's lease time reaches half the lease length, it will attempt to renew the existing address information.

- **ip dhcp excluded-address** Specifies the IP addresses that the DHCP server should not assign to DHCP clients based on the network numbers you've defined for the DHCP pool or pools. These addresses are already used in the subnet, such as static addresses assigned to the switches and routing device. If you are defining network numbers for your pool, make sure you exclude the network number and the directed broadcast address from the pool. Notice that this command is not part of the pool configuration, but is a Global Configuration command.

NOTE Typically, Cisco routers are configured as DHCP servers for small networks, such as branch offices. In large corporate or campus networks, a dedicated DHCP server or servers are usually set up in the data center and/or distribution layers of the network.

To view the DHCP pool information, use the **show ip dhcp pool** command:

```
IOS# show ip dhcp pool
Pool 1:
 Utilization mark (high/low)    : 85 / 15
 Subnet size (first/next)       : 24 / 24
 Total addresses                : 254
 Leased addresses               : 11
 Pending event                  : none
 1 subnet are currently in the pool :
 Current index        IP address range          Leased addresses
 10.1.1.12            10.1.1.1 - 10.1.1.254     11
```

With this command, you can view the total number of available addresses, the configured address range, and the number of currently leased addresses.

To view the current IP addresses assigned to DHCP clients, use the **show ip dhcp binding** command:

```
IOS# show ip dhcp binding
Bindings from all pools not associated with VRF:
IP address      Client-ID/          Lease expiration      Type
                Hardware address/
                User name
10.1.1.1/24     0063.6973.636f      Mar 29 2014 04:36 AM  Automatic
```

This command lists the IP addresses assigned to the clients: the IP-to-MAC address bindings.

When assigning IP addresses to clients, IOS will first ping the IP address to ensure that it hasn't been assigned to anyone else; additionally, IOS will examine its ARP table to ensure that the IP address isn't in use by any other device. To view these conflicts, use the **show ip dhcp conflict** command:

```
IOS# show ip dhcp conflict
IP address      Detection method     Detection time          VRF
172.16.1.32     Ping                 Feb 16 1998 12:28 PM
172.16.1.64     Gratuitous ARP       Feb 23 1998 08:12 AM
```

If an address conflict is detected, the address is removed from the DHCP pool and an administrator must manually resolve the problem. Use the **clear ip dhcp conflict** command to clear a conflicted address from the list. Optionally, you can use the **debug ip dhcp server** command to troubleshoot problems with the operation of DHCP on an IOS device.

EXAM TIP If an address conflict is detected, the address is removed from the DHCP pool and an administrator must manually resolve the problem. Be familiar with the output of the **show ip dhcp conflict** command.

VIDEO   13.02. The digital resources that accompany this book contain a multimedia demonstration of configuring and verifying a DHCP server on a Cisco router.

DHCP Relay Configuration

In larger networks, networking devices that need addresses via DHCP may not reside on the same broadcast domain as the DHCP server and therefore are unable to reach a DHCP server. In most companies, the DHCP servers are centralized at the distribution layer or in the data center. Therefore, by default, the DHCP servers will not see the DHCP requests that the clients are advertising; routers don't forward broadcast messages to solve this issue.

The solution to this problem is to use the IOS feature *DHCP relay*: the Cisco router acts as a relay agent with the DHCP REQUEST message. The process is shown in Figure 13-4. In the figure, when the router receives the broadcasted addressing request from the client, it changes it to a unicast message, with the router as the source and the DHCP server as the destination. The agent includes the network number to help the DHCP server choose the correct addressing pool. All messages between the agent and the DHCP server are delivered using unicast. From the client's perspective, it thinks it's actually communicating locally with the DHCP server.

To configure the router as a DHCP relay agent, use the following:

```
Router(config)# service dhcp
Router(config)# interface g0/0
Router(config-if)# ip helper-address DHCP_server_IP_address
```

The **service dhcp** command is enabled by default—you need to execute this only if the DHCP service has been manually disabled. You then navigate to the interface you

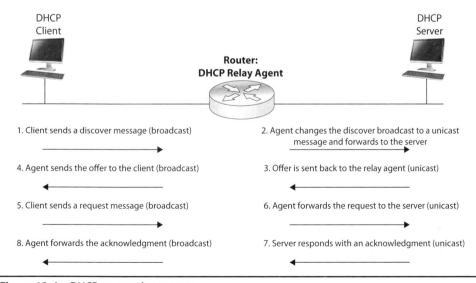

Figure 13-4   DHCP agent relay process

want to configure to listen for DHCP messages. The **ip helper-address** command is used to configure the router as a DHCP relay agent and defines the DHCP server to forward DHCP messages to. You can configure this command multiple times if you have redundant DHCP servers.

If you want to verify that the DHCP relay operation is configured properly and identify the address of the DHCP server that the DHCP messages are forwarded to, you can use the **show ip interface** command:

```
VAN-R1#show ip interface
GigabitEthernet0/0 is up, line protocol is up (connected)
  Internet address is 12.0.0.1/8
  Broadcast address is 255.255.255.255
  Address determined by setup command
  MTU is 1500 bytes
  Helper address is 14.0.0.10
  Directed broadcast forwarding is disabled
(output omitted for briefness)
```

 VIDEO   13.03. The digital resources that accompany this book contain a multimedia demonstration of configuring and verifying DHCP relay on a Cisco router.

Exercise 13-2: Configuring DHCP Services

In this exercise you will configure VAN-R1 as a DHCP server to provide IP addresses of 12.100.0.1 up to 12.100.0.50. We are using the same network topology for this exercise as the last exercise.

1. Ensure that all physical components such as routers and switches are connected as per the network diagram, and then power on the devices.

2. Connect your workstation to the console port of VAN-R1. Then launch PuTTY, choose Serial Connection, and set the correct COM port. Then click Open.

3. In the PuTTY window, press ENTER to get a prompt on your Cisco device.

4. Access VAN-R1's privileged EXEC mode and create a DHCP pool with the following information:

   - Use the name VAN_Pool.

   - Assign the IP addresses of 12.0.0.0 network.

   - Reserve the first 120 of those addresses, because they are already used by devices that needed static addresses.

   - Set the router address to 12.0.0.1.

   - Set the domain name to Exer13-2.loc.

   - Set the DNS server address to 12.0.0.100.

```
VAN-R1>enable
VAN-R1#config term
VAN-R1(config)#ip dhcp pool VAN_Pool
VAN-R1(dhcp-config)#network 12.0.0.0 255.0.0.0
VAN-R1(dhcp-config)#default-router 12.0.0.1
VAN-R1(dhcp-config)#domain-name exer13-2.loc
VAN-R1(dhcp-config)#dns-server 12.0.0.100
VAN-R1(dhcp-config)#exit
VAN-R1(config)#ip dhcp excluded-address 12.0.0.1 12.0.0.120
```

5. Connect a client to the network and verify that it receives an IP address from the router's DHCP service.

6. On VAN-R1 use the **show ip dhcp binding** command to view the addresses that have been given out:

```
VAN-R1#show ip dhcp binding
IP address      Client-ID/           Lease expiration      Type
                Hardware address
12.0.0.121      0030.F2E8.4203       --                    Automatic
VAN-R1#
```

Network Address Translation

Address translation was originally developed to solve two problems: to handle a shortage of IPv4 addresses and to hide network addressing schemes. Most people think that address translation is used primarily to solve the first problem. However, network address translation provides solutions for many problems and has many advantages.

Running Out of Addresses

After the huge Internet explosion during the early and mid-1990s, it was foreseen that the current IP addressing scheme would not accommodate the number of devices that would need public addresses. A long-term solution was conceived to address this; it called for the enhancement of the TCP/IP protocol stack, including the addressing format. This new addressing format is called IPv6. Whereas the current IPv4 addressing scheme uses 32 bits to represent addresses, IPv6 uses 128 bits for addressing, creating billions of extra addresses. IPv6 is discussed in Chapter 14.

Private Addresses

It took a while for IPv6 to become a standard, and on top of this, its adoption early on was quite slow, even with ISPs on the Internet backbone. The main reason that this standard wasn't embraced for a long time is the success of the two short-term solutions to the address shortage problem: schemes to create additional addresses, called *private addresses*, and translation of these addresses to public addresses using address translation.

RFC 1918, by the Internet Engineering Task Force (IETF), is a document that was created to address the shortage of addresses. When devices want to communicate, each device needs a unique IP address. RFC 1918 created a private address space that any company can use internally. Table 13-2 shows the range of private addresses that RFC

Table 13-2	Class	Range of Addresses
RFC 1918 Private Addresses	A	10.0.0.0–10.255.255.255
	B	172.16.0.0–172.31.255.255
	C	192.168.0.0–192.168.255.255

1918 set aside. As you can see from this table, you have 1 Class A, 16 Class B, and 256 Class C addresses at your disposal. Just the single Class A address of 10.0.0.0 has more than 17 million IP addresses, which is more than enough to accommodate your company's needs.

 EXAM TIP Remember the private addresses listed in Table 13-2. Private addresses are a scheme developed by IETF to overcome the limited number of available public IP addresses. However, private addresses cannot be placed in packets that will be routed to a public network; they must be translated first. Translation typically takes place on a perimeter device, such as a router or security appliance (such as the Cisco Adaptive Security Appliance [ASA]).

One of the main issues addressed in RFC 1918 is that private addresses can be used only internally within a company and cannot be used to communicate to devices in a public network, such as the Internet. If you send packets with RFC 1918 addresses in them to your ISP, for instance, your ISP will either filter them or not be able to route this traffic back to your devices. Obviously, this creates a connectivity problem, since many of your devices with private addresses need to send and receive traffic to and from public networks.

Address Translation

A second standard, RFC 1631, was created to solve the connectivity problem of RFC 1918. It defines Network Address Translation (NAT), which enables you to change an IP address in a packet to a different address. When communicating to devices in a public network, your device needs to use a source address that is a public address. Address translation enables you to translate your internal private addresses to public addresses before these packets leave your network.

 NOTE Common devices that can perform address translation include firewalls, routers, and servers. Typically address translation is done at the perimeter of the network by either a router or (more commonly) a firewall.

Actually, RFC 1631 doesn't specify that the address you are changing has to be a private address—it can be *any* address. This is useful if you randomly chose someone else's public address space but still want to connect to the Internet. Obviously, you don't own this address space, but address translation enables you to keep your current addressing scheme and have those source addresses translated to your ISP-assigned addresses before your packets enter the Internet.

Here are some common reasons for using address translation:

- You have to use private addressing because your ISP didn't assign you enough public IPv4 addresses.

- You are using public addresses but have changed ISPs, and your new ISP won't support these public addresses.

- You are merging two companies and they are using the same address space—for instance, 10.0.0.0—which creates routing and reachability issues.

- You want to assign the same IP address to multiple machines so that users on the Internet see this offered service as a single logical computer.

 EXAM TIP   Remember the reasons why you may want to use address translation in your network.

Address Translation Types

Address translation comes in a variety of types, such as NAT, Port Address Translation (PAT), dynamic address translation, and static address translation. Because of the many terms used, the concept of address translation can be confusing, especially because many people use the address translation terms incorrectly. The following sections cover these different types of address translation.

Terms and Definitions

Table 13-3 shows some common terms used in address translation, and Table 13-4 shows some terms used for types of address translation.

Term	Definition
inside	Addresses located inside your network
outside	Addresses located outside your network
local	IP address physically assigned to a device
global	Public IP address physically or logically assigned to a device
inside local IP address	Inside device with an assigned private IP address
inside global IP address	Inside device with a registered public IP address
outside global IP address	Outside device with a registered public IP address
outside local IP address	Outside device with an assigned private IP address

Table 13-3   Common Address Translation Terms

Translation Type	Explanation
simple	One IP address is translated to a different IP address.
extended	One IP address and one TCP/UDP port number are mapped to a different IP address and, possibly, port number.
static	A manual address translation is performed between two addresses and possibly port numbers.
dynamic	An address translation device automatically performs address translation between two addresses and possibly port numbers.
Network Address Translation (NAT)	Only IP addresses are translated (not port numbers).
Port Address Translation (PAT)	Many inside IP addresses are translated to a single IP address, where each inside address is given a different TCP or UDP port number for uniqueness.

Table 13-4 Common Address Translation Types

 EXAM TIP Remember the terms and definitions in Tables 13-3 and 13-4 for the exam.

Implementing NAT

NAT translates one IP address to another. This can be a source address or a destination address. Two basic implementations of NAT can be used: *static* and *dynamic*. The following sections cover the mechanics of these implementations.

Static NAT

With static NAT, a manual translation is performed by an address translation device, translating one IP address to a different one. Typically, static NAT is used to translate destination IP addresses in packets as they come into your network, but it's also used to translate source addresses as they leave your network. Figure 13-5 shows a simple example of outside users trying to access an inside web server. In this example, you want Internet users to access an internal web server, but this server is using a private address (10.1.1.1). If an outside user were to enter this private address in the destination IP address field, that would create a problem, because the user's ISP would drop the packet. Therefore, the web server needs to be presented as having a public address. This is defined in the address translation device (in this case, it is a Cisco router).

In the figure, the web server is assigned an inside global IP address of 200.200.200.1 on the router, and your DNS server advertises this address to outside users. When outside users send packets to the 200.200.200.1 address, the router examines its translation table for a matching entry. In this case, it sees that 200.200.200.1 maps to 10.1.1.1. The router then changes the destination IP address to 10.1.1.1 and forwards the packet to the inside web server. Note that if the router didn't do the translation to 10.1.1.1, the web server wouldn't know this information was meant for itself, since the outside user sent the traffic originally to 200.200.200.1. Likewise, when the web server sends traffic out to

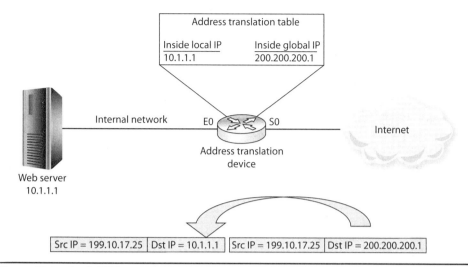

Figure 13-5 Static NAT example

the public network, the router compares the *source* IP address to entries in its translation table, and if it finds a match, it changes the inside local IP address (private source address, 10.1.1.1) to the inside global IP address (public source address, 200.200.200.1). Static translations are always present in the translation table.

 EXAM TIP Remember that static translation is commonly used to enable connections that initiate from the outside to access inside resources. Static translations are always present in the translation table.

Dynamic NAT

With static address translation, you need to build the translations manually. So if you have 1000 devices, you need to create 1000 static entries in the address translation table, which is a lot of work. Typically, static translation is done for inside resources that outside people want to access. When inside users access outside resources, dynamic translation is typically used. In this situation, the global address assigned to the internal user isn't that important, since outside devices don't directly connect to your internal users—they just return traffic to them that the inside user requested.

With dynamic NAT, you must manually define two sets of addresses on your address translation device: one set defines which inside addresses are allowed to be translated (the local addresses), and the other defines what these addresses are to be translated to (the global addresses). When an inside user sends traffic through the address translation device, say a router, it examines the source IP address and compares it to the internal local address pool. If it finds a match, it determines which inside global address pool it should use for the translation. It then dynamically chooses an address in the global address pool that is not currently assigned to an inside device. The router adds this entry in its address translation table, the packet is translated, and the packet is then sent to the outside world. If no matching entry is found in the local address pool, the address is not translated and is forwarded to the outside world in its original state.

When returning traffic enters your network, the address translation device examines the destination IP address and checks it against the address translation table. Upon finding a matching entry, the address translation device converts the global inside address to the local inside address in the destination IP address field of the packet header and forwards the packet to the inside network.

Dynamic NAT translations are added to the translation table when a source matches the dynamic NAT policy configuration and are removed once an idle timer is reached. All traffic from a source is translated to the same destination, no matter how many connections are opened from the source.

Port Address Translation

One problem with static or dynamic NAT is that it provides only a one-to-one address translation. Therefore, if you have 5000 internal devices with private addresses, and all 5000 devices try to reach the Internet simultaneously, you need 5000 public addresses in your inside global address pool. If you have only 1000 public addresses, only the first 1000 devices are translated and the remaining 4000 won't be able to reach outside destinations. To overcome this problem, you can use *address overloading*. Many other terms are used to describe this process, including Port Address Translation (PAT) and Network Address Port Translation (NAPT).

Dynamic PATs are added to the translation table when a new connection matches the dynamic PAT policy configuration and are removed once an idle timer is reached or the connection ends. For example, with TCP, the connection ends when the FIN and FIN-ACK segment messages are seen, or a hard reset (RST) is performed. Most translation devices are smart enough to use the same PAT address for multiple connections opened to the same destination. For example, if you download a web page from a web server, that typically takes dozens of connections. In this situation, most translation devices, including Cisco IOS devices, will use the same source address for all these translations. This ensures that the destination server is seeing all these connections from the same source.

EXAM TIP　For the exam remember that PAT, or dynamic NAT address overloading, enables you to use the same global IP address for all internal devices, where the source port in a TCP or UDP header is used (possibly changed) to differentiate among the different translated connections. Dynamic NAT with overload is used when more devices need to access the Internet than you have public IP addresses assigned by your ISP.

Same IP Address, Different Port Numbers

With PAT, all devices that go through the address translation device have the same global IP address assigned to them, so the source TCP or UDP port numbers are used to differentiate the different connections. If two devices have the same source port number, the translation device changes one of them to ensure uniqueness. When you look at the translation table in the address translation device, you'll see the following items when PAT is performed on a packet:

- Inside local IP address (original source private IP)
- Inside local port number (original source port number)
- Inside global IP address (translated public source IP)
- Inside global port number (new source port number)
- Outside global IP address (destination public address)
- Outside global port number (destination port number)

One main advantage of NAT over PAT is that NAT will basically work with most types of IP connections. Since PAT relies on port numbers to differentiate connections, PAT works only with TCP and UDP; however, many vendors, including Cisco, also support Internet Control Message Protocol (ICMP) with PAT using a proprietary translation method.

NOTE Most vendors use the sequence number in an ICMP echo message, along with the source address, to uniquely identify a translation for ICMP traffic.

Example Using PAT

Let's take a look at an example using PAT. In Figure 13-6, both PCs execute a telnet to 199.199.199.1, and both of these connections use a source port number of 50,000. When these connections reach the address translation device, the device performs its PAT translation. For the first connection, say PC-A, the source IP address (inside local) is changed to 200.200.200.7 (inside global). Since this is the first connection and the source port is not found in the translation table, the source port number is left as is. When PC-B makes a telnet connection to the remote device, since it is using a source port number (50,000) already in the table for a connection to the telnet server, the address translation device changes it from 50,000 to an unused number in the translation table—here, for example, it's 50,001. Therefore, when traffic is sent from the telnet server to the inside PCs, the address translation device will be able to differentiate the two connections and undo the translation correctly by examining both the destination IP address *and* port number in the telnet reply packets: the destination port of 50,000 will be redirected to PC-A and the destination port of 50,001 will be changed back to 50,000 and redirected to PC-B. In both cases, the destination IP address is also changed to the inside local address of the device to which the packet will be forwarded.

NOTE Note that you don't have to restrict yourself to one type of address translation process. For instance, PAT is typically used for inside-to-outside connections, while static NAT is used for outside-to-inside connections.

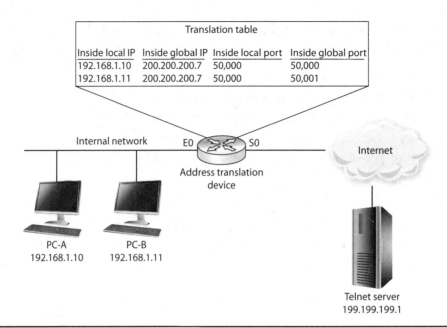

Figure 13-6 PAT example

Port Address Redirection

The previous example showed PAT being carried out dynamically by the address translation device. In some situations, however, this will not work. For instance, your ISP may assign you a single public IP address. You need to use this with PAT to enable inside users to access outside resources. However, you'll have a problem if you want outside users to access an internal service, such as a web server. Dynamic PAT, unfortunately, won't work in this situation.

Another solution to this problem is available: static PAT, often called *port address redirection* (PAR). Let's look at a simple example to illustrate how PAR works. Assume that your ISP has assigned you a single public IP address: 199.199.199.1. You need to use this address for inside users to access the outside world, but you still need the outside world to access an internal web server. With static PAT, you set up your address translation device to look not only at the destination IP address (199.199.199.1), but also at the destination port number (80 for a web server). You create a static PAT entry such that when the address translation device sees this combination of address and port numbers, the device translates it to the inside local IP address and, possibly, the port number used for the service on this inside device.

For example, assume you are given the network shown back in Figure 13-5. In this example, your ISP has assigned you a single IP address, 200.200.200.1, and this address must be configured on your router's S0 interface. This presents a problem in this example, since you have an internal web server that you want external users to access. Port address redirection can be used to overcome this problem. You would set up a static PAT entry on your router that would take TCP traffic sent to 200.200.200.1 on port 80 and redirect it to 10.1.1.1 on port 80. Without PAR, the router would try to process the web connection itself since this IP address is assigned to its own local interface.

 EXAM TIP For the exam, you should remember that port address redirection enables you to redirect application traffic directed to one address to a different address.

Advantages of Address Translation

As mentioned, network address translation devices are typically used to give you an almost inexhaustible number of addresses as well as to hide your internal network addressing scheme. Another advantage of address translation is that if you change ISPs or merge with another company, you can keep your current addressing scheme and make any necessary changes on your address translation device or devices, making your address management easier.

Another big advantage of address translation is that it gives you tighter control over traffic entering and leaving your network. For example, if you are using private addresses internally, all traffic entering and leaving must pass through an address translation device. Because of this restriction, it is much easier to implement your security and business policies.

 EXAM TIP Remember the advantages of network address translation: conservation of public addresses, protection of resources (security) with private addresses from external devices, and no need for readdressing of devices when switching from one ISP to another.

Disadvantages of Address Translation

Even though network address translation solves many problems and has many advantages, it also has its share of disadvantages. Here are three main issues:

- Each connection has an added delay.
- Troubleshooting is more difficult.
- Not all applications work with address translation.

Because address translation changes the contents of packets and, possibly, segment headers, as well as computing any necessary new checksum values, extra processing is required on each packet. This extra processing, obviously, will affect the throughput and speed of your connections. The more packets that pass through your address translation device needing translation, the more likely your users will notice the delay. Therefore, choosing the appropriate product for address translation becomes very important.

 EXAM TIP Remember the disadvantages and limitations of address translation for the exam.

Whenever problems arise with connections involving address translation, it can be difficult to troubleshoot them. It is difficult to track down the real source and destination of a connection—you have to log into your address translation device and look at your translation tables. And if the packet is going through multiple layers of translation, possibly at both the source and destination sites, this can be a hair-pulling experience. Also, even though one of the advantages of address translation is that it hides your internal addressing scheme, it also creates security issues—an external hacker can more easily hide his identity and IP address by sending his packets through a translation device or multiple translation devices.

Probably the most difficult issue with address translation is that not all applications will work with it. For instance, some applications embed IP addressing or port information in the actual data payload (such as FTP), expecting the destination device to use this addressing information in the payload instead of what is in the packet and segment headers. This can pose a problem with address translation, since address translation, by default, doesn't translate data payload information, only header information. Multimedia and NetBIOS applications are notorious for embedding addressing information in data payloads. In some instances, some vendors' address translation devices can detect this process for certain applications and fix it when building the appropriate translation in the translation table. For instance, Cisco routers with the IOS firewall feature set and ASA security appliances support a fix-up process that covers many of these application issues, including embedded addressing information. However, if your product doesn't support this feature, you'll need to disable address translation for the affected devices.

NAT Configuration

As mentioned, NAT can be static or dynamic. The configuration process is similar for both types. Probably the most difficult thing about configuring address translation is understanding the difference between the terms *inside* and *outside*. These terms refer to where your devices are located (inside) and where the external network (the Internet, for instance) is (outside). This is important when it comes to the configuration of address translation. On the IOS device, you must perform two basic configuration steps:

- Define the address translation type (Global Configuration mode commands).
- Define the location of devices (Interface Subconfiguration mode commands).

The following sections cover the configuration of both static and dynamic NAT.

Configuring Static NAT

As mentioned, static NAT is typically used when devices on the outside of your network want to access resources, such as web, DNS, and e-mail servers, on the inside. Here are the two commands used to define the static translations for NAT:

```
Router(config)# ip nat inside source static
                    inside_local_source_IP_address
                    inside_global_source_IP_address
Router(config)# ip nat outside source static
                    outside_global_destination_IP_address
                    outside_local_destination_IP_address
```

The **inside** and **outside** parameters specify the direction in which translation will occur. For instance, the **inside** keyword specifies that the inside source local IP addresses are translated to an inside global IP address when *leaving* the network; and the destination global IP addresses are translated to inside local IP addresses when *entering* your network. The **outside** keyword changes the outside *destination* global IP address to an outside local address (the **ip nat outside source static** command is used when you are connecting two company networks together and their addresses overlap).

 EXAM TIP For the exam, remember how to create a one-to-one static translation with the **ip nat inside source static** and **ip nat outside source static** commands.

After you configure your translations, you must specify which interfaces on your router are considered to be on the inside and which are on the outside with the following configuration:

```
Router(config)# interface type [slot_#/]port_#
Router(config-if)# ip nat {inside | outside}
```

Specify **inside** for interfaces connected to the inside of your network and **outside** for interfaces connected to external networks, such as your ISP.

Let's take a look at a simple static NAT example. I'll use the network shown in Figure 13-7 for this example. In this example, an internal web server (192.168.1.1) will be assigned a global IP address of 200.200.200.1.

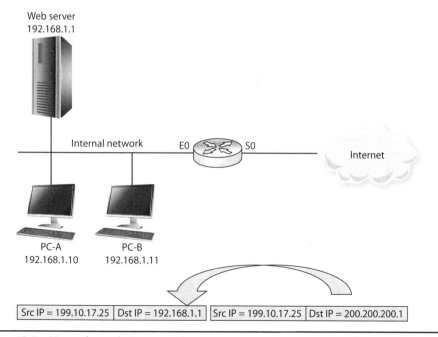

Figure 13-7 Network translation example

Here's the router's configuration to accomplish this static translation:

```
Router(config)# ip nat inside source static
                         192.168.1.1 200.200.200.1
Router(config)# interface ethernet 0
Router(config-if)# ip nat inside
Router(config-if)# exit
Router(config)# interface serial 0
Router(config-if)# ip nat outside
```

The **ip nat inside source static** command defines the translation. The **ip nat inside** and **ip nat outside** commands specify what interfaces are on the inside (E0) and what interfaces are on the outside (S0). Note that any packets that don't match the address translation rule will pass between these two interfaces untranslated. If you want only translated packets to pass between these interfaces, you'll need to configure an appropriate ACL or ACLs.

EXAM TIP Use the **ip nat inside** or **ip nat outside** Interface Subconfiguration mode command to specify which interfaces are considered inside and which are outside.

Configuring Dynamic NAT

When you are configuring dynamic NAT, you'll need to configure three things: what inside addresses are to be translated, what global addresses will be used for the dynamic translation, and what interfaces are involved in the translation. To specify what internal devices will have their source address translated, use the following command:

```
Router(config)# ip nat inside source
                     list standard_IP_ACL_name_or_#
                     pool NAT_pool_name
```

The **ip nat inside source list** command requires you to configure a standard IP ACL that has a list of the inside source addresses that will be translated—any addresses listed with a **permit** statement will be translated, and any addresses listed with a **deny**, or the implicit deny, statement will not be translated. Following this is the name of the address pool: this ties together the address pool you'll use that contains your global source IP addresses.

To create the pool of source inside global IP addresses, use this command:

```
Router(config)# ip nat pool NAT_pool_name
                     beginning_inside_global_IP_address
                     ending_inside_global_IP_address
                     netmask subnet_mask_of_addresses
```

The pool name that you specify references the inside addresses that will be translated from the **ip nat inside source list** command. Next, list the beginning and ending IP addresses in the pool, followed by the subnet mask for the addresses. Once you have done this, the last thing you need to configure is which interfaces are considered to be on the inside and outside of your network. Use the **ip nat inside** and **ip nat outside** Interface Subconfiguration mode commands discussed earlier.

EXAM TIP The **ip nat inside source list** command specifies which internal addresses will be dynamically translated. Remember that translation takes place only when a packet matches a **permit** statement in the ACL: matching a **deny** statement or the implicit deny exempts the packet from translation. The **ip nat pool** command specifies the global addresses to use when performing dynamic translation of local addresses.

Look at the network shown in Figure 13-7 to illustrate how dynamic NAT is configured. In this example, the two PCs will have dynamic NAT performed on them:

```
Router(config)# ip nat inside source list 1 pool nat-pool
Router(config)# access-list 1 permit host 192.168.1.10
Router(config)# access-list 1 permit host 192.168.1.11
Router(config)# ip nat pool nat-pool 200.200.200.2
                         200.200.200.3 netmask 255.255.255.0
Router(config)# interface ethernet 0
Router(config-if)# ip nat inside
Router(config-if)# exit
Router(config)# interface serial 0
Router(config-if)# ip nat outside
```

The **ip nat inside source list** command specifies the inside source IP addresses that will be translated. Notice that these are addresses in ACL 1—192.168.1.10 and 192.168.1.11. They are associated with the global address pool called nat-pool. The **ip nat pool** command specifies the global addresses that the inside source addresses will be translated to. And finally, ethernet 0 is specified as being on the inside and serial 0 is on the outside.

 VIDEO 13.04. The digital resources that accompany this book contain a multimedia demonstration of configuring dynamic NAT on a router.

PAT Configuration

The previous example showed an example of dynamic NAT. This section covers how to configure PAT on your router. This configuration, which is very similar to configuring dynamic NAT, requires three basic translation commands. The first thing you specify is which inside devices will have their source addresses translated. You'll use the same command that you used in dynamic NAT, but you'll add the **overload** parameter to specify that PAT is to be performed:

```
Router(config)# ip nat inside source
                    list standard_IP_ACL_#
                    pool NAT_pool_name overload
```

Next, you specify the global pool to use. Again, you'll use the same command you used in dynamic NAT:

```
Router(config)# ip nat pool NAT_pool_name
                    beginning_inside_global_IP_address
                    ending_inside_global_IP_address
                    netmask subnet_mask_of_addresses
```

You can specify more than one address to use in PAT, or you can specify a single IP address (use the same address for the beginning and ending addresses). And last, you have to tell the IOS which interfaces are inside and outside, respectively, in terms of the **ip nat inside** and **ip nat outside** commands.

Now we'll use Figure 13-7 to see how PAT is configured. In this example, 200.200.200.1 is being used in the static translation for the internal server. Only a single, additional, IP address is placed in the address pool (200.200.200.2) and the address translation is restricted to performing PAT for only two devices: 192.168.1.10 and 192.168.1.11. Here's the configuration:

```
Router(config)# ip nat inside source list 1 pool
                      nat-pool overload
Router(config)# access-list 1 permit host 192.168.1.10
Router(config)# access-list 1 permit host 192.168.1.11
Router(config)# ip nat pool nat-pool 200.200.200.2
                      200.200.200.2
                      netmask 255.255.255.0
Router(config)# interface ethernet 0
Router(config-if)# ip nat inside
Router(config-if)# exit
Router(config)# interface serial 0
Router(config-if)# ip nat outside
```

Address Translation Verification

Once you have configured address translation, you can use many different commands to verify and troubleshoot the operation of address translation on your router. For instance, if you want to see the address translation table on your router, use the **show ip nat translations** command:

```
Router# show ip nat translations
Pro  Inside global   Inside local   Outside local  Outside global
---  200.200.200.1   192.168.1.1    ---            ---
---  200.200.200.2   192.168.1.2    ---            ---
```

In this example, two addresses are being translated: 192.168.1.1 (inside local) to 200.200.200.1 (inside global) and 192.168.1.2 (inside local) to 200.200.200.2 (inside global). Notice that no protocol is listed (Pro) or port numbers, indicating that these are NAT translations, not PAT.

Here's an example of the **show** command with PAT translations in the translation table:

```
Router# show ip nat translations
Pro Inside global      Inside local      Outside local Outside global
tcp 200.200.200.1:1080 192.168.1.1:1080 201.1.1.1:23  201.1.1.1:23
tcp 200.200.200.1:1081 192.168.1.2:1080 201.1.1.1:23  201.1.1.1:23
```

In this example, both 192.168.1.1 and 192.168.1.2 are accessing the same outside device (201.1.1.1) using telnet. Notice that both also use the same source port number (1080 under the Inside local column). The IOS has noticed this and changed the second connection's source port number from 1080 to 1081 to differentiate the two connections.

You can even see address translations statistics on your router with this command:

```
Router# show ip nat statistics
Total translations: 2 (0 static, 2 dynamic; 0 extended)
Outside interfaces: Serial0
Inside interfaces: Ethernet0
Hits: 98 Misses: 4
Expired translations: 1
Dynamic mappings:
-- Inside Source
access-list 1 pool nat-pool refcount 2
pool nat-pool: netmask 255.255.255.255
start 200.200.200.10 end 200.200.200.254
type generic, total addresses 12, allocated 1 (9%), misses 0
```

In this example, there are currently two dynamic translations in the translation table. Hits refers to the number of times the IOS looked into the translation table and found a match (an existing translation that can be used for the packet), while Misses indicates the number of times the IOS looked in the table for a translation, didn't find one, and had to create an entry in the translation table for the packet.

For dynamic entries in the translation table, you can clear all of the entries, or specific entries, using the following commands:

```
Router# clear ip nat translation *
Router# clear ip nat translation inside
                    global_IP_address local_IP_address
Router# clear ip nat translation outside
                    global_IP_address local_IP_address
Router# clear ip nat translation protocol inside
                    global_IP_address global_port
                    local_IP_address local_port
```

The first command clears all dynamic entries in the table. Note that to clear static entries, you need to delete your static NAT configuration commands from within configuration mode.

In addition to **show** commands, you can also use **debug** commands for troubleshooting. The **debug ip nat** command, for instance, will show the translations the IOS is doing on every translated packet. This is useful in determining whether the IOS is translating your packet and segment header addressing information correctly. Please note that on a busy network, this command will require a lot of CPU cycles on your router.

 EXAM TIP   Remember these commands for the exam. Use the **show ip nat translations** command to display the router's translations. Use the **clear ip nat translation** command to clear dynamic translations from the translation table. The **debug ip nat** command shows the router performing address translation in a real-time fashion.

Here's an example of the **debug ip nat** command:

```
Router# debug ip nat
05:32:23: NAT: s=192.168.1.10->200.200.200.2, d=201.1.1.1 [70]
05:32:23: NAT*: s=201.1.1.1, d=200.200.200.2->192.168.1.10 [70]
```

In the first line of this example, an internal machine (192.168.1.10), which is the source address in the packet (s=), is having its address translated to 200.200.200.2 where the packet is being sent to the destination of 201.1.1.1 (d=). The second line shows the returning traffic from 201.1.1.1 and the translation from the global to the local inside address. An asterisk (*) indicates that the packet was fast-switched. The number in the brackets ([ ]) is an identification number of the packet and can be used to correlate this information to packet traces done with an external protocol analyzer or sniffer product.

TIP You can add the **detailed** parameter to the **debug ip nat** command to display a description of each packet that is a candidate for translation, as well as any errors, such as no more addresses in the global pool to assign to an outbound user.

VIDEO 13.05. The digital resources that accompany this book contain a multimedia demonstration how to monitor NAT on a router.

Exercise 13-3: Configuring NAT Overloading

In this exercise you will use a different network topology to practice configuring NAT overloading on your Cisco router. The following network topology is used by this lab exercise:

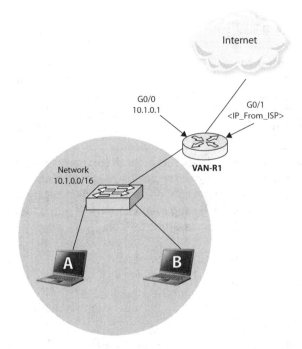

1. Ensure that all physical components such as routers and switches are connected as per the network diagram, and then power on the devices.

2. Connect your workstation to the console port of VAN-R1. Then launch PuTTY, choose Serial Connection, and set the correct COM port. Then click Open.

3. Press ENTER in the PuTTY window to get a prompt on your Cisco device.

4. Configure each of the interfaces on VAN-R1 with the appropriate IP address.

5. Create an access list that includes all of the IP addresses on the 10.1.0.0/16 network that will be permitted to use NAT:

   ```
   VAN-R1(config)#access-list 1 permit 10.1.0.0 0.0.255.255
   ```

6. Enable NAT and apply the access list. Overload the interface connected to the Internet (in this example g0/1):

   ```
   VAN-R1(config)#ip nat inside source list 1 interface g0/1 overload
   ```

7. Configure the inside interface:

   ```
   VAN-R1(config)#interface g0/0
   VAN-R1(config-if)#ip nat inside
   ```

8. Configure the outside interface:

   ```
   VAN-R1(config-if)#interface g0/1
   VAN-R1(config-if)#ip nat outside
   ```

9. Ensure that a client system is using an IP address in the 10.1.0.0/16 network and has 10.1.0.1 set as the default gateway.

10. From the client system enter **ping 8.8.8.8**.

11. To view the translations on VAN-R1, use the **show ip nat translations** command.

Address Translation Troubleshooting

Troubleshooting problems of traffic flowing through a router is not necessarily an easy task. It can become complicated depending on what features you have enabled, as you can see from the preceding two sections. Follow these steps when troubleshooting problems you think are related to address translation:

1. Verify your NAT commands to ensure that your configuration is correct, including the ACL, with the **permit** statements that specify traffic that should be dynamically translated.

2. Check to see whether the router is actually translating the packets for the user with the **show ip nat translations** command.

3. Use the **show ip nat statistics** command to see whether translations are actually occurring—remember that the output is static and you'll need to re-execute it multiple times to update the statistics. For example, by sending five ICMP echoes through the router that match a NAT translation rule, you should see the hit count increment by 5.

4. Use the **debug ip nat [detailed]** command to see if translation is occurring or not; make sure enough addresses are available in a corresponding global NAT pool when performing dynamic NAT.

5. Verify that you have correctly configured the router's interfaces for NAT as inside or outside with the **ip nat inside** or **ip nat outside** Interface Subconfiguration mode command.

6. Use the **show access-lists** command to see if hit counts appear on the **permit** statements for packets that should be translated.

7. Make sure the router can route the packet to the destination by looking at the routing table with **show ip route**.

8. If the packet is being translated, but you are not getting any replies for the user traffic, such as echo replies when using ping, examine any ACLs on the router to make sure that the traffic can get back through the router with the **show access-lists** command: look for incrementing hit counts on **deny** statements.

EXAM TIP   Be comfortable with the troubleshooting steps listed here in troubleshooting address translation problems.

Quality of Service

Networks today require the capabilities to carry different types of traffic, such as regular data, voice, and video, and must somehow ensure that all the data reaches the destination in a timely manner. Network administrators have to ensure that adequate bandwidth is given to critical business applications or applications that require more bandwidth, such as voice and video applications.

Quality of service (QoS) has a set of mechanisms that enable network devices to make decisions related to bandwidth and performance in order to optimize network traffic. In Figure 13-8, you can see a router with three Gigabit interfaces connected to LANs. Let's assume there are many hosts on each of these LANs that need to send lots of traffic out to the Internet on the Fast Ethernet interface. The problem is that you have all this traffic coming from three Gigabit interfaces trying to funnel through the lower bandwidth of the 100 Mbps connection going to the Internet. As the administrator for this network you may need to optimize traffic to ensure that critical application data gets a higher priority over other traffic.

Figure 13-8
QoS scenario

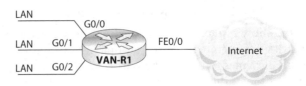

The general idea of QoS is that when a packet is received by a router, or a frame is received by a switch, it can be marked for a particular type of service that is read by networking devices in order to determine the level of priority to give to the packet or frame.

Forwarding Per-Hop Behavior and QoS Terminology

Cisco uses differentiated services, or *DiffServ*, as a tool to achieve QoS on the network. DiffServ as a technology uses *per-hop behavior* (PHB), which is used to determine the priority assigned to a packet when traveling through a router (a hop).

You should be familiar with a number of terms and concepts when discussing DiffServ (and QoS). Let's take a look at the QoS process and terminology.

Classification and Marking

The first step to implementing QoS is that packets or frames must be classified as a particular type of traffic and then marked so that the networking devices can perform QoS actions on those packets. *Classification* of packets is done by the QoS features of a device analyzing the header of the packet to determine the type of traffic it is. For example, QoS can use an ACL to identify packets coming from a specific network as being high priority traffic.

After the packet or frame has been classified, it is then *marked* to achieve a type of service. The packet or frame is marked by adding information to the header of the packet or frame. With IP packets, there is a *Type of Service* (ToS) field in the packet that is marked with a *Differentiated Services Code Point* (DSCP). DSCP codes are used by DiffServ to indicate what type of actions network devices should take with a packet.

Here are some examples of the DiffServ DSCP codes:

- **Expedited Forwarding (EF)** This code is applied to packets that require low latency and low packet loss. For example, voice traffic would use EF and note that IP phones mark their VoIP packets with EF by default.

- **Assured Forwarding (AF)** These codes are used to mark queues for a packet and their drop priority. The format for the code is AF*XY*, where *X* is the queue (1 to 4) for the packet, and *Y* is the drop priority value of 1 to 3.

- **Class Selector (CS)** This field applies the packet to a class. The class is identified with a value of CS*n*, where *n* is a number from 0 to 7.

In a layer 2 frame, a field in the 802.1Q header, the *Class of Service* (CoS) field, is marked by a layer 2 device using trunking to indicate any actions that devices should take with the frame. Note that wireless traffic is layer 2 traffic as well, but it uses a ToS field instead of CoS.

Queuing

When a device needs to deliver a message and the interface is busy, the device will need to place the message in a queue. With QoS, each classification of traffic can be placed into different queues, with a scheduler determining when the traffic in a queue can be forwarded, typically based on priority.

Congestion

QoS offers features that enable you to avoid congestion on a network link. *Congestion* occurs, for example, when traffic coming from three Gigabit interfaces is trying to go out one Fast Ethernet interface at 100 Mbps. To handle congestion on a link, such as a WAN link, you can use priority features and queueing features to ensure that delay-sensitive traffic is handled first on a congested link.

Policies

You can use policies to limit the bit rate of a link—like the way ISPs limit the bit rate of your Internet traffic based on what you paid for. Using policies, you can monitor traffic and compare it against a traffic contract, typically referred to as the *committed information rate* (CIR). When traffic exceeds the contracted bit rate, you can drop the extra traffic. When monitoring the traffic bit rate, you can take a number of actions, such as enabling the packet to continue, dropping the packet, or marking the packet with a different DSCP value.

Shaping

Shaping is a QoS feature that enables administrators to enforce lower bit rates on an interface than what it is capable of handling. Shaping is typically used by ISPs to enforce bandwidth utilized by customers based on their subscription. Shaping can be used by administrators to limit bandwidth used by different departments. Shaping is similar to policies, except with shaping, you typically buffer the over-usage traffic for later delivery instead of dropping it.

Logging and Syslog

An *event* is something that happens (such as someone logging in); an *incident* is an issue with what happened (an unauthorized login access was detected). Logging plays a key role in your management and security solution. Even though SNMP supports traps, the number of traps you can use is limited: logging supports many more types and kinds of messages than SNMP traps.

Logging to a syslog server makes it easier for you to manage and keep a historical record of your logging information from a multitude of devices. Syslog uses UDP and runs on port 514. Unfortunately, all logging information is sent in clear text, it has no packet integrity checking, and it is easy for a hacker to send false data to the syslog server. Therefore, it is highly recommended that you encrypt information between your networking devices and the syslog server and that you set up a filter on the syslog server to accept only logging information from particular IP addresses.

By default, logging messages are sent to the router's console port; however, the following locations are also supported: terminal lines, internal memory buffer, SNMP traps, and a syslog server. Common destinations used by administrators are the logging buffer (RAM), the console terminal, and syslog servers. Syslog is the most common, since it enables you to centralize (aggregate) logging messages easily on a server. The advantage of using syslog is that messages can be stored on a hard drive on the syslog server instead of on the router itself, freeing up router resources. The following sections introduce you to logging as well as how to configure logging from the CLI.

NOTE   Common logging destinations used by administrators are the logging buffer (RAM), the console terminal, and syslog servers. The advantage of using syslog is that messages can be stored on a hard drive on the syslog server instead of on the router itself, freeing up router resources. Even though SNMP supports traps, the number of traps is limited: logging supports many more types and kinds of messages than SNMP traps. Syslog enables you to centralize (aggregate) logging messages easily on a server.

Logging Messages

All of Cisco's log messages can contain the following information:

- **Timestamp**   The date and time of the occurrence (optional)
- **Log message name**   The name of the message
- **Severity level**   The severity level of the log message, embedded in the log name (such as %SYS-5-CONFIG_I, where 5 is the severity level)
- **Message text**   A very brief description of the event

Here's an example of a log message:

```
Nov 19 12:30:00 EST: %SYS-5-CONFIG_I: Configured from
    console by vty0 (10.0.11.11)
```

In this example, the timestamps have been enabled (they are disabled by default). This is followed by the category of logging (SYS indicates a system message), the severity level (5), and the subcategory (CONFIG indicates a change on the router). Last is the message text.

Logging Severity Levels

Table 13-5 summarizes the severity levels of log messages, as well as the importance of the severity levels.

EXAM TIP   Be familiar with these logging level numbers *and* names for the exam. In addition, remember that the logging level indicates any message at that level or higher. For example, if you set the level to 3, messages from levels 1 to 3 would be logged. The default facility level is local7.

Level	Name	Description
0	Emergency	The router is unusable (IOS can't load).
1	Alerts	The router needs immediate attention; for instance, the temperature is too high.
2	Critical	There is a critical condition; for instance, the router is running out of memory.
3	Errors	An error condition exists, such as an invalid memory size.
4	Warnings	A warning condition exists; for instance, a crypto operation failed.
5	Notifications	A normal event occurred; for instance, an interface changed state.
6	Informational	This is an informational message; for instance, a router dropped a packet because of an ACL filter.
7	Debug	This is the output of **debug** commands.

Table 13-5 Logging Levels

Logging Configuration

Here are the basic commands for setting up logging:

```
Router(config)# logging [host] {hostname | IP_address}
Router(config)# logging trap level_name_or_#
Router(config)# logging console level_name_or_#
Router(config)# logging buffered level_name_or_#
Router(config)# logging monitor level_name_or_#
Router(config)# logging facility facility_type
Router(config)# logging source-interface interface_name
Router(config)# logging on
```

Here's a description of each command:

- **logging [host]**   Defines a syslog server to which log messages are sent.
- **logging trap**   Defines the severity level at which to log messages. This command must specify the name or number of the level, as shown in the first two columns of Table 13-5. The level indicates any message at that level or higher. For example, if you set the level to 3, messages from levels 1 to 3 would be logged.
- **logging console**   Defines the logging level for the console line.
- **logging buffered**   Defines the logging level for the log messages stored in the router's RAM.
- **logging monitor**   Defines the logging level for log messages sent to the router's other lines, such as virtual type terminals (VTYs).
- **logging facility**   Directs logging information to the appropriate file on the syslog server. The default is local7, but this can be changed. The facility type enables you to keep different log files for different devices on the same syslog server, making it easier to find log messages.

- **logging source-interface**   Specifies which interface on the router will be used to reach the syslog server. By default, the router will use its routing table to determine what interface, and thus what source IP address to use, when sending a log message. You may want to configure this command if the router can use multiple interfaces to reach the log server, with the possibility that multiple source IP addresses could be used, but the syslog server is allowing log messages only from one of the router's IP addresses.

- **logging on**   You must enable logging with this command. However, this is not necessary for log messages sent to the console, which is enabled by default.

 NOTE   There are many other parameters to the **logging** command, but the ones I've discussed are the most commonly configured parameters.

By default, Cisco IOS devices do not include the local timestamp (date and time) with the syslog messages sent to the syslog server: they rely on the server attaching its time to the message. To have the IOS device include its own local time, configure the following command:

```
Router(config)# service timestamps {log | debug} datetime [msec]
```

You can add timestamps to log messages or the output of **debug** commands. The **msec** parameter specifies that the current millisecond value should be included in the router's timestamped log message.

 EXAM TIP   You'll need to be familiar with the syntax of the **service timestamps** command for the exam.

Logging Verification

Use the **show logging** command to verify your configuration. If logging to the router's RAM (buffered) is enabled, you'll see these log messages at the bottom of the display:

```
Router# show logging
    Syslog logging: enabled (0 messages dropped, 1 messages
                rate-limited, 0 flushes, 0 overruns, xml disabled,
                filtering disabled)
No Active Message Discriminator.
No Inactive Message Discriminator.
    Console logging: level debugging, 32 messages logged, xml
                disabled, filtering disabled
    Monitor logging: level debugging, 0 messages logged, xml
                disabled, filtering disabled
    Buffer logging:  level informational, 2 messages logged,
                xml disabled, filtering disabled
```

```
    Logging Exception size (4096 bytes)
    Count and timestamp logging messages: disabled
    Persistent logging: disabled
No active filter modules.
ESM: 0 messages dropped
    Trap logging: level notifications, 27 message lines logged
        Logging to 10.0.0.1  (udp port 514,  audit disabled,
            authentication disabled, encryption disabled, link up),
            1 message lines logged,
            0 message lines rate-limited,
            0 message lines dropped-by-MD,
            xml disabled, sequence number disabled
            filtering disabled

Log Buffer (51200 bytes):
*Jan 29 16:39:25.991: %SYS-5-CONFIG_I: Configured from console by
    console
*Jan 29 16:39:26.991: %SYS-6-LOGGINGHOST_STARTSTOP: Logging to host
    10.0.0.1 port 514 started - CLI initiated
```

Logging CLI Example

I'll use the network example shown in Figure 13-9 to illustrate how to set up a router to send log messages to a syslog server (10.0.0.1). Here's the configuration:

```
Router(config)# logging 10.0.0.1
Router(config)# logging trap 5
Router(config)# logging source-interface fa0/0
Router(config)# logging on
```

Notice that the router will send log messages only from level 5 and lower and that the router sources log messages from the FA0/0 interface.

 VIDEO 13.06. The digital resources that accompany this book contain a multimedia demonstration of configuring and verifying syslogging on a Cisco router.

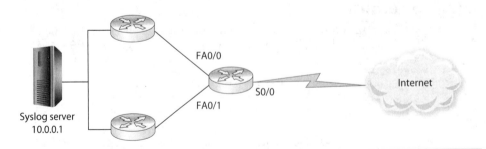

Figure 13-9 Logging example

Working with NetFlow

NetFlow is a Cisco-proprietary technology used to classify and identify traffic and to provide statistics for the traffic. Originally it was meant for QoS and traffic management purposes, but it can be used to detect attacks by looking for anomalies in traffic sessions. Common uses for NetFlow include

- Network traffic accounting
- Usage-based network billing
- Network capacity and planning
- Security
- Denial-of-service (DoS) monitoring capabilities
- Network monitoring and troubleshooting

NOTE NetFlow enables administrators to identify applications causing network congestion, diagnose slow performance, and verify that an application receives the appropriate amount of bandwidth based on its class of service (CoS). Benefits include network, application, and user monitoring, network planning, and accounting/billing.

NetFlow is like a telephone bill: it shows you who (source) is connecting to whom (destination), what application and/or protocol they are using, how long the connection lasted, how much information was transmitted across the connection (source versus destination), and much, much more.

NOTE Cisco relies on the use of NetFlow, but there are other, similar solutions in the marketplace. The open standard sFlow is commonly supported by other vendors.

NetFlow Architecture

A *flow* is basically a session between two devices: the parameters associated with a connection involving information in the layer 3 and layer 4 headers, as well as some other components, to identify a flow. A flow may involve the following:

- Layer 3 protocol
- Source and destination IP addresses
- Source and destination port numbers
- CoS or ToS information
- Input interface name

- Flow timestamp
- Next-hop IP address
- TCP flags

Minimally, a flow must contain a source IP address, a destination IP address, and an ingress interface. Cisco uses application-specific integrated circuits (ASICs) to capture the flow information. The technology used by the ASICs, Cisco Express Forwarding (CEF), implements many features to offload processing of the CPU to an interface or a card. The most common feature of CEF is to offload forwarding of the traffic from the CPU to the ASIC. Another function of CEF is to create flow information for NetFlow. Even though ASICs capture the flow information, the IOS device's CPU must be involved in forwarding the flow information to a NetFlow collector: this can be very CPU-intensive.

Some NetFlow information can be examined locally on the IOS device; however, to gather and examine NetFlow information over long periods of time, you need a NetFlow collector (basically a logging server that understands NetFlow flow information). The following versions are supported by Cisco:

1	Original version of NetFlow
5	The standard and most common implementation
7	Specific to the 6500, 6800, and 7600 products
8	Reduces resource usage (summarized flow information)
9	Flexible file format to support additional fields and use for IPv6, multiprotocol label switching (MPLS), Border Gateway Protocol (BGP), and multicast

The most common implementation of NetFlow is version 5, but the most flexible is version 9. When sending NetFlow information to a collector, you must identify the version used on both the IOS device and collector so that both can understand the flow information. The NetFlow information is sent using UDP as a transport protocol.

Many, many products in the marketplace can perform the function of a NetFlow collector. NetFlow Collector is a Cisco product that provides a GUI to examine flow information and statistics in a visual format, including bar charts, pie charts, and histograms, to name a few. One concern with a collector is the number of devices and amount of flow information the collector will receive: you can quickly overburden a collector if you send too much information to it.

 EXAM TIP Remember for the exam that, minimally, a flow must contain a source IP address, a destination IP address, and an ingress interface. Traffic is considered in the same flow if the packets contain the same IP addressing, port numbers, and layer 3 protocol information. Sending flow information to a collector can be CPU-intensive. One concern with a collector is the number of devices and amount of flow information the collector will receive. Version 5 is the most common implementation of NetFlow.

NetFlow Configuration

To configure NetFlow, you must perform the following four tasks:

1. Enable data capturing on an interface: ingress is incoming and egress is outgoing.

2. Define the IP address and UDP port of the NetFlow collector.

3. Optionally identify the version of NetFlow to export the flow information.

4. Verify the NetFlow configuration, operation, and statistics.

NOTE Even though ASICs capture the flow information using CEF, the flow information must be stored in RAM. IOS enables you to define memory limits for NetFlow if you have limited memory on your IOS device. The default cache size depends on the particular Cisco product and platform.

The following commands show how to enable NetFlow from the CLI and how to export the information to a NetFlow collector:

```
IOS(config)# ip cef
IOS(config)# interface type number
IOS(config-if)# ip flow {ingress | egress}
IOS(config-if)# exit
IOS(config)# ip flow-export version {1 | 5 | 9}
IOS(config)# ip flow-export destination mgmt_IP UDP_port
```

NetFlow versions vary based on device and code. As of IOS 12.4, for example, routers support only versions 1, 5, and 9.

Most Cisco management stations, acting as collectors, listen on UDP port 9997, by default. Flow monitors are NetFlow components that enable you to define global NetFlow parameters, such as the cache size and the number of unique flow records to collect. This configuration is then applied to a respective interface (the configuration of flow monitors is beyond the scope of this book).

TIP Flow monitors are NetFlow components that enable you to define global NetFlow parameters, such as the cache size and the number of unique flow records to collect. This configuration is then applied to a respective interface.

NetFlow Verification

You can use two commands to verify the NetFlow configuration on your IOS device. First, you verify that it is enabled on the respective interface:

```
IOS# show ip interface g1/0/1
.
.
.
 Input features: Ingress-NetFlow, MCI check
 Output features: Egress-NetFlow
```

To verify the NetFlow configuration and get an overall status of the NetFlow operation, use the **show ip flow export** command:

```
Router# show ip flow export
Flow export v5 is enabled for main cache
  Exporting flows to 10.51.12.4 (9991)
  Exporting using source IP address 10.1.97.17
  Version 5 flow records
  11 flows exported in 8 udp datagrams
  0 flows failed due to lack of export packet
  0 export packets were sent up to process level
  .
  .
  .
```

In this example, 11 flows were exported to the NetFlow collector at 10.51.12.4.

To view a summary of the flow information captured by the IOS device, use the **show ip cache flow** command:

```
Router# show ip cache flow
IP packet size distribution (44027 total packets):
 1-32   64   96  128  160  192  224  256  288  320  352  384  416  448
 .119 .800 .000 .000 .000 .000 .000 .000 .000 .000 .000 .000 .000 .000
  480  512  544  576 1024 1536 2048 2560 3072 3584 4096 4608
 .000 .000 .000 .039 .000 .039 .000 .000 .000 .000 .000 .000
IP Flow Switching Cache, 278544 bytes
  51 active, 4045 inactive, 173 added
  84752 ager polls, 0 flow alloc failures
  Active flows timeout in 3 minutes
  Inactive flows timeout in 60 seconds
IP Sub Flow Cache, 25800 bytes
  153 active, 871 inactive, 451 added, 173 added to flow
  0 alloc failures, 0 force free
  1 chunk, 1 chunk added
  last clearing of statistics never
Protocol    Total    Flows   Packets Bytes   Packets Active(Sec) Idle(Sec)
--------    Flows    /Sec     /Flow  /Pkt     /Sec    /Flow       /Flow
TCP-FTP         8    0.0       871    40       3.4    1394.5       0.4
TCP-FTPD        8    0.0       872    40       3.4    1394.9       0.1
TCP-WWW         4    0.0       871    40       1.7    1393.3       1.1
TCP-SMTP        4    0.0       871    40       1.7    1393.3       1.4
TCP-other      16    0.0       871    40       6.8    1393.3       1.1
UDP-other      72    0.0         1    53       0.0       0.0      15.4
ICMP           10    0.0       871   427       4.3    1394.6       0.3
Total:        122    0.0       357   117      21.6     571.3       9.4

SrcIf     SrcIPaddress   DstIf      DstIPaddress    Pr SrcP DstP Pkts
Et0/0.1   192.168.67.6   Et1/0.1*   172.16.10.200   01 0000 0C01    7
Et0/0.1   192.168.67.6   Et1/0.1    172.16.10.200   01 0000 0C01    7
Et0/0.1   172.16.6.1     Null       224.0.0.9       11 0208 0208    1
  .
  .
  .
```

Using this command, you can see which protocols/applications use the highest volume of traffic and between which hosts these sessions occur.

EXAM TIP   For the exam, remember that the **show ip cache flow** command visualizes the general NetFlow data captured by an IOS device.

 VIDEO   13.07. The digital resources that accompany this book contain a multimedia demonstration of configuring and verifying NetFlow on a Cisco router.

Chapter Review

The date and time on your router are important for message logging, digital certificates, and many other things. Common methods of accessing NTP information is via multicast messages from a server or unicast query messages from a client. NTPv3 supports authentication of messages using a digital signature created from MD5. It is recommended that you set up your own local master time source.

Many Cisco IOS devices support DHCP server and relay agent features. When setting up a server, you create a DHCP pool, which has IP addresses, a DNS server(s), a domain name, a default gateway address, and a lease time. An addressing conflict occurs when a server checks to see if an unused address in the pool is being used and determines that it's currently in use by another device. Conflicts must be manually cleared by an administrator on an IOS device. DHCP relay is used when the clients and the DHCP server are in different subnets (VLANs); an IOS device can act as a relay between the two devices, interacting with the DHCP server using unicast messages.

SNMP is used to manage devices remotely. The three components of SNMP are the management station (NMS), the agent, and the MIBs. Get, send, and trap/inform messages are used between the NMS and the agent. SNMPv2c supports community strings for security, which are in clear text. SNMPv3 supports message validation, authentication, and encryption of messages, and is thus more secure than SNMPv2c.

Private addresses are defined in RFC 1918: 10.0.0.0/8, 172.16.0.0/16–172.31.0.0/16, and 192.168.0.0/24–192.168.255.0/24. If you use private addresses, you must have them translated to a public address before packets reach a public network. Address translation is used when you don't have enough public addresses, you change ISPs but keep your existing addresses, you are merging companies with overlapping address spaces, or you want to assign the same IP address to multiple machines.

The term *inside local IP address* refers to packets with a private or original IP address. The term *inside global IP address* refers to packets with a public, or translated, address. NAT translates one IP address to another, while PAT (address overloading) translates many IP addresses to the same global address, where the source port numbers are changed to ensure the translation device can differentiate the connections. PAR redirects traffic destined to a port on one device to a different device.

Address translation provides access to an almost inexhaustible group of addresses and enables you to hide your internal network design from outsiders. It also gives you tighter control over traffic entering and leaving your network. However, address translation adds some delay to your traffic, makes troubleshooting more difficult, and won't work with all applications, especially multimedia applications.

The **ip nat inside source static** command sets up static NAT. The **ip nat inside source list** and **ip nat pool** (add **overload** to do PAT) commands set up dynamic translations. The **ip nat inside | outside** Interface Subconfiguration mode command defines which interfaces are considered internal and external for address translation.

Use the **show ip nat translations** command to view the router's address translation table. The **clear ip nat translation** * command clears all dynamic address translation entries in the router's translation table. The **debug ip nat** command will show the translations the IOS is doing on every translated packet.

Logging is used to record events that occur on a device. Logging information can be viewed locally on a device or forwarded to a syslog server. The logging level of a message indicates its severity, where logging levels range from 0 (emergency) to 7 (debugging). Logging provides much more information than what is available with SNMP traps and informs. By default, logging is enabled for the console of IOS devices, but it must be manually enabled for other destinations. Timestamps for logging and debug messages are disabled by default but can be enabled with the **service timestamps** command.

NetFlow, a proprietary Cisco technology, captures information about flows that can be used for network traffic accounting, accounting/billing based on amount of traffic sent, network capacity planning, network monitoring, and many other network management functions. A flow is basically a session between two devices and must minimally contain a source IP address, a destination IP address, and an ingress interface. Cisco uses ASICs to capture the flow information. Cisco supports multiple versions of NetFlow, where version 5 is the most common. The **show ip cache flow** command displays a summary of the session flows, but to gather information historically, an external NetFlow collector is necessary.

Quick Review

Understanding Network Services

- NTP has three methods of delivering time messages: broadcast, unicast, and multicast.

- NTPv3 supports authentication of messages using MD5 signatures.

- You should set up your own time server, commonly referred to as a local master clock, and implement MD5 authentication with NTPv3—don't use SNTP, because Cisco doesn't support authentication with it.

- The three components of SNMP are a manager, an agent, and MIBs.

- An SNMP trap/inform is an alert generated by an agent.

- SNMPv2c uses community strings and added the use of inform and get bulk requests. SNMPv3 adds message integrity, authentication, and encryption.

Configuring DHCP Services

- A DHCP server assigns IP address parameters to a requesting host. On Cisco IOS DHCP servers, addresses are defined in a pool.

- If you are defining network numbers for your pool, make sure you exclude the network number and the directed broadcast address from the pool.

- IP addresses are leased to hosts, typically on a temporary basis. When a client's current address lifetime reaches the half-life of the lease time, it will attempt to renew the existing addressing information it obtained previously.

- If an address conflict is detected, the address is removed from the DHCP pool and an administrator must manually resolve the problem. Conflicts can be seen by executing the **show ip dhcp conflict** command.

Network Address Translation

- Reasons to use address translation include not having enough public addresses, changing ISPs, merging networks with overlapping addresses, and representing multiple devices as a single logical device.

- An inside local IP address is a private address assigned to an inside device. An inside global IP address is a public address associated with an inside device.

- NAT does a one-to-one address translation. PAT translates multiple IP addresses to a single address, using the source TCP/UDP port number to differentiate connections.

- Port address redirection is a form of static PAT, where traffic sent to a specific address and port is redirected to another machine (and possibly a different port).

- To define inside and outside, use the **ip nat inside | outside** Interface Subconfiguration mode command.

- To configure static NAT, use the **ip nat inside | outside source static** command.

- To set up dynamic NAT, use the **ip nat inside source list** command, with a standard ACL specifying the inside local addresses. Add **overload** to this command to do PAT. Use the **ip nat pool** command to specify the global addresses.

- Use the **show ip nat translations** command to view the static and dynamic address translations. Use the **clear ip nat translation** * command to clear the dynamic translations from the address translation table. Use **debug ip nat** to see the actual translation process.

- When troubleshooting address translation problems, first verify your address translation configuration. Examine the translation table with the **show ip nat translations** command. Use the **show ip nat statistics** command to see whether translations are actually occurring.

- Use the **debug ip nat [detailed]** command to see whether translation is occurring or not. Verify that you have correctly configured the router's interfaces for NAT as inside or outside. Use the **show access-lists** command to see whether hit counts appear on the permit statements for packets that should be translated.

Logging and Syslog

- Common logging destinations used by administrators are the logging buffer (RAM), the console terminal, and syslog servers. The advantage of using syslog is that messages can be stored on a hard drive on the syslog server instead of on the router itself, freeing up router resources. Syslog enables you to centralize (aggregate) logging messages easily on a server.

- Even though SNMP supports traps, the number of traps is limited: logging supports many more types and kinds of messages than are supported by SNMP traps.

- Logging levels are emergency (0), alerts (1), critical (2), errors (3), warnings (4), notifications (5), informational (6), and debug (7). The logging level indicates any message at that level or higher. For example, if you set the level to 3, messages from levels 1 to 3 would be logged.

- The default facility level is local7.

- The **service timestamps** commands enable the addition of the local date, time, and, optionally, milliseconds to the logging or debug records.

Working with NetFlow

- NetFlow enables administrators to identify applications causing network congestion, diagnose slow performance, and verify that an application receives the appropriate amount of bandwidth based on its class of service (CoS).

- NetFlow benefits include network, application, and user monitoring; network planning; and accounting/billing.

- Minimally, a flow must contain a source IP address, a destination IP address, and an ingress interface. Traffic is considered in the same flow if the packets contain the same IP addressing, port numbers, and layer 3 protocol information.

- Sending flow information to a collector can be CPU-intensive.

- One concern with a collector is the number of devices and amount of flow information the collector will receive.

- Flow monitors are NetFlow components that enable you to globally define NetFlow parameters, such as the cache size and the number of unique flow records to collect, which are then applied to a respective interface.

- The **show ip cache flow** command displays the general NetFlow data captured by an IOS device.

Questions

The following questions will help you measure your understanding of the material presented in this chapter. Read all the choices carefully because there may be more than one correct answer. Choose the correct answer(s) for each question.

1. Which IOS command defines an NTP server?

   A. **ip ntp server**

   B. **ntp server**

   C. **ntp-server**

   D. **ip ntp-server**

2. Which IP addresses should be excluded from a DHCP server pool? (Choose two.)

   A. All the DHCP server's IP addresses

   B. The subnet number

   C. The directed broadcast address

   D. DHCP client address

3. The _____ IOS command must be executed to enable the DHCP server and/or relay agent features if they were previously disabled.

4. Which of the following are components of SNMP? (Choose three.)

   A. Agent

   B. Manager

   C. NetFlow

   D. Syslog

   E. MIB

5. Enter the IOS command to enable logging to destinations other than the console:
   _____.

6. What are two of the common logging destinations used by administrators on Cisco devices? (Choose two.)

   A. TFTP server

   B. Terminal sessions

   C. Syslog servers

   D. RAM

   E. Flash

7. A NetFlow flow must minimally contain which items? (Choose two.)

   A. IP address

   B. Port numbers

   C. Ingress interface

   D. CoS

8. Version _____ is the most common implementation of NetFlow.

9. _____ translates one (and only one) IP address to another.

   A. NAT

   B. PAT

   C. PAR

   D. NAT and PAT

10. An _____ is a public IP address associated with an inside device.

   A. Inside global IP address

   B. Inside local IP address

   C. Outside global IP address

   D. Outside local IP address

11. Which command is used to define the local addresses that are statically translated to global addresses?

   A. **ip nat inside source static**

   B. **ip nat inside**

   C. **ip nat inside source list**

   D. **ip nat pool**

12. You have 30 internal machines that need to access the Internet: 192.168.1.32/27. You've been given six public IP addresses for this access: 199.1.1.41–199.1.1.46. Interface fastethernet0/0 is connected to the inside and serial1/0 to the ISP on your router. Enter the commands to perform PAT with this information.

13. When configuring the **ip nat inside source** command, which parameter must you specify to perform PAT?

   A. **pat**

   B. **overload**

   C. **load**

   D. **port**

14. When working with QoS, which DiffServ value is placed in the DSCP field by the IP phone for VoIP traffic by default?

A. AF22

B. ToS

C. CS0

D. EF

Performance-based Questions

In the Cisco exams, performance-based questions require you to drag a box from the left side of the screen to its proper place on the right side of the screen to answer the questions. The following are some sample performance-based questions.

1. Using the following exhibit, write each characteristic listed on the left into the appropriate box on the right.

Resolves FQDNs to IP addresses
Used to automatically assign IP addresses to hosts
Uses UDP ports 67 and 68
Uses UDP port 53

2. Using the following exhibit, place the DHCP phases in the correct order.

DHCP Request
DHCP Offer
DHCP Acknowledge
DHCP Discover

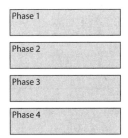

Answers

1. B. Use the **ntp server** command to define an NTP server.

2. B and **C.** The network and directed broadcast addresses should be excluded as well as statically assigned IP addresses, including the default gateway address of the subnet/VLAN (the subnet number).

3. The **service dhcp** IOS command must be executed to enable the DHCP server and/or relay agent features if they were previously disabled.

4. A, B, and **E.** The agent, the NMS (manager), and MIBs are the three components of SNMP.

5. The **logging on** command enables logging to destinations other than the console.

6. **C** and **D.** Common logging destinations used by administrators are the logging buffer (RAM), the console terminal, and syslog servers.

7. **A** and **C.** Minimally, a flow must contain a source IP address, a destination IP address, and an ingress interface.

8. Version 5 is the most common implementation of NetFlow.

9. **A.** NAT translates only one IP address to another.

10. **A.** An inside global IP address is a public IP address assigned to an inside device.

11. **A.** The **ip nat inside source static** command configures static NAT translations.

12. Here are the commands to enter:

```
ip nat pool mypool 199.1.1.41 199.1.1.46
    netmask 255.255.255.248
  access-list 1 permit 192.168.1.32 0.0.0.31
  ip nat inside source list 1 pool mypool overload
  interface fastethernet0/0
    ip nat inside
  interface serial1/0
    ip nat outside
```

13. **B.** Use the **overload** parameter with the **ip nat inside source** command to set up PAT.

14. **D.** The DiffServ Expedited Forwarding (EF) value is placed in the DSCP field to indicate that the data needs low latency.

Performance-based Answers

1. The following identifies the characteristics of DNS and DHCP.

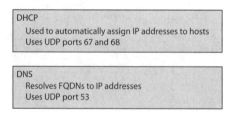

2. The following is the correct order of the DHCP process.

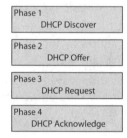

CHAPTER 14

IPv6

In this chapter, you will

- Learn about the need for IPv6
- Learn about IPv6 enhancements and addressing
- Learn how to configure IPv6 on an interface
- Learn how to configure routing with IPv6

This chapter introduces you to the next generation of TCP/IP: IP version 6 (IPv6). Because of the many deficiencies found in IPv4, as well as the poor scalability for hierarchical addressing in IPv4, IPv6 was developed to meet the rapidly growing needs of small companies, corporations, and the explosive growth of the Internet, especially in emerging markets such as China and India. In this chapter you'll discover why IPv6 is necessary, the different kinds of IPv6 addresses, routing with IPv6, and how to configure a basic IPv6 setup. The CCNP certification goes into much more depth than what you'll find in this chapter.

Necessity of IPv6

An IPv4 address is 32 bits in length; that means there are 2^{32} actual IP addresses, which equals 4.3 billion addresses. Not all of these are usable, however: only 3.7 billion of these are actually usable. Many addresses are reserved, such as research (239–254), broadcast (255), multicast (224–239), private (10, 172.16, and 192.168), and loopback addresses (127). And, of course, many of the usable addresses are already assigned, leaving very, very few addresses for new growth.

Unlike 32-bit IPv4 addresses, IPv6 uses a 128-bit address. This allows for 3.4×10^{38} addresses, which is enough for many IP addresses for each person on Earth, and probably on multiple planets.

Growth Issues

During the early-to-mid-1990s, concern began to grow about the diminishing number of IPv4 addresses. The temporary solution to this problem was to set aside an address space, called *private addresses*, which anyone could use in a public network. Recall from Chapter 4 that these addresses are defined in IETF RFC 1918: 10.0.0.0/8, 172.16.0.0–172.31.255.255, and 192.168.0.0–192.168.255.255. To access a public network, address translation is used to translate the private addressing information to a public address, commonly with static Network Address Translation (NAT) translations for internal services and dynamic overloading (in particular, Port Address Translation, or PAT) for user connection.

Many changes in the marketplace, however, are quickly reaching the point where address translation won't be enough: there won't be any public addresses left to translate to. Here are some valid reasons why companies are beginning to migrate to an IPv6 environment:

- Currently more than 3 billion people are connected to the Internet, and this is exponentially increasing based on fast-emerging technical markets such as China and India.

- More than 2 billion smart phones, tablets, and similar devices offer common data services such as e-mail and web browsing, and this number is expected to grow as more and more businesses implement mobile applications.

- More data services are being offered on consumer products, such as automobiles, household appliances, and industrial devices, and this number is expected to grow into the billions.

As you can see, it's not a matter of *if* public addresses are going to be depleted, and not even *when* it's going to happen, but *how soon* in the near future this is going to happen. Because IPv4 is only a 32-bit address, and because the designers did not foresee the growth of the Internet, we have run out of IPv4 address. The goal of IPv6 is to increase the address space (it is a 128-bit address space), which gives us more than enough IPv6 address for everyone in the world to use and handles future growth.

Think about the technology revolution that has occurred in the past decade: you can now use your smart phone to change the channels on your TV, call home and program the microwave to turn on, or stream content from your TV provider to your PC and then to a network storage device that your TV can quickly access. And this revolution is still in its early stages. For communication to take place among all these devices, they need an addressing structure, and most companies are basically relying on TCP/IP to provide this.

IPv6 Features

Obviously, the replacement for IPv4 needs to support enough addresses for this growing demand, but it also needs to provide ease of use and configuration, enhanced security, and the ability to interoperate with IPv4 as the transition takes place. Here are some features built into IPv6:

- **Very large address space** IPv6's large address space deals with global growth, where route prefixes can be easily aggregated in routing updates. Support for multihoming to Internet service providers (ISPs) with a single address space is easily accomplished. Autoconfiguration of addressing information, including the capability of including Media Access Control (MAC) addresses in the IP address, as well as plug-and-play options, simplifies address management. Renumbering and modification of addresses is easily accommodated, as is public-to-private readdressing, without involving address translation.

- **Security** IP security (IPsec) is built into IPv6, whereas it is an awkward add-on in IPv4. With IPv6, two devices can dynamically negotiate security parameters and build a secure tunnel between them with no user intervention.

- **Mobility** With the growth of mobile devices, such as smart phones and tablets, devices can roam between wireless networks without breaking their connections.

- **Streamlined encapsulation** The IPv6 encapsulation is simpler than that of IPv4, providing faster forwarding rates by routers and better routing efficiency. No checksums are included, reducing processing on endpoints. No broadcasts are used, reducing utilization of devices within the same subnet. Quality of service (QoS) information is built into the IPv6 header, where a flow label identifies the traffic; this alleviates intermediate network devices from having to examine contents inside the packet, the TCP/UDP headers, and payload information to classify the traffic for QoS correctly.

- **Addressing capabilities** As with IPv4, addresses can be assigned statically or obtained via Dynamic Host Control Protocol (DHCPv6). However, unlike IPv4, IPv6 supports stateless autoconfiguration, which enables a device to acquire addressing automatically without implementing a DHCP server solution.

- **Transition capabilities** Various solutions exist to enable IPv4 and IPv6 to coexist successfully when migrating between the two. One method, dual stack, enables you to run both protocols simultaneously on an interface of a device. A second method, tunneling, enables you to tunnel IPv6 over IPv4, and vice versa, to transmit an IP version of one type across a network using another type. Cisco supports a third method, Network Address Translation-Protocol Translation (NAT-PT), to translate between IPv4 and IPv6 (sometimes the term *Proxy* is used instead of Protocol).

 EXAM TIP For the exam, make sure you are familiar with the enhanced features of IPv6 in the bulleted list.

IPv6 Addressing

What scares most administrators about IPv6 addresses is how different they appear when compared to IPv4 addresses. Learning to deal with an address four times longer seems impossible; however, as you will see in this chapter, the standards body for TCP/IP has simplified it as much as possible.

IPv6 Address Format

Whereas IPv4 addresses use a dotted-decimal format, in which each byte ranges from 0 to 255, IPv6 addresses use eight sets of four hexadecimal addresses (16 bits in each set), separated by a colon (:), like this: *xxxx:xxxx:xxxx:xxxx:xxxx:xxxx:xxxx:xxxx* (*x* would be a hexadecimal value). This notation is commonly called *string* notation. Each hexadecimal value ranges from 0 to 9 and A to F (0–F).

Here are some important items concerning IPv6 addresses:

- Hexadecimal values can be displayed in either lower- or uppercase for the characters A–F.

- A leading zero in a set of numbers can be omitted; for example, you could enter either *0012* or *12* in one of the eight fields—both are correct.

- If you have successive fields of zeroes in an IPv6 address, you can represent them as two colons (::). For example, *0:0:0:0:0:0:0:5* could be represented as *::5*; and *2000:C67:0:0:8888:9999:1111:0* could be represented as *2000:C67::8888:9999:1111:0*. However, you can do this only *once* in the address: *2000::C67::891::00* would be invalid, since *::* appears more than once in the address. The reason for this limitation is that if you had two or more repetitions, you wouldn't know how many sets of zeroes were being omitted from each part.

- An unspecified address is represented as *::*, since it contains all zeroes.

 EXAM TIP For the exam, you'll need to remember the format of IPv6 addresses: eight sets of four hexadecimal numbers (16 bits). If you have successive fields of zeroes in an IPv6 address, you can represent them as two colons (::). However, you can do this only once in the address; so 2000::C67::891::00 would be invalid since :: appears more than once in the address.

Calculating Hex Addresses

Let's take a look at how an IPv6 address is converted from binary to make the hexadecimal address. Figure 14-1 displays the structure of a typical IPv6 address and denotes the bit structure.

Let's break down the figure. At the top left of the figure you can see an IPv6 address that starts with fe80. Each character in the IPv6 address is made up of 4 bits. This means that each block in the address separated by a colon (:) is 16 bits in length. There are eight blocks, so 8 × 16 bits = 128 bits.

The pattern of 4 bits that each character makes can be easily figured out using a quick conversion table, shown in the top-right corner of Figure 14-1. You can see that the values of each of the 4 bits are 8, 4, 2, and finally 1 on the far right side. Just like figuring out the value of an octet with IPv4, you can calculate the 4 bits used by taking the decimal number (7 is the example in the figure) and turning on (set the bit to 1) the 4-, 2-, and 1-bit placeholders. This will create a decimal value of 4 + 2 + 1 = 7. Looking at the chart in the figure, you'll see that the decimal value of 7 is also the hex value of 7, which has a binary value of 0111. Knowing that each character is based off a 4-bit value, you could use a conversion table to help you figure out what each hex value is in binary.

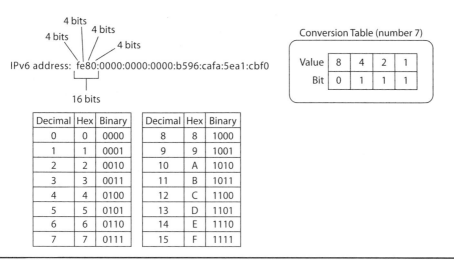

Figure 14-1 Converting hex to binary

To start the table, I list 16 decimal numbers in order from 0 through 15 (because hexadecimal address is 16 based). I then list each hexadecimal value in order, from 0 to 9 (that is only 10 numbers; we need 6 more), then the tenth hex value is A and continues to F to make the 16 values in the hex system. Finally, I create a third column, which is the binary value of each of those hex values—you can cheat and use the corresponding decimal number of a hex value to figure out what the binary should be. For example, the hex value of "C" corresponds to a decimal value of 12, and to calculate 12 in binary is 1100 (8 + 4 + 0 + 0).

This means that the first block in the IPv6 of fe80 has the 16-bit pattern of

```
1111 1110 1000 0000
```

Types of IPv6 Addresses

Recall from Chapter 4 that many types of IPv4 addresses exist: unicast, broadcast, multicast, research, private, and so on. IPv6 also has different types of addresses. Following are the three main types:

- **Anycast** This is very different from an IPv4 broadcast. An anycast address is used for one device to talk to the nearest device that has that address assigned to its interface (one-to-the-nearest address), where many interfaces can share the same address. These addresses are taken from the unicast address space but can represent multiple devices, such as multiple default gateways. For example, using an anycast address as a default gateway address on your routers, user devices have to know of only one address, and you don't need to configure a protocol such as Hot Standby Router Protocol (HSRP) or Virtual Router Redundancy Protocol (VRRP).

- **Multicast** This is similar to a multicast in IPv4.

- **Unicast** This represents a single unique address used for direct communication.

EXAM TIP   Make sure that you are able to compare and contrast anycast, multicast, and unicast IPv6 addresses for the exam, and remember that IPv6 doesn't support broadcast addresses.

Anycast

One of the problems with addressing in IPv4 is the use of broadcasts, which every device has to process on a segment (even when the broadcast isn't ultimately destined to a device). IPv4 relies heavily on broadcasts to discover devices on a segment, such as Address Resolution Protocol (ARP), and to acquire addressing, such as Dynamic Host Control Protocol (DHCP). In IPv6, broadcasts no longer exist: they've been replaced with anycast and multicast addresses.

EXAM TIP   Remember that anycast addresses are used for one device to talk to the nearest device that has that address assigned to its interface (one-to-the-nearest). An anycast address is an IPv6 address from the global address pool configured on multiple devices.

An anycast address identifies one or more *interfaces*. Notice that I don't use the term *device*, since a device can have more than one interface. Sometimes people use the term *node* to designate an interface on a device. Basically, an anycast is a hybrid of a unicast and multicast address. With a unicast, one packet is sent to one destination; with a multicast, one packet is sent to all members of the multicast group; and with an anycast, a packet is sent to any one member of a group of devices that are configured with the anycast address. By default, packets sent to an anycast address are forwarded to the closet interface (node), which is based on the routing process employed to get the packet to the destination. Given this process, anycast addresses are commonly referred to as *one-to-the-nearest* addresses. And, interestingly enough, anycast addresses are allocated from the global pool of unicast addresses in IPv6, making a unicast address and an anycast address indistinguishable from each other when you look at them in a packet. And since multiple devices can be configured with the same anycast address, anycast addresses are commonly used when there is a need to load-balance traffic such as web content to two different destinations.

Multicast

Multicasts in IPv6 serve a function similar to their counterpart in IPv4: they represent a group of interfaces interested in seeing the same traffic. A multicast packet example for IPv6 is shown in Figure 14-2. The first 8 bits are set to FF. The next 4 bits are the lifetime of the address: 0 is permanent and 1 is temporary. The next 4 bits indicate the scope of the multicast address (how far the packet can travel): 1 is for a node, 2 is for a link, 5 is for the site, 8 is for the organization, and E is global (the Internet). For example, a multicast address that begins with FF02::/16 is a permanent link address, whereas an address of FF15::/16 is a temporary address for a site. FF02::1 represents all IPv6 devices (similar to a broadcast in IPv4). FF02::2 represents all routers on an IPv6 segment or VLAN.

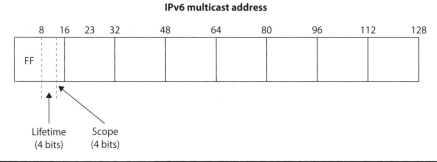

Figure 14-2 IPv6 multicast address

EXAM TIP For the exam, you'll need to remember that FF02::1 is a multicast address that represents all IPv6 devices (similar to a broadcast address in IPv4). FF02::2 is a multicast address that represents all routers on an IPv6 segment or VLAN. Also note that all multicast addresses start with FF in IPv6.

Unicast

IPv6 unicast addresses are assigned to each node (interface), and their uses are discussed in RFC 4291. The five types of unicast addresses are listed in Table 14-1. Interestingly enough, multiple addresses of any type can be assigned to a device's interface: unicast, multicast, and anycast.

Private Addresses As mentioned in Table 14-1, private addresses are used for devices that don't need to access a public network such as the Internet. There are two kinds of private addresses:

- **Site-local/unique-local** A site-local address (aka unique-local address) is considered a private IP address, similar to the 10.0.0.0/8 private IP with IPv4. This address is used for local communication within a site. A site-local address always starts with FEC:: through FFF::.

- **Link-local** A link-local address is similar to an APIPA address in IPv4 and is used for communication on the network link. A link-local address starts with FE80::/10 (FE8:: through FEB::).

Site-local addresses are similar to the RFC 1918 addresses and represent a particular site or company. These addresses can be used within a company without having to waste any public IP addresses—not that this is a concern, given the large number of addresses available in IPv6. However, by using private addresses, you can set up address translation policies for IPv6 to easily control who is allowed to leave your network and receive returning traffic.

Address	Value	Description
Global	2000::/3	Global unicast addresses are IPv6 public IP addresses that are routable on the Internet, and which are assigned by the Internet Assigned Numbers Authority (IANA). They are equivalent to IPv4 public IP addresses. ISPs summarize these to provide scalability in the Internet.
Reserved	(range)	Reserved addresses are used for specific types of anycast as well as for future use. Currently about 1/256th of the IPv6 address space is reserved.
Private	FE80::/10	Like IPv4, IPv6 originally supported private addressing, which is used by devices that don't need to access a public network. The first two digits are FE, and the third digit can range from 8 to F.
Loopback	::1	Like the 127.0.0.1 address in IPv4, 0:0:0:0:0:0:0:1, or ::1, is used for local testing functions; unlike IPv4, which dedicates a complete Class A block of addresses for local testing, only one address is used for local testing in IPv6.
Unspecified	::	0.0.0.0 in IPv4 means "unknown" address. In IPv6, this is represented by 0:0:0:0:0:0:0:0, or ::, and is typically used in the source address field of the packet when an interface doesn't have an address and is trying to acquire one dynamically.

Table 14-1   IEEE Ethernet Components

Link-local addresses are a new concept in IPv6. These kinds of addresses have a smaller scope as to how far they can travel—that is, no farther than the local link (the data link layer). Routers will process packets destined to a link-local address, but they will not forward them to other links. Their most common use is for a device to acquire unicast site-local or global unicast addressing information, discover the default gateway, and discover other layer 2 neighbors on the segment. When a device is using link-local addresses, it must specify an outbound interface, since every interface is connected to a "link."

 EXAM TIP   For the exam, remember the starting values for each of the types of addresses. Site-local addresses start with FEC:: through FFF::, link-local addresses start with FE8:: through FEB:: (usually FE80). The loopback address is ::1, which is equivalent to IPv4's 127.0.0.1.

Global Unicast Addresses   With the exception of the multicast address space of FF00::/8, unicast and anycast addresses make up the rest of the address types. Global unicast addresses have the first three bits of the first hex value always set to 001, so this means a global unicast address always starts with a 2 or a 3, such as 2000 or 2001. However, IANA has currently assigned only 2000::/3 addresses to the global pool, which is about 1/6th of the available IPv6 addresses. Of these addresses, only 2001::/16 are assigned to various Internet address registries. Global unicast addresses are made up of two components, shown in Figure 14-3: a subnet ID (64 bits) and an interface ID (64 bits). The subnet ID contains the registry of the address (which is responsible for assigning it, such as IANA),

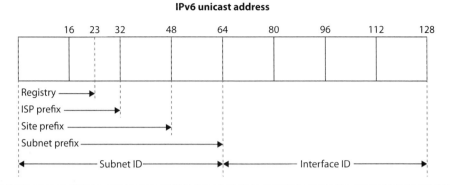

Figure 14-3 IPv6 unicast address

the ISP prefix (which ISP is associated with the address), the site prefix (which company is assigned the address space), and a subnet prefix (subnets within the site). ISPs are assigned an ISP prefix range that enables them easily to aggregate their prefixes, advertising just a single route to the Internet backbone; this alleviates one main problem today with how the Internet grew and how ISPs, initially, were assigned IPv4 address spaces that could not be summarized easily. Another advantage of this address allocation is that the subnet prefix is 16 bits in length. Therefore, with a single global site address, a company can address up to 65,536 subnets.

The last half of the IPv6 address, the interface ID, represents a particular interface within the site. One requirement with addresses from 2000::/3 through E000::/3 is that the interface ID must have a 64-bit value in it to be considered valid. Therefore, addresses that have 0s for the last 64 bits are considered invalid IPv6 unicast addresses. For example, 2004:1234:5678:90AB:: is invalid, since the interface ID (the last 64 bits—that is, the last four sets of numbers) is binary zeroes.

EXAM TIP For the exam, remember that global addresses have a first digit of a 2 or 3, and are currently usually 2000 or 2001. An interface can be assigned multiple IPv6 addresses—this includes link-local, global unicast, and/or anycast addresses.

Modified EUI 64 The interface ID is typically composed of a part of the MAC address of the interface. When this is done, the interface ID is commonly called an *extended unique identifier 64* (EUI-64). Figure 14-4 shows an example of the frame with an EUI-64 format. The *organizationally unique identifier* (OUI), which is the first 24 bits of the MAC address on a network card, is mapped into the first 24 bits of the interface ID. The seventh bit in the highest order byte is set to 1, indicating that the interface ID is unique across the site, or 0, indicating that it is unique within the local scope only. The OUI mapping is followed by the 16-bit value of FFFE. The last 24 bits of the MAC address are then mapped into the last part of the interface ID.

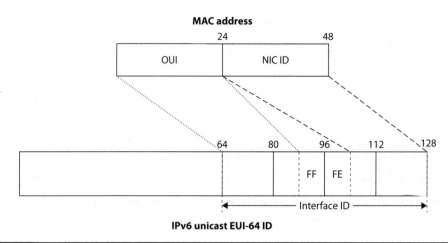

Figure 14-4 EUI-64 interface ID

 EXAM TIP Remember that addresses that have 0s for the interface ID part of a unicast IPv6 address are invalid. For example, this would be an invalid IPv6 unicast address: 2001:5005::. Also, remember that with the EUI-64 method, 0xFFEE is inserted between the upper 3 bytes and the lower 3 bytes of the MAC address, which then becomes the host ID of the address.

IPv6 Enhancements

IPv6 has made some enhancements and changes over IPv4 that make it more network-friendly and scalable. These enhancements include the IPv6 header, ICMPv6, and neighbor discovery.

IPv6 Header

Figure 14-5 shows the IPv4 header and its fields. This header contains 12 fields, followed by the Options field, which, if present, is of variable length. Without any options, the IPv4 header is 20 bytes, and with options, it is at most 40 bytes.

In IPv6, six of these header fields are no longer part of the new IPv6 header. These are indicated by the lighter shading in Figure 14-5:

- **Header Length** This is no longer necessary in IPv6 because all IPv6 headers are fixed-length.
- **Identification** This function hasn't been used for a long time in IPv4 and has been deprecated in IPv6.
- **Flags** This function hasn't been used for a long time in IPv4 and has been deprecated in IPv6.

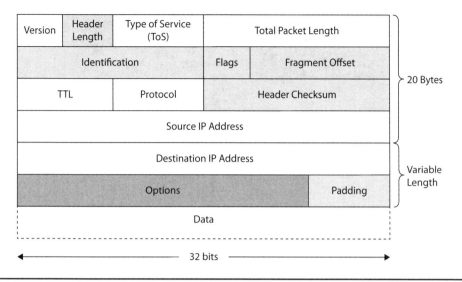

Figure 14-5 IPv4 header

- **Fragment Offset** Fragmentation is processed differently in IPv6 and doesn't need fields in the IPv6 header for this process (this has been moved to the Extension Header Information field in IPv6).

- **Header Checksum** Today's data link layer technologies are reliable, so this field is no longer necessary in IPv6.

- **Padding** This field is no longer necessary in IPv6.

Figure 14-6 displays the fields of the IPv6 header. Here is an explanation of the eight fields in the IPv6 header:

- **Version** This 4-bit field contains the number 6 instead of 4.

- **Traffic Class** This 8-bit field is similar to the ToS field in the IPv4 header.

- **Flow Label** This 20-bit field is new to IPv6 and has no IPv4 equivalent. It is used to mark individual traffic flows for additional policy functions performed by the routing device.

- **Payload Length** This 16-bit field indicates the size of the payload. In IPv4, the Total Packet Length field is the size of the entire packet, but in IPv6, the Payload Length field doesn't include the size of the IPv6 header.

- **Next Header** This 8-bit field performs the same function as the Protocol field in the IPv4 header.

- **Hop Limit** This 8-bit field performs the same function as the TTL field in the IPv4 header.

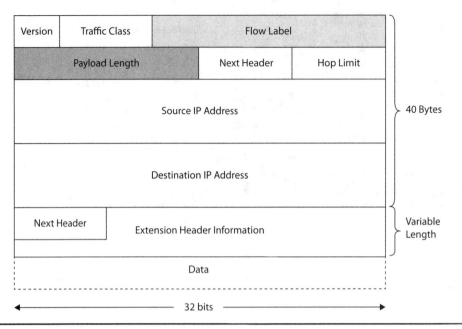

Figure 14-6 IPv6 header

- **Source IP Address** This 128-bit (16-byte) field indicates the source IPv6 address.
- **Destination IP Address** This 128-bit (16-byte) field indicates the destination IPv6 address.

Following these eight fields are the extension headers, if any exist. These replace the IPv4 Options field. The number of extensions is not fixed, so the total length of the Extension Header Information field (list of extensions) is variable. As you can see from Figures 14-5 and 14-6, the IPv6 header has been simplified (with fewer fields).

ICMPv6

ICMPv6 has a protocol number of 58. Like ICMP in IPv4, ICMPv6 is used to help perform diagnostic tests and identify problems (echo, echo reply, destination unreachable, hop count exceeded, and so forth). However, a lot more functionality has been added to ICMPv6.

In a sense, ICMPv6 is like the "Swiss Army knife" of IPv6 protocols. It takes over the responsibility that other, separate, protocols in IPv4 perform:

- **Address Resolution Protocol (ARP)** IPv4 uses ARP to resolve IP addresses to MAC addresses. ARP no longer exists as a separate protocol in IPv6; ICMPv6 now performs its functions.

- **Internet Group Management Protocol (IGMP)** IPv4 uses this protocol so that routing devices can learn if there are multicast devices in a VLAN that want to receive a multicast stream and to forward the necessary stream or streams to the VLAN. IGMP no longer exists as a separate protocol in IPv6; ICMPv6 now performs its functions.

ICMPv6 has taken over the role of other protocols as well and also has new functionality. Here are some examples of the new functions performed in ICMPv6:

- **Router solicitation and advertisement** Enables devices to query routing devices on a segment using a multicast message or routing devices to advertise themselves via multicast messages; also allows for the redirection of end stations to the best gateway for a destination network
- **DNS solicitation and advertisement** Enables devices to query for DNS servers on a segment using a multicast message or DNS server to advertise themselves via multicast messages
- **Neighbor solicitation and advertisement** Commonly referred to as *neighbor discovery*, determines the data link layer address for neighbors on the same link (the replacement of IPv4's ARP), finds neighboring routers, and keeps track of the reachability of neighbors via multicast messages

 EXAM TIP For the exam, remember that IPv6 does not have broadcast traffic, so ICMPv6 uses unicast and multicast traffic.

Address Assignment

You can use four methods to assign an IPv6 address to an interface: two are done statically and two dynamically. The following three sections discuss these four options.

Static Address Assignment

One option you have is to statically assign a unicast address to a device's interface using either of these two approaches:

- Specify all 128 bits manually.
- Specify the first 64 bits manually and use EUI-64 to acquire the last 64 bits.

You can manually specify the entire 128-bit address, or you can specify the subnet ID and have the device use the EUI-64 method to create the interface ID part of the address. If you're manually entering the entire address, remember that sets of fields that have 0s in them can be abbreviated with a double colon (::). The EUI-64 method is the approach more commonly used by most network administrators.

DHCPv6

DHCPv6 is an update of DHCP in IPv4 and works similarly to the previous version, with a few differences. In IPv6, DHCPv6 is referred to as *stateful autoconfiguration*. Before the client can begin, it must first detect a router on the link via a neighbor discovery process. If the client detects a router, the client examines the router advertisement messages to determine whether DHCPv6 has been set up. If the router specifies that DHCPv6 is supported, or no router advertisement messages are seen, the client will begin to find a DHCPv6 server by generating a DHCP solicit message. This message is sent to the ALL-DHCP-Agents multicast address, using the link-local scope to ensure that the message isn't forwarded, by default, beyond the local link. An agent is either a DHCPv6 server or a relay, such as a router.

In DHCPv4 (IPv4 addressing), you configured the IP Helper feature on Cisco routers when the DHCP server was not on the same segment as the requesting clients. IP Helper has the router redirect a DHCP request either to a particular server or a directed broadcast address of the segment that had one or more DHCP servers. This is no longer necessary in DHCPv6: if no server is on the link, a relay can forward the request to the ALL-DHCP-Agents multicast address with the site-local scope. You still have the option of doing this statically, and this is necessary if you want to control which DHCPv6 server or servers should process the request.

Stateless Autoconfiguration

Stateless autoconfiguration is an extension of DHCPv6. As with DHCPv6, clients can acquire their addressing dynamically; however, with stateless autoconfiguration, no DHCP server is necessary to assign IPv6 addressing information to the clients. Instead, the client uses information in router advertisement messages to configure an IPv6 address for the interface. This is accomplished by taking the first 64 bits in the router advertisement source address (the prefix of the router's address) and using the EUI-64 process to create the 64-bit interface ID. Stateless autoconfiguration was designed primarily for cell phones and home network and appliance equipment to assign addresses automatically without having to manage a DHCP server infrastructure. Devices will verify that their address is unique before using it via neighbor query messages using ICMPv6.

 EXAM TIP For the exam remember the term stateless autoconfiguration. Stateless autoconfiguration assigns addresses dynamically without needing a DHCP server. The device learns the IPv6 prefix from a router advertisement and uses EUI-64 to create the interface ID part of the address dynamically.

Normally, routers generate periodic router advertisement (RA) messages the client can listen to and then use to generate its link address automatically; however, when the client is booting up, waiting for the RA may take awhile. In this situation, the client will generate a router solicitation message, asking the router to reply with an RA so the client can generate its interface address.

Information that can be obtained via stateless autoconfiguration include

- The network numbers (prefixes)
- The lifetime of the prefixes
- A flag that indicates the kind of autoconfiguration the end stations can perform (stateless or stateful)
- The default router for the prefix(es) and the lifetime for this value
- The default maximum transmission unit (MTU) size for the segment
- The maximum hop count allowed

Other information can also be obtained, but this list comprises the most common parameters.

Routing and IPv6

As in IPv4, routers in IPv6 find best paths to destinations based on metrics and administrative distances; and like IPv4, IPv6 routers look for the longest matching prefix in the IPv6 routing table to forward a packet to its destination. The main difference is that the IPv6 router is looking at 128 bits when making a routing decision instead of 32 bits.

 NOTE RFC 2461 requires that a router must be able to identify the link-local address of each neighboring router, which is used in the routing process. Because of this, the use of global unicast addresses as a next-hop address is not recommended by the RFC.

Supported Routing Protocols

IPv6 supports both static and dynamic routing protocols. IPv6 supports these routing protocols: static, Routing Information Protocol next generation (RIPng), Open Shortest Path First (OSPFv3), Intermediate System-Intermediate System (IS-IS) for IPv6, Multiprotocol Border Gateway Protocol (MP-BGP4), and Enhanced Interior Gateway Routing Protocol (EIGRP) for IPv6. This book covers only an introduction to static, RIPng, and OSPFv3 routing; the other dynamic routing protocols are covered in more depth in Cisco's CCNP curriculum and certification.

RIPng

RIPng is defined in RFC 2080. It is actually similar to RIP for IPv4, with these characteristics:

- It's a distance vector protocol.
- The hop-count limit is 15.
- Split horizon and poison reverse are used to prevent routing loops.
- It is based on RIPv2.

NOTE Cisco routers running 12.2(2)T and later support RIPng.

These are the enhancements in RIPng:

- An IPv6 packet is used to transport the routing update.
- The all RIP routers multicast address (FF02::9) is used as the destination address in routing advertisements and is delivered to UDP port 521.
- Routing updates contain the IPv6 prefix of the router and the next-hop IPv6 address.

EXAM TIP You'll be expected to know that RIPng uses UDP port 521 for its connections, and its destination multicast address is FF02::9.

OSPFv3

OSPFv3 is the version of OSPF to support IPv6 and has been enhanced with many features, making it just as scalable as other interior gateway protocols. The protocol number for OSPFv3 is 89. Here are some of the enhancements:

- The OSPFv3 process requires a router ID, just as in OSPFv2 (IPv4). This is a 32-bit number that must statically be configured; it cannot be acquired by an IPv4 address on the routing device, since you may not even be using IPv4 on the routing device.
- When forming adjacencies, the routers use their link-local addresses as their source. The link-local addresses appear in the link state database and routing table for next-hop addresses.
- Because link-local addresses are used, conflicting global addresses on the interfaces will not prevent adjacencies from being formed: in other words, the global addressing structure has been abstracted from the interface. In OSPFv2, this would cause routers to fail building an adjacency, but it doesn't cause a problem in OSPFv3.
- Any router within an area can perform summarization or filtering. This was one of the biggest weaknesses of OSPFv2 compared to EIGRP. In OSPFv2, only area boundary routers (ABRs) and autonomous system boundary routers (ASBRs) could do summarization or filtering, whereas an EIGRP router could do this. This greatly limited the scalability of OSPFv2. OSPFv3 no longer has this issue.

EIGRP for IPv6

EIGRP has been updated to support IPv6 routing and is now referred to as EIGRP for IPv6. EIGRP for IPv6 is a stand-alone process and not part of the EIGRP for IPv4 configuration. It supports the same features as its older EIGRP implementation for IPv4: diffusing update algorithm (DUAL), rich metric structure, load balancing, and many others.

Implementation Strategies

One nice feature of moving your network to IPv6 is that you don't have to do it all in one step. Various migration strategies support both IPv4 and IPv6 as you migrate from the former to the latter. Table 14-2 briefly lists these. The next two sections discuss dual stacking and manual IPv6 tunneling, the two most common methods.

 EXAM TIP Be familiar with the information in Table 14-2 for the exam. Remember that routers running both IPv6 and IPv4 are referred to as being "dual stacked." Connecting IPv6 networks by tunneling IPv6 packets within IPv4 packets is referred to as "6to4 tunneling."

Dual Stacking   In dual stacking, a device runs both protocol stacks: IPv4 and IPv6. Of all the transition methods, this is the most common one. Dual stacking can be accomplished on the same interface or different interfaces of the device. The top part of Figure 14-7 shows an example of dual stacking on a router, where NetworkA has a mixture of devices configured for the two different protocols, and the router is configured in dual stack mode. Older IPv4-only applications can still work while they are migrated to IPv6 by supporting newer APIs to handle IPv6 addresses and DNS lookups with IPv6 addresses.

Transition Method	Description
Dual stacking	Devices such as PCs and routers run both IPv4 and IPv6, and thus have two sets of addresses.
Manual IPv6-over-IPv4 (6to4) tunneling	IPv6 packets are tunneled across an IPv4 network by encapsulating them in IPv4 packets. This requires routers configured with dual stacks.
Dynamic 6to4 tunneling	Enables IPv6 localities to connect to other IPv6 localities across an IPv4 backbone, such as the Internet, automatically. This method applies a unique IPv6 prefix to each locality without having to retrieve IPv6 addressing information from address registries or ISPs.
Intra-Site Automatic Tunnel Addressing Protocol (ISATAP) tunneling	Uses virtual links to connect IPv6 localities together within a site that is primarily using IPv4. Boundary routers between the two addressing types must be configured with dual stacks.
Teredo tunneling	Instead of using routers to tunnel packets, the hosts perform the tunneling. This requires the hosts to be configured with dual stacks. It is commonly used to move packets through an IPv4 address translation device.
NAT Proxying and Translation (NAT-PT)	Has an address translation device translate addresses between an IPv6 and IPv4 network, and vice versa.

Table 14-2   IPv4-to-IPv6 Transition Options

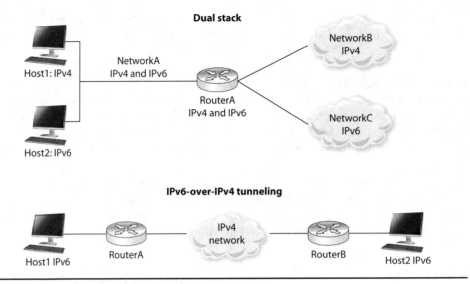

Figure 14-7 Dual stack and IPv6 tunneling

NOTE The main disadvantage of dual stacking on a segment is that devices configured using only one stack must forward their traffic to a dual stacked device, such as a router, which must then forward the traffic back to the same segment using the other stack. This is an inefficient use of bandwidth, but it does enable devices using both protocol stacks to coexist on the same network segment.

IPv6 Tunneling IPv6 tunneling enables you to tunnel IPv6 packets by carrying them as payloads in an IPv4 packet, as shown at the bottom of Figure 14-7. Using tunneling, you can connect IPv6 networks together across an intermediate IPv4 network. When tunneling IPv6 packets in an IPv4 payload, the IPv4 Protocol field contains a value of 41, indicating that IPv6 tunneling is occurring. The two routers performing the tunneling must be configured using dual stacking, since they need to communicate with both IPv6 and IPv4 devices on different segments.

If you are configuring the tunnel manually, you'll need to configure both the IPv4 and IPv6 addresses statically. You'll also need to ensure that routing is performing normally to tunnel the IPv6 packets across the IPv4 network, as well as allowing the two IPv6 networks, as shown in Figure 14-7, to see each other's routes.

TIP Cisco recommends against using the IP Unnumbered feature for the tunnel endpoints, since this can make it more difficult for you to troubleshoot problems when tunneling doesn't work.

IPv6 Configuration

This section covers the basics of enabling IPv6 on your router, assigning IPv6 addresses to your interfaces, and enabling basic routing functions.

Enabling IPv6 and Assigning Addresses

To use IPv6 on your router, you must, at a minimum, enable the protocol and assign IPv6 addresses to your interfaces, like this:

```
IOS(config)# ipv6 unicast-routing
IOS(config)# interface type [slot_#/]port_#
IOS(config-if)# ipv6 address ipv6_address_prefix/prefix_length
                    [eui-64]
```

The **ipv6 unicast-routing** command globally enables IPv6 and must be the first IPv6 command executed on the router. The **ipv6 address** command assigns the prefix, the length, and the use of EUI-64 to assign the interface ID. Optionally, you can omit the **eui-64** parameter and configure the entire IPv6 address.

To use stateless autoconfiguration, use the following configuration:

```
IOS(config)# interface type [slot_#/]port_#
IOS(config-if)# ipv6 address autoconfig [default]
```

If a default router is selected on this interface, the **default** parameter causes a default route to be installed using that default router. The **default** parameter can be specified only on one interface.

You can use the **show ipv6 interface** command to verify an interface's configuration. Here's an example configuration, with its verification:

```
IOS(config)# ipv6 unicast-routing
IOS(config)# interface fastethernet0/0
IOS(config-if)# ipv6 address 2001:1cc1:dddd:2::/64 eui-64
IOS(config-if)# end
Router# show ipv6 interface fastethernet0/0
FastEthernet0/0 is up, line protocol is up
  IPv6 is enabled, link-local address is FE80::207:EFF:FE46:4070
      [TEN]
  No Virtual link-local address(es):
  Global unicast address(es):
    2001:1CC1:DDDD:2:207:EFF:FE46:4070, subnet is
      2001:1CC1:DDDD:2::/64 [EUI/TEN]
  Joined group address(es):
    FF02::1
    FF02::2
  .
  .
  .
```

In this example, notice that the link-local address is FE80::207:EFF:FE46:4070. Also notice the global address: 2001:1CC1:DDDD:2:207:EFF:FE46:4070.

You can use the **ping** and **traceroute** commands to test connectivity with IPv6. Execute the command and immediately follow it with the IPv6 address you want to test. Here's an example:

```
IOS# ping 2001:DB8:D1A5:C800::5
Type escape sequence to abort.
Sending 5, 100-byte ICMP Echos to 2001:DB8:D1A5:C800::5, timeout is
  2 seconds:
.!!!!
Success rate is 100 percent (5/5), round-trip min/avg/max = 0/0/4 ms
```

Remember that you can test connectivity to link-local addresses only in the same VLAN; however, you can test access to global addresses in the same or different VLANs.

To set up a static DNS resolution table on the router, use the **ipv6 host** command; you can also specify a DNS server with the **ip name-server** command:

```
IOS(config)# ipv6 host hostname [port_#] ipv6_address1
                        [ipv6_address2…]
IOS(config)# ip name-server DNS_server_IPv6_address
```

The **ip name-server** command can be used to assign both IPv4 and IPv6 DNS servers.

 EXAM TIP For the exam know the steps to configure IPv6 on your router. First, enable IPv6 with the **ipv6 unicast-routing** command. Then create IPv6 addresses on the interfaces with the **ipv6 address *ipv6_address_prefix/prefix_length*** command.

 VIDEO 14.01. The digital resources that accompany this book contain a multimedia demonstration of configuring IPv6 addresses on a Cisco router.

IPv6 Static Routing

Configuring an IPv6 static route is similar to configuring an IPv4 static route. Here is the syntax:

```
IOS(config)# ipv6 route prefix/bits IPv6_next_hop_address
                        administrative_distance
```

The *prefix* is the network number, with the corresponding number of bits of the network number, you want to reach. For a default route, use **::/0** as the prefix.

To view the IPv6 routes in the routing device's routing table, use the **show ipv6 route** command:

```
Router# show ipv6 route
IPv6 Routing Table - default - 19 entries
Codes:C - Connected, L - Local, S - Static, R - RIP, B - BGP
      U - Per-user Static route, I1 - ISIS L1, I2 - ISIS L2,
      IA - ISIS interarea, IS - ISIS summary, O - OSPF intra,
      OI - OSPF inter, OE1 - OSPF ext 1, OE2 - OSPF ext 2
```

```
IPv6 Routing Table - 8 entries
L   4000::2/128 [0/0]
     via ::, Ethernet1/0
C   4000::/64 [0/0]
     via ::, Ethernet1/0
LC  4001::1/128 [0/0]
     via ::, Loopback0
L   5000::2/128 [0/0]
     via ::, Serial6/0
C   5000::/64 [0/0]
     via ::, Serial6/0
S   5432::/48 [1/0]
     via 4000::1, Null
L   FE80::/10 [0/0]
     via ::, Null0
L   FF00::/8 [0/0]
     via ::, Null0
```

The formatting of the output is slightly different from that of the IPv4 routing table. Like the IPv4 routing table, a **C** indicates a directly connected route (network) and an **S** indicates a static route. The **L** is new—it's a host route. This is an IPv6 address of a host connected to that interface. Also notice that you can see the administrative distance and metric for each route ([*X*/*Y*]).

 VIDEO   14.02. The digital resources that accompany this book contain a multimedia demonstration of configuring static routing with IPv6 on a Cisco router.

RIPng

You enable RIPng a little differently than RIP for IPv4. First, you use the **ipv6 router rip** *tag* command to enable RIPng globally:

```
IOS(config)# ipv6 unicast-routing
IOS(config)# ipv6 router rip tag
```

If you haven't enabled IPv6 unicast routing, you must do this first. When executing the **ipv6 router rip** command, this takes you into a subcommand mode, where you can change some of the global values for RIPng, such as disabling split horizon, changing the administrative distance, and adjusting timers. The *tag* is a locally significant identifier used to differentiate between multiple RIP processes running on the router.

Unlike RIP for IPv6, RIPng has no **network** command to include interfaces. Instead, you must enable RIPng on a per-interface basis with the **ipv6 rip** *tag* **enable** command:

```
IOS(config)# interface type [slot_#/]port_#
IOS(config-if)# ipv6 rip tag enable
```

The *tag* parameter associates the interface with the correct RIPng routing process.

EXAM TIP For the exam, you'll be expected to know how to use these commands. Use the **ipv6 router rip** *tag* command to enable RIPng globally and the **ipv6 rip** *tag* **enable** command to enable it on an interface.

To view the routing protocol configuration, use the **show ipv6 rip** command:

```
Router# show ipv6 rip
RIP process "RIPPROC1", port 521, multicast-group FF02::9,
    pid 187
    Administrative distance is 120. Maximum paths is 16
    Updates every 30 seconds, expire after 180
    Holddown lasts 0 seconds, garbage collect after 120
    Split horizon is on; poison reverse is off
    Default routes are not generated
    Periodic updates 2, trigger updates 0
  Interfaces:
    FastEthernet0/0
  Redistribution:
    None
```

In this example, the tag is RIPPROC1 for the name of the RIPng routing process and RIPng is enabled on FastEthernet0/0. To view the IPv6 routing table for RIPng, use the **show ipv6 route** or **show ipv6 route rip** command.

OSPFv3

Enabling OSPFv3 for IPv6 is a little different from enabling OSPFv2 for IPv4. The following sections briefly introduce you to a basic OSPFv3 configuration and verification.

OSPFv3 Global Configuration

As in OSPFv2, in OSPFv3 you enable a process globally and can perform certain functions within the process, such as assigning the router ID and defining the areas:

```
IOS(config)# ipv6 router process_ID
IOS(config-router)# router-id router_ID
IOS(config-router)# area area_number
```

The process ID, as in OSPFv2, uniquely identifies the OSPF process locally running on the routing device (it is locally significant and is not shared with other OSPFv3 routing devices). The router ID is a 32-bit number typically represented using a dotted-decimal format. The area number is also a 32-bit number, which can be represented by a decimal (12) or a dotted-decimal (0.0.0.12) format. Here's a simple example:

```
IOS(config)# ipv6 unicast-routing
IOS(config)# ipv6 router process_ID
IOS(config-router)# router-id router_ID
IOS(config-router)# area area_number
```

TIP Typically, when creating router IDs, I use the first digit to represent the area that the router is in. For area border routers (ABRs), the first number would be 0 and the second number (and possibly the third number) would represent an area the device is located within. The last octet I reserve for the identity of the router within the area. For example, if I had a backbone router with all its interfaces within area 0, its router ID might be 0.0.0.1. If I had an ABR connected to area 1, its router ID might be 0.1.0.5. This helps me quickly identify who the router is and what its role is. You must hard-code the router ID in OSPFv3, and it's optional in OSPFv2. However, even in OSPFv2, I sometimes use this method for certain customers.

OSPFv3 Interface Configuration

Once you set up the global properties for OSPFv3, you must place interfaces into the local process. Unlike OSPFv2, where you used the **network** command within the OSPFv2 routing process configuration, IPv6's configuration is like RIPng, where you perform the configuration under an interface:

```
IOS(config)# interface type [slot_#/]port_#
IOS(config-if)# ipv6 ospf process_ID area area_number
```

Simple OSPFv3 Configuration Example

Here's an example configuration placing two interfaces in area 0:

```
IOS(config)# ipv6 unicast-routing
IOS(config)# ipv6 router ospf 1
IOS(config-router)# router-id 0.0.0.1
IOS(config-router)# exit
IOS(config)# interface g1/0/1
IOS(config-if)# ipv6 ospf 1 area 0
IOS(config-if)# exit
IOS(config)# interface g1/0/2
IOS(config-if)# ipv6 ospf 1 area 0
IOS(config-if)# exit
```

As you can see, the configuration is fairly simple. Remember that your Cisco device does not need a global IPv6 address on an interface in order to participate in OSPFv3—it needs only a link-local address, which it will automatically acquire, assuming IPv6 is globally enabled and the interface is enabled.

OSPFv3 Verification

Once you've configured OSPFv3, you can verify the operation of OSPFv3 by using **show** commands similar to those used in OSPFv2. To display general information about OSPFv3 routing processes, use the **show ipv6 ospf** command. Here's an example:

```
IOS# show ipv6 ospf
Routing Process "ospfv3 1" with ID 10.10.10.1
 SPF schedule delay 5 secs, Hold time between two SPFs 10 secs
 Minimum LSA interval 5 secs. Minimum LSA arrival 1 secs
 LSA group pacing timer 240 secs
```

```
Interface flood pacing timer 33 msecs
Retransmission pacing timer 66 msecs
Number of external LSA 0. Checksum Sum 0x000000
Number of areas in this device is 1. 1 normal 0 stub 0 nssa
   Area BACKBONE(0)
        Number of interfaces in this area is 2
        MD5 Authentication, SPI 1000
        SPF algorithm executed 2 times
        Number of LSA 5. Checksum Sum 0x02A005
        Number of DCbitless LSA 0
        Number of indication LSA 0
        Number of DoNotAge LSA 0
        Flood list length 0
```

In this example, the router's ID is 10.10.10.1 and two interfaces are connected to area 0.

To display IPv6 neighbor discovery (ND) cache information (the actual neighbors), use the **show ipv6 neighbors** command. You can also use the show **ipv6 ospf neighbor** command to show neighbor information for OSPFv3 specifically, as shown here:

```
Router# show ipv6 ospf neighbors
Neighbor ID  Pri  State      Dead Time   Interface ID   Interface
172.16.4.4    1   FULL/  -   00:00:31    14             Serial1/0/1
172.16.3.3    1   FULL/BDR   00:00:30    3              FastEthernet0/0
172.16.5.5    1   FULL/  -   00:00:33    13             Serial1/0/2
```

Use the **show ipv6 route** command to view the routing table. To view only the OSPF routes, add the **ospf** parameter: **show ipv6 route ospf**.

EIGRP for IPv6

The scalability features available in EIGRP for IPv4, neighbor discovery, the DUAL algorithm, metrics, load balancing, multicast, and incremental updates, are also available in EIGRP for IPv6. Like EIGRP for IPv4, EIGRP for IPv6 uses hello packets to discover and become neighbors with other local EIGRP for IPv6 routers. Also like EIGRP for IPv4, EIGRP for IPv6 uses multicasts, but the FF02::A IPv6 multicast link-local address is used. This section provides a cursory introduction to the configuration of EIGRP for IPv6.

EIGRP for IPv6 Global Configuration

Here are the basic global commands to enable EIGRP for IPv6:

```
IOS(config)# ipv6 unicast-routing
IOS(config)# ipv6 router eigrp autonomous_system
IOS(config-rtr)# eigrp router-id router_ID
IOS(config-rtr)# [no] shutdown
```

The first command enables IPv6 on the routing devices. The second command specifies the autonomous system that the routing device is associated with. As with EIGRP for IPv4, the autonomous system number must match between two routers or they will not form a neighbor relationship. The **eigrp router-id** command defines the router's 32-bit ID. You can represent this as a decimal or dotted-decimal number, such as 10.1.1.1. The **shutdown** command disables or enables the EIGRP process. Depending on IOS version, the default can vary (this was discussed in Chapter 11).

EIGRP for IPv6 Interface Configuration

Once you set up the global properties for EIGRP for IPv6, you must place interfaces into the local process. Unlike EIGRP for IPv4, where you use the **network** command within the EIGRP routing process configuration, IPv6's configuration is similar to that of RIPng and OSPFv3, where you perform the configuration under an interface:

```
IOS(config)# interface type [slot_#/]port_#
IOS(config-if)# ipv6 eigrp autonomous_system
```

EIGRP for IPv6 Simple Configuration

Here's an example configuration placing two interfaces in autonomous system 100:

```
IOS(config)# ipv6 unicast-routing
IOS(config)# ipv6 router eigrp 100
IOS(config-router)# eigrp router-id 100.1.1.1
IOS(config-router)# no shutdown
IOS(config)# interface g1/0/1
IOS(config-if)# ipv6 eigrp 100
IOS(config-if)# exit
IOS(config)# interface g1/0/2
IOS(config-if)# ipv6 eigrp 100
IOS(config-if)# exit
```

As you can see, the configuration is fairly simple and very similar to OSPFv3's configuration. Remember that your Cisco device does not need a global IPv6 address on an interface in order to participate in EIGRP for IPv6—it needs only a link-local address, which it will automatically acquire, assuming IPv6 is globally enabled and the interface is enabled.

EIGRP for IPv6 Verification

To verify the neighbor relationships for EIGRP for IPv6, use the **show ipv6 eigrp neighbors** command:

```
IOS# show ipv6 eigrp neighbors
IPv6-EIGRP neighbors for AS (100)
H Address                Intf   Hold   Uptime    SRTT  RTO   Q    Seq
                                (sec)  (ms)                  Cnt  Num
0 Link-local address:    Et0/0  14     00:00:13  11    200   0    2
FE80::A8BB:CCFF:FE00:200
```

In this example, one neighbor is connected to interface E0/0 in autonomous system 100.

To display entries in the EIGRP IPv6 topology table, use the **show ipv6 eigrp topology** command:

```
IOS# show ipv6 eigrp topology
IPv6-EIGRP Topology Table for AS(1)/ID(2001:0DB8:10::/64)
Codes: P - Passive, A - Active, U - Update, Q - Query, R - Reply,
r - reply Status, s - sia Status
P 2001:0DB8:3::/64, 1 successors, FD is 281600
   via Connected, Ethernet1/0
```

In this example, there is one successor route in the topology table.

To view the EIGRP routes in the routing table, use the **show ipv6 route eigrp** command. As in IPv4, EIGRP for IPv6 routes are denoted by a **D**. The output of all these **show** commands is very similar to the IPv4 corresponding commands.

Exercise 14-1: Configuring IPv6 Static Routing

In this exercise, you will configure IPv6 addresses on the VAN-R1 and LA-R1 routers and then configure IPv6 static routes on the routers so that data can pass through the networks. The network diagram for all of the exercises in this chapter is shown in the following illustration:

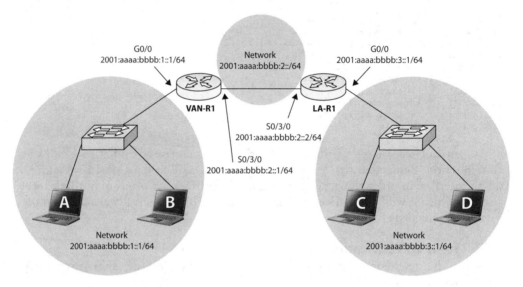

1. Ensure all network devices are booted up.

2. Connect to the console port of VAN-R1.

3. On the VAN-R1 router, verify that the Gig0/0 and Serial0/3/0 interfaces are up by viewing their statuses.

4. To enable IPv6 routing on VAN-R1, type the following commands:

```
VAN-R1>enable
VAN-R1#config term
Enter configuration commands, one per line.  End with CNTL/Z.
VAN-R1(config)#ipv6 unicast-routing
```

5. To assign an IPv6 address to Gig0/0 and Serial0/3/0, use the following commands:

```
VAN-R1(config)#interface g0/0
VAN-R1(config-if)#ipv6 address 2001:aaaa:bbbb:1::1/64
VAN-R1(config-if)#no shutdown
VAN-R1(config-if)#interface s0/3/0
VAN-R1(config-if)#ipv6 address 2001:aaaa:bbbb:2::1/64
VAN-R1(config-if)#no shutdown
```

Note the IP addresses of each interface.

6. To verify the IPv6 addresses on each of the interfaces, use the **show ipv6 interface brief** command:

```
VAN-R1(config-if)#exit
VAN-R1(config)#exit
VAN-R1#show ipv6 interface brief
GigabitEthernet0/0        [up/up]
    FE80::209:7CFF:FE04:AB01
    2001:AAAA:BBBB:1::1
Serial0/3/0               [up/up]
    FE80::209:7CFF:FE04:AB01
    2001:AAAA:BBBB:2::1
```

Note the global unicast address and the link-local address assigned to each of the interfaces.

7. Switch to the console port of the LA-R1 router and navigate to global configuration mode.

8. Enable IPv6 routing on the LA-R1 router.

9. Configure the IPv6 address of 2001:aaaa:bbbb:2::2/64 on the serial interface of the LA-R1 router.

10. Configure the IPv6 address of 2001:aaaa:bbbb:3::1/64 on the Gigabit interface of the LA-R1 router.

11. The following summarizes all of the commands you should have used:

```
LA-R1>enable
LA-R1#config term
LA-R1(config)#ipv6 unicast-routing
LA-R1(config)#interface s0/3/0
LA-R1(config-if)#ipv6 address 2001:aaaa:bbbb:2::2/64
LA-R1(config-if)#no shutdown
LA-R1(config-if)#interface g0/0
LA-R1(config-if)#ipv6 address 2001:aaaa:bbbb:3::1/64
LA-R1(config-if)#no shutdown
LA-R1(config-if)#exit
LA-R1(config)#exit
LA-R1#
```

Verify your IPv6 addresses on LA-R1 by entering the **show ipv6 interface brief** command.

12. Verify the IPv6 routing table on LA-R1 by running the **show ipv6 route** command.

13. To test the connectivity between the WAN link of routers LA-R1 and VAN-R1, use the following **ping** command, which should be successful:

```
LA-R1#ping 2001:aaaa:bbbb:2::1
Type escape sequence to abort.
Sending 5, 100-byte ICMP Echos to 2001:aaaa:bbbb:2::1, timeout is 2 seconds:
!!!!!
Success rate is 100 percent (5/5), round-trip min/avg/max = 1/3/12 ms
```

14. To test the connectivity between the LA-R1 and the Vancouver network by pinging the Gigabit interface, run the following commands (note that the ping should not be successful because LA-R1 does not know how to reach the :1 subnet):

```
LA-R1#ping 2001:aaaa:bbbb:1::1
Type escape sequence to abort.
Sending 5, 100-byte ICMP Echos to 2001:aaaa:bbbb:1::1, timeout is 2 seconds:
.....
Success rate is 0 percent (0/5)
```

15. To be able to ping each of the networks, you need to add a static IPv6 route to the routing tables. On LA-R1, add a static route to the :1 subnet by entering the following command:

```
LA-R1>enable
LA-R1#config term
LA-R1(config)#ipv6 route 2001:aaaa:bbbb:1::/64 2001:aaaa:bbbb:2::1
```

Note that the this statement is saying, "If there is any data for the 2001:aaaa:bbbb:1 subnet, send it over to 2001:aaaa:bbbb:2::1 address," which is VAN-R1's WAN interface.

16. View the IPv6 routing table on LA-R1, and you should see the entry for the :1 subnet.

17. Now you need to add a static route to the VAN-R1 router so it knows how to reach the :3 subnet. Go to the CLI of VAN-R1.

18. Enter the following commands to add an IPv6 route to reach the :3 subnet:

```
VAN-R1>enable
VAN-R1#config term
Enter configuration commands, one per line.  End with CNTL/Z.
VAN-R1(config)#ipv6 route 2001:aaaa:bbbb:3::/64 2001:aaaa:bbbb:2::2
```

19. Verify that the route for the :3 subnet was added by using the **show ipv6 route** command.

20. Switch back to the LA-R1 router and try to ping the WAN interface of VAN-R1 by its IPv6 address:

```
LA-R1#ping 2001:aaaa:bbbb:2::1
Type escape sequence to abort.
Sending 5, 100-byte ICMP Echos to 2001:aaaa:bbbb:2::1, timeout is 2 seconds:
!!!!!
Success rate is 100 percent (5/5), round-trip min/avg/max = 1/3/12 ms
```

21. Now try to ping the IPv6 address of the Gigabit port on VAN-R1 from LA-R1. (It should be successful this time because we have IPv6 static routes configured.)

```
LA-R1#ping 2001:aaaa:bbbb:1::1
Type escape sequence to abort.
Sending 5, 100-byte ICMP Echos to 2001:aaaa:bbbb:1::1, timeout is 2 seconds:
!!!!!
Success rate is 100 percent (5/5), round-trip min/avg/max = 1/4/17 ms
```

Exercise 14-2: Configuring OSPFv3 Routing

In this exercise, you will remove the IPv6 static routes created in the previous exercise and then configure the OSPFv3 routing protocol to share the IPv6 routing tables between the two routers.

1. Ensure that all Cisco routers are up and running.

2. Console into VAN-R1 and remove the static route by entering the following commands:

```
VAN-R1>enable
VAN-R1#config term
VAN-R1(config)#no ipv6 route 2001:aaaa:bbbb:3::/64
```

3. Verify that the route has been removed with the **do show ipv6 route** command.

4. Connect to the console port of LA-R1 and remove the static route with the following commands:

```
LA-R1#enable
LA-R1#config term
LA-R1(config)#no ipv6 route 2001:aaaa:bbbb:1::/64
```

5. From the LA-R1 router, see if you can ping the address of 2001:aaaa:bbbb:1::1. (You should not be able to, because the route is gone that gives the router knowledge of how to reach that system.)

6. To configure OSPFv3 on VAN-R1, enter the following commands:

```
VAN-R1(config)#ipv6 unicast-routing
VAN-R1(config)#ipv6 router ospf 1
VAN-R1(config-rtr)#router-id 0.0.0.1
VAN-R1(config-rtr)#exit
```

7. To configure the interfaces for area 0, enter the following commands:

```
VAN-R1(config)#interface g0/0
VAN-R1(config-if)#ipv6 ospf 1 area 0

VAN-R1(config-if)#interface s0/3/0
VAN-R1(config-if)#ipv6 ospf 1 area 0
VAN-R1(config-if)#exit
VAN-R1(config)#exit
```

8. To configure OSPFv3 on LA-R1, enter the following commands:

```
LA-R1>enable
LA-R1#config term
LA-R1(config)#ipv6 unicast-routing
LA-R1(config)#ipv6 router ospf 1
%OSPFv3-4-NORTRID: OSPFv3 process 1 could not pick a router-id, please
configure manually
LA-R1(config-rtr)#router-id 0.0.0.2
LA-R1(config-rtr)#exit
```

```
LA-R1(config)#interface g0/0
LA-R1(config-if)#ipv6 ospf 1 area 0
LA-R1(config-if)#interface s0/3/0
LA-R1(config-if)#ipv6 ospf 1 area 0
LA-R1(config-if)#exit
LA-R1(config)#exit
LA-R1#
01:51:40: %OSPFv3-5-ADJCHG: Process 1, Nbr 0.0.0.1 on Serial0/3/0 from
LOADING to FULL, Loading Done
LA-R1#
```

9. From LA-R1, enter **ping 2001:aaaa:bbbb:1::1** to test connectivity to the :1 subnet. It should be successful, because OSPF has shared the routing tables between the two routers.

10. Use the following commands to verify the configuration of OSPFv3 on both routers:

```
show ipv6 interface brief
show ipv6 route
show ipv6 ospf
```

Chapter Review

This chapter focused on an introduction to IPv6. Because of the limited number of remaining addresses in IPv4, IPv6 was designed to bring the Internet into its next generation. IPv6 addresses use eight sets of four hexadecimal addresses (16 bits in each set), separated by a colon (:), like this: *xxxx:xxxx:xxxx:xxxx:xxxx:xxxx:xxxx:xxxx*. If you have successive fields of zeroes in an IPv6 address, you can represent them by using two colons (::). However, you can use this shorthand only *once* in the address.

IPv6 addresses come in three basic types: anycast, multicast, and unicast. An anycast address is very different from an IPv4 broadcast: it represents a one-to-the-nearest interface, where many interfaces can share the same address. A multicast address is similar to a multicast in IPv4: one-to-many. A unicast address represents a single interface. Global unicast addresses are 2000::/3. A loopback is ::1. Site-local private addresses range from FEC:: through FFF::, and link-local addresses range from FE8:: through FEB::.

Many of the IPv4 fields in the IP header have been deprecated and are no longer used today. The IPv6 header has been simplified and streamlined to make it more efficient for today's networks. Some protocols, such as ARP and IGMP, have also been deprecated. Their functions are now performed by IMCPv6, which also has some new functions, including router, DNS server, and neighbor discovery.

The most common way of assigning static addresses to an interface is to use the EUI-64 method. DHCPv6 and stateless autoconfiguration enable a device to acquire an address dynamically. Stateless autoconfiguration accomplishes this by requesting that a router give the subnet ID and the device using EUI-64 to acquire an interface ID dynamically.

Routing protocols supported in IPv6 include static, RIPng, OSPFv3, IS-IS for IPv6, MP-BGP4, and EIGRP for IPv6. RIPng uses UDP port 521 for its connections. Its destination multicast address is FF02::9. The most common transition methods to move from IPv4 to IPv6 include dual stacking and 6to4 tunneling. In dual stacking, a device runs both protocol stacks. In 6to4 tunneling, IPv6 packets are encapsulated in an IPv4 packet to move across an IPv4 backbone to another IPv6 network.

You must first execute the **ipv6 unicast-routing** command to enable IPv6. An address must be assigned to each interface, typically using the EUI-64 method, for it to process IPv6 packets. RIPng must be configured globally and then enabled on a per-interface basis. A tag is used to specify the RIPng routing process to which an interface belongs. Like RIPng, OSPFv3 and EIGRP must be configured globally and then enabled on a per-interface basis. In the OSPFv3 Global Configuration, you define the router ID and the area numbers; you then associate the interfaces to the areas for an OSPF process. For EIGRP for IPv6, the Global Configuration requires you to configure an autonomous system number and, possibly, bring up the routing process with the **no shutdown** command.

Quick Review

Necessity of IPv6

- IPv6 addresses are 128 bits in length.
- IPsec is built into the IPv6 protocol and allows for device roaming without losing connectivity.

IPv6 Addressing

- IPv6 addresses use eight sets of four hexadecimal addresses (16 bits in each set), separated by a colon (:), like this: *xxxx:xxxx:xxxx:xxxx:xxxx:xxxx:xxxx:xxxx*.
- If you have successive fields of zeroes in an IPv6 address, you can represent them using two colons (::), but this can be used only once in an address.
- An anycast address represents the nearest interface to a device, where many devices can share an anycast address. Multicast addresses begin with FF.
- Global unicast addresses are public addresses, similar in purpose to IPv4 public addresses. Global unicast addresses begin with 2 or 3, for example 2000 or 2001.
- Site-local/unique local addresses are similar in purpose to IPv4 private addresses and always start with FEC:: through FFF::. It is common to see reference to FEC0 for site-local/unique local addresses.

- Link-local addresses are similar in purpose to APIPA addresses in IPv4 and start with FE80.
- The subnet ID is the first 64 bits and the interface ID is the last 64 bits. EUI-64 enables dynamic creation of the interface ID portion by using the MAC address on the interface.

IPv6 Enhancements

- The IPv6 header has been updated and simplified because some of the fields in the IPv4 header have no relevance today.
- ICMPv6 has been enhanced. ICMPv6 takes over the responsibilities of the IPv4 ARP and IGMP protocols, and it also performs neighbor, router, and DNS server discovery services.

Address Assignment

- DHCPv6 and stateless autoconfiguration enable interfaces to acquire their addressing dynamically.
- Stateless autoconfiguration enables an interface to learn the subnet ID from a router and dynamically create the interface ID using the EUI-64 method.

Routing and IPv6

- Supported routing protocols for IPv6 include static, RIPng, OSPFv3, IS-IS for IPv6, MP-BGP4, and EIGRP for IPv6.
- RIPng is based on RIPv2. The all RIP routers multicast address is FF02::9 and is sent via UDP to port 521.
- In dual stack, a device runs both the IPv4 and IPv6 protocol stacks. And 6to4 tunneling tunnels IPv6 packets in an IPv4 payload to connect two IPv6 networks via an intermediate IPv4 network.

IPv6 Configuration

- The **ipv6 unicast-routing** command globally enables IPv6 and must be the first IPv6 command executed on the router. The **ipv6 address** command assigns the prefix, the length, and the use of EUI-64 to assign the interface ID.
- The **ipv6 router rip** *tag* command enables an RIPng routing process on the router. The **ipv6 rip** *tag* **enable** command associates an interface to a particular RIPng routing process. The **show ipv6 rip** command displays the configuration of the RIPng routing process. The **show ipv6 route rip** command displays the RIPng routes in the IPv6 routing table.

- The **ipv6 router ospf** *process_ID* command takes you into the OSPFv3 routing process, and the **router-id** and **area** commands define the router's ID and the areas the router is connected to. The **ipv6 ospf** *process_ID* **area** *area_number* command associates an interface to a particular OSPF routing process and area.

- The **ipv6 router eigrp** *autonomous* command takes you into the EIGRP for IPv6 routing process, and the **no shutdown** command enables the EIGRP for IPv6 process (this is required in certain versions of IOS). The **ipv6 eigrp** *autonomous_system* command associates an interface to a particular EIGRP for IPv6 autonomous system.

Questions

The following questions will help you measure your understanding of the material presented in this chapter. Read all the choices carefully, as there may be more than one correct answer. Choose the correct answer(s) for each question.

1. You are configuring OSPF for IPv6 on your router that has the following interfaces configured:

G0/0: 192.168.2.1/24
S0/3/0: 192.168.3.1/24

You would like to configure OSPF to route traffic for the G0/0 interface only. What commands would you use to enable routing of IPv6 with OSPF on the G0/0 interface?

A. R1(config)#**ipv6 unicast-routing**
  R1(config)#**ipv6 ospf 10**
  R1(config-rtr)#**router-id 0.0.0.1**

B. R1(config)#**ipv6 ospf 10**
  R1(config)#**router-id 0.0.0.1**

C. R1(config)#**ipv6 ospf 10**
  R1(config)#**network 192.168.2.0**

D. R1(config)#**ipv6 unicast-routing**
  R1(config)#**ipv6 router ospf 10**
  R1(config-rtr)#**router-id 0.0.0.1**
  R1(config)#**interface G0/0**
  R1(config-if)#**ipv6 ospf 10 area 0**

2. Which of the following are valid IPv6 unicast addresses? (Choose two.)

A. 2001::567::891::

B. 2000::57

C. 2000:FFEE:7878:1111:1:2:7:E

D. 2001::

3. Which of the following best describes an anycast address?

   A. One-to-all

   B. One-to-many

   C. Single interface

   D. One-to-nearest

4. Which of the following represents a global unicast address?

   A. 2001:FFEE:7880::

   B. FF80::9868:1122:ABCD:1234

   C. ::1

   D. None of the above

5. Which of the following IPv4 protocols have been replaced by functions performed by ICMPv6? (Choose two.)

   A. ARP

   B. RIP

   C. DHCP

   D. IGMP

6. Which of the following enables a router to forward a DHCP request to a remote DHCP server?

   A. DHCP solicit

   B. Stateless autoconfiguration

   C. Stateful autoconfiguration

   D. IP Helper

7. Which of the following is true concerning RIPng?

   A. Uses 6to4 to share routing information with neighboring routers

   B. Uses a multicast address of FF02::9

   C. Uses TCP as a transport

   D. Uses port 520

8. Match the transition method with its description:

Transition method	Description
dual stack	host-to-host tunneling
6to4 tunneling	virtual links connect IPv6 localities
ISATAP	IPv6 packets are encapsulated in IPv4 payloads
Teredo tunneling	both protocol stacks are operational on a device

9. Which IPv6 command must be the first one entered on a Cisco router?

A. router ipv6-unicast

B. ipv6 address

C. ipv6 unicast-routing

D. ipv6 support enable

10. What command would you use to configure your router to use a global IPv6 address based on the modified EUI-64 format?

A. Ipv6 address 2001:aaaa:bbbb:1::1/64

B. ipv6 enable

C. ipv6 address autoconfig

D. Ipv6 address FE80::/EUI-64

11. Which router command enables RIPng on an interface?

A. ipv6 rip *tag* enable

B. network

C. ipv6 router rip *tag*

D. ripng enable *tag*

12. Which of the following address types represents an IPv6 private address that is not routable on the Internet?

A. Global

B. Multicast

C. Loopback

D. Unique-local

Performance-based Question

1. Looking at the following IPv6 network, what commands would you use to configure a primary route from router R3 to the Loopback interface on R1, and use the pathway of R2 as an alternate route?

From the available commands on the left, draw a line from the appropriate commands on the left, into the two configuration spots of router R3 (on the real exam you would drag and drop for this type of question).

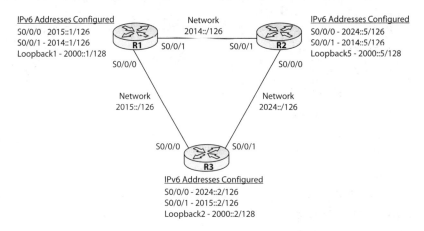

Available Commands

ipv6 route 2000::1/128 2014::1

ipv6 route 2000::1/128 2015::1

ipv6 route 2000::1/128 2014::5 10

ipv6 route 2000::1/128 2024::2 10

ipv6 route 2000::1/128 2015::2

ipv6 route 2000::1/128 2024::5 10

Desired Router R3 Configuration

Command 1:

Command 2:

Answers

1. D. To enable OSPF for IPv6, you first must enable IPv6 routing, and then start the OSPFv3 routing process and give it an ID. You then assign a router ID to the router, and finally configure each desired interface for OSPF.

2. B, C. 2000::57 and 2000:FFEE:7878:1111:1:2:7:E are valid IPv6 unicast addresses. As a reference, **A** is incorrect because it has multiple :: representations, making it invalid. The problem with choice **D** is it has the interface ID value of all 0s, which is also invalid.

3. D. An anycast is one-to-nearest type of address.

4. A. A global unicast address always has the first three bits set to 001, which means they will always start with a 2 (0010) or a 3 (0011). Therefore, 2001:FFEE:7880:: is correct.

5. A, D. IPv4's ARP and IGMP have been deprecated in IPv6; these functions are now performed by ICMPv6.

6. D. IP Helper is the feature that enables the router to forward a DHCP solicit message to a remote DHCP server. For reference, **A**, DHCP solicit, is what a DHCP client generates to acquire its addressing information. **B**, stateless autoconfiguration, is what a client performs when DHCP is not configured but the client still wants to acquire its addressing dynamically.

7. B. RIPng uses a multicast address of FF02::9.

8. Dual stack: both protocol stacks are operational on a device.
6to4 tunneling: IPv6 packets are encapsulated in IPv4 payloads.
ISATAP: virtual links connect IPv6 localities.
Teredo tunneling: host-to-host tunneling.

9. C. The **ipv6 unicast-routing** command globally enables IPv6 and must be the first IPv6 command executed on the router.

10. C. Use the **ipv6 address autoconfig** command to auto-assign a modified EUI-64 format to the host ID portion of the address.

11. A. The **ipv6 rip** *tag* **enable** command enables RIPng on an interface.

12. D. The **unique-local** IPv6 address type is a private address similar to the 10.0.0.0/8 IPv4 private address type. A unique-local address is also known as a site-local address and has an address that typically starts with FE80.

Performance-based Answer

1. This looks like a complex question, but really it is just a simple routing question using your knowledge of IPv6 you learned in this chapter, plus the static routing knowledge from Chapter 11. In this example, you need to add two routes to the address of 2000::1/128. The first route must use the direct pathway to R1 so you specify that the static route is to send to 2015::1, while the backup route is to use a static floating route that has the administrative distance set to a higher value (in this case 10). The backup route will send the data to R2, so you must point to the interface on R2 closest to R3.

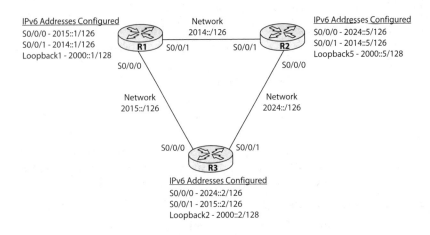

IPv6 Addresses Configured
S0/0/0 - 2015::1/126
S0/0/1 - 2014::1/126
Loopback1 - 2000::1/128

Network
2014::/126

IPv6 Addresses Configured
S0/0/0 - 2024::5/126
S0/0/1 - 2014::5/126
Loopback5 - 2000::5/128

R1   S0/0/1   S0/0/1   R2
S0/0/0   S0/0/0

Network
2015::/126

Network
2024::/126

S0/0/0   R3   S0/0/1

IPv6 Addresses Configured
S0/0/0 - 2024::2/126
S0/0/1 - 2015::2/126
Loopback2 - 2000::2/128

Available Commands

ipv6 route 2000::1/128 2014::1

ipv6 route 2000::1/128 2014::5 10

ipv6 route 2000::1/128 2024::2 10

ipv6 route 2000::1/128 2015::2

Desired Router R3 Configuration

Command 1:

ipv6 route 2000::1/128 2015::1

Command 2:

ipv6 route 2000::1/128 2024::5 10

Wireless Networking

In this chapter, you will

- Learn about wireless network concepts such as radio frequency, SSIDs, and channels
- Learn about wireless standards and protocols
- Understand wireless architectures, positioning of WLC, and AP modes
- Understand management access connections

Networks are no longer limited to using cabled, or wired, devices. Today's networks use a mix of wired systems along with wireless systems that use radio frequencies (RFs) to transmit data to a *wireless access point* (WAP). The WAP may have a connection to the wired network, which enables the wireless devices to communicate with the entire network.

This chapter introduces you to the world of wireless networks! It's important that you understand the various aspects of wireless networks for your CCNA certification exam, so be sure to study this chapter well. This chapter introduces you to wireless basics, will discuss some security concerns around wireless, and will then show you how to set up a wireless network.

Introducing Wireless

In a wireless network, radio frequencies (RFs) transmit data from one device to another through the air. Wireless networks are especially useful in offices, where they enable workers to use laptops anywhere throughout the location to connect to the network instead of using only desktop computers hardwired to the network. Most laptops have wireless network cards installed to enable wireless.

As you know, computers work with data in the form of 1s and 0s. With wireless, the transceiver in the wireless network device is responsible for encoding that data into RF waves. If you could look at an RF wave, you'd see that the low frequency parts of the wave are 0s, while the high frequency parts of the wave are 1s (see Figure 15-1).

Figure 15-1
Radio waves
represent data
(1s and 0s) being
delivered.

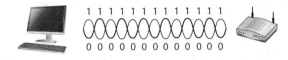

When a system sends data on a wireless network, the transceiver built into the computer's wireless network card encodes the data (1s and 0s) into radio waves. The transceiver then passes the data to the wireless antenna on the device to send the radio waves through the air to the receiving device, where its antenna picks up the radio waves and passes them to the transceiver. Then the transceiver converts the radio waves to data (1s and 0s) for the receiving device to read.

Wireless Concepts

A number of network components are used to create a wireless network. In this section we look at the common components you need to be familiar with.

Wireless Access Point

The WAP device, commonly referred to as just *access point*, adds wireless capabilities to your network. It is responsible for sending and receiving radio waves to enable wireless devices to communicate with other devices on the local area network (LAN). A wireless device (such as a laptop) sends data to a device on the LAN (such as a printer), by first sending the data wirelessly to the wireless access point, which then passes the data on to the device that is connected to the wired network (the printer). Figure 15-2 displays a typical setup of a network that uses a WAP.

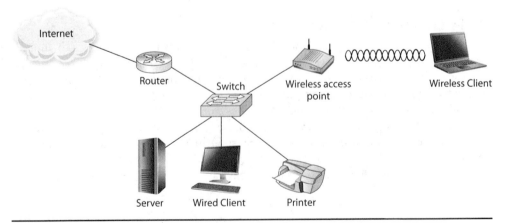

Figure 15-2   A WAP enables wireless devices to talk to the LAN.

Wireless Clients

A wireless client is any device that has a wireless network card installed and that communicates with an RF signal. Examples of wireless clients are laptops, smart phones, tablets, and any other device that has a wireless network card installed. The wireless client, also known as a wireless station, typically connects to the network via the WAP.

To connect your wireless clients to a wireless network, you need a WAP, which has antennas that send and receive the wireless signal between the wireless client and access point, but the access point also has a connection to the wired network so that wireless clients can access resources on the wired network. Most home users have a wireless router, which performs the function of an access point, but also includes other features such as Network Address Translation (NAT), a network firewall, and Dynamic Host Configuration Protocol (DHCP) services. Although most IT folks interchange the terms of wireless access point and wireless router, they are technically different devices. The wireless access point is focused on providing connectivity to wireless clients, while a wireless router does that, but also provides the additional services just mentioned.

Wireless LAN Controller

Enterprise networks that have a number of access points (APs) can have multiple APs configured from a central point by using a wireless LAN controller (WLC). The WLC can also provide centralized authentication for all your network's APs if you configure the WLC to use a central Remote Authentication Dial-In User Service (RADIUS) server.

The WLC connects to the network in the same way the AP does—they both connect to a network switch, which is a wired device on the network (that is, it's not connected wirelessly). Once all of the APs and the WLC are connected to the network, the WLC can be used to deploy configuration settings to the APs or to perform other administrative tasks such as software upgrades.

Figure 15-3 shows an example of how the WLC and the APs may be positioned on a network. Notice the APs on floors 2, 3, and 4 that provide wireless access to the devices on those floors. Also notice that each AP has a wired Ethernet connection to a switch; this switch is known as the *distribution system* (DS). The DS could be a dedicated switch for WAPs to connect to, or it could be a switch for your wired network that all other wired devices connect to. Note that the Cisco 9300 switch can have the WLC controller software installed on it, so that if you were using a 9300 switch in a branch office, you could then deploy a branch WLC without using any additional hardware.

Each of the APs will have its own management IP address, and you can remotely connect to that AP and change the configuration settings. Or you can add a WLC to the network that is used to centrally manage the configuration of all the APs. Notice in Figure 15-3 that the WLC is located on floor 1 and is connected to the switch, or distribution system, as well.

The port on the WLC that connects to the switch (the distribution system) is the *distribution port*. Because the WLC sends a lot of data through that port, including traffic destined for the APs in the CAPWAP (Control and Provisioning of Wireless Access Points) tunnel and traffic from the wireless clients, it is common for a WLC to have multiple distribution ports that connect the WLC to the distribution system (the switch).

Figure 15-3
Access points
and a wireless
LAN controller
connect to the
switch.

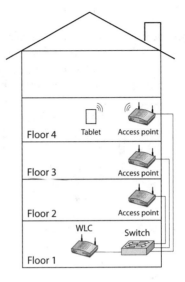

These distribution ports always operate as trunk ports (instead of access ports) because they need to carry traffic for all of the virtual LANs (VLANs). It is also common to combine the distribution ports together in a *link aggregation group* (LAG), which combines the bandwidth of all ports in the group. The LAG also provides load balancing on the ports so that no one port is over-utilized and fault tolerance on the link can handle the workload if one port fails the other ports in the group.

Putting It All Together

Let's take a look at a typical setup for a wireless network using an AP to provide network access to clients on the network that are part of different VLANs. In Figure 15-4, you can see a Cisco switch that contains two VLANs: VLAN 10 for the accounting department and VLAN 20 for the marketing department.

To give each department wireless access, we connect an access point to the switch, but notice in the figure that the access point is connected to a port that is outside the two VLANs. This is because we need the AP to deliver traffic for both VLANs. So we connect the AP to the switch, and then configure the port that the AP is connected to as a trunk port, so that it can carry traffic for VLAN 10 and VLAN 20.

To configure the AP, you connect to the AP, either through the CLI or the web GUI and configure two *Service Set Identifiers* (SSIDs). The SSID is the name of the wireless network that the clients will choose when they see a list of available networks; this is the wireless network that the clients will connect to. Each AP can provide multiple wireless networks or multiple SSIDs. In our example, we configure an SSID for accounting (ACCT_WLAN) and an SSID for marketing (MKT_WLAN) and then assign each SSID to the appropriate VLAN.

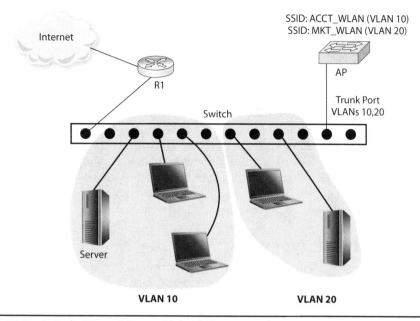

SSID: ACCT_WLAN (VLAN 10)
SSID: MKT_WLAN (VLAN 20)

Internet

R1

AP

Switch

Trunk Port
VLANs 10,20

Server

VLAN 10   VLAN 20

Figure 15-4   A single AP providing multiple wireless networks

Antenna Types

The typical wireless network environment involves using a WAP with connected antennas that transmit the radio signal through the air. The new CCNA exam expects you to understand these types of wireless antennas that are used by wireless technologies:

- **Omnidirectional**   Sends the radio signals in all directions to cover a broad range or area.

- **Semi-directional**   Sends radio signals in a single direction, but the signal has a wide range of coverage in that direction. You can compare this to a streetlight that shines downward but covers a wide area below. An example of a semi-directional antenna is a hallway wireless antenna in a facility.

- **Highly directional**   Also known as *unidirectional*, this antenna sends radio signals in a single direction covering a very small area. Back to the light analogy—you can compare this to the way that a spotlight covers a small area when the light shines. A highly directional antenna could be used in a long hallway in a hospital or warehouse and would cover the long, narrow, confined space.

In addition, a few common practices can help cover the area needed by the wireless network and control connections to your wireless network. Several methods can help with area coverage and security with your wireless network by manipulating characteristics of the antenna.

For better performance and area coverage, try maintaining line of sight between antennas. Although this is not required, remember that the more objects the signal has to pass through, the weaker the signal will get. Also ensure that the antennas on the WAP are a reasonable distance from the wireless clients. If a client is too far away, it may not be able to connect. From a security point of view, you want to limit who is connecting to your wireless network by placing the WAP (and its antennas) in the center of the building. And remember that if you place the AP close to an outer wall of the building, it is possible that someone outside the building could connect to your wireless network.

You can also change the power levels on the AP to control how strong the signal is. If clients cannot connect to the AP because they are too far away, you may solve the problem by increasing the AP power level, which strengthens the signal so it can travel farther. From a security point of view, be aware that it's better to *lower* the power levels so that the range of the signal does not go beyond the building walls.

Wireless Network Types

You can create two major modes of wireless networks: ad hoc mode or infrastructure mode. Each of these is known as a wireless mode, and each has its advantages.

With *ad hoc mode*, the wireless device, such as a laptop, is connected to other wireless devices in a peer-to-peer environment without the need for a WAP. With *infrastructure mode*, the wireless clients are connected to a central device, which is a WAP. The wireless client sends data to the AP, which then sends the data on to the destination (as shown in Figure 15-5). As mentioned, the wireless client can access network

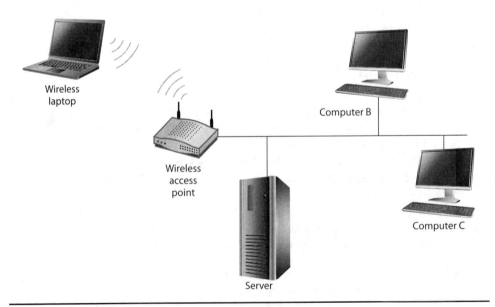

Figure 15-5   A typical wireless network running in infrastructure mode

resources on the wired network once connected to the AP because the AP is connected to the wired network.

The advantage of ad hoc mode is that you don't need to purchase the AP; the benefit of infrastructure mode is that when you use the WAP, you get to control who can connect to the wireless network, and many devices can connect to the AP at one time to share information.

Wireless Terminology

You need to be familiar with a number of other wireless terms and concepts for the Cisco CCNA exam. Some of these terms have already been mentioned in the chapter:

Basic Service Set (BSS) This refers to a wireless network that has a single AP. All wireless clients connect to the single AP to gain access to the network.

Basic Service Set Identifier (BSSID) This is the MAC address of the WAP. When you use wireless security tools to assess the security of a wireless network, you will notice that the tools identify the AP MAC with the label "BSSID." When you use many of the command line security tools, you usually specify the AP you are testing with the --**bssid** switch.

Service Set Identifier (SSID) This is the name of the wireless network. When configuring the AP, you will need to configure the name of the wireless network by setting the SSID setting.

Distribution System (DS) This is the network switch that connects the AP to the LAN.

Extended Service Set (ESS) In larger organizations with office environments that span large areas, such as multiple floors or multiple buildings, you'll probably not be able to have a single AP service (aka BSS) for all the wireless clients because they are physically spread out. In this case you need to set up an ESS, which comprises a number of access points, configured with the same SSID, that are positioned at different points throughout the building to service wireless clients within that area.

Creating an ESS requires the following:

- Each AP must be configured with the same SSID.
- Each AP must be configured with a different, non-overlapping, channel.
- The AP must cover areas that overlap by 10 percent, so that roaming wireless clients do not lose a connection.

Figure 15-6 compares a BSS with an ESS.

 EXAM TIP Be sure to know the wireless terms discussed in this section for the CCNA exam.

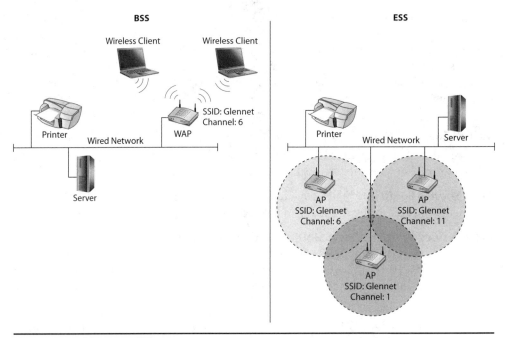

Figure 15-6 BSS versus ESS

Wireless Standards

The Institute of Electrical and Electronics Engineers (IEEE) committee has developed wireless standards in the 802 project models for wireless networking. Wireless and several standards are defined by the 802.11 project model.

802.11a

The 802.11a wireless standard is an older standard that runs at the 5 GHz frequency. 802.11a devices can transmit data at 54 Mbps and are incompatible with 802.11b and 802.11g devices.

 EXAM TIP For the exam, remember that 802.11a was an early wireless standard that ran at a different frequency than 80211.b and 802.11g. This makes it incompatible with 802.11b/g. Remember that 802.11a defines wireless environments running at 54 Mbps while using a frequency of 5 GHz.

802.11b

The 802.11b wireless standard has a transfer rate of 11 Mbps while using a frequency of 2.4 GHz. These devices are compatible with 802.11g/n devices because they run at the same frequency and follow the Wi-Fi standard.

EXAM TIP Note that 802.11b runs at 11 Mbps, and 802.11g runs at 54 Mbps. The 802.11n standard is designed to reach up to 600 Mbps!

802.11g

The 802.11g wireless standard is a newer standard that was designed to be compatible with 802.11b, but it also increases the transfer rate. The transfer rate of 802.11g devices is 54 Mbps using a frequency of 2.4 GHz.

All 802.11g devices are compatible with 802.11b/n devices because they all follow the Wi-Fi standard and run at the same frequency of 2.4 GHz.

802.11n

The 802.11n wireless standard is a wireless standard that came out in late 2009. The goal of 802.11n is to increase the transfer rate beyond what current standards such as 802.11g support. 802.11n supports transfer rates up to 600 Mbps.

To help accomplish this, 802.11n introduced two new features: multiple input, multiple output (MIMO) and channel bonding. MIMO uses multiple antennas to achieve more throughput than can be accomplished with only a single antenna. Channel bonding enables 802.11n to transmit data over two non-overlapping channels to achieve more throughput. 802.11n is designed to be backward compatible with 802.11a, 802.11b, and 802.11g and can run at the 2.4 GHz or 5 GHz frequency.

EXAM TIP Wireless networks today are called *Wi-Fi*, which stands for *wireless fidelity*. 802.11b, 802.11g, and 802.11n are all part of the Wi-Fi standard and, as a result, are compatible with one another.

802.11ac

The 802.11ac wireless standard was approved in 2014 and is considered a high-throughput wireless standard that runs on the 5 GHz frequency range. The 802.11ac standard offers throughput of potentially 1 Gbps by increasing the channel width and offering similar features to the 802.11n standard, such as MIMO and multi-user MIMO (MU-MIMO), which involves enabling multiple transmitters to send separate signals and multiple receivers to receive separate signals at the same time.

Most 802.11ac wireless routers have a universal serial bus (USB) 3.0 port, where you can connect an external hard drive to the wireless router and stream high-definition video to clients.

It is important to note that 802.11a was an early implementation of wireless networking and is not compatible with early Wi-Fi networks such as 802.11b and 802.11g. As an example of the compatibility, my home wireless network has an AP that is an 802.11g device, but one of my old laptops has an 802.11b wireless network card. My old laptop can communicate on the network because the two standards are 100 percent compatible with one another. In this example, the laptop with the 802.11b card connects only at 11 Mbps, while my new laptop with the 802.11g card connects at 54 Mbps.

	802.11	802.11	802.11	802.11n	802.11ac
Frequency	5 GHz	2.4 GHz	2.4 GHz	5/2.4 GHz	5 GHz
Transfer Rate	54 Mbps	11 Mbps	54 Mbps	Up to 600 Mbps	1 Gbps
Range	150 feet	300 feet	300 feet	300 feet	300 feet, but more throughput
Compatibility	802.11	802.11g/n	802.11b/n	802.11a/b/g	802.11a/b/g/n

Table 15-1 Comparing the Different Wireless Standards

Key Points About Wireless Standards to Remember

Table 15-1 summarizes key points you need to be familiar with about the different wireless standards for the CCNA certification exam.

 EXAM TIP   Remember that wireless transmission speeds decrease as your distance from the WAP increases.

Channels

You've read that 802.11b/g/n/ac all run at the 2.4 GHz frequency, but you should also understand that 2.4 GHz is a frequency range. Each frequency in the range is known as a *channel*. This discussion focuses on the 2.4 GHz frequency, which also uses channels, but we'll focus on the 2.4 GHz frequency first, because there are channels that overlap with one another. Using channels that overlap with one another could cause interference and instability with the wireless network.

Most wireless devices enable you to specify which channel you want to use. This is important because if you are having trouble with your wireless network failing a lot, it could be that the wireless devices are conflicting or interfering with other wireless devices in your area. A good example of this is cordless phones; they may run at the 2.4 GHz range and could cause issues with your wireless network. As a solution, you could change the channel on your WAP and clients, which changes the frequency—hopefully preventing any conflicts with other household items. Note that modern cordless phones follow the DECT 6 standard, which moves the communication to the 1.9 GHz band, solving the problem of interference from cordless phones.

Table 15-2 lists the different frequencies used by the different channels.

When looking at a diagram of overlapping channels in the 2.4 GHz frequency, you can see that you can use three main channels that do not overlap—channels 1, 6, and 11.

Looking at Figure 15-7, you can see that channels 1, 6 and 11 do not overlap with one another. So if you were to create multiple wireless networks within the 2.4 GHz frequency, you could start by placing one network on channel 1 and another on channel 6 or 11. Keep in mind that there are other wireless networks around you, so if you are getting interference on your wireless network, it could be because the other wireless

	Channel	Frequency Range
Table 15-2	1	2.3995 GHz–2.4245 GHz
Different Wi-Fi Channels and	2	2.4045 GHz–2.4295 GHz
Their Operating	3	2.4095 GHz–2.4345 GHz
Frequency Ranges	4	2.4145 GHz–2.4395 GHz
	5	2.4195 GHz–2.4445 GHz
	6	2.4245 GHz–2.4495 GHz
	7	2.4295 GHz–2.4545 GHz
	8	2.4345 GHz–2.4595 GHz
	9	2.4395 GHz–2.4645 GHz
	10	2.4445 GHz–2.4695 GHz
	11	2.4495 GHz–2.4745 GHz
	12	2.4545 GHz–2.4795 GHz
	13	2.4595 GHz–2.4845 GHz

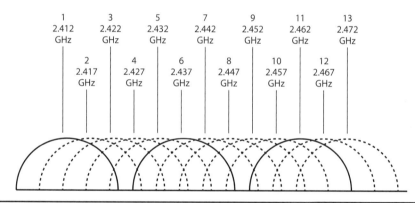

Figure 15-7   Channels 1, 6, and 11 do not overlap.

networks close to you are using the same channel. Experiment with changing the channel on your wireless network to increase the stability of the network.

Use Non-overlapping Channels

Remember when troubleshooting wireless networks that you could be getting interference from other wireless devices and household devices such as cordless phones or Bluetooth devices running on the same channel. To resolve this, experiment by changing the channel your wireless network uses to reduce the amount of interference received. As noted in Table 15-2, adjacent channels have overlapping frequencies and will interfere with one another, so changing from channel 2 to channel 1 will not solve interference problems, but changing from channel 2 to channel 6 might.

TIP To avoid interference on your wireless network from other household items, try to purchase items such as cordless phones that run on a different frequency than 2.4 GHz. If you are experiencing problems on the wireless network, you could try changing the channel on the wireless equipment and see if a different channel is more reliable. Also note that other non-wireless devices such as microwaves can cause interference by generating noise signals in the 2.4 GHz frequency range.

A channel has a specific "width" to it, and that width allows for a specific amount of data to pass through the channel (called *bandwidth*). The point to make here is that a wireless standard that has a larger channel bandwidth will be able to deliver more data and give better performance. For example, 802.11g has a channel bandwidth of 20 MHz, while 802.11n can have a channel bandwidth of 40 MHz (when running on 5 GHz frequency). Increasing the channel bandwidth is the way newer wireless standards are providing better transfer rates. The following lists the channel bandwidth per standard:

- 802.11a: 20 MHz
- 802.11b: 22 MHz
- 802.11g: 20 MHz
- 802.11n: 20 or 40 MHz
- 802.11ac: 20, 40, 80, or 160 MHz

Wireless Security Protocols

A number of wireless authentication and encryption protocols have been developed over the years to help secure your wireless network. You should consider them for implementation on your wireless network.

Wired Equivalent Privacy

Wired Equivalent Privacy (WEP) was designed to give the wireless world a level of security that could equate to that of the wired networking world. In the wired world, someone would have to be in your office to connect a cable to your network, but with wireless networking, this is, of course, not the case. Someone could sit outside your building in a parked car and connect to your wireless network.

To configure your wireless network with WEP, you simply specify a shared key, or passphrase, on the WAP. The theory is that if anyone wants to connect to your wireless network, they'd need to know the shared key and would need to configure their workstation with that key. When you configure the shared key on the AP and client, any data sent between the client and the AP is encrypted with WEP. This will prevent unauthorized individuals from capturing data in transit and reading it.

Note that there were huge flaws in how WEP implemented its encryption and key usage, and as a result, both 64-bit and 128-bit WEP are easily cracked. For security reasons, you should not use WEP unless you have older APs that do not support WPA or WPA2.

Wi-Fi Protected Access

Wi-Fi Protected Access (WPA) was designed to improve upon wireless security and fix some of the flaws in WEP. WPA uses a 128-bit key and the Temporal Key Integrity Protocol (TKIP), which is used to change the encryption keys for every packet that is sent. This will make it far more difficult for hackers to crack the key, which is very easy to do with WEP. WPA uses RC4 as the symmetric encryption algorithm, which is why WPA is sometimes referred to as TKIP-RC4, as in the CCNA objectives.

WPA has a number of other improvements over WEP; for example, it has improved integrity checking, and it supports authentication using the Extensible Authentication Protocol (EAP), a very secure authentication protocol that supports a number of authentication methods such as Kerberos, token cards, certificates, and smartcards.

EAP messages are encapsulated inside IEEE 802.1X packets for network access authentication with wired or wireless networks. When IEEE 802.1X is used to control access to the wireless network, the wireless client attempts to connect to a WAP; the AP asks the client for proof of identity and then forwards that to a RADIUS server for authentication.

Many variations of EAP have developed over time:

- **LEAP**   Lightweight Extensible Authentication Protocol is Cisco's proprietary EAP solution created before the IEEE created 802.1X.

- **PEAP**   Protected Extensible Authentication Protocol is used to encapsulate EAP messages over a secure tunnel that uses Transport Layer Security (TLS). Because EAP assumes the packets are sent over a secure network, with PEAP, TLS is used to create a secure tunnel between two points.

- **EAP-FAST**   EAP-FAST is an authentication protocol designed by Cisco to replace LEAP. EAP-FAST is typically used to provide authentication services to wireless networks.

- **EAP-TLS**   EAP-TLS is the EAP protocol that uses TLS security for secure authentication on wireless networks. The EAP-TLS solution typically involves the use of client certificates to perform the authentication.

- **EAP-TTLS**   EAP-TTLS (EAP-Tunneled Transport Layer Security) builds on EAP-TLS by having the capabilities to authenticate both the client and the server, although the client does not need to use certificates for authentication. The server can authenticate the client after a secure channel is set up using the server's certificate.

When configuring WPA on the wireless network, note that WPA operates in three different modes—WPA Personal, WPA Enterprise, and Open:

- **WPA Personal**   With WPA Personal, aka WPA-PSK (WPA preshared key), you can configure the AP with a starting key value, known as the preshared key, which is then used to encrypt the traffic. This mode is used most by home users and small businesses.

- **WPA Enterprise**   WPA Enterprise, aka WPA-802.1X, is a WPA implementation that uses a central authentication server such as a RADIUS server for authentication and auditing features. WPA Enterprise is used by larger organizations so that they can use their existing authentication server to control who has access to the wireless network and to log network access.

- **Open**   An open wireless network does not require any password to connect and does not use any form of encryption to keep the wireless data secret from prying eyes. Naturally, it is not recommend to leave your wireless network open (you should implement WPA2) or to connect your client system to an open network that you are not familiar with.

 EXAM TIP   The CCNA certification exam will test your knowledge of the different security protocols such as WPA, WPA2, WPA3, and open networks. Always be sure to implement the most secure method supported by your devices; this is usually WPA2.

WPA2

WPA2 improves upon the security of WPA and should be used instead of WPA if you have the choice. WPA2 uses Counter Mode with Cipher Block Chaining Message Authentication Code Protocol (CCMP or CCM Mode Protocol) for data privacy, integrity, and authentication on a WPA2 wireless network. WPA2 uses CCMP with the Advanced Encryption Standard (AES) protocol (which is sometimes referred to as CCMP-AES) for the encryption of wireless traffic instead of TKIP and supports additional features, such as added protection for ad hoc networks and key caching. Because WPA2 uses AES as its encryption protocol, it supports 128-bit, 192-bit, and 256-bit encryption.

WPA2 also supports the TLS and the TTLS protocols through the use of the EAP. Known as EAP-TLS and EAP-TTLS, these protocols offer secure methods of performing authentication on a wireless network.

WPA3

WPA3 is the newest version of WPA, which was developed in 2018 and is slowly being adopted by manufacturers. Because WPA3 is fairly new, you may have it as an option only on newer wireless devices. WPA3 has improved security over WPA2 by introducing some new features:

- It improves the encryption by using 256-bit Galois/Counter Mode Protocol (GCMP-256) for data encryption.

- Simultaneous Authentication of Equals (SAE) is a feature of WPA3 that increases security by enabling the access point to authenticate the client, and the client to authenticate the access point. This stronger authentication method helps prevent eavesdropping and cracking of handshake traffic that was common with WPA2.

- The encryption process with WPA3 uses session keys, which are designed to protect a user from decrypting another user's traffic even if they both have used the same Wi-Fi key.

EXAM TIP Be sure to be familiar with the different wireless security protocols for the CCNA exam.

Wireless Security Practices

Authentication and Authorization

The CCNA exam expects you to be familiar with techniques used to control who gains access to a wireless network via *authentication* and *authorization*.

Shared or Open   An open wireless network, also known as a shared network, does not implement any method to control who gains access to the network. It is the least secure of all the wireless network types.

Preshared Key   You can control who gains access to the wireless network by configuring an encryption protocol such as WPA2 or WPA3 in personal mode, and then specify the encryption key, also known as the preshared key. This encryption key would need to be configured on any device that wants to connect to your wireless network.

MAC Filtering   In addition to using a preshared key, you can configure MAC filtering, which authorizes who is allowed to access the network by their MAC address. Keep in mind that a number of tools can be used to monitor wireless traffic and view the MAC addresses of authorized clients connected to the access point. An attack could then spoof the MAC address to bypass the MAC filtering feature.

802.1X   When using WPA2/WPA3 in enterprise mode, you must specify the IP address of the RADIUS or TACACS+ server in the configuration of the access point or WLC. This means that the access point/WLC will forward the client to the RADIUS server to be authenticated before being granted access to the network. The benefit of 802.1X is that you can authenticate users by more than just a preshared key—they can be authenticated using a username and password against a central authentication service.

Cisco Wireless Architectures

You can use different Cisco wireless architectures while designing your wireless network, as well as the different Cisco WAP modes. And you can connect to APs to perform remote management.

Wireless Architectures

You can set up your Cisco wireless network in different ways: each setup is known as a wireless architecture. Some wireless architectures are simple and involve only a WAP, while other architectures have WLC to help manage the wireless settings across multiple APs.

Autonomous Architecture

With the autonomous architecture model, your Cisco wireless network is made up of independent APs that you manage individually, typically with the GUI of the AP. Each AP could supply one or more SSIDs, with each SSID associated with a different VLAN.

With this model, each SSID is associated with a single VLAN, and the AP has a connection to a switch using a trunk port. The trunk port is configured to carry all traffic for each of the VLANs.

In this scenario, if you need to add a new wireless network (SSID) to all the APs, you must configure each AP individually, because they each operate independently.

Split-MAC Architecture

The split-MAC architecture offers a more centralized model in which a WLC is used to deploy the configuration to each of the APs. In this scenario, the APs are known as *lightweight access points* (LAPs) because they receive their configuration from the WLC and are not configured directly.

In this model the WLC is used to deploy configuration settings such as the radio frequency to use, quality of service (QoS) settings, any authentication, authorization, and accounting (AAA) settings that deal with configuration of a TACACS+/RADIUS server, and policy settings.

In the split-MAC architecture model, Control and Provisioning of Wireless Access Points (CAPWAP) is a secure private tunnel used to carry communication between the WLC and the LAP. All communication between the WLC and LAP travels through the CAPWAP. There are actually two tunnels: one for control communication and another for the data:

- The control channel carries the commands and is encrypted by default. The CAPWAP control channel uses UDP 5246.
- The data channel is not encrypted by default, but it can be encrypted. The CAPWAP data channel uses UDP 5247.

Cloud-based Architecture

In a cloud-based architecture, the WLC is not a device on your physical network, but is provided by a cloud provider and resides in the cloud. The cloud-based WLC provides the same functions as a WLC connected to your LAN, but you have the benefit of it being a cloud device that is managed by the cloud provider. Cloud-based architecture models include a Cisco Meraki license and a Cisco Catalyst 9800-CL, which provide WLC capabilities to a wireless network.

Positioning of WLC

You need to understand the role that the WLC plays on your network to understand where you should physically position the WLC. Types of architectures include centralized WLAN, Cisco FlexConnect mode, and converged WLAN.

Centralized WLAN Architecture

In a centralized WLAN architecture, you are using a WLC to manage your LAPs. All communication to the LAP must pass through the WLC to verify that the communication is authorized (remember that the WLC can provide AAA functionality). This means that communication between two wireless clients connected to the LAP must travel the network path to the WLC (and then back) when data goes from one wireless device to another. This could cause issues with delay or even outages if the WLC is physically distanced from the LAPs.

Placement of the WLC should be carefully considered. If you place the WLC on the opposite end of the network from the LAPs, then the CAPWAP tunnel that carries traffic between the LAP and the WLC must travel across the network, causing delays. Also, because the LAPs must be able to communicate with the WLC, if the WLC or the CAPWAP tunnel goes down in a centralized WLAN architecture, the wireless devices are dropped from the network (even if the LAP is functioning). You can solve this by either changing the mode on the AP (more on this in a bit) or by placing the WLC closer to the LAPs.

Cisco FlexConnect

The Cisco FlexConnect mode on the LAP enables the LAP to pass data to the LAN directly and is not required to pass the data through the WLC. Also, the LAPs can authenticate clients in order for the client to gain wireless access, whereas in the centralized model all authentication was done by the WLC. With the Cisco FlexConnect mode, if the CAPWAP tunnel fails, the LAPs still function because they have their configuration and are authorized to pass traffic on to the network and authenticate wireless clients. The Cisco FlexConnect mode is a popular choice when your WLC is located in the head office and you have LAPs in branch offices.

Converged WLAN Architecture

To ensure that communication between the WLC and the LAPs is efficient and reliable, the WLC and LAPs are connected to the same switch in a converged WLAN architecture. These could be access layer switches or distribution layer switches. This enables the LAPs to communicate with the LAPs through the switch quickly, without needing the traffic to travel across the entire network. In the converged WLAN architecture, you would need multiple WLCs for different parts of the network. The benefit is the CAPWAP tunnel would be a shorter distance between the LAP and its WLC. This topology results in faster Wi-Fi access with less delays.

AP Modes

You just learned that you can change the AP mode to modify how it is being used and how it operates. For the CCNA exam, you need to be familiar with a number of different access point modes, listed here.

Local Mode   This is the default mode for the LAPs and involves what we describe earlier: the LAP has a CAPWAP tunnel to the WLC in which all traffic must pass through the CAPWAP to the WLC. If the CAPWAP fails, all wireless clients are disconnected from that LAP.

Bridged Mode   This mode is used when you want the AP to be used to connect two networks together, such as the networks of two buildings separated by a bit of distance. With this scenario, the AP acting as a bridge is authenticated to the remote wireless network, but the devices in the remote building are not.

FlexConnect Mode   In this mode, the LAPs are in branch offices and the WLC is located in the head office. The LAPs can pass traffic directly between clients and to the LAN, while normally the traffic would need to be sent to the WLC. This is an important feature, because it reduces network delay that would have been caused by sending traffic over the WAN to reach the WLC. With FlexConnect mode, the LAP can be used to authenticate and authorize wireless clients as well. Remember that in FlexConnect mode, the LAPs still function even if the CAPWAP tunnel fails.

Mesh Mode   This mode represents another special scenario mode in which a WAP connects to another WAP, essentially acting as an extender to the wireless network. When a wireless client connects and sends data to the LAN, it is possible that the data will travel through multiple mesh nodes before reaching the LAN. A mesh node (an AP in a mesh topology), also known as a mesh access point (MAP), uses the Adaptive Wireless Path Protocol (AWPP) to determine the best path to the root access point (RAP).

Monitor Mode   This mode is used to monitor activity for rogue APs that are connected to the network. An AP running in monitor mode does not transmit wireless signals, but only receives wireless signals in order to detect the rogue AP.

Sniffer Mode   To perform analysis of the wireless traffic, you can configure the AP in sniffer mode. Once sniffer mode is configured, the AP will capture wireless traffic and send the traffic to a remote computer for analysis.

 EXAM TIP   Be sure to know the AP modes for the Cisco CCNA certification exam.

Management Access Connections

When it comes to managing or configuring the WAP or the wireless LAN controller, you can use the CLI or a web interface.

Managing from the CLI

You can manage the AP or WLC through the CLI either by using the console port on the device for local administration or, if you have enabled remote management with telnet or Secure Shell (SSH), you can use those protocols. With many APs and wireless controllers, you can connect to a local console port to configure the device from the CLI. This, of course, assumes that you have local access to the device. You can also enable telnet or SSH on the AP or wireless LAN controller to manage the device remotely from across the network. As you will learn in later chapters, you should use SSH over telnet, because SSH encrypts the communication.

Managing from a Web Interface

If you'd rather not use the CLI for configuration of the WAP or WLC, you can use the web interface by connecting to the management IP address of the device. Use HTTP (non-secure) or HTTPS (secure) to configure the AP or WLC, including configuring telnet or SSH, configuring RADIUS for central authentication, or creating wireless networks, to name just a few configuration settings.

TACACS+/RADIUS

You can configure your AP or WLC to use an authentication service such as TACACS+ or RADIUS. You will learn more about authentication services in the next few chapters, but for now, know that you can have the AP or WLC require someone that is connecting to be authenticated by an external authentication system (the TACACS+ or RADIUS server).

Configuring Wireless with a GUI

The new Cisco CCNA exam expects you to know the steps to create and configure a wireless LAN and settings such as security settings and QoS settings. In this section you will learn the steps to configure wireless networks on a WLC.

I should note that many WLCs have a *service port*, which is an out-of-band management port you can use to connect to the WLC and configure the device. There is also a management interface with an IP address assigned that you can also use to remotely manage the WLC device. The service port is a good backup method to manage the device should you not be able to connect to the management interface.

WLAN Creation

The first step to configuring a WLAN controller is to create the WLAN. You will need to connect the WLAN to the dynamic interface on the WLC that enables the WLAN to bind to the VLAN on the wired network.

Create a Dynamic Interface

Our first task is to create a dynamic interface, which is used to link the WLAN to a VLAN on the switch. Here are the steps:

1. Log into the WLC using the web interface.
2. Choose Controller at the top of the page.
3. Choose Interfaces from the left navigation pane.
4. Click the New button in the top-right corner to create a new interface.

5. Enter an interface name, such as ACCT.

6. Specify the VLAN ID you want to connect the interface to. For example, you can specify 10 (for VLAN ID 10).

7. Configure the interface for an IP address within the network range of the VLAN.

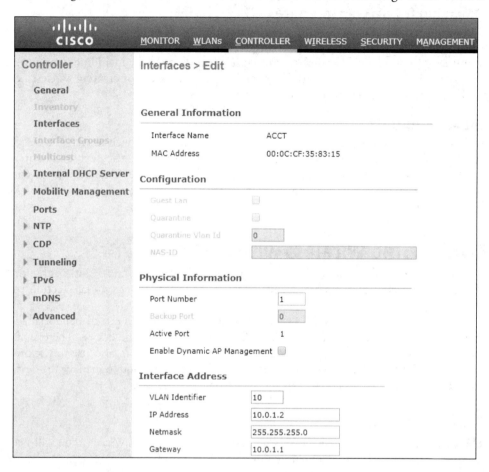

Create a WLAN

Your next task is to create the WLAN object within the WLC that will be bound to that interface. Follow these steps:

1. Click the WLANs link from the top navigation.

2. Choose Create New from the drop-down list at the upper-right and then click Go.

3. Enter the profile name for the WLAN, such as ACCT.

4. Enter the SSID for the wireless LAN, such as ACCT.

5. The WLAN is assigned a unique ID within the WLC. Click Apply.

After you click Apply, you'll see the configuration screen of the WLAN, where you can change common settings such as the SSID, the dynamic interface on the WLC the WLAN is assigned to, and whether or not you want to broadcast the SSID. Notice in the following illustration that I have assigned the ACCT wireless network to the dynamic interface, also called ACCT, that was created in the previous step.

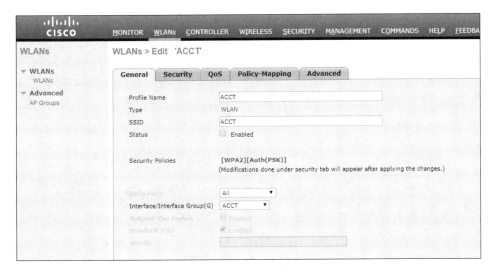

Security Settings

You can change the security settings for the WLAN by choosing the Security tab while modifying the configuration of your WLAN.

1. Choose the Security tab at the top of the screen.

2. Choose WPA+WPA2 as the Layer 2 security protocol.

3. Choose WPA2 Policy in the WPA+WPA2 Parameters section.

4. You can then choose AES as the WPA2 Encryption type.

5. Choose PSK (preshared key) as the Authentication Key Management type.

6. Choose ASCII as the PSK Format.

7. Enter your desired preshared key (wireless password).

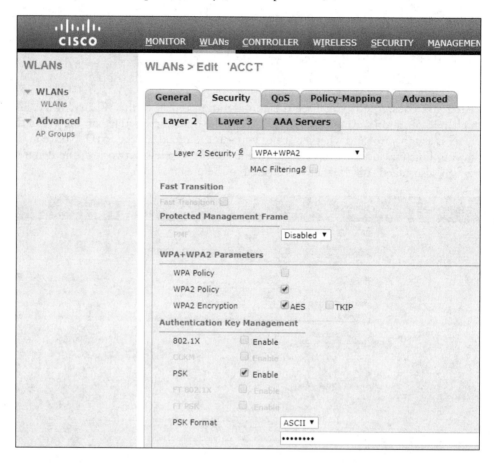

QoS Profiles

After configuring the wireless security settings, you can choose to configure the QoS settings for the wireless network. Choosing the QoS profile will specify how the WLC should handle and prioritize traffic from this wireless network. You can select one of the following QoS profiles:

- Platinum (used to ensure high quality of service for voice traffic)
- Gold (used to ensure high quality of service for video traffic)

- Silver (used for regular traffic—the default and considered a best effort profile)
- Bronze (used for background traffic as it is given the lowest bandwidth)

Choose the profile that best suits your needs. Remember for the certification exam that VoIP traffic should be using the Platinum QoS profile.

Advanced Wireless LAN Settings

After choosing the QoS profile, click the Advanced tab to set the advanced settings for the wireless network. Here you can specify settings such as the session timeout value, which is how frequent clients must reauthenticate to WLAN; configure features such as peer-to-peer (P2P) blocking, URL filtering to control URLs that are accessed by the clients, and the maximum number of clients that can connect.

1. Select the desired advanced settings.
2. Click Apply to complete the configuration.

Configuring RADIUS/TACACS+

If you would like to configure the wireless network to use a RADIUS server or TACACS+ server as an authentication service for clients who connect to your wireless network, you have a few steps to the configuration. First, you must add the RADIUS/TACACS+ server to the configuration, and then you can select the server when configuring your wireless LANs.

To add the RADIUS/TACACS+ server to the controller:

1. From the top navigation bar, choose the Security link.
2. Click the New button to add a new RADIUS server.
3. Type the IP address of the RADIUS server and fill in the Shared Secret/Confirm Shared Secret. The shared secret is the password needed to connect to the RADIUS server.

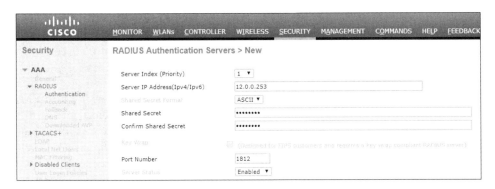

4. Choose Apply.

Now that you have added the RADIUS server, you can go back to your WLAN and configure the WLAN to use that RADIUS server. Follow these steps to configure your WLAN to use the RADIUS server:

1. Choose the WLANs link in the top navigation bar.

2. Click the link for the WLAN you wish to edit.

3. Choose the Security tab within the WLAN settings.

4. Choose the AAA Servers tab.

5. Select the RADIUS server's IP address from the Server 1 drop-down list.

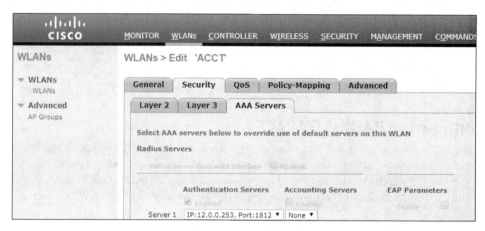

6. Choose Apply in the top-right corner.

Chapter Review

In this chapter you learned about wireless networks and their components. You learned about how radio waves are used to deliver data and the components of a wireless network, such as wireless access points (WAPs) and wireless LAN controllers (WLCs).

You read about the difference between a Basic Service Set (BSS) and Extended Service Set (ESS) and the three core requirements for configuring an ESS: multiple access points with the same SSID, different channels, and overlapping areas of coverage of at least 10 percent. You also learned about the different wireless standards such as 802.11g, 802.11n, and 802.11ac.

You then read about the different wireless security protocols and how WPA2 or WPA3 (if possible) should be used on your wireless network to encrypt wireless communication. Finally, you learned about the Cisco wireless architectures such as an autonomous architecture, where each access point is configured individually, or a Split-MAC architecture that involves using a wireless LAN controller to configure all access points from a central point.

Quick Review

Introducing Wireless

- Wireless clients connect to the wireless access point (AP) to access the network. Wireless communication uses radio waves to transmit the data.

- In an enterprise environment, you can centrally manage multiple APs with a wireless LAN controller (WLC). The AP and WLC communicate using a private tunnel known as the CAPWAP.

- A BSS is a wireless network with a single AP, whereas an ESS is a wireless network that has multiple APs to cover a larger area. With an ESS, each AP uses the same SSID, but different channels.

- The 802.11b and 802.11g wireless standards run on the 2.4 GHz frequency. The 802.11b standard runs at 11 Mbps, while 802.11g runs at 54 Mbps. The 802.11n standard can run on the 2.4 GHz or 5 GHz frequencies, and 802.11ac runs on the 5 GHz frequency. The 802.11n standard provides a transfer rate of up to 600 Mbps and 802.11ac can provide 1 Gbps.

- The WEP security protocol uses RC4 as the encryption algorithm, WPA uses TKIP, and WPA2 uses AES. You can run the WPA/WPA2/WPA3 in enterprise mode, which means that you configure the AP to use an authentication service such as TACACS+ or RADIUS.

Cisco Wireless Architectures

- Autonomous architecture involves each AP being configured individually. Split-MAC architecture uses a WLC to configure all of the APs from a central location. With a cloud-based architecture, the WLC is located in the cloud.

- Configure the AP for FlexConnect mode to enable the LAPs to pass traffic directly between clients and to the LAN and to allow the AP to still function if the CAPWAP fails.

- The CAPWAP is a private tunnel that carries communication between the LAP and the WLC.

- There are two channels in the CAPWAP tunnel: the control channel and the data channel. The control channel transmits control information such as commands and uses UDP 5246. The data channel transmits all other information between the LAP and WLC and uses UDP 5247.

Questions

The following questions will help you measure your understanding of the material presented in this chapter. Read all the choices carefully because there may be more than one correct answer. Choose the correct answer(s) for each question.

1. Your manager is wondering why you have purchased a wireless LAN controller (WLC). Which of the following would you use to describe the benefit of a WLC?

   A. It can be used with autonomous and lightweight access points.

   B. It requires the use of a RADIUS server.

   C. It enables you to centrally manage all access points.

   D. It allows configuration only via a console port.

2. Which access point solution would you use if you wanted to ensure that the access point could still serve clients when communication to the WLC has failed?

   A. Mesh

   B. FlexConnect

   C. Local

   D. CAPWAP

3. What type of access points are managed by the WLC?

   A. Autonomous

   B. CAPWAP

   C. Heavyweight

   D. Lightweight

4. When designing an Extended Service Set (ESS) wireless network, which of the following represents a design best practice?

   A. Configure each access point with a unique non-overlapping channel and the same SSID.

   B. Configure each access point with the same channel and the same SSID.

   C. Configure each access point with a unique non-overlapping channel and a unique SSID.

   D. Configure each access point with the same channel, but different SSIDs.

5. Which of the following is the encryption algorithm used by WPA2 with a preshared key?

   A. RC4

   B. AES

   C. TKIP with RC4

   D. TKIP with WEP

6. You are configuring the wireless network using the GUI of the wireless LAN controller. While configuring the WPA2 PSK, which two data formats can you use? (Choose two.)

    A. Hexadecimal

    B. Decimal

    C. Binary

    D. ASCII

    E. Base10

7. Which wireless standard runs at 54 Mbps?

    A. 802.11ac

    B. 802.11n

    C. 802.11g

    D. 802.11b

8. Which wireless encryption protocol uses AES as the encryption algorithm?

    A. WEP

    B. WPA2

    C. RC4

    D. WPA

9. You are using a wireless scanner that reports the BSSID of each of the wireless networks. What does the BSSID represent?

    A. The MAC address of the access point

    B. The name of the wireless network

    C. The channel for the wireless network

    D. The IP address of the access point

Performance-based Question

    1. Using the following exhibit, match the wireless term with its definition.

	Used to centrally manage access points
WPA2	
Service Port	Used to map a WLAN to a VLAN
Wireless LAN Controller	
Dynamic Interface	Used by wireless clients to access the wired network
Access Point	
	An interface used for out-of-band management
	A wireless encryption protocol

Answers

1. **C.** A WLC is used to manage configuration settings on multiple lightweight access points (LAPs) from a single point.

2. **B.** FlexConnect access points can service wireless clients even if the WLC or CAPWAP tunnel fails.

3. **D.** The WLC manages the configuration of lightweight access points (LAPs).

4. **A.** To configure an ESS you must configure each access point with the same SSID but different, non-overlapping channels.

5. **B.** The WPA2 wireless encryption protocol uses the Advanced Encryption Standard (AES) symmetric encryption algorithm to perform the encryption.

6. **A, D.** When inputting the preshared key for WPA2, you can input the key as either an ASCII value or a hexadecimal value.

7. **C.** The 802.11g wireless standard runs at 54 Mbps.

8. **B.** The WPA2 wireless encryption protocol uses AES as its symmetric encryption algorithm.

9. **A.** The BSSID is the MAC address of the wireless access point.

Performance-based Answer

1. The following is the mapping of wireless terms with their definition. Keeping in mind the real exam, you would need to drag items on the left side and drop them on the matching item on the right side.

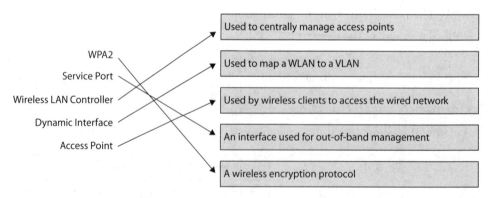

CHAPTER 16

Security Fundamentals

In this chapter, you will

- Be introduced to threats and attack types
- Compare authentication and authorization
- Understand the importance of password policy elements
- Learn about remote access and VPNs
- Learn best practices for implementing a security program

One of the new focus points of the Cisco CCNA certification is the addition of security topics. In this chapter you will learn about basic security concepts such as threats, vulnerabilities, and exploits. You will also learn about common reasons systems get attacked and ways to mitigate those attacks by following common security best practices.

You will also learn about the difference between authentication and authorization, as well as concepts related to authentication, authorization, and accounting (AAA) services and centralized authentication with RADIUS and Terminal Access Controller Access-Control System Plus (TACACS+).

Understanding Threats and Attack Types

For our first topic in this chapter, we'll introduce you to basic terminology related to security concepts and the different threats against a system. A bit later in this section, we will identify the different attack types that are common nowadays.

Fundamentals of Security

Information security is big business today as companies seek to protect their assets from some form of attack. As an IT professional, you will be asked to protect these assets, but how do you know what type of protection mechanism to use? The answer depends on what fundamental element of security you are trying to protect: confidentiality, integrity, or availability (CIA).

Confidentiality

The first goal of information security is to keep information confidential, which means not allowing unauthorized individuals to access the information. You can use a number of methods to maintain confidentiality:

- You can configure permissions on files and/or folders to block unauthorized individuals from accessing these files and/or folders.
- You can encrypt the data in storage so that only people with the decryption key can gain access to the data. This is known as *encrypt-in-storage*.
- You can encrypt the data as it travels across the network or Internet. This is known as *encrypt-in-transit*.

Integrity

Integrity deals with being able to ensure the integrity of the data that is being read. If, for example, an employee stores a file on the server and the next month accesses that file, how does she know that the file has not been tampered with or altered? You can use technologies that offer integrity services to identify whether the file has been altered.

A common technique to prove the integrity is *hashing*. With hashing, the data (in this case, a file) is run through a hashing algorithm to generate an answer (known as a *hash value*). This hash value is then stored for reference at a later time. The next time you read the file, you run the file through the same hashing algorithm to generate a new hash value. You then compare the two hash values: if the two hash values are the same, the file has not been altered. Common examples of hashing algorithms are Message Digest 5 (MD5) and Secure Hashing Algorithm 1 (SHA-1) and 256 (SHA-256).

Availability

The third goal of information security is availability. If an employee stores a report on the server, for example, he expects the report to be there later when he needs it. We can use a number of technologies to increase the chances that a company asset, such as that report, is available, such as the following:

- **Backups**   If we make backups of the file server and the server crashes, we can restore the company data from the backups. As a network professional, you back up your Cisco device configuration and IOS using the commands you learned in Chapter 8.
- **RAID**   Servers have multiple drives configured in a RAID array, so that if a drive fails, employees will still be able to access the company data.
- **Clustering**   Servers are placed in a highly available cluster, so that if one server fails, the other server can handle the workload.
- **FHRP**   As you learned in Chapter 11, you can configure your Cisco router in a first hop redundancy protocol (FHRP) topology, so that if a router fails, another router can take over and employees can still gain Internet or WAN access.

Vulnerabilities and Exploits

Before we jump into a big list of different types of attacks, it is important for you to understand some common security terms that you will hear about when discussing topics related to attacks. Following are some key terms you should remember as you learn more about security and attacks:

- **Threat**   An action that exposes a compromise to confidentiality, integrity, or the availability of an asset. Example threats include denial-of-service (DoS) attacks (which violate availability) or an attacker hacking a database and retrieving credit card numbers (which violates confidentiality).

- **Threat actor**   The person or group causing the threat to occur. Common examples are hackers and disgruntled employees.

- **Vulnerability**   A weakness in a product that could enable someone to bypass the security of the product and gain access to or cause damage to the system. Every product has vulnerabilities, which is why we need to patch systems regularly. As the product vendor learns of a vulnerability, it ships out the fix in a software patch.

- **Exploit**   An activity that takes advantage of a system or a software vulnerability to compromise security. Individuals take advantage of system or software vulnerabilities in order to compromise security, leading to an exploit.

- **Mitigation technique**   The method used to reduce the likelihood or impact of a threat or to remove it entirely. For example, to mitigate a DoS attack, we could create multiple servers in a highly available solution. Or to mitigate a potential attacker's access to credit card numbers, we could encrypt the credit card numbers included in the database.

 EXAM TIP   For the exam, know that a *vulnerability* is a weakness in a product, and an *exploit* occurs when someone leverages that vulnerability to compromise the system.

Common Vulnerabilities

A number of common configuration mistakes can lead to vulnerabilities on your systems and devices. As a network administrator, you should be aware of these common vulnerabilities that can lead to your systems being attacked:

- **Unnecessary running services**   Be sure to assess the services running on a computer and then disable any unnecessary ones. The more software running on a system, the more likely vulnerabilities exist that the hacker can use to gain access to it.

- **Open ports**   A Transmission Control Protocol (TCP) or User Datagram Protocol (UDP) port open on the system is an invitation for a hacker to gain access to the system. Close any open ports on the system that are not needed, and use a firewall to block access to ports that must remain open.

- **Unpatched systems**   Be sure to keep your systems up-to-date with patches and security fixes. That way, any software on the system is less likely to have vulnerabilities that a hacker can exploit.

- **Unencrypted channels**   Ensure that any communication channels between systems are encrypted as much as possible. Using unencrypted communication enables hackers to capture the traffic and read the information.

- **Clear-text credentials**   Ensure that the authentication protocols being used are encrypting the passwords when users are authenticating to the systems. Replace any unsecure authentication protocols with a secure authentication protocol.

- **Unsecure protocols**   Be sure to encrypt all communication. Most Internet protocols we use daily, such as telnet, HTTP, File Transfer Protocol (FTP), Trivial File Transfer Protocol (TFTP), and Simple Network Management Protocol (SNMPv1 and v2), send traffic in an unencrypted format. If an attacker captures unencrypted traffic using a sniffer program, he can view the details of the traffic, access any sensitive information in that traffic, and potentially learn the username and password being used to authenticate to the system. Be sure to investigate each protocol used on the network; if it is not encrypting communication, find a secure replacement for that protocol. For example, instead of using telnet for remote administration of your Cisco devices, use Secure Shell (SSH).

Malicious Software

Another common form of hacker attack is through malicious software. Malicious software is any software that is designed to harm a system, and it comes in many forms. Following are some of the malicious software you should be familiar with for the CCNA exam:

- **Virus**   The traditional virus is attached to a file, so that when you open the file, the virus is activated and infects your system. Viruses can delete files from the system or modify the boot sector so that the computer no longer boots.

- **Worm virus**   Today, we usually deal with worm viruses—a lot. A worm virus is a self-replicating virus, which means that it can infect your system without you opening a file. Worms can arrive as attachments in e-mails, instant messages, or through software vulnerabilities. Or it may be present on a flash drive that infects your system when you connect the flash drive to your computer. A worm virus infects one computer and then spreads across your entire network.

- **Trojan virus**   A Trojan virus is a program that you are tricked into installing because you believe the application does something useful; in reality, however, the program is a virus that infects your system. The Trojan virus typically modifies your system by opening a TCP/IP port, which allows a hacker to connect to the system and take control of it.

- **Spyware**   This hidden software monitors and collects information about you and your Internet surfing habits. Spyware has also been known to do more than just monitor for information: it can make changes to your system through browser redirection (sending you to a different web page) or slow down your network connection.

- **Adware**   This software automatically loads advertisements on your screen, typically in the form of pop-up windows. The advertisements are designed to entice you into purchasing products or subscribing to particular web sites.

- **Logic bomb**   This type of virus is planted on your system with the intention of infecting it later. After an infected application is installed, the logic bomb waits until a particular condition is satisfied, such as a specific date, and then the virus performs its malicious purpose.

- **Keylogger**   A keylogger is either a piece of software or a hardware device installed on your system that is designed to capture all of your keystrokes in an attempt to learn your passwords and other information.

- **Spam**   Spam refers to unsolicited commercial e-mails. These e-mail messages typically are mass mailed, and their purpose is to convince you to purchase their products or services. The spammers (people who send the spam messages) usually get your e-mail address from a web site or newsgroup after you have posted a comment to the group.

- **Ransomware**   This malicious software takes control of your system and does not give control back until you pay a fee. In a recent common scenario, ransomware encrypts your drive, and you must pay a fee to get the encryption key.

Mitigating Attacks

You've learned about mitigation techniques—actions you can take to reduce or eliminate threats. The following outlines some security best practices you can employ to help protect your company assets. Here are some common mitigation techniques that can help you prevent attacks or reduce the impacts of attacks:

- *Patch systems.* The first step you can take to protect your systems is to ensure that you have a patch management strategy in place. Make sure that you keep all systems up-to-date with patches, because they remove known vulnerabilities from your system. Most operating systems and applications have an automatic update feature that you can enable so that updates are downloaded and applied automatically as they are released.

- *Encrypt network traffic.* To protect your data from prying eyes, ensure that you are encrypting all network communication. This includes encrypting web, e-mail, and FTP traffic, if need be.

- *Encrypt data stored on mobile devices.* Ensure that you are encrypting data that is stored on laptops and other mobile devices. Employees may lose their devices, or their mobile devices may be stolen at some point, so it is critical that data stored on these devices is encrypted and that the devices are password protected.

- *Install antivirus software.* To protect your systems from malware, be sure to install antivirus software on all systems and keep the virus definitions up-to-date.

- *Use strong passwords.* Ensure that you are using strong passwords for all user accounts and devices.

- *Educate employees.* It is important to educate your employees on security best practices and to ensure that they understand what can happen if they do not follow them.

- *Run hashing algorithms.* You can verify the integrity of data by running it through a mathematical hashing algorithm, which generates a hash value. The server uses a key to create a hash value with a password stored on the server and then compares the resulting value with the hash value sent by the client. If the two hash values are the same, the client has supplied the correct password. If the hash values are different, this indicates that the data has been changed in some way. Examples of hashing algorithms are MD5 and SHA.

Exercise 16-1: Matching Security Terms

In this exercise, you will match the security term to its description.

Term	Description
___ Threat	A. Used to ensure that data has not been maliciously altered
___ Vulnerability	B. A person or group that is causing the threat to occur
___ Confidentiality	C. Used to reduce the likelihood or impact of the threat or remove it entirely
___ Exploit	D. An action that exposes a compromise to confidentiality, integrity, or availability of an asset
___ Threat actor	E. Used to take advantage of a vulnerability in order to compromise security
___ Integrity	F. Ensures that information is kept private with controls such as encryption
___ Mitigation technique	G. A weakness in a product

Attack Types

Now it is time to look at some of the different types of threats and attacks that can occur against systems. Understanding the different types of attacks and methods that hackers are using to compromise systems is essential to understanding how to secure your environment. This section will introduce you to a number of different types of attacks.

Social Engineering Attacks

With a social engineering attack, the attacker compromises the network or system through social interaction with an individual through an e-mail message or phone call, tricking the victim into divulging information that can be used to compromise security. The information that the victim divulges to the hacker would most likely be used in a subsequent attack to gain unauthorized access to a system or network.

Education is the key to protecting yourself and fellow employees from social engineering attacks. Keeping all personnel aware of the popularity of social engineering attacks and the different scenarios that could be examples of such attacks will help raise the security level of the organization.

Following are some of the most common social engineering attack scenarios:

- **Attacker impersonates administrator** The attacker may call an employee and impersonate the company's network administrator. The hacker will try to convince the employee to change his or her password or divulge password information so that the attacker can use the information to access the system.

- **Attacker impersonates user** The attacker calls an unsuspecting network administrator and plays the role of a frustrated user who cannot log on to the network. The network administrator naturally helps the "user" by resetting his or her password and helping the person log on, which results in giving the attacker access to the system.

- **Attacker impersonates vendor** The attacker may e-mail a customer and pretend to be a vendor of a piece of software. The attacker tries to convince the user to install an update, but the user doesn't realize the update is actually a Trojan virus that gives the attacker access to the system.

Phishing Attack

A common type of social engineering attack in use these days, a phishing attack occurs when the hacker creates a fake web site that looks exactly like a popular web site, such as a site for a bank or online merchant. The attacker sends an e-mail message trying to trick the user into clicking a link that leads to the fake site (called "phishing"). When the user attempts to log on to the fake site with his or her account information, the attacker records the username and password and then tries using that information to log on to the real site, potentially gaining access to the user's account.

There are several forms of phishing attacks. *Spear phishing* is focused on a specific victim or group of victims. In general, phishing attacks are sent to random e-mail addresses, but in spear phishing, the attacker poses as a known or trusted sender and targets specific individuals or groups. A *whaling attack* is a form of phishing attack that is targeted at company executives, such as a CEO. Whaling targets the "whales," or the "big fish," in the organization.

Network-Based Attacks

Most types of attacks are considered network-based attacks, in which the hacker performs the attack from a remote system. There are a number of different types of network attacks:

- **Eavesdropping attack**   Also known as *packet sniffing,* eavesdropping involves the use of a network monitoring tool known as a sniffer, which is used to capture and analyze network traffic. If the traffic is not encrypted, the hacker could read confidential data, including usernames and passwords.

- **Spoofing**   In a spoof attack, the hacker modifies the source address of the packets he or she is sending so that the packet appears to be coming from someone else. Spoofing is a common method to bypass access controls placed on switches, routers, or firewalls. There are a few different types of spoofing:

    - *MAC spoofing* involves altering the source MAC address of a packet. It is common for an attacker to spoof the MAC address so that he can bypass the MAC filtering features on a wireless network or attempt to bypass the port security features of a switch.

    - *IP spoofing* involves altering the source IP address of a packet. An attacker may use IP spoofing to attempt to bypass access control lists (ACLs) on a router or firewall.

    - *E-mail spoofing* involves altering the source e-mail address of an e-mail message. E-mail spoofing is typically used by an attacker in a phishing attack to make the e-mail look like it is coming from someone else (a trusted party).

- **Man-in-the-middle (MITM) attack**   With an MITM attack, the hacker inserts himself in the middle of two systems that are communicating. He then passes the information back and forth between the two, with neither party knowing all the communication is passing through the hacker's system. The benefit of this is the hacker can then view any sensitive data sent between the two systems.

- **Hijack attack**   A hacker takes over a session between you and another individual and disconnects the other individual from the communication. You still believe that you are talking to the original party and may send private information to the hacker instead of the original party.

- **Denial of service**   A denial-of-service (DoS) attack causes the system or its services to either crash or become unresponsive. As a result, the system cannot fulfill its purpose and provide those services. For example, your web server sells products to your customers. An attacker performs a DoS by sending so many request to your web server that it becomes overwhelmed and too busy to service valid request from your customers.

- **Distributed denial of service**   With a DDoS, the hacker uses multiple systems to attack a single target system. A good example is the smurf attack, in which the hacker pings a number of computers but modifies the source address of those packets so that they appear to come from another system (the victim, in this case). When all of these systems receive the ping request, they will reply to the same address, essentially overburdening that system with data.

- **Buffer overflow**   In a buffer overflow attack, the attacker sends more data to a buffer than it can hold. The data may include malicious code that may corrupt data or cause private information to be revealed, providing the attacker the ability to gain administrative access to the system in a command prompt or shell.

- **Exploit attack**   In this type of attack, the attacker knows of a security problem (a vulnerability) within an operating system or a piece of software and leverages that knowledge by exploiting the vulnerability.

- **Botnet**   A botnet is a group of systems that a hacker takes over and uses in a DDoS attack.

- **DNS poisoning**   With DNS poisoning, a hacker alters (or poisons) your DNS data in order to redirect clients to the wrong system. In another common attack against DNS, a hacker tries to do a zone transfer (copy your DNS data) in order to map out your network.

- **Smurf attack**   In a smurf attack, the hacker sends a ping message to a number of systems but spoofs the IP address so that it looks like the ping messages are coming from different systems. The result is that all the systems send ping replies to the victim, essentially performing a DDoS.

- **Friendly/unintentional DoS**   Some scenarios can lead to an unintentional DoS attack. For example, an account lockout policy could lead to a DoS, preventing the user from logging on once the account is locked. Users may also unintentionally cause a DoS if they delete a file by accident.

- **Physical attack**   Physical attacks occur when the attacker gains physical access to your facility and is able to cause damage to your equipment or even the facility. Implementing physical security controls, such as locking mechanisms and guards, can help prevent these attacks.

- **ARP poisoning**   A hacker can insert herself in the middle of communication by altering the Address Resolution Protocol (ARP) cache on a victim's system and causing all communication to pass through the hacker's system, enabling her to capture all traffic. This is a common method to perform an MITM attack.

- **VLAN hopping**   VLAN hopping is an exploit against virtual local area networks (VLANs) that enables an individual to gain access to a VLAN when he is not connected to it. Hackers accomplish this by double-tagging the frames for different VLANs, or they can imitate a trunking port so that they receive all traffic.

- **Deauthentication**   A deauthentication attack is common in wireless attacks. The hacker sends a command to disconnect or deauthenticate the client from the wireless network. As a result, the client is forced to reauthenticate with the wireless network where the hacker can capture the reauthentication traffic. The authentication packets can be replayed by the attacker in order to generate more traffic in hopes of cracking the wireless encryption.

- **Zero-day attacks**   In a zero-day attack, a vulnerability unknown by the software developer is exploited before the developer realizes the problem and issues a patch. Companies can have a team in place to test software and identify vulnerabilities not yet known.

Password Attacks

An attacker may try to crack the passwords stored in a network account database or a password-protected file. There are three major types of password attacks: a dictionary attack, a brute-force attack, and a hybrid attack:

- **Dictionary attack**   This attack involves the use of a word list file, which is a list of potential passwords. The attacker uses a program to read and try each of the passwords from the file to break into a system. This is a very quick form of password attack, because no calculations are required: the attacker is simply reading a file.

- **Brute-force attack**   In a brute-force attack, the attacker uses a program that tries every possible combination of characters to guess a password. This attack is slower than a dictionary attack because a file is not read; instead, the program calculates each possible password.

- **Hybrid attack**   Like a dictionary attack, a hybrid attack involves a word list file, but it also places numbers at the end of the words to catch passwords that are not dictionary words, in case a password contains a number at the end, which is common. For example, a dictionary attack would not find the password *pass1*, but a hybrid attack might.

 EXAM TIP   Be sure that you know all of the different types of attacks before taking the Cisco exams. Be most familiar with denial of service, spoofing, password attacks, and social engineering attacks.

Authentication and Authorization Concepts

There are differences between authentication and authorization processes and differences in how these processes are used to allow or deny access to network resources. When securing network resources, you should first have users log on to the network with their own private usernames and passwords; once logged on, they will be able to access network resources to which they have been given permission. The process of logging on to the network is known as *authentication*, whereas controlling what network resources users may access once they have logged on to the network is known as *authorization*.

Authentication

Authentication is the process whereby users or computers identify themselves to the network so that they can start accessing network resources or a network device (in the case of managing the device). The method used to authenticate a user depends on the network environment and can assume forms such as the following:

- **Username and password**   When the user starts the computer or connects to the network, she types a username and password that are associated with the user's particular network account.

- **Smartcard** Using a smartcard for logon is similar to accessing your bank account at an ATM. To log on to the network, you insert a smartcard, which is similar to a debit card, into a smartcard reader and then supply a PIN. To be authenticated, you must have the smartcard and know its password. Smartcards are also known as PKI cards because they are used to authenticate the client in a public key infrastructure (PKI) environment; the card contains the employee's private key.

- **Biometrics** In this case, the user provides a retina scan or fingerprint as a credential. Biometrics is becoming a very popular solution in highly secure environments where special biometric devices are used.

Whatever method is used to provide the necessary credentials, the outcome is the same, in the sense that the credentials are sent to a directory service such as Microsoft Active Directory, where they are verified. For example, if the username and password are correct, the user is authenticated and allowed to access network resources. Network servers also have the ability to authorize users to access different resources, depending on how they are authenticated—for example, authentication through biometrics may give a user access to more resources than simple username and password authentication can provide. If the credentials are incorrect, authentication fails and the user is denied access to the network, as shown in Figure 16-1.

When users provide credentials such as a username and a password, the credentials are passed to the server using an authentication method. A number of authentication methods are used in the Microsoft world, as described in the following list:

- **Anonymous authentication** You are not required to log on. Windows uses an account for the actual service, and you are passed through as that account. Whatever permissions the anonymous account has are the permissions you will have while you are connected anonymously. This is a popular authentication method for web sites or FTP servers.

- **Basic authentication** You are required to log on, and the username and password are sent to the server in clear text. This means that if someone has a packet sniffer between you and the server, that person will be able to capture your password and view it because it is not encrypted.

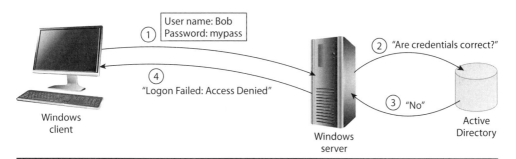

Figure 16-1 Logging on to a network

- **Integrated Windows authentication** You are required to log on to the server, but your username and password are sent to the server in an encrypted format. This authentication method is more secure than basic authentication if users are required to log on.

- **Kerberos** This popular mutual authentication protocol is used by default with Microsoft Active Directory environments. Active Directory adheres to the Lightweight Directory Access Protocol (LDAP) standard, which is the Internet protocol for accessing and querying a directory. Kerberos uses a key distribution center (KDC) server that is responsible for issuing tickets that are needed for a client to request a service from any other server on the network (known as a realm). The Kerberos process starts when the client logs on to the network. The KDC authentication server issues the client a ticket-granting ticket that gives the client permission to request a service ticket, which is required to request service from a server on the network. When the client wants to connect to a specific server on the network, it must request a ticket from the ticket-granting service (TGS), which is another component of the KDC. The TGS grants the ticket to the client so the client can access the required server on the network.

These authentication methods are very "Microsoft-ish," but there are standard protocols used to perform authentication as well. The standard authentication protocols used by various network services, such as remote access service (RAS) and virtual private networks (VPNs), include the following:

- **Password Authentication Protocol (PAP)** PAP sends the user's credentials in plain text and is very insecure, because it is easy for someone to analyze and interpret the logon traffic. This is the authentication protocol used by the basic authentication method mentioned previously.

- **Challenge Handshake Authentication Protocol (CHAP)** With CHAP, the server sends a client a challenge (a key), which is combined with the user's password. Both the user's password and the challenge are run through the MD5 hashing algorithm (a formula), which generates a hash value, or mathematical answer, and that hash value is sent to the server for authentication. The server uses the same key to create a hash value with the password stored on the server and then compares the resulting value with the hash value sent by the client. If the two hash values are the same, the client has supplied the correct password. The benefit is that the user's credentials have not been passed on the wire at all.

- **Microsoft Challenge Handshake Authentication Protocol (MS-CHAP)** MS-CHAP is a variation of CHAP and uses the MD4 hashing algorithm rather than MD5, which is used by CHAP. MS-CHAP also uses the Microsoft Point-to-Point Encryption (MPPE) protocol along with MS-CHAP to encrypt all traffic from the client to the server.

- **MS-CHAPv2** With MS-CHAP version 2, the authentication method has been extended to authenticate both the client and the server. MS-CHAPv2 also uses stronger encryption keys than CHAP and MS-CHAP.

- **Extensible Authentication Protocol (EAP)**   EAP allows for multiple logon methods, such as smartcard logon, certificates, Kerberos, and public-key authentication. EAP is also frequently used with Remote Authentication Dial In User Service (RADIUS), which is a central authentication service that can be used by RAS, wireless, or VPN solutions.

Password Alternatives

Other authentication techniques can be used outside of typing a username and/or password:

- **Biometrics**   With biometric authentication, you will need to present an aspect of yourself to authenticate to the system. For example, the system may scan your fingerprint, take a retina scan, or use facial or use voice recognition.
- **Certificates**   You may be required to have a certificate to authenticate to a system. A certificate is an electronic file that contains encryption keys and other properties, such as the owner's ID and who created the certificate. The certificate is typically stored on a PKI card (smartcard), or it could be on a USB stick. Certificates can be used as a password-less form of authentication that can be configured on your Cisco device for SSH remote access.

Authentication Factors

The CCNA exam expects you to know the different methods, or factors, of authentication. An individual can be authenticated using any of the following authentication factors:

- **Something you know**   This is the most common authentication factor, where you know information to prove your identity. An example of this authentication factor is knowing a password or a PIN.
- **Something you have**   Also a common authentication factor, this is based on your having something in your possession that enables you to gain access to the environment. For example, you use a swipe card or physical token to enter a building. In today's day and age with web site logins, you can have the web site send a code to your phone after you type a correct username and password. This would be an example of something you have, because in order to receive the code, you need to have your phone in your possession.
- **Something you are**   You can gain access to a system by using this more advanced authentication factor. This authentication factor involves biometrics: you use a characteristic of yourself for authentication, such as a retina scan, fingerprint, or voice recognition, to prove your identity. This is considered the most secure method of authentication.

 EXAM TIP   The CCNA exam expects you to know these different authentication factors, but it also expects you to identify *single-factor authentication*, *two-factor authentication*, and *three-factor authentication* schemes.

In addition to the preceding factors, you should be familiar with several other factors of authentication. If you are authenticating to a system by using only one of the authentication factors, you are using a *single-factor authentication* scheme. For example, knowing the username and password is a single-factor authentication scheme because they are both examples of something you know.

A *two-factor authentication scheme* is based on two authentication factors, such as something you know and something you have. For example, you have a bank card (something you have) and you know the PIN to use the bank card in an ATM. This authentication scheme is much stronger than simply needing to have the bank card to gain access to your account. If that were the case, then anyone with the bank card could withdraw money from the account. The following are common examples of two-factor authentication schemes:

- **Physical token and password**   You authenticate with something you have and something you know.

- **Smartcard and PIN**   You authenticate with something you have and something you know.

- **Biometrics and password**   You authenticate with something you are and something you know.

- **Logon credential, and then access code from mobile phone notification**   In this example you would log on with your username and password, and then a notification is sent to your phone with a one-time access code you will need to type when logging into the application. This is an example of something you know (username and password), and something you have (the phone).

Multifactor authentication (MFA) requires you to log in with two or more factors. Suppose you need an authentication code to log into a site. You enter your username and password (something you know), and you use your phone (something you have) to receive an authentication code. Once you receive the code, you enter that on the site to complete the login process. This is an important feature that should be used with any web site login to ensure that if someone is able to get your password they cannot log into the site as you because they do not possess your phone.

Although two-factor authentication is the more common form of MFA, you can have more such as three-factor authentication. An example of three-factor authentication is if you are required to do a retina scan (something you are), swipe a card (something you have), and then insert the PIN associated with that card (something you know).

EXAM TIP   For the exam, know that a smartcard is an example of two-factor authentication, because you need to have the smartcard and you need to know a PIN to gain access. Another example of two-factor authentication is a fingerprint scan and a password. Notice that in this example, the two factors are something you are and something you know.

Single Sign-On

Single sign-on (SSO) is an important concept regarding authentication. When you authenticate to the network that offers SSO, you can access multiple systems based on that single authentication information. So with SSO, you are not required to authenticate with each different system you access—you authenticate once and then can gain access to multiple systems without authenticating again.

Using SSO, you don't have to authenticate with each server individually. Years ago, before SSO was available, logging on to each system required a separate username and password, so users had to remember various passwords to access more than one server. With SSO, the user logs on with one set of credentials, a token is generated, and the token is then presented to the other trusted servers on the network to enable the user to access resources on the network.

 EXAM TIP For the Cisco CCNA exam, remember that authentication occurs when someone identifies herself to the system and her identity is verified.

Authorization

Once you have been authenticated to the network, you will be authorized to access network resources. There are various types of authorization, depending on what it is that you are trying to be authorized for. For example, if you are trying to access a file on the network, authorization is determined according to the permissions assigned to the file. If you are trying to change the time on the server, authorization is determined by your privileges, or rights. From a Cisco networking point of view, authorization is implemented as access control lists, which are configured on the router to allow or deny traffic from entering or leaving the network.

Permissions vs. Rights

Permissions and rights are examples of authorization used on endpoints such as workstations and servers. (This is not a Cisco example, but I wanted to mention it because it is an example of authorization, and one that you will come across on the network if you are responsible for managing security on servers.)

A *permission* is your level of access to a resource such as a file, folder, or object. The permission is a characteristic of the resource and not a characteristic of the user account. For example, if an administrator wanted to give Bob read permission to a file, the admin would go to the properties of that file and set the permissions. Notice that the admin does not go to the user's account to assign the permissions.

In Windows operating systems, a *right* is your privilege within the operating system to perform a particular task. For example, when companies deploy Windows to all client systems on the network, users may be surprised that they cannot change the time on their computers. This is because they do not have the Change System Time rights. A user (or a group to which a user is a member) must be assigned the appropriate right to configure a particular aspect of the operating system. Rights are a significant security feature of the Microsoft OS. It is important to note that administrators can configure the OS because the group that they are a member of (Administrators) is assigned all the rights.

The goal here is not to make this too much of a Windows discussion, but just to offer examples of authorization. After you log on to a computer, you are authorized, or not authorized, to access different files or perform different actions because of the permissions and rights that have been configured for you as a user.

Controlling Traffic

A Cisco example of authorization is the access control list (ACL). To authorize which traffic is allowed to enter or leave different parts of your network, you will configure rules on your firewall or Cisco routers. The ACL is a list of these rules that either permit or deny different types of traffic from entering or leaving your network. (You will learn more about ACLs in Chapter 17). The router receives a packet and then typically allows or denies the packet based on the protocol, the source or destination IP address (IP filtering), or the source and destination port (port filtering).

Network Access Control

Network access control (NAC) is a hot technology today that enables you to authorize who can gain access to a wired or wireless network based on the state of the connecting system, known as *posture assessment.* With NAC, you can specify conditions that a system must meet in order to gain access to the network. If those conditions are not met, the user can be sent to a restricted network, where he can take actions to remedy the problem.

For example, you may require that for a system to connect to the network, it must have antivirus software installed, and the antivirus definitions must be up-to-date. You may also require that the system have a personal firewall enabled. If any of these conditions is not met, the NAC system places the client on a restricted network, where the user can typically apply patches or, in this case, perform an update of the virus definitions.

When connected to the restricted network, the client has no access to network resources because communication to the private company network from the restricted network is controlled. Figure 16-2 displays a network access control environment.

Figure 16-2
NAC is used to place health requirements on systems connecting to the network.

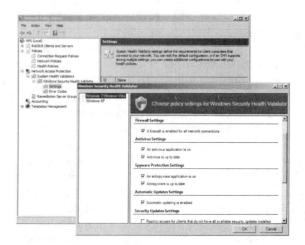

Today, NAC is used in many scenarios, as demonstrated in the following examples:

- **Connecting to wireless** When connecting to a wireless network, the NAC system may require you to accept the terms of wireless network usage before you are given access to the network.

- **Patch status** A client connects to a network, either locally or through VPN, and the client's health is checked to ensure that it has antivirus software installed, that virus definitions are up-to-date, and that the system is up-to-date with patches before the client is allowed to connect to the network.

- **Connecting to a switch** If the switch is 802.1x-compliant, it can be configured to ensure that the connecting client is authenticated by an authentication service (such as RADIUS) before allowing the client access to the network.

Port Security

Another common method used to authorize who can gain access to the network is to implement *port security* on your Cisco switches. The port security feature of a switch enables you to control which systems can connect to individual ports on the switch according to their MAC addresses. To refresh your memory on port security, review Chapter 9.

 EXAM TIP For the CCNA exam, be sure to be familiar with ACLs and port security, and be able to identify scenarios in which they are being used.

Network Segmentation

It is important to ensure that you separate different types of systems, or environments, from one another to help increase security. For example, a hotel that provides wireless access to its guests would ensure that the systems from the wireless network are not connected with the hotel's corporate systems. You typically segment systems by not providing a physical connection between the two networks, or, if you need to have a physical connection, you use a router or firewall to control communication between the types of systems using ACLs. VLANs are also a great Cisco switch feature to help implement different network segments.

In the following scenarios, it is important to implement network segmentation:

- **Legacy systems** You may want to separate a legacy system from the rest of the network because the legacy system is running older software or protocols. Or you may want to segment the legacy system because it is older and potentially not as secure as newer systems, because patches for the old system are no longer being provided. Having the older system connected to the same network with newer systems would lower the security of the newer systems. For example, you could place a Windows 7 system running a legacy application, or a Windows Server 2012, in the category of a legacy system.

- **Separate private/public networks**   You should separate the private network (your LAN) from any untrusted public network (such as the Internet) to help reduce chances of attacks from the Internet.

- **Honeypots/honeynets**   A honeypot is a system or network designed to attract a hacker to attack it instead of attacking a production system or network. You want to ensure that you segment the honeypot environment from the production environment so that a hacker who is tricked into trying to hack into the honeypot does not see the production system or network.

- **Testing labs**   Any test environment should be segmented from the production network. One good reason to do this is a test lab typically uses the same IP addresses and computer names that the production systems are using, so you want to make sure that the systems are not on the same network to prevent IP and name conflicts.

- **Performance optimization and load balancing**   You may choose to segment systems as a way to load balance some of the work. For example, instead of having all users connect to one server for service, you can place that service on two different servers, which are each on a different network. This way, each network is being serviced by one server with half the traffic. You could also load balance traffic by having a separate switch or wiring closet for each floor and have that floor connect to a layer 3 switch to segment the traffic of each floor from traffic of the others.

- **Compliance**   You may need to separate systems using different segments to comply with regulations or other requirements. For example, a vendor may not support a product unless it is separated from different types of systems. Regulations governing your organization may also have compliance requirements that involve controlling communication to systems that store sensitive data. For example, the Payment Card Industry Data Security Standard (PCI DSS) requires isolating any system storing or processing credit card data on its own network segment.

Accounting

After the individual authenticates to the system, she is then authorized (or not authorized) to perform different actions on the system or network. *Accounting* then kicks in, tracking and logging the actions that the user performs while accessing the system or network. Accounting is very important to security; by logging user actions, the user is held accountable for all of her actions.

Following are some examples of activity that may be tracked:

- **Internet usage**   Log each web site that the user visits.
- **File access**   Log each time a user accesses certain files on a server or, more importantly, each time a user deletes or copies a file.
- **Database access**   Log when a user accesses certain data in a database or changes or deletes data in the database.

AAA Services

The services of authentication, authorization, and accounting are collectively known in the industry as AAA services.

- **Authentication**   The authentication service is responsible for validating the credentials presented by the user and typically involves having an authentication database of criteria. For example, when a user logs on with a username and password, that information is verified against an account database.

- **Authorization**   Once the account information has been verified, the user is granted access to the network. The authorization component may need criteria other than account information before granting access. For example, the authorization service may require that the authentication request come from a specific subnet.

- **Accounting**   Accounting deals with logging activity performed by users and administrators, so that users can be held accountable for their actions. Accounting can also be used to help determine how much money each department should be paying for the service (the security solution).

Many AAA solutions have been released over the years, such as RADIUS and TACACS+. These services offer the benefit of a central system that can offer authentication, authorization, and accounting for many types of environments, such as wired network, wireless networks, and VPNs.

RADIUS

Remote Access Dial-In User Service (RADIUS) is a central authentication service that has been popular for many years. The client computer that needs access to the network connects to the network by attempting to connect to a switch or a wireless access point, or by making a connection to a VPN server from across the Internet. In this case, the switch, wireless access point, or VPN server is known as the RADIUS client, because it sends the authentication request to the RADIUS server that is running in the background. This RADIUS server verifies the credentials and sends back a reply that indicates whether the network client is to be granted or denied access (see Figure 16-3).

   NOTE   IEEE 802.1x is the standard for devices that can use a RADIUS server for authentication services. When purchasing network devices such as switches and access points, be sure to verify that they are 802.1x compliant if you need to use a central authentication server.

TACACS and XTACACS

TACACS originated as an authentication service that ran on UNIX systems. TACACS services used TCP and UDP port 49. A few years after TACACS was introduced, Cisco created its own proprietary authentication service called *Extended TACACS* (XTACACS), which worked as a central authentication service for Cisco devices.

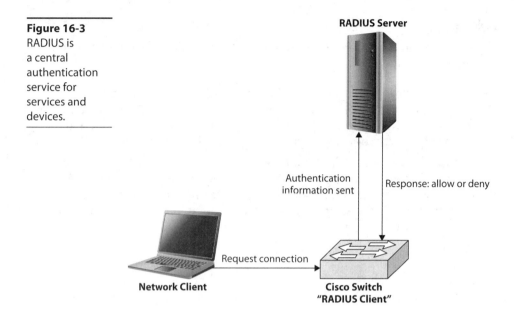

Figure 16-3
RADIUS is a central authentication service for services and devices.

RADIUS Server

Authentication information sent

Response: allow or deny

Request connection

Network Client

Cisco Switch "RADIUS Client"

TACACS+

The TACACS+ protocol is the AAA protocol used by Cisco networks and supersedes the original TACACS and XTACACS protocols. TACACS+ uses TCP for communication and uses the same topology used by RADIUS in the sense that the client tries to connect to the Cisco switch, and the switch, which is the TACACS client in this case, sends the authentication request to the TACACS server. TACACS+ has been improved over RADIUS from a security standpoint, because it encrypts all information between the TACACS client and the TACACS server, whereas RADIUS encrypts only the password between the RADIUS client and the RADIUS server.

Password Policy Elements

The CCNA exam expects you to understand the importance of policies in securing the environment. In this section you will learn more about password complexity, password policy, account lockout policy, and the management of accounts and passwords.

Password Complexity

One of the most important concepts related to passwords is ensuring that users understand the importance of having a complex password. A *complex password* is a password that is at least eight characters long and requires the inclusion of lowercase letters, uppercase letters, numbers, and symbols. For example, *jT94q$ym4C* would be a complex password.

The problem with using complex passwords, however, is that they are difficult to remember. When discussing complex passwords, I encourage users to take a familiar phrase and choose which characters to include from the phrase in the password. For example, you might base a password on the entire phrase or on the first or second character from each word in the phrase.

Let's take a look at an example using the common phrase *"the best of both worlds"* as the basis for our password:

- First, we can join the words together and capitalize the first letter of each word (to satisfy the need for lowercase and uppercase characters): *TheBestOfBothWorlds*

- Next, we may want to do some character replacement to use a combination of letters, numbers, and symbols. For example, the *O* can be replaced with a 0 (zero), the *e* can be replaced with a *3*, and the *s* can be replaced with a *$* (dollar sign). So now we have a password that looks like this: *Th3B3stOfB0thW0rld$*

This is just a small example to give you the idea of how you can educate your users on creating complex passwords, while also making it easy for them to remember.

Password Policy

To enforce strong passwords and good password practices, you will need to configure a password policy to control how passwords are used on your systems. Figure 16-4 shows the elements of a password policy on a Windows 10 workstation.

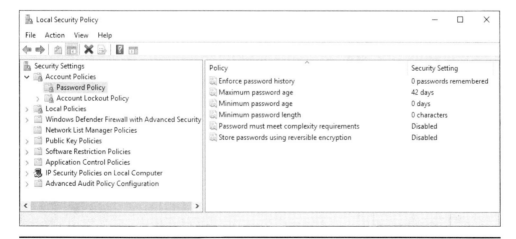

Figure 16-4 Password policy elements

The following list outlines the common password policy elements that should be configured in any environment:

- **Minimum password length**   Specify how long a password must be. I recommend setting this to at least eight characters.
- **Maximum password age**   Specify how frequently (in days) users will need to change their passwords. I recommend 30 to 90 days at the most for password changes.
- **Password history**   Specify that a user cannot change a password to a password they've already used. I recommend setting the password history to 24 passwords remembered; this means the user cannot reuse the last 24 passwords they used in the past.
- **Minimum password age**   Specify how long users must keep a password before they are allowed to change it again. The purpose of this policy is to stop someone from voluntarily changing his password a large number of times in a row to remove a password from the password history, which would enable him to reuse an old password, bypassing the password history requirement. I recommend a value of one or two days here.
- **Complexity requirements**   Specify that the password include uppercase letters, lowercase letters, numbers, and symbols.

Account Lockout Policy

An account lockout policy helps you protect user accounts from being hacked. With an account lockout policy (see Figure 16-5), you specify that after a certain number of bad logon attempts, an account will be locked and cannot be used. You also specify for how long the account is locked; typically, the account is locked until the administrator unlocks it.

Figure 16-5   Account lockout policy elements

The following are the account lockout policy settings on a Windows system:

- **Account lockout threshold**   The number of bad logon attempts that will be tolerated before the account is locked.
- **Account lockout duration**   The number of minutes that the account will be locked. For example, it could be locked for a number of minutes or set to 0 (zero), which means the account would be locked until an administrator unlocks it.
- **Reset account lockout counter after**   How long before the bad logon threshold resets back to zero.

Account and Password Management

As a network administrator, you'll perform a number of tasks to manage user accounts and passwords to help create a secure environment. Your first two steps are to create a password policy and an account lockout policy, but you may need to perform other actions as well.

Password Expiration

Password policies are set to expire after a maximum amount of time. Suppose, for example, that you set a user's password expiration to 30 days. This means that after a user has used a password for 30 days, it will expire. The next time the user logs on, she'll be asked to change her password. If anything goes wrong with a password reset, you may need to reset the password for a user with your user account management tool.

Disable Accounts

If an employee takes a leave from work, such as a parental leave, or quits his job, the first thing you should do is disable the user's account so that the employee cannot log on and use that account. This is important today, especially, as employees may access their work e-mail from anywhere via the Internet or they may work remotely, off-premises. If an employee leaves the company, he should not be able to log on to access company e-mail or use the company network. It's important that you disable the user's account as soon as possible.

Remove Unnecessary Accounts

Every so often, you should audit the user accounts that exist in your environment and identify those that are no longer needed and can be removed. I recommend that, to be on the safe side, you disable an account that is not needed for a period of time at first (to see if anyone complains), and then, if you are sure the account is no longer necessary, you can delete the account.

Remote Access and VPNs

Remote access concepts such as virtual private networks (VPNs), remote access protocols such as Cisco AnyConnect, site-to-site VPNs, and remote administration protocols such as telnet, SSH, and RDP are common in network environments today. For the Cisco CCNA certification exam, you'll need to have a fundamental understanding of remote access concepts, specifically the purpose of VPNs and the different remote access protocols that are used by companies to remotely access network devices.

VPN Overview

Once the Internet became popular, allowing users in remote (off-premises) locations to communicate with distant networks was an obvious solution. For example, if you had an office in New York and a user in a hotel room in Boston needed to access the New York network, what better solution than to use the Internet? Of course, many security issues are involved in sending data across the Internet, because the entire world of hackers may tap into your network!

Virtual private networks (VPNs) offer a solution. With a VPN, the user in the Boston hotel can connect to the Internet using a Wi-Fi connection provided by the hotel. Once the Internet connection is achieved, the user can use the IP address of the VPN server in New York to create a "secure tunnel" between her laptop (the client system) and the VPN server in New York. With a VPN, any data that travels between the two systems will be encrypted and therefore will be considered secure.

VPNs offer two major benefits: they provide secure communication across an unsecure medium, and no costs are incurred to communicate between the two locations. Once all systems have an Internet connection, VPN solutions leverage that connection and add security to it.

 EXAM TIP Remember that a VPN is designed to establish a secure (encrypted) tunnel over an untrusted network, such as the Internet, and is used to encrypt traffic that travels across that untrusted network.

VPN Protocols

For the CCNA certification exam, you'll need to understand the purpose of a VPN and the main protocols used to encrypt communication with a VPN. Following are common protocols used to secure VPN traffic:

- **Point-to-Point Tunneling Protocol (PPTP)** This older VPN protocol is used to encrypt Point-to-Point Protocol (PPP) traffic and is common in older Microsoft environments. PPTP uses the Generic Routing Encapsulation (GRE) protocol to transport the PPP packets, but it uses the Microsoft Point-to-Point Encryption (MPPE) protocol to encrypt the traffic. To allow PPTP traffic to pass through the firewall, you will need to open TCP port 1723 (control port) and protocol ID 47 (carries the data) on the firewall.

- **Layer 2 Tunneling Protocol (L2TP)** L2TP has been around for quite a few years now, but it's a newer VPN protocol than PPTP. L2TP uses the more secure IPsec (Internet Protocol Security) for encryption of traffic instead of MPPE. To allow L2TP traffic through your firewall, you will need to open UDP port 500 (for key exchange), UDP port 5500 (for IPsec NAT), and UDP port 1701 on the firewall.

- **Secure Socket Transport Protocol (SSTP)**   The SSTP protocol is a common VPN protocol today and is the newest of the three protocols listed. SSTP has a benefit in that it uses Secure Sockets Layer (SSL) to encrypt the VPN traffic, making it easy to configure the firewall to allow VPN traffic to pass through— you simply need to open the SSL port 443.

In addition to these protocols, you should be familiar with three other security protocols: GRE, IPsec, and ISAKMP.

- **Generic Routing Encapsulation (GRE)**   GRE is a networking protocol that is designed to create a point-to-point tunnel between two devices. As a tunneling protocol, GRE is used to establish the point-to-point link and then encapsulate other types of traffic, such as IPv4 or IPv6 packets, into the GRE packet. GRE is a common protocol used to set up a VPN tunnel between two Cisco routers.

- **IPsec**   This protocol is used to encrypt all IP traffic once IPsec has been configured on the system or device. The IPsec protocol uses Encapsulation Security Payload (ESP) to encrypt traffic, Authentication Header (AH) protocol for message integrity and authentication, and Internet Key Exchange (IKE) to exchange encryption keys between systems.

- **ISAKMP**   The Internet Security Association and Key Management Protocol (ISAKMP) is responsible for setting up a secure channel (known as a security association) and exchanging keys. ISAKMP is used by IKE for authentication before key exchange.

Remote Access VPNs

Users (or an administrator) can install VPN software on a laptop to connect over the Internet to a VPN server at work through a secure tunnel from the laptop to the company network. This helps ensure the security of data traveling through the tunnel. The VPN software running on the company laptop uses one of the VPN protocols mentioned earlier to encrypt data from the laptop, across the Internet, and to the company network. For example, a laptop user may have Cisco AnyConnect installed on his laptop to establish a VPN connection to the corporate network using SSL.

Site-to-Site VPNs

Another common topology in use is the site-to-site VPN solution. In this case, a VPN appliance, typically a router with VPN capabilities, is installed at each location that is used to create the encrypted tunnel from one location to another. The clients are not establishing the tunnel, so they do not need a configured VPN connection to the remote location from their own system. Instead, they will go through a network device such as a router that will create the VPN tunnel to the other location.

Site-to-site VPNs are commonly used to connect branch offices to a head office. Figure 16-6 compares a remote access VPN used by an employee with a laptop at home to connect to the office, and a site-to-site VPN used to connect different office locations together in a secure manner. The key point to remember is that with a remote access VPN, the endpoint device has VPN software installed to create the secure tunnel, while

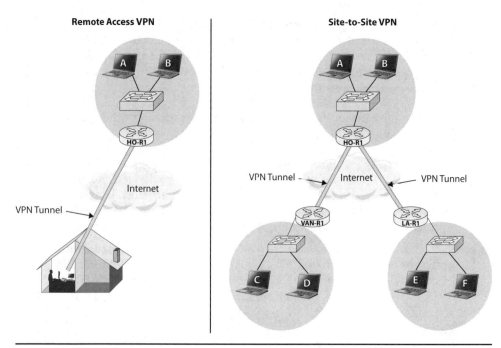

Figure 16-6   A remote access VPN versus a site-to-site VPN

with a site-to-site VPN, the Cisco routers or ASA firewalls create the secure tunnel for that network location.

EXAM TIP   For the CCNA exam know the difference between a remote access VPN and a site-to-site VPN. With a remote access VPN solution, a user has VPN software installed on their system that they use to remote into the office using a secure tunnel. With a site-to-site VPN, the edge devices at each network location (the routers) create the VPN tunnel.

Remote Administration Protocols

You'll often need to administer a device on the network from an offsite location. In *remote administration*, you will not be connected directly to the device through the console port, and you'll need to make administration changes from another part of the network or from across the Internet.

To manage these devices remotely, you will use a remote administration protocol. The following are some common remote administration protocols in use:

- **Telnet**   You learned earlier in this book that telnet is a common remote administration protocol that enables you to connect to your switch or router and make administrative changes remotely. The problem with telnet, however, is that it sends data in clear text, including the authentication traffic (username and password). For this reason, you should not use telnet for remote administration; instead, use SSH to access onsite switches and routers securely. You will learn how to configure SSH in the next chapter.

- **SSH**   SSH sends all data in an encrypted format, including the authentication traffic (username and password). If you need to manage your Cisco switches and routers, remotely ensure that SSH is the only protocol being used.

- **RDP**   The Remote Desktop Protocol is used for remote administration of workstations and servers on the network. You can use RDP to administer a computer located somewhere else on the network or on the Internet.

Implementing a Security Program

The last security topic is an important one: how to a security program. Simply put, a security program is a set of procedures that are created within the company to help improve security. A good security program involves a number of elements, such as user awareness, training programs for company employees, and the implementation of physical access control methods.

User Awareness

A key to improving security in any organization is to have a user awareness program that communicates the importance of maintaining security to protect the company's assets. The user awareness program should explain the responsibility of each employee to uphold the organization's security policies.

Employees should be aware of a number of secure practices:

- **Not sharing passwords**   Ensure that employees understand the importance of not sharing their password with anyone.

- **Using strong passwords**   Ensure that employees know that the stronger the password, the harder it is for an attacker to crack the password and gain access to the network.

- **Keeping doors shut and locked**   Ensure that employees know that a secure facility has locked doors in some areas to prevent unauthorized individuals from gaining physical access to the facility and its equipment.

- **Keeping a clean desk**   A clean desk policy is designed to help keep information confidential. Employees should not leave confidential paperwork unattended on their desks for everyone to see.

- **Not clicking links from untrusted sources**   Employees should be aware of phishing attacks to help them understand that clicking a link from an unknown source can give a malicious person access to the company's system and data.

Employee Training

Security training should be designed to improve the company's overall security. The security program should have a training element to it that identifies the different levels of training that each type of employee should have that is designed to improve overall security to the company. For example, all employees should take a one-day security awareness clinic that introduces the core security best practices that all users should be following. The employee training program can provide additional security training appropriate to each job role in the company. For example, management should be trained on how they can manage their staff to help them best maintain a secure work environment, while the technical team will require specialized training that demonstrates how to implement different security controls to protect the company's assets.

Physical Access Control

Physical security is one of the most important security concepts in any organization. A variety of physical security measures can be used to ensure that unauthorized individuals cannot gain physical access to computers or devices.

Perimeter Security

The first line of defense in physical security is at the perimeter of the facility premises. Especially in highly secure environments, it is critical that you control who is allowed to enter the company's property, even outside the building. Two popular methods of controlling access to company property are fences and security guards.

Perimeter Fencing In highly secure environments, installing a fence around the perimeter of the property can deter intruders from trespassing. A fence around the premises can force individuals who want to access the facility to go through the main gates, where security guards monitor everyone who enters or leaves the facility.

   The height of the fence depends on your organization's specific security requirements. To deter a casual intruder, a fence height of 3 to 4 feet would be sufficient. Keep in mind, however, that a 4-foot fence is easy to climb, so perhaps a fence height of 5 to 7 feet would be more appropriate. A determined intruder, however, would have no problem figuring out how to climb a 7-foot-tall fence; to deter such an intruder, the recommended fence height is 8 feet with three lines of barbed wire on top, tilted at a 45-degree angle toward the outside.

 EXAM TIP   For the certification exam, know that the recommended fence height to deter a determined intruder is 8 feet plus three strands of barbed wire on top, facing the intruder at a 45-degree angle.

Security Guards   A fenced property requires a main gate, where guards monitor everyone who enters or leaves the premises. Security guards will verify that a visitor is expected at the facility and typically provide a visitor ID badge that is to be worn at all times. Employees entering the facility will need to display their employee ID badges to gain access. ID badges usually include the employee's name and photo.

The security guard can monitor persons leaving the facility to ensure that equipment is not being stolen. A security guard can also watch for any abnormal activities. (I talked to a customer who said that if employees remove a company laptop or some other equipment to use remotely, the security guard verifies that the employee is allowed to leave with the equipment and makes him or her sign out the equipment. This process is intended to eliminate internal theft of company assets.)

If warranted by your company, security guards may be positioned throughout the facility to help ensure that no security incidents occur. The guards should be trained to watch for ID badges on all persons walking through the facility, and to stop and question anyone who does not have a proper ID badge. (At one customer's facility, I was given a visitor badge, and as I put it on, the gentleman who had authorized me said, "No, you have to attach it on your left side." The organization required that all personnel and visitors wear their ID badge on their left side so that security guards could easily see it.)

Mantraps No physical security discussion would be complete without including mantraps. A typical *mantrap* is a small area between two doors. It provides access security because the second door will not unlock until the first door is closed. This helps prevent *piggybacking* or *tailgating*, when an unauthorized person tries to slip in behind you after you have unlocked a door. A mantrap ensures that only one person at a time can pass through a secured entrance. After entering the first door, you should not open the second door if someone entered the mantrap area behind you (unless you are sure the person is authorized to enter).

Another form of mantrap is a C-shaped cylinder, about the size of an old-fashioned telephone booth, that rotates between two openings and can be stopped halfway to prevent an intruder from proceeding. Mantraps can also be revolving doors that rotate enough to allow only a single person to pass through.

Depending on the environment, the mantrap area may include a secure window. On the other side of that window, a security guard monitors anyone who enters or leaves the facility.

 EXAM TIP A mantrap is used to help prevent tailgating by trapping individuals in an area between two doors. The second door will not unlock until the first door is closed.

Detective Controls

A variety of detective controls can be employed to help provide or support physical security on the organization's premises. These include motion detectors, video surveillance cameras, asset tracking tags, and tamper protection.

Motion Detection and Video Surveillance Cameras Organizations can install motion detectors throughout the facility to detect moving objects or persons in areas where no activity should be occurring. When movement is detected, some detectors trigger alerts that are sent to a designated individual's phone. Or the detector may turn on lights to illuminate the area, or maybe start recording video with video surveillance equipment. Some motion detectors emit infrared light and send an alert notification when there is a break in the light beam. Other detectors send out rays of microwave radiation and are triggered if any of those waves reflects an object in its path.

Physical security may involve using closed-circuit television (CCTV) or other video surveillance technologies such as IP cameras. In CCTV, cameras are installed to monitor areas of the facility. The video feed is sent to computer screens in a central security area, where security personnel can monitor for suspicious activity. Older CCTV monitoring systems sent the video to VHS tapes or to other recording equipment; today's video surveillance cameras record to a personal video recorder (PVR), which stores the data on a hard drive.

EXAM TIP Remember that CCTV systems capture video and send it to a *specific* system or set of displays. It is popular to send these video feeds to a control room, where security personnel monitor the screens for suspicious activity.

Many of today's video surveillance systems are a little more advanced and are not really considered CCTV, because equipment owners can now connect to a camera via the Internet and view the captured video live on a smart phone. Most modern monitoring systems can also record the captured video to remote locations across the network, such as to a central server.

Asset Tracking Tags Another part of physical security is the ability to track company assets and maintain an inventory of each asset and its location. For example, companies should place asset tracking tags on laptops, printers, computers, monitors, and projectors, and then store information about that device and its asset number in a database. Items should be inventoried on a regular basis to ensure that the database is up-to-date.

Tamper Detection Devices such as computers and servers have tamper-detection features that can detect when a computer case is opened. On bootup, the system notifies the user if any of these actions has occurred. When reviewing BIOS settings on a system, you should verify that tamper detection features are enabled.

Incident Prevention Controls

An incident prevention control is a mechanism that helps prevent a security incident from occurring. In this section, you will learn about incident prevention controls that relate to physical security, including badges, biometrics, smartcards, proximity readers and key fobs, and locks.

Badges To ensure physical security, organization personnel can be required to wear ID badges that typically contain the employee's name and photo. Other types of ID badges identify nonpersonnel, such as facility visitors. In highly secure environments, the visitor badge is typically a color that easily differentiates it from an employee badge that uses a different color. Some companies take that a bit farther and require two different colors of ID badges for visitors: one color for a visitor who must be accompanied by an escort while on premises, and another color ID badge for an unescorted visitor.

Biometrics   Biometrics involves a user's personal characteristics that must be authenticated to unlock a door or access a piece of equipment. Examples of biometrics include a retinal scan, fingerprint scan, or voice recognition. Many laptops and mobile devices use fingerprint scanners to authenticate a person before allowing them access to the device.

Smartcard   This credit-card-sized plastic card contains a computer chip that stores information about the cardholder who is authorized to use the card for access. A smartcard can contain authentication information within the chip, which can be used to control access to different areas of the building.

Proximity Reader and Key Fob   A proximity reader is a sensor device that reads an access code from a token or card. Proximity readers can be user-activated or system-sensing. With a user-activated proximity reader, the employee would key in a code or swipe an access card by the sensor to gain access to a locked door. A system-sensing proximity reader system continuously sends out an interrogating signal that the user's access device would respond to by sending the access code to the sensor to unlock a door.

A key fob is a keychain-like device that is used to swipe across a sensor to gain access to an area, a network closet, or a server room. There are also forms of key fob token devices, such as an RSA token, which continually regenerates codes that last for 60 seconds. The code is used in conjunction with a user's password to authenticate to the network.

Locks   One of the most popular methods of controlling access to a facility or room is to implement a locking system on the doors. Conventional locks are easy to pick and susceptible to a bump key attack. A *bump key* is a normal key that has been filed down to fit into a lock; the key is inserted into the lock and pulled out one notch. When the key is tapped, it causes the pins in the lock to align and then unlock the door.

You can purchase pick-resistant locks (at a higher cost), which offer added security and cannot be easily compromised, but most companies use electronic locking systems, also known as electronic key systems, in today's high-security environments. Two popular electronic locking systems are listed here:

- **Keycard readers and swipe cards**   Some electronic locking systems involve token devices or swipe cards that are used with a proximity or swipe reader to unlock a door. Each device or card includes the holder's access code encoded within it. When the employee swipes the token or card past the reader's electronic sensor, the door unlocks.

- **Cipher locks**   With a cipher lock, also known as an electronic combination lock, the employee enters a personal identification number (PIN) or key code sequence on a keypad to gain access. The lock may sometimes require the user to press multiple number keys at the same time. For example, the code may require the user to press 3, then 2 and 4 at the same time, followed by 7. (I have seen electronic keypads that do not show numbers on the buttons until you press a start button. Once you press the start button, the system randomly generates the placement of the numbers so that if someone watches your finger position, they will not be able to determine your access code.)

By using either of these electronic locking systems, a company can control which areas an employee can access based on an access code. These systems can also log access, including the date and time that an employee accesses the facility or different areas of the facility.

Network Closet or Server Room

Once you have controlled access to the building, you also want to ensure that you control who has access to the network closet or server room. To ensure physical security, the network closet containing communication equipment should be locked, and only a limited number of personnel should have access to the network closet. A server room, which contains servers, routers, and switches, is also locked, with limited access.

Most server rooms and communications closets also use rack systems that support locking the door to the rack to prevent someone from gaining access to the network equipment mounted on the rack. This is a great additional layer of security to protect your equipment from someone who may have gotten access to the room.

Chapter Review

In this chapter you were introduced to a number of security concepts that should be practiced in any environment.

You were first introduced to the importance of confidentiality, integrity, and availability (CIA) as the fundamental goals of security. You then learned of different types of attacks that can occur and some common techniques you can use to help prevent attacks from occurring.

You also learned about the AAA services—authentication, authorization, and accounting. These are important concepts to know for the exam. You also learned about RADIUS or TACACS+ as a central authentication service on the network.

Ensuring that users have good password practices is critical to the security of the environment. You learned about password policies and account lockout policies and other user account and password management concepts.

You also learned the importance of remote access concepts with virtual private networks (VPNs) and remote administration protocols. VPNs are used to create an encrypted tunnel across an unsecure network, such as the Internet. You also learned that you should configure SSH on your routers and switches for remote administration needs.

Finally, you were introduced to the concept of a security program and the types of elements that go into a security program.

Quick Review

Understanding Threats and Attack Types

- The fundamental goals of security are confidentiality, integrity, and availability. This is often referred to as CIA.
- A vulnerability is a weakness in a product, while an exploit is something that takes advantage of that weakness.
- Social engineering is when the attacker tries to trick you into compromising security through social contact (e-mail message, phone call, or in person conversation).

Authentication and Authorization Concepts

- Authentication is the verification of the credentials, while authorization is checking if someone is permitted to do something.
- Accounting is tracking actions performed by individuals.

Password Policy Elements

- A password policy should ensure that passwords are complex (mix of letters, numbers, and symbols) and meet a minimum number of characters (such as 8).
- An account lockout policy is used to lock an account after a certain number of bad logon attempts.

Remote Access and VPNs

- A remote access VPN is when the user runs VPN software on their system to create a secure connection from their workstation to the VPN server.
- A site-to-site VPN is when the branch office router creates a secure connection to the main office. Employees do not need VPN software on their workstations with a site-to-site VPN.

Implementing a Security Program

- Create a security program that educates employees on the importance of their role with company security.

Questions

The following questions will help you measure your understanding of the material presented in this chapter. To help you better prepare for the exams, read all choices carefully before selecting your answer. Choose the correct answer(s) for each question.

1. What is the difference between authentication and authorization services?

   A. Authentication determines what the user can do, while authorization identifies and verifies the user.

   B. Authorization tracks user activity, while authentication identifies and verifies the user.

   C. Authentication identifies and verifies the user, while authorization determines what the user can do.

   D. Authorization determines what the user can do, while authentication tracks the user activity.

2. What is the purpose of accounting with AAA services?

   A. Accounting is designed to determine what the user can do.

   B. Accounting is designed to track the activities of the user.

   C. Accounting is used to identify and verify the user.

   D. Accounting is used to authenticate the user with a characteristic of himself.

3. Which of the following authentication actions satisfies the requirements of multifactor authentication?

   A. An employee types her username and password to log on to the system.

   B. An employee logs on with a username and PIN.

   C. A user must have a key fob and a driver's license to log on.

   D. An employee logs on with a username and password, and then enters an access code she received as a notification on her smart phone.

4. Which of the following accurately defines AAA?

   A. Authentication tracks user activity, accounting verifies the user, and authorization determines tasks allowed to be performed by the user.

   B. Authentication verifies the user, accounting tracks user activity, and authorization determines tasks allowed to be performed by the user.

   C. Authentication tracks user activity, accounting determines tasks allowed to be performed by the user, and authorization verifies the identity of the user.

   D. Authentication determines tasks allowed by the user, accounting tracks user activity, and authorization verifies the identity of the user.

5. Which of the following would be part of a company's user awareness training program?

    A. Having an e-mail sent to all users from an unknown source that asks them to click a link

    B. Configuring SSH on the router

    C. Requiring mantraps at highly secure facilities

    D. Disabling unused ports on a switch

6. What type of attack is a smurf attack?

    A. Phishing attack

    B. Password attack

    C. Buffer overflow attack

    D. DDoS attack

7. What is the difference between RADIUS and TACACS+?

    A. RADIUS was created by Cisco, while TACACS+ is an IEEE AAA service.

    B. TACACS+ encrypts only the username and password, while RADIUS encrypts all of the traffic.

    C. RADIUS encrypts only the username and password, while TACACS+ encrypts all of the traffic.

    D. They are the same service.

8. What technology is used to encrypt communication across an untrusted network?

    A. RADIUS

    B. TACACS+

    C. NAC

    D. VPN

9. You are configuring a site-to-site VPN. What protocol is responsible for encrypting the data between the two sites?

    A. SHA1

    B. IPsec

    C. IKE

    D. WPA2

10. What type of attack involves the attacker altering the source IP address of the packet so that it can bypass your access control list?

    A. Spoofing

    B. DDoS

    C. Phishing

    D. Password

Performance-based Questions

The Cisco exams include performance-based questions that ask you to drag a box from the left side of the screen to its proper place on the right side of the screen in order to answer the question. The following are some sample performance-based questions related to topics in this chapter.

1. Looking at the description on the left side of the exhibit, identify the term as being a characteristic of accounting, authentication, or authorization.

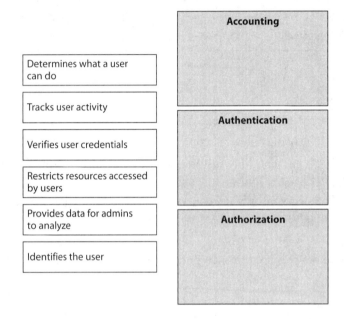

2. Looking at the types of attacks on the left side of the screen, draw a line to connect each attack type to the description that best matches it.

DoS attack	Hacker sends an e-mail trying to trick user into clicking a link
Spoofing attack	A form of password attack that uses a password list file
Keylogger	Used in an MITM attack so victim sends data to hacker
Phishing attack	Hacker uses multiple systems to cause victim to crash
DDoS attack	Malware used to capture what a user is typing
Dictionary attack	Involves hacker altering the source address
ARP	Causes a system to crash or become unresponsive

Answers

1. **C.** Authentication involves the user submitting credentials and those credentials being verified by the system. After the user is authenticated, authorization allows or denies the user the ability to perform actions.

2. **B.** Accounting services, which is part of AAA services, is designed to track or log the activities performed by the user.

3. **D.** Multifactor authentication requires that the user log on with at least two of the following: something you know, something you have, and something you are. The username and password are *something you know*, while having the phone in your possession so that you can receive the access code is the *something you have* factor.

4. **B.** Remember for the exam that authentication verifies the user, accounting tracks user activity, and authorization determines the actions allowed to be performed by the user.

5. **A.** User awareness involves educating users on security topics that directly affect them, such as phishing attacks, which involves an e-mail being received from an unknown source asking the user to click a link. Sending them an example of a phishing attack would help users understand how e-mail can be used to deceive them.

6. **D.** A smurf attack is an older attack that involved sending ping messages to a large number of systems, but altering the source IP address of the ping message to be that of the intended victim. This is an example of a DDoS attack because all of the replies would overwhelm and crash the victim's system.

7. **C.** RADIUS is an industry standard authentication service that encrypts only the username and password, while TACACS+ is a Cisco proprietary authentication service that encrypts all the traffic.

8. **D.** Virtual private networks (VPNs) are used to create a secure tunnel between two points so that data can travel across an untrusted network in a secure manner.

9. **B.** IPsec is an encryption protocol that is used to encrypt communication within a VPN.

10. **A.** In a spoofing attack, the attacker alters the source address. This could be the source MAC address, the source IP address, or the source e-mail address of an e-mail message.

Performance-based Answers

Following are the correct answers to the performance-based questions in this chapter.

1. The CCNA exam expects you to understand the difference between authentication, authorization, and accounting. The following is the answer to the performance-based question. On the real exam, you are expected to drag-and-drop the boxes on the left side of the screen onto the matching description on the right side of the screen.

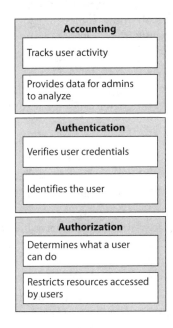

2. The following shows the matching of each attack type to the description that best matches the attack type:

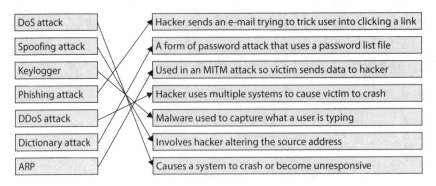

Implementing Security on Cisco Devices

In this chapter, you will

- Review device password configuration
- Learn how to configure layer 2 security features
- Focus on access control lists
- Learn about access control list placement

The new CCNA exam expects you to understand the security features of Cisco devices. The last chapter introduced you to security terminology, which you will be tested on as well, but this chapter focuses more on the hands-on configuration settings that you should be aware of that affect the security of your device.

In this chapter we will review the password configuration options and the configuration of Secure Shell (SSH) on the Cisco device before looking at layer 2 security features to help prevent attacks on the network. You will then learn about access control lists, which you can use to allow or block traffic from entering or leaving a network.

Configuring Device Passwords

Securing your Cisco device starts with configuring the different passwords that may exist on the device. In this section you will learn about the different passwords that should be configured on your Cisco device. The Cisco CCNA exam will have a few questions on device passwords and the content included in this section.

Enable Password and Secret

The first password to discuss is the password that an administrator will need to enter when navigating from user EXEC mode to privileged EXEC mode using the **enable** command. Two types of enable passwords can be configured: the *enable password,* which is not encrypted in the configuration file, and the *enable secret,* which is encrypted in the configuration file. If both the enable password and the enable secret are set, you will need to use the secret to access privileged EXEC mode.

VIDEO 17.01. The digital resources that accompany this book contain a multimedia demonstration of configuring an enable password and an enable secret.

You can configure the enable password with the **enable password** command and the enable secret with the **enable secret** command, as shown here:

```
VAN-R1>enable
VAN-R1#config term
VAN-R1(config)#enable password ciscopass
VAN-R1(config)#enable secret ciscosecret
```

Now if you display your configuration with the **do show running-config** command, you will see that the enable password is not encrypted, but the secret is:

```
VAN-R1(config)#do show running-config
Building configuration...
(output cut for briefness)
enable secret 5 $1$mERr$wZMkJsj2RVk4hay2C4T32.
enable password ciscopass
```

 TIP Remember that with Cisco you can remove a feature by adding a **no** at the beginning of a command. So if you want to remove the enable secret, you can use the **no enable secret** command, and if you want to remove the enable password, you can use the **no enable password** command.

Securing the Console and Auxiliary Port

The next password to configure on your device is the console password, which is an additional password required when someone connects to the console port of the device. Keep in mind that an administrator would need to supply the console port password before even entering privileged EXEC mode and would need to supply the enable password or enable secret as well. To configure a console password, navigate to the line con 0 port from global configuration mode and then set the password, as shown here:

```
VAN-R1>enable
VAN-R1#config term
VAN-R1(config)#line con 0
VAN-R1(config-line)#password conpass
```

The next step is very important. With the preceding commands configured, if you connect to the console port on your device, you will notice that you are not prompted for a password. This is because after setting the password, you must use the **login** command to indicate to the Cisco device that authentication is required on the port and to prompt for the password:

```
VAN-R1(config-line)#login
```

EXAM TIP For the Cisco CCNA exam, remember that you need to use the **login** command after setting the password in order to require authentication on that port.

Your Cisco router may have an auxiliary (AUX) port next to the console port. The auxiliary port is used as a backup line, where a modem can be connected to enable you to access your router remotely and perform administration changes. Typically, you would remotely access the router with SSH using the IP address of the router, but if something went wrong with the interface and you could not connect from across the network, you could connect a modem to the router's auxiliary port and then dial into the router. Note that if you do not connect a modem to the auxiliary port, it acts like another console port, and you can connect to it locally to administer the device.

TIP The important point here is that, no matter whether you do or don't connect a modem to the auxiliary port, you need to configure a password on the port. I see many network administrators who do not configure a password on the auxiliary port because they are not aware that someone could connect to it as though it were a second console port.

To configure a password on the auxiliary port, navigate to the AUX line from global configuration mode and then set the password with the commands shown next. Note that the **login** command is used here as well; if you forget this command, the configured password has no effect, because the device will not require authentication on that port.

```
VAN-R1>enable
VAN-R1#config term
VAN-R1(config)#line aux 0
VAN-R1(config-line)#password auxpass
VAN-R1(config-line)#login
```

VIDEO 17.02. The digital resources that accompany this book contain a multimedia demonstration of configuring a console password and auxiliary password on a Cisco device.

Securing VTY Ports

If you want to administer the device remotely with telnet or SSH, you will need to configure a password on the virtual type terminal (VTY) ports. To configure a password on the VTY ports, navigate to the VTY lines and then use the **password** command. You are required to use the **login** command here as well to force the device to require authentication by prompting for a password when connecting to those ports.

```
VAN-R1>enable
VAN-R1#config term
VAN-R1(config)#line vty 0 15
VAN-R1(config-line)#password telnetpass
VAN-R1(config-line)#login
```

CAUTION I have said it before within the text of this book, and I will say it again here: You should use SSH instead of telnet, because telnet sends all communication in clear text from the administrator's machine to the device. This includes the authentication traffic, so someone who can tap into that communication can grab your username and password for the device. SSH encrypts all communication from the administrator's machine to the device, including the authentication traffic. You will learn how to configure SSH on your device later in the chapter.

VIDEO 17.03. The digital resources that accompany this book contain a multimedia demonstration of configuring VTY passwords on the Cisco device.

Exercise 17-1: Configuring Passwords on the Cisco Routers

In this exercise you will configure console, auxiliary, and VTY passwords for the VAN-R1 and LA-R1 routers. The following illustration shows the network setup to use for the exercises in this chapter:

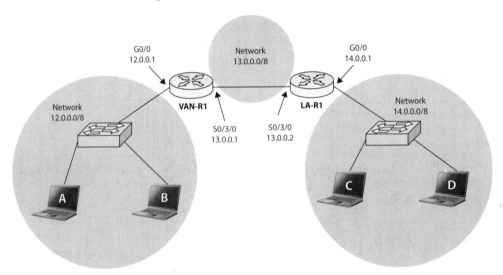

1. Ensure that you have all physical components such as routers and switches connected as per the network diagram, and then power on the devices.
2. Connect your workstation to the console port of VAN-R1. Then launch PuTTY, choose Serial connection, set the correct COM port, and choose Open.
3. Press ENTER in the PuTTY window to get a prompt on your Cisco device.

4. Access VAN-R1's privileged EXEC mode and configure the following passwords. Ensure that the router is configured to prompt for these passwords when a connection is attempted:

Console port password: **labconpass**
Auxiliary port password: **labauxpass**
VTY passwords: **labvtypass**

```
VAN-R1>enable
VAN-R1#config term
Enter configuration commands, one per line.  End with CNTL/Z.
VAN-R1(config)#line con 0
VAN-R1(config-line)#password labconpass
VAN-R1(config-line)#login
VAN-R1(config-line)#line aux 0
VAN-R1(config-line)#password labauxpass
VAN-R1(config-line)#login
VAN-R1(config-line)#line vty 0 15
VAN-R1(config-line)#password labvtypass
VAN-R1(config-line)#login
```

5. Configure the following enable password and secret values:

Enable password: **labenablepass**
Enable secret: **labenablesecret**

```
VAN-R1(config-line)#exit
VAN-R1(config)#enable password labenablepass
VAN-R1(config)#enable secret labenablesecret
VAN-R1(config)#
```

6. Save your changes to NVRAM with the **do write** command.

7. Verify your configuration with the **do show running-config** command.

8. Configure the same passwords on the LA-R1 router. Use the preceding commands as a guide.

9. On the VAN-R1 router, exit out of the console connection and then connect again. Supply the passwords as needed (note that you must supply the console password before the enable secret password).

Note that you have configured the enable password and enable secret, but you must supply the enable secret value as the password when you now enter privileged EXEC mode.

Configuring Users

When setting up the security for the console port, auxiliary port, or the VTY ports, you can increase security by requiring a username and password instead of just a password. In this section you will learn how to manage a user list on your Cisco device, and you will learn about privilege levels.

Creating User Accounts

You can create a list of user account names and passwords that are stored locally on your Cisco device. To do this, you use the **username** command and fill in the username and password parameters as shown here:

```
VAN-R1>enable
VAN-R1#config term
VAN-R1(config)#username edtetz password edpass
VAN-R1(config)#username glenclarke password glenpass
```

 VIDEO 17.04. The digital resources that accompany this book contain a multimedia demonstration of configuring user accounts on the Cisco device.

Next, use the **login local** command on each of the port types that will use that list for authentication. In the **login local** command, **login** means force authentication (just like with the password option in the previous discussion), but **local** means use the local database of usernames and passwords for the authentication (not just the port password). For example, the following commands would configure the console port to require someone to log on with a username and password to get local access to the device:

```
VAN-R1(config)#line con 0
VAN-R1(config-line)#login local
```

You would use the **login local** command on the VTY ports and the auxiliary port if you wanted to require authentication that is verified against the username and password list.

 EXAM TIP For the CCNA exam, remember that the **login local** command is used on the console, auxiliary, and VTY ports to force authentication by using the local username and password database.

Privilege Levels

There are 16 privilege levels on Cisco devices, numbered 0 to 15, with 0 being the lowest amount of privilege and 15 being the highest amount of privilege. To give you an idea of the capabilities of the levels, when you are in user EXEC mode, you have privilege level 1, which is why you cannot make changes to the device. When you move to privileged EXEC mode, your privilege level is raised to 15 (full administrative capabilities). This is why you have to move to privileged EXEC mode to make changes to the device.

The exciting part of privilege levels is that you can assign a privilege level to a user, and then associate that privilege level to a command so that the user can execute that command. To associate a privilege level to a user, use the **privilege** parameter with the **username** command, as shown here:

```
VAN-R1(config)#username adminguy privilege 3 password adminpass
```

If you want to change the privilege level of a command so the user can execute that command, you assign the command the same privilege level with the **privilege exec** command:

```
VAN-R1(config)#privilege exec level 3 show running-config
```

In this example, I have assigned the **show running-config** command to level 3 so that a user needs to have a privilege level of at least level 3 to run that command.

If you are unsure of your privilege level, you can use the **show privilege** command:

```
VAN-R1>show privilege
Current privilege level is 1
VAN-R1>enable
VAN-R1#show privilege
Current privilege level is 15
```

Notice that when I am in user EXEC mode, my privilege level is 1, but when I move to privileged EXEC mode, my privilege level changes to 15.

Exercise 17-2: Creating Users on Cisco Devices

In this exercise you will configure a few user accounts in the local user account database on the Cisco device and then modify the console port to require a username and password when logging on to the Cisco device.

1. Ensure that you have completed the previous lab exercise before continuing with this exercise.

2. Connect your workstation to the console port VAN-R1. Then launch PuTTY, choose Serial connection, set the correct COM port, and choose Open.

3. Press ENTER in the PuTTY window to get a prompt on your Cisco device.

4. Access VAN-R1's privileged EXEC mode and configure the following usernames and passwords on the router:

   Username: **bob** / password: **bobpass**
   Username: **sue** / password: **suepass**

5. Disconnect and reconnect to the console port. Are you prompted for a username and password? _____

6. Log in to the router with the console password of *labconpass* and enter privileged EXEC mode by providing the secret of *labenablesecret*.

7. To force the router to use the username and password list for console access, auxiliary port access, and VTY access, navigate to each of those ports and use the **login local** command:

```
VAN-R1(config)#line con 0
VAN-R1(config-line)#login local
VAN-R1(config-line)#line aux 0
VAN-R1(config-line)#login local
VAN-R1(config-line)#line vty 0 15
VAN-R1(config-line)#login local
```

8. Save the configuration changes and then disconnect from the console port and reconnect. Are you asked for a username and password? _____

9. Log in with a username of *bob* and a password of *bobpass*.

10. For additional practice, configure the same usernames and passwords on the LA-R1 router. Ensure that you log in with a username and password when connecting to the console port, auxiliary port, and VTY ports.

11. Save all changes to both routers and keep them running for the next exercise.

Encrypting Passwords

Now that we have configured all of the passwords for the Cisco device, let's save those to startup-config by using the **write** command. Let's take a look at the configuration file with the **show startup-config** command.

```
VAN-R1#show startup-config
Using 1385 bytes
version 15.1
(output cut for briefness)
enable secret 5 $1$mERr$wZMkJsj2RVk4hay2C4T32.
enable password ciscopass
username adminguy privilege 3 password 0 adminpass
line con 0
 password conpass
 login
line aux 0
 password auxpass
 login
line vty 0 4
 password telnetpass
 login
line vty 5 15
 password telnetpass
 login
VAN-R1#
```

When you look at the configuration file, you can see that all of the passwords, except the secret, are stored in plain text. This means that if someone can gain physical access to your router, he or she can view the configuration file and see the passwords you are using. From a security point of view, this is a very bad configuration!

You can encrypt all passwords in your Cisco configuration files with a quick, simple command, **service password-encryption**:

```
VAN-R1#config term
VAN-R1(config)#service password-encryption
VAN-R1(config)#do write
```

When the command executes, it encrypts any plain-text passwords in the configuration file so that someone viewing the configuration file does not know what your passwords are. After executing the command, you can view the configuration file to verify that the passwords are encrypted:

```
VAN-R1(config)#do show startup-config
Using 1444 bytes
version 15.1
(output cut for briefness)
service password-encryption
```

```
enable secret 5 $1$mERr$wZMkJsj2RVk4hay2C4T32.
enable password 7 0822455D0A1615160118
username adminguy password 7 08204843001715160118
line con 0
 password 7 0822434019181604
 login
line aux 0
 password 7 0820595619181604
 login
line vty 0 4
 password 7 08354942071C110713181F
 login
line vty 5 15
 password 7 08354942071C110713181F
 login
VAN-R1(config)#
```

Notice in the output that **service password-encryption** is shown in the configuration file and that it is turned on. Also notice in the highlighted areas that the passwords are no longer viewable in the configuration.

 VIDEO 17.05. The digital resources that accompany this book contain a multimedia demonstration of configuring password encryption on a Cisco device.

The value of having all of your passwords encrypted in the configuration file is that if someone does get physical access to your device and is able to view the configuration file, he will not know what your passwords are. For example, if someone gained physical access to my router, bypassed the password with the password recovery procedures (you learned about in Chapter 8), and I was not encrypting the passwords, he could view my VTY passwords and then remote into my network at a later time using that password. Please remember this: encrypt the passwords!

 EXAM TIP For the exam, remember that the **service password-encryption** command is used to encrypt all passwords in the configuration file.

Exercise 17-3: Encrypting Passwords on Cisco Devices

In this exercise you will view the passwords that are configured on a Cisco device and then encrypt them within the Cisco configuration files.

1. Ensure that you have completed the previous lab exercise before continuing with this exercise.

2. Connect your workstation to the console port of VAN-R1. Launch PuTTY, choose Serial connection, set the correct COM port, and choose Open.

3. Press ENTER in the PuTTY window to get a prompt on your Cisco device.

4. Access VAN-R1's privileged EXEC mode and view the running configuration with a **show running-config** command. Record which passwords are encrypted:

	Yes	No
Enable password		
Enable secret		
Console password		
Auxiliary password		
VTY password		
Bob's password		
Sue's password		

5. Navigate to global config and use the **service password-encryption** command to encrypt all passwords. Then view the running configuration.

6. Record which passwords are now encrypted:

	Yes	No
Enable password		
Enable secret		
Console password		
Auxiliary password		
VTY password		
Bob's password		
Sue's password		

7. Save your changes with the **do write** command.

8. Switch over to the LA-R1 router and ensure that all passwords are encrypted on that router by using the **service password-encryption** command.

9. On the LA-R1 router, verify that the passwords are encrypted and then save the configuration.

Configuring SSH

Another security feature that you should configure on your Cisco devices is to configure the device to use SSH instead of telnet. Here's a quick review of each: Telnet uses TCP port 23 and does not encrypt the communication. SSH uses TCP port 22 and encrypts all communication including the username and password that are transmitted from the administrator's computer to the Cisco device.

Configuring SSH requires a few preparation steps:

1. Configure a hostname on your router if one does not already exist.

2. Create a username and password that administrators will use to authenticate to the device when they connect using SSH.

3. Configure a domain name on the device, as this domain name is used to generate the cryptographic key used for the encryption.

Here's an example:

```
Router>enable
Router#config term
Router(config)#hostname VAN-R1
VAN-R1(config)#username glenclarke password glenpass
VAN-R1(config)#ip domain-name gleneclarke.com
```

You will also need to verify that the Cisco device is using a crypto-supported IOS version, such as one that has *K9* at the end of the IOS image filename.

After you have completed the preparation steps, you are ready to generate the encryption key with the **crypto key generate rsa** command:

```
VAN-R1(config)#crypto key generate rsa
The name for the keys will be: VAN-R1.gleneclarke.com
Choose the size of the key modulus in the range of 360 to 2048 for your
  General Purpose Keys. Choosing a key modulus greater than 512 may take
  a few minutes.
How many bits in the modulus [512]: 512
% Generating 512 bit RSA keys, keys will be non-exportable...[OK]
VAN-R1(config)#
```

Notice that the name for the key is based on the hostname and the domain name that you configured. When you are asked the bit strength to use, accept the default of 512.

Now that you have the encryption key you can configure the VTY ports to only accept a connection if it is using SSH. In the following code example, notice we are configuring authentication using the local usernames on the device. You can then use the **transport input ssh** command to specify that the only protocol to be used on these ports is SSH.

```
VAN-R1(config)#line vty 0 15
VAN-R1(config-line)#login local
VAN-R1(config-line)#transport input ssh
```

At this point, the Cisco device will no longer accept telnet connections for remote administration. You can take this one step further and use access control lists to limit which IP addresses can SSH into the device, but we will save that discussion for later in the chapter in the section, "Implementing Access Control Lists."

 EXAM TIP   For the CCNA exam, remember the commands to restrict the VTY ports to only accept connections from SSH clients (and not telnet clients).

Exercise 17-4: Enforcing SSH for Remote Administration

In this exercise you will configure the Cisco routers of VAN-R1 and LA-R1 for remote administration using the SSH protocol only.

1. Ensure that you have completed the previous exercise before continuing with this exercise.

2. Connect your workstation to the console port of VAN-R1. Launch PuTTY, choose Serial connection, set the correct COM port, and choose Open.

3. Press ENTER in the PuTTY window to get a prompt on your Cisco device.

4. Access VAN-R1's privileged EXEC mode and create a username *exer174user* with a password *Pa$$w0rd*. Configure a domain name *exer17-4.loc*:

```
VAN-R1>enable
VAN-R1#config term
VAN-R1(config)#username exer174user password Pa$$w0rd
VAN-R1(config)#ip domain-name exer17-4.loc
```

5. Create an encryption key for SSH by using the following command. Set the bit strength to *512* when prompted:

```
VAN-R1(config)#crypto key generate rsa
```

6. Configure the VTY ports for authentication using a username and password by using the **login local** command on the VTY ports:

```
VAN-R1(config)#line vty 0 15
VAN-R1(config-line)#login local
```

7. Ensure that only SSH is used as a protocol by the VTY ports:

```
VAN-R1(config-line)#transport input ssh
```

8. Go to the CLI of LA-R1 and verify that you cannot telnet into the VAN-R1 router using the **telnet 13.0.0.1** command. You should receive an error.

9. On the LA-R1 router, perform the same steps in this exercise to ensure that SSH can be used only as a remote administration protocol.

 VIDEO 17.06. The digital resources that accompany this book contain a multimedia demonstration of requiring SSH as the remote administration protocol for your Cisco device.

Configure Layer 2 Security Features

In this section you will learn about the layer 2 security features supported by layer 2 and layer 3 switches. This section will first review some of the basic practices for hardening your switches and will then look at some of the common layer 2 attacks and how to mitigate them.

Disable Unused Ports

The first security best practice for hardening your switch is to disable any unused ports on the switch. This will help prevent an unauthorized person from connecting to an empty port and gaining network access. To disable the port, use the **shutdown** command on the port:

```
VAN-SW1>enable
VAN-SW1#config term
VAN-SW1(config)#interface g0/10
VAN-SW1(config-if)#shutdown
```

If you wanted to shut down a number of ports on your switch at one time, you could use the **interface range** command to select the ports, and then follow that up with the **shutdown** command:

```
VAN-SW1>enable
VAN-SW1#config term
VAN-SW1(config)#interface range g0/12 - 24
VAN-SW1(config-if)#shutdown
```

VIDEO   17.07. The digital resources that accompany this book contain a multimedia demonstration of disabling an unused port on a switch.

Port Security

After disabling any unused ports on the switch, your next step in hardening the switch is to configure port security on the used ports. As you learned in Chapter 9, port security is a feature that enables you to specify which MAC addresses are authorized to use a port. If an unauthorized device connects to the port, the port security feature can shut down the port until the administrator enables it.

To review port security, navigate to the port and place the port in access mode, which means that an endpoint device, such as a workstation, is going to connect to the port to use it:

```
VAN-SW1>enable
VAN-SW1#config term
VAN-SW1(config)#interface g0/7
VAN-SW1(config-if)#switchport mode access
```

Next, you'll enable the port security feature on the port and then specify the MAC address that is authorized to use the port. To save you having to know and type in the MAC address, you can use the *sticky option*, which means that the switch will dynamically configure port security with whatever connects to the port. If you set the maximum number of addresses to learn to *1*, then **sticky** will learn only the address of the currently connected device and will configure port security with that MAC address:

```
VAN-SW1(config-if)#switchport port-security
VAN-SW1(config-if)#switchport port-security mac-address sticky
VAN-SW1(config-if)#switchport port-security maximum 1
```

EXAM TIP   For the CCNA exam, remember that the **sticky** option with port security is used to restrict the port to the system that is currently connected to that port. It saves the administrator from having to learn the MAC address of that client and then inputting it into the port security command.

Lastly, specify what happens when an unauthorized device connects to the port on the switch with the violation mode. Look back to Chapter 9 for a review of the violation modes; here we'll disable the port by using the shutdown mode:

```
VAN-SW1(config-if)#switchport port-security violation shutdown
```

VIDEO   17.08. The digital resources that accompany this book contain a multimedia demonstration of configuring port security on the switch.

DHCP Snooping

A common problem encountered on enterprise networks today occurs when a rogue DHCP server is placed on the network and gives out bogus IP addresses to network clients. This causes the client computers to be unable to access network resources, because the address the client is assigned is typically on a different subnet.

A rogue DHCP server presents great security risk to the organization, as a hacker could have placed the rogue DHCP server on the network to give out her own IP address range, including the default gateway and DNS server settings. This gives the attacker the ability to perform a man-in-the-middle attack, because she can have the default gateway set to her own system, causing all traffic to flow through her system.

You can use a layer 2 switch feature called *DHCP snooping* to mitigate rogue DHCP servers. With DHCP snooping, you can categorize a port as either a *trusted port* or an *untrusted port*. You configure the port that your DHCP server is connected to as a trusted port, indicating that the port is under your control and is authorized to generate DHCP server messages. You then configure all other ports as untrusted ports, because the DHCP server is not connected to them. Then, if someone connects a rogue DHCP server to one of the untrusted ports, the switch will drop the DHCP server–related messages such as DHCPOFFER, DHCPACK, and DHCPNACK, protecting the network from the rogue DHCP server.

Configuring DHCP Snooping

The DHCP snooping feature is disabled by default and must be enabled globally and then enabled for each VLAN on the switch. For example, the following commands enable DHCP snooping on the switch and then for VLAN 1:

```
Switch>enable
Switch#config term
Switch(config)#ip dhcp snooping
Switch(config)#ip dhcp snooping vlan 1
```

Keep in mind that these two commands should be the last commands you run, although from a teaching point of view, they are the first commands I like to discuss. The reason these should be the last two commands is because now DHCP snooping has been enabled, but we did not specify any trusted ports, which means that your real DHCP server on the network is currently not allowed to give addresses out to clients until you configure it in a trusted port.

 EXAM TIP For the CCNA exam, remember how to configure DHCP snooping, and note that it can be enabled on a per-VLAN basis.

To enable your DHCP server to give addresses out on the network, you configure the switch interface that the DHCP server is connected to as a trusted port by navigating to the interface and using the **ip dhcp snooping trust** command:

```
Switch(config)#interface g1/0/2
Switch(config-if)#ip dhcp snooping trust
```

 EXAM TIP For the CCNA exam, remember that the port on the switch that has the DHCP server connected is to be configured as a trusted port.

DHCP Snooping Binding Database
As the switch is intercepting DHCP messages, it is building up the *DHCP snooping binding database*, which is a listing of the untrusted hosts (hosts connected to untrusted ports) that have received IP addresses from the DHCP server. The DHCP snooping binding database contains an entry for each untrusted interface that has a system connected with details such as the interface ID, the MAC address of the client, the IP address of the system connected to that port, and the VLAN the interface is a part of. If you want to view the DHCP snooping binding database, you can use the **show ip dhcp snooping binding** command.

The DHCP snooping binding database is maintained by the switch, so as DHCPACK messages are seen by the switch, it adds the entry to the database, and as DHCPRELEASE messages are seen, it removes the entries from the database.

Dynamic ARP Inspection
Before looking at dynamic ARP inspection as a layer 2 security feature, let's first discuss what problem it solves. When a device talks to another device on the network, it must first learn the MAC address of that device so that it can send data to that device. You learned in Chapter 3 that devices use ARP to learn the MAC addresses of devices on the network by broadcasting an ARP request message out saying, "Whoever has this IP address, I need to know your MAC address." The broadcast is seen by all systems but ignored by all except the one system that has that specific MAC address. That system sends an ARP reply, which says something to the effect of, "That is my IP address, and

here is my MAC address." This is the important part from a security point of view: when a device receives the ARP reply, it stores that information in an area of memory known as the ARP cache, which is a listing of IP addresses and corresponding MAC addresses. The important thing to note here is that devices on the network will trust any information in the ARP cache by default.

Attackers have learned to perform ARP poisoning attacks, which enable them to put incorrect information in the ARP cache unknowingly that your system will trust. For example, if the attacker wants to perform a man-in-the-middle attack, he could poison your ARP cache by specifying that his MAC address corresponds to the IP address of the default gateway. Then, when you surfed the Internet, all traffic would be sent to the attacker's system, where he could capture the traffic and then forward it to the real default gateway.

To improve security and help prevent ARP poisoning attacks (and man-in-the-middle attacks), Cisco switches include the *Dynamic ARP Inspection* (DAI) feature. If you enable the DAI feature on the switch, the switch will intercept all ARP messages and then compare the information in the ARP message with the data stored in the DHCP snooping binding database (which has a list of IP addresses and MAC addresses). For example, after you enable DAI, if an attacker sends out an ARP poison message that says he is using the IP address of the default gateway and gives the MAC address of his system, the switch will look up that IP address in the DHCP snooping binding database and verify that it is the correct MAC address to go with that IP address. If it is not, the packet is dropped, which means that the attacker would not be successful in poisoning the ARP cache.

 EXAM TIP   For the CCNA exam, remember that dynamic ARP inspection is designed to prevent man-in-the-middle attacks and ARP poisoning attacks.

Keep in mind that DAI performs checks only on untrusted ports, because it uses the DHCP snooping binding database, which stores information only on untrusted ports. Also, like DHCP snooping, DAI is configured on a per-VLAN basis. To configure dynamic ARP inspection on the switch for VLAN 1, you would use the following commands:

```
Switch>enable
Switch#config term
Switch(config)#ip arp inspection vlan 1
```

If you have a number of switches connected together, you would configure the connected ports of the switches (trunk ports) as trusted ports so that your switches do not verify the ARP messages coming from those ports. For example, if port 24 on my switch is connected to another switch, I would specify that the port is trusted with the following commands:

```
Switch(config)#interface g1/0/24
Switch(config-if)#ip arp inspection trust
```

EXAM TIP   For the exam, remember that trunk ports are configured as trusted ports so that the switch does not check all ARP messages coming from the other switch.

Implementing Access Control Lists

The last few chapters introduced you to routing protocols and their basic configurations. By default, once you set up routing, your router will enable any packet to flow from one interface to another. You may want to implement policies to restrict the flow of traffic, for security or traffic policy reasons. Cisco enables you to control the flow of traffic from one interface to another by using access control lists (ACLs). ACLs, pronounced *ackles*, are a powerful feature of Cisco IOS. Cisco actually supports ACLs for protocols other than IP, including Internetwork Packet Exchange (IPX), AppleTalk, layer 2 traffic, and others. This chapter focuses only on IP ACLs.

ACL Overview

ACLs, known for their ability to filter traffic as it either enters or leaves an interface, can also be used for other purposes, including restricting remote access (VTY) to an IOS device, filtering routing information, prioritizing traffic with queuing, triggering phone calls with dial-on-demand routing (DDR), changing the administrative distance of routes, and specifying traffic to be protected by an IPsec VPN, among many other purposes. This chapter focuses on restricting the flow of traffic to or through a router.

EXAM TIP   Remember that ACLs can be used for filtering of traffic through the IOS device as well as for filtering remote-access traffic to IOS's VTY lines.

Definition

ACLs are basically a set of commands, grouped together by a number or name, which are used to filter traffic entering or leaving an interface. ACL commands define specifically which traffic is permitted and which is denied. ACLs are created in Global Configuration mode.

Once you create your group of ACL statements, you must activate them. For filtering traffic between interfaces, the ACL is activated in Interface Subconfiguration mode. This can be a physical interface, such as ethernet0 or serial0, or a logical interface, such as ethernet0.1 or serial0.1. When activating an ACL on an interface, you must specify in which direction the traffic should be filtered:

- **Inbound**   As the traffic comes into an interface from an external source, IOS compares the packet to the interface ACL before IOS forwards the packet to another interface.

- **Outbound**   The packet is received on an interface and forwarded to the exit interface; before the traffic exits an interface to the network, IOS compares the packet to the ACL.

One restriction that ACLs have is that they cannot filter traffic that the router itself originates. For example, if you execute a ping or traceroute from the router, or if you telnet from the router to another device, ACLs applied to the router's interfaces cannot filter these connections outbound. However, if an external device tries to ping, traceroute, or telnet *to* the router or *through* the router to a remote destination, the router can filter these packets.

 EXAM TIP You'll be tested on ACLs, so remember that for inbound ACLs, the ACL is processed before any further processing by IOS; with outbound ACLs, the packet is routed to the interface and then the outbound ACL is processed. ACLs applied outbound to interfaces cannot be used to filter traffic IOS originates itself.

Types

ACLs come in two varieties: *numbered* and *named*. Numbered and named ACLs define how the router will reference the ACL. You can think of this as being similar to an index value. A numbered ACL is assigned a unique number among all ACLs, whereas a named ACL is assigned a unique name among all named ACLs. These are then used by the router to filter traffic.

Each of these references to ACLs supports two types of filtering: *standard* and *extended*. Standard IP ACLs can filter only on the source IP address inside a packet, whereas extended IP ACLs can filter on the source and destination IP addresses in the packet, the IP protocol (TCP, UDP, ICMP, and so on), and protocol information (such as the TCP or UDP source and destination port numbers or ICMP message types). With an extended ACL, you can be very precise in your filtering. For example, you can filter a specific telnet session from a user's PCs to a remote telnet server. Standard ACLs do not support this form of granularity. With a standard ACL, you can either permit or deny all traffic from a specific source device. Table 17-1 compares the two types of ACLs and identifies the parameters that can be used to filter traffic for each type.

The two types of ACLs can be statically defined on the IOS device or dynamically downloaded via an authentication server. Dynamic ACLs are typically used when a user authenticates to the network, such as via a switch port using IEEE 802.1X; once a user is successfully authenticated, the switch downloads an ACL from an authentication server and applies it to the user's switch port. The ACL is then used to filter the traffic.

Filtered Information	Standard IP ACL	Extended IP ACL
Source address	Yes	Yes
Destination address	No	Yes
IP protocol (IP, TCP, or UDP)	No	Yes
Protocol information (port number)	No	Yes

Table 17-1 Standard and Extended ACL Comparison

Once the user leaves the network, the dynamic ACL is removed from the switch port. The use and configuration of dynamic ACLs is beyond the scope of this book, which focuses on the configuration of static ACLs on IOS devices themselves.

 EXAM TIP   Remember the filtering abilities of standard versus extended ACLs in Table 17-1. Be able to describe the use of a dynamic ACL.

ACL Processing

ACLs are basically statements that are grouped together by either a name or a number. Within this group of statements, when a packet is processed by an ACL, IOS will go through certain steps in finding a match against the ACL statements. ACLs are processed *top-down* by IOS. A packet is compared to the first statement in the ACL, and if IOS finds a match between the packet and the statement, IOS will execute one of two actions included with the statement: *permit* or *deny*.

If IOS doesn't find a match of packet contents to the first ACL statement, IOS will proceed to the next statement in the list, again going through the same matching process. If the second statement matches the packet contents, IOS executes one of the two actions. If there is no match on this statement, IOS will keep on going through the list until it finds a match. If IOS goes through the entire list and doesn't find a match in the ACL statements to the ACL contents, the router will *drop* the packet.

The top-down processing of ACLs brings out the following very important points:

- Once a match is found, no further statements are processed in the list.
- The order of statements is important, since after the first match, the rest of the statements are not processed.
- If no match is found in the list, the packet is dropped.

Statement Ordering

If a match is found on a statement, no further statements are processed. Therefore, the order of the statements is *very* important in an ACL. If you have two statements, one denying a host and one permitting the same host, whichever one appears *first* in the list will be executed and the second one will be ignored. Because order of statements is important, you should always place the most specific ACL statements at the top of the list and the least specific at the bottom of the list.

Let's take a look at an example to illustrate this process. In this example, you have an ACL on your router with two statements in this order:

1. Permit traffic from subnet 172.16.0.0/16.

2. Deny traffic from host 172.16.1.1/32.

Remember that the router processes these statements from the *top down*. Let's assume that a packet is received on the router with a source IP address of 172.16.1.1. Given the preceding ACL, the router compares the packet contents with the first statement. Does the packet have a source address from network 172.16.0.0/16? Yes. Therefore, the result indicates that the router should permit the packet. Notice that the second statement is never processed once the router finds a match on a statement. In this example, any traffic from the 172.16.0.0/16 subnet is permitted, even traffic from 172.16.1.1.

Let's reverse the order of the two statements in the ACL and see how this reordered ACL will affect traffic flow:

1. Deny traffic from host 172.16.1.1.

2. Permit traffic from subnet 172.16.0.0/16.

If 172.16.1.1 sends traffic through the router, IOS first compares these packets with the first ACL statement. Since the source address matches 172.16.1.1, the router drops the packet and stops processing statements in the ACL. In this example, it doesn't matter what traffic 172.16.1.1 is sending, because it's dropped. If another device, say 172.16.1.2, sends traffic through the router, the router compares the packet contents to the first ACL statement. Since the source address in the packet doesn't match the source address in the ACL statement, the router proceeds to the next statement in the list. Comparing the packet contents to the statement, there is a match. Therefore, the router will execute the results, permitting the traffic from 172.16.1.2. As you can see from both of these ACL examples, the order of statements in the ACL is very important and *definitely* impacts what traffic is permitted or denied.

EXAM TIP   Be able to reorder statements in an ACL to provide the desired outcome.

Implicit Deny

Another important aspect of the top-down process is that if the router compares a packet to every statement in the list and does not find a match against the packet contents, the router will *drop* the packet. This process is referred to as *implicit deny*. At the end of every ACL is an invisible statement that drops all traffic that doesn't match any of the preceding statements in the ACL. Given this process, it makes no sense to have a list of only deny statements, since the implicit deny drops all traffic anyway. Therefore, every ACL should have at least *one permit* statement; otherwise, an ACL with only deny statements will drop all traffic, given the deny statements and the hidden implicit deny statement.

EXAM TIP   For the exam, you'll need to remember a few things about ACL statements. An ACL can take two actions: permit or deny. Statements are processed top-down. Once a match is found, no further statements are processed; therefore, order is important. If no match is found, the invisible implicit deny statement at the end of the ACL drops the packet. An ACL should have at least one permit statement; otherwise, all traffic will be dropped because of the hidden implicit deny statement at the end of every ACL.

Important Configuration Guidelines

Configuring an ACL is not a simple process. To get the configuration process right, you should be guided by the following list:

- Statement order is important. Put the most restrictive statements at the top of the list and the least restrictive at the bottom.

- ACL statements are processed top-down until a match is found, and then no more statements in the list are processed.

- If no match is found in the ACL, the packet is dropped (implicit deny).

- Each grouping of ACL statements needs either a unique number or a unique name.

- The router cannot filter traffic that it, itself, originates.

- Only one IP ACL can be applied to an interface in each direction (inbound and outbound)—two or more ACLs cannot be applied inbound or outbound to the same interface. (Actually, one ACL for each protocol, such as IP and IPX, can be applied to an interface in each direction.)

- Applying an empty ACL to an interface permits all traffic by default. In order for an ACL to have an implicit deny statement, you need at least one actual permit or deny statement in the ACL.

As you can see from this list of guidelines, ACLs are not a simple matter. ACLs are one of IOS's more complex, yet powerful, features. The configuration, management, and troubleshooting of ACLs can become very complex and create many headaches for you. Therefore, it is important for you to understand the process the router uses when it compares packets to ACLs and how to create and maintain them. The following sections cover the basic configuration of ACLs on your router.

 EXAM TIP   For the CCNA exam, remember the list of important ACL configuration guidelines.

Creating an ACL

This section provides a brief introduction to the two basic commands you'll use to configure IP ACLs. The sections following this cover the actual details of configuring numbered versus named ACLs and standard versus extended ACLs.

To create a numbered ACL, use the following general syntax:

```
Router(config)# access-list ACL_# permit|deny conditions
```

Prior to IOS 11.2, you could give an ACL only a number as an identifier. Starting with IOS 11.2, an ACL can be referenced by a number or name. The purpose of the *ACL_#* is to group your statements together into a single list or policy. You cannot choose just any number for an ACL. Each layer 3 protocol is assigned its own range or ranges of numbers.

Table 17-2 ACL Types and Numbers	ACL Type	ACL Numbers
	IP Standard	1–99, 1300–1999
	IP Extended	100–199, 2000–2699

Table 17-2 shows the valid ACL numbers for IP ACLs. As you can see from this table, numbered ACLs give you a limited number of lists that you can create, which is based on the range of numbers assigned to a protocol type. However, named ACLs do not have this restriction. Basically, the number of named ACLs on a router is restricted only by the amount of RAM and NVRAM your router has.

 EXAM TIP For the CCNA exam, remember the numbers you can use for IP ACLs. Standard ACLs can use numbers ranging from 1 to 99 and 1300 to 1999, and extended ACLs can use numbers ranging from 100 to 199 and 2000 to 2699.

The *conditions* in an ACL statement tell the router what contents in the packet need to match in order for the router to execute the action (**permit** or **deny**). The conditions can include matching of IP addresses and protocol information. When IOS compares a packet to the conditions, if it finds a match, no more ACL statements are processed; if it doesn't find a match, IOS proceeds to compare the packet to the next ACL statement in the list.

Matching on Addresses: Wildcard Masks

When dealing with IP addresses in ACL statements, you can use *wildcard masks* to match on a range of addresses instead of manually entering every IP address that you want to match on.

First, a wildcard mask is *not* a subnet mask. Like an IP address or a subnet mask, a wildcard mask is composed of 32 bits. Table 17-3 compares the bit values in a subnet mask and a wildcard mask. With a wildcard mask, a *0* in a bit position means that the corresponding bit position in the address of the ACL statement *must* match the same bit position in the IP address in the examined packet. A *1* in a bit position means that the corresponding bit position in the address of the ACL statement does *not* have to match the bit position in the IP address in the examined packet. In other words, the wildcard mask and the address in the ACL statement work in tandem. The wildcard mask tells the router which addressing bits in the address of the ACL statement must match the bits in the packet to which it is being compared.

Table 17-3 Subnet Mask versus Wildcard Mask	Bit Value	Subnet Mask	Wildcard Mask
	0	Host component	Must match
	1	Network component	Ignore

In reality, a wildcard mask is more like an *inverted* subnet mask. For instance, if you want to match on any address in a subnet or network, you can simply take the subnet mask, invert its bit values (change the 1s to 0s and the 0s to 1s), and you have a corresponding wildcard mask.

Let's look at a simple example of performing a binary conversion of a subnet mask to a wildcard mask. Assume that you have a subnet mask of 255.255.0.0. Its binary representation is 11111111.11111111.00000000.00000000. When you convert this to a wildcard mask, invert the bits, like this: 00000000.00000000.11111111.11111111. Then convert this to decimal: 0.0.255.255. This is the corresponding wildcard mask for the subnet mask of 255.255.0.0. In this example, the wildcard mask tells the router that the first 16 bits of the corresponding IP address in the ACL statement must match the first 16 bits in the IP address of the examined packet for the router to continue processing the statement; otherwise, the router will proceed to the next ACL statement. As you can see, this example was easy to convert.

Let's look at a more difficult example. Assume that you want to match on a subnet that has a subnet mask of 255.255.240.0. Here's the entire subnet mask in binary: 111 11111.11111111.11110000.00000000. In this example, the first, second, and fourth octets are easy to convert: the difficult conversion is in the third octet. To convert the subnet mask to a wildcard mask, invert all the bits, as shown here: 00000000.000000 00.00001111.11111111. Next convert this back to decimal. This results in a wildcard mask of 0.0.15.255.

As you can see, if a subnet mask has 0 in an octet, the wildcard mask has a value of 255; if the subnet mask has 255 in an octet, the wildcard mask has a value of 0. However, the third octet in the second example makes this process more difficult.

Here's a shortcut to alleviate the conversion of a subnet mask to a wildcard mask. When doing the conversion, subtract each byte in the subnet mask *from* 255. The result will be the corresponding byte value for the wildcard mask. Going back to the 255.255.240 example, here is the shortcut:

- First byte: 255 – 255 (first subnet byte value) = 0 (wildcard mask value)
- Second byte: 255 – 255 (second subnet byte value) = 0 (wildcard mask value)
- Third byte: 255 – 240 (third subnet byte value) = 15 (wildcard mask value)
- Fourth byte: 255 – 0 (fourth subnet byte value) = 255 (wildcard mask value)

As you can see, this results in a wildcard mask of 0.0.15.240. This simple trick makes converting subnet masks to wildcard masks (and vice versa) very easy.

 EXAM TIP Wildcard masks are used to match a rule against bits in a packet. A *0* in a bit position means match, and a *1* means ignore. If you want to match against a subnet, invert the subnet mask to create the wildcard mask. The trick is to subtract each octet in the subnet mask from 255, resulting in the wildcard mask. Don't be surprised if you have to use this trick for a handful of ACL questions on the CCNA exam.

Special Wildcard Masks

Two special types of wildcard masks exist: 0.0.0.0 and 255.255.255.255. A wildcard mask of 0.0.0.0 tells IOS that all 32 bits of the address in the ACL statement must match those found in the IP packet in order for IOS to execute the action for the statement. A 0.0.0.0 wildcard mask is called a *host mask*. Here's a simple example of this information in an ACL statement: 192.168.1.1 0.0.0.0. This statement tells IOS to look for the exact same IP address (192.168.1.1) in the IP packet. If IOS doesn't find a match, IOS will go to the next ACL statement. If you configure 192.168.1.1 0.0.0.0, the IOS will covert this to the following syntax: *host 192.168.1.1* (note the keyword *host* that precedes the IP address).

A wildcard mask of 255.255.255.255 tells the router the exact opposite of a 0.0.0.0 mask. In this mask, all of the bit values are *1s*, which tells IOS that it doesn't matter what is in the packet that it is comparing to the ACL statement—*any* address will match. Typically, you would record this as an IP address of 0.0.0.0 and a wildcard mask of 255.255.255.255, like this: 0.0.0.0 255.255.255.255. If you enter this, IOS will convert the address and mask to the keyword *any*. Actually, the IP address that you enter with this mask doesn't matter. For instance, if you enter 192.168.1.1 255.255.255.255, this still matches any IP address. Remember that it's the wildcard mask that determines what bits in the IP address are *interesting* and should match.

 TIP Some wildcard masks can be confusing, such as 0.0.1.255. For masks like this, it's sometimes easier to look at them from a subnet mask perspective. In this example, the corresponding subnet mask would be 255.255.254.0. You can use a simple trick here by subtracting the wildcard mask from a local broadcast address (255.255.255.255) to come up with the correct wildcard mask. Based on this little trick, it's easier to see why the fourth row of Table 17-4 matches on a range of addresses from 172.16.2.0 to 172.16.3.255.

Wildcard Mask Examples

Since the concept of a wildcard mask can be confusing, let's look at some examples. Table 17-4 shows some examples of IP addresses and wildcard masks.

IP Address	Wildcard Mask	Matches
0.0.0.0	255.255.255.255	Match on any address (keyword *any* in an ACL statement).
172.16.1.1	0.0.0.0	Match only if the address is 172.16.1.1 (preceded by the keyword *host*).
172.16.1.0	0.0.0.255	Match only on packets that are in 172.16.1.0/24 (172.16.1.0–172.16.1.255).
172.16.2.0	0.0.1.255	Match only on packets that are in 172.16.2.0/23 (172.16.2.0–172.16.3.255).
172.16.0.0	0.0.255.255	Match only on packets that are in 172.16.0.0/16 (172.16.0.0–172.16.255.255).

Table 17-4 Wildcard Mask Examples

EXAM TIP For the CCNA exam, be familiar with how wildcard masks work, as well as the special notation Cisco uses for a match on all devices or a specific host, as shown in Table 17-4. A wildcard mask of 0.0.1.255 matches on a range of two Class C networks.

Activating an ACL

Once you have built your IP ACL, it will do nothing until you apply it to a process in IOS. This chapter focuses primarily on filtering traffic through interfaces; to have IOS filter traffic between interfaces, you must enter the appropriate interface or interfaces and activate your ACL. Here's the command to activate an ACL on an interface:

```
Router(config)# interface type [slot_#]port_#
Router(config-if)# ip access-group ACL_# in|out
```

At the end of the **ip access-group** command, you must specify which ACL you are activating and in which direction:

- **in** As traffic comes into the interface
- **out** As traffic leaves the interface

EXAM TIP For the CCNA exam, remember that you use the **ip access-group** command to activate an ACL on an interface. You must specify the ACL number or name and the direction: either **in** or **out**. For an inbound ACL, the ACL is processed first before being forwarded to an exit interface. ACLs can even be applied to subinterfaces: LAN (VLAN traffic) and WAN. You can have one ACL applied per direction, per protocol on an interface.

Note that you can apply the same ACL to multiple interfaces on a router, or you can activate the same ACL twice on the same interface: inbound and outbound. You can also apply a nonexistent ACL to an interface. A nonexistent ACL is an ACL that has no statements in it—an empty ACL will permit *all* traffic. For an ACL to have an implicit deny, it needs at least one **permit** or **deny** statement. It is highly recommended that you do *not* apply nonexistent ACLs to a router's interface. In this situation, when you create the very first statement in the list, the implicit deny is automatically placed at the bottom, which might create reachability issues for your router.

Let's take a look at an example that has a nonexistent ACL and examine the kinds of problems that you might experience. Assume that you have applied an ACL (#10) to a router's ethernet0 interface and this ACL currently doesn't have any **permit** or **deny** statements (it's empty). You are connected to the router via telnet on this interface, and your PC has an IP address of 192.168.1.1. You create an entry in ACL #10 that permits traffic from 172.16.0.0/16. As soon as you do this, you lose your telnet connection. If you guessed that the implicit deny caused the router to drop your connection, you guessed correctly. As soon as the router has one statement in it, the implicit deny is added at the bottom. In this example, since your PC had a source address of 192.168.1.1, and this wasn't included in the first statement, the router dropped your connection because it couldn't find any matching statements in ACL #10.

 NOTE A lot of confusion exists among published authors about an empty ACL: some say an empty ACL drops all traffic, some say it permits all traffic, and some say that it depends on the IOS version. I've worked with ACLs since they first came out in version 7 of IOS. An empty ACL has always allowed traffic to and through the interface. I encourage you to test this by applying an inbound ACL to the router's interface that has no statements and then ping that interface: the ping will work.

Now that we have some of the basics of ACLs, we want to look at standard ACLs and extended ACLs. The following sections cover standard and extended ACLs as numbered ACLs and named ACLs.

Standard Numbered ACLs

Standard IP ACLs are simple and easy to configure. First, standard IP ACLs filter on only the *source IP address* in an IP packet. Use the following command to create an entry in a standard numbered IP ACL:

```
Router(config)# access-list {1-99 | 1300-1999} {permit | deny}
                        source_IP_address [wildcard_mask] [log]
```

With a standard numbered IP ACL, you can use list numbers of 1–99 and 1300–1999. Following this is the action the router should take if there is a match on the condition. The condition is based solely on the source IP address. You follow up the source IP address parameter with an optional wildcard mask. If you omit the mask, it defaults to 0.0.0.0—an exact match is required in order to execute the action.

 EXAM TIP For the CCNA exam, be very familiar with the syntax of a standard ACL, as well as the fact that it can filter only on source addresses in a packet. If you omit the wildcard mask in a standard ACL, it defaults to 0.0.0.0 (an exact match of the entire address is required).

Next is the optional **log** parameter, which was introduced to standard ACLs in IOS 12.0. This parameter will cause any match of this statement to be printed to the console port of the router. These messages, by default, will not appear on a *non-console* connection, such as a VTY or TTY, to the IOS device unless you execute the following:

```
Router# terminal monitor
```

 NOTE The **terminal monitor** command is good only for your current session: when you log out and then log back into the IOS device, you'll need to re-execute the command to see logging output on your VTY or TTY session.

You can also forward these ACL logging messages to a syslog server. This setup is useful for debugging and security purposes. Once you have created your ACL, you can proceed to activate it on an interface with the **ip access-group** *ACL_#* **in|out** command.

Standard IP ACL Examples

Now that you have been introduced to the two basic commands to create and activate a standard numbered IP ACL, let's look at some examples to help you further your understanding. Here's the first example:

```
Router(config)# access-list 1 permit 192.168.1.1
Router(config)# access-list 1 deny 192.168.1.2
Router(config)# access-list 1 permit 192.168.1.0 0.0.0.255
Router(config)# access-list 1 deny any
Router(config)# interface serial 0
Router(config-if)# ip access-group 1 in
```

In this example, the first ACL statement in ACL #1 says that in order to execute the **permit** action, the IP packet must have a source address of 192.168.1.1—if it doesn't, IOS proceeds to the second statement. Remember that if you omit the wildcard mask on a standard ACL, it defaults to 0.0.0.0—an exact match of the corresponding address in the ACL statement. The second ACL statement says that in order to execute the **deny** action, the IP packet must have a source address of 192.168.1.2; if it doesn't, IOS proceeds to the third statement. The third ACL statement says that in order to execute the **permit** action, the IP packet must have a source address between 192.168.1.0 and 192.168.1.255—if it doesn't, IOS proceeds to the fourth statement. The fourth statement is actually not necessary: it drops any packet. You don't need this statement since an invisible implicit **deny any** statement occurs at the end of every ACL. The last two commands in the ACL example activate ACL #1 on serial 0 as traffic comes into the interface.

Actually, you could have written the preceding ACL like this:

```
Router(config)# access-list 1 deny 192.168.1.2
Router(config)# access-list 1 permit 192.168.1.0 0.0.0.255
Router(config)# interface serial 0
Router(config-if)# ip access-group 1 in
```

This example reduces your configuration from four ACL statements in the list down to two.

 VIDEO   17.09. The digital resources that accompany this book contain a multimedia demonstration of configuring a standard numbered ACL on a router.

Here's another example of a standard ACL:

```
Router(config)# access-list 2 deny 192.168.1.0
Router(config)# access-list 2 deny 172.16.0.0
Router(config)# access-list 2 permit 192.168.1.1
Router(config)# access-list 2 permit 0.0.0.0 255.255.255.255
Router(config)# interface ethernet 0
Router(config-if)# ip access-group 2 out
```

This ACL example has a few problems. Examine it and see if you can spot them.

The first ACL statement appears to deny all traffic from 192.168.1.0/24. In reality, it will accomplish nothing. Remember that if you omit the wildcard mask for the address, it defaults to 0.0.0.0—an exact match. The problem is that you'll never have a packet with a source address of 192.168.1.0, since this is a network number, and not a host address. The second statement has the same problem. The third and fourth statements are okay.

As you can see, configuring ACLs can be tricky. For the preceding example, here's the updated configuration:

```
Router(config)# access-list 2 deny 192.168.1.0 0.0.0.255
Router(config)# access-list 2 deny 172.16.0.0 0.0.255.255
Router(config)# access-list 2 permit 192.168.1.1
Router(config)# access-list 2 permit 0.0.0.0 255.255.255.255
Router(config)# interface ethernet 0
Router(config-if)# ip access-group 1 out
```

In this example, the first statement now says that any packet with a source address from network 192.168.1.0/24 should be dropped. The second statement will drop any traffic from the Class B network 172.16.0.0/16. The third statement will permit traffic from 192.168.1.1. The fourth statement will permit traffic from anywhere. Actually, there is *still* a problem with this configuration—look at the first and third statements. Will the third statement ever be executed? If you answered *no*, you are correct. In this situation, you need to put the more specific entry before the less specific one. Another minor point to make is that the fourth statement in the list could represent the address as the keyword **any**. Here's the updated configuration:

```
Router(config)# access-list 2 permit 192.168.1.1
Router(config)# access-list 2 deny 192.168.1.0 0.0.0.255
Router(config)# access-list 2 deny 172.16.0.0 0.0.255.255
Router(config)# access-list 2 permit any
Router(config)# interface ethernet 0
Router(config-if)# ip access-group 1 out
```

There's actually one more problem with this ACL. If you guessed the ACL number used on the interface is not correct, then you guessed correctly. Notice that the ACL created has a number of *2*, while the application of the ACL on the interface uses *1*. To fix this, use the following configuration:

```
Router(config)# interface ethernet 0
Router(config-if)# no ip access-group 1 out
Router(config-if)# ip access-group 2 out
```

Note that you must first remove the old ACL from the interface before applying the new ACL.

 EXAM TIP   For the CCNA exam, be able to troubleshoot ACL configurations by examining the order of statements in the list. The preceding example with misconfigured ACL statements is an excellent example of issues to look for in configuring ACLs.

Restricting VTY Access to the Router

In addition to using standard IP ACLs to filter traffic as it enters and/or leaves an interface, you can also use them to restrict VTY access (telnet and SSH) to your router. You may want to do this to allow only network administrators to access the CLI of your IOS device remotely. Setting this up is almost the same as setting up restricted access on an interface.

First, you need to create a standard ACL that has a list of **permit** statements that allow your corresponding network administrators remote access; include the IP addresses of their PCs in this list. Next, you need to activate your ACL. However, you will not do this on any of the router's interfaces. If you were to activate this ACL on an interface, it would allow any type of traffic from your administrators but drop *all* other traffic. Remember that when someone accesses your router via telnet or SSH, the router associates this connection with a VTY line. Therefore, you'll apply your standard ACL to the VTYs, like this:

```
Router(config)# line vty 0 4
Router(config-line)# access-class standard_ACL_# in|out
```

Remember that your router supports five telnets by default (0–4), and more on certain IOS devices. You can configure all VTYs simultaneously by specifying the beginning and ending line numbers after the **vty** parameter. If you don't apply the restriction to all of your VTYs, you are leaving a back-door into your router, which may cause a security problem.

Also notice the command used to apply the ACL to the line: **access-class**. This is different from activating an ACL on a router's interface. If you use the **in** parameter, you are restricting telnet and SSH access to the router itself. The **out** parameter is kind of unique. By using this parameter, you are restricting what destinations this router can telnet or SSH to when someone uses the **telnet**, **connect**, or **ssh** command. This creates an exception to a standard ACL and has the router treat the address in the ACL statements as a destination address; it causes the router to compare this address to the address in the **telnet** command before allowing the user on the router to telnet to the specified destination.

Here's a simple example of using a standard ACL to filter telnet traffic to a router:

```
Router(config)# access-list 99 permit 192.168.1.0 0.0.0.255
Router(config)# line vty 0 4
Router(config-line)# access-class 99 in
```

In this example, only traffic from 192.168.1.0/24 is allowed to telnet or SSH into this router. Because of the implicit deny at the end of **access-list 99**, all other connections to this router (via the VTYs) will be dropped.

 VIDEO 17.10. The digital resources that accompany this book contain a multimedia demonstration of configuring a standard numbered ACL to restrict remote access to a router.

As you will see in the next section, you can also use extended ACLs to restrict access to the IOS device, but this configuration is much more complex. Second, extended ACLs are applied to interfaces and thus won't be able to restrict telnet access *from* the router to a remote destination. And third, whenever you apply an ACL to an interface on the router, you'll affect the performance of the router on that interface. Depending on the router model, the IOS version, and the features you have enabled, the degradation in performance will vary (today's most current IOS versions take a very small performance hit when using ACLs on interfaces). Therefore, if you only want to restrict telnet or SSH access to or from the router, using a standard ACL and the **access-class** statement on your VTYs is the best approach.

 EXAM TIP For the CCNA exam, remember that you can restrict remote access to your IOS device by requiring user login, using only SSH, and applying a standard ACL to the VTY lines. You need to apply the ACL with the **access-class** mode command on the VTY lines. Note that you can also do this with an extended ACL, but this requires more configuration on your part.

Exercise 17-5: Configuring Standard Numbered ACLs

In this exercise you will create two standard access lists on the VAN-R1 router. The first ACL will block all traffic from the 14.0.0.0 network except traffic from one IP address, and the second ACL will be used to limit from which remote workstation the administrator is allowed to administer the router.

1. Ensure that you have completed the previous exercise before continuing with this exercise.

2. Connect your workstation to the console port of VAN-R1. Then launch PuTTY, choose Serial connection, set the correct COM port, and choose Open.

3. Press ENTER in the PuTTY window to get a prompt on your Cisco device.

4. Access VAN-R1's privileged EXEC mode and create a standard access list numbered *1* that permits the entire 12.0.0.0/8 IP address range and applies this to the VTY ports as the only authorized IP addresses for remote administration:

```
VAN-R1>enable
Password: labenablesecret
VAN-R1#config term
VAN-R1(config)#access-list 1 permit 12.0.0.0 0.255.255.255
VAN-R1(config)#line vty 0 15
VAN-R1(config-line)#access-class 1 in
VAN-R1(config-line)#exit
```

5. Create another standard access list, numbered *2*, that permits only traffic from the IP address of 14.0.0.5 and the IP address of 14.0.0.1, and denies traffic from all other traffic from the 14.0.0.0 network. Apply the access list to the WAN interface for inbound:

```
VAN-R1(config)#access-list 2 permit 14.0.0.5 0.0.0.0
VAN-R1(config)#access-list 2 permit 14.0.0.1 0.0.0.0
VAN-R1(config)#access-list 2 deny 14.0.0.0 0.255.255.255
VAN-R1(config)#interface g0/0
VAN-R1(config-if)#ip access-group 2 out
VAN-R1(config-if)#exit
```

NOTE   We applied the access list to the internal network card instead of the one connected to the WAN so that Open Shortest Path First (OSPF) packets coming from the LA-R1 can be received. Any traffic from the 14.0.0.0 network will not be delivered into the 12.0.0.0 network unless it is coming from 14.0.0.1 or 14.0.0.5.

6. Go to the computer with the IP address of 14.0.0.5 and try to ping 12.0.0.5. Were you successful? _____

7. Go to another computer on the 14.0.0.0 network and try to ping 12.0.0.5. Were you successful? _____

Extended Numbered ACLs

Extended IP ACLs are much more flexible in what you can match on than standard ACLs. Extended ACLs can match on all of the following information:

- Source *and* destination IP addresses
- TCP/IP protocol (IP, TCP, UDP, ICMP, and so on)
- Protocol information, such as port numbers for TCP and UDP, or message types for ICMP

The following sections cover the configuration and use of extended numbered IP ACLs.

EXAM TIP   For the CCNA exam, remember that extended IP ACLs can filter on source and destination IP addresses, protocol, and protocol data such as source and destination ports. Because extended ACLs are very specific in what they filter, Cisco recommends placing them as close as possible to the source that is being filtered.

Command Syntax

Here is the generic command to configure an extended numbered IP ACL:

```
Router(config)# access-list {100-199 | 2000-2699} {permit | deny}
                IP_protocol
                source_address source_wildcard_mask
                    [protocol_information]
                destination_address destination_wildcard_mask
                    [protocol_information] [log]
```

As you can see from this command, the configuration of an extended ACL is more complicated than that of a standard one. Extended IP numbered ACLs can use list numbers in the ranges 100–199 and 2000–2699. After the action (**permit** or **deny**) comes the IP protocol that you want to match on. This is the first major difference between an extended ACL and a standard one. These IP protocols include the following: **ip**, **icmp**, **tcp**, **gre**, **udp**, **igrp**, **eigrp**, **igmp**, **ipinip**, **nos**, and **ospf**. If you want to match on any IP protocol—TCP, UDP, ICMP, and so on—use the **ip** keyword for the protocol. If Cisco doesn't have a name for the IP protocol you want to specify, use the number of the protocol instead, such as **6** for TCP.

The second major difference is that you must specify both the source and destination addresses and their respective wildcard masks. With a standard ACL, you can specify only the source address, and the wildcard mask is optional. Depending on the IP protocol, you may be able to add protocol information for the source and/or destination. For example, TCP and UDP enable you to specify both source and destination port numbers, and ICMP enables you to specify ICMP message types. As with standard ACLs, you can log messages to the console or a syslog server with the **log** parameter.

Once you have created your extended numbered IP ACL, you must activate it on your router's interface with the **ip access-group** command. Note that this is the same configuration used with a standard ACL. Once you activate the ACL, the router will begin filtering traffic on the interface.

 EXAM TIP Be very familiar with the general syntax of an extended ACL statement: you may have to configure an extended ACL on the exam.

TCP and UDP

Use the following syntax to configure an extended ACL for TCP or UDP:

```
Router(config)# access-list {100-199 | 2000-2699} {permit | deny}
                {tcp | udp} source_address source_wildcard_mask
                [operator source_port_#]
           destination_address destination_wildcard_mask
                [operator destination_port_#]
           [established] [log]
```

After specifying the action (**permit** or **deny**), you configure the IP protocol: **tcp** or **udp**.

Operators With TCP and UDP, you can specify the source, destination, or both source and destination port numbers or names. To specify how to perform the match, you must configure an operator. The operator tells the router how to match on the port number(s) or names. Table 17-5 lists the valid operators for TCP and UDP ACL entries. Note that these operators apply only to TCP and UDP connections. Other IP protocols do not use them. If you omit the port number or name, the ACL looks for a match on all TCP or UDP connections.

Table 17-5
TCP and UDP
Operators

Operator	Explanation
lt	Less than
gt	Greater than
neq	Not equal to
eq	Equal to
range	Range of port numbers

Port Name	Command Parameter	Port Number
FTP Data	**ftp-data**	20
FTP Control	**ftp**	21
Telnet	**telnet**	23
SMTP	**smtp**	25
WWW	**www**	80
POP3	**pop3**	110

Table 17-6 Common TCP Port Names and Numbers

Ports Numbers and Names   For TCP and UDP connections, you can list either the name or the number of the port. For example, if you wanted to match on telnet traffic, you could use either the keyword **telnet** or the number **23**. Table 17-6 lists some of the most common port names and numbers for TCP connections.

Table 17-7 shows some of the common UDP port names and numbers.

EXAM TIP   One common problem that occurs when setting up an ACL is that the administrator specifies the wrong protocol for the application, such as TCP for TFTP, RIP, or DNS queries, instead of UDP. This is also true of port numbers or names. You need to be familiar with the TCP/IP protocols and their ports when setting up filtering policies. Remember the TCP and UDP application names and numbers in Tables 17-6 and 17-7 for the exam.

The established Keyword   The **established** keyword is used only for TCP connections. The assumption behind the use of this keyword is that you are originating TCP traffic on the inside of the network and filtering the returning traffic as it comes back into your network. In this situation, this keyword allows (or denies) any TCP traffic that has a certain flag or flag bits set in the TCP segment header, indicating that this is returning traffic back into your network.

EXAM TIP   For the Cisco CCNA exam, understand the use of the **established** keyword with TCP ACL statements.

Port Name	Command Parameter	Port Number
DNS Query	**dns**	53
TFTP	**tftp**	69
SNMP	**snmp**	161
IP RIP	**rip**	520

Table 17-7 Common UDP Port Names and Numbers

VIDEO 17.11. The digital resources that accompany this book contain a multimedia demonstration of configuring an extended numbered ACL to allow telnet traffic through a router.

ICMP

The following command shows the syntax of filtering ICMP traffic:

```
Router(config)# access-list 100-199|2000-2699 {permit | deny} icmp
                source_address source_wildcard_mask
                destination_address destination_wildcard_mask
                [icmp_message] [log]
```

Unlike TCP and UDP, ICMP doesn't use ports. Instead, ICMP uses message types. And where TCP and UDP extended ACLs enable you to specify both source and destination ports, ICMP enables you to enter an ICMP message. Table 17-8 shows some of the common ICMP messages and brief descriptions. You can enter the ICMP message by either its name or its number. If you omit the ICMP message type, all message types are included.

 TIP If you execute the **no access-list** command, followed by the ACL number, the entire ACL and its referenced commands are deleted. What most administrators don't realize, or forget, is that if you preface any numbered ACL statement with the **no** parameter, it has exactly the same effect: the entire ACL is deleted. For example, executing the **no access-list 100 permit tcp any any** command causes the router basically to ignore everything after the **100** parameter, causing the router to execute the command as if it were **no access-list 100**!

 EXAM TIP Use an extended ACL with the ICMP protocol to filter ping application traffic. For the exam, remember the ICMP message types in Table 17-8.

Message Type	Message Description
administratively-prohibited	Indicates the packet was filtered
echo	Used by ping to check a destination
echo-reply	Response to an echo message created by ping
host-unreachable	Subnet is reachable, but the host is not responding
net-unreachable	Network/subnet is not reachable
traceroute	Filters on traceroute information when ICMP is used

Table 17-8 Common ICMP Messages

Extended IP ACL Example

Now that you have seen the syntax for creating extended numbered IP ACLs, take a look at a configuration example:

```
Router(config)# access-list 100 permit tcp
                    any 172.16.0.0 0.0.255.255
                    established log
Router(config)# access-list 100 permit udp
                    any host 172.16.1.1 eq dns log
Router(config)# access-list 100 permit tcp
                    172.17.0.0 0.0.255.255
                    host 172.16.1.2 eq telnet log
Router(config)# access-list 100 permit icmp
                    any 172.16.0.0 0.0.255.255
                    echo-reply log
Router(config)# access-list 100 deny ip any any log
Router(config)# interface GigabitEthernet 0/0
Router(config-if)# ip access-group 100 in
```

The assumption behind this example is that it is restricting what traffic can come into a network. The first statement says that if any TCP session has any source address and is destined to 172.16.0.0/16, it will be permitted if certain TCP flag bits are set (**established**) in the TCP segment header, indicative of returning traffic. Remember that the keyword **any** is the same as 0.0.0.0 255.255.255.255. Also, the **log** keyword will cause a match on this statement to be printed on the console. Since a TCP port isn't specified, all TCP connections will match on this statement.

The second line of this example allows a DNS query from any source device to be sent to an internal DNS server (172.16.1.1). Remember that the 0.0.0.0 wildcard mask is removed and the keyword **host** is inserted in the front of the IP address. A match on this statement is also logged.

The third line allows any telnet connection from devices in the 172.17.0.0/16 network if the destination device is 172.16.1.2. Remember that telnet uses TCP. A match on this statement is also logged.

The fourth line allows any replies to a ping to come back to devices with an address of 172.16.0.0/16. Note that only the echo replies are allowed—echoes are not allowed, preventing someone from this interface from executing pings. A match on this statement is also logged.

The fifth line isn't necessary because all traffic not matching on the previous **permit** statements will be dropped. However, if you want to log what is dropped, you'll need to configure this statement with the **log** parameter, as shown in the example. The last part of the configuration shows the ACL applied inbound on ethernet0.

 EXAM TIP   Go back and look at the extended IP ACL example again and make sure you understand how the ACL functions. You'll need to understand how the ACL functions in similar examples on the exam.

Named ACLs

Starting with IOS 11.2, Cisco routers support both numbered and named ACLs. One of the original limitations of numbered ACLs was that you could create only so many of them. Originally, you could have only 99 standard IP ACLs and 100 extended IP ACLs. Starting back with IOS 11.2, Cisco enabled you to use names to reference your ACLs instead of, or in combination with, numbered ACLs. Unlike in numbered ACLs, in named ACLs you can delete a single entry in the ACL without deleting the entire ACL. No need to worry about when the named ACLs came into play, just know that it was a welcome feature because it meant we were not limited by numeric values.

Creating Named ACLs

To create a named IP ACL, use the following command:

```
Router(config)# ip access-list {standard | extended} ACL_name
```

The first thing you must specify is the type of ACL: standard or extended. Second, you must give the ACL a name that groups the ACL statements together. This name must be unique among all named ACLs.

After you enter this command, you are taken into the appropriate ACL Subconfiguration mode, as is shown here:

```
Router(config-std-acl)#
```

or

```
Router(config-ext-acl)#
```

Once you are in Subconfiguration mode, you can enter your ACL commands. For a standard named ACL, use the following configuration:

```
Router(config)# ip access-list standard ACL_name
Router(config-std-acl)# permit|deny source_IP_address
                          [wildcard_mask]
```

For an extended named ACL, use the following configuration:

```
Router(config)# ip access-list extended ACL_name
Router(config-ext-acl)# permit|deny IP_protocol
                          source_IP_address wildcard_mask
                              [protocol_information]
                          destination_IP_address wildcard_mask
                              [protocol_information] [log]
```

As you can see, creating a standard or extended named IP ACL is similar to creating a numbered one. Once you have created your extended numbered IP ACL, you must activate it on your IOS device's interface with the **ip access-group** command, referencing a name instead of a number.

 EXAM TIP Be familiar with how to create a named ACL and the two different Subconfiguration modes you are taken into, depending on whether the ACL is standard or extended.

Example of a Named Access List

This example converts the extended IP numbered ACL from the "Extended IP ACL Example" section earlier in this chapter to a named ACL:

```
Router(config)# ip access-list extended do_not_enter
Router(config-ext-acl)# permit tcp any 172.16.0.0 0.0.255.255
                        established log
Router(config-ext-acl)# permit udp any
                        host 172.16.1.1 eq dns log
Router(config-ext-acl)# permit tcp 172.17.0.0 0.0.255.255
                        host 176.16.1.2 eq telnet log
Router(config-ext-acl)# permit icmp any 176.16.0.0 0.0.255.255
                        echo-reply log
Router(config-ext-acl)# deny ip any any log
Router(config)# interface GigabitEthernet 0/0
Router(config-if)# ip access-group do_not_enter in
```

Both this example and the numbered example do the *exact same thing*. Therefore, it is a matter of personal preference whether you use a named ACL or a numbered ACL. (My preference is to use numbered ACLs, if only because I've been using them since they first came out in IOS version 7.)

VIDEO 17.12. The digital resources that accompany this book contain a multimedia demonstration of configuring a named IP ACL on a router.

ACL Remarks

Starting in IOS 12.0(2)T, you can embed remarks or comments within your ACL statements. Remarks work with named or numbered ACLs. Here's the configuration, based on whether you're using a numbered ACL or a named ACL:

```
Router(config)# access-list ACL_# remark remark
```

or

```
Router(config)# ip access-list standard|extended ACL_name  Router(config-
{std|ext}-acl)# remark remark
```

The remark can be up to 100 characters in length.

TIP Go ahead and use copious remarks in your ACLs, since some ACLs can have thousands of statements in them! Without the remark feature, you would have an almost impossible task of determining what a statement or group of statements was doing when you are confronted with so many ACL entries.

Access List Verification

Once you have created and activated your ACLs, you can verify their configuration and operation with various **show** commands. One common command that you can use is the Privilege EXEC **show running-config** command, which will display your ACL and the interface or interfaces on which it is activated. However, you can use many other commands as well.

If you simply want to see which ACLs are activated on your router's interfaces, you can use the **show ip interfaces** command:

```
Router# show ip interfaces
GigabitEthernet0/0 is up, line protocol is up
  Internet address is 172.16.1.1/24
  Broadcast address is 255.255.255.255
  Address determined by setup command
  MTU is 1500 bytes   Helper address is not set
  Directed broadcast forwarding is disabled
  Outgoing access list is not set
  Inbound  access list is 100
  Proxy ARP is enabled
  .
  .
  .
```

From the output of this command, you can see that ACL 100, an extended numbered IP ACL, is applied inbound on ethernet0.

 VIDEO 17.13. The digital resources that accompany this book contain a multimedia demonstration of using the **show ip interfaces** command on a router to verify the activation of your ACLs.

To view the statements in your ACLs, use either of the following two commands:

```
Router# show access-lists [ACL_#_or_name]
Router# show ip access-list [ACL_#_or_name]
```

Here is an example of the **show access-lists** command:

```
Router# show access-lists
Extended IP access list 100
    permit tcp 172.16.0.0 0.0.255.255 any established
          (189 matches)
    permit udp host 172.16.1.39 any eq domain
          (32 matches)
    permit icmp host 199.199.199.1 any
IPX sap access list 1000
 deny FFFFFFFF 7
 permit FFFFFFFF 0
```

First, notice that the router keeps track of matches on each statement. The first statement in ACL 100 has had 189 matches against it.

 TIP It is recommended that you put a **deny ip any any** command at the end of an extended ACL, even though the implicit deny statement will drop the traffic. By putting this statement at the end of your ACL, you can see the hit counts of all the denied traffic: since the implicit deny command is invisible, you can't see the hit counts for it.

You can clear these counters with this command:

```
Router# clear access-list counters [ACL_#_or_name]
```

 EXAM TIP   For the Cisco CCNA exam, know the commands you can use to troubleshoot ACLs. Use the **show ip interfaces** command to see whether or not an IP ACL is applied to your router's interfaces. Use the **show access-lists** command to view all of the ACLs on your router. The **show ip access-list** command lists only the IP ACLs on your router.

Also notice that using the **show access-lists** command displays all ACLs from all protocols on your router. From the preceding output, two ACLs are shown: an extended numbered IP ACL and an IPX SAP ACL. If you want to view only ACLs for IP, use the following command:

```
Router# show ip access-list
Extended IP access list 100
    permit tcp 172.16.0.0 0.0.255.255 any established  (189 matches)
    permit udp host 172.16.1.39 any eq domain  (32 matches)
    permit icmp host 199.199.199.1 any
```

If you want to view only a particular ACL, use either of the following two commands:

```
Router# show access-lists 100
Extended IP access list 100
    permit tcp 172.16.0.0 0.0.255.255 any established  (189 matches)
    permit udp host 172.16.1.39 any eq domain  (32 matches)
    permit icmp host 199.199.199.1 any
```

or

```
Router# show ip access-list 100
.
.
.
```

 VIDEO   17.14. The digital resources that accompany this book contain a multimedia demonstration of using the **show ip access-list** or **show access-lists** command on a router to verify the activation of your ACLs.

ACL Changes

Prior to the addition of the sequenced ACL feature, you basically had to make ACL changes in an external text editor such as Windows Notepad, delete the old ACL on the router, and paste in the new commands. However, starting in IOS 12.3, you can edit ACLs on your IOS device on-the-fly with the *sequenced ACL* feature. Sequenced ACLs enable you to insert and delete statements and remarks in an existing ACL.

With sequenced ACLs, each ACL command is given a unique sequence number. By default, the sequence numbers start at 10 and increment by 10. You know that your IOS device supports sequenced ACLs if you display them with the **show access-lists** command and you see sequence numbers in front of the ACL statements:

```
Router# show access-lists
Extended IP access list 101
    10 permit ip host 192.168.101.69 any
    20 permit ip host 192.168.101.89 any
```

As you can see from this example, ACL 101 is using sequenced ACLs. The sequence numbers are added when the router boots up and loads the ACL or when you add or change the ACL from the CLI or Cisco Configuration Professional (CP). Whenever you save the IOS's configuration to NVRAM, the sequence numbers are not stored with the ACL statements: Cisco implemented this feature for backward compatibility with older IOS versions that do not support sequenced ACLs.

Sequenced ACLs work with both named and numbered ACLs; however, to edit a numbered ACL, you must treat it as though it were a named ACL. Once you enter the ACL subcommand mode, you can delete an entry by prefacing the sequence number with the **no** command:

```
Router(config)# ip access-list {standard|extended} ACL_name_or_#
Router(config-{std|ext}-nacl)# no sequence_#
```

To insert a statement in an ACL, enter the ACL subcommand mode and preface the ACL statement with a sequence number that does not currently exist in the list of statements, like this:

```
Router(config)# ip access-list {standard|extended} ACL_name_or_#
Router(config-{std|ext}-nacl)#  sequence_# {permit | deny}
                    ACL_condition
```

Since sequence numbers increment by 10, if you need to insert more than nine statements in the same place in your ACL, you'll first need to resequence the entries in the list:

```
Router(config)# ip access-list resequence ACL_name_or_number
                    starting_seq_#   increment
```

With this command, you need to specify the initial sequence number, and then the increment. In the following example, the initial sequence number is 100 and the increment is 100:

```
Router(config)# ip access-list resequence 101 100 100
Extended IP access list 101
    100 permit ip host 192.168.101.69 any
    200 permit ip host 192.168.101.89 any
```

 VIDEO 17.15. The digital resources that accompany this book contain a multimedia demonstration of the sequenced ACL feature.

Understanding ACL Placement

This section covers design issues with ACLs—that is, where you should place ACLs of a given type (standard or extended). Given the source and destination that you are filtering, on what router and what interface on that router should you activate your ACL? This section covers some of the important points you should consider when determining where to put your ACLs.

First, don't go crazy with ACLs and create dozens and dozens of them across all of your routers. This makes testing and troubleshooting your filtering rules almost impossible. In a campus network, for example, ACL configuration and filtering is on the layer 3 switch or router at the distribution layer that connects a building or floor to the campus backbone. This model was discussed in Chapter 1—the core, distribution, and access layers.

The second point is that you will want to limit the number of statements in your ACL. An ACL with hundreds of statements is almost impossible to test and troubleshoot. It's not unusual to see an ACL have a lot of unnecessary and overlapping commands that have been carried over from years past.

As to where you should place your ACLs, the following two rules hold true in most situations:

- Standard ACLs should be placed as close to the destination devices as possible.
- Extended ACLs should be placed as close to the source devices as possible.

 TIP   Remember that standard ACLs should be placed as close to the destination device as possible, and extended ACLs should be placed as close to the source device as possible.

Standard ACLs

You want to place standard ACLs as close to the destination that you want to prevent the source from reaching, since they enable you to filter only on the source IP address in the packet headers. If you put the standard ACL too close to the source, you could be preventing the source from accessing other valid services in your network. By putting the standard ACL as close to the destination as possible, you are still enabling the source to access other resources, while restricting it from accessing the remote destination device or devices.

Let's take a look at an example to illustrate the placement of standard ACLs. Use the network shown in Figure 17-1. In this example, the user (192.168.5.1) should be prevented from accessing the server (192.168.1.1). Here is the ACL configuration:

```
Router(config)# access-list 1 deny host 192.168.5.1
Router(config)# access-list 1 permit any
```

As you can see from this example, the goal is to prevent 192.168.5.1 from accessing the server at 192.168.1.1, and to allow everyone else to access the server. Let's discuss the options for placing this ACL. Your first choice is to place this ACL on RouterC. If

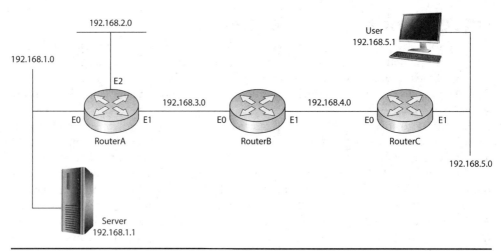

Figure 17-1   Placement of ACLs

you placed it here, 192.168.5.1 would not be able to reach 192.168.1.1, but the user wouldn't be able to access anything else either. If you placed the ACL on RouterB, the user would be able to access the 192.168.4.0 network, but nothing else. You actually have two choices for placing the ACL on RouterA: interfaces E0 and E1. If you placed it inbound on E1, the user wouldn't be able to access network 192.168.2.0. Therefore, you would have to place it outbound on E0 of RouterA.

Note that there is still an issue with using standard ACLs—any traffic from 192.168.5.1 is dropped as it attempts to leave this interface. So the user is prevented from reaching not only the server but anything else on this segment. Another issue with standard ACLs, since you typically place them as close to the destination as possible, is that they are not very network-friendly: packets travel almost all of the way to the destination and *then* they are dropped. This wastes bandwidth in your network, especially if the source is sending a lot of traffic to the destination.

Extended ACLs

Given the preceding example, it would be much better to place the standard ACL as close to the source as possible to prevent unwanted traffic from traversing almost the whole network before being dropped. With a standard ACL, though, you would be preventing the user from accessing most of the resources in the network.

Extended ACLs, however, don't have this limitation, since they can filter on *both* the source and destination addresses in the IP packet headers. Given this ability, it is recommended that you place extended ACLs as *close* to the source as possible, thus preventing unwanted traffic from traversing your network. With an extended ACL, since you can filter on both addresses, you can prevent a source from accessing a particular destination or destinations but still allow it to access others.

With the preceding example, your configuration would look like this when using an extended ACL:

```
Router(config)# access-list 100 deny ip host 192.168.5.1
                                   host 192.168.1.1
Router(config)# access-list 100 permit ip any any
```

This configuration example is preventing only traffic from 192.168.5.1 to 192.168.1.1. Now the question is, where should you place this ACL? Again, you want to put this extended ACL as close to the source as possible. This means that you should place it on RouterC. RouterC has two interfaces, though. In that case, placing the extended ACL as close to the source as possible means placing it on RouterC's E1 interface in the inbound direction. If you were to place it on E0, and the router had another interface that it could use to reach the destination, the source still might be able to get around the filter. If you place it on RouterC's E1 interface, 192.168.5.1 can access every location except 192.168.1.1. Likewise, any other traffic is permitted to go anywhere in the network.

You can be more specific with your filtering in this example. For example, if you want to restrict just telnet access, but allow other types of access from 192.168.5.1 to 192.168.1.1, then you should specify the IP protocol (**tcp**) and the destination port name or number (**telnet** or **23**).

 NOTE Standard ACLs are very rarely used to filter traffic between interfaces. In much older versions of IOS, there was a large performance difference between using standard versus extended ACLs, where standard ACL processing was much faster. Today there is no difference on current router platforms with newer versions of IOS. Knowing this information, you should focus on using extended ACLs to filter traffic to or through the router.

Chapter Review

In this chapter you learned about a number of security best practices when configuring Cisco devices. You learned about configuring device passwords such as the enable password and the enable secret, and you learned how to configure passwords on the console port, auxiliary port, and the VTY port.

You also learned how to create user accounts and configure authentication to the different port types with the **login local** command. You learned about encrypting all passwords on the Cisco device and how to restrict access of remote administration to SSH and not allow telnet communication because it is insecure.

You learned about layer 2 security features such as disabling unused ports. If you enable a port, you can use the port security feature to associate a MAC address with the port so that an unauthorized device cannot connect to the port. You learned about DHCP snooping features that allow the switch to prevent rogue DHCP servers on the network. The final layer 2 security feature was dynamic ARP inspection, which helps prevent man-in-the-middle attacks via ARP poisoning by checking the IP address and MAC address of any ARP message against the DHCP snooping binding database.

The final topic of the chapter discussed using access control lists (ACLs) to control what traffic is allowed to enter or leave the device. Standard access list are used for creating rules based off of the source IP address of the packet only, while extended access lists can create rules based on source and destination IP addresses, source and destination ports, and protocol information.

Quick Review

Configuring Device Passwords

- You can configure either an enable password or enable secret, which is used to authenticate someone when entering privileged EXEC mode. The enable secret is encrypted within the configuration file and takes precedence if both passwords are set.
- Configure passwords on each of the types of ports (console, auxiliary, and VTY) so that someone must authenticate to the system when they connect. You can prompt for a password by using the **login** command on the port type.
- You can create a user account and password list and force authentication with the user list by using the **login local** command on the console, auxiliary, or VTY ports.
- You can encrypt all passwords in the configuration file by using the **service password-encryption** command.
- To prepare for the configuration of SSH on your device, set the hostname and the domain name of the device. This information is used when you generate the encryption key.
- To force SSH as a remote administration protocol and not allow telnet, you must use the **transport input ssh** command on the VTY port.

Configure Layer 2 Security Features

- Disable unused ports on the switch with the **shutdown** command.
- In highly secure environments, look to using the port security feature, which locks down an enabled port so that can be used only by an authorized device. Port security associates the MAC address with the port of the authorized system.
- To prevent rogue DHCP servers from sending out DHCPOFFER messages on the network, use DHCP snooping.
- To prevent ARP poisoning attacks on the network, use dynamic ARP inspection, which validates the IP address and MAC address in an ARP message against the DHCP snooping binding database.

Implementing Access Control Lists

- Standard ACLs are used to filter traffic by the source IP address only and have an ACL number assigned to them that ranges from 1 to 99 or 1300 to 1999.

- Extended ACLs are used to filter traffic based on the source and destination IP addresses, source and destination ports, and protocol information as well. Extended ACLs have an ACL number ranging from 100 to 199 or 2000 to 2699.

- Each ACL has an implicit deny at the end of the ACL, so if a rule does not match the packet being evaluated, the packet is dropped.

- You can create an access list with the **access-list** command (for example, **access-list 1 permit 192.168.2.0 0.0.0.255**).

- After creating the access lists, you apply it to the interface by navigating to the interface and then using the **ip access-group** command (for example, **ip access-group 1 in**).

- You can apply an access list to the VTY ports with the **access-class** command.

Understanding ACL Placement

- Standard ACLs should be placed as close to the destination devices as possible.

- Extended ACLs should be placed as close to the source devices as possible.

Questions

The following questions will help you measure your understanding of the material presented in this chapter. Read all the choices carefully because there may be more than one correct answer. Choose the correct answer(s) for each question.

1. What command would you use on a Cisco device to ensure that passwords are encrypted within the configuration files?

   A. **password-encryption**

   B. **service password-encryption**

   C. **password encrypt on**

   D. **enable secret**

2. You have configured an enable password and an enable secret on your Cisco device. Which one will you need to use when you navigate to privileged EXEC mode?

   A. The enable password

   B. The strongest password of the two

   C. The enable secret

   D. The one that was configured first

3. Looking at the following configuration performed by one of your network administrators, why are admins not prompted for a password when connecting to the console port?

```
VAN-R1>enable
VAN-R1#config term

VAN-R1(config)#line con 0
VAN-R1(config-line)#password conpass
```

   A. Need to configure an enable password

   B. Need to configure an enable secret

   C. Must add the **authenticate** command

   D. Missing the **login** command

4. You want to create an access list that filters traffic by the source IP address of the packet only. What type of access list would you use?

   A. Extended

   B. Standard

   C. Extension

   D. Basic

5. Your manager is concerned with rogue DHCP servers being added to the network. What switch feature would you use to prevent rogue DHCP servers?

   A. DHCP snooping

   B. Dynamic ARP inspection

   C. Access control list

   D. Port security

6. You are configuring SSH on a Cisco switch. What two conditions must exist for your configuration to be successful?

   A. The switch must be running a crypto-supported IOS image.

   B. You must have configured a console password.

   C. Routing must be disabled.

   D. You must have run the **ip domain-name** command.

   E. You must have OSPFv2 running on the switch.

7. You want to configure an access list that ensures only HTTP traffic is allowed to reach the system with the IP address of 10.0.45.10/24. What type of access list would you use?

   A. Extended

   B. Standard

   C. Extension

   D. Basic

8. You have created an access list numbered 100 that you would like to apply to the GigabitEthernet 0/0 interface for inbound traffic. What commands would you use?

   A. Use the following:
   ```
   Router(config)# interface GigabitEthernet 0/0
   Router(config-if)# ip access-group 100 ingress
   ```

   B. Use the following:
   ```
   Router(config)# interface GigabitEthernet 0/0
   Router(config-if)# ip access-group 100 egress
   ```

   C. Use the following:
   ```
   Router(config)# interface GigabitEthernet 0/0
   Router(config-if)# access-class 100 in
   ```

   D. Use the following:
   ```
   Router(config)# interface GigabitEthernet 0/0
   Router(config-if)# ip access-group 100 in
   ```

Use the following configuration to answer questions 9 and 10.

```
VAN-R1>enable
VAN-R1#config term
VAN-R1(config)#enable password ciscopass
VAN-R1(config)#enable secret ciscosecret

VAN-R1(config)#username edtetz password edpass
VAN-R1(config)#username glenclarke password glenpass

VAN-R1(config)#line con 0
VAN-R1(config-line)#password conpass

VAN-R1(config)#line vty 0 15
VAN-R1(config-line)#password telnetpass
VAN-R1(config-line)#login
```

9. In the configuration, administrators are not prompted for usernames and passwords when they try to administer the Cisco device remotely. What can you do to remedy this?

   A. Add the **login** command to **con 0**.

   B. Use stronger passwords on the user accounts.

   C. Change the **login** command to the **login local** command.

   D. Add the **service password-encryption** command.

10. What password will administrators need to use to enter into privileged EXEC mode?

   A. **glenpass**

   B. **ciscosecret**

   C. **conpass**

   D. **ciscopass**

Performance-based Questions

The Cisco exams have performance-based questions where you must drag an item from the left side of the screen to its proper place on the right side of the screen to answer the question. Following are some sample performance-based questions related to security.

1. You have configured an extended access list with the following rules:

```
access-list 120 deny tcp 145.13.45.100 0.0.7.255 any eq 23
access-list 120 deny tcp 145.13.45.100 0.0.7.255 any eq http
access-list 120 permit ip any any
```

Using the following exhibit, identify which packets would be denied and which packets would be permitted by writing the packet information in the boxes on the right. On the real exam, you would need to drag the box representing the packet to the appropriate category on the right.

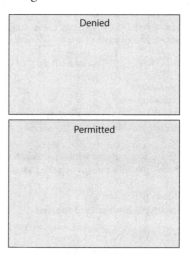

Source IP: 145.13.15.29
Destination Port: 23

Source IP: 145.13.42.110
Destination Port: 23

Source IP: 145.13.45.10
Destination Port: 21

Source IP: 145.13.47.15
Destination Port: 80

Source IP: 145.13.51.12
Destination Port: 80

Denied

Permitted

2. Draw a line from the command on the left side to the appropriate description on the right side. Not all descriptions are used.

Description

Restrict VTY access to the SSH protocol

Command

Deny the usage of SSH

service password-encryption

Encrypt passwords within the configuration file

switchport port-security violation shutdown

Disable the port when a security violation occurs

ip arp inspection vlan 1

Configured on the port your DHCP server is connected to

transport input ssh

Configured on the port that DHCP clients are connected to

ip dhcp snooping trust

Designed to prevent MiTM attacks

Answers

1. **B.** The **service password-encryption** command is used to encrypt all plain text passwords in the configuration file. It is highly recommended that you do this to prevent someone from viewing your passwords when looking at the configuration on the Cisco device.

2. **C.** Both the **enable password** and **enable secret** commands are used to configure a password that is required by administrators if they enter privileged EXEC mode. It is recommended, however, that you use the enable secret, because it is encrypted within the configuration file. If both are set, the secret is the password that must be used by administrators, because it takes precedence.

3. **D.** After configuring a password on any of the connection lines such as the console port, auxiliary port, or VTY ports, you must use the **login** command to tell the Cisco device you want authentication on the port.

4. **B.** A standard access list is used to filter packets based on the source IP address only.

5. **A.** You can prevent rogue DHCP servers from being added to the network by using DHCP snooping features on the switch. When DHCP snooping is enabled, you must configure the port that the authorized DHCP is connected to as a trusted port. All other ports are untrusted, which means the switch will block DHCP-related messages such as the DHCPOFFER message.

6. **A, D.** To configure a switch for SSH, it must have a crypto-supported IOS image so that you can use the **crypto** command to generate an encryption key. Crypto-supported IOSs have a *K9* in the name of the IOS image file. You also need to set the hostname of the device and the IP domain name, because those names are used when the encryption key is generated.

7. **A.** Extended access lists can filter traffic based on the source and destination IP addresses, source and destination ports, and protocol information. Remember that a standard access list can filter traffic based on only the source IP address in the packet.

8. **D.** To apply an access list to an interface, you must first navigate to the interface and then use the **ip access-group** command to specify the access list number and the direction of traffic the access list is to filter (either in or out). The following code is correct:

```
Router(config)# interface GigabitEthernet 0/0
Router(config-if)# ip access-group 100 in
```

9. **C.** For remote administration, the administrators would be connecting to the VTY ports. Looking at the configuration, you can see that there is a list of usernames and passwords, but the VTY port is missing the **login local** command, which tells the Cisco device you want to authentication using local user accounts.

10. **B.** When entering privileged EXEC mode, the enable secret value is used to log in if one is configured; otherwise, the enable password value would be used.

Performance-based Answers

1. The following illustration shows which packets would be permitted and which would be denied. To answer this question, you first need to figure out what the subnet is that the rules are dealing with. The best way to do that is with this calculation: 255.255.255.255 – 0.0.7.255 (the wildcard mask). This gives you a subnet mask of 255.255.248.0. This means each network block is determined by the increment of 8 in the third octet. This places the subnet in question as 145.13.40.0–145.13.47.255, so any addresses in that range that are using port 80 or port 23 will be denied.

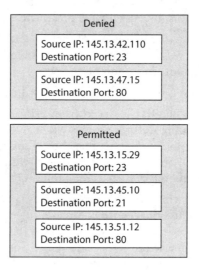

2. The following shows the correct matching of the command with the description of what the command is designed to achieve.

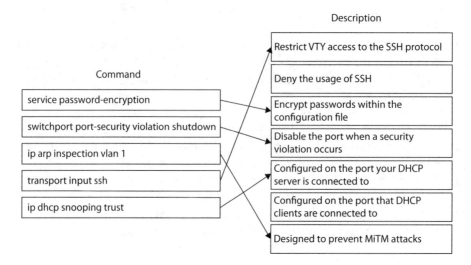

CHAPTER 18

Automation and Programmability

In this chapter, you will

- Learn about the difference between traditional network management and controller-based automation
- Learn about software-defined networking (SDN) and the Cisco Digital Network Architecture (DNA)
- Learn about data exchange formats such as XML and JSON

Our last chapter is a new topic for the Cisco CCNA exam and provides an introduction to automation and software-defined networking (SDN). I am sure that SNA will be a big focus in future versions of the CCNA exam; for the current version of the exam, however, you just need to know the purpose of automation and the related concepts.

Introduction to Automation

In this section you are introduced to the benefits of automation of networking devices by first reviewing how traditional networks are managed and then comparing that to the use of automation.

Traditional vs. Controller-based Networking

The new Cisco CCNA expects you to understand and be able to compare traditional networking environments with controller-based networking, which is the networking environment of the future.

Traditional Network Management

In traditional networking environments, you manage each of your networking devices, such as your Cisco routers and switches, one-by-one. This is, of course, labor intensive, and administrators are prone to making mistakes to the configuration of a device because they must manually input each command.

With traditional networking environments, you typically take the following actions for each network device over the lifetime of the device:

1. Install the network device into the networking environment.
2. Apply an initial configuration to the device so that it functions as needed.
3. Over time, apply updates to the configuration.
4. Upgrade the software on the device as needed.
5. Monitor the overall performance of the device and events that occur on the device with protocols such as Simple Network Management Protocol (SNMP) and NetFlow.

Those five actions may not seem like a lot of work, but remember that you are taking these steps with each device on the network. So, for example, if a new IOS becomes available that needs to be applied to all your switches, you are looking at quite a bit of time to perform the upgrade: you have to back up the configuration of the device, back up the old IOS of the device, add the new IOS to the device, and ensure that the device is booting to that IOS.

Also keep in mind that, for each configuration change that needs to be made to your network devices, you need to console into or remote into the device with telnet or Secure Shell (SSH), and then apply the configuration change. Then you must disconnect and then connect to the next device to apply the configuration change. And you must do this for all your devices.

Here are some key points to remember about management of traditional networks:

- The focus of the network administrator is on each individual device. The administrator must connect to each device and apply the change to that device.
- The configuration change is inputted manually by the administrator. This means that there is high potential for configuration errors.
- Finally, traditional management involves using blacklisting as the security model, which means that everything is allowed unless you disallow it.

Controller-based Networking

Controller-based networking takes advantage of automation technologies that are used to apply configuration changes to multiple devices at one time. The *controller* software component or appliance automates configuration changes on the network and handles the deployment of configuration changes to multiple devices simultaneously.

With automation, when a new device is added to the network, it locates an initial configuration that needs to be applied and then applies the configuration, without needing the administrator's intervention. Configuration can also be applied based on *profiles*, such as a quality of service (QoS) profile or an authentication, authorization, and accounting (AAA) profile. You can also automate changes to devices through the use of scripts such as Cisco TLC or Python scripts executing on the devices.

You can use automation for a number of different tasks. For example, if you needed to perform an upgrade on a device, you could use automation to check what software image exists on the device, and if it determines that the old version needs replacing, you can automate the upgrade procedures to execute on that device. Again, this is all done without the administrator actually visiting the device. You can also use automation to schedule specific tasks or operations on the device and automate troubleshooting procedures if there is a problem with a device.

For the CCNA exam, you'll need to remember these key points about controller-based network management:

- The focus of the administrator is on the entire network. Changes can be applied to multiple devices at once.

- The administrator inputs changes into policy elements that are then applied to multiple devices automatically.

- A whitelisting security model is used: everything is blocked unless you allow it.

Benefits of Automation

Automation offers huge benefits. First, companies can reduce their support staff and save on staffing funds by automating the many tasks that technicians would traditionally need to perform by visiting each device. This does not mean we are out of a job! It simply means our job changes a bit in the sense that, as technicians, we would focus on the creation of the automation procedures and scripts.

Second, automation offers time savings. With traditional networking, it takes quite some time to apply configuration changes to multiple devices. In most cases administrators would need to travel to the location of each device to apply the change (unless it was a simple change that could be performed remotely).

Finally, one of the more important benefits of automation is that you can guarantee consistency in your configurations. With automation, you create the script and then instruct the controller to deploy that to the devices; each device receives the same configuration. This not only helps ensure that you are familiar with the configuration of each device, but it also means that less configuration errors occur, because an administrator is not typing the same configuration commands over and over on each device.

Understanding Planes

Before getting into automation architectures and software-defined networking (SDN), I want to discuss the different *planes* that are part of the architecture of each Cisco device and what types of actions each plane is responsible for. This is important because, with automation environments, you can move some of the planes off the device and into the cloud if you want. But you first need to know what planes are.

All Cisco devices have three planes within the architecture of the device, with each plane performing a specific function on the device. The planes are known as the *control plane*, *data plane*, and *management plane*.

Control Plane

The control plane is responsible for running the different protocols on the device, such as routing protocols, layer 2 protocols, and protocols such as Dynamic Host Control Protocol (DHCP), if it is configured. By running these protocols, the control plane learns information about the network and then stores that information in tables. For example, while running a routing protocol such as Open Shortest Path First (OSPF), the control plane would learn of routes and then store those routes in the routing table. The control plane could populate the MAC address table, routing tables, and the ARP table, among others.

The control plane runs the routing protocols, handles the exchange of routing information, and makes decisions as to what goes into the routing table. Although the control plane executes logic to create and populate these tables, the tables are physically stored close to where they used—in the data plane.

Data Plane

The data plane is responsible for storing the information in the tables and making decisions based on the information contained in the tables. The data plane is also known as the forwarding plane, because this plane contains all logical and physical components that control the forwarding of a frame or packet. For example, when a packet enters the router, the data plane looks at the routing table to determine where to forward the packet before forwarding it to its destination. Note that features such as packet inspection, classifications for QoS, and access control lists (ACLs) would be processed in the data plane.

Management Plane

The management plane runs the components we use to manage the devices, such as the management protocols of telnet or SSH. It also contains the management ports, such as the console port and the auxiliary port used to manage the device. The management plane is also responsible for AAA functionality if it is being used. For example, the management plane authenticates anyone who tries to access the device, authorizes actions of individuals, and provides accounting features.

Software-Defined Networking

To achieve automation (controller-based networking), you use software-defined networking (SDN). In SDN, software is responsible for applying configuration changes to devices on the network. Through this software, you are able to administer all devices on the network from a central point. The *SDN controller* drives the automation and applies the changes to the devices on the network.

The SDN controller can be implemented in a number of ways:

- As software installed on a server
- As an appliance that contains the controller inside
- As a remote controller located in the cloud

No matter how the controller is implemented, the controller uses tools such as Puppet, Chef, and Ansible to help automate changes on the network. You will learn more about Puppet, Chef, and Ansible later in this chapter in the section "Configuration Management Technologies."

Here's how the controller is used: You launch the GUI and then choose the devices you want to make changes to. Then select the settings to be applied to each of the devices. The controller then applies those changes to those devices.

Software-Defined Architectures

The Cisco CCNA exam expects you to understand and describe the SDN architecture components such as the underlay network, the overlay network, and the SDN fabric.

Underlay Network

The underlay network contains all of your regular network components, such as routers. When building an SDN environment, your first step is to ensure that all network devices have the appropriate protocols and features configured to enable network communication to occur and to enable access to the network devices. This means that you must configure all IP addresses on the interfaces, ensure that the interfaces are enabled, and configure routing between the broadcast domains of the network. You must use an open standard protocol such as OSPF, Border Gateway Protocol (BGP), or Intermediate System-Intermediate System (IS-IS) as the routing protocols.

Overlay Network

The overlay network is the logical network that runs on top of the traditional network devices (the underlay network). The overlay network includes the *virtual networks* that are created on top of the underlay network that uses virtual technologies such as virtual routing and forwarding (VRF), multiprotocol label switching virtual private network (MPLS VPN), and Virtual Extensible LAN (VXLAN).

 EXAM TIP Although you are not required to be familiar with these virtual technologies for the CCNA exam, you should know that there are virtual protocols to go with virtual networking. It is also important to remember that the underlay network acts as the physical connectivity that is used by the overlay network, which is considered the logical network.

SDN Fabric

The *SDN fabric* includes all the components that make up the SDN environment, including the underlay network and overlay network. The SDN fabric is made up of the physical network devices that are contained within the underlay network and are controlled by the SDN controller, which is also part of the SDN fabric.

Separation of Planes

When implementing an SDN model, you are making changes to the location of the control plane. With traditional networking, the control plane resides on the device with the data plane, but with SDN networking, the control plane follows a centralized model by which it is run on the SDN controller. The SDN application will communicate with the SDN controller for two reasons: to send out configuration changes to the networking devices, and to receive updated information on the configuration of the devices so that the configuration can be mapped in the SDN application.

As changes are made through the SDN application, they are communicated to the controller, which then sends those changes to each of the networking devices. Separating these components enables administrators to deploy changes throughout the network in a timely fashion.

 NOTE If the SDN controller goes down, you will be unable to make new changes, but the devices can still make forwarding decisions based on the current state of the data plane on the devices.

Campus Device Management vs. Cisco DNA Center

When many of us think of *campus device management*, we think of the traditional methods used to manage configuration changes to our Cisco devices. We console into the device or remotely manage the device via SSH, then apply the configuration changes needed, and then disconnect from the device. If we need to apply the configuration change to ten different devices, we repeat those steps with each device.

The Cisco *Digital Network Architecture* (DNA) Center is a physical appliance you can purchase that provides SDN capabilities (automation). The DNA Center offers a central point to manage your network devices, automate configuration changes, and perform analysis of the devices. SDN and the DNA Center offer *intent-based networking*, which means that they use software to control the networking environment.

When you purchase the Cisco DNA Center appliance, it contains a built-in *Application Policy Infrastructure Controller* (APIC), which is the SDN controller component built into the DNA Center. The DNA Center also includes a built-in *Network Data Platform* (NDP) component, which is responsible for analyzing problems, displaying information about the problems, and then offering solutions to the problems.

North-bound and South-bound APIs

An *application programming interface* (API) is application logic that contains a number of functions that perform different actions. In SDN networking, APIs are critical to move information from the application you use to manage changes to the controller, and then to move data from the controller to the network devices. The API is the *logic* of how to move the data, but the data itself is in a *data format* that enables it to be shared across applications and devices. (You'll read more about data format in a bit.)

For the Cisco CCNA exam, you need to be familiar with the two APIs with SDN networking: the *north-bound API* and the *south-bound API*. As shown in Figure 18-1, the north-bound API is responsible for moving data between the application and the controller, while the south-bound API is responsible for moving data between the controller and the network devices.

APIs use a client/server architecture in which each execution requires a client and a server. The client is the component receiving the data, and the server is the component sending the data. So with the north-bound API, the server is the application and the client is the controller. With the south-bound API, the server is the controller and the client is the network device.

 EXAM TIP For the Cisco CCNA exam, be familiar with the north-bound API and the south-bound API.

There are two different types of APIs: *internal APIs* and a *web service APIs*. An internal API is used to share data between applications on a system, while a web service API is used to exchange data between devices across the network or Internet.

Figure 18-1
North-bound
and south-bound
APIs

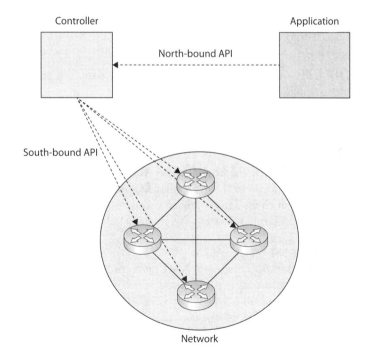

Exchanging Data

In SDN networking, configuration settings need to be exchanged between the applications you use to apply configuration settings to the devices, the SDN controller, and the network devices. In this section you will learn about how that data exchange occurs and the format of the data.

REST-based APIs

One of the most common types of APIs is the *Representational State Transfer* (REST) API. This web-service API is used mostly in the north-bound API. In REST-based APIs, HTTP methods perform create, read, update, and delete (CRUD) actions against the data. For example, the HTTP **GET** verb (aka method) is used to read data, while the HTTP **POST** verb is used to create data. Following are some of the HTTP verbs used by REST APIs:

- **GET** Used to perform a call that *reads* data from the source. For example, the following URL may retrieve details about customer 5:

  ```
  GET http://www.gleneclarke.com/customers/5
  ```

- **PUT** Used to *update* an existing record within the data. For example, the following URL would update customer 2:

  ```
  PUT http://www.gleneclarke.com/customers/2/Glen/Clarke/Halifax
  ```

- **POST** Used to *create* a new record within the data. For example, the following URL would create customer 10:

  ```
  POST http://www.gleneclarke.com/customers/10/Bob/Smith
  ```

- **DELETE** Used to *delete* a record from the data. For example, the following URL would delete customer 10:

  ```
  DELETE http://www.gleneclarke.com/customers/10
  ```

Data Formats

As mentioned earlier in the chapter, the API is the action that is performed on data, but the data needs to be in a format that facilitates it being shared between platforms, applications, and devices. This is where two common data formats, also known as data encoding methods, come into play: XML and JSON.

XML Data Format

The Extensible Markup Language (XML) is a common format for data that needs to be exchanged so that the data is understood at the destination. XML got really popular in the early 2000s and is still used today to exchange data.

XML is easy to read because it uses tags, similar to HTML tags, to describe the data. Looking at the following XML code, you can see that there are multiple books in the data, with the title of the first book being *CompTIA Security+ Certification Study Guide* and the second book being *CompTIA Network+ Certification Study Guide*:

```
<Books>
  <Book ISBN="1260026051">
    <Title>CompTIA Security+ Certification Study Guide</Title>
    <Author>Glen E. Clarke</Author>
    <Price>34.76</Price>
  </Book>
  <Book ISBN="1260122042">
    <Title>CompTIA Network+ Certification Study Guide </Title>
    <Author>Glen E. Clarke</Author>
    <Price>37.26</Price>
  </Book>
</Books>
```

Notice that it is very clear that the author of both books is Glen E. Clarke. The use of the tags ensures that the receiver of the data does not misinterpret the information (in other words, the receiver will not confuse author *Glen E. Clarke* with the titles of the books).

JSON Data Format

XML was the data format for exchanging information between environments for many years, but all of the opening and closing of the tags added to the amount of data that was being transmitted. As mobile applications became popular, a new data format was needed in order to minimize the amount of data being delivered, especially over the cellular phone network: enter JavaScript Object Notation (JSON).

JSON is considered a lightweight data exchange protocol compared to XML. It is now used by many applications and APIs to share data between environments. The following is an example of our book data in the JSON format:

```
{"books":[
    { "isbn":"1260026051",
      "title":"CompTIA Security+ Certification Study Guide",
      "author":"Glen E. Clarke",
      "price":"34.76"},
    { "isbn":"1260122042",
      "title":"CompTIA Network+ Certification Study Guide",
      "author":"Glen E. Clarke",
      "price":"37.26"}
]}
```

Notice a few things about the JSON format—because you do need to know these for the exam: The data is represented in name–value pairs, with the label inside quotation marks, then a colon, and then the value for that data within quotes. Each piece of data is separated by a comma, and each record is in curly brackets, { }. For example, notice that the information about each book is within a set of curly brackets. Also notice that the entire list is inside two sets of brackets: curly brackets and square brackets, {[ ]}. This is because JSON data needs the curly brackets, { }, but because there are multiple books in this listing, an array is used and identified by square brackets, [ ].

 EXAM TIP For the CCNA exam, know the JSON data format.

Configuration Management Technologies

As we talked about SDN environments, I mentioned that applications communicate with SDN controllers, which then send the configuration changes to network devices. These applications are called *configuration management systems*, and they are used to automate the configuration changes to the network devices. The configuration management system uses scripts that you develop to apply configuration changes to multiple devices simultaneously. Once the script is created, you can use the GUI of the configuration management system to schedule a task that runs the script on the devices, or you can manually apply the configuration change to be applied to the devices. Three major players in the configuration management system world that you should remember are Puppet, Chef, and Ansible.

Note that these programs all use the APIs we discussed earlier to communicate the changes that are needed. For example, the configuration management application (Puppet, Chef, or Ansible) uses the north-bound API to send the configuration changes to the controller, and then the controller sends the changes to the device using the south-bound API.

Puppet

Puppet uses a master/agent topology, in which the master is the controller and you install an agent on each network device that you want to manage. Puppet uses a *pull model*, which means that the agent checks with the master (controller) at regular intervals to see if any tasks need to be run. If it finds such tasks, the agent pulls the script (known as a *manifest file*) from the master and runs it on the device. The scripting language that is used with Puppet is Ruby, and the communication channel for the master to talk to the devices is TCP port 8140.

Chef

Chef is similar to Puppet in the sense that it is a master/agent topology as well and also checks for tasks that need to be run. Again, if it finds such tasks, the agent pulls the script of changes (known as a *cookbook* in this example) from the master (controller) and applies the configuration changes. Chef uses Ruby as a scripting language as well, with network communication using TCP port 10002.

Ansible

Ansible is a little different from Puppet and Chef because it is agentless. You do not need to install an agent on the device because Ansible uses a push model, where the master (the controller) pushes the configuration change to the device. Ansible is a Python tool that uses the YAML language to create a *playbook,* which is the file that contains the instructions that need to be executed on the device after it is pushed to the device by the master. It is important to know for the exam that Ansible uses SSH to communicate with the device and apply the configuration, so SSH needs to be configured on the devices.

 EXAM TIP For the CCNA exam, be familiar with the differences between Puppet, Chef, and Ansible. Also remember when the north-bound API is used and when the south-bound API is used.

Chapter Review

In this chapter you learned about network configuration concepts such as traditional network management versus controller-based networking used for automation. You learned about software-defined networking and its architecture. You also learned how SDN separates the control plane from the data plane.

You learned about the Cisco DNA Center and the use of APIs to exchange data between components. You learned about the importance of JSON as a data format, with an example of the JSON data format. And, finally, you learned about configuration management technologies Puppet, Chef, and Ansible.

Quick Review

Introduction to Automation

- Traditional network management involves applying a configuration change to each device one at a time. This is time-consuming and prone to administration errors.

- Controller-based networking involves using automation technologies to send a change to the controller and have it apply the change to all devices simultaneously.

- The control plane is responsible for running routing and features to collect information to populate into tables used by the device.

- The data plane, also known as the forwarding plane, uses the information in tables to make forwarding or routing decisions.

- The management plane handles management access and AAA functions of authentication, authorization, and accounting.

Software-Defined Networking

- In SDN, software is used to apply configuration changes to devices on the network.

- The SDN controller applies the configuration changes to devices on the network.

- There are three components to the SDN architecture: the underlay network, which is the network devices with protocols and features configured such as IP addresses and routing protocols; the overlay network, which is the virtual networks that are created in software; and the SDN fabric, which is all network devices and the SDN controller.

Campus Device Management vs. Cisco DNA Center

- A Cisco DNA Center is an appliance you purchase that contains the SDN controller for your network.

- The north-bound API is used to send the configuration information from the application to the controller.

- The south-bound API is used to send the configuration information from the controller to the device.

Exchanging Data

- The JSON data format is used to exchange information between environments.
- The REST API is the application logic that executes tasks over HTTP.
- The REST API uses HTTP verbs to perform operations.

Questions

The following questions will help you measure your understanding of the material presented in this chapter. Read all the choices carefully because there may be more than one correct answer. Choose the correct answer(s) for each question.

1. Which of the following is a valid format for JSON data?
   A. "empid":"126","name":"Bob Smith","phone":"555-5555"
   B. {"empid":"126","name":"Bob Smith","phone":"555-5555"}
   C. empid: "126",name: "Bob Smith",phone: "555-5555"
   D. {empid: "126",name: "Bob Smith",phone: "555-5555"}

2. What API is used to communicate configuration information between the controller and the network device?
   A. REST API
   B. Web API
   C. South-bound API
   D. North-bound API

3. What component within the software-defined networking architecture contains the virtual networks?
   A. South-bound API
   B. Underlay network
   C. Overlay network
   D. Puppet

4. Which of the following are characteristics of traditional network management? (Choose three.)
   A. The administrator focuses on the device.
   B. The administrator focuses on the network.
   C. The administrator inputs the configuration manually.
   D. The administrator places configuration in policies.
   E. It uses a whitelisting security model.
   F. It uses a blacklisting security model.

5. Which configuration management application uses YAML as the scripting language?

    A. Ansible

    B. Puppet

    C. Chef

    D. Cisco DNA Center

6. Which of the following are characteristics of controller-based networking? (Choose three.)

    A. The administrator focuses on the device.

    B. The administrator focuses on the network.

    C. The administrator inputs the configuration manually.

    D. The administrator places configuration in policies.

    E. It uses a whitelisting security model.

    F. It uses a blacklisting security model.

Performance-based Question

The Cisco exams have performance-based questions in which you must drag a box from the left side of the screen to its proper place on the right side of the screen to answer the questions. The following is a sample performance-based question related to this chapter:

1. Using the following exhibit, write each of the characteristics listed on the left side of the screen into the correct category on the right.

Puppet

Communicates using TCP port 8140

Communicates using SSH

Chef

Communicates using TCP port 10002

Uses Ruby as a language

Stores configuration elements in a manifest file

Ansible

Uses YAML as the configuration language

Answers

1. **B.** Each record within the JSON format is contained within curly brackets, { }. Each label is in quotes, followed by a colon, and followed by the value representing the data in quotes. Therefore, {"empid":"126","name":"Bob Smith","phone":"555-5555"} is correct.

2. **C.** The south-bound API is used to communicate configuration changes between the controller and the network device.

3. **C.** The overlay network contains the virtual network components for the SDN architecture.

4. **A, C, F.** With traditional network management, the administrator is focused on each individual device and connects to each device individually to apply changes manually. Traditional networking also uses a blacklisting model, where everything is allowed, and the administrator must block unwanted traffic.

5. **A.** Ansible uses YAML as the scripting language.

6. **B, D, E.** With controller-based networking, the administrator focuses on the network and making changes throughout the network at one time. This involves placing the configuration change into a policy element, and then applying the policy element to the network devices that need that change. Controller-based networking follows a whitelisting security model, in which everything is blocked until the administrator allows it.

Performance-based Answer

The following are the answers to the performance-based question for this chapter. Remember that on the actual exam, you will need to drag and drop items to place them in their correct locations.

1. The following shows the correct mapping of characteristics for Puppet, Chef, and Ansible.

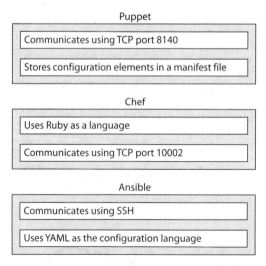

Puppet

Communicates using TCP port 8140

Stores configuration elements in a manifest file

Chef

Uses Ruby as a language

Communicates using TCP port 10002

Ansible

Communicates using SSH

Uses YAML as the configuration language

Exam Readiness Checklists: 100-490 & 200-301

CCT Certification Exam (100-490)

Objective	Ch#
1.0 General Networking Knowledge	**1, 2, 3, 4, 6, 8, 14**
1.1 Use the OSI and TCP/IP models and their associated protocols to explain how data flows in a network	2, 3
1.2 Describe the basic functionality and key differences of this hardware: LAN switch, router, and wireless access points	1
1.3 Differentiate between these Layer 2 technologies: Ethernet, Fast Ethernet, Gigabit Ethernet, Serial, and Optical	1
1.4 Describe LAN cabling	1
1.5 Describe the function of CSU/DSU	1, 6
1.6 Describe Telco termination point	1
1.7 Describe an IPv4 and IPv6 address and subnet	4, 14
1.8 Describe the function of FTP, TFTP, and PING	1, 8
1.9 Describe the function of Telnet and SSH	1, 8
2.0 Cisco Equipment and Related Hardware	**6**
2.1 Identify the Cisco equipment including the Cisco Nexus 9000 Series, Nexus 7000 Series, Nexus 3000 Series, MDS 9000 Series, Catalyst 9000 Series, Catalyst 6800 Series, Catalyst 6500 E-Series, Catalyst 3850, 3650, 2960, 1000 Series and Meraki switches and Cisco 8000 Series, Cisco ASR 9000 Series, Cisco ASR 1000 Series, NCS 5500 Series, NCS 5000 Series routers and Cisco 4000, 1100, 900, 800 Series Integrated Service routers	6
2.2 Identify Cisco products by logo marking and model number (including, but not limited to, locations on chassis, line card, module, or adapter)	6
2.3 Identify Cisco Transceiver Modules	6

CCNA Certification Exam (200-301)

Objective	Ch#
1.0 Network Fundamentals	**1, 3, 4, 5, 9, 14, 15**
1.1 Explain the role and function of network components	1
1.1.a Routers	1
1.1.b L2 and L3 switches	1
1.1.c Next-generation firewalls and IPS	1
1.1.d Access points	1
1.1.e Controllers (Cisco DNA Center and WLC)	1
1.1.f Endpoints	1
1.1.g Servers	1
1.2 Describe characteristics of network topology architectures	1
1.2.a 2 tier	1
1.2.b 3 tier	1
1.2.c Spine-leaf	1
1.2.d WAN	1
1.2.e Small office/home office (SOHO)	1
1.2.f On-premises and cloud	1
1.3 Compare physical interface and cabling types	1
1.3.a Single-mode fiber, multimode fiber, copper	1
1.3.b Connections (Ethernet shared media and point-to-point)	1
1.3.c Concepts of PoE	1
1.4 Identify interface and cable issues (collisions, errors, mismatch duplex, and/or speed)	1
1.5 Compare TCP to UDP	3
1.6 Configure and verify IPv4 addressing and subnetting	4, 5
1.7 Describe the need for private IPv4 addressing	4
1.8 Configure and verify IPv6 addressing and prefix	14
1.9 Compare IPv6 address types	14
1.9.a Global unicast	14
1.9.b Unique local	14
1.9.c Link local	14
1.9.d Anycast	14
1.9.e Multicast	14
1.9.f Modified EUI 64	14

Objective	Ch#
5.0 Security Fundamentals	**15, 16, 17**
5.1 Define key security concepts (threats, vulnerabilities, exploits, and mitigation techniques)	16
5.2 Describe security program elements (user awareness, training, and physical access control)	16
5.3 Configure device access control using local passwords	17
5.4 Describe security password policies elements, such as management, complexity, and password alternatives (multifactor authentication, certificates, and biometrics)	16
5.5 Describe remote access and site-to-site VPNs	16
5.6 Configure and verify access control lists	17
5.7 Configure Layer 2 security features (DHCP snooping, dynamic ARP inspection, and port security)	17
5.8 Differentiate authentication, authorization, and accounting concepts	16
5.9 Describe wireless security protocols (WPA, WPA2, and WPA3)	15
5.10 Configure WLAN using WPA2 PSK using the GUI	15
6.0 Automation and Programmability	**18**
6.1 Explain how automation impacts network management	18
6.2 Compare traditional networks with controller-based networking	18
6.3 Describe controller-based and software-defined architectures (overlay, underlay, and fabric)	18
6.3.a Separation of control plane and data plane	18
6.3.b North-bound and south-bound APIs	18
6.4 Compare traditional campus device management with Cisco DNA Center enabled device management	18
6.5 Describe characteristics of REST-based APIs (CRUD, HTTP verbs, and data encoding)	18
6.6 Recognize the capabilities of configuration management mechanisms Puppet, Chef, and Ansible	18
6.7 Interpret JSON encoded data	18

About the Online Content

This book comes complete with TotalTester Online customizable practice exam software with more than 290 practice exam questions for the CCT and CCNA exams and other book resources including:

- Video training from the author
- Bonus searchable glossary of key terms from the book
- PDF lab book containing all the lab exercises and lab solutions from the book

System Requirements

The current and previous major versions of the following desktop browsers are recommended and supported: Chrome, Microsoft Edge, Firefox, and Safari. These browsers update frequently, and sometimes an update may cause compatibility issues with the TotalTester Online or other content hosted on the Training Hub. If you run into a problem using one of these browsers, please try using another until the problem is resolved.

Your Total Seminars Training Hub Account

To get access to the online content you will need to create an account on the Total Seminars Training Hub. Registration is free, and you will be able to track all your online content using your account. You may also opt in if you wish to receive marketing information from McGraw Hill or Total Seminars, but this is not required for you to gain access to the online content.

Privacy Notice

McGraw Hill values your privacy. Please be sure to read the Privacy Notice available during registration to see how the information you have provided will be used. You may view our Corporate Customer Privacy Policy by visiting the McGraw Hill Privacy Center. Visit the **mheducation.com** site and click **Privacy** at the bottom of the page.

Single User License Terms and Conditions

Online access to the digital content included with this book is governed by the McGraw Hill License Agreement outlined next. By using this digital content you agree to the terms of that license.

Access   To register and activate your Total Seminars Training Hub account, simply follow these easy steps.

1. Go to this URL: **hub.totalsem.com/mheclaim**

2. To register and create a new Training Hub account, enter your e-mail address, name, and password. No further personal information (such as credit card number) is required to create an account.

    If you already have a Total Seminars Training Hub account, enter your e-mail and password on the **Log in** tab. Otherwise, follow the remaining steps.

3. Enter your Product Key: **4wpw-cqpw-p0sq**

4. Click to accept the user license terms.

5. For new users, click the **Register and Claim** button to create your account. For existing users, click the **Log in and Claim** button.

You will be taken to the Training Hub and have access to the content for this book.

Duration of License   Access to your online content through the Total Seminars Training Hub will expire one year from the date the publisher declares the book out of print.

Your purchase of this McGraw Hill product, including its access code, through a retail store is subject to the refund policy of that store.

The Content is a copyrighted work of McGraw Hill, and McGraw Hill reserves all rights in and to the Content. The Work is © 2021 by McGraw Hill.

Restrictions on Transfer   The user is receiving only a limited right to use the Content for the user's own internal and personal use, dependent on purchase and continued ownership of this book. The user may not reproduce, forward, modify, create derivative works based upon, transmit, distribute, disseminate, sell, publish, or sublicense the Content or in any way commingle the Content with other third-party content without McGraw Hill's consent.

Limited Warranty   The McGraw Hill Content is provided on an "as is" basis. Neither McGraw Hill nor its licensors make any guarantees or warranties of any kind, either express or implied, including, but not limited to, implied warranties of merchantability or fitness for a particular purpose or use as to any McGraw Hill Content or the information therein or any warranties as to the accuracy, completeness, correctness, or results to be obtained from, accessing or using the McGraw Hill Content, or any material referenced in such Content or any information entered into licensee's product by users or other persons and/or any material available on or that can be accessed through the licensee's product (including via any hyperlink or otherwise) or as to non-infringement of third-party rights.

Any warranties of any kind, whether express or implied, are disclaimed. Any material or data obtained through use of the McGraw Hill Content is at your own discretion and risk and user understands that it will be solely responsible for any resulting damage to its computer system or loss of data.

Neither McGraw Hill nor its licensors shall be liable to any subscriber or to any user or anyone else for any inaccuracy, delay, interruption in service, error or omission, regardless of cause, or for any damage resulting therefrom.

In no event will McGraw Hill or its licensors be liable for any indirect, special or consequential damages, including but not limited to, lost time, lost money, lost profits or good will, whether in contract, tort, strict liability or otherwise, and whether or not such damages are foreseen or unforeseen with respect to any use of the McGraw Hill Content.

TotalTester Online

TotalTester Online provides you with a simulation of both the CCT and CCNA exams. Exams can be taken in Practice Mode or Exam Mode. Practice Mode provides an assistance window with references to the book, explanations of the correct and incorrect answers, and the option to check your answer as you take the test. Exam Mode provides a simulation of the actual exam. The number of questions, the types of questions, and the time allowed are intended to be an accurate representation of the exam environment. The option to customize your test in Practice Mode allows you to create custom exams from selected exam domains or book chapters, and you can further customize the number of questions and time allowed.

To take a test, follow the instructions provided in the previous section to register and activate your Total Seminars Training Hub account. When you register you will be taken to the Total Seminars Training Hub. From the Training Hub Home page, select **CCT/CCNA All-in-One Exam Guide (100-490 & 200-301) TotalTester** from the Study drop-down menu at the top of the page, or from the list of Your Topics on the Home page. You can then select the option to customize your quiz and begin testing yourself in Practice Mode or Exam Mode. All exams provide an overall grade and a grade broken down by domain.

Other Book Resources

The following sections detail the other resources available with your book. You can access these items by selecting the Resources tab, or by selecting **CCT/CCNA All-in-One Exam Guide (100-490 & 200-301) Resources** from the Study drop-down menu at the top of the page or from the list of Your Topics on the Home page. The menu on the right side of the screen outlines all of the available resources.

Video Training from the Author

Video clips from author Glen E. Clarke provide detailed examples of key certification objectives in audio/video format. You can access these videos by navigating to the Resources tab and selecting Videos. The videos are set up to display in a Web browser and are not available for download.

Downloadable Content

The Resources tab also includes links to view or download additional content that accompanies this book. The downloadable content for this book includes: a bonus glossary and a PDF lab book containing all the labs from the book in addition to a lab solutions PDF.

Glossary

A bonus PDF glossary from the book has been included for your review. You can access the glossary by navigating to the Resources tab and selecting Glossary from the Downloads section of the menu. You can also choose to view the glossary online using the link provided.

Lab Exercises and Solutions

A PDF lab book containing all the lab exercises from the book, and a separate PDF containing all the lab solutions, are provided for download. The corresponding lab files and sample website files for use in the labs have been provided as well. All of the lab content is included under the Downloads section of the menu on the Resources tab. These files can also be viewed online using the link provided.

Technical Support

For questions regarding the TotalTester or operation of the Training Hub, visit **www.totalsem.com** or e-mail **support@totalsem.com**.

For questions regarding book content, visit **www.mheducation.com/customerservice**.

100BaseT An Ethernet architecture using CAT 5 twisted-pair cable to transmit at 100 Mbps, also known as Fast Ethernet. The maximum distance per segment is 100 meters.

1000BaseT An Ethernet architecture using CAT 5e twisted-pair cable to transmit at 1000 Mbps, also known as Gigabit Ethernet. The maximum distance per segment is 100 meters.

802.1Q This IEEE trunking standard that supports two types of frames: tagged and untagged. An untagged frame does not carry any VLAN identification information in it—basically, this is a standard Ethernet frame. 802.1Q tagging modifies the original Ethernet frame. A 4-byte field, called a tag field, is inserted into the middle of the original Ethernet frame header, and the original frame's FCS (checksum) is recomputed in accordance with this change. Tagging is done to help other connected switches keep the frame in the source VLAN.

802.2 IEEE has split the OSI Reference Model's data link layer into two components: Media Access Control (MAC) and Logical Link Control (LLC). The LLC, performed in software, is defined in 802.2 and is responsible for identifying the upper layer protocol that is encapsulated. There are two implementations of LLC: Service Access Point (SAP) and Subnetwork Access Protocol (SNAP). The MAC is performed in hardware. Examples of different types of MAC are 802.3 Ethernet and 802.5 Token Ring.

802.3 This IEEE standard defines how Ethernet is implemented. It is responsible for defining the framing used to transmit information between two network interface cards (NICs). A frame standardizes the fields in the frame and their lengths so that every device understands how to read the contents of the frame. 802.3 has a length field, while Ethernet II has a type field. 802.2 LLC frames are encapsulated in an 802.3 frame before being sent out of an Ethernet interface.

AAA (Authentication Authorization and Accounting) An authentication service that enables users to log on, controls who can log on, and tracks usage of the system.

access control list (ACL) Known for their ability to filter traffic as it either comes into or leaves an interface, ACLs can also be used for other purposes, including the following: to restrict telnet (virtual type terminal [VTY]) access to a router, filter routing information, prioritize WAN traffic with queuing, trigger phone calls with dial-on-demand routing (DDR), and change the administrative distance of routes. An ACL is a list of statements. Cisco's IOS processes ACLs top-down: once a packet's contents matches the condition, the action is executed (permit or deny). If no match is found, the implicit deny rule is enacted.

access layer The bottom layer of Cisco's three-layer hierarchical model. The access layer is at the periphery of your campus network, separated from the core layer by the distribution layer. The main function of the access layer is to provide the user an initial connection to your network. Typically, this connection is provided by a switch.

access-link connection This connection to a device has a standardized Ethernet NIC that understands only standardized Ethernet frames—in other words, a normal NIC that understands IEEE 802.3 and/or Ethernet II frames. Access-link connections can be associated with only one VLAN. It is sometimes referred to as an access port.

access methods These are rules that govern the use of the physical network by various devices. An access method determines how data is submitted on the wire. Two examples of access methods are token passing and carrier-sense multiple access with collision detection (CSMA/CD).

access point Also known as a wireless access point; wireless clients connect to a wired network through the access point.

access rate The speed of the physical connection between your router and the Frame Relay switch (such as a T1).

account A location on a network that stores information regarding access to the network. It contains the information that enables a person to use the network, including username and logon specifications, password, and rights to directories and resources.

account lockout A feature that locks out an account after a certain number of unsuccessful logon attempts (three bad attempts is a common choice). Typically, a locked account can no longer be used until the administrator unlocks it. This helps prevent hackers from breaking into accounts.

acknowledgment (ACK) A packet of information sent from the recipient computer to the sending computer for the purpose of verifying that a transmission has been received. An unsuccessful transmission will generate a negative acknowledgment (NACK).

adapter A card that is inserted into the system to provide functionality, such as a network adapter, which provides connectivity to the network.

address overloading *See* Port Address Translation (PAT).

Address Resolution Protocol (ARP) An Internet layer protocol that helps TCP/IP devices find other devices in the same broadcast domain. ARP uses a local broadcast to discover neighboring devices. Basically, ARP resolves a layer 3 IP address of a destination to the layer 2 MAC address of the destination.

administrative distance A Cisco-proprietary mechanism used to rank the IP routing protocols. It is used as a tie-breaker if a router is learning the same route from two different routing protocols, such as Open Shortest Path First (OSPF) and Enhanced Interior Gateway Routing Protocol (EIGRP).

alternate port   New in Rapid Spanning Tree Protocol (RSTP), an alternate port has an alternative path or paths to the root but is currently in a discarding state. When the root port fails, the switch can speed up convergence by using the alternate port.

American Standard Code for Information Interchange (ASCII)   A representation of standard alphabetic and other keyboard characters in a computer-readable, binary format.

analog modem   A device used to connect to a remote network via a standard public switched telephone network (PSTN) line. Although there are many different types and makes of modems, they can be categorized into three groups: single external, single internal, and multiline rack mounted.

anycast address   This IPv6 address identifies one or more interfaces (not devices), sometimes called nodes. An anycast is a hybrid of a unicast address and a multicast address. With a unicast, one packet is sent to one destination; with a multicast, one packet is sent to all members of the multicast group; and with an anycast, a packet is sent to any one member of a group of devices that are configured with the anycast address. By default, packets sent to an anycast address are forwarded to the closest interface (node), which is based on the routing process employed to get the packet to the destination. Given this process, anycast addresses are commonly referred to as one-to-the-nearest addresses.

application layer   The seventh layer, or topmost layer, of the OSI Reference Model, the application layer provides the interface that a person uses to interact with the application.

application-specific integrated circuit (ASIC)   These specialized processors can do very few tasks but do them extremely well. Processors, on the other hand, can perform many tasks but are not necessarily optimized for these tasks. Many types of networking hardware, including switches, use ASICs.

asynchronous communication   Communication that does not require both the sender and the receiver to be online and participating in the communication at the same time.

Asynchronous Transfer Mode (ATM)   A packet-switching network technology for LANs and WANs that can handle voice, video, and data transmissions simultaneously.

authentication   The process of a user proving her identity to a system so that she can then access a system and its resources. Users are typically authenticated to the network after supplying correct username and password information.

authorization   The process by which the system grants a user access to a resource such as a file or printer. Authorization follows authentication.

Automatic Private IP Address (APIPA)   This IP address has the first two octets of 169.254.x.y and is automatically assigned by the system when a Dynamic Host Control Protocol (DHCP) server cannot be found on the network.

autonomous system (AS)   A group of networks under a single administrative control, which could be your company's network, a division within your company, or a group of companies' networks.

AutoSecure   An IOS feature on newer model routers, such as the Cisco ISR series, that enables you to add a basic security configuration on your router. It is a privileged EXEC script similar to the System Configuration Dialog: where the latter creates a basic configuration for a router, AutoSecure focuses only on security functions for securing a router.

backbone   The main cable that interconnects networks.

backdoor   A method a hacker uses to gain access to an unauthorized system. This backdoor may be available because of a vulnerability in the system or as a result of a previous attack.

backup   The process of saving files to a separate location, usually an offline storage location, such as a different system or the cloud.

backup port   Used in RSTP, a backup port on a segment could be used to leave a segment, even though there is already an active designated port for the segment. When a designated port fails, you can use a switch with a backup port to speed up convergence.

bandwidth   The amount of data that the media can transfer. Bandwidth is usually measured in bits per second (bps).

bandwidth domain   All of the devices on the same layer 2 physical segment are said to be in the same bandwidth domain. The more devices you have on a physical segment, the less bandwidth each device has. You can use routers or switches to create separate bandwidth domains.

baseband transmission   A technique used to transmit encoded signals over cable using digital signaling at the same frequency. *See also* broadband transmission.

Basic Service Set Identifier (BSSID)   This is the wireless network name—commonly known as the SSID. When the network is made up of one access point, it is referred to as the BSSID, but if multiple access points make up the wireless network, it is known as an Extended Service Set Identifier (ESSID).

binary representation   Any value represented with just 0s and 1s.

bits   A basic binary representation of information as a single protocol data unit (PDU). Two bit values—on (1) and off (0)—are used by computers to encode information. Bits are physical layer (layer 1) PDUs.

blocking state   When STP is enabled, ports go into a blocking state under one of three conditions: when a root switch is elected, when a switch receives a Bridge Protocol Data Units (BPDU) on a port that indicates a better path to the root than the port the switch is currently using, and when a port is not a root port or a designated port. A port in a blocking state will remain there for 20 seconds by default. During this state, the only thing the port is doing is listening to and processing BPDUs on its interfaces.

bootstrap program   This program brings the router or switch up and determines how IOS image and configuration files will be found and loaded, based on the configuration register and/or the existence of any **boot** commands in the configuration file.

BPDU Guard   A feature used on ports configured with the PortFast feature. If a PortFast port receives a BPDU, the switch's BPDU Guard feature immediately disables the port. Remember that PortFast is used on non-switch ports to keep them in a forwarding state; the assumption is that a PortFast port is not connected to a switch and therefore shouldn't be receiving BPDUs.

bridge   A device that solves the layer 2 bandwidth and collision problem by performing a switching function in software. A bridge supports only half-duplex connections. It typically supports 2–16 ports and performs store-and-forward switching.

bridge (or switch) ID   Each layer 2 device running STP is assigned a unique identifier, which is also used in the BPDUs that the layer 2 devices advertise. The bridge ID has two components: the bridge's or switch's priority (2 bytes) and the bridge's or switch's MAC address (6 bytes).

Bridge Protocol Data Unit (BPDU)   For STP to function, the switches need to share information with each other. BPDUs are sent out as multicasts every 2 seconds by default, and only other layer 2 devices are listening to this information. Switches use BPDUs to learn the topology of the network, including loops.

broadband transmission   A technique used to transmit encoded signals over differing frequencies using analog signaling. *See also* baseband transmission.

broadcast   A PDU sent to all devices. The destination MAC address denotes all devices on a segment (FFFF.FFFF.FFFF). A destination IP address of 255.255.255.255 represents all devices.

broadcast domain   A group of systems that can receive one another's broadcast messages.

broadcast storm   An issue that occurs when there are so many broadcast packets on the network that the capacity of the network bandwidth approaches or reaches saturation.

bus topology   A network topology that connects all computers to a single shared cable. In a bus topology, if one computer fails, the network fails. *See also* star topology.

cable modem   A network device that connects to a network or the Internet using standard TV coaxial cable.

Carrier Sense Multiple Access/Collision Detection (CSMA/CD)   A media access control method used in an Ethernet environment, where only one NIC can successfully send a frame at a time but all NICs can simultaneously listen to information on the wire. Before an Ethernet NIC puts a frame on the wire, it will first sense the wire to ensure that no other frame is currently on it. The NIC must go through this sensing process because the Ethernet medium supports multiple access—another NIC may already have a frame on the wire. If the NIC doesn't sense a frame on the wire, it will transmit its own frame; if it detects a frame on the wire, the NIC will wait for the completion of the transmission for the frame on the wire and then transmit its own frame. If two or more machines simultaneously sense the wire and see no frame, and both place their frames on the wire, a collision will occur. When a collision occurs, the systems will detect the collision and resend their data at varying intervals.

Challenge Handshake Authentication Protocol (CHAP) An identity verification protocol that uses a three-way handshake process to perform authentication for a Point-to-Point Protocol (PPP) connection. First, the source sends its username (not its password) to the destination. The destination sends back a challenge, which is a random value generated by the destination. Both sides then run the source's username, the matching password, and the challenge through the MD5 hashing function. The source will then send the result of this function to the destination. The destination compares this value to the hashed output that it generated—if the two values match, the password used by the source must be the same password used by the destination, and thus the destination will permit the connection.

channel service unit/data service unit (CSU/DSU) A piece of hardware that sits between a network and a digital telephone line to translate data between the two formats. A CSU/DSU is most commonly used to attach a network router to a T1 or other digital telephone line.

circuit-switched connection Dialup connections that include analog modem and digital Integrated Services Digital Network (ISDN) connections.

classful routing protocols A routing protocol that understands only class subnets. Routing Information Protocol version 1 (RIPv1) and IGRP are examples. A classful protocol does not send subnet mask information in routing updates. RIP and IGRP can have subnet masks other than the default, but the subnet mask used must be the same for all subnets of a class address.

Classless Interdomain Routing (CIDR) An extension to VLSM and route summarization. With VLSM, you can summarize subnets back to the Class A, B, or C network boundary. CIDR takes this one step further and enables you to summarize a block of contiguous Class A, B, and C networks. This is commonly referred to as supernetting, which is supported by today's classless protocols.

classless routing protocol These protocols do not have any issues accepting routing updates with any bit value for a subnet mask and allow nonconforming subnet masks, such as a default route. Classful routing can also accept a default route but requires the configuration of the **ip classless** command. However, this overrides the classful protocols' mechanics. Classless routing protocols include RIPv2, EIGRP, OSPF, IS-IS, and BGP.

coaxial (or coax) cable One of three types of physical media that can be used at the OSI physical layer. In a coaxial, one strand (a solid-core wire) runs down the middle of the cable, surrounded round by insulation. There are two different types of commonly used Ethernet coaxial cables: thickwire and thinwire. *See also* twisted pair cable and fiber optic cable.

collision domain A segmented group of networked systems in which simultaneous data transmissions can collide with one another.

command line A character-mode interface for computer applications that relies on commands instead of a graphical interface to process information.

committed burst rate (B$_c$)   The average data rate (over a smaller period of fixed time than CIR, defined next) that a provider guarantees for a Frame Relay VC; in other words, the data rate is for a smaller time period yet yields a higher average data rate than CIR. This allows for small bursts in data streams.

committed information rate (CIR)   The average data rate, measured over a fixed period of time, which the carrier guarantees for a Frame Relay VC.

Common Spanning Tree (CST)   A single instance of a spanning tree protocol (STP) running for an entire switched network (all VLANs).

computer virus   A computer program built to sabotage or destroy a computer or network.

configuration register   A four-digit hexadecimal value used by the bootstrap program to determine from where the IOS image and configuration file should be loaded. Once the IOS device is booted up, you can view the configuration register value with the **show version** command.

connected route   The interface route through which a router will connect to a subnet or network. A router will look at its active interfaces, examine the addresses configured on the interface and determine the corresponding network number, and populate the routing table with the routes and interfaces. These interface routes are referred to as connected routes, since the router is directly connected to the subnet or network.

connection-oriented communication   A form of communication that ensures reliable delivery of data from the sender to the receiver, without intervention required by either. Error correction and flow control are provided at various points from the source to the destination.

connectionless communication   A form of communication in which the destination computer does not notify the source when the information is received. This can be unreliable because there is no notification to guarantee delivery. Connectionless communication can be faster than connection-oriented communication, because there is no overhead in the initial setup of the dialog, like with connection-oriented communication, and no overhead of notifying the sender that the information was received.

content-addressable memory (CAM) table   An old bridging term, also referred to as a port or MAC address table, that describes the table that holds the MAC addresses of devices and the ports to which they are connected. The layer 2 device uses this table to make switching decisions.

core layer   The backbone of the network that provides a very high-speed connection between the different distribution layer devices. Because of the need for high-speed connections, the core consists of high-speed switches and will not, typically, perform any type of packet or frame manipulations, such as filtering or quality of service. Because switches are used at the core, the core is referred to as a layer 2 core. The traffic that traverses the core is typically intended to access enterprise corporate resources, such as the Internet, gateways, e-mail servers, and corporate applications.

counting to infinity   A problem with a routing loop. When a routing loop occurs and a packet or packets are caught in the loop, they continuously circle around the loop, wasting bandwidth on the segments and wasting CPU cycles on the routers that are processing the packets. To prevent packets from circling around the loop forever, distance vector protocols typically place a hop count limit on how far a packet is legally allowed to travel.

crossover cable   An Ethernet cable that crosses over two sets of wires: pin 1 on one side is connected to pin 3 on the other side, and pin 2 is connected to pin 6. Crossover cables should be used when connecting a data terminal equipment (DTE) device to another DTE or a data communications equipment (DCE) device to another DCE. Use a crossover cable to connect a hub to another hub, a switch to another switch, a hub to a switch, or a PC, router, or file server to another PC, router, or file server.

customer premises equipment (CPE)   Your network's equipment, which includes the DCE (modem, NT1, CSU/DSU) and DTE (router, access server). This equipment is located onsite and connects to the carrier's WAN.

cut-through switching   A process by which a switch reads only the very first part of the frame before making a switching decision. Once the switch device reads the destination MAC address, it begins forwarding the frame (even though the frame may still be coming into the interface).

data communications equipment (DCE)   A device that terminates a physical connection and provides clocking and synchronization of a connection between two sites. It connects to a DTE device. DCEs include such equipment as CSU/DSUs, NT1s, and modems.

data link layer   The second layer in the OSI Reference Model, the data link layer provides for physical, or hardware, addresses, commonly called Media Access Control (MAC) addresses. The data link layer also defines how a networking device accesses the media to which it is connected by defining the media's frame type. This includes the fields and components of the data link layer, or layer 2, frame.

data terminal equipment (DTE)   An end-user device, such as a router or PC, which connects to the WAN via the DCE.

datagram   *See* packet.

default gateway   A router that knows how to get the local broadcast domain's traffic to remote destinations. If devices on a segment want to reach devices in a different broadcast domain—that is, a different network—they must know to which default gateway to forward their traffic.

default route   A special type of static route. Whereas a static route specifies a path a router should use to reach a specific destination, a default route specifies a path the router should use if it doesn't know how to reach a destination.

demarcation point   The point at which the responsibility of the WAN carrier is passed on to you; it could be inside or outside your local facility. Note that this is a logical boundary and not necessarily a physical boundary.

demilitarized zone (DMZ)   An area between the Internet and a private LAN that can be used to place servers that are available to the Internet. Servers such as web servers, FTP servers, e-mail servers, and DNS servers are typically placed in a DMZ.

denial of service (DoS)   A form of attack that causes a system to crash or become unresponsive.

designated port   With STP, each segment can have only one port on a single layer 2 device in a forwarding state, called a designated port. The layer 2 device with the best accumulated path cost will use its connected port to the segment as the designated port.

designated router (DR)   An OSPF router will not form adjacencies to just any router. Instead, a client/server design is implemented in OSPF. For each network multi-access segment, there is a DR and a backup designated router (BDR) as well as other routers. As an example, if you have ten VLANs in your switched area, you'll have ten DRs and ten BDRs. The one exception of a segment not having these two routers is on a WAN point-to-point link. When an OSPF router comes up, it forms adjacencies with the DR and the BDR on each multi-access segment to which it is connected. Any exchange of routing information is between these DR/BDR routers and the other OSPF neighbors on a segment (and vice versa). An OSPF router talks to a DR using the IP multicast address of 224.0.0.6. The DR and the BDR talk to all routers using the 224.0.0.5 multicast IP address.

DHCP relay   In larger networks, networking devices that need addresses via DHCP and the DHCP servers are typically not in the same subnet (broadcast domain). The solution to this problem is to use an IOS feature called DHCP relay, where an IOS routing device acts as a relay agent with the DHCP REQUEST message. When the router receives the broadcasted addressing request from the client, it changes it to a unicast message, with the router as the source and the DHCP server as the destination. The agent includes the network number to help the DHCP server choose the correct addressing pool. All messages between the agent and the DHCP server are delivered using unicast. The client thinks it's communicating locally with the DHCP server.

directed broadcast address   If all the host bits in an IP network number are set to 1s, which means this address is the very last, it is the directed broadcast address. This address represents all the hosts on the segment and can be routed by a router.

discard eligibility (DE)   The DE bit is used to mark a Frame Relay frame as a low-priority frame. You can do this manually, or the carrier will do this for a frame that is nonconforming to your traffic contract (exceeding CIR/Bc values).

distance vector routing protocols   These protocols use the distance (metric) and direction (vector) to find paths to destinations. Sometimes this is referred to as routing by rumor, since the routers learn routing information via broadcasts from directly connected neighbors, and these neighbors may have learned these networks from other neighboring routers. Some examples of IP distance vector routing protocols are RIPv1 and IGRP.

distribution layer   As opposed to the core and access layers, the distribution layer performs most of the connectivity tasks. Typically routers are used at the distribution layer to connect the access layers to the core. The responsibilities of this layer include the following: containing broadcasts, securing traffic, providing a hierarchy through layer 3 logical addressing and route summarization, and translating between media types.

Domain Name System (DNS)   A database that maps Internet domain names to IP addresses. DNS is a TCP/IP application that other applications, such as FTP, telnet, web browsers, and e-mail, use to resolve the names a user enters to real IP addresses.

dotted decimal   A format of an IP address that is converted to make it understandable to people. IPv4 addresses are 32 bits in length. To make the addresses readable, they are broken into 4 bytes (called octets), with a period (decimal) between each byte. So that the address is understandable to humans, the four sets of binary numbers are then converted to decimal.

dual stacking   Devices such as PCs and routers run both IPv4 and IPv6, and thus have two sets of addresses, called dual stacking.

duplex   The method of transmitting and receiving frames. With a *half-duplex* configuration, an interface can either send or receive frames—it can't do both simultaneously. Half-duplex connections are used in shared environments such as when a hub was used on the network. With a *full-duplex* configuration, an interface can both send and receive simultaneously. Full-duplex connections are used when a device is connected to a switch.

Dynamic Host Configuration Protocol (DHCP)   This protocol enables devices to acquire their IP addressing information dynamically. It is built on a client/server model and defines two components: a server (delivering host configuration information) and a client (requesting and acquiring host configuration information).

dynamic routing protocols   These protocols advertise the routes they are familiar with and pass on the metrics, the number of other routers, or the number of hops required to get from their host to another network, either directly or indirectly through another router.

Dynamic Trunk Protocol (DTP)   A protocol used to form and verify a trunk connection dynamically between two Cisco switches. DTP is Cisco-proprietary and is supported on both 802.1Q and ISL trunks.

Easy VPN   A Cisco design feature that makes it easy to deploy a VPN, scale it to a large number of users, and centralize policy configurations for remote access. The Easy VPN Server centralizes the policy configurations for the Easy VPN Remotes and provides access to corporate resources. The Easy VPN Remote enables the user or users to access corporate resources securely via the Easy VPN Server. Very little configuration is required on Easy VPN Remote to bring up a tunnel—another reason the term "easy" is used to describe this solution.

encryption   An algorithm that hides the contents of a message, or other file or communication, by deliberately scrambling the elements that compose the item. The item must then be decrypted to its original form before it can be read.

Enhanced IGRP (EIGRP)   A Cisco-proprietary routing protocol based on IGRP that includes many built-in enhancements. Because it has its roots in IGRP, the configuration is similar; however, it has many added link state characteristics that enable EIGRP to scale to enterprise network sizes. These characteristics include fast convergence, loop-free topology, Variable Length Subnet Masking (VLSM) and route summarization, multicast and incremental updates, and routing for multiple routed protocols (IP, Internetwork Packet Exchange [IPX], and AppleTalk). EIGRP is a hybrid protocol.

EtherChannel   A layer 2 solution that enables you to aggregate multiple layer 2 Ethernet-based connections between directly connected devices. Basically, an EtherChannel bundles together multiple Ethernet ports between devices, providing what appears to be a single logical interface. STP views the EtherChannel as a single logical connection between the connected devices, which means that you can actually use all of the individual connections, simultaneously, in the channel you've created.

Ethernet   A LAN media type that functions at the data link layer. Ethernet uses the Carrier Sense Multiple Access/Collision Detection (CSMA/CD) mechanism to send information in a shared environment. Ethernet was initially developed with the idea that many devices would be connected to the same physical piece of wiring.

extended access control list   An ACL that can match on all of the following information: source and destination IP addresses, IP protocol (IP, TCP, UDP, ICMP, and so on), and protocol information, such as port numbers for TCP and UDP or message types for ICMP.

Extended Service Set Identifier (ESSID)   Multiple access points used to create a single wireless network with the same name. The SSID in this case is known as an ESSID.

Exterior Gateway Protocol (EGP)   A protocol that handles routing between different autonomous systems. Today, only one EGP is active: the Border Gateway Protocol (BGP). BGP is used to route traffic across the Internet backbone between different autonomous systems.

extranet   An extended intranet, in which certain internal services are made available to known external users or business partners at remote locations. The connections that are used by these external users and the internal services are typically secured via a firewall and VPN.

fiber optic cable   Fiber optic cable is a form of network cabling that uses a glass core to carry pulses of light. Fiber optic cabling is able to reach distances over 10 KM.

File Transfer Protocol (FTP)   A protocol designed primarily for transferring data across a network. FTP denotes both a protocol and a utility used for this purpose. It was created to transfer data files quickly and efficiently from one host to another without affecting the remote host's resources.

firewall   Software or hardware that prevents unauthorized traffic between two networks by examining the packets that travel on both networks. A firewall looks at the address and port information in the packet and then determines whether that type of traffic is allowed.

forwarding state   In STP, ports that are in a learning state after the forward delay timer expires are placed in a forwarding state. In a forwarding state, the port will process BPDUs, update its content addressable memory (CAM) table with frames that it receives, and forward user traffic through the port. Only root and designated ports will end up in a forwarding state.

fragment-free switching   A modified form of cut-through switching. Where cut-through switching reads up to the destination MAC address field in the frame before making a switching decision, fragment-free switching makes sure that the frame is at least 64 bytes long.

frame   A PDU used at the data link layer. With IEEE, two PDUs are used: one for LLC (802.2) and one for MAC (802.2 or 802.5).

full-duplex   A type of communication that enables data to flow in both directions simultaneously.

fully qualified domain name (FQDN)   An Internet-style name used to refer to a system or device, such as *www.gleneclarke.com*.

Gateway Load Balancing Protocol (GLBP)   A Cisco-proprietary protocol that is similar to Cisco's Hot Standby Router Protocol (HSRP). One of the limitations of HSRP and Virtual Router Redundancy Protocol (VRRP) is that only one router in the HSRP group is active and can forward traffic for the group—the rest of the routers sit idle. This is not an efficient process, because one or more routing devices are not processing any traffic, and it does not take advantage of the bandwidth of the connections that these other routing devices are connected to. Cisco designed GLBP to rectify this issue. GLBP enables the dynamic assignment of a group of virtual addresses to end stations. With GLBP, up to four routing devices in the group can participate in the forwarding of traffic. Plus, if a GLBP routing device fails, fault detection occurs automatically and another GLBP routing device picks up the forwarding of packets for the failed routing device.

Generic Route Encapsulation (GRE) tunnel   This point-to-point tunnel is a logical connection between two routers that is used to carry all types of IP and non-IP traffic. GRE tunnels are commonly used with IPsec site-to-site VPN solutions to provide for scalability and flexibility. Originally developed by Cisco and then standardized in RFCs 1701 and 1702, GRE provides a logical connection (subnet) between two routers across either a private or a public network. To provide the logical connection between devices, Cisco IOS uses a logical tunnel interface. When "tunneling" packets, information is added to the original data (either a packet or frame) to indicate that GRE is being used and the destination GRE device to forward it to. Cisco supports the encapsulation of either layer 3 packets (such as IPv4 or IPv6, IPX, and so on) or layer 2 frames (bridging traffic).

gigabit network   A network that operates at 1000 Mbps, or 1 gigabit per second (Gbps).

gratuitous ARP   An ARP reply that is generated without a corresponding ARP request. This is commonly used when a device may change its IP address or MAC address and wants to notify all other devices on the segment about the change so that the other devices have the correct information in their local ARP tables.

half-duplex   Used by the OSI session layer to enable data to flow in two directions, but in only one direction at a time. With half-duplex dialogs, replies and acknowledgments are possible.

handshaking   Connection-oriented services must ensure that data is sent reliably across the network. Handshaking takes place at the beginning of a communication session, when the two computers determine the rules for communication, such as transmission speed and which ports to use. Handshaking also determines the proper way to terminate the session when finished to ensure that communication ends in an orderly manner.

hardware address   *See* Media Access Control (MAC) address.

hierarchical addressing   Used to set up a network so that routing information can be summarized. IP addresses are laid out such that as you go up each layer in the hierarchy, routes can be summarized into a smaller set of routes.

high availability (HA)   Refers to an environment that can withstand components failing, because duplicate components are available in case any components fail.

High-Level Data Link Control (HDLC)   This protocol is based on ISO standards. It can be used with synchronous and asynchronous connections and defines the frame type and interaction between two devices at the data link layer. Cisco's implementation of HDLC is based on ISO standards, but Cisco has made a change in the frame format, making it proprietary. In other words, Cisco's HDLC will work only if the remote end also supports Cisco's protocol. HDLC is the default encapsulation on synchronous serial interfaces on a Cisco router.

host   A system or device that participates on the network.

host ID   The portion of the 32-bit address that identifies the device on a TCP/IP network.

HMAC function   Hashed message authentication code functions are commonly used to validate that a packet is coming from a trusted source and that the packet hasn't been tampered with. The source runs information from the packet being sent, along with the symmetric key, through the HMAC function, creating a digital signature. The signature is then added to the original packet and sent to the destination. The destination repeats the process: it considers the original packet input along with the same symmetric key and should be able to generate the same signature that was sent in the packet. If the signature generated is the same, that means the packet came from someone who knows the symmetric key and the packet hasn't been tampered with; if the computed signature is not the same, the packet is dropped, since the signature in it is a fake or the packet was tampered with between the source and destination.

hold-down timer   This mechanism is used to give routers running a distance vector protocol enough time to propagate a poisoned route and to ensure that no routing loops occur while propagation is occurring. During this period, the routers will freeze the poisoned route in their routing tables for the period of the hold-down timer, which is typically three times the interval of the routing broadcast update.

Hot Standby Routing Protocol (HSRP)   This Cisco-proprietary protocol provides a single definition of a default gateway on the end station and layer 3 redundancy. With HSRP, a group of routing devices represents a single virtual default gateway that has a virtual IP address and a virtual MAC address. If the primary routing device fails, another routing device in the HSRP group takes over and processes the frames sent by the end stations to the virtual MAC address. An advantage of HSRP groups is that different subnets (VLANs) can have different default gateways, thus providing load balancing. Also, within each HSRP group, there is a primary default gateway and the capability to use multiple routers to perform a backup function.

hub   A physical layer device that provides a logical bus structure for Ethernet. A hub will replicate a physical layer signal from one interface to all of its other interfaces.

hybrid routing protocol   A protocol that merges advantages of both distance vector and link state routing protocols into a new protocol. Typically, hybrid routing protocols are based on a distance vector protocol but contain many of the features and advantages of link state protocols. Examples of hybrid routing protocols include RIPv2 and EIGRP.

Hypertext Transfer Protocol (HTTP)   The unsecure protocol used on the Internet or an intranet to deliver web pages from the web server to the client using a web browser.

Hypertext Transfer Protocol Secure (HTTPS)   The secure version of HTTP that delivers web pages in an encrypted format to the client using a web browser.

implicit deny   With an ACL, if the router compares a packet to every statement in the list and does not find a match against the packet contents, the router will drop the packet, based on the invisible implicit deny statement at the end of every ACL.

inside global IP address   An IP address in an inside network that has an associated public IP address.

inside local IP address   An IP address in an inside network that has an associated private IP address.

Interior Gateway Protocol (IGP)   A routing protocol that handles routing within a single autonomous system. IGPs include RIP, IGRP, EIGRP, OSPF, and IS-IS.

Internet   The global network that enables specific internal resources in your network to be accessed by unknown external users via a web browser. For example, your company may enable external users to access its web site to purchase products via the Internet.

Internet Control Message Protocol (ICMP)   A protocol used to send error and control information between TCP/IP devices. Defined in RFC 792, it includes many different messages that devices can generate or respond to.

Internet layer   A TCP/IP protocol stack layer that equates to the network layer (layer 3) of the OSI Reference Model.

Internet Protocol (IP)   A common protocol that sets up the mechanism for transferring data across a network. IP provides packet delivery for all other protocols within the TCP/IP suite.

Internet Protocol (IP) address   A unique numeric label that identifies a computer on the network. It is 32 bits long, with four octets separated by dots. This number is converted to binary and used as a unique identifier.

Internetwork Operating System (IOS)   A Cisco proprietary operating system that provides a function similar to that of Microsoft Windows XP or Linux: it controls and manages the hardware on which it is running. Basically, IOS provides the interface between you and the hardware, enabling you to execute commands to configure and manage your Cisco device.

intranet   A network that is local to a company. In other words, users from within a company can find internal resources and information without having to access a network outside the company, such as the Internet.

Inverse ARP   A protocol that enables you to discover the layer 3 protocol address at the other end of a Frame Relay virtual circuit (VC). It is similar to Reverse ARP in TCP/IP.

IP Security (IPsec)   An open standard defined across quite a few different RFCs. IPsec functions at the network layer and protects IP packets. IPsec can be used for LAN-to-LAN (L2L) VPNs as well as remote access. Compared to all other VPNs, IPsec is the most secure commercial solution today and the most widely used, but it's also the most difficult to set up and troubleshoot.

IPv6-over-IPv4 (6to4) tunneling   A process by which IPv6 packets are tunneled across an IPv4 network by encapsulating them in IPv4 packets. This requires routers configured with dual stacking.

learning state   In STP, from a listening state, a port moves into a learning state. During the learning state, the port is still listening for and processing BPDUs on the port; however, it differs from the listening state in that the port begins to process user frames: The switch examines the source addresses in the frames and updates its CAM table, but the switch is still not forwarding these frames out destination ports. Ports stay in this state for the length of the forward delay time (which defaults to 15 seconds).

leased line   A dedicated circuit or point-to-point connection in a WAN.

light-emitting diode (LED)   Cisco uses these semiconductor diodes that light up to show the status of various physical components of its products. For instance, LEDs are commonly used to display the status of an interface. In Cisco's equipment, LEDs can change to various colors, such as green, amber or orange, red, or off, to indicate various states.

Link Control Protocol (LCP)   A protocol whose primary responsibility is to establish, configure, authenticate, and test a PPP connection. Some of the things that LCP will negotiate when setting up a PPP connection include the authentication method used (PAP or CHAP), the compression algorithm used, the callback phone number to use, and multilink.

link-local address   IPv6 link-local addresses have a smaller scope than site-local addresses as to how far they can travel: just the local link (the data link layer). Routers will process packets destined to a link-local address, but they will not forward them to other links. Their most common use is for a device to acquire unicast site-local or global unicast addressing information, enabling the device to discover the default gateway and to discover other layer 2 neighbors on the segment.

link state advertisement (LSA)   OSPF routers use LSAs to communicate with each other. One type of LSA is a hello, which is used to form neighbor relationships and as a keepalive function. Hellos are generated every 10 seconds. When sharing link information (directly connected routes), links are sent to the designated router (DR, at 224.0.0.6), and the DR disseminates this to other routers (224.0.0.5) on the segment.

link state protocols   These protocols use the Shortest Path First (SPF) algorithm, invented by Dijkstra, to find the best layer 3 path to a destination. Whereas distance vector protocols rely on rumors from other neighbors about remote routes, link state protocols will learn the complete topology of the network: which routers are connected to which networks. OSPF is an example of a link state protocol.

listening state   After the 20-second blocking timer expires, a root or designated port in STP will move to a listening state. Any other port will remain in a blocking state. During the listening state, the port is still listening for BPDUs and double-checking the layer 2 topology. The only traffic that is being processed in this state consists of BPDUs—all other traffic is dropped. A port will stay in this state for the length of the forward delay timer. The default for this value is 15 seconds.

local area network (LAN)   A network used to connect networking devices that are all located within a very close geographic area, such as a floor of a building, a building itself, or a campus environment.

local loop   The connection from the carrier's switch to the demarcation point in a WAN connection.

local management interface (LMI)   A mechanism that defines how the Frame Relay DTE, such as a router, interacts with the Frame Relay DCE, such as a switch. LMI is local and is not sent to the destination DTE.

logical address   The network layer is responsible for the logical address scheme. All layer 3 addressing schemes have two components: network and host (or node). Each segment (physical or logical) in your network needs a unique network number. Each host on these segments needs a unique host number from within the assigned network number. The combination of the network and host numbers assigned to a device provides a unique layer 3 address throughout the entire network.

Logical Link Control (LLC)   *See* 802.2.

logical topology   Describes how devices communicate with each other across the physical topology.

loopback address   Any address that starts with 127.x.x.x in IPv4 or the address of ::1 in IPv6. The loopback address is used to test and verify that the TCP/IP software stack has been loaded and is functional on the system.

loopback interface   A logical, virtual interface on a router. These interfaces are treated as physical interfaces on a router: you can assign addressing information to them, include their network numbers in routing updates, and even terminate IP connections on them, such as telnet and SSH. Loopback interfaces are commonly used for assigning a router ID to an OSPF router, for testing purposes, and for terminating tunnel connections such as GRE and IPsec.

Media Access Control (MAC) address   The data link layer uses MAC, or hardware, addresses for communication. For LAN communications, each machine on the same connected media type needs a unique MAC address. A MAC address is 48 bits in length and is represented as a 12-digit hexadecimal number. To make it easier to read, the MAC address is represented in a dotted-hexadecimal format, like this: FF:FF:FF:FF:FF:FF.

metric   A routing protocol will use a measurement called a metric to determine which path is the best path. Examples of metrics include hop count, cost, bandwidth, and delay.

multicast frame   With a multicast frame, the destination MAC address denotes a group of devices, which could include no device, some devices, or all devices.

Nagle   An algorithm that handles TCP congestion by enabling multiple characters to be sent in the same TCP segment instead of different segments, like telnet. This is useful for devices running at high CPU utilization to allow for remote CLI access to still be responsive.

native VLAN   802.1Q trunks support two types of frames: tagged and untagged. An untagged frame does not carry any VLAN identification information in it—basically, this is a standard, unaltered Ethernet frame. The VLAN that supports untagged frames is the native VLAN.

NetFlow   A Cisco-proprietary technology that classifies and identifies traffic, and provides statistics for the traffic. Originally it was meant for QoS and traffic management purposes, but it can be used to detect attacks by looking for anomalies in traffic sessions. Common uses for NetFlow include network traffic accounting, usage-based network billing, network capacity and planning, security, denial of service (DoS) monitoring capabilities, and network monitoring and troubleshooting. NetFlow is like a telephone bill, where you can see who (source) is connecting to whom (destination), what application and/or protocol they're using, how long the connection lasted, how much information was transmitted across the connection (source versus destination), and much, much more.

network   All of the components (hardware and software) involved in connecting computers across small and large distances. Networks are used to provide easier access to information, thus increasing productivity for users.

Network Address Translation (NAT)   A technique that translates one IP address to another, typically private to public and vice versa.

Network Control Protocol (NCP) A protocol that defines the process for how two PPP peers will negotiate the network layer protocols, such as IP and IPX, which will be used across the PPP connection.

network layer The third layer of the OSI Reference Model, the network layer provides for a logical topology of your network using logical, or layer 3, addresses.

Network Time Protocol (NTP) An open standard that enables you to periodically synchronize your device's time with a centralized time server for the current date and time. NTP uses UDP on port 123. The reliability of the server refers to its stratum level of clock source. The most accurate is an atomic clock, but most networks typically don't need that kind of precision and instead obtain time from a GPS source. NTP has three basic methods of delivering time messages between the time server and the NTP client: unicast, broadcast, and multicast.

non-broadcast multi-access (NBMA) A term used to describe WAN networks that use VCs for connectivity. With WAN networks that use VCs, each device is connected to another device via a point-to-point VC—only two devices can be connected to a VC. This poses a problem with partially meshed NBMA environments where devices are located in the same subnet.

nonvolatile RAM (NVRAM) A form of persistent RAM: when the device is turned off, the contents of NVRAM are preserved. This is where the IOS startup-config file is stored.

Open Shortest Path First (OSPF) A link state protocol that handles routing for IP traffic. It uses the SPF algorithm, developed by Dijkstra, to provide a loop-free topology. It also provides fast convergence with triggered, incremental updates via link state advertisements (LSAs). OSPF is a classless protocol and allows for a hierarchical design with VLSM and route summarization. It uses cost as a metric.

Open Systems Interconnection (OSI) Reference Model The International Organization for Standardization (ISO), an international standards body, developed the OSI Reference Model to help describe how information is transferred from one machine to another: from the time at which a user enters information using a keyboard and mouse to its conversion to electrical or light signals to be transferred across an external medium. It is important to understand that the OSI Reference Model describes concepts and terms in a general manner, and that not every network protocol will fit nicely into the scheme explained in ISO's model (IP and IPX, for example, do not). Therefore, the OSI Reference Model is most often used as a teaching and troubleshooting tool.

outside global IP address An outside device with a registered public IP address.

oversubscription When you add up all of the committed information rates (CIRs) of your VCs on an interface and they exceed the access rate of the interface, the result is oversubscription; you are betting that all of your VCs will not run, simultaneously, at their traffic-contracted rates.

packet   A PDU used at the network layer. It is also referred to as a datagram in the TCP/IP protocol stack.

packet-switched connection   A connection, such as Frame Relay and X.25, that uses virtual circuits across the carrier's network to provide for WAN connections.

path cost   In STP, the accumulated port costs from a switch to the root switch path. When a BPDU comes into a port, the path cost value in the BPDU is incremented by the port cost of the incoming port. This value is incremented from layer 2–to–layer 2 device. The path cost value helps the layer 2 device determine which ports should be root and designated ports.

Per-VLAN Spanning Tree Protocol (PVST)   A protocol in which each VLAN has its own instance of STP, with its own root switch, its own set of priorities, and its own set of BPDUs. Based on this information, each VLAN will develop its own loop-free topology.

permanent virtual circuit (PVC)   A virtual connection similar to a leased line. PVCs must be manually configured on each router and built on the carrier's switches before you can send any data. One disadvantage of PVCs is that they require a lot of manual configuration up front to establish the VC. Another disadvantage is that they aren't very flexible: if the PVC fails, there is no dynamic rebuilding of the PVC around the failure. However, once you have a PVC configured, it will always be available, barring any failures between the source and destination.

physical layer   The first, or bottommost, layer of the OSI Reference Model. The physical layer is responsible for the physical mechanics of a network connection, which includes the following: type of interface used on the networking device, type of cable used for connecting devices, the connectors used on each end of the cable, and the pinouts used for each of the connections on the cable.

physical topology   Describes how devices are physically cabled together.

Point-to-Point Protocol (PPP)   A protocol based on a set of WAN standards. PPP performs the dynamic configuration of links, allows for authentication, compresses packet headers, tests the quality of links, performs error detection, multiplexes network layer protocols across the same link, and enables multiple PPP physical connections to be bound together as a single logical connection. PPP works with asynchronous and synchronous serial interfaces as well as High-Speed Serial Interfaces (HSSIs) and ISDN interfaces (BRI and PRI).

point-to-point topology   A topology with a single connection between two devices, in which two devices can directly communicate with each other without interference from other devices.

poison reverse   When a router advertises a poisoned route to its neighbors, its neighbors break the rule of split horizon and send back to the originator the same poisoned route, called a poison reverse. This ensures that everyone received the original update of the poisoned route. This process is used by distance vector protocols to prevent routing loops.

poisoned route   A derivative of split horizon. When a router detects that one of its connected routes has failed, the router will poison the route by assigning an infinite metric to it. It is used by distance vector protocols to prevent routing loops.

port address redirection (PAR)   Static Port Address Translation (PAT) is often called port address redirection. An address translation device configured with PAR will take a packet headed for a certain destination address and port number and redirect it to another destination address and a possibly different port number. This differs from NAT, which does only a one-to-one IP address translation.

port address table   *See* content-addressable memory (CAM) table.

Port Address Translation (PAT)   A process by which inside IP addresses are translated to a single IP address, where each inside address is given a different port number for uniqueness.

port cost   In STP, each port is assigned a cost that is inversely proportional to the bandwidth of the interface. The lower the port cost, the more preferred it is. When a BPDU comes into a port, the path cost value in the BPDU is incremented by the port cost of the incoming port. This helps the layer 2 device figure out which ports should be root and designated ports.

port security   A switch feature that enables you to lock down switch ports based on the MAC address or addresses associated with the interface, preventing unauthorized access to a LAN.

PortFast   A feature that enables a port to be always placed in a forwarding state—this is true even when STP is running and the root and designated ports are going through their different states. So, when STP is running, PortFast ports on the same switch can still forward traffic among themselves, somewhat limiting your STP disruption. PortFast should be configured only on ports not connected to other switches, such as ports that have PCs, servers, and routers connected to them.

power-on self test (POST)   A process that performs hardware tests when a Cisco device is booting up. These tests can include interfaces, lines, and memory components. For many components, if a failure occurs, the Cisco device will fail to boot up.

PPP Authentication Protocol (PAP)   The simplest, but least secure, of PPP's authentication protocols. During the authentication phase, PAP will go through a two-way handshake process. In this process, the source sends its username and password, in clear text, to the destination. The destination compares this information with a list of locally stored usernames and passwords. If it finds a match, the destination sends back an accept message. If it doesn't find a match, it sends back a reject message.

presentation layer   The sixth layer of the OSI Reference Model, which is responsible for defining how information, such as text, graphics, video, and/or audio information, is presented to the user in the interface being used.

private IP address RFC 1918 is a document that was created to address the shortage of IP addresses. When devices want to communicate with each other, each device needs a unique address. RFC 1918 created a private address space that any company can use internally. These addresses include 10.0.0.0/8, 172.16.0.0/16–172.31.0.0/16, and 192.168.0.0/24–192.168.255.0/24. Private IP addresses are non–Internet routable. You must use address translation to translate a private address to a public one if you want to communicate with devices on a public network, such as the Internet.

privileged EXEC mode An access level for Cisco devices that provides high-level management access to IOS, including all commands available at user EXEC mode. This mode enables detailed troubleshooting and is also a stepping-stone to configuration mode. If you see a # character at the end of the prompt information, you know that you are working in privileged EXEC mode.

protocol A system that defines the rules to be used in a technology. Some protocols are open standard, meaning that many vendors may use the protocol, while others are proprietary, meaning that they work only with one particular vendor. For example, common protocols used to implement e-mail functionality in a system include Simple Mail Transfer Protocol (SMTP), Internet Message Access Protocol version 4 (IMAP4), and Post Office Protocol 3 (POP3).

protocol data unit (PDU) A term generically used to describe data and its overhead, including items such as segments, packets, and frames.

proxy ARP A form of ARP that enables a router to respond with its own MAC address in an ARP reply for a device on a different network segment. Proxy ARP is used when you need to move a device from one segment to another but cannot change its current IP addressing information.

RADIUS (Remote Authentication Dial-In User Service) A central authentication service that can be used to force users to log on when accessing a wireless network, connecting to a switch, or connecting to a VPN server.

Rapid Spanning Tree Protocol (RSTP) An IEEE standard, 802.1w, which is interoperable with 802.1d and an extension to it. The problem with 802.1d, however, is that it was designed back when waiting for 30 to 50 seconds for convergence wasn't a problem. However, in today's networks, this can cause serious performance problems for networks that use real-time applications, such as Voice over IP (VoIP). RSTP enables almost instantaneous convergence in most situations.

read-only memory (ROM) Nonvolatile memory: when you turn off your device, the contents of ROM are not erased. ROM contains the necessary firmware to boot up your router and typically has the following four components: POST, bootstrap program, ROMMON, and possibly a Mini-IOS.

ready/not ready signals   These signals can be used at the transport layer to implement flow control. With ready/not ready signals, when the destination receives more traffic than it can handle, it can send a not ready signal to the source, indicating that the source should stop transmitting data. When the destination has a chance to catch up and process the source's information, the destination will respond with a ready signal. Upon receiving the ready signal, the source can resume the sending of data.

reconnaissance attack   A threat that occurs when an adversary tries to learn information about your network. He will do this by discovering network components and resources and the vulnerabilities that exist in them.

remote-access VPN   An extension of the classic circuit-switching network, such as POTS or ISDN. This VPN securely connects remote users or a small office/home office (SOHO) to a corporate or branch office. With a remote-access VPN, the VPN provides a virtualization process, making it appear that the remote-access user or office is physically connected to the corporate office network. Common protocols used for remote-access VPNs include IPsec, SSL, PPTP, and L2TP.

repeater   A physical layer device that will amplify a signal so that the signal can travel a farther distance. Repeaters are typically used when you need to extend the distance of a cable.

Reverse Address Resolution Protocol (RARP)   Sort of the reverse of an ARP. In an ARP, the device knows the layer 3 address, but not the data link layer address. With a RARP, the device doesn't have an IP address and wants to acquire one. The only address that this machine has is a MAC address. Common protocols that use RARP are Bootstrap Protocol (BOOTP) and DHCP.

RJ-45   This connector is located on the end of twisted-pair cables. It looks like a telephone connector but is wider, because there are eight pins instead of the four pins found with telephone cable (which uses an RJ-11 connector).

rollover cable   A type of cable used for console connections that resembles an Ethernet CAT 5 cable; however, a rollover cable is proprietary to Cisco and will not work for other types of connections. The rollover cable has eight wires inside its plastic shielding. Each side of the rollover cable reverses the wires compared to the other side: pin 1 on one side is wired to pin 8 on the other side; pin 2 is wired to pin 7, and so on.

ROM Monitor (ROMMON)   On a Cisco router or switch, the ROM Monitor loads a bootstrap program that allows for low-level diagnostic testing of the IOS device, performs the password recovery procedure, and can perform an emergency upgrade if the IOS image is corrupted or missing in flash.

root bridge or switch   When STP is running, a spanning tree, which is basically an inverted tree structure, is first created. At the top of the tree is the root bridge. From the root bridge are branches (physical Ethernet connections) connecting to other switches, and branches from these switches connect to other switches, and so on. The layer 2 device with the lowest bridge ID (bridge priority + MAC address) is elected as the root.

root port   In STP, each non-root switch needs to select a single port it will use to reach the root switch. This is the root port, which has the best accumulated path cost to the root bridge or switch.

router   A networking device that functions at the network layer. Because routers operate at a higher layer than layer 2 devices and use logical addressing, they provide many advantages. Routers perform the following functions: define logical addressing schemes, contain broadcasts and multicasts, find layer 3 paths to destinations, connect different media types, switch packets on the same interface using VLANs, and use advanced features such as filtering and quality of service (QoS).

router-on-a-stick   A router with a single trunk connection to a switch; it routes between the VLANs on this trunk connection.

Routing Information Protocol (RIP)   An older distance-vector protocol that uses hop count as a routing metric. RIP comes in two versions: Version 1 is a distance vector protocol. Version 2 is a hybrid protocol. RIPv1 uses local broadcasts to share routing information. These updates are periodic in nature, occurring, by default, every 30 seconds. To prevent packets from circling around a loop forever, both versions of RIP use counting to infinity, placing a hop count limit of 15—any packet that reaches the 16th hop will be dropped. Instead of using broadcasts, RIPv2 uses multicasts. And to speed up convergence, RIPv2 supports triggered updates. RIPv1 is classful, and RIPv2 is classless.

routing table   Routers use network numbers to make routing decisions: how to get a packet to its destination. They build a routing table, which contains path information, including the network number, which interface the router should use to reach the network number, the metric of the path, and how the router learned about this network number.

runtless switching   *See* fragment-free switching.

segment   A PDU used at the transport layer.

Service Access Point (SAP)   The LLC performs its multiplexing by using SAP identifiers. When a network layer protocol is encapsulated in the 802.2 frame, the protocol of the network data is placed in the SAP field. The destination uses this to determine which layer 3 protocol should process the frame.

session layer   The sixth layer of the OSI Reference Model, the session layer is responsible for initiating the setup and teardown of connections. To perform these functions, the session layer must determine whether or not data stays local to a computer or must be obtained or sent to a remote networking device.

Simple Mail Transfer Protocol (SMTP)   A protocol used to send mail over the Internet.

Simple Network Management Protocol (SNMP)   A protocol commonly used to manage (configure and/or monitor) a networking device remotely. SNMP is composed of three components: The network management station (NMS) is a device that accesses and manages agents. The agent is a device managed by an NMS. The Management Information Base (MIB) defines how information (configuration, operational, and statistical) is stored on an agent. The interaction is between the NMS and the agent, which can involve two types of connections. The NMS sends a "get" or "set" command to the agent: get commands are used for retrieving MIB information, and set commands are used to change MIB information. The agent sends "traps" or "informs" to the NMS, which are a form of a log message, indicating an important condition on the device. Information stored on an agent is located in a MIB. Each MIB is uniquely identified with an object identifier (OID). Get, send, and trap messages are based on the MIB information identified by a particular OID.

site-local address   These IPv6 addresses are similar to the RFC 1918 IPv4 addresses and represent a particular site or company. They can be used within a company without having to waste any public IP addresses—not that this is a concern, given the large number of addresses available in IPv6. However, by using private addresses, you can set up address translation policies for IPv6 to easily control who is allowed access to leave your network and who can receive returning traffic.

Site-to-Site VPN   Sometimes called a LAN-to-LAN or L2L VPN, this VPN connects two locations or sites together, basically extending a classical WAN design. Two intermediate devices, commonly called VPN gateways, actually protect the traffic between the two LANs. This type of VPN tunnels packets between the locations: the original IP packet from one LAN is encrypted by one gateway, forwarded to the destination gateway, and then decrypted and forwarded to the local LAN at its end to the destination.

small office/home office (SOHO)   A network that includes a small number of people working from a home or small office.

Spanning Tree Protocol (STP)   A protocol whose main function is to remove layer 2 loops from your topology. DEC originally developed STP; IEEE enhanced the initial implementation of STP in 802.1d.

split horizon   A method used by distance vector protocols to prevent routing loops in a network. With split horizon, if a neighboring router sends a route to a router, the receiving router will not propagate this route back to the advertising router on the same interface.

standard IP access control list (ACL)   An ACL that enables you to match packets based only on the source IP address.

star topology   A network setup that involves systems connecting to a central device, such as a switch.

stateless autoconfiguration   Using this functionality, an extension of DHCPv6, clients can still acquire their addressing dynamically; however, no server is necessary to assign IPv6 addressing information to the clients. Instead, each client uses information in router advertisement messages to configure an IPv6 address for the interface. This is accomplished by taking the first 64 bits in the router advertisement source address (the prefix of the router's address) and using the EUI-64 (extended unique identifier) process to create the 64-bit interface ID. Stateless autoconfiguration was designed primarily for cell phones, PDAs, and home network and appliance equipment to assign addresses automatically without having to manage a DHCP server infrastructure.

static route   A route that is manually configured on the router.

sticky learning   A port security feature that enables a switch to dynamically learn which MAC addresses correspond to particular ports, and then set up permanent CAM table entries for these.

store-and-forward switching   The most basic form of switching, in which the layer 2 device must pull the entire frame into the buffer of the port and check the cyclic redundancy check (CRC) of the frame before that device will perform any additional processing on the frame.

straight-through cable   An Ethernet cable on which pin 1 on one side is connected to pin 1 on the other side, pin 2 is connected to pin 2, and so on. A straight-through cable is used for DTE-to-DCE connections. A DTE is a router, PC, or file server, and a DCE is a hub or switch.

subinterface   A logical interface associated with a single physical interface. A physical interface can support many subinterfaces. Cisco routers treat subinterfaces just as they do physical interfaces. You can shut down a physical interface, which shuts down all of its associated subinterfaces, or you can shut down a single subinterface while keeping the remaining subinterfaces operational.

subnet mask   Each TCP/IP address has three components: a network component, a host component, and a subnet mask. The function of the subnet mask is to differentiate between the network address, the host addresses, and the directed broadcast address for a network or subnet.

subnet zero (subnet 0)   When performing subnetting, the first and last subnets created are referred to as subnet zero. Some older TCP/IP stacks didn't support the use of subnet zero, but this is not true of today's current operating systems.

subnetting   A local subdivision of an IP address range into multiple IP address ranges.

Subnetwork Access Protocol (SNAP)   Two frame types are supported by 802.2: SAP and SNAP. One of the issues of the original SAP field in the 802.2 SAP frame is that even though it is 8 bytes in length, only the first 6 bits are used for identifying upper layer protocols, which enables up to 64 protocols. Back in the 1980s, many more protocols than 64 were available, plus there was the expectation that more protocols would be created. SNAP overcomes this limitation without having to change the length of the SAP field. To indicate a SNAP frame, the SAP fields are set to hexadecimal 0xAA, the control field is set to 0x03, and the OUI field is set to 0x0. The type field identifies the upper layer protocol that is encapsulated in the payload of the 802.2 frame. AppleTalk is an example of a protocol that uses an 802.2 SNAP frame.

subset advertisement   When a server responds to a VTP client's or VTP server's request, it generates a subset advertisement, which contains detailed VLAN configuration information, including the VLAN numbers, names, types, and other information.

summary advertisement   This is generated by a switch in VTP server mode. Summary advertisements are generated every 5 minutes by default, or when a configuration change takes place on the server switch. Unlike a subset advertisement, a summary advertisement contains only summarized VLAN information.

supernetting   *See* Classless Interdomain Routing (CIDR).

switch   A layer 2 device that is used to solve bandwidth and collision problems. Switches perform their switching in application-specific integrated circuits (ASICs) hardware. All switches support store-and-forward switching, and some switches also support cut-through and fragment-free switching. Switches typically support both half- and full-duplexing. Switches come in many sizes, and some have more than 100 ports.

switched virtual circuit (SVC)   In a process similar to how a telephone call works, each SVC device is assigned a unique address, similar to a telephone number. To reach a destination device using an SVC, you'll need to know the destination device's address. In WAN environments, this is typically configured manually on your SVC device. Your device sends the SVC address to the carrier switch, which sets up the connection. Once you are done using the circuit, your device signals the carrier switch to tear it down. SVCs are used for intermittent data or for backup purposes.

Synchronous Optical Network (SONET)   A fiber-optic network communications link that supports rates up to 13.22 Gbps.

syslog   A method of logging device information to a remote server. Logging to a syslog server makes it easier to manage and keep a historical record of your logging information from a multitude of devices. Syslog uses UDP and runs on port 514. All logging information is sent in clear text and has no packet integrity checking, making it easy for a hacker to send false data to the syslog server. Therefore, it is highly recommended that you encrypt information between your networking devices and the syslog server, as well as set up a filter on the syslog server to accept logging information only from particular IP addresses.

System Configuration Dialog   When a router boots up, runs its hardware diagnostics, and loads IOS software, IOS then attempts to find a configuration file in NVRAM. If it can't find a configuration file to load, IOS will run the System Configuration Dialog, commonly referred to as Setup mode, which is a script that prompts you for configuration information. The purpose of this script is to ask you questions that will enable you to set up a basic configuration on your device.

T1   A widely used digital transmission link that uses a point-to-point transmission technology with two-wire pairs: one pair is used to send and one is used to receive. T1 can transmit digital, voice, data, and video signals at 1.544 Mbps.

T3   Similar to T1 but designed for transporting large amounts of data at high speeds. T3 is a leased line that can transmit data at 45 Mbps.

telnet   A terminal emulation program used to connect remotely to an application or server.

three-way handshake   With reliable TCP sessions, before a host can send information to another host, a three-way handshake process must take place to establish the connection: SYN, SYN/ACK, and ACK.

Time Division Multiplexing (TDM)   Channelized services, such as a T1 or E1, use TDM to create many logical channels on a single piece of wire. Each channel, or timeslot, is given its own amount of bandwidth and time on the wire. Each channel does not simultaneously transmit its information along with other channels. Instead, each must take its own turn in sending a small bit of information. All channels are given the same amount of bandwidth and time, and after all of the channels have been given their chance to send information, the first channel begins again.

transceiver   The portion of the network interface that actually transmits and receives electrical signals across the transmission media. It is also the part of the interface that actually connects to the media.

Transmission Control Protocol (TCP)   A protocol responsible for providing a reliable logical connection between two devices within TCP/IP. It uses windowing to implement flow control so that a source device doesn't overwhelm a destination with too many segments.

Transmission Control Protocol/Internet Protocol (TCP/IP)   A standard that includes many protocols. It defines how machines on an internetwork can communicate with one another. It was initially funded by and developed for DARPA (Defense Advanced Research Projects Agency). Originally designed in RFC 791, TCP/IP has become the de facto standard for networking protocols. The Internet uses TCP/IP to carry data between networks, and most corporations today use TCP/IP for their networks.

transport layer   The fourth layer of the OSI Reference Model, the transport layer is responsible for the actual mechanics of a connection. It can provide both reliable and unreliable delivery of data on a connection. For reliable connections, the transport layer is responsible for error detection and correction: when an error is detected with the sending of information, the transport layer will resend the data. For unreliable connections, the transport layer provides only error detection—error correction is left up to one of the higher layers (typically the application layer).

trunk connection   This type of connection is capable of carrying traffic for multiple VLANs. To support trunking, the original Ethernet frame must be modified to carry VLAN information to ensure that the broadcast integrity is maintained.

twisted pair cable   A common network cable type that uses eight copper wires made up of four pairs of wires. Each pair of wires are twisted around one another to help prevent crosstalk from neighboring pairs of wires in the cable. The copper wires carry an electrical signal from one end of the cable to another.

unicast frame   With a unicast frame, the destination MAC address denotes a single device.

unshielded twisted pair (UTP)   A four-pair copper wire, where each pair is periodically twisted. It is cheap to install and troubleshoot, but it is susceptible to electromagnetic interference (EMI) and radio frequency interference (RFI), and cable distances are limited to a short haul.

User Datagram Protocol (UDP)   This protocol provides an unreliable connection at the transport layer. UDP doesn't go through a three-way handshake to set up a connection—it simply begins sending the information. Likewise, UDP doesn't check to see if sent segments were received by a destination; in other words, it doesn't have an acknowledgment process. Typically, if an acknowledgment process is necessary, the application layer will provide this verification.

user EXEC mode   An access level for Cisco devices that provides basic access to IOS, with limited command availability (basically simple monitoring and troubleshooting). If you see a > character at the end of the prompt information, you know that you are in user EXEC mode.

variable-length subnet masking (VLSM)   A subnet design strategy that enables you to have more than one mask for a given subnet when subnetting the original class A, B, or C network address. Classful protocols such as RIPv1 and IGRP do not support VLSM. Deploying VLSM requires a routing protocol that is classless, such as BGP, EIGRP, IS-IS, OSPF, or RIPv2. VLSM provides two major advantages: more efficient use of addressing and the ability to perform route summarization.

virtual circuit (VC)   A logical connection between two devices. Therefore, many VCs can exist on the same physical connection. VCs can provide full connectivity at a much lower price than using leased lines. VCs are used in Asynchronous Transfer Mode (ATM), Frame Relay, and X.25.

virtual LAN (VLAN)   A group of networking devices in the same broadcast domain that are not restricted to any physical boundary in the switched network, assuming that all the devices are interconnected via switches and that there are no intervening layer 3 devices. Logically speaking, VLANs are also subnets.

virtual private network (VPN)   A special type of secure network that is used to provide a secure, protected tunnel or connection across a public network, such as the Internet. The network part of the term refers to the use of a public network, such as the Internet, to implement the WAN solution. The virtual part of the term hides the public network from the internal network components, such as users and services. The private part of the term specifies that the traffic should remain private—not viewable by eavesdroppers in the network. This is accomplished using encryption to keep the data confidential.

Virtual Router Redundancy Protocol (VRRP)   This protocol performs a function similar to Cisco's proprietary HSRP. The one major downside to HSRP is that it is a proprietary protocol; VRRP, however, is an open standard and is defined in IETF RFC 2338. Like HSRP, VRRP has end stations that use a virtual router for a default gateway. One main difference between VRRP and HSRP is that HSRP uses a virtual IP address for the default gateway, whereas VRRP can use either a virtual IP address or the interface address of the master router. If a virtual IP address is used, an election process takes place to choose a master router. VRRP is supported for Ethernet media types as well as in VLANs and MPLS VPNs.

virtual type terminal (VTY)   A logical line on a Cisco device that is used to manage telnet and SSH connections.

VLAN Trunk Protocol (VTP)   A proprietary Cisco protocol used to share VLAN configuration information between Cisco switches on trunk connections. VTP enables switches to share and synchronize their VLAN information, which ensures that your network has a consistent VLAN configuration.

voice over IP (VoIP)   A group of technologies that are designed to carry voice and video over an IP network.

VTP client mode   A switch in VTP client mode cannot make changes to its VLAN configuration itself—it requires a switch in VTP server mode to tell it about the VLAN changes. When a client switch receives a VTP message from a server switch, it incorporates the changes and then floods the VTP message out its remaining trunk ports. An important point to make is that a client switch does not store its VLAN configuration information in NVRAM—instead, it learns this from a server switch every time it boots up.

VTP pruning   A Cisco VTP feature that enables your switches to dynamically delete or add VLANs to a trunk, creating a more efficient switching network.

VTP server mode   A switch configured in VTP server mode can add, modify, and delete VLANs. A VTP server switch, when making a change, propagates the VTP message concerning the change on all of its trunk ports. If a server switch receives a VTP update message, it will incorporate the update and forward the message out its remaining trunk ports.

VTP transparent mode   A switch configured in VTP transparent mode can add, modify, and delete VLANs. Configuration changes made to a transparent switch affect only that switch, and no other switch in the network. A transparent switch ignores VTP messages—it will accept them on trunk ports and forward them out its remaining trunk ports, but it will not incorporate the message changes.

WebVPN   SSL VPNs, even though they use SSL as their protection protocol, are implemented differently by each vendor, making them proprietary. Cisco's SSL VPN solution is called WebVPN and provides three secure connection methods: clientless, thin client, and the SSL VPN Client. The clientless and thin client implementations use a normal web browser, with JavaScript installed, to provide the VPN solution. The SSL VPN Client provides network layer protection and enables users to use their day-to-day applications without any modifications.

wide area network (WAN)   A network that connect LANs, typically when the LANs that need to be connected are separated by a large distance. Where a corporation provides its own infrastructure for a LAN, WANs are leased from carrier networks, such as telephone companies. Four basic types of connections, or circuits, are used in WAN services: circuit-switched, cell-switched, packet-switched, and dedicated connections.

wildcard mask   When dealing with IP addresses in ACL statements, you can use wildcard masks to match on a range of addresses instead of having to manually enter every IP address that you want to match on. A wildcard mask is not a subnet mask, but like an IP address or a subnet mask, a wildcard mask consists of 32 bits. With a wildcard mask, a 0 in a bit position means that the corresponding bit position in the address of the ACL statement must match the bit position in the IP address in the examined packet. A 1 in a bit position means that the corresponding bit position in the address of the ACL statement does not have to match the bit position in the IP address in the examined packet. OSPF **network** statements also use wildcard masks.

windowing   TCP and other transport layer protocols provide for the regulation of the flow of segments, ensuring that one device doesn't flood another device with too many segments. TCP uses a sliding windowing mechanism to assist with flow control. For example, with a window size of 1, a device can send only one segment, and then it must wait for a corresponding acknowledgment before receiving the next segment.

wireless access point (WAP)   A network device that enables wireless clients to connect to the wireless network. Wireless clients connect to the WAP and send data to other hosts on the network through it.

INDEX